Critical Race Realism

Critical Race Realism

INTERSECTIONS OF PSYCHOLOGY, RACE, AND LAW

Edited by

GREGORY S. PARKS, SHAYNE JONES,
AND W. JONATHAN CARDI

THE NEW PRESS

NEW YORK

Requests for permission to reproduce selections from this book should be mailed to:
Permissions Department, The New Press, 38 Greene Street, New York, NY 10013.

Published in the United States by The New Press, New York, 2008
Distributed by W. W. Norton & Company, Inc., New York

LIBRARY OF CONGRESS CATALOGING-IN-PUBLICATION DATA

Critical race realism : Intersections of psychology, race, and law / edited by Gregory S.
Parks, Shayne Jones, and W. Jonathan Cardi.
    p. cm.
Includes bibliographical references.
ISBN 978-1-59558-146-4 (hc.)
    1. Race discrimination—Law and legislation—United States.   2. Discrimination in
justice administration—United States.   3. Race discrimination—United States.
4. African Americans—Civil rights.   5. United States—Race relations.   I. Parks,
Gregory, 1974–   II. Jones, Shayne E.   III. Cardi, W. Jonathan.
KF4755.C749 2008
342.7308'73—dc22   2007037608

The New Press was established in 1990 as a not-for-profit alternative to the large, commercial publishing houses currently dominating the book publishing industry. The New
Press operates in the public interest rather than for private gain, and is committed to publishing, in innovative ways, works of educational, cultural, and community value that are
often deemed insufficiently profitable.

www.thenewpress.com

Composition by NK Graphics
This book was set in Adobe Caslon

Printed in the United States of America

2 4 6 8 10 9 7 5 3 1

CONTENTS

PART TWO: CIVIL LAW

PART THREE: CRIMINAL LAW

PERMISSIONS

An expanded version of Gregory S. Parks's *Towards a Critical Race Realism*, 18 CORNELL JOURNAL OF LAW AND PUBLIC POLICY (2008).

Jody Armour's *Stereotypes and Prejudice: Helping Legal Decisionmakers Break the Prejudice Habit*, 83 CALIFORNIA LAW REVIEW 733 © 1995 California Law Review, Inc. and Jody Armour. Reprinted by permission of the California Law Review, Inc. and the author.

Theodore Eisenberg and Sheri Lynn Johnson's *Implicit Racial Attitudes of Death Penalty Lawyers*, 53 DEPAUL LAW REVIEW 1539 © 2004 DePaul University, Theodore Eisenberg, and Sheri Lynn Johnson. Reprinted by permission of the authors.

Gary Blasi's *Advocacy Against the Stereotype: Lessons from Cognitive Social Psychology*, 49 UCLA LAW REVIEW 1241 © 2002 Regents of the University of California and Gary Blasi. Reprinted by permission of the author.

Jerry Kang's *Trojan Horses of Race*, 118 HARVARD LAW REVIEW 1489 © 2006 by the Harvard Law School and Jerry Kang. Reprinted by permission of the author.

Linda Hamilton Krieger and Susan T. Fiske's *Behavioral Realism in Employment Discrimination Law: Implicit Bias and Disparate Treatment*, 94 CALIFORNIA LAW REVIEW 997 © 2006 California Law Review, Inc. Reprinted by permission of the California Law Review, Inc.

Christine Jolls and Cass R. Sunstein's *The Law of Implicit Bias*, 94 CALIFORNIA LAW REVIEW 969 © 2006 by California Law Review, Inc. Reprinted by permission of the California Law Review, Inc.

Richard R.W. Brooks's *Fear and Fairness in the City: Criminal Enforcement and Perceptions of Fairness in Minority Communities*, 73 SOUTHERN CALIFORNIA LAW REVIEW 1219 © 2000 University of Southern California and Richard R.W. Brooks. Reprinted by permission of the University of Southern California and the author.

FOREWORD

Richard Delgado

This interdisciplinary volume is a welcome and long overdue addition to scholarship on race, racism, and American law.

To be sure, the movement it inaugurates, critical race realism, has forerunners, for example, in Supreme Court Justice Louis Brandeis's famous brief in *Muller v. Oregon* or the Supreme Court's citation of Kenneth and Mamie Clark's doll studies in *Brown v. Board of Education*.

It also builds on earlier movements, such as law and society (Wisconsin) and legal realism (Harvard and Yale) that, like it, placed a high value on empirical research. Even today, Mark Galanter, a law and society scholar at Wisconsin, uses empirical methods to study the behavior of large law firms or how repeat players constantly come out ahead in the game of litigation.

And legal realism, while no longer a formal movement, lives on through a host of successors, including critical legal studies, critical race theory, and feminist jurisprudence, which build on its insights about the role of power and knowledge.

Perhaps because of their common origins, the essays in this volume and those in these related schools of thought exhibit a great deal in common. With narrative jurisprudence and legal storytelling—key elements in critical race theory—these essays share a skepticism of conventional wisdom and a desire to go beyond "what everyone knows."

Also like their critical race counterparts, the new writers emphasize particularity and context. Distrusting broad generalization, they set out to discover what happens in specific settings, such as when black women buy automobiles at dealerships or a white law student interviews a Latina client in a law school clinic.

Critical race theory seeks to understand unconscious and institutional racism; the essays in this collection do the same. Critical race theory holds that race is a social construction; most critical race realists would agree—indeed, one of their objectives is to understand how society goes about constructing and inventing racial differences. (See, for example, the essays by Gary Blasi and Jerry Kang in this volume.)

All these movements have been receptive to a wide range of social science knowledge. Indeed, a classic critical race theory anthology devotes an entire chapter to critical social science, while the latest edition of Catharine MacKinnon's casebook, *Sex Equality*, uses social science information to explain how sexual inequality persists in a society ostensibly dedicated to treating men and women equally.

The essays in this volume, then, build on a legacy of progressive lawyers who employ the tools of social science to reform the law and persuade judges to rule their way. But these essays go further than that, especially when one considers them cumulatively. For example, the chapter by Jody Armour suggests a simple way legal decisionmakers can surmount their own prejudices. Other chapters discuss how the legal system could build on studies of implicit associations or the new science of cognitive psychology to devise more effective remedies for discrimination. Still other contributors explore how defense lawyers can counteract their own biases, challenge those inherent in eyewitness identification, or identify those that come into play when an expert witness of color testifies in front of a white jury. One discusses ingroup prejudice against blacks with stereotypically African American features.

Do tort doctrines such as the reasonable man incorporate a white standard, and, if so, does this explain blacks receiving smaller awards than whites for the same injuries? Why do whites and nonwhites see many issues, such as affirmative action, white-collar crime, racial profiling, or police conduct, in such different terms? All these issues are the subject of much uninformed speculation, but the essays in this volume offer concise, testable knowledge drawing on the latest findings from the world of research.

Since exposing racism, identifying its source, and revealing how it hides its face are vital issues for a system of adjudication that strives to be even-handed, every legal reader (indeed, every reader) should take the opportunity to read these essays.

This book, then, marks an impressive beginning. Still, it is not too early to ask what topics could be on the new movement's future agenda. What might readers look for in this book's second edition, perhaps five or ten years hence?

Critical race realism as a movement may profit from examining more closely its relation to critical race theory, with which it shares two-thirds of its name. Although I have highlighted a few continuities between the two movements, a number of potential differences invite attention.

Among these are the tension between being critical and being empirical. Scientific findings, a critical race theorist might say, rarely speak for themselves; they require an act of interpretation. For example, imagine that a social scientist discovers that law students of color, on average, do worse than their white counterparts. Does this mean that affirmative action harms them by placing them in elite schools where they are in over their heads? Or does it mean that legal educators should try harder to achieve a "critical mass" of minority students so as to increase their comfort level? In other words, more affirmative action, not less.

If facts and narratives come mixed up in complex ways so that facts alone do not explain, while narratives unmoored in reality are treacherous, how should critical race theory's storytellers and critical race empiricists find common ground? It would seem that the world needs both, but how do they relate to each other?

A second issue that critical race realism may want to place on its agenda is the relationship between knowledge and power.

History shows that scientific certitudes replace each other with unsettling regularity. Much like judges steeped in particular legal traditions (realism, legal process, strict construction, etc.), scientists in different fields work within separate paradigms, more or less blind to evidence falling outside their area of specialization. Just as troubling is the question of which paradigm—which social science—best maps onto the law in a particular area.

Consider, for example, how defenders of race-conscious school assignments, like those who appeared before the Supreme Court recently in the Seattle-Louisville case, need to produce a "compelling state interest." (The current color-blind Court requires one whenever the law draws an explicitly racial classification.) Educational psychologists wishing to support diversity in the public schools might marshal evidence that black and Latino students who attend integrated schools do better—and white students no worse—when school districts mix students by race.

But *sociological* evidence shows that introducing diversity into a workplace, school, nation, or other group, at least in the short run, is apt to cause everyone (including the minorities) to "hunker down"—to distrust their neighbors, stay at home, volunteer less, and enjoy less social capital than in settings that are homogeneous. So is diversity a compelling *state* interest or not? If diversity is good for individuals (both white and nonwhite) but may be bad for societies (at least in the short run), which paradigm—psychology or sociology—is the apt one for law and its peculiar grid?

The new movement may also wish to consider the complex nature of racism, in particular the extent to which it is merely a kind of mistake or cognitive error. It is tempting to believe that discrimination is the product of faulty information (or schemas, or stereotypes, or cognitive categories, or automatic associations between color and good or evil) and that once we realize how much incorrect information we carry around in our heads, we will of course want to change how we think, speak, and act.

But suppose that racism is not entirely a mistake but also a strategy for hoarding resources and preserving the best jobs, schools, and neighborhoods for our kind. If preserving group advantage lies at the heart of racism, as one school of critical race scholars holds, then straightening out our fellow citizens' ideas, thoughts, concepts, unconscious desires, cognitive categories, and implicit associations will leave much racism unaddressed.

A final issue that critical race realism may wish to explore concerns the perspective or standpoint from which to address issues of race and class. A classic article by Alan Freeman calls attention to the difference that a perpetrator, rather than a victim, perspective makes in cases of discrimination. A perpetrator perspective looks at discrimination from the perspective of the perpetrator, often a white person, while a victim perspective looks at the same set of events from the perspective of the persons of color who are on the receiving end. Freeman argued that current antidiscrimination law placed an excessive valuation on whites' experiences and racial sins and too little on those of racism's victims.

Might social scientists replicate the same error? Essays exploring racism's ubiquity, the large number of whites who have trouble associating good qualities with blacks on timed tests, and how white law students in legal clinics may overcome their racial preconceptions when working with nonwhite clients address legitimate concerns. But after exhausting them, many issues remain: How does racism feel to its victim? What happens to a black student's aspiration level when all of his or her teachers or professors are white? Can a black man serve as a role model for a black woman? Why do Latinos report a greater social distance from blacks than the blacks do from them?

A new movement cannot address every issue at once, and it is no criticism of critical race realism that an initial volume leaves a few issues unexplored. As with the arrival of a newborn infant, being present at the birth of a new scholarly movement is a rare pleasure. Speculating what the newcomer may become is just as great a source of wonder. In the meantime, the essays in this volume are an auspicious beginning that everyone interested in race and its working should welcome.

Pittsburgh, Pennsylvania
October 2007

INTRODUCTION

A historical account of American law shows a dramatic irony. The law has served as a tool to both oppress and liberate people of color. In the face of such oppression, a handful of legal practitioners and academics have used the law for progressive, social change. Among the latter, critical race theorists have been in the vanguard of providing "a race-based, systematic critique of legal reasoning and legal institutions." In 2002, Temple University Press published *Crossroads, Directions, and a New Critical Race Theory*. In one of the commentaries on the book, University of California at Berkeley law professor Rachel Moran noted that it captures a discipline at a crossroads, struggling to define its substantive mission, methodological commitments, and connection to the world outside of academia. Almost five years after *Crossroads'* publication, critical race theory continues to grapple with these same issues.

This book sets out to address these issues by proposing a particular methodology called critical race realism—a synthesis of critical race theory, empirical social science, and public policy. This methodology has both academic and applied components. Furthermore, its mission is to provide a more systematic race-based evaluation and critique of legal doctrine, institutions, and actors (e.g., judges, juries, etc.). By employing social science, critical race theory should (1) expose racism where it may be found, (2) identify its effects on individuals and institutions, and (3) put forth a concerted attack against it, in part, via public policy arguments.

There are a number of individuals and movements that inform us as to what critical race realism is or could be. First, the growth of interdisciplinarity in early American legal education signified that other academic disciplines could be fruitfully brought to bear on the law. Second, the insights of Supreme Court justices Holmes, Brandeis, and Cardozo and Harvard Law School dean Pound made way for the acceptance of social science within

American jurisprudence, the study of law in action, and the use of law to advance public policy. Third, the work of academics at both Columbia and Yale law schools—that is, the legal realists, the law science policy movement, and Yale's Divisional Studies Program—firmly ushered in a new way of looking at the law, one that is functional in its approach, debunks commonly held legal ideologies, and integrates social science with the law, and law with public policy. Fourth, the development of the "law and" movement and its progeny—for example, law and society, law and economics, critical legal studies, critical race theory—extended our understanding of law and social science and critiques of legal doctrine, institutions, and actors.

It is not our contention that the contributors to this book subscribe to this notion of critical race realism. They are simply a group of social science and legal academics who appreciate and are engaged in scholarship at the nexus of social science, race, and law. However, their work provides a sampling of how other academics and activists might begin to bridge the gaps between these areas for progressive social change.

Critical Race Realism

1

Toward a Critical Race Realism

Gregory S. Parks

INTRODUCTION

Several intellectual movements, schools of thought, and individuals have contributed, in various ways, to what can be defined as critical race realism. Here, critical race realism consists of (1) a deconstructive element, a systematic, race-based evaluation and critique of the law and legal institutions, and (2) a constructive element, a racially progressive policy agenda. Both elements rely heavily on empirical social science. With this in mind, there is a long history of liberal activism that has employed social science to end the racial status quo in America. There has also been a conservative effort to shore up that status quo. The twentieth century provides a number of instances where the legal battle over racial equality in America has been fought employing social science. For instance, just as social science was employed to advance the aims of the *Brown v. Board of Education* decisions to end school racial segregation,[1] there was also a scientific ef-

fort to reverse the legal gains of those decisions.[2]

Charles Houston fought on the progressive side of that battle by employing social science and seeking to effectuate change in law and public policy. As such, Houston embodied and put into practice realist philosophy; he was the exemplar of critical race realism. Just as Houston and his efforts provide a template for critical race realism, contemporary efforts and movements help situate it. Houston's work and *Brown*'s effect was to create an increasingly interdisciplinary approach to the law.[3] Contemporary court cases dealing with race issues such as *Griggs v. Duke Power Co.*, *McCleskey v. Kemp*, and *Grutter v. Bollinger* reflect such interdisciplinarity.[4] In addition to this interdisciplinary legacy, Houston and *Brown* also pointed a way toward a synthesis of social science and the law directed at changing public policy. It is this legacy that may be relied upon in looking at how critical race realism may currently be conceptualized.

I. CONTIGUOUS MODELS: EMPIRICAL LEGAL STUDIES, THE NEW LEGAL REALISM PROJECT, AND BEHAVIORAL REALISM

In light of efforts by the legal realists and the law and society movement, recent efforts to integrate law and social science are afoot. A new and rigorous empiricism, with its substantial benefits, has found its place within legal academia. First, empiricism arguably leads to objective knowledge, unfettered by personal prejudices.[5] Second, it has incredible potential to affect public policy.[6] As such, it is no surprise that empirical legal scholarship has taken firm root within legal academia in recent years. For instance, the conference theme in 2006 for the annual meeting of the Association of American Law Schools was "Empirical Scholarship: What Should We Study and How Should We Study It?"[7] Additionally, empirical legal scholarship is the "discernible emerging trend" in hires among law faculty, and law schools have hired an increasing number of J.D./Ph.D.'s as faculty.[8] Arguably, a significant number of these dual-degree hires are trained in economics, psychology, sociology, or political science and presumably trained in empirical methodologies. In addition to hires, recent legal academia trends suggest that law professors are increasingly interested in and producing more empirical scholarship.[9]

Moreover, there is a growing infrastructure for producing and publishing empirical legal scholarship. Several law schools offer courses in empirical methods to train their students.[10] A number of institutions have programs or initiatives designed to increase the output of empirical legal scholarship.[11] Washington University in St. Louis has a Workshop on Empirical Research in the Law. The law school at the University of California, Los Angeles, has an Empirical Research Group. Harvard Law School has a Program on Empirical Legal Studies. Wake Forest Law School has a Center for Student Empirical Studies sponsored by its law review. Additionally, the Institute for Legal Studies at the University of Wisconsin Law School, the Center for the Study of Law and Society at Boalt Law School, and the Baldy Center at the University of Buffalo all support empirical and interdisciplinary scholarship.

Additionally, traditional law reviews are publishing more empirical scholarship. Faculty-edited, peer-reviewed journals such as the *Journal of Empirical Legal Studies*, *Journal of Legal Studies*, *Journal of Law and Economics*, *Law & Society Review*, and *Journal of Law, Economics & Organization* have emerged and rank among some of the most prestigious law journals.[12] Cyberspace too has become a repository for empirical legal scholarship. The Social Science Research Network's Legal Scholarship Network includes a section on empirical legal scholarship. The recently launched Empirical Legal Studies blog serves as a Web site where empirical legal scholars discuss research and contemporary issues in the field. There has also been a growth in the number of conferences focused on empirical legal scholarship. These range from small conferences, such as the empirical legal scholarship conference at Northwestern Law School, to national conferences, such as the empirical legal scholarship conference at the University of Texas–Austin Law School. Beyond law schools, agencies such as the National Science Foundation's Law and Social Science division and the National Institute of Justice aid in the development of empirical legal scholarship.

Recent efforts have attempted to create a formalized movement among empirical scholars: the New Legal Realism Project. How this movement differs from the law and society movement seems unclear at this point.[13] Nonetheless, for the past ten years, academics have debated the need for a "new legal realism."[14] Finally, in 2005, the American Bar Foundation and the University of Wisconsin Law School's Institute for Legal Studies sponsored the first New Legal Realism Symposium,[15] which resulted in the publication of several articles.[16] The new legal realism agenda consists of five points. First, it takes both a bottom-up and top-down approach. A bottom-up approach necessitates that empirical research must support assertions about the law's impact on everyday people's lives.[17] Additionally, there must be a continued effort to study decision makers and institutions at the top. Furthermore, this bottom-up approach requires an appreciation of "power arrangements and hierarchies" within our legal system.[18] Second, new legal realists seek to facilitate some translation between law and social science—bridge the gap between "epistemolog[ies], methods, operating assumptions and overall goals. . . ."[19] Third, new legal realists attempt to reconcile issues related to potential researcher subjectivity.[20] Fourth, new legal realism must broaden its horizon and focus on international as well as national issues.[21] Finally, new legal realism not only incorporates empirical research and legal theory but also must address policy issues. In doing so, new legal realism cannot simply be a method of critique; it must also point the way toward "positive social change."[22]

Over the past several years, the topic of race has taken some root within areas of empirical legal scholarship and social science and law literature. Maybe the clearest indication of this is the New Legal Realism Symposium issue of the *Wisconsin Law Review*. With the launching of this new effort to put forth a serious integration of empirical methods and legal scholarship, more than one-quarter of the articles focused on race issues.[23] Furthermore, half of the articles from its Law & Social In-

quiry Symposium focused on race issues.[24] This suggests that there is at least some effort on the part of empirical legal scholars to substantively address issues of race.

In addition to efforts by empirical legal scholars and participants in the New Legal Realism Project, a number of scholars have come together to advance what they term behavioral realism. According to this perspective, people have schemas for various categories, including racial categories. Individuals in these racial categories are then automatically ascribed some meaning. It can be difficult to ascertain what these meanings are; for example, people often lack introspection or actively conceal their feelings about racial categories. Behavioral realists employ the Implicit Association Test as a measure of unconscious racial attitudes. Furthermore, their goal is to identify latent processes or assumptions in the law related to human decision making and assess new scientific understanding about human behavior from the mind sciences. As articulated by Jerry Kang, the law must then take into account models of human decision making or state clearly that it will not take this new science into account. Kang further notes that the future of behavioral realism consists of answering a number of descriptive and normative questions. With regard to the former, does implicit racial bias exist? If it does, is there any real-world impact of implicit racial bias? If there is a real-world impact, can it be rectified? With regard to the latter, should implicit racial bias be countered? If it should, does countering implicit racial bias respect notions of individual autonomy? If it does, is the intervention lawful? Ultimately, as Kang notes, social science and legal scholarship should help us answer these questions. Social science journals should decide if the science is correct, and law reviews should decide if the science is being validly employed.[25] This burgeoning area of scholarship has produced fruitful works in the *Harvard Law Review*[26] and collaborative efforts between psychology and law professors featured in the *California Law Review* Behavioral Realism Symposium.[27]

II. CRITICAL RACE REALISM: CRITICAL RACE THEORY AND CONTEMPORARY MOVEMENTS

Narrowly conceptualized, critical race realism is not new. Charles Houston employed social science in a litigation strategy as a means to legally end school segregation, which in turn had policy reverberations. Contemporarily, law professors have also demonstrated growing interest in the intersection of race and social science. Thus, my contention is simply that critical race theorists should employ empirical modes of understanding race and racism among legal actors and within legal institutions and doctrine more often. Quite possibly, it should be the dominant strand of critical race scholarship.

Critical race theorists may argue any of the conventional points against engaging in empirical research.[28] Additionally, they may also make arguments, more particular to critical race theory, against synthesizing critical race theory and empirical legal scholarship. First, quite like their critical legal studies predecessors, many critical race theorists may insist that facts are irrelevant, maybe even pretextual, to judicial decision outcomes.[29] Employing statistical data supports the idea that such data are neutral and objective. This is fundamentally antithetical to critical race theory doctrine. Second, the use of quantitative methods might undermine the power of narrative, a central critical race theory methodology.[30]

My attempt is not to cast aside this dominant strand of critical race scholarship. I concur wholeheartedly with Richard Delgado's analysis that

[t]he stories of outgroups aim to subvert the ingroup reality. In civil rights, for example, many in the majority hold that any inequality between blacks and whites is due either to cultural lag, or inadequate enforcement of currently existing beneficial laws—both of which are easily correctable. For many minority persons, the principal instrument of their subordination is neither of these. Rather, it is the prevailing mindset by means of which members of the dominant group justify the world as it is, that is, with whites on top and browns and blacks on the bottom.

Stories, parables, chronicles, and narratives are powerful means for destroying mindset—the bundle of presuppositions, received wisdoms, and shared understandings against a background of which legal and political discourse takes place.[31]

In a nutshell, narrative is a rich descriptive method. It may serve as a cathartic tool for the narrator. It may also allow the "other" to gain a sense of perspective,[32] maybe even empathy.[33]

However, narrative has its share of weaknesses—ones that would be substantially buttressed if employed in conjunction with empiricism. As noted by Daniel Farber and Suzanna Sherry, there are concerns about the validity of narratives.[34] This is likely to be particularly so among those naive about issues of race or those who are outright antagonists to the critical race theory agenda of racial progress. Farber and Sherry cite four validity concerns. The first is that fictional narrative creates a "spurious aura of empirical authority."[35] The second deals with the degree to which the narrative is truthful. Similarly, the third focuses on the difficulty of actually discerning if truth is being spoken—a methodological issue. Finally, the fourth concern is the degree to which the narrative account is representative of any population of people.[36]

Indeed, it is quite possible to be both critical and empirical.[37] Moreover, the benefits of synthesizing critical race theory with empirical legal scholarship are manifold. First, empirical legal scholarship methods allow for theory development, empirical testing, and theory refinement.[38] Furthermore, employing empirical research methods leads to reasonably objective knowledge that is relatively unfettered by personal prejudices.[39] Additionally, empirical methods have the "propensity to sharpen our focus on the normative questions that may be concealed by factual complexity and by the willingness of [some] to avoid responsibility for [their] value choices."[40] For example, though empirical research may impact powerful people's attitudes and actions, such individuals also have "defenses to ward off offensive or inconvenient knowledge."[41] However, when individuals or institutions can no longer employ empirical uncertainties to continue to engage in conscious or unconscious racist conduct, they must ultimately state their normative preferences.[42]

Second, it has long been noted that empirical legal scholarship is of value to critical race theory. Derrick Bell noted that "empiricism is a crucial aspect of Racial Realism. By taking into consideration the abysmal statistics regarding the social status of black Americans, their oppression is validated."[43] As such, empirical legal scholarship can be a more useful tool in highlighting racial disparities in the law's application vis-à-vis traditional case analysis.[44] As such, it allows critical race theorists to reach out to individuals who are less willing to accept a central principle of critical race theory—that people of color are subordinated in America. This is done by revealing that although blatant racism may be significantly diminished in America, unconscious racism exists and still adversely impacts the lives of African Americans and other people of color.[45] As Karl Llewellyn noted, "[W]e need improved machinery for making the facts

about such effects—or about needs and conditions to be affected by a decision—available to the courts."[46] Empirical social science is just such machinery.

With these factors in mind, an empirical analysis of race and law issues has some general yet substantive benefits. These benefits are evinced whether empirical methodology is employed alone or in conjunction with the narrative approach. Furthermore, these benefits speak directly to the concerns raised by Farber and Sherry. First, empiricism bolsters claims made by theory or personal narrative. Second, empiricism provides a method to validate the narrative. Relatedly, empiricism addresses Farber and Sherry's final validity concern. It allows one to test the degree to which a theory or a personal account of reality is true for others. Where it is generalizable, especially for a vast number of similarly situated individuals, public policy may be implicated.[47]

Thus, the third benefit of synthesizing empirical legal scholarship and critical race theory should be concerned with what Robert Summers described as pragmatic instrumentalism—a means-end relationship to law.[48] Legal scholarship, more readily than any other type of research, has the potential to shape public policy.[49] In this vein, the benefit of critical race theory's employment of social science is that social science may help shape courts', legislatures', and administrative agencies' policy decisions.[50] Policy goals, and the best methods for pursuing them, necessitate data about the "policies and about empirical assumptions underlying the policies and about the likely effect of various routes for achieving them."[51] Social science can provide those data.[52] As such, law must be seen both as a response to social needs and as having an impact on social issues.[53] Charles Houston's efforts at Howard Law School to create a "laboratory for civil rights and a nursery for civil rights lawyers" demonstrates an effort to create such policy changers—social engineers.[54] Both practicing attorneys and law professors have demonstrated a long history of serving in this role.[55] Thus, legal policy may be shaped by a number of actors, involve substantive or procedural law, and relate to public or private law.[56] Thus, the legal scholar, legal policy maker, or practicing lawyer may shape public policy. A legal academic may employ social science through her research by providing a more systematic approach to understanding the role of race within the legal system. A legal policy maker may employ social science either procedurally or substantively.[57] Procedurally, he may employ social science to get the legislature or courts to function in a more racially fair manner. Substantively, the policy maker may employ social science to look at the underlying racial fairness of a rule of law. A practicing lawyer may employ social science by introducing it into evidence to advance certain arguments in a case.[58]

Ultimately, the challenge to the broader goal of using social science to shape public policy with regard to race may be how, and by whom, it would be implemented. For example, judges may not be well suited to understand the significance of the social science evidence. Courts are not well equipped to respond to changes in the social science literature. Social science evidence, once accepted as persuasive by courts, becomes precedent. Such precedent becomes difficult to alter when additional research alters the conclusions of previous social science. Compared to courts, however, legislatures can adapt to changes in social science more quickly and act without there being a live controversy before them.[59]

A number of legal actors could be deemed critical race realists. However, law professors may be in the best position to actually formulate a critical race realism

agenda. This is largely because they can actually produce critical race realism scholarship. What is problematic is that their training likely makes them ineffective empirical legal scholars. First, law schools are not particularly good at teaching their students, some of whom go on to be law professors, how to systematically "find, interpret, prove, and rebut" facts.[60] Second, social scientists are taught to subject their hypotheses to "every conceivable test and data source" in an attempt to disconfirm the hypothesis. However, a lawyer attempts to marshal all possible evidence in support of her hypothesis and "distract attention" from any possible contradictory information.[61] A critical race realist should utilize the best of both of these approaches. Third, legal scholars largely do their academic work isolated from their social science counterparts and suffer from a failure to dialogue.[62] Fourth, law professors, unlike their social scientist counterparts, do not have a stable group of graduate students trained in empirical methodology and statistical analysis.[63] Thus, legal academics are likely at a handicap in developing an empirical agenda.

Thus, to develop a critical race realism, law schools might consider offering not only courses in empirical legal scholarship[64] but also empirical legal scholarship courses focused on critical race theory topics.[65] Critical race theorists may also take any of three steps to advance critical race realism. First, they might retool.[66] Several universities offer programs to train faculty in empirical research methodology. For example, the University of Michigan, through its Inter-university Consortium for Political and Social Research (ICPSR) Summer Program in Quantitative Methods, offers courses in basic and advanced quantitative analysis. Harvard University, through its Institute for Quantitative Social Science, offers a variety of degree and training programs, conferences, and seminars and workshops. In addition, Northwestern recently offered an Empirical Scholarship Workshop. Second, critical race theorists could also collaborate with social scientists in other departments[67] or the growing number of law professors who are also social scientists.[68] An additional source of collaboration could be social science graduate students interested in the intersection of race and law issues. Critical race theorists might also actively recruit graduate students engaged in social science, race, and law scholarship to law school. Such an approach would possibly add to the pool of minority law students and provide law pro-fessors with a research assistant, trained in research methodology, for three years. Finally, critical race theorists could simply import social science and empirical scholarship into their own work.

CONCLUSION

Critical race theory was founded as "a race-based, systematic critique of legal reasoning and legal institutions."[69] It has been critiqued, however, as struggling to define its substantive mission, methodological commitments, and connection to the world outside of academia.[70] This chapter attempts to provide a specific methodology that is consistent with critical race theory's overarching mission and that has both applied and academic components. Empirical social science is this methodology, which should ultimately (1) expose racism where it may be found, (2)

identify its effects on individuals and institutions, and (3) put forth a concerted attack against it, in part, via public policy arguments. This is critical race realism.

Critical race realism is drawn from a long and rich intellectual history. This history started with the growth of interdisciplinarity in American legal education and traversed its way through intellectual movements at Columbia, Yale, Chicago, and Wisconsin law schools. The recent explosion in empirical legal scholarship and the New Legal Realism Project provide contemporary efforts with which critical race realism must square itself. Ultimately, the intersection of social science, race, and law, or of race and empirical legal scholarship, is not a new nexus. The efforts of Charles Hamilton Houston in ending school segregation point to this fact. Furthermore, there has been growing interest in these areas within recent years. However, given this history and contemporary movement, we advocate that critical race theory incorporate more empirical social science. We do not think that there is an incompatibility between being critical and being empirical. Furthermore, we do not think that such an approach need supplant critical race theory's narrative approach. We do, however, think empirical social science can greatly enhance critical race theorists' arguments and advance critical race theory's goals. Thus, we hope critical race theorists take steps to indeed make critical race theory more systematic.

Part One

LEGAL ACTORS AND PARTICIPANTS

2

Stereotypes and Prejudice:
Helping Legal Decisionmakers Break the Prejudice Habit

Jody Armour

INTRODUCTION

A certain brand of judicial formalism promotes the very discrimination it purports to eliminate. Such self-defeating formalism typically takes the following form: A court forbids references during formal legal proceedings to a social characteristic such as race, gender, or sexual orientation, because that trait historically has been a basis for invidious discrimination. As a result, legal decisionmakers are less able to control their discriminatory responses than they would be if they confronted and dealt with their antagonism toward the characteristic in question. A dramatic cinematic depiction of this type of judicial formalism appears in several courtroom scenes in the movie *Philadelphia*. The

film—inspired by a true story—concerns a successful gay attorney, Andrew Beckett, who is wrongfully discharged by his law firm because of his sexual orientation. In the following scene, Beckett's attorney is cross-examining a firm employee who was involved in the conspiracy to discharge Beckett wrongfully:

PLAINTIFF'S ATTORNEY: Are you a homosexual?

WITNESS: What?

PLAINTIFF'S ATTORNEY: Are you a homosexual? Answer the question. Are you a homo? Are you a faggot? . . . fairy . . . booty snatcher . . . rump-roaster? Are you gay?

DEFENSE ATTORNEY: Where did this come from? [The witness's] sexual orientation has nothing to do with this case.

PLAINTIFF'S ATTORNEY: Your honor, everybody in this courtroom is thinking about sexual orientation, you know, sexual preference, whatever you want to call it. Who does what to whom, and how they do it. I

Editors' Note: This chapter is an abridged version of Jody Armour, *Stereotypes and Prejudice: Helping Legal Decision-makers Break the Prejudice Habit*, 83 CAL L. REV. 733 (1995), reprinted by permission of the California Law Review and the author.

mean, they're looking at Andrew Beckett [plaint.], they're thinking about it. They're looking at Mr. Wheeler [senior partner], Ms. Cornini [defense counsel], even you, your honor. They're wondering about it. I mean, hey, trust me, I know that they are looking at me and thinking about it. So let's just get it out in the open, let's, let's get it out of the closet, because this case is not just about AIDS, is it? So let's talk about what this case is really all about, the general public's hatred, our loathing, our fear of homosexuals, and how that climate of hatred and fear translated into the firing of this particular homosexual, my client, Andrew Beckett.

JUDGE: In this courtroom, justice is blind to matters of race, creed, color, religion, and sexual orientation.

PLAINTIFF'S ATTORNEY: With all due respect, your honor, we don't live in this courtroom though, do we?

JUDGE: No, we don't. However, as regards this witness, I'm going to sustain the defense's objection.

Unfortunately, the formalism exemplified by this fictional judge's reaction to references to sexual orientation reflects real life judicial resistance to attorneys' attempts to bring the issue of prejudice into the open at trial. For example, in *Jackson v. Chicago Transit Authority*, a black plaintiff brought a negligence action against a municipal corporation for personal injuries sustained when the bus he boarded collided with a truck.[1] During his closing argument, the plaintiff's counsel "alluded to the fact that his client was Negro, as contrasted to the jurors, the attorneys and the court itself, who were all Caucasians." The jury returned a verdict for the plaintiff, but the appellate court granted the defendants a new trial on the ground that such a racial reference "should not be made before any tribunal. It is an unmitigated appeal to prejudice and its effect could only be de-

structive of the proper administration of justice."

In characterizing the reference by the plaintiff's counsel to his client's racial identity as a case of playing to the prejudices of the jury, the *Jackson* court ignores a critical distinction between racial references that subvert the rationality of the fact-finding process and racial references that actually enhance the rationality and fairness of the fact-finding process. Worse still, this court's superficial analysis has gained legitimacy and wide currency through its use and endorsement by the authors of *The Torts Process*, a popular torts casebook.[2] Citing *Jackson* as authority, the casebook authors, James Henderson, Richard Pearson, and John Siliciano, assert that "a lawyer's effort to invoke jury sympathy for a client based on such characteristics (as race, nationality, or ethnic background) is as objectionable as an appeal to be unsympathetic to the other side for the same reason."[3] Henderson, Pearson, and Siliciano point to several professional responsibility standards that are relevant to determining whether the attorney in *Jackson* acted appropriately in adverting to his client's racial identity.

Despite Henderson, Pearson, Siliciano, and *Jackson*, however, attorneys frequently challenge fact finders explicitly to resist succumbing to bias in making judgments about members of stereotyped groups. For example, in the trial of those accused in the 1993 World Trade Center bombing case, defense attorney Austin Campriello asked the jury to avoid associating stereotypes of Arab and Muslim violence and terrorism with his client. And in a recent capital murder trial, defense attorney Paul Nugent urged the jury not to allow homophobia to distort their deliberations about his client's guilt or innocence. Thus we have a legal process issue that is neither pro-prosecution nor pro-defense: Do arguments based on race, sexual preference, or any other characteristic widely used to stereotype individuals necessarily "appeal to prejudice," or instead can some such arguments actually promote the rationality and fairness of the fact-finding process?

I argue that in many situations it may enhance the rationality of the decision-making process for attorneys explicitly to challenge fact finders to confront their biases against blacks and members of other stereotyped groups. In arguing that bias reduction among legal decisionmakers is feasible, I must frame a model of prejudice that goes beyond the "unconscious racism" model that informs much of the current legal analyses of prejudice. For although the unconscious racism model certainly does not endorse the kind of color-blind formalism espoused in *Jackson*, neither does it provide theoretical leverage for developing legal strategies aimed at helping decisionmakers to resist unconscious discrimination. Perhaps for this reason, commentators working within the unconscious racism framework have not developed proactive strategies for promoting bias reduction among white legal decisionmakers, but instead have focused on after-the-fact constitutional review of decisions by whites or on techniques to increase the number of black decisionmakers. Race shield laws (modeled after rape shield laws) have also been proposed to prevent the exploitation of racial imagery in criminal trials. Such proposals, however, still presuppose high baseline levels of prejudice in white jurors that racial imagery serves to exacerbate. There is little discussion of techniques for lowering the high baseline level of anti-black bias itself.

I contend that current legal commentators have not explored bias reduction strategies because they have not explored the utility of consciously endorsed, nonprejudiced beliefs in the fight against biased judgments by legal decisionmakers.

Current discussions of prejudice in the legal literature view people who report nonprejudiced personal beliefs as either hypocritical or self-deluded. The model of prejudice I will frame, however, posits that many people who report nonprejudiced personal beliefs actually do hold such beliefs. For many, these nonprejudiced personal standards are well internalized, and techniques that encourage people to activate their nonprejudiced beliefs are the key to reducing discriminatory social judgments about blacks and members of other stereotyped groups. Although I do not dispute the contention of many legal commentators that unconscious discrimination routinely distorts the judgments of legal decisionmakers (to the contrary, I discuss compelling empirical proof that unconscious discrimination frequently biases the social judgments of all Americans), I develop an empirically grounded framework for fashioning techniques that can help legal decisionmakers combat even their unconscious discriminatory tendencies. This framework focuses on the conscious and unconscious responses that Americans have to people from stereotyped groups and on the interplay between these two distinct kinds of responses. Specifically, I suggest ways of activating nonprejudiced beliefs in jury members to counteract their unconscious bias.

In [section] I, I analyze the claim by legal commentators that people who profess nonprejudiced personal beliefs are either hypocritical racists or unconscious racists. I argue that these rather pessimistic interpretations of contemporary racial attitudes result from a failure of commentators carefully to distinguish between two distinct sources of responses to blacks and other marginalized social groups—namely, stereotypes and personal beliefs. Conceptualizing stereotypes and personal beliefs as distinct sources of responses to blacks differs from the long-standing tradition of essentially equating the two; that is, a stereotype is often defined as "a set of beliefs about the personal attributes of a group of people."[4] Yet, drawing upon recent developments in social cognition, which adopts an information-processing model as a means of understanding social judgments, feelings, and behaviors, I argue that the distinction is important because the activation of stereotypes and personal beliefs is governed by different cognitive processes: automatic and controlled processes, respectively. Controlled processes are the key to escaping unconscious discrimination.

In [section] II, I elaborate a new model of unconscious discrimination rooted in compelling empirical research. This discussion considers the close relationship between stereotypes and automatic processes and shows how negative responses to members of stereotyped groups are essentially "bad habits," at least for people who hold nonprejudiced personal beliefs. In [section] III, I consider the potential for legal decisionmakers to control (at least temporarily) the discrimination habit by activating their nonprejudiced— or at least egalitarian—personal beliefs. I conclude that it is crucial for courts to distinguish between rationality-enhancing and rationality-subverting uses of racial references to prevent color-blind formalism from promoting discrimination by fact finders against litigants from stereotyped groups.

I. HYPOCRITICAL RACISTS AND AVERSIVE RACISTS

Ethnic attitudes are a part of the social heritage of the developing child. They are transmitted across generations as a component of the accumulated knowledge of society. No person can grow up in a society without learning the prevailing attitudes concerning the major ethnic groups. In fact, given the polarization of ethnic atti-

tudes, we ought to consider the question of how some people escape being prejudiced.[5]

This suggestion that some people in our society escape prejudice conflicts with many current discussions of prejudice in the legal literature. Many legal commentators view prejudice as an inevitable outgrowth of our cultural belief system. For example, in an often-quoted passage from his seminal article, "The Id, the Ego, and Equal Protection: Reckoning with Unconscious Racism," Professor Charles Lawrence III states:

> Americans share a common historical and cultural heritage in which racism has played and still plays a dominant role. Because of this shared experience, we also inevitably share many ideas, attitudes, and beliefs that attach significance to an individual's race and induce negative feelings and opinions about nonwhites. To the extent that this cultural belief system has influenced all of us, we are all racists.[6]

This view of prejudice as inevitable and ubiquitous, however, does not square with the survey literature on racial attitudes indicating that prejudice has been declining steadily over the past forty years. Citing a series of reports on attitudes of white Americans toward black Americans appearing in *Scientific American* between 1956 and 1978, Charles E. Case and Andrew M. Greeley conclude that "there has been a continuous increase in the percent of whites who favor equal treatment for blacks in all areas of American society" since 1942.[7] Furthermore, responding to commentaries suggesting a resurgence of racism in the late 1980s, Charlotte Steeh and Howard Schuman reviewed surveys conducted between 1984 and 1990 on young white adults and concluded that the survey data show that there is "no widespread, systematic decline in liberal racial attitudes among those people entering adulthood from 1960 to 1990."[8]

Legal commentators have reconciled reports indicating diminishing prejudice with the claim that prejudice remains ubiquitous by attacking the validity of the self-evaluations that form the basis of these reports. Specifically, commentators in effect characterize people who report nonprejudiced personal beliefs as either hypocritical, sub rosa racists or unconscious, aversive racists. I will first consider the hypocrisy reading of the survey literature and argue that this rather pessimistic interpretation of the surveys results from a failure to carefully distinguish between stereotypes and prejudice. The distinction between responses based on stereotypes and responses based on prejudiced personal beliefs provides a crucial theoretical tool for understanding how jurors' discriminatory responses to blacks and members of other marginalized groups may be overcome. I will then turn to the aversive racism interpretation of the surveys, examine empirical and conceptual shortcomings of this model of prejudice, and suggest how the dissociation of stereotypes and prejudice helps in the resolution of these shortcomings and in the development of prejudice reduction strategies.

A. Hypocritical Racists

In "Black Innocence and the White Jury," Professor Sheri Lynn Johnson offers the hypocrisy interpretation of self-evaluation prejudice reports.[9] According to Johnson, "any encouragement that might be drawn from the initial decrease in extreme negative stereotypes must be qualified by the likelihood that newer data reflect some fading of stereotypes—but also some faking."[10] From this viewpoint, prejudice has not decreased nearly as much as it seems; it just has become less socially acceptable. Thus, merely to appear socially desirable, many survey respondents profess racial liberalism. Although Johnson does not give a concrete estimate of how much "faking" the newer data reflect, she does suggest that "it now may be quite common to underreport prejudiced attitudes" by faking racial tolerance.[11]

To support this interpretation of the survey literature, Johnson points to the findings of an experiment in which white subjects were asked to report their responses to blacks under a normal (control) condition and under a "bogus pipeline" condition. In the pipeline condition, a researcher wires his subjects to a machine that the subjects believe will give him an accurate physiological measure of (i.e., a pipeline to) their automatic or "covert" reactions.[12] The researchers then asked these subjects to estimate what the machine was telling the experimenter about their uncontrolled responses to blacks, as the experimenter asked them to rate blacks on various personality traits, such as ignorance, stupidity, honesty, and sensitivity. Researchers assumed that these estimations would correspond to the subjects' "honest" beliefs about blacks. Subjects' estimates of their uncontrolled responses to blacks in the pipeline condition were significantly more negative than the responses to blacks reported by subjects who did not believe that their uncontrolled responses were being monitored.

Johnson characterizes these automatic, uncontrolled physiological responses in this experiment as the subjects' "true feelings"[13] and "pure" attitudes.[14] She interprets these findings as proof of prejudice's persistence notwithstanding survey data to the contrary. This interpretation, however, rests on a failure to distinguish between two distinct sources of negative responses to blacks (and other marginalized social groups)—namely, stereotypes and prejudice. Once this critical distinction is understood, it becomes evident that the bogus pipeline results prove only the persistence of stereotypes, not prejudice, and therefore are perfectly consistent with the proposition that prejudice has decreased significantly over the last forty years.

Stereotypes consist of well-learned sets of associations among groups and traits established in children's memories at an early age, before they have the cognitive skills to decide rationally upon the personal acceptability of the stereotypes.[15] For example, Phyllis Katz reports a chilling case of a three-year-old child who, upon seeing a black infant, said to her mother, "Look mom, a baby maid."[16] By the time the child turned three, before she had developed the cognitive ability to judge the appropriateness of the stereotypic ascription, the associational link between black women and certain social roles was already forged in her memory.

In contrast, prejudice consists of derogatory personal beliefs. As Anthony R. Pratkanis points out, beliefs are propositions that people endorse and accept as being true.[17] Thus, prejudiced personal beliefs are the "endorsement or acceptance of the content of a negative cultural stereotype."[18] That a person has a negative stereotype established in her memory does not necessarily mean that she endorses that stereotype. As [Patricia G.] Devine points out, "[A]lthough one may have knowledge of a stereotype, his or her personal beliefs may or may not be congruent with the stereotype."[19] For example, if the three-year-old child described above grows up and decides that the stereotype of a maid is an inappropriate basis for responding to black women, she may experience a fundamental conflict between the previously established stereotype and the more recently established nonprejudiced personal belief. In such a case, her responses to black women and to blacks generally will turn on whether those responses are based on the well-established stereotype or her more recently adopted nonprejudiced beliefs.

Of course, some people's stereotypes and personal beliefs overlap; that is, some people not only have knowledge of the cultural stereotypes from years of socialization but endorse and accept them as well. Research literature classifies these individuals as high-prejudiced.[20] However, many people have thought about the cultural stereotypes, recognized them as inappropriate bases for responding to others, and deliberately rejected them. Researchers refer to these individuals as low-prejudiced. Although high- and low-prejudiced persons differ in their personal beliefs about blacks, common socialization experiences have firmly entrenched the cultural stereotype of blacks in the memories of both.

The failure to distinguish between stereotypes and prejudiced personal beliefs leads Johnson and other commentators to take an all-or-nothing approach to prejudice: if a person experiences any stereotype-congruent responses in any situation, she is prejudiced. This view fails to recognize that a change in a person's beliefs does not instantly extinguish habitual responses derived from well-learned stereotypes. Because stereotypes are established in children's memories at an early age and constantly reinforced through the mass media and other socializing agents, stereotype-congruent responses may persist long after a person has sincerely renounced prejudice. As Devine and colleagues point out, non-prejudiced beliefs and stereotype-congruent thoughts and feelings may coexist within the same individual. Dr. Thomas Pettigrew, a leading authority on stereotypes and prejudice, has described one example of this conflict: "Many Southerners have confessed to me . . . that even though in their minds they no longer feel prejudice against blacks, they still feel squeamish when they shake hands with a black. The feelings are left over from what they learned in their families as children."[21]

There is strong empirical evidence that

the vast majority of low-prejudiced people realize that they are prone to stereotype-congruent responses, that is, that their actual reactions to out-group members sometime conflict with their personal standards for how they should respond. In one recent study, researchers gave a sample of several hundred white subjects (college students, very few of whom were high-prejudiced) a questionnaire, the first section of which asked them to report their personal standards for how they should respond in five different situations involving black people.[22] For example, one situation read as follows: "Imagine that a Black person boarded a bus and sat next to you. You should feel uncomfortable that a Black is sitting next to you."

The subjects were asked to circle the number between 1 (strongly disagree) and 7 (strongly agree) that best reflected their personal standard for how they should respond in each situation. The second section of the questionnaire asked the subjects to report on the 1-to-7 scale how they believed they actually "would" respond in the same five situations. Out of the 101 cases, 71 percent of the subjects reported actual "would" responses that were more negative than their "should" responses, which reflected their personal standards for how they should respond. Separate studies found similar should-would discrepancies in responses to homosexual men. These studies also investigated whether the subjects' personal standards (shoulds) were well internalized (i.e., viewed by the subjects as highly important and as central to their personal identity or merely derived from society's standards). Researchers found that low-prejudiced subjects strongly internalized their personal standards, and that these subjects felt compunction (guilt and self-criticism) when they transgressed the standards.

These findings, which several later studies have replicated,[23] suggest a less

pessimistic interpretation of the bogus pipeline results than Johnson adopts. That a subject reports more negative responses about blacks when he believes an experimenter can monitor his autonomic nervous system (or what Johnson refers to as his "true attitudes") does not prove that he is truly prejudiced or that he is faking his more positive responses on questionnaires. It may show only that he realizes, as most low-prejudiced people do, that he is prone to stereotype-congruent responses. Although he may not endorse these responses and may feel compunction about experiencing them, he may believe that the pipeline will detect their presence. In other situations, however, such as responding to a questionnaire, the low-prejudiced person may inhibit his stereotype-congruent responses and replace them with responses based on his nonprejudiced personal standards. A model of prejudice that recognizes the distinction between stereotypes and prejudiced personal beliefs—a model I shall call the "dissociation model"—points to the possibility of inhibiting and replacing stereotype-congruent responses with nonprejudiced responses derived from nonprejudiced personal beliefs. If nonprejudiced personal beliefs can counteract stereotypes in this way, perhaps there is hope for combatting the influence of ubiquitous derogatory stereotypes.

Studies support the proposition that responses derived from nonprejudiced personal beliefs can inhibit and replace responses derived from stereotypes. Research has demonstrated that low- and high-prejudiced people are equally prone to stereotype-congruent responses when they cannot consciously monitor their responses to questions. However, low- and high-prejudiced people have given very different responses when they have had to think consciously about what their responses imply about their self-image. For example, one study asked subjects to list all of their own thoughts (e.g., beliefs, feelings, expectations) about blacks under strictly anonymous conditions, thus eliminating any reason to manufacture "correct" responses.[24] Researchers found that the high-prejudiced subjects listed primarily negative stereotypical thoughts about blacks and were inclined to stereotype. In contrast, the low-prejudiced subjects wrote few pejorative thoughts; they reported beliefs that contradicted the stereotype and emphasized the importance of racial equality. These results make intuitive sense. For low-prejudiced people, writing stereotype-congruent thoughts would contradict their personal beliefs and threaten their nonprejudiced identity. But because beliefs of high-prejudiced people overlap with stereotypes, conscious reflection should not inhibit their stereotype-congruent responses. Thus, if personal beliefs really matter, if low-prejudiced subjects can counteract the stereotype-congruent responses to which research shows high- and low-prejudiced people are equally prone, then the thoughts that those subjects anonymously list about blacks should be very different from the thoughts anonymously listed by high-prejudiced subjects.

The findings of this thought-listing study, which are strongly confirmed and extended by other research that I discuss below, reveal that much more than semantics is at stake in the distinction between stereotypes and prejudice. Inasmuch as negative stereotypes and personal beliefs diverge, as they do in low-prejudiced people, they imply different responses to stereotyped groups. This insight enables us to investigate the interplay between the two conceptually distinct sets of responses and to develop strategies for activating the responses based on nonprejudiced personal beliefs and inhibiting the stereotype-congruent responses. However, before elaborating a framework for working out the full implications of the interplay between stereotypes and nonprejudiced personal beliefs, I will consider the other major attack on the validity and efficacy of nonprejudiced personal beliefs: aversive racism.

B. Aversive Racists

The dominant model of prejudice in current legal literature is the theory of aversive racism. Whereas the hypocritical racist model posits that people who express nonprejudiced personal beliefs are manipulating their self-presentation to appear more socially desirable, the aversive racist model holds that ostensibly nonprejudiced people are not so much deceiving others as fooling themselves. The two models are not mutually exclusive but complementary. Commentators freely switch from one to the other by dismissing the validity of people's racially liberal self-descriptions and nonprejudiced personal beliefs.

The theory of aversive racism begins with the proposition that most Americans are highly committed to egalitarian values. Therefore, they desire to maintain an egalitarian, nonprejudiced self-image. This desire causes them to express nonprejudiced personal beliefs.[25] Such professed nonprejudiced beliefs are not to be confused with genuine—that is, well-internalized—nonprejudiced beliefs, for deep down "aversive racist[s] believe[ ] in white superiority"[26] and "do not want to associate with blacks."[27] Desperately clinging to their egalitarian, nonprejudiced values and self-image, aversive racists repress their negative feelings and beliefs about blacks. Lawrence refers to these repressed anti-black beliefs as "hidden prejudice"[28] and offers a Freudian theory of unconscious motivation to explain how "we all harbor prejudiced attitudes that are kept from our consciousness."[29]

Moreover, since aversive racists do not recognize their anti-black attitudes, the prospects for prejudice reduction are particularly dim. Here the pessimism of the aversive racism model asserts itself. Writing from this perspective, Professor Peggy Davis observes, "It is difficult to change an attitude that is unacknowledged. Thus, 'like a virus that mutates into new forms, old-fashioned prejudice seems to have evolved into a new type that is, at least temporarily, resistant to traditional . . . remedies.'"[30]

Commentators contend that proof of aversive racism lies in the discrepancy between responses to blacks that are consciously monitored and those that are not consciously monitored. Whenever aversive racists consciously monitor their responses to blacks, they do not discriminate against them since discrimination would undermine their egalitarian self-images. For example, verbal responses to questionnaires designed to measure racial prejudice can be monitored consciously by the respondents and therefore cannot identify aversive racists. More generally, if the situation clearly calls for a nonprejudiced response, or if a nonracial justification or rationalization for engaging in a prejudiced response cannot be generated, the response will be positive because it cannot escape being consciously monitored.

In contrast, when the situation is normatively ambiguous, or when a non-race-related justification is handy, the covert anti-black attitudes and beliefs of aversive racists find expression in racial discrimination. For example, white research subjects led to believe that a person was in distress helped black victims as often as white victims when there was no ostensible justification for a failure to help.[31] However, if the subjects knew that someone else was available to help, they "helped black victims much less frequently than they helped white victims (38% vs. 75%)."[32] Ac-

cording to proponents of the aversive racism model, the availability of other potential rescuers provided subjects with a convenient nonracial excuse for not helping the black victims. This interpretation of the helping behavior study carries very discouraging implications for racially fair dispute resolution, for in formal legal proceedings, finding a nonracial reason to discriminate against a black litigant is especially easy to do—one simply gives more weight to the evidence favoring the opposing litigant.

The aversive racism model, however, is empirically and conceptually incomplete. One empirical problem with the model concerns its assumption that aversive racists—who, according to commentators, now include most Americans—are not aware of their conflicting reactions to blacks; their anti-black thoughts and feelings are supposedly excluded from consciousness. If this assumption were accurate, most survey respondents would not report discrepancies between their standards for how they should respond to blacks and how they actually would respond, since they are unaware. Yet the vast majority of subjects in several studies recognized and acknowledged that they sometimes experience such discrepancies. Thus, although the aversive racism framework may describe some white Americans, it almost certainly does not account for most.

Another empirical problem with the aversive racism theory concerns the Freudian theory of unconscious motivation to which it is often wedded. As Lawrence frankly admits, psychoanalytic theory presents real difficulties for empirical verification. A model, such as aversive racism, whose theoretical underpinnings are not empirically demonstrable demands an intellectual leap of faith that many may be unwilling to make. Alternatively, commentators have attempted to explain aversive racism by drawing on research in cognitive psychology. Although this research, unlike Freudian psychoanalysis, provides a rich lode of empirical findings on the inherent tendency of the human mind to prejudge and overgeneralize (a lode I mine actively in [section] II of this article), commentators writing from this perspective never adequately explain how the prejudgments and overgeneralizations resulting from this tendency escape a person's awareness. On the contrary, commentators suggest that we are aware of the resulting stereotypes, but that we experience them as rational reflections of objective reality rather than as figments of our distorted cognitive processes. Thus, neither the Freudian [perspective] nor the cognitive framework gives an empirically grounded account of how fact finders could fall into negative responses to blacks and members of other stereotyped groups without being aware of those responses as they are occurring. To convince courts to factor psychological propositions about unconscious discrimination into their formulation and application of legal rules, it is important to frame a model of such discrimination that is firmly rooted in empirical research.

The conceptual problem with the prevailing aversive racism model concerns its tendency to conflate stereotype and prejudice. Recall Lawrence's often quoted assertion that "[t]o the extent that this cultural belief system has influenced all of us, we are all racists." Since ethnic attitudes and stereotypes are part of a society's social heritage and no one can escape learning the prevailing attitudes and stereotypes assigned to the major ethnic groups, Lawrence's position states that we are all racists. Lawrence does not, however, explore the implications of the fact that people do not always endorse the knowledge structures that socialization has established in their memories. For example, although socializing forces un-

doubtedly have entrenched the cultural stereotype of women in the memory of feminists as well as every other American, feminists could be called sexists only in a Pickwickian sense. One reason it seems so anomalous to apply the value-laden term *sexist* to feminists is because feminists have both renounced the cultural stereotype about women and developed egalitarian personal beliefs about women. Thus, feminists have two distinct and conflicting cognitive structures concerning women: the cultural stereotype and their egalitarian personal beliefs. Similarly, low-prejudiced people have two conflicting cognitive structures concerning blacks: the black cultural stereotype and their non-prejudiced personal beliefs. Calling feminists "sexists" and low-prejudiced persons "racists" identifies them more with the well-learned cultural stereotype than with their personal beliefs, and implies that the stereotype is somehow the more compelling of the two knowledge structures.

Instead of debating which cognitive structure—stereotypes or nonprejudiced personal beliefs—is the defining feature of a low-prejudiced person's mental processes, or which is the more important determinant of her responses to members of stereotyped groups, I argue that both types of responses occur and that both can influence decisionmakers' behavior. In developing this analysis, I draw extensively on recent research in social cognition, a defining characteristic of which is its emphasis on the type of social information that is stored in memory. Following Devine and colleagues, I argue that stereotypes and personal beliefs (or attitudes) represent conceptually distinct and potentially conflicting subsets of information about ethnic or racial groups, and that a different cognitive process governs each distinct subset of information. Further, understanding the interplay between these different types of information and processes both accounts for unconscious discrimination and suggests strategies for combatting it. Perhaps most importantly, I will try to ground each step of my analysis of unconscious discrimination and discrimination reduction techniques in empirically demonstrated propositions. Thus, I hope to lay down a solid empirical foundation for the claim that unconscious discrimination routinely infects legal decisionmaking, without ignoring the utility of nonprejudiced personal standards in the fight against such discrimination.

II. AN EMPIRICALLY DEMONSTRABLE MODEL OF UNCONSCIOUS DISCRIMINATION

[G]iven a sensory input with equally good fit to two nonoverlapping categories, the more accessible of the two categories would "capture" the input.[33]

It is widely believed that our judgments and memories of others turn on whatever information about them has been made available to us. But if information alone were sufficient to determine our social judgments, then reasonable people who are exposed to the same information about someone should form the same judgments. Yet people often form different judgments and recollect different facts, even when exposed to the same information. Thus, in addition to information from the environmental and social context, the perceiver's cognitive structures and processes must also determine his or her social judgments. The following question therefore arises: What are these processes, and what implications do they carry for social judgments of blacks and other stereotyped groups?

Following Jerome Bruner, social cognition researchers conceptualize the process that underlies the perception of persons as a categorization process. In Lawrence's apt summary of this perspective, "[a]ll humans tend to categorize in order to make sense of experience. Too many events occur daily for us to deal successfully with each one on an individual basis; we must categorize in order to cope."[34] Thus, a person who is asked to judge another's behavior must first take whatever information she receives about the other's behavior and interpret, or encode, this behavior by assigning it to a category. According to social psychologists E. Tory Higgins and Gillian King, social and personal categories include information about social groups (e.g., blacks, women, gays and lesbians), social roles and occupations (e.g., spouses, maids, police officers), traits and behaviors (e.g., hostile, crime-prone, patriotic, intelligent), and social types (e.g., intellectual, social activists, rednecks).[35] Once the behavior is assigned to one of these categories, it is stored in memory, from which it subsequently can be retrieved to make further inferences and predictions about the person.

When individuals must judge another's behavior, however, they are unlikely to perform an exhaustive search of memory for all potentially relevant categories, compare the behavior to each such category, and then characterize the behavior in terms of the category with the best "fit." Rather, they are likely to base their judgment on the category that happens to be the most readily accessible at the time the information is received. Steven L. Neuberg explains this phenomenon with the following example:

[J]ust after viewing an extremely violent film in which a heartless mugger preys upon innocent travelers of the city streets, a moviegoer would have a greater than usual tendency to perceive the behavior of a stranger who bumps into him or her as reflecting hostility or aggressiveness. Alternatively, after viewing a comedy featuring the inept Inspector Clouseau, the moviegoer might be more likely to perceive the identical social interaction in terms of the stranger's clumsiness. In each example, the film preceding the interaction "primed" particular cognitive categories that subsequently influenced the interpretation of the incident.[36]

Numerous studies confirm this intuitive account of the centrality of category accessibility in social perceptions and judgments. In one classic study, E. Tory Higgins, William E. Rholes, and Carl R. Jones posited that unobtrusively exposing subjects to certain personality trait terms in one exercise would activate, or prime, the categories to which these terms referred, making it more likely the subjects would use the categories to characterize a person in an unrelated context.[37] To test this hypothesis, Higgins, Rholes, and Jones asked subjects to perform a complex cognitive task that momentarily exposed them to several trait terms. Later, in what ostensibly was an unrelated experiment on reading comprehension, the subjects read a paragraph about a target person, which was ambiguous as to his likability. After reading the passage, subjects characterized the target person in their own words. As predicted, subjects unobtrusively exposed to favorable trait terms tended to use those terms or their synonyms in characterizing the target, while subjects exposed to unfavorable terms tended to use those terms or their synonyms in their characterizations. In contrast, control subjects that researchers exposed to trait terms that were not applicable to interpreting the target's behavior did not vary systematically in their characterizations.

These results carry enormous implications for judgments and evaluations of stereotyped groups. If cues of group membership such as race serve to prime trait categories such as hostility, people will systematically view behaviors by members of certain racial groups (e.g., blacks) as more

menacing than the same behaviors by members of other racial groups (e.g., whites).

Birt L. Duncan's research provides background for understanding these implications. Duncan found that whites interpreted the same ambiguous shove as hostile or violent when the actor was black and as "playing around" or "dramatizing" when the actor was white.[38] He assumed that category accessibility best explains this differential perception of violence as a function of the protagonist's race. Duncan assumed that the presence of the black actor primed the stereotype of blacks, and since the stereotype associates blacks with violence, the violent behavior category was more accessible when interpreting behavioral information about blacks than whites. [H. Andrew] Sager and [Janet Ward] Schofield replicated Duncan's findings in studies of schoolchildren.[39] They found that both black and white children rated ambiguously aggressive behaviors (e.g., bumping in the hallway) of black actors as being more mean or threatening than the same behaviors of white actors.

Although Duncan's study provides compelling evidence that race influences category accessibility, it does not determine whether the influence is unconscious or conscious. It is possible that upon noticing the racial identity of the black protagonist, the subjects (or some percentage of them) formed a conscious expectation for instances of trait categories stereotypically associated with blacks (e.g., hostile, prone to violence). Indeed, research indicates that expecting to see an instance of a trait category increases the likelihood that a person will process ambiguous information by putting it into that category.

On the other hand, Duncan's subjects (or some percentage of them) could have been sincerely nonprejudiced and refrained from consciously forming any race-based expectation of hostility, yet the mere presence of the black protagonist may have automatically (i.e., unconsciously) activated the black stereotype, including the hostility trait category that figures so prominently in that stereotype. Thus, the subjects could have sincerely renounced racial prejudice and still unconsciously practiced discrimination against the black actor. To understand how a knowledge structure such as a stereotype can operate outside a person's awareness and determine his or her responses to others, it is necessary to understand the distinction between habits and decisions, a distinction cognitive psychologists characterize in terms of automatic versus controlled processes. Since this distinction also sheds light on the interplay of stereotypes and personal beliefs in responses to members of stereotyped groups, and ultimately points to strategies for discrimination reduction, I will discuss it in detail.

A habit is "an action that has been done many times and has become automatic. That is, it is done without conscious thought."[40] In contrast, a decision to take or not to take an action involves conscious thought. The distinction between habit and conscious decision is one of the oldest concepts in psychology. In his *Principles of Psychology*, William James described the origins and consequences of habit as follows:

> [A]ny sequence of mental action which has been frequently repeated tends to perpetuate itself; so that we find ourselves automatically prompted to think, feel, or do what we have been before accustomed to think, feel, or do, under like circumstances, without any consciously formed purpose, or anticipation of results.[41]

James concluded that it is necessary to free limited consciousness from the many mundane requirements of life by removing frequently used or habitual mental sequences from conscious awareness.

The current model of habits and decisions employed by cognitive psychologists is not appreciably different from that outlined by James over a century ago, except that the current model expresses the distinction in terms of automatic versus controlled processes. According to D.L. Ronis and colleagues, "[h]abits are the results of automatic cognitive processes."[42] As Patricia G. Devine points out, "[a]utomatic processes involve the unintentional or spontaneous activation of some well-learned set of associations or responses that have been developed through repeated activation in memory."[43] Controlled processes, on the other hand, "are intentional and require the active attention of the individual."[44] Learning to drive a car provides a useful illustration of this distinction. When you first get behind the wheel, virtually every maneuver is a controlled response. Deciding when and how to apply your foot to the pedals as you turn the steering wheel or manually shift gears demands concentration and effort. After enough practice, however, these maneuvers become automatic. You can accelerate, brake, and steer while contemplating health care reform or talking to a traveling companion. The well-learned motor responses occur without conscious effort.

A critical characteristic of habits or automatic processes is that they can operate independently of conscious decisions to break with old patterns of responses and adopt new ones. Thus, attitudes and beliefs can change without a corresponding change in established habits, resulting in a conflict between currently endorsed responses and old habitual responses. Anyone who has ever tried to break a bad habit knows the persistence of habitual responses in the face of decisions to adopt new ones.

Applied to the relationship between stereotypes and personal beliefs, the habit-decision/automatic-controlled processes distinction provides critical theoretical support for understanding the more and less conscious aspects of responses to blacks (and members of other stereotyped groups). As discussed earlier, the black stereotype is established in children's memories before children develop the cognitive ability to critically evaluate and decide on the stereotype's acceptability. Further, the social environment, including the mass media, incessantly reactivates this stereotype. Thus, the stereotype is an ingrained set of associations (i.e., a habit) that involves automatic processes. Nonprejudiced personal beliefs, on the other hand, are necessarily newer cognitive structures that result from a low-prejudiced person's conscious decision that stereotype-based responses to blacks are unacceptable.

It follows that these decisions to renounce the already established stereotype do not come to mind (i.e., are not reactivated) nearly as frequently as the social environment automatically activates the stereotype. Because the stereotype has a longer history and greater frequency of activation than the more recently acquired personal beliefs, even people with well-internalized nonprejudiced beliefs are likely to experience a fundamental conflict between the stereotype and their personal beliefs. The discrepancies that most low-prejudiced subjects report between how they believe they should respond and how they actually would respond in contact situations with blacks (as well as gays) reflect this conflict. That these subjects also report feeling compunction (i.e., guilt and self-criticism) as a result of these discrepancies implies that they regard the stereotype-congruent responses as essentially a bad habit.

This analysis assumes that just as habitual responses (like putting on a seat belt) may be triggered automatically by the presence of relevant environmental cues (like sitting in a car), stereotype-congruent responses may be triggered automatically by a group membership cue such as a person's racial identity (or its symbolic equivalent). This means that for a person who rejects the stereotype to avoid stereotype-congruent responses to blacks (i.e., to avoid falling into a bad habit), she must intentionally inhibit the automatically activated stereotype and activate her newer personal belief structure. As Devine points out, "[S]uch inhibition and initiation of new responses involves controlled processes."[45] That is, "nonprejudiced responses take intention, attention, and effort."[46]

A particularly illuminating implication of this model is that unless a low-prejudiced person consciously monitors and inhibits the activation of a stereotype in the presence of a member (or symbolic equivalent) of a stereotyped group, she may unintentionally fall into the discrimination habit. For example, the whites in Duncan's study who interpreted the same ambiguous shove as hostile when the actor was black and as innocuous when the actor was white could have had well-internalized nonprejudiced beliefs. However, they may not have consciously monitored the automatic activation of the black stereotype. Because blacks are stereotypically viewed as hostile, activation of the stereotype would have primed the hostility category, making it more accessible for social judgments about the black actor. Since the black stereotype is automatically activated, it could have biased subjects' judgment of the black actor unconsciously.

One strength of this model, then, is that it explains how even people with well-internalized nonprejudiced standards are capable of unconscious discrimination against blacks. Patricia Devine designed an experiment whose results provide empirical support for this model. This research examined how automatic processes affected responses to members of a stereotyped group. The experiment involved presenting stereotype-related information to people below their perceptual threshold, so that subjects could not consciously process the information. Thus, any effects of such subliminally presented information on subsequent social judgments would necessarily result from automatic processes. As discussed below, Devine found that the effects of automatic stereotype activation are equally strong and inescapable for high- and low-prejudiced subjects.

In Devine's study, both high- and low-prejudiced subjects performed a task that exposed them to either a low concentration (20 percent of a 100-word list) or a high concentration (80 percent of a 100-word list) of black stereotype labels (e.g., afro, lazy, musical, athletic, poor, etc.) in a manner determined to be effectively outside their conscious awareness. For example, to prevent subjects from having conscious access to the labels, the labels were presented very rapidly (within a time frame of 80 milliseconds) and were followed immediately by a mask (i.e., a series of jumbled letters). None of these labels, or "primes," was related to hostility. In an ostensibly unrelated second experiment, subjects read a behavioral description of a person named Donald, whose race was not specified, and who was engaging in a series of ambiguously hostile behaviors. For example, Donald demands his money back from a store clerk immediately after a purchase and refuses to pay his rent until his apartment is repainted. Devine found that both high- and low-prejudiced subjects' ratings of the target's hostility were significantly higher (i.e., indicated more hostility) when subliminally exposed to a high, rather than low, concentration of black-stereotype labels.

These findings demonstrate that well-learned sets of associations such as stereotypes can be activated automatically in perceivers' memories and can affect subsequent social judgments. The effects of automatic stereotype priming on subjects' evaluation of the target person's hostility are especially revealing in Devine's experiment because no hostility-related traits were used as primes. Thus, it seems that the black stereotype must be constructed cognitively in such a way that activating one component of the stereotype simultaneously primes or activates the remaining closely associated components as well. These findings also suggest that even low-prejudiced subjects who have well-internalized nonprejudiced beliefs about blacks have cognitive structures (i.e., stereotypes) that automatically produce stereotype-congruent evaluations of ambiguous behaviors when subjects cannot monitor stereotype activation consciously.

In this sense, Lawrence and other commentators are correct in pointing out that we are all prone to stereotype-congruent or prejudice-like responses to blacks and other stereotyped groups. However, the research demonstrating disassociation of stereotypes and personal beliefs in low-prejudiced people argues against the conclusion that we are all racists. Instead, I suggest that it is more accurate and useful to say that we are all creatures of habit.

III. COMBATTING UNCONSCIOUS DISCRIMINATION IN THE COURTROOM

Perhaps the most important strength of the dissociation model of automatic and controlled processes I have outlined is that it suggests a strategy for resisting unconscious discrimination. Thus far, the model has focused on how people who are firmly committed to their low-prejudiced beliefs remain prone to automatic activation of stereotypes. According to the model, for such individuals to resist falling into the discrimination habit, they repeatedly recall their personal beliefs so that their social judgments become based on these beliefs rather than the stereotypes. Reminding decisionmakers of their personal beliefs, therefore, may help them to resist falling unconsciously into the discrimination habit. This section describes evidence that this approach can be effective.

A. Empirical Support for the Strategy

The range of discrimination-reduction strategies that courts will countenance and lawyers will employ may turn significantly on which model of prejudice they adopt. Whereas the unconscious-racism model fails to explore the utility of conscious processes and nonprejudiced beliefs in the fight against racial discrimination, the present model views such processes and beliefs as valuable weapons in the fight against discrimination.

There is considerable empirical evidence supporting the dissociation model's assumption that responses based on automatic processes can be inhibited and replaced by responses based on controlled processes. Focusing on the effect of gender stereotypes on memory, for example, Higgins and King demonstrated that when gender was not brought situationally to subjects' attention, or made "salient," subjects' descriptions of self and others reflected more traditional views of gender-linked attributes. Higgins and King have suggested that under such conditions, traditional gender stereotypes, with their longer history and greater frequency of activation, are activated automatically and influence recall. When gender was brought to the subjects' attention or made salient, however, they apparently inhibited the traditional stereotype, and descriptions were more consistent with their more recently developed, modern views of gender-linked attributes. In other words, when the subjects were reminded of gender, they checked their stereotype-

congruent responses more assiduously than when gender was less salient.

This dissociation model is also consistent with the findings, described earlier, concerning the proclivity of white rescuers to help white but not black victims in distress. Recall that white research subjects led to believe that a person was in distress helped black victims as often as white victims when there was no ostensible justification for a failure to help. On the other hand, if the subjects knew of the availability of another who might help, they "helped black victims much less frequently than they helped white victims."[47] According to the dissociation model, when the subjects believed they were the only potential rescuer, they were required consciously to think about what their responses to the black victim's call of distress implied about their nonprejudiced self-conceptions. When the conflict between their nonprejudiced personal beliefs and the stereotype of blacks is made salient in this way, the dissociation model predicts that low-prejudiced persons are likely to resolve the conflict by inhibiting their prejudice-like responses and reaffirming their nonprejudiced self-conceptions. On the other hand, when the subjects believed that there were others who might help, the conflict between stereotype and personal belief was less salient and the low-prejudiced subjects were therefore less likely to monitor and inhibit responses based on the negative black stereotype.

B. A Narrative of Hope

"YOU'RE ALL PREJUDICED" DARROW TELLS JURY [headline, *Detroit Free Press*, May 12, 1926].[48]

Clarence Darrow, one of the most famous lawyers in American history, directly challenged jurors to confront their own prejudices in a dramatic murder trial early in this century. The case involved a black family who moved into a middle-class white Detroit neighborhood in 1925. When Dr. Ossian Sweet and his wife moved into the neighborhood with their baby daughter, they knew other blacks who had bought homes in white neighborhoods had been forced to move by "improvement associations." Accordingly, Dr. Sweet brought along his brothers, several friends, and an ample supply of guns and ammunition. Two nights after his arrival, a large white crowd, estimated at several hundred, gathered around the house and began throwing stones at the house amid cries of "niggers." Although police officers were present to maintain order, they stood idly by as the barrage of rocks increased. Seeing a big stone crash through an upstairs window and the crowd make a sudden movement, both Sweet and his younger brother fired a warning shot over the heads of the boisterous mob. One of the mob's members was killed.

Everyone in the house was arrested and charged with murder. The NAACP asked Darrow to come out of retirement to defend the Sweets. Darrow agreed. In his summation to the jury, Darrow challenged them to confront their own racial biases directly:

> I haven't any doubt but that every one of you is prejudiced against colored people. I want you to guard against it. I want you to do all you can to be fair in this case, and I believe you will. . . .
>
> . . .
>
> You need not tell me you are not prejudiced. I know better. We are not very much but a bundle of prejudices anyhow. We are prejudiced against other people's color. Prejudiced against other men's religions; prejudiced against other people's politics. Prejudiced against people's looks. Prejudiced about the way they dress. We are full of prejudices. . .
>
> . . .
>
> . . . Here were eleven colored men, penned up in the house. Put yourselves in

their place. Make yourselves colored for a little while. It won't hurt, you can wash it off. They can't, but you can; just make yourself black for a little while; long enough, gentlemen, to judge them, and before any of you would want to be judged, you would want your juror to put himself in your place. That is all I ask in this case, gentlemen. They were black, and they knew the history of the black. . .

> . . .
>
> . . . Supposing you had your choice, right here this minute, would you rather lose your eyesight or become colored? Would you rather lose your hearing or be a Negro? Would you rather go out there on the street and have your leg cut off by a streetcar, or have a black skin? . . .
>
> . . . Life is a hard game anyhow. But, when the cards are stacked against you, it is terribly hard. And they are stacked against a race for no reason but that they are black.[49]

The jury returned a not-guilty verdict for Dr. Sweet, and the prosecution decided not to proceed further against any of the remaining defendants.

Dr. Sweet's case provides a compelling narrative of hope and redemption that stands in marked contrast to the pessimism of many current discussions of prejudice in the courtroom. Clarence Darrow, in the heyday of Jim Crow, successfully urged a jury of white males to resist succumbing to their discriminatory impulses in judging the reasonableness of a black man's use of lethal force against a white man. Darrow's feat was especially remarkable because it required Darrow to combat the influence of both stereotypes and prejudice on the fact finders. In the 1920s, just as today, American culture was replete with derogatory images of blacks. Thus, negative black stereotypes that could be triggered automatically by the presence of a black person were well established in the fact finders' memories. Moreover, the percentage of whites who accepted or endorsed the prevailing black stereotypes was much greater in the past than it is today. Many of Dr. Sweet's jurors, therefore, probably also formed a conscious expectation for instances of trait categories stereotypically associated with blacks (e.g., D.W. Griffith's popular and celebrated 1915 film, *Birth of a Nation*, presented a Ku Klux Klan view of blacks as lawless savages). Because automatic (stereotype-driven) and controlled (prejudice-driven) processes can operate simultaneously on the same underlying categories, the two processes likely were mutually reinforcing in many of these jurors; that is, both processes combined additively to make the underlying negative categories about blacks more accessible. Confronting fact finders whose personal beliefs and stereotypes about blacks overlapped, Darrow's strategy was based on the assumption that even high-prejudiced people personally endorse general egalitarian beliefs. Dr. Sweet's life hinged on whether the jurors—prompted by Darrow's race-conscious appeals—could resist their discriminatory impulses and respond to Dr. Sweet on the basis of their egalitarian ideals. Fortunately for Dr. Sweet and those of us who find relief from despair in what his case says about the capacity of jurors to resist even their most entrenched biases, the jury responded to Darrow's plea by activating their egalitarian responses and checking their prejudiced and stereotype-congruent ones.

Today, although more people espouse nonprejudiced personal beliefs than in Darrow's time, the black stereotype is probably no less entrenched in the memories of Americans than in Darrow's day. Indeed, with the advent of an omnipresent mass media and its incessant manipulation of stereotypes, it may be more entrenched. Thus, habitual stereotype-congruent responses to blacks, even by sincerely racially liberal whites, may distort legal judgments concerning blacks as much in contemporary America as in the America Darrow

knew. If so, these distorted judgments are more insidious than before because they result from automatic processes, which often (but not necessarily always) escape conscious detection. Nevertheless, Darrow's strategy of explicitly engaging our egalitarian responses and urging us consciously to substitute them for our more habitual responses squares with modern empirical research on discrimination reduction techniques. As the recent research in social cognition demonstrates, avoiding stereotype-congruent responses requires conscious effort by the decisionmaker.

A more recent trial, the infamous New York subway vigilante case of *People v. Goetz*, is an example of a case in which the failure to give direct and explicit consideration to racial factors may have resulted in less fair deliberations by the fact finders.[50] In this case, the defendant, Bernhard Goetz, successfully claimed that his shooting of four black teenagers after one of them requested five dollars was justified as an act of self-defense. Professor George Fletcher, a legal theorist who witnessed the entire trial, identified numerous unmistakable instances of the defense "indirectly and covertly . . . play[ing] on the racial factor."[51] For example, the defense "relentlessly attack[ed]" the black victims as "savages," "vultures," the "predators" on society, and the "gang of four." According to the dissociation model developed in [section] II, the use of such racial imagery automatically activates and reactivates the black stereotype. This activation renders negative thoughts and feelings associated with that stereotype acutely accessible for social judgments about the black victims. The fact finders may not experience these judgments as stemming from their knowledge of the black stereotype, but instead as rational, evenhanded evaluations of objective reality. The only way to combat the effect of covert appeals to racial imagery may be to challenge explicitly the fact finders to monitor consciously their responses to avoid unconscious stereotyping. In considering the impact on the jury of the defense's use of racial imagery, Fletcher reaches conclusions about the need to openly address the racial factor that are consistent with this analysis:

> In the end, Slotnick's [Goetz's attorney] covert appeal to racial fear may have had more impact on the jury precisely because it remained hidden behind innuendo and suggestion. It spoke to that side of the jurors' personality that they could not confront directly. Paradoxically, Slotnick may have gained more from not [explicitly playing on the racial factor] than from bringing the racial issue out into the open. Openly talking about racial fear in the courtroom might have helped the jury to deal more rationally with their own racial biases.[52]

C. A Blueprint for Applying the Dissociation Model

References to stereotyped groups in legal proceedings vary in both content and subtlety. The content of a group reference concerns the specific aspect of the stereotype that the reference invokes. For example, fairly recent cases record attorneys playing on stereotypes of blacks, Italians, and Native Americans as more prone to violence and criminality than other Americans. Other cases describe attorneys invoking stereotypes of blacks as subhuman, sexually predatory, and dishonest, to name a few. As the earlier analysis revealed, playing on any particular aspect of a stereotype may activate the entire stereotype, thus distorting a wide range of social judgments about the stereotyped litigant.

The subtlety of group references ranges from blatant to covert and indirect. Although recent case law contains numerous examples of references from both ends of this continuum, the dissociation model suggests that the more subtle references

may be particularly pernicious because subtle references inconspicuously may activate the relevant stereotypes. This deprives jurors of the opportunity to monitor consciously their responses for convergence with their personal beliefs. Moreover, for courts concerned with policing inappropriate group references, subtle references pose special problems of identification. For example, Goetz's attorney, Barry Slotnick, did not explicitly mention race in his characterization of the black youths his client shot as "savages" and "predators," but his statements arguably constituted subtle racial references.

To identify the covertly racial tenor of such statements, courts need a test of the symbolic significance that the culture attaches to them. For to the extent that certain references carry racial connotations, they constitute symbolic equivalents of members of that race and thus serve as cues that activate (often unconsciously) racial stereotypes. Thoughtful formulations of tests for identifying subtle racial symbolism have been developed by Professor Lawrence (the cultural meaning test)[53] and Professor Johnson (the racial imagery shield law).[54] Whatever test for identifying references a court adopts, fairness and accurate fact-finding require that once the court identifies an inappropriate reference, it should give the opposing party the choice of a mistrial or corrective instructions. Given the enormous societal interest in racially fair legal proceedings, courts must follow a policy of zero tolerance with respect to inappropriate racial references.

1. ADMISSION OF RATIONALITY-ENHANCING GROUP REFERENCES
The central thesis of this article, however, is that not all references to blacks or other stereotyped groups are inappropriate. I therefore turn now to the critical distinction between rationality-enhancing and

rationality-subverting group references. Group references that exploit, exacerbate, or play on the prevailing stereotypes that fact finders carry with them into the jury box subvert the rationality of the fact-finding process. But references that challenge the fact finders to reexamine and resist their discriminatory responses enhance the rationality of the fact-finding process. For example, referring to blacks as animal-like or subhuman (e.g., "savages," "monsters," and "Tasmanian devils") resonates so strongly with prevailing black stereotypes as to constitute rationality-subverting racial references. In contrast, Darrow's plea for jurors consciously to monitor and resist their anti-black prejudices and stereotypes is an example of rationality-enhancing uses of group references.

I propose that courts recognize and apply this distinction as follows. Once a court identifies a group reference made by one litigant's counsel, it should give the opposing side the choice of a mistrial or corrective instructions. This general proscription of group references should be subject to very limited exceptions. One such exception would be that the reference enhances rationality, in that it challenges fact finders to monitor and inhibit their stereotype-congruent responses. To fall under this exception, the attorney making or seeking to make the reference in litigation would have to represent the interests of the member of that group and hold a good-faith belief in the rationality-enhancing value of the reference. Inasmuch as courts seek to protect the truth-seeking function of the trial process, I argue that they should maintain the same goal in cases involving litigants from other stereotyped groups.

Especially sensitive are those cases in which an attorney representing a member of a stereotyped group makes an ostensibly derogatory reference to that group. The attorney may claim that such a reference actually helps fact finders resist prejudice-like responses when making judgments about the group member whom she represents. For example, on one level Darrow's statement that the white jurors would rather lose their eyesight and have their legs cut off by a streetcar than have black skin makes a very invidious statement about the negative social value of his client's racial identity. (Today white college students regularly report that if they were suddenly to become outwardly black while they inwardly remain who they were, reasonable compensation would be $1 million a year for life!)[55] On another level, however, it was clear from the context in which Darrow used these ostensibly invidious racial references that they actually constituted an appeal to the jurors to rise above their prejudices on that occasion.

Similarly, in the movie *Philadelphia*, the attorney's use of the epithets associated with gay men—"faggot," "fairy," "booty snatcher," "rump-roaster"—were calculated to challenge the fact finders to confront and inhibit their habitual stereotype-congruent responses to gays, not to encourage such responses. Not mentioning race or sexual orientation at all, when cues that automatically trigger the stereotypes associated with these characteristics abound, promotes unconscious discrimination against members of these stereotyped groups. To control a bad habit, a person first must recall it consciously and then intentionally inhibit it as he or she responds in ways consistent with his or her personally endorsed beliefs and attitudes.

2. TIMING OF RATIONALITY-ENHANCING GROUP REFERENCES

Assuming that an attorney representing a member of a stereotyped group seeks to make rationality-enhancing group references for her client, what is the best setting for such references? Salutary group references may be made in a variety of settings, including voir dire, opening statements, presentation of the case in chief, closing arguments, and jury instructions. All these settings present opportunities for legal actors to encourage prospective or sitting fact finders to guard against their prejudice-like responses. Voir dire, for example, may present an excellent opportunity to search not only for avowedly prejudiced venirepersons, but also to signal to prospective jurors the importance of consciously monitoring their habitual responses to the stereotyped litigant.

Another favorable setting for rationality-enhancing group references may be during opening statements. A striking illustration of both a lawyer's efforts to activate a jury's nonprejudiced impulses in this setting, and a court's misguided application of color-blind formalism to his efforts, comes from a tort case pitting a pharmaceutical company against a low-income black infant and her mother.[56] The mother and child sought damages for serious injuries the child suffered from using the pharmaceutical company's allegedly defective drug. In his opening statement to a mostly white jury, plaintiffs' counsel characterized the case as "a test of our judicial system to see if a child who is at the lower end of our society . . . can come before a jury and receive fair and just compensation for [her] injuries."[57] He then directly addressed the racial dimension of the case:

> [W]e were concerned about the effect of having black people come to an area where there are not many black people and expecting to get justice from a jury which is mostly white people. We decided to confront this issue and we asked you the questions this morning, and we were really pleased with the responses that we got and we think that this is an impartial jury and everyone here has sworn that they will try this case not on the basis of passions, or prejudice, or economic basis, but on the basis of the facts and the law.[58]

Criticizing counsel's comments, the Third Circuit warned that "the remarks should not be repeated in the opening statement at the retrial."[59] According to the court, the counsel's remarks were "beyond the realm of appropriate advocacy '[T]here must be limits to pleas of pure passion and there must be restraints against blatant appeals to bias and prejudice.'"[60]

In this case, the Third Circuit elided the crucial distinction between rationality-enhancing and rationality-subverting racial references that I have been developing. A large and compelling body of social science research—including case studies, laboratory findings in mock jury studies, and general research on racial prejudice—establishes that racial bias affects jury deliberations.[61] Perhaps the best chance for litigants such as this low-income black infant and her mother to receive a fair trial from a mostly white jury is for courts to recognize this distinction and permit rationality-enhancing racial references by a black litigant's attorney in settings likely to maximize the salutary effects of such references.

What settings are most favorable for rationality-enhancing group references? While this important question requires detailed consideration that is beyond the reach of this article, I suggest a few ideas to serve as a starting point for examining this issue. Confronting individuals about their biased, unconscious reflexes may produce different results at different stages of the litigation process. Jury studies suggest that many jurors already have made up their minds before the closing argument. This suggests that perhaps voir dire and opening statements (and even pretrial publicity) are the most important settings for rationality-enhancing comments and confrontations. In Darrow's celebrated defense of Dr. Sweet, for example, one wonders whether, in addition to his closing argument, he also confronted the jurors' stereotypes and prejudices at earlier stages of the proceeding, and if so, whether these earlier confrontations significantly contributed to Sweet's acquittal. Perhaps the acquittal resulted from the cumulative effect of a multiplicity of factors, including Darrow's repeated salutary racial references (perhaps throughout the trial), the makeup of that particular jury and the dynamics of their group decisionmaking, the judge's demeanor, and the pretrial publicity and media coverage. Future research will have to try to parse each of these variables and weigh its influence on the accuracy and fairness of the factfinding process. My analysis has aimed not to provide a ready answer to these crucial questions but to provide a theoretical framework for approaching them. Above all, I have attempted to establish that justice often will be better promoted in litigation if we consciously confront stereotypes than if we take a color-blind, ostrich-like head-in-the-sand approach.

CONCLUSION

Early in the twentieth century, W.E.B. Du Bois prophesied, in his monumental book *The Souls of Black Folk*, that "[t]he problem of the twentieth century is the problem of the color-line,—the relation of the darker to the lighter races of men in Asia and Africa, in America and the islands of the sea."[62] Over a hundred years later, race continues to be an American obsession and racial discrimination continues to pervade every aspect of the American experience. I have argued that on one level there has been significant progress in race relations since the publication of *The Souls of Black Folk*—the percentage of Americans who personally accept and endorse the black stereotype has decreased. On the other hand, as a well-learned set of associations, stereotypes continue to be well established in the memories of all Americans. Hence, as Professors Lawrence, Johnson, Davis, and others have pointed out, we are all prone to stereotype-congruent or prejudice-like responses to blacks (and members of other stereotyped groups), especially in unguarded moments. But research and experience suggest that in some circumstances it is possible to resist falling into the discrimination habit. Further progress in eliminating discrimination will require a deeper understanding of the habitual nature of our responses to stereotyped groups and the development of strategies for helping people inhibit their habitual and activate their endorsed responses to these groups.

3

Implicit Racial Attitudes of Death Penalty Lawyers

Theodore Eisenberg and Sheri Lynn Johnson

INTRODUCTION

Defense attorneys commonly suspect that the defendant's race plays a role in prosecutors' decisions to seek the death penalty, especially when the victim of the crime was white.[1] When the defendant is convicted of the crime and sentenced to death, it is equally common for such attorneys to question the racial attitudes of the jury. These suspicions are not merely partisan conjectures; ample historical,[2] statistical,[3] and anecdotal[4] evidence supports the inference that race matters in capital cases. Even the General Accounting Office of the United States concludes as much.[5] Despite *McCleskey v. Kemp*,[6] in which the United States Supreme Court concluded that strong, well-controlled statistical correlations with race do not

demonstrate causation, half of all Americans believe that race does influence the administration of the death penalty.[7]

In investigating the influence of racial bias, commentators (ourselves included) have focused on prosecutors and jurors,[8] generally neglecting the question of whether bias affects the representation defense counsel provides his or her client. In part, this may be due to the greater difficulty in uncovering evidence of bias in the ranks of defense counsel; most of the evidence of bias of other death penalty actors has been uncovered through the efforts of defense counsel, a class one might suspect would be less likely to scrutinize itself. It may also be faith in the adversary system that disinclines observers to suspect bias on the part of defense counsel: one would hope that those who represent capital defendants (or at least African American capital defendants) would themselves be free of racialized thinking as they establish trust with their clients, direct both fact and mitigation investigations, select experts,

Editors' Note: This chapter first appeared as Theodore Eisenberg & Sheri Lynn Johnson, *Implicit Racial Attitudes of Death Penalty Lawyers*, 53 DePaul L. R. 1539 (2004), reprinted by permission of the authors.

choose witnesses to call, and decide what arguments to make. A final reason for this inattention to defense lawyers may be the apparent sincerity of the ideological commitment of most such lawyers to racial equality; not only do they proclaim that commitment, but the poor pay and low status of their work suggest some amount of sacrifice for those ideological commitments. But ideological commitment need not translate into racially unbiased evaluations, as a large accumulation of literature discussing social and cognitive psychology demonstrates.[9] Indeed, the defense lawyer's commitment to the formal norm of equality is probably shared with most prosecutors and jurors. So the question should be asked, better late than not at all: what do we know about the capital defense lawyer's racial attitudes?

Nothing. Virtually nothing is known about the racial attitudes of lawyers in general, let alone defense lawyers or capital defense lawyers specifically. The demographic characteristics, compensation patterns, career paths, and occasionally the daily activities of lawyers are studied, but researchers to date have expressed little interest in their attitudes, with the exception of attitudes concerning job satisfaction.

In contrast, quite a lot is known about the racial attitudes of the general population. The prevalence of hostile, overt racism has been declining at least since the 1960s.[10] Some researchers have observed that polls may overstate this trend, given the growing social unacceptability of racial hostility. Indeed, when experiments have tried to weed out social desirability effects, they do find greater levels of conscious stereotyping and hostility, though still clearly lesser levels than in the past.[11] For the most part, however, old-fashioned, Bull Connor–style racism has been replaced not with color blindness but with subtler manifestations of racial bias. Some social psychologists have labeled this newer racism "aversive racis[m]," documenting the prevalence of subjects who subscribe to a formal norm of equality but desire to keep their distance from other racial groups and often covertly disparage those groups.[12] Cognitive psychologists have focused more on stereotypes, observing how thinking and judgment may be altered by stereotypes that the subject would not endorse, and often consciously rejects.

Both of these (related) conceptions of modern racism raise the troubling possibility that defense counsel, who are charged with undivided loyalty to their clients and presumed to serve as a shield against racial bias on the part of other criminal justice system actors, may in fact experience both compromised loyalty and judgment when they serve African American or Latino clients. On the other hand, perhaps capital defense attorneys, either by self-selection or by training, are different from the rest of the population in this regard. This article describes preliminary data suggesting that they are not. That they exhibit similar automatic racial attitudes does not, of course, prove that their performance is impaired by those attitudes; we leave the implications of our findings for the discussion section.

I. GATHERING THE DATA

A. The Instrument

The Implicit Association Test (IAT) was developed to measure the relative strength with which groups (or individuals) are associated with positive and negative evaluations. It has been used to measure attitudes about a variety of issues, including race, gender, age, and political candidates, and is accepted as a valid research tool. All variations of the IAT use some form of response latency to assess those attitudes that are "automatic," as opposed to attitudes that are subject to intention or control, and operate on the principle that it should be easier to make the same behavioral response to concepts that are associated than to concepts that are not associated. Computerized versions of the IAT achieve these pairings by assigning a keyboard key to be pressed in response to items from categories such as "old" or "bad," and another key to be pressed in response to items from the opposite categories, such as "young" or "good." Then the pairings are switched, with the subject being asked to press one key in response to either "old" or "good," and another key in response to items from either the "young" or "bad" category. The differential speed required to complete these two opposite pairings is measured, yielding information both about the direction of the implicit attitude and the strength of the association; thus, if it takes longer for a subject to complete the pairings of "old" and "good" than the pairings of "young" and "good," then the researcher infers that "young" is automatically associated with "good" for that subject, and "old" with "bad."

More than 500,000 IATs that focus on race have been taken online using this format. In the race IAT, subjects are first asked to pair "good" words with pictures of white faces and "bad" words with pictures of black faces, and then to reverse the pairings. Here, if the subject can more quickly complete the task when "white" and "good" (and "black" and "bad") are paired than when "black" and "good" (and "white" and "bad") are paired, it means that the subject automatically pairs "white" with "good"—and "black" with "bad."

A paper-and-pencil version of the race IAT is also available and was used in collecting these data because of time and computer accessibility constraints. In the paper-and-pencil version, subjects are faced with a column of words and faces, which they are asked to categorize "as quickly as possible without making too many mistakes" in twenty seconds. Before doing this, the subjects complete two practice tests; the first test pairs "flowers" with "good" and "insects" with "bad," and the second pairs "insects" with "good" and "flowers" with "bad." This practice is designed to make the subject familiar with the pairing and check-off process, and accustomed to the idea of switching which items are paired. Then the subjects are asked to familiarize themselves with four new categories. One category is "good," which is composed of the words *flower*, *pretty*, and *love*; a second category is "bad," composed of the words *ugly*, *vomit*, and *hate*; the third category is "white," which is composed of five white faces; and the fourth category is "black," which is composed of five black faces. A short column of these words and pictures appears, and the subjects are instructed to go down the column checking the items that are "white" or "good" on the left of the item and items that are "black" or "bad" on the right of the item. After being allowed to ask questions, the subjects are told that when they turn the next page, they will be asked to check "white" or "good" on the left, and "black" or "bad" on the right, completing as many as possible in the allotted time, as the (shorter) sample on page 36, top, indicates:

After completing this task, the subjects are asked to turn the page, and the new pairing of "black" with "good" and "white" with "bad" is explained. Subjects then complete the same task with the new pairing, as the sample on page 36, bottom, indicates.

The number of items correctly completed on each test is then counted; it is not the number of items a particular subject can complete that is of significance, but the difference in the number of items he or she completes when "white" is paired with "good" and "black" with "bad," as contrasted with the number completed when "black" is paired with "good" and "white" with "bad."

White Good		Black Bad
○	happy	○
○		○
○	love	○
○		○
○	evil	○
○		○
○	poison	○
○		○
○	terrific	○
○		○

White Good		Black Bad
○	bad	○
○		○
○	poison	○
○		○
○	good	○
○		○
○	love	○
○		○
○	evil	○
○		○

Black Good		White Bad
○	vomit	○
○		○
○	hatred	○
○		○
○	good	○
○		○
○	love	○
○		○
○	poison	○
○		○

Black Good		White Bad
○	joy	○
○		○
○	vomit	○
○		○
○	terrific	○
○		○
○	hatred	○
○		○
○	love	○
○		○

B. The Subjects

Two of the three data sets are the product of presentations made by one of the authors at training sessions for capital defense lawyers. The first was obtained at an annual gathering of lawyers who represent death row inmates in federal habeas corpus proceedings. Most of these attorneys are experienced capital litigators, but some novices were invited. The training session was held in Nashville, Tennessee, but the attorneys came from all over the country. These subjects we will call the "habeas lawyers." The second data set was collected at a training session for Georgia trial lawyers involved in representing defendants charged with capital crimes; these subjects we will call the "trial lawyers." We asked all of these subjects for their race. For the trial lawyers, we also collected the age and gender of each subject. The third data set is composed of most of the students in a first-year constitutional law class at Cornell Law School; we will call them the "law students." For the law students we collected race, age, and gender data.

II. RESULTS

As shown in Table 3.1, on average, the subjects in all three groups completed more items when "white" was paired with "good" and "black" with "bad" than when "black" was paired with "good" and "white" with "bad," and in all three groups these differences are statistically significant. For example, the table's first row shows that, for all subjects combined, an average of 16.4 correct responses were given when "white" was paired with "good" and "black" with "bad" compared to 13.5 correct responses when "black" was paired with "good" and "white" with "bad." A test of the statistical significance of the

difference in means, computed using a t-test, yields a p-value of less than 0.0001 for our 321 subjects, as reported in column 4. The difference in means is significant at that level for each group as well as for all groups combined.

To eliminate the possibility that the significance of the difference is the product of a few extreme individuals and to ensure that the results are not sensitive to the distributive assumptions associated with the t-test, we also tested the statistical significance of the differences in median correct scores. Column 5 shows that the median differences are also significant beyond the 0.0001 level for all groups and for the groups aggregated into a single sample. Thus, the probability of observing by chance differences as large as, or larger than, those observed is vanishingly small.

As shown in the Table 3.5 regression models reported below, differences between the three groups—habeas lawyers, trial lawyers, and law students—are not statistically significant. Within each group, however, the differences between black and white subjects are highly significant. Table 3.2 expands on Table 1 by reporting the results broken down by race within each subject group. Table 3.2 shows that, for all groups combined, as well as for each subject group, the average white subject completed

TABLE 3.1. Number of Items Completed When "Good" Is Paired with White Faces Versus When "Good" Is Paired with Black Faces, by Subject Group

	Average Number of Correct Responses When "Good" Is Paired With:		Difference = (1) – (2) (3)	Significance of Difference		N (6)
	(1) White Faces	(2) Black Faces		(4)	(5)	
All subjects	16.4	13.5	2.8	<.0001	<.0001	321
Habeas lawyers	14.4	12.1	2.3	<.0001	<.0001	146
Trial lawyers	16.7	13.6	3.0	<.0001	<.0001	92
Law students	19.5	15.9	3.6	<.0001	<.0001	83

more items when "white" was paired with "good" than when "black" was paired with "good," while the average black subject completed more items when "black" was paired with "good."[13] For example, for all white subjects combined, an average of 16.6 correct responses were given when "white" was paired with "good" and "black" with "bad" compared to 13.2 correct responses when "black" was paired with "good" and "white" with "bad." In contrast, for all black subjects combined, an average of 14.4 correct responses were given when "white" was paired with "good" and "black" with "bad," compared to 15.8 correct responses when "black" was paired with "good" and "white" with "bad."

Column 3 of Table 3.2, which is the difference in correct responses between columns 1 and 2, shows that this racial difference persists for all three groups. White subjects in all these groups provided more correct responses when "white" was paired with "good." Black subjects in all three groups provided more correct responses

when "black" was paired with "good." For the most part, we limited our analysis to white and black subjects because the subjects in the two lawyer groups were almost exclusively black and white. In the constitutional law class, however, there were fourteen Asian subjects, enough to make analysis of their results potentially meaningful. We found that the Asian subjects were not significantly different from the white subjects, but were significantly different from the black subjects.

Columns 4 and 5 show that for all groups of white subjects, the differences in the numbers of correct responses between "white" being paired with "good" and "black" being paired with "good" are highly statistically significant. In part because of the smaller number of black subjects in each group, and in part because the mean difference in their "white"/"good" and "black"/"good" scores is smaller, differences in black subjects' performance on the "white"/"good" pairing as compared to the "black"/"good" pairing are not statisti-

TABLE 3.2. **Number of Correct Responses When "Good" Is Paired with White Faces Versus When "Good" Is Paired with Black Faces, by Race of Subjects**

	Average Number of Correct Responses When "Good" Is Paired With:		Difference = (1) – (2)	Significance of Difference		N
	(1)	(2)	(3)	(4)	(5)	(6)
	White Faces	Black Faces		Means	Medians	
All subjects	16.4	13.5	2.8	<.0001	<.0001	321
Whites	16.6	13.2	3.4	<.0001	<.0001	281
Blacks	14.4	15.8	−1.4	.097	.039	40
Habeas lawyers	14.4	12.1	2.3	<.0001	<.0001	146
Whites	14.5	12.0	2.4	<.0001	<.0001	140
Blacks	12.7	14.0	−1.3	.669	.399	6
Trial lawyers	16.7	13.6	3.0	<.0001	<.0001	92
Whites	17.4	13.1	4.3	<.0001	<.0001	70
Blacks	14.4	15.5	−1.1	.112	.086	22
Law students	19.5	15.9	3.6	<.0001	<.0001	83
Whites	20.2	15.6	4.5	<.0001	<.0001	71
Blacks	15.4	17.3	−1.8	384	.432	12

cally significant for the three subgroups considered separately. When the three groups are combined, however, the differences in the median numbers of correct responses for black subjects between "white" being paired with "good" and "black" being paired with "good" are statistically significant at the .039 level, and the means differ at the .097 level.

Thus, both white and black subjects score higher when their own racial group is paired with "good." But Table 3.2 indicates that the difference is not of the same magnitude. Table 3.3 explores this difference by reorganizing some of the data in Table 3.2. Table 3.3 again shows that both black and white subjects on average scored higher when their own racial group was paired with "good" than when it was paired with "bad." In all three groups, white subjects' scores were more affected by which race was paired with "good" than were the scores of black subjects. Column 3 reports these differences in differences for each subject group.

Columns 4 and 5 show that for the groups combined (as well as for the trial lawyers taken individually), the differences in differences are statistically significant. For the two other groups, the direction of the effect is the same, but the effect is not statistically significant at traditional levels, a result likely attributable to the small number of black subjects. The races' different reactions also emerge in another measure. Only a quarter of white subjects scored the same or better on the "black"/"good" pairing as on the "white"/"good" pairing, while almost half of the black subjects scored the same or better on the "white"/"good" pairing as on the "black"/"good" pairing.

We also examined the effect of gender on the performance, holding race constant. Table 3.4 below reports the results. (Its sample is smaller than the samples in the other tables because we did not record the gender of the subjects for the first group we sampled, the habeas lawyers.) Table 3.4 can be used to explore two separable questions. First, do the results in Tables 3.1 and 3.2 hold when the sample is disaggregated by gender? That is, do males and females separately confirm the pattern of more correct responses when white faces are paired with "good" than when black faces are paired with "good"? Second, Table 3.4 explores whether the pattern of responses varies not only by race, as suggested in Tables 3.2 and 3.3, but also by gender.

TABLE 3.3. **Difference Between Number of Items Completed When "Good" Is Paired with Own-Race Faces Versus When "Good" Is Paired with Other-Race Faces, by Subject Group**

	Mean Difference Between Number of Correct Responses When "Good" Is Paired with Subject's Own Race Versus When "Good" Is Paired with Other Race		Difference = (1) – (2) (3)	Significance of Difference		N (6)
	(1) Whites	(2) Blacks		(4) Means	(5) Medians	
All subjects	3.4	1.4	2.1	.008	.018	321
Habeas lawyers	2.4	1.3	1.1	.548	.839	146
Trial lawyers	4.3	1.1	3.2	.0003	.001	92
Law students	4.5	1.8	2.7	.130	.123	83

Theodore Eisenberg and Sheri Lynn Johnson

Table 3.4 shows that the core result of significantly different reactions to "white"/"good" pairings and "black"/"good" pairings holds for black males, white females, and white males. However, for white females and males the significant advantage is in "white"/"good" pairings, while for black males, the significant advantage is in "black"/"good" pairings. For black females, the tendency is toward easier "black"/"good" pairings, but the difference, as reported in columns 3 through 5, is not statistically significant.

Column 6 explores whether the difference in differences varies statistically significantly across the race/gender groups. White women (as well as black women and black men) are significantly different from white men. For both blacks and whites, the tendency is for men to reflect a greater own-race advantage than women, but for black subjects, the difference is smaller and not significant.

Note that column 6, which shows the level of significance of difference from white males, reports a test of the difference in the median number of "good" characteristics correctly associated with one's own race and the other race. A t-test of the difference in means is also statistically significant.

The analysis so far explores subject group differences and race/gender differences in isolation from one another. To assess all factors simultaneously, we employ regression analysis and report the results in Table 3.5, including age in the models for those subjects for whom age is known. Models reported in columns 1 and 2 explore the differences described in Tables 3.1 and 3.2—the difference between subjects' scores when whites are paired with "good" characteristics and when blacks are paired with "good" characteristics. We report both ordinary least-squares models and negative binomial models. Negative binomial models are appropriate because the dependent variables in our models are count data—the difference in the number of correct responses.[14] Columns 3 and 4 report models that explore the difference in differences between the "white"/"good" and "black"/"good" scores. It thus assesses whether the explanatory variables in the model help explain the degree of within-race favoritism.

Table 3.5 confirms the results in the earlier tables. Models 1 and 2 show that black females, black males, and white females all tend to have less extreme differences between the "white"/"good" and "black"/"good" conditions than do white males. The results are all significant at or beyond the 0.05 level. The results do not depend on the functional form, least-squares, or negative binomial of the models used. The

TABLE 3.4. **Number of Items Correctly Completed When "Good" Is Paired with White Faces Versus When "Good" Is Paired with Black Faces, by Race and Gender**

	Average Number of Correct Responses When "Good" Is Paired With:		Difference = (1) − (2)	Significance of Difference (1) − (2) from White Males' Difference			N
	(1)	(2)	(3)	(4)	(5)	(6)	(7)
	White Faces	Black Faces		Means	Medians		
Black females	15.0	16.1	−1.1	.365	.397	.002	22
Black males	14.3	16.1	−1.8	.020	.025	.010	12
White females	18.1	15.1	2.9	.0001	.0002	.041	55
White males	18.6	13.8	4.8	<.0001	<.0001		100

TABLE 3.5. **Regression Models of Differences in Scores Between Pairings**

	(1)	(2)	(3)	(4)
	Dependent Variable = Difference Between Subject's "White"/"Good" and "Black"/"Good" Scores		Dependent Variable = Difference Between Subject's Own-Race/"Good" and Other-Race/"Good" Scores	
	OLS	Negative Binomial	OLS	Negative Binomial
Black female	−6.465**	−0.344**	−4.272**	−0.285**
	(4.88)	(4.30)	(3.37)	(3.06)
Black male	−7.001**	−0.381**	−3.149**	−0.206**
	(8.59)	(7.99)	(3.50)	(3.39)
White female	−2.035*	−0.098*	−2.099*	−0.133
	(2.51)	(2.50)	(2.59)	(2.54)
White male = reference category				
Trial lawyers	0.802	0.041	0.645	0.045
	(0.91)	(0.95)	(0.73)	(0.78)
Habeas lawyers	−2.437	−0.128	−1.947	−0.136
	(1.02)	(0.98)	(0.81)	(0.79)
Law students = reference category				
Age	−0.620	−0.031	−0.835*	−0.054*
	(1.56)	(1.59)	(2.12)	(2.13)
Age missing	−1.613	−0.075	−2.794	−0.178
	(0.58)	(0.51)	(0.98)	(0.90)
Gender missing	0.166	0.014	0.344	0.035
	(0.12)	(0.19)	(0.25)	(0.35)
Constant	6.278**	3.154**	6.912**	2.954**
	(6.43)	(69.42)	(7.12)	(51.01)
Observations	321	321	321	321
R-squared or pseudo R-squared	0.16	.030	0.10	.017

Robust t statistics in parentheses
*Significant at 5%; **significant at 1%

story is constant across models 1 and 2. Similarly, models 3 and 4 show that the difference between the number of "good" characteristics correctly associated with one's own race and the other race is associated with a race/gender effect. White males again differ statistically significantly from the other three race/gender combinations. They tend to record greater differences between own-race/"good" and other-race/"good" pairings than do the other race/gender combinations. The result is statistically significant and persists in both least-squares and negative binomial models.

Again, differences between the three subject groups—habeas lawyers, trial lawyers, and law students—are not significant. The only surprise is that age, which viewed in isolation was not a significant predictor of performance, is slightly but significantly correlated, and in a negative direction, with size of mean "white"/"good" and "black"/"good" differences.

III. DISCUSSION

Because speed at these tasks reflects relative ease in associating two categories of items, the creators of the IAT describe a subject who is more adept at pairing "white" with "good" than "black" with "good" as having an "automatic preference" for "white." In adopting this terminology, we note that *preference* as used here does not imply a conscious choice, but merely an automatic association; when we say that subjects have an automatic preference for "white," we mean nothing more than that they automatically associate "white" with "good" and "black" with "bad."[15] [Section] II of this article reported both the direction of the automatic associations and their relative strength for each professional group (ha-beas lawyers, trial lawyers, and law students) and for demographic subgroups of each group (dividing the groups by race, gender, and age). Because we used a paper-and-pencil version of the IAT, we are unable to compare the strength of observed preferences with those found in the larger IAT databases,[16] but we can compare the direction of those preferences with those observed in the larger, more diverse (and overwhelmingly lay) subject pool, as well as relative differences between the demographic subgroups in each data set. After making these comparisons, we will turn to the question of what behavioral implications, if any, these observed automatic preferences entail.

The direction and demographic distribution of the automatic preferences we observed are strikingly consistent with those observed in the larger trials not targeted at occupational subgroups.[17] Data from the Web sites, like our data, reflect significant automatic preference for whites among white subjects; this is true when "good" and "bad" are in turn paired with black and white faces, and it is also true when they are paired with first names that are associated with black people or white people. Black Web subjects, on the other hand, show an automatic preference for black faces or names, but that preference,

like the preference of our defense lawyer and law student subjects, is weaker than is white subjects' automatic preference for white faces or names. Our responses and the Web responses both mimic earlier laboratory results with college student subjects. Moreover, the Web researchers found, as we find, that Asian respondents show a pro-white bias level comparable to that of white respondents. Finally, while our regression reflected that white women showed slightly, but significantly less, negativity toward black faces than did white men, Web researchers reported that women subjects (not broken down by race, but predominantly white) showed slightly less automatic preference for whites.

The reader will recall that our results on age were of marginal significance in the regression, with older age predicting slightly less of an automatic preference for whites. This is the only place our results differ even slightly from those of the Web research; there, older participants did not differ at all from younger ones on the analogous face test. Several explanations for these disparate findings are possible. While it is possible that our older capital defense attorneys, unlike their age peers in the general population, actually do harbor weaker automatic preferences for whites than do otherwise similar subjects, Web research on the performance of various measuring algorithms suggests that our results may be an artifact of our scoring method, which does not account for the fact that older subjects perform all of the tasks more slowly.

Thus, our capital defense attorneys, both trial and postconviction (trial lawyers and habeas lawyers), look like our law students in their implicit attitudes about race and, as far as we can tell, pretty much like the rest of the population. White men have the strongest automatic preference for whites, followed by white women. The responses of Asian subjects look like those of white subjects. In contrast, black subjects have an automatic preference for blacks, but it is significantly smaller than the preference white and Asian subjects have for whites. If one imagines that automatic reactions are the combined product of culture and individual experience, these patterns are not surprising.

Looking at other empirical evidence concerning lawyers, the observed similarities between defense lawyers, law students, and the lay population are also not surprising. Popular impression to the contrary, comparisons between judges and juries generally find little difference in the damages they award.[18] And, most relevantly, judges appear to be just as susceptible as are jurors to three cognitive illusions that hinder accurate decision making: anchoring, hindsight bias, and egocentric bias.[19] Finally, judges' political orientation has been shown to have some influence in politically charged cases.[20] As is slowly being recognized across the field, "lawyers are like other people and suffer from the same human failings as those not admitted to the bar."[21] Though we have presented evidence that white capital defense lawyers, like the rest of the population, have automatic reactions that make associating "white" with "good" easier than associating "white" with "bad," we have by no means proved that they treat black clients (or witnesses, jurors, attorneys, or judges, for that matter) differently than they treat their white counterparts. Indeed, even the evidence on the relationship between explicit prejudice and discrimination is complex. Subjects who acknowledge negative attitudes toward vulnerable groups do not always discriminate against them; either lack of opportunity or social disapproval may inhibit the expression of those attitudes.[22] Likewise, subjects who disavow negative attitudes toward a vulnerable group may nonetheless discriminate against that group for a variety of reasons, including

social pressure to do so and covert or unconscious stereotypes about the target group. Because measurement of implicit racial attitudes is quite new, even less is known about how those attitudes affect behavior.

It is, however, possible to note what external factors are known to make discrimination more likely and consider their presence or absence in the context of capital representation of a minority-race defendant. As already mentioned, social approval (or even the absence of social disapproval) enhances the likelihood of discrimination. The factor of social approval must vary widely in capital representation, depending in part on whether the relevant audience is the local prosecutor (with whom the next case must be plea-bargained), the local judge (who may be the source of the next appointment as counsel), the local defense bar (whose attitudes differ by area), the jurors (who in some small localities are potential clients), or the national capital defense bar. Stereotypes are more likely to alter judgment when a task is complex[23] or a decision difficult,[24] or when the context activates stereotypes.[25] Certainly the task of representing a capital defendant or habeas pe-titioner is complex and involves many difficult decisions. Moreover, the capital litigation context—in which the defendant is accused of heinous crimes—seems especially likely to activate stereotypes of violence and criminality.

There is some evidence that awareness of automatic reactions can trigger attempts to counteract them, and that such attempts are sometimes successful.[26] Here we have no clear indication of whether capital defense attorneys struggle against their own automatic reactions. On the one hand, we would predict from their ideological commitments that they would be inclined to do so, if they were aware that they had such reactions; on the other hand, anecdotal experience in administering these tests leads us to believe that many capital defense attorneys were surprised at their own automatic preferences and, therefore, would not have previously realized that they should struggle against those preferences.

CONCLUSION: WHO IS POLICING THE BIAS POLICE?

Our initial foray into the racial attitudes of capital defense lawyers permits us a modest conclusion: as with the rest of the population, race influences their automatic reactions. This proves neither that race does nor that it does not, often influence the quality of representation afforded the black clients of these attorneys. For judges reviewing the effectiveness of the assistance of counsel provided to capital defendants, our data suggest that they should not assume that race has not influenced the actions of defense counsel, and that they should not assume that counsel will be sensitive to the racial bias of other criminal justice system actors. For the capital defense lawyers themselves, it suggests that introspection about racial stereotypes and reactions, as well as vigilance concerning those effects on others, is necessary. For the public, it may be yet another reason to doubt the evenhandedness of capital punishment.

4

Advocacy Against the Stereotype:
Lessons from Cognitive Social Psychology
Gary Blasi

The problem of the Twentieth Century is the problem of the color line.
—W.E.B. Du Bois[1]

INTRODUCTION

Two anniversaries approach. Next year will mark the centennial of W.E.B. Du Bois's famous assessment and prediction. The year following will see the fiftieth anniversary of *Brown v. Board of Education* and the beginning of an era of hope, including the hope that the law might help us finally transcend the bitter residue of slavery and begin an ending to racial discrimination.[2] The grim truth, however, is that in our public schools and in many other settings, "the color line" is the problem of the twenty-first century as well. *Brown* promised public education "available to all on equal terms."[3] Five months into the millennium, on the forty-sixth anniversary of *Brown*, civil rights and pro bono lawyers filed a statewide class action

Editors' Note: This chapter is an abridged version of Gary Blasi, *Advocacy Against the Stereotype: Lessons from Cognitive Social Psychology*, 49 UCLA L. Rev. 1241 (2002), reprinted by permission of the author.

on behalf of approximately one million California students, the great majority of them children of color, consigned to woefully substandard public schools.[4] Discovery and investigation in that case have revealed a public education system still marked by the grossest racial disparities. To cite but one example, in California public schools in which more than half of teachers lack full credentials, 98 percent of the students are nonwhites.[5] As a matter of cold statistical fact, many of California's public schools more closely resemble those one would expect from the era of *Plessy v. Ferguson*[6] than those promised by *Brown*. The plaintiffs' lawyers persist in an effort to realize concretely in the classrooms of California the abstract promise of *Brown*. They work with all that any lawyer has: facts, legal doctrine, and their own ingenuity and advocacy skills. The lawyers are able and the facts are powerful, but legal doctrine has evolved to a more uncertain place, pervaded by the faint hope that if we now try hard to ignore race, racial discrimination and the persisting effects of past injustice will simply fade away.

The current "color-blind" jurisprudence of the U.S. Supreme Court rests on an implicit theory of stereotyping and prejudice, the central premise of which is that prejudice is a matter of motivation and intent. Borrowing from quite different traditions in psychology, Charles Lawrence and Linda Krieger demonstrate in two seminal articles that this implicit theory is wrong: the behavior of real human beings is often guided by racial and other stereotypes of which they are completely unaware.[7] Since these articles were published, scientific knowledge of how stereotypes operate in the human mind has accumulated steadily. Striking recent experimental results have required science to build new models of human thinking and behavior. New theories explain—and sophisticated computer models now simulate—a broad range of experimental findings. Researchers in the new field of social cognitive neuroscience have developed techniques for illuminating not only how but where in the brain race is processed.[8] Many of the most recent scientific discoveries have significant implications for how lawyers and legal scholars should think about stereotypes and prejudice. With a handful of exceptions, however, legal scholars and practicing lawyers have generally ignored these developments. As a result, advocates are often operating on the basis of an implicit theory of prejudice that is as flawed as the theory guiding the evolution of constitutional doctrine. Indeed, as I explain, it is in some ways the same theory. Persisting inequality and discrimination may therefore partially reflect, in addition to unsound legal principles and political failure, the results of antidiscrimination advocacy conducted on the basis of incorrect assumptions about people and prejudice.

*   *   *

The purpose of this article is to . . . [draw] on recent advances in social psychology and cognitive science in understanding how race (and other stereotypes) function in the human mind. The fundamental questions here are these: What would it mean to take these scientific findings seriously? More particularly, if lawyers and public policy advocates rigorously engaged this scientific literature, how might lawyering and policy advocacy be reshaped? In addition to unrealized potential benefits, would the approaches suggested by science entail certain costs? Although my ultimate intended audience is advocates and lawyers, scholars and law teachers have an especially important role to play in exploring these questions, as potential intermediaries between psychological science and advocacy practice. Just as engineers constructing bridges need access to the best metallurgical science, so too must lawyers and advocates understand as accurately as possible the cognitive and motivational processes of judges, jurors, policy makers, and voters. Unfortunately, both legal scholarship and practice too often rest on implicit theories of prejudice and stereotyping that are, if not entirely wrong, now known to be seriously incomplete.

Just as most of us proceed in the world on the basis of "folk theories" of physics that are sometimes at odds with scientific findings, most of us act in the social world on the basis of implicit theories about how people think and act. The only problem with these theories is that they are often wrong. In [section] I, I offer a sampling of recent scientific findings, some of which run strikingly against folk theories, and then provide a brief overview of some of the major scientific theories that account for these results. On the basis of this science, I explain in [section] II why advocacy derived from folk theories of social psychology is likely to be ineffective and what the recent science suggests in the way of additional or alternative advocacy strategies, as well as the limits of any kind of advocacy that does not attend to institutional and structural social change.

*   *   *

I. A QUICK SURVEY OF CURRENT RESEARCH

I introduce here a sample of some of the more striking experimental results obtained by cognitive scientists and social psychologists in the past decade or so, and then present a condensed summary of some of the contemporary theories that account for these results. Limitations of both space and the author will ensure that this account is incomplete. In addition, the study of stereotyping and associated behavior is a rapidly evolving field with contending schools of thought and theoretical models. I have tried to steer clear of the major controversies, but any of the intellectual combatants may well disagree. The controversies generally concern explanations. What I find most compelling are the experimental results, a sampling of which are set out in summary form below.

A. A Sampling of Experiments

I begin with a recent series of experiments by Samuel R. Sommers and Phoebe C. Ellsworth that suggests that stereotypes affect jurors in ways that contradict conventional assumptions. Sommers and Ellsworth studied the reactions of mock jurors, all of whom were white, to narratives describing trial testimony. For example, in one experiment, the trial narrative concerned a locker room fight between high school basketball players. In all of the narratives the fight was cross-racial—involving either a black defendant and a white victim, or vice versa. In one version of the narrative, an additional sentence was added suggesting that the de-

fendant had been the subject of racial remarks and unfair criticism from teammates of the other racial group earlier in the season. In that race-salient version of the trial evidence, mock jurors showed no racial bias: they were as likely to convict the white defendant as the black defendant on the same facts. When that one sentence was removed, however, and the only reference to race was a single mention of the race of each of the two athletes, mock jurors "convicted" the black defendant 90 percent of the time and the white defendant only 70 percent of the time.[9] Moreover, when asked to recommend a sentence for the defendant, mock jurors reading the trial summary in which race was not salient recommended a significantly harsher sentence for the black defendant. Sommers and Ellsworth conclude, "White jurors are more likely to demonstrate racial prejudice in cases without salient racial issues."[10] Plainly, something not predicted by conventional notions of prejudice is going on in these studies. The experiments summarized below suggest that those conventional notions are wrong in multiple ways.

I. AUTOMATICITY OF STEREOTYPING AND EFFECTS ON BEHAVIOR

Two sets of subjects appear at a laboratory. All are told that they will be asked to solve some scrambled word puzzles and will be timed on their performance. Half of the subjects are given scrambled sentences including a few words associated with the "elderly" stereotype, words like *gray*, *wrinkled*, *wise*, and *Miami*. The control group receives similar scrambled sentence puzzles that do not contain these words. After solving several puzzles, subjects in the first group are asked whether they noticed any themes or recurring topics in the puzzles. None of the subjects reports noticing any theme or any particular reference to the concept of "elderly." Subjects are then excused and leave the experiment room, thinking that their participation is complete. But now the key part of the experiment actually begins: as subjects leave the room, another experimenter secretly measures the time it takes each of them to walk down a corridor to the elevator. Remarkably, those subjects who have merely been exposed to words associated with the "elderly" stereotype—but not including words about speed, pace, or gait—walk substantially more slowly down the hall.[11] A short explanation is that the scrambled word puzzles have activated the "elderly" stereotype in the minds of experimental subjects and that the activated stereotype has influenced their behavior in a way consistent with the stereotype.

[*Editors' Note: In several deleted paragraphs, Professor Blasi reports on John Bargh's "computer crash" study, B. Keith Payne's "gun or tool" experiment, and Margaret Shih's "math test" research. Each of these studies is described in Jerry Kang's "Trojan Horses of Race," reprinted in this anthology.*]

*   *   *

The implications of these experimental results are distressing. If racism and other stereotype-driven phenomena are located so deeply in human cognition, if we are all affected by stereotypes of which we have no conscious awareness, stereotypes about others as well as ourselves, what can we do to control stereotyping and to reduce prejudice? To be sure, people do display differences in these effects. Stereotypes are more easily activated in people who display more conscious prejudice.[12] Stereotype activation also varies according to the parts of the stereotype that are used to prime activation. Words associated with the negative features of a stereotype will activate the stereotype in people of both low and high prejudice. Associated words that are positive or neutral will activate the stereotype only in more prejudiced people. All people are less likely to activate stereotypes during

periods in which exceptional demands are placed on cognitive resources and people are being kept "cognitively busy."[13]

Despite these variations, however, all of us behave in ways that demonstrate that we are subject to the effects of stereotypes, including those we expressly disavow. Many readers will believe otherwise. Most of us would prefer to believe that we do not, for example, differentially associate "good" and "bad" with members of stereotyped groups, including racial groups. I encourage skeptical readers to spend the few minutes on the Internet necessary to take the extensively validated Implicit Association Test, which uses reaction times to measure implicitly held stereotypes and attitudes toward stereotyped groups.[14]

2. ALTERED JUDGMENTS

It may also be possible under some circumstances for people to activate, but not to act upon, stereotypes. Psychologists distinguish between activation (a stereotype being on one's mind) and stereotype application (using the stereotype to make judgments or to guide behavior). Whether we activate stereotypes and whether we make judgments based on them is not determined entirely by cold cognitive processes, but is also affected by emotion and by our sense of ourselves. For example, our assessments of other people are affected by their apparent assessments of us. Experiments demonstrate that students who have received high grades from female professors rate them as highly as male professors, but assess as less competent female professors who have given them poor grades. Recipients of praise from a black doctor tend to activate the stereotype of "doctor," while people disparaged by the same physician tend to activate the stereotype for "black." Although these phenomena take place below the level of conscious processing, it is almost as if basic cognitive processes are looking out for our subjective sense of well-being: we feel better if we can admire our admirers and disparage our critics, subconsciously telling ourselves to consider the source.

One way to make people feel better about themselves is to ask them to write about those values they have identified as being most important to them.[15] Subjects asked to write about values they have previously indicated as unimportant do not experience the same temporary increase in self-esteem. Using this method of manipulating feelings of self-esteem, experimenters assessed how the self-concept affected stereotyping. Experimental subjects were divided into two groups. Half went through the self-affirming essay-writing exercise; the other half did not. All the subjects were then asked to evaluate two nearly identical videotaped interviews with a young woman described as an applicant for a job as personnel manager. Although the same woman appeared in the two videos, cues concerning her ethnicity (hairstyle, dress, jewelry, purported name, and background facts) were varied, in order to potentially prime a "Jewish American princess" stereotype prevalent in the population from which the subjects were drawn. In the control situation, cues were changed to suggest that the young woman was an Italian Catholic. Subjects were asked to rate the applicant in terms of her personality and qualifications for the job. Those subjects who had gone through the self-affirming preparation were much less likely to rate the purported "Jewish" applicant negatively and in ways consistent with the Jewish American princess stereotype.[16]

The same experimenters then demonstrated that events that reduce self-esteem can increase the likelihood that negative stereotypes are applied. They manipulated subjects' feelings of self-worth by manipulating their scores on a phony reasoning and verbal acuity test, and then asked high-scoring and low-scoring subjects to evaluate a man described in a written narrative containing ambiguous clues that he might fit a "gay male" stereotype. Those subjects who had been misled into feeling somewhat bad about themselves were significantly more likely to apply a homophobic stereotype to the fictional character in the story. In another experiment, nonblack subjects were selected randomly, given bogus intelligence tests, and then told on a randomly assigned basis that they had either done very poorly or very well on the test. All subjects were then primed subliminally, by the methods already described, with black or white faces, under conditions of cognitive load that ordinarily suppress stereotype activation. Those subjects who had failed the bogus test nevertheless activated the black stereotype. Those who had done well did not.[17]

Across a range of experiments, it appears that the motivation to boost self-worth affects the activation and application of negative group stereotypes. As John Bargh has argued, repeated experiences of failure and negative stereotype activation can produce a strong psychological association between personal failure and negative stereotypes.[18] Although there are other explanations, this process may help account for the prevalence of some of the most virulent forms of racism, sexism, and homophobia among white males who are failures according to social convention.

3. COUNTERING STEREOTYPES

On a more hopeful note, it is also possible for motivational processes to lead to the inhibition of stereotypes.[19] Under circumstances in which activating or applying a negative stereotype would tend to diminish our self-concept—as when white males react to praise from a black doctor or a female teacher—we are less likely to do so. These effects raise the question of whether egalitarian norms themselves can inhibit stereotype activation and application. For if part of our self-concept is that we are unprejudiced, fair, and egalitarian, then knowing that we have acted on the basis of a stereotype may diminish our view of ourselves. That connection may tend to inhibit the effects of stereotypes among people who adhere consciously to egalitarian norms—provided they are aware of their reliance on stereotypes. In part, this means that we must accept that it is not only anonymous subjects described in psychology journals who suffer from the irrational processes described above. These processes are universal, and they apply to each of us.

A general awareness of our frail rationality, however, is not sufficient. In order to inhibit judgments and behavior based on stereotypes, we must be aware of the specific stereotype at the time it is activated. The entire thrust of the research reported above is that stereotype activation often takes place at a preconscious or subconscious level. Assuming we do have some specific and timely awareness, we must also have both the motivation and the ability to control stereotype activation and application. Motivation can be supplied by social norms or our own moral values and personal will. The ability to control these otherwise automatic processes means devoting time and cognitive resources to focusing on individuating information. One of the reasons stereotypes persist is that they are easy to maintain; overcoming them requires significant effort. Whether all these conditions can obtain is, ultimately, an empirical matter. John Bargh contends that "[t]he odds that all of these necessary conditions will be met in a given situation . . . becomes vanishingly small."[20]

Other psychologists are more optimistic. Galen Bodenhausen and C. Neil Macrae have elaborated a theory of stereotyping and behavior that emphasizes potential inhibitory as well as activating processes.[21] For example, all individuals belong to more than one potential category. Causing subjects to think of a person as a member of one category inhibits the activation of stereotypes associated with another category. For example, priming subjects to react to a video of an apparently Chinese woman as "woman" actually inhibits their ability to later recognize Chinese words, compared either to subjects primed with the "Chinese" association or to unprimed controls.[22] And people who are sufficiently motivated to avoid discrimination can in fact do so. For example, in another experiment subjects were shown a picture of a "skinhead" and asked to write an essay about his probable qualities. The half of the subjects who were instructed to try to avoid stereotypes in their essays successfully did so. There was, however, a catch: when subjects who had successfully suppressed the stereotype in their essays were later exposed to a skinhead image, they were more likely than controls to activate the stereotype.[23]

This is but one of many studies that demonstrate a "rebound effect," in which the active suppression of stereotypes leads to increased stereotyping at the next opportunity.[24] Of course, even people who have prejudiced thoughts may still be able to control their behavior, at least in terms of what would appear blatantly prejudiced, either to themselves or to others. As noted above, Sommers and Ellsworth demonstrated that white jurors behaved as if they were "on guard" against racism in race-salient cases, but not in cases in which race was not so apparently at issue. Apparently, controlling more subtle expressions of prejudice requires conscious awareness that behavior may be affected by stereotypes.

Finally, one line of recent experiments suggests that people can develop habits of mind that work to suppress stereotyping. Having and frequently expressing the chronic goal of egalitarianism can suppress the degree to which we automatically activate stereotypes.[25] And a recent study by

Bargh and his colleagues suggests that it is possible to counter stereotypes at the same preconscious level at which they are activated. They exposed subjects to scrambled word puzzles containing words associated with achievement (*win, compete,* or *attain*). These subjects were more persistent than controls in trying to solve puzzles, suggesting that the priming had altered their motivational level.[26] Perhaps more relevantly, subjects exposed to scrambled sentences with words priming cooperation such as *helpful, support, fair,* or *friendly* were more likely to cooperate in potentially competitive games. These results suggest that priming subjects with fairness or egalitarian goals might activate unconscious cognitions that would counter the effects of the automatic activation of stereotypes, leaving the entire battle between fairness and prejudice to be played out at a subconscious level. In a recent presentation, Bargh suggested that we might think of this approach as "fighting automatic fire with automatic fire."[27]

B. Theories

In order to make sense of experimental results such as those described above, cognitive and social psychologists have developed a range of explanatory theories and models. As before, limitations of both space and the author prevent a comprehensive summary. I offer in this part a summary of the theories that this law professor has found persuasive.

1. SOCIAL CATEGORIES, DATA, AND PROTOTYPES

We know that a significant part of prejudice is bound up in the ordinary cognitive processes of categorization. If we ask people to describe a category of furniture (for example, chairs) or a category of people (people from Oklahoma), we are likely to get back a list of features. In the case of furniture, the list might resemble the dictionary definition. But there are many good reasons to believe that we do not understand concepts or process memories with regard to lists of category features. Among the best evidence is the fact that people do not treat all formally equivalent members of a category as being the same. A stork and a robin are both birds, by any dictionary definition or list of defining features. Yet, if we measure how long it takes people to decide whether the animal in a picture is a bird, they decide much more quickly in the case of robins. If we ask people to list all the birds they can think of, robins come up much more frequently than storks. By these methods, we can map out the category of "bird" and determine that it has something like a "radial" structure: some birds are perceived as more "birdlike" than others, with robins (for North Americans) being nearest the "center" of the category.[28] From these and many other experiments, cognitive scientists now believe that people understand and process information about most categories not with reference to features but by means of prototypes, sets of particular exemplars, or "idealized cognitive models."[29]

When it comes to making sense of people's categories of other people, there is little reason to believe that an entirely different cognitive process comes into play. Presumptively, we understand categories of people not in terms of feature lists, but with reference to prototypical individuals or groups of exemplars.[30] Readers can conduct a simple experiment themselves at this point: First, try to imagine a carpenter. When you have that image settled in your mind, describe the color of her hair. On reading the last two sentences, some readers will miss the feminine pronoun. Others (perhaps most) will be a bit taken aback, and then answer "brown." Of course nothing in the word *carpenter* specifies a gender or a hair color. Some would say that we take account of statistical base rates and that, at least in some places, most carpenters are male and the most common hair color is brown. It is considerably more likely, however, that we do not store information about human categories with regard to statistical base rates, but by reference to prototypes or sets of exemplars. Whereas we may be aware of the general fact of variation among people in every category, our prototypes have particular rather than scalar or fuzzy characteristics. For example, Devon Carbado has described how scholars and activists have written and acted as if the prototype for "black" is heterosexual and the prototype for "gay" is white.[31] What we sometimes refer to as "essentialism" may be less the result of flawed thinking than a by-product of quite ordinary thinking about human categories. Those categories are represented by prototypes that invariably have features beyond those necessary, as a matter of logic, to define the category. Here again, readers can conduct their own further experiment: try to imagine, in sequence, a baseball player, a trial lawyer, a figure skater, and a U.S. Supreme Court justice—without a specific gender or race, but rather with a statistical distribution based on empirical facts. Prototype effects are pervasive. That these effects exist does not mean that we cannot consciously correct for false implications prototypes sometimes suggest, but it does mean that conscious effort is required to do so. [. . .]

2. MOTIVATED COGNITION

[. . .] Experiments exploring the connection between emotion and cognition have given rise to the concept of "motivated cognition" or "hot cognition."[32] The experiments in this area are in many ways as striking as those demonstrating the automaticity of stereotype activation, and demonstrate that stereotype activation itself is impacted by affect. People whose moods are elevated by a seemingly insignificant intervention (receiving an unexpected gift worth twenty-nine cents) rate more highly the performance of their cars and television sets. Counterintuitively, people who are happy are more likely than sad people to use stereotypes in social judgment.[33] Along with mood, motivation also affects both the activation of stereotypes and their application in judgments.[34] Given any ambiguity in a situation, our perceptions are shaded toward consistency with our emotional set, as well as our existing stock of social categories. Finally, most people most of the time like to think of themselves as reasonable, coherent, moral people. We tend to reinterpret the social world so as to maintain that self-affirming view, for reasons explained in the next [section].

3. DISSONANCE, CONSISTENCY, AND SELF-AFFIRMATION

In the classic studies that gave rise to the term "cognitive dissonance," Leon Festinger and his colleagues induced subjects to act in ways that were contrary to their beliefs—for example, to write essays advocating positions with which the subjects strongly disagreed.[35] Experimenters then measured the attitudes of the subjects on the same issues and found that subjects' attitudes had changed systematically in the direction of the positions they had taken in their assigned essays. Festinger theorized that the shift resulted from a basic psychological need to reduce the tension, or dissonance, between concurrently held cognitions or beliefs. Writing an essay that argues against our principles induces just such a tension—which can be reduced by unconsciously adjusting our principles in the direction of the stance we have been induced to take.

Such dissonance can involve beliefs or cognitions about anything. When they relate to our conceptions of ourselves, however, the effects can be particularly strong. One of the progeny of cognitive dissonance theory is Claude Steele's self-affirmation theory, according to which "thought and action are guided by a strong motivation to maintain an overall self-image of moral and adaptive adequacy."[36] Steele demonstrated that the attitude-shifting consequences of dissonance could be reduced by giving subjects a self-affirming experience after writing their counterattitudinal essays but before retesting their attitudes. In other words, it seems that we may be troubled by inconsistencies between what we believe and what we do, but we can live with that result so long as we have other reasons to be satisfied with ourselves. [. . .]

4. CONNECTIONIST MODELS

Given that what seems most odd and unacceptable about the experimental results is the inappropriate ways in which logically unrelated elements appear to be connected in the mind, it is appropriate that the leading contending models of human thinking that explain (and predict) many of the phenomena described thus far are called connectionist models, described by Dan Simon as follows:

> In connectionist models, the elements that constitute thought processes are not evaluated or processed individually, but are activated in relation to other elements in the network. Each cognitive element exerts influence on all those elements to which it is connected, and is influenced by them in return. Such relationships are said to impose a constraint on each of the related elements. In aggregate, a complex thought-task can be expressed as a large set of interconnected constraints, through which all elements affect the related elements, and through these constraints they affect and are affected by the entire set.[37]

In other words, the architectural design for human thinking is not linear and logical like some Newtonian machine, but is embedded in a messy web of connections more like the biological brain than any digital computer. Research in the 1970s established that people behave as if concepts are stored in associational networks, such that activation of one concept (for example, "fire engine") leads more readily to the activation of closer concepts (for example, "red") than more remote concepts (for example, "apple"), and such that activation can spread through the network (for example, from fire engine to red to apple). These networks of concepts can be mapped experimentally by measuring the time it takes subjects to recognize or classify stimuli, or the instances of categories that first come to mind. For example, if subjects are primed by being shown a black-and-white photo of a fire engine, they will be able to recognize a red apple more quickly than a green apple. Or, on being shown a picture of a yellow canary and then asked to name a fruit, experimental subjects are more likely than control subjects to name lemons or bananas. The associational models of concepts extend to the connections between concepts and attitudes. Our implicit attitudes can also be assessed by reaction time experiments. For example, the general cultural preference for youth over age is revealed in how quickly and accurately subjects can match pictures of young people or positive words (*happy* or *friend*) to the category "young or good," compared to their speed and accuracy in matching pictures of older people to the same category. The same methods are used to assess reactions to various stereotyped groups in the Implicit Association Test.

What makes connectionist models particularly promising are discoveries in the mathematical understanding of how large numbers of interconnected elements behave when they interact subject to specified constraints, and in the development of computer simulations of those interactions that allow modeling the behavior of the entire web of interconnected elements. Needless to say, a full exposition of this theory is beyond the scope of this article. However, some examples may help convey at least an impression of the ways in which connectionist models operate.

First, consider two categories that for most people lack much emotional valence: carpenters and Harvard graduates. Now, consider a Harvard-educated carpenter. What do you imagine such a person to be like? For many people, the combination creates a mild sense of dissonance in a way that "Harvard-educated lawyer" does not. Experiments demonstrate that when people encounter conceptual combinations they find incoherent, they tend to invent causal stories that restore a sense of coherence, narratives with new information that "explains away" the apparent inconsistency between the components of the concept. For example, some people will suggest that possibly the carpenter went to Harvard in the 1960s and has an anti-establishment/anti-materialist orientation, or that she is not merely a carpenter but an exquisite craftsman of fine art objects.[38] In effect, the introduction of the causal theory serves to explain—and thus render coherent—the membership of the same person in both categories. Notably also, once the incoherence of the initial combination causes us to activate the "anti-materialist" prototype, that prototype may have other, logically unrelated features. We may, for example, think of a Harvard-educated carpenter as having pacifist or anti-war views.

*   *   *

One can easily imagine similar basic processes taking place in a context more closely related to the subject at hand. Brent Staples, a black columnist for the *New York Times*, has described how, as a young male graduate student in Chicago, he sought to disrupt the stereotypes of

whites he encountered on the street by whistling the music of Vivaldi.[39] Staples's intuition was that a stereotyping white person would deal with the resulting dissonance by introducing a counterstereotypical or exceptionalist explanation, just as subjects attributed counterstereotypical or exceptional qualities to a carpenter when told the carpenter attended Harvard.

[. . .] Connectionist models would [ ] predict that the kind of music playing when a witness sees an ambiguous object may affect whether the witness "sees" a gun or a pair of pliers in the first few moments of perception. [. . .]

Connectionist models can also account for how people understand the causes of social problems. For example, despite the obvious close link between homelessness and poverty, most people blame homelessness on society but blame poverty on the poor.[40] These results are likely explained by the hidden role of race in prototypes of homeless people and poor people, through the following mechanisms: First, in attributing the causes of social problems, people tend to blame individual members of out-groups for their plight, while attributing the difficulties of in-group members to circumstances or society. Most European Americans overestimate the percentage of African Americans among the poor and underestimate the prevalence of African Americans among the homeless.[41] The differential racial associations, combined with the tendency to attribute the problems of out-group members to individual problems, explain the differences in attributions of causation[. . . .]

[. . . D]eveloping some sense of the connectionist processes that describe how stereotypes affect judgment and behavior, particularly at the level of unconscious or preconscious thought, can inform more sophisticated advocacy in areas in which stereotypes are relevant. One of the most important implications of the new social cognitive science is that there are likely to be very few situations in which stereotypes are not—through webs of intermediate connections—relevant to social judgment and behavior. The same body of science helps account for the failures of advocacy based on a folk psychology of prejudice and suggests new advocacy strategies and tactics, based on better theories of how stereotypes operate.

II. RETHINKING ADVOCACY

*　　*　　*

A. Limitations of Advocacy Based on Folk Theories of Prejudice

We now have an adequate basis for evaluating some conventional advocacy strategies that ignore the science described above and rely instead on folk theories of stereotyping and prejudice. Just as we cannot get by in the physical world without implicit theories about the movement of objects, we cannot exist in the social world without implicit theories of human behavior. In most areas of human knowledge, there are both folk and scientific theories. Folk theories (also known as lay theories or implicit theories) are those upon which most laypeople seem to operate. For example, most people without formal training in physics seem to have a theory of momentum that predicts the course of a stone on the end of a string swung around in a circle and then released. That folk theoretic prediction is that the stone will follow a curved path, as if the stone possesses a kind of curving dispositional momentum. In physics as in many other areas of knowledge, contemporary folk theories bear a remarkable resemblance to those of Aristotle. Untrained people also generally have an Aristotelian theory of categories, including categories

of people. If we ask the average person to define or describe a "chair," we are likely to get back a list of necessary and sufficient features—the dominant folk theory of concepts and categories. If a dispute arises about the "chairness" of a particular object, we may turn to a dictionary, which operationalizes folk theory in a list of features. While we have no analogous dictionary of human types, if we ask someone to characterize a group, the typical response also includes a list of features—the contents of which will often reveal something about stereotypes.

I. STEREOTYPING AS INCORRECT EMPIRICAL BELIEF AND ADVOCACY AS INSTRUCTION

Applying this folk psychology of categories to stereotypes, a stereotype consists of beliefs about the features that characterize a social group, and applying a stereotype means assuming that an apparent member of the group has those features. People using stereotypes thus may be making two kinds of errors. The first is an error of fact about the base rates of characteristics in the categorized population in the absence of evidence. For example, despite stereotypes to the contrary, there has never been a time when most people on welfare in the United States were African American, nor a time when most African Americans were on welfare. The second kind of error is ignoring variation within the category, thus assuming that an individual will have a characteristic attributed to the group. Thus, stereotypes notwithstanding, other than lacking a Y chromosome, there are very few features shared by all women. Indeed, we can know virtually nothing meaningful about a person based on group membership—other than the fact, perhaps, that the person has had the experience of being assessed by others on the basis of apparent group membership.

If the "false empirical belief" theory of stereotypes in folk psychology were correct, what strategy would an advocate pursue when targets are relying on stereotypes? If the problem is false beliefs about base rates, the cure would seem to be more accurate information. For example, a welfare advocate wanting to challenge a racial stereotype might present statistical information demonstrating that most people on welfare are, in fact, white. If the error is too ready a willingness to attribute group characteristics to an individual, a slightly different strategy is required. [Albert J.] Moore, [Paul Bruce] and [David A.] Bergman, and Binder advise responding to "silent arguments" reflecting stereotypes in the same manner we respond to overt arguments of the same form, by introducing information that suggests why the individual is exceptional.[42] Thus, without acknowledging a juror's hidden prejudice that the group to which her client belongs is lazy, a lawyer can introduce evidence of the long hours worked by the client. The limitation of this strategy is that it leaves the stereotype intact and deals with only those particular implications of the stereotype of which the advocate is aware and which she is able to address.

The principal limitation of the more general base-rate correction strategy is that it relies on the wrong medium of discourse. If our beliefs about social categories are embedded in discrete prototypes, then data about base rates are the wrong form in which to provide information. Information about demographic data should cause the race of our prototypical welfare recipient to change. But our prototype was not constructed out of data in the first place, but from a long series of exemplars and prototypes provided by culture, including the cultural residue of propaganda wars of the past. It will be changed not by statistics, but by other exemplars. The race of the prototype for welfare recipients might

change, for example, if we are provided with numerous additional exemplars of white welfare recipients. There are, however, powerful psychological forces that tend to prevent this from happening. As many experiments have demonstrated, when people encounter a person who differs from a previously held stereotype, they tend not to change their stereotype, but to create a new subtype to accommodate the exception.[43]

This is particularly the case if we provide people with information about a person that even conceivably might make the person unrepresentative of the stereotyped group. For example, Ziva Kunda and Kathryn Oleson presented subjects with a story about an introverted lawyer, which countered the commonly held stereotype that lawyers are extroverted. Those subjects who were told that the lawyer worked in a small firm developed a subtype stereotype of "small firm lawyers" as introverts. Subjects who were told he worked in a large firm developed a subtype stereotype of "big firm lawyers" as introverts. The result was two new subtype stereotypes but no change in the underlying general stereotype about lawyers. Only when the counterstereotypical instances are introduced without any information to justify a subtype does there seem to be any effect at all on the underlying stereotype. For example, subjects who admitted to a stereotype about gay men being promiscuous altered those views when they read a story about a gay man in a long-term relationship—provided they were not given other information. Subjects reading the same story with one additional piece of information—that the man in the story was an accountant—did not change their stereotype. Rather, they merely created a new stereotype for "gay male accountants" as being less promiscuous. As we saw in the case of the Harvard-educated carpenter, people are quite adept at constructing information that will allow them to maintain preexisting stereotypes.

But not all the current research points in the same dismal direction. Nilanjana Dasgupta and Anthony Greenwald have shown that we can in some cases alter automatic responses to instances of negatively stereotyped groups.[44] They used the Implicit Association Test to assess the implicit racial attitudes of subjects. They then exposed subjects to images of well-known and highly regarded African Americans such as Denzel Washington and to images of well-known but despised European Americans such as Jeffrey Dahmer. This was enough to significantly alter, for at least twenty-four hours, the automatic reactions to black-associated and white-associated names, as measured in the Implicit Association Test. Significantly, explicit attitudes were unaffected.

Many of the implications of stereotype research place lawyers, advocates, and their clients and constituents in something of a bind: One way to avoid having a stereotype applied is to highlight information that will give decision makers some reason to generate a subtype and to view the client as exceptional. At the same time, this strategy is known to ensure the preservation of stereotypes. In other words, by pointing out that a black male client listens to classical music, a lawyer can pander to (and perhaps thereby reinforce) the prejudices of the audience. Obviously, whether to pursue an exceptionalist strategy is not therefore merely a technical question to be decided by lawyers and advocates without consulting clients and constituencies. The science provides no clear guidance for resolving the implicit conflicts. What is clear from the science is that informational strategies that rely on providing empirical data are ineffective because expressed in the wrong form. Informational strategies that do take account of the fact that stereotypes are

bound up in prototypes can be effective, but are limited by the tendency to generate subtype stereotypes in order to preserve the general stereotype. Plainly, more is required than information, even when the information is presented in the correct form.

2. STEREOTYPING AS IMMORALITY AND ADVOCACY AS MORAL SUASION

Another folk theory of stereotyping has particular force regarding prejudices that have resulted in the gravest human harm. For most of us, for example, racism or anti-Semitism reflects not merely cognitive or informational error, but moral failure as well. It may be that the same cognitive processes underlie all stereotyping, but there are powerful moral differences between actions based on stereotypes about people from Oklahoma and actions based on stereotypes bound up in histories of brutality and oppression, of slavery and the Holocaust. Indeed, even to speak of the cognitive errors connected with lynchings and death camps seems to trivialize immorality of literally unspeakable proportions. Moral repugnance overwhelms other reactions. It is no accident that the contestation of these stereotypes has taken place in substantial part in those arenas where morality is most often spoken of, in religious gatherings and discourse, from the early abolitionists to the former National Conference of Christians and Jews.

If prejudice is, at bottom, a moral failing, then what are advocates to do in situations where these particularly morality-laden stereotypes obtain? One approach rooted in this folk theory of prejudice is confrontation. If we confront a person with the evident immorality of his or her prejudice, prejudice should yield to internal moral pressure. There is an underlying assumption that the target shares a moral framework, which may in fact often be the case, at least on the level of stated beliefs and values. But there is also an assumption that confronting an individual with evidence of his or her immoral prejudice will lead to a diminution of the latter. Unfortunately, as we have seen, people have many ways of dealing with apparent contradictions between their asserted values and their actions that enable them to resist the notion that there is a contradiction.

Moralizing strategies are ineffective because they require the target to accept the almost unacceptable: that she or he is an immoral person. As we have seen, the seemingly universal drive to maintain our self-image plays a role in generating stereotypes and prejudice, because our self-image is to some degree socially relative. Moralizing strategies attack the self-image of the target directly. There is no doubt that some psychological mechanism causes people to be able to confess their transgressions. People do, after all, confess their sins. But in the religious rituals in which these psychological processes play out, redemption and restoration of the self-image is immediately available by those means provided by the religion. Moralizing confrontational arguments, by contrast, come unaccompanied by an offer of redemption. Not surprisingly, these arguments are often simply turned aside, most commonly by denial and by reinterpretation of the facts. For this reason, frontal assaults on prejudice tend to be as ineffective as they are common.

There may be an explanation for the prevalence of advocacy strategies that rely on explicitly characterizing a target's views as racist, sexist, homophobic, and so on, even in the face of the experience that these strategies are so rarely effective. Ironically, the pull toward this advocacy strategy is supported by two of the same psychological processes that promote racial stereotyping and prejudice in some people. First, the strategy rests on a false stereotype of stereotypers and an incomplete prototype of prejudice. In a sense it shares with the Supreme Court's defective equal protection jurisprudence much of the same implicit prototype of "individuals who intentionally discriminate." Second, confrontational moralizing strategies also promote in advocates who use them a feeling of superiority with regard to a disfavored group: prejudiced people. Characterizing an argument or attitude as racist, for example, may be accurate in some sense, but it also carries with it the implicit notion that the advocate is without prejudice. In making the argument, the advocate thus acquires a certain sense of superiority, at least in relative moral terms. This is not to say that there is not a place for moral argument, especially with regard to those stereotypes that have resulted in so much that is evil and wrong. But if the pragmatic aim is to persuade rather than to judge, the strategy of moralizing confrontation is likely doomed to failure. There is a place for an appeal to morality and to norms of egalitarianism, even as a pragmatic matter, as we shall see. But a less direct approach is required.

B. Aspects of a Rethought Strategy

[. . .] Although none of us may be able to control our deeply held attitudes as revealed in the Implicit Association Test, all of us can resist relying on stereotypes in making important decisions—under the right conditions. As summarized in a recent article:

> Current models of prejudice and stereotype reduction argue that prejudice-free responses require perceivers to be aware of their biases; to be motivated to change their responses because of personal values, feelings of guilt, compunction, or self-insight; and to possess cognitive resources necessary to develop and practice correction strategies.[45]

The simultaneous confluence of all these conditions is rare but not impossible.

One of the jobs of an advocate is to see that these conditions obtain at the right time with the right targets, and in light of what we know about how stereotypes function in the mind.

[. . .] Although advocacy strategies depend on context, the recent scientific findings suggest some approaches worth considering in any context.

I. RECOGNIZING THE
PERVASIVENESS OF THESE PROCESSES

As a foundational matter, advocates must take account of phenomena such as the automaticity of stereotype activation and the consequences of subconscious associations modeled in connectionist networks. [. . .] Because implicit attitudes are the product of webs of association rather than logical entailment, the effects of stereotyping are likely to be found in a range of situations seemingly far removed from issues of race. In other words, the very notion of "playing the race card" is misleading. By virtue of the automatic and connectionist processes described above, "race cards" are always present and having an effect, even when they are facedown or still in the deck. Racial minorities and others in stereotyped groups suffer silent consequences even when, and sometimes it appears especially when, group identity is unmentioned or unmentionable.

Some social issues are well understood to have become race-coded. Martin Gilens has demonstrated that that it is the stereotypes whites have about the laziness of African Americans that largely determine white attitudes toward welfare, much more so than variables such as economic self-interest, egalitarianism, or attributions of blame for poverty.[46] Lucy Williams[47] and Naomi Cahn,[48] among others, have demonstrated convincingly the ways in which welfare law and regulations are driven by "gendered and raced images." Linda Ammons has described

the role of racial stereotypes in domestic violence cases involving women of color.[49] Similarly, there is powerful evidence that it is the stereotypes whites possess of black men as violent that drive white attitudes about crime.[50] It is fairly evident that issues such as these have become so thoroughly racialized that every conversation about them is a conversation about race.[51] The basic research on stereotyping suggests that such issues are only the most obvious instances of race-coding. For example, any debate about placing restrictions on song lyrics will be affected by the indirect connection to race through rap music. Any reference to an urban issue, including such apparently neutral issues as parks or mass transit, will be affected by the underlying association of "urban" to "minority." Indeed, research suggests that race may be doing the most work in those public policy arenas in which it has not been explicitly mentioned. The lawyers working on the California public schools case I mentioned at the outset must contend with the fact that, at least in California, any reference to "substandard public schools" will trigger associations to inner cities and racial minorities, even if many of those schools are in rural areas and attended by many white children, and perhaps particularly if public discourse about school conditions has become "colorblind."

In the end, of course, the existence and intensity of these remote associations with racial or other stereotypes raises empirical questions that can only be tested through experiments and survey analytic techniques. My point here is that advocates cannot deal with the consequences of these remote associations with stereotypes unless they are aware that they potentially exist. In any advocacy episode involving significant resources, lawyers and advocates might be well advised to devote the resources necessary to map empirically the webs of connection that may affect how jurors, voters, or other targets of advocacy respond to varying presentations.

2. PROMOTING AWARENESS AMONG TARGETS

OF UNIVERSAL STEREOTYPING PROCESSES

Just as advocates cannot deal with the consequences of automatic processes and hidden prejudice unless conscious of their presence, neither can the targets of advocacy. Awareness by targets of these paths to prejudice is generally a condition precedent to reducing their effects. Whatever our motivations, none of us can do much about prejudices of which we are completely unaware. As previously noted, most of us are resistant to believing that our own thinking could be marred by irrational processes. The most direct approaches may therefore be the least effective. But a less confrontational approach may have a better chance. For example, when I teach the material about automaticity of stereotypes to law students, I find less resistance if I begin with the experimental evidence in the contexts of stereotypes of the elderly, rather than experiments about race or gender. A different approach might be required in China, where older people are generally viewed in a more positive way.

Connectionist models suggest an explanation. Stereotypes about the elderly are much less affect-laden in U.S. culture than stereotypes about race, perhaps especially for relatively young people. Most of us, after all, will become elderly at some point, and although our policies toward the elderly may not be ideal, there has never been anything like slavery or Jim Crow with regard to older people. The connections among our self-image, sense of morality, and stereotypes are such that we are less threatened by the implication that we stereotype the elderly than by the notion that we are unconscious racists or sexists. Having accepted the implications of automaticity in a less affect-laden context, we may then be more willing to generalize—to accept that these same mechanisms may drive at least some of our behavior and attitudes about race, sexual orientation, or other affect-laden categories.

One of the consequences of getting to this point is rethinking who is affected by racism and stereotype-driven processes. In conventional usage, the term *racist* is usually reserved for people who subjectively adhere to prejudiced views and behave accordingly. But if we mean to apply the term to people whose behavior is to some degree driven, however unconsciously, by racial stereotypes, then to be a racist is to be an American. [. . .]

3. MOTIVATING CORRECTIVE ACTION: VOLITION, PRECONSCIOUS PROCESSES, AND NORMS

To the extent that there is good news in the current science about stereotypes, it is that while we may be unable to do much about their automatic activation, we can nevertheless behave in substantially nonprejudiced ways if we are so motivated. The effects of motivation can be introduced in many different ways. What seems to matter most is whether antidiscrimination norms are activated, either directly or indirectly. This might be done by argument, by jury instruction, or by implicit invocation of anti-prejudice norms. As Sommers and Ellsworth showed, mock jurors seem effectively to instruct themselves in cases in which race is a salient issue, though not in more ordinary cases.[52] More recently, John Conley and his colleagues demonstrated that the "racial ecology of the courtroom" (for example, a black defendant facing white accusers in an all-white courtroom) may activate antidiscrimination norms: under these conditions, white jurors are less likely to convict a black defendant, even without explicit instructions.[53] These studies, along with the connectionist models we have considered, suggest that there is good reason explicitly to instruct juries in every case, stereotype-salient or not, about the specific potential stereotypes at work in the case.

Obviously, it is not only when we are explicitly ordered by a judge, or persuaded by an advocate, that we can avoid stereotyping. All of us carry around internalized versions of such imperatives, whether we have ever heard the word *norm* or not. Most people like to think of themselves as true to their values, whatever they are. If our values include fairness and treating people as individuals, then anything that increases self-awareness should decrease our application of stereotypes. And, indeed, there is very interesting empirical support for this notion. In a rather remarkable series of experiments, Macrae and his colleagues demonstrated that subjects exposed to a potential stereotype stimulus (a photo of a male construction worker) generated significantly fewer stereotypic associations if a closed-circuit television in the experiment room showed an image of the subject rather than a stranger.[54] Perhaps jury deliberation rooms, as well as the halls of the U.S. Congress, should be furnished with more mirrors.

As noted earlier, John Bargh and his colleagues have recently demonstrated that goals such as fairness can, in effect, be "injected" into people by the same simple priming processes that produce automatic stereotyping effects.[55] For example, it appears that merely seeing or hearing words such as *fairness* can cause people to behave as if they are more committed to being fair, entirely without the conscious knowledge of the subjects. This suggests that lawyers or others interested in countering the effects of automatic stereotyping

should insert into their presentations as many contrarian priming words, pictures, and other stimuli as possible. Although there is a certain Orwellian irony to the idea, our system of justice might be more evenhanded if the televisions in jury assembly rooms were programmed with both apparent and subliminal fairness primes amid the usual fare of soap operas and reruns of *Judge Judy*.[56]

4. COUNTERING "SILENT ARGUMENTS" WITH EXPLICIT ARGUMENTS, CROSS-CATEGORIZATION, AND COUNTERSTEREOTYPICAL EXEMPLARS

My colleagues Moore, Binder, and Bergman advise treating stereotypes as if they were generating "silent arguments" and responding to them by the same means one responds to explicit arguments. For example, the prosecutor in a reckless-driving case may introduce evidence that at the time the defendant was observed speeding, he was late for a doctor's appointment, relying on an explicit generalization about people who are late for appointments. In response, the defense lawyer can undermine the generalization with what Moore and his co-authors call "except whens": for example, by pointing out that the generalization may be true except when the doctor is a friend of the defendant and likely to be more accommodating. Stereotypes give rise to unstated inferences in the same form. Moore and his co-authors use the example of a judge whose prejudice leads him to believe that Iranian Americans are more likely to stage accidents. They advise a lawyer for an Iranian American plaintiff to introduce evidence undermining that inference: for example, that the plaintiff has never made a prior claim—evidence that would not be relevant to an explicit claim or argument in the case. This approach deals with one inference that flows from the stereotype, as applied to the particular individual, without challenging the stereotype itself. Undermining all of the effects of the stereotype, even in the limited context of a single trial, would require introducing "except when" evidence as to every relevant implication of the stereotype.

One can think of cross-categorization strategies as responding to the same problem in a more general way. These strategies rely on the fact that every person falls into more than one category, including categories associated with stereotypes. Sometimes the stereotypes have conflicting implications: recall the experiment regarding the mathematical performance of Asian American women. Whether the stereotypes are in direct conflict or not, there is considerable evidence that drawing attention to additional categories to which a person belongs can reduce prejudice based on a salient, stereotype-laden category.[57] Rather than engaging in explicit arguments, by highlighting other group membership we can deploy silent arguments of our own, based on generalizations or stereotypes associated with other categorizations. By simply drawing attention to another category, we implicitly suggest something like "she may be an X and therefore have quality A—an assumption I do not at this moment contest— but she is also a Y, and for that reason more likely to have quality B." Advocates are often counseled to humanize their clients. In part this means conveying the multidimensional complexity of human beings who may otherwise be understood by reference to one label or group.

Introducing counterstereotypical exemplars of the stereotyped category is another way of affecting, through information, the stereotypes of advocacy targets. As noted above, this strategy is limited by the fact that people tend to respond by creating subtypes for the exemplars rather than modifying their

preexisting stereotypes. This is one of the reasons that the "contact hypothesis"—the notion that prejudice can be reduced simply through contact with members of the stereotyped groups—has proven wildly overoptimistic.[58] Only under very limited, and often counterintuitive, conditions does increased exposure to counterstereotypical individuals seem to have any effect on stereotypes. For example, the more strikingly divergent the exemplar is from the stereotype, the more likely the exception is simply subtyped and the smaller the effect on the basic stereotype. On the other hand, there is evidence that stereotype change can result from exposure to "people who moderately disconfirm perceivers' stereotypes of their group."[59]

Cognitive social psychologists attribute the decline in stereotypes about Irish Americans, for example, to the effects of these processes over time. Advocates must develop and implement strategies to deal with episodes on a much shorter time scale. In the shorter run, advocates designing public education efforts intended, in part, to counter the effects of stereotypes should rely more on images of people who will be seen as less exceptional than Denzel Washington or Edward James Olmos.

*   *   *

CONCLUSION

In the end, there is something odd and incomplete about an article on what might be characterized as the pragmatics of prejudice. Coming to grips with the universality and mechanisms of stereotyping and prejudice is much less cathartic than denunciation and calls to higher moral purpose and action. In the lives of those who daily pay the personal price of prejudice, however, it is action that matters more. To return to where I began, in the public school classrooms of California, we might explain to the million children of color whose futures are slipping away from them that no one really intends them any harm. No one is intentionally depriving them of books or teachers with some minimal training while ensuring that other children have everything they need and more. We might also explain that for a half century lawyers have been fighting to re-duce these disparities, as they now are in *Williams v. California*,[60] and that other lawyers and advocates are opposing discrimination in other ways. It would be harder, however, to explain advocacy failures occasioned by our ignoring what science now knows about how prejudice actually works.

5

Individual and Intergroup Processes to Address Racial Discrimination in Lawyering Relationships

Carwina Weng

INTRODUCTION

Imagine you are a criminal defense attorney. You will interview two men today, both accused of unlawful sexual assault. Each client admits that he had sex with the respective complainant—in each case a young woman the client met casually at a party—but contends that the sex was consensual. Each also suggests that the complainant might claim to have minor injuries caused when the sex got a bit rough.

What are your initial reactions to each client? To his situation?

What if you are told that in the first case the accused is white and that in the second case the accused is black?

For the first two questions, most of us would probably report that our reactions to each client and his situation would be the same: nonjudgmental, open to hearing the client's narrative, open to assessing credibility. That is, after all, part of our training as lawyers. For the next two questions, again most of us would probably make the same report.

But might there be a split second's hesitation about the black client?

There well might be. Even the best-intentioned among us might experience a moment of hesitation about a black client accused of a violent crime, if only because we are exposed to news stories that suggest that young black men are violent and dangerous.[1] Research shows that this kind of exposure and innate processes of social categorization along race lines affect the way we think about crime, including who commits it and what society's response should be.[2]

This is not to say that the lawyer would then not do her best to represent the black client zealously and competently, as she would for any client. But even a lawyer with low levels of prejudice might unintentionally allow bias to affect her relationship with and her representation of a black client. That bias could cause misunderstandings of the client's narrative, credibility judgments, conflict over strategy, and general mistrust and conflict—even if the client prevails.

An example of such misunderstanding is eloquently documented by clinical law professor Clark D. Cunningham. Cunningham describes his experience, along with legal clinic students, in representing an African American man stopped for allegedly running a stop sign. The police briefly searched the driver and then charged him with disorderly conduct for statements he made. The lawyers' theory of the case focused on the reasons for the search (whether it was justified), whereas the client's theory was about why he was stopped, namely, racial harassment, what might now be called "driving while black." The lawyers' lack of recognition for or development of the client's theory and the personal value he placed on his perspective of the stop contributed to the client's profound dissatisfaction with the representation he received, even after the charges against him were dropped.[3]

So, what's a lawyer who, like Cunningham, wants to work with clients in a racially appropriate manner to do? This chapter offers some understanding of how unintentional racial discrimination can occur and suggests some ways to combat unintentional racial discrimination on individual and institutional bases, based on current research in social cognition.

I. CATEGORIZATION, RACIAL STEREOTYPES, AND PREJUDICE

I begin with a brief overview of the cognitive process of categorization and its relationship to racial stereotypes and prejudice.[4] Categorization is a process people undertake automatically, like breathing, to make sense of our world. We sort information into categories of people, objects, places, events, and so on. We then develop cognitive structures called schemas that contain the knowledge we hold about a category, associations of traits, characteristics, or attributes, and examples of the category. A schema helps us to identify who or what we see and to explain and predict events and behaviors. When a person's schema includes a generalized conception of the category into which the perceiver sorts an individual and the attributes the perceiver attributes to that category, the schema might be a stereotype. And if the links between the category and stereotyped attributes are made frequently or consistently, then the links associated with the category might become stronger, so that the stereotype might be more readily activated, even subconsciously.[5]

So when a lawyer meets a client, she undergoes a series of cognitive processes starting with automatic categorization: in which category, including race, does this client fit? From that category, the lawyer will then activate schemas associated with the category, and these schemas will affect her interaction with the client cognitively and affectively. Which schemas, including stereotypes, influence the interaction depends on factors such as primacy (which schemas are activated first), salience (which schemas seem more relevant), and accessibility. Racial schemas are particularly accessible because people pay more attention to physical characteristics such as skin color. Thus in the example at the beginning of this chapter, the schemas might trigger thoughts about the client's criminality, socioeconomic background, aggressiveness, violence, and credibility, and emotional reactions to the client.[6] Note that the holding of such knowledge or reacting negatively to the client does not entail endorsement of their content.[7]

Typically, a lawyer will apply her schemas to interpret and evaluate the client consistently with the schema. Thus, if a lawyer activates a stereotype of a black male as generally hostile and aggressive, she might hesitate to shake his hand upon greeting him. And if she activates a stereotype of a black male as sexually violent, she might evaluate the client's claim of consensual rough sex with more skepticism than she might evaluate the white client's claim. This behavior could occur without volition by the lawyer, resulting in aversive or implicit discrimination. Aversive or implicit discrimination occurs when a person who consciously endorses egalitarian values unconsciously holds biased beliefs.[8]

Such implicit bias does not mean, however, that our lawyer is doomed to reinforce race discrimination throughout her representation of this or another client. Research has shown that stereotype activation can decrease over time, as the perceiver's attention moves to other information about the target individual. Indeed, exposure to a racially different target for even less than fifteen minutes can decrease stereotype activation.[9] In an ongoing relationship, as between a lawyer and client, the lawyer will receive more information about the client, and her efforts to understand the client, whether because the client behaves in ways inconsistent with the schemas activated by the lawyer or because of the lawyer's need for accuracy, can push the lawyer to rely less on the schema and more on individuating information about the client.[10]

In addition, although a person may still hold knowledge of stereotypes, recent research has shown that activation and application of stereotypes, even unconsciously, is by no means inevitable, especially when an individual is motivated to act in a nonbiased manner and can bring cognitive resources to bear on the task. It

also helps to operate in an environment constructed to reinforce and promote egalitarian values and behavior.[11]

II. TACKLING RACE BIAS ON AN INDIVIDUAL LEVEL

Because techniques for individual efforts at acting without bias in lawyer-client relationships have been covered extensively elsewhere,[12] this chapter focuses on more general social cognition principles and processes. In particular, Patricia Devine has described a multistep process for reducing bias on an individual basis:

1. An individual must first decide that biased and nonegalitarian behavior is inappropriate and adopt nonprejudiced beliefs and personal standards.
2. Next, the individual must internalize these standards and integrate them into his self-concept.
3. Third, the individual must self-regulate his behavior based on his egalitarian personal standards. This last step entails recognizing that his behavior may reflect implicit bias that conflicts with his avowed standards.[13]

In other words, a person who wants to act in a nonbiased manner learns that her behavior falls short, experiences guilt and compunction, and is further motivated to change her behavior. Time and practice eventually make nonbiased behavior a habit and can result in the inhibition of stereotypes consciously and unconsciously.[14]

Empirical research has tested the validity of this model. For example, Kerry Kawakami and her colleagues tested the effects of training to negate automatic stereotype activation. In a series of studies, she trained participants to ignore stereotyped associations with the category "skinhead,"[15] such as "aggressive," even after the stereotype had been primed. In the first study, participants performed a primed Stroop color-naming task to determine whether the skinhead stereotype had been activated both before and after training to negate the stereotype.[16] The training consisted of 480 trials in which participants were instructed to say no to presentations of skinhead stereotypes. Comparisons of the participants' pre- and posttraining Stroop task results indicated that activation of the skinhead stereotype after training did not interfere with color naming. The second study replicated the methodology of the first but repeated posttraining Stroop task testing at two, six, and twenty-four hours subsequent to the first session to test the duration of the stereotype-negation training. The study demonstrated that the participants were able to respond with a no to category-stereotype presentations for at least twenty-four hours following the training. The third study replicated these results for a race-based stereotype, thereby demonstrating that the results of the first two studies were potentially generalizable.[17]

Devine, Ashby Plant, and David Amodio studied the bias-reduction process from the lens of motivation. Participants first completed an evaluation of their explicit race bias levels and then engaged in a variety of tests to measure their implicit bias. The study found that the source of motivation—internally held egalitarian values versus external motivation based on concern for the approval of others—determined how well a participant was able to act without prejudice. Individuals with high internal motivation to be egalitarian were most adept at acting without explicit and implicit race bias. Individuals who were motivated externally did less well.[18]

John Dovidio, Kerry Kawakami, and Samuel Gaertner tested whether the Devine model applied to internally motivated changes of implicit stereotypes. In this study, white participants first completed explicit and implicit measures of prejudice and an implicit measure of attribution of stereotyped black traits to another person, after being subliminally primed with racially stereotypic characteristics. Next, they were exposed to discrepancies between how they wanted to behave and how they thought they would behave toward blacks, and their emotional reactions to these discrepancies were measured. Three weeks later, the participants again performed the two implicit stereotyping tasks and the behavior discrepancy evaluation. Among participants who at the initial session had a greater discrepancy between desired and likely behavior, the level of guilt was greater, especially for participants who were lower in prejudice. At the second session, all participants showed a reduced gap, regardless of their prejudice levels. Thus, awareness of discrepancies between their personal values and actual behavior seemed to motivate whites in general to behave publicly in a more egalitarian fashion, and, in whites with lower levels of prejudice, this awareness further demonstrated greater internalization of egalitarian behavior in implicit bias measures.[19]

These studies hold out hope for bias reduction, but the crux of this process is figuring out whether one's behavior is biased. Explicit bias is easier to tackle in this age of public egalitarianism and diversity training. At least in public, it is rare, for example, to hear racial epithets, regardless of how much prejudice an individual actually holds, because social norms now dictate against such language.[20] In addition, diversity training at its most basic level conveys knowledge about and appreciation for people of different races, ethnicities, and other subordinate groups.[21]

Implicit bias is harder to address. One first must become aware that one is subconsciously accessing and applying stereotypes about people from different racial/ethnic groups. This can of course be done by readings in social cognition. In addition, though, anyone with access to the Internet and an e-mail account can participate in Project Implicit, a large-scale study about automatic preferences and biases. The project invites participants to take an Implicit Association Test (IAT) on subjects ranging from pets to racial/ethnic groups, politics, and celebrities. As the researchers explain:

> The IAT asks you to pair two concepts (e.g., *young* and *good*, or *elderly* and *good*). The more closely associated the two concepts are, the easier it is to respond to them as a single unit. So, if *young* and *good* are strongly associated, it should be easier to respond faster when you are asked to give the same response . . . to these two. If *elderly* and *good* are not so strongly associated, it should be harder to respond fast when they are paired. This gives a measure of how strongly associated the two types of concepts are. The more associated, the more rapidly you should be able to respond.[22]

The IAT thus can allow a test taker to learn whether she has implicit attitudes toward an out-group that she might not realize she had and may not want.

The next task is developing the motivation to change behavior. Individuals with low prejudice may have more internalized motivation to change their behavior to comply with their standards of egalitarianism. Thus, a person with low prejudice, who is aware of her implicit biases, might engage in self-regulation to bring her behavior and implicit attitudes in line with her egalitarian values and explicit attitudes.[23] Regular practice can help make her egalitarian values more accessible than stereotypes and might make clearer the signs of bias and situations in which bias occurs so that the lawyer can better avoid problems in the future.[24]

For an individual with high prejudice, success in reducing biased behavior also will depend on the mix of internal and external reasons for achieving the goal. Research has shown that societal pressure to avoid prejudice can lead to backlash, accompanied by anger and a less favorable attitude toward egalitarian policies. Thus, in a study conducted by Devine and Plant, blatant efforts were made to develop support for an affirmative action policy by exposing participants to a communication designed to change negative attitudes toward affirmative action. Individuals who had high levels of prejudice and low motivation to change their attitude reported strong resistance to the policy, as the policy was perceived as an attack on their specific anti-affirmative-action and general racial attitudes. In a second study, more subtle efforts at influencing attitudes were made, by having individuals opposed to affirmative action write an essay in support of the policy. Participants who were more highly motivated internally to be egalitarian reported more positive reactions to the task and the policy—a change in their attitudes. Participants with high external motivation to be egalitarian but low internal motivation continued to show anger about the task, perhaps because they were looking for external pressure to change their attitudes. But individuals with low external and internal motivation were less angry.[25]

Given the likelihood of backlash from individuals who are more prejudiced and less internally motivated to change, efforts to change their biased behavior must proceed more carefully to build internal motivation and to decrease anger. Devine suggests a two-pronged approach: to increase external motivation, using a respected person to endorse egalitarian norms in an effort to decrease resistance, and to increase internal motivation, creating space for private self-confrontation about values. The latter can be achieved by increasing empathy, which makes it harder to feel anger and resentment toward a member of the out-group, and by appealing to the individual's general values, rather than focusing on specific race-based beliefs, so that the individual can discover for himself how his values affect people of other races and his own reactions to such people.[26] Over time, then, perhaps a high-prejudiced, low-motivated individual would be able to internalize more the goal of acting in a nonbiased manner.

Transitioning from these theories to practical lawyering is not easy. It requires the lawyer to recognize that race affects his lawyering and to explore those effects. Two examples of ways to address race in lawyer-client interactions come from my clinical teaching. As part of my teaching, students learn to recognize and address multicultural lawyering and are graded on their client interactions, including their handling of race and other cultural issues. This evaluation provides external motivation for students to lawyer in an egalitarian manner.

First, a Latina student had been assigned to work with a white woman seeking to end shared legal custody and to stop visits between her ex-husband and their two children. The basis for the mother's action was revelations by her son of sexually inappropriate behavior by the father and the parents' history of domestic violence. The student evinced skepticism of the mother's claims of domestic violence and sexual abuse against the children. As we explored the basis for her skepticism, the student talked a lot about the family's background: Both parents were highly educated, having met in graduate school at an Ivy League institution. The mother had not completed her Ph.D. because of the marriage, but the father remained well employed as a scientist.

In the student's world, white people with this socioeconomic status did not experience domestic violence and sexual abuse. I noted that the fact that the client presented against the stereotype of an abused woman was one reason I was glad the clinic was representing her. The student and I explored the stereotype of an abused woman, talked about signs of abuse and patterns of behavior that a survivor might exhibit, and considered whether the client might be credible based on these traits. We also looked critically at the record of the initial divorce to see whether the court system might also have acted on the stereotype of abused women as poor women of color. This discussion about the client herself and her experience of the family court system enabled the student to connect with the client, especially regarding the client's desire to protect her children, for the student herself had been abused as a child.

In the second example, a white male student was assigned to the case of a Guatemalan client seeking unpaid overtime wages. The client was undocumented. The student had very strong anti-immigration views and ironically had been opposing a proposed guest worker program just before he reviewed the client's file. In this instance, the student and I did not consider his concerns specifically as a race issue but looked closely at his immigration stance and his general background and values. We found strong beliefs in zealous advocacy (a professional rule for lawyers), in the sanctity of law, in a general idea of justice as well as a very strong work ethic. From these beliefs, we determined points of convergence with the client and his situation: given the number of hours of overtime he reported, he was clearly a hard worker; the client's employer was breaking laws in hiring the client and in not paying overtime wages to the point of exploiting the client's immigration status; and the client had a clear sense of justice and fairness, being unwilling to demand the legal overtime rate of time and a half when he had contracted only for his regular hourly wage. In considering these points, the student turned into an enthusiastic advocate for this particular individual and actually moved his case forward more than the previous students had.

III. TACKLING RACE BIAS ON AN INTERGROUP LEVEL

Focusing solely on an individual's biases is not, of course, enough to decrease prejudiced behavior on a broad basis. Indeed, too great a focus on group identity instead of individuating traits can even increase prejudice, as group focus can increase the sense of difference on a group level. Accordingly, efforts to reduce prejudice must also target intergroup interaction.[27]

I start with a summary of basic principles that affect intergroup interaction: (1) the intergroup accentuation principle—we see members of the same group as more similar; (2) the in-group favoritism principle—we trust or like other members of our own social group more than members of an out-group; and (3) the social competition principle—we see interdependence with other groups negatively and compare other groups negatively to our own.[28]

Because of the operation of these basic principles, mere intergroup contact is not enough to reduce prejudice. Rather, to reduce prejudice, such contact must occur in a setting that minimizes the effects of these negative intergroup principles.[29] A suitable setting espouses egalitarian norms; promotes positive and equal interactions among members of dominant and subordinate groups, including the forma-

tion of personal relationships; and permits open and truthful discussions among members of different groups.[30]

The emphasis on equal interactions is important because power differentials in a relationship skew the ways in which each person views the other. The person with power has less need to view the subordinate person as an individual rather than as a member of a racial out-group because the subordinate may be less important to her own success. Thus, she may not realize or care that she is using stereotypes in her interactions with her subordinate. By contrast, a person who feels dependent on another will be motivated to decategorize the other person—to understand the person on whom he is dependent as an individual, not just as a member of an out-group—because individualization allows each dependent person to better predict how the other person will behave and therefore to better control their progress to achieve common goals.[31] So, a person of color who is a supervisor is treated more as an individual by her underlings than a person of color who is a subordinate is treated by his supervisor.[32]

Studies have shown that it is possible to make pairings interdependent, even when a power differential appears to exist. Susan T. Fiske, for example, reviews studies of interviewers and job applicants, which demonstrate that interviewers who realize that their outcomes are contingent upon the applicants are more likely to treat the applicants as individuals. For example, interviewers are reminded that they too must sell their employer to the applicant and that they must conduct a good interview of an applicant to get the best information possible to determine whether an offer should be made.[33]

Indeed, the ideal interdependent situation would seem to be one in which successful cooperation among members of different racial groups prevails.[34] Decategorization focuses on reducing favoritism toward in-group members, as individual identity as opposed to group identity becomes salient.[35] Cooperative intergroup interaction can go further, not only decreasing the significance of racial group differences but also promoting the extension of in-group favoritism to members of a different group. The extension of in-group favoritism occurs as cross-category similarities are found or created.[36]

There are two ways in which cross-category similarity result. The first is recategorization, in which a common group identity develops, and the second is mutual differentiation, in which individuals maintain their own group identities while finding common ground or subordinate group identity with others.[37] Neither of these methods is exclusive of the other or of decategorization.

With recategorization, members of different racial groups may maintain their subgroup identities while developing a superordinate, common group identity. If the different subgroups (for example, Asian and Latino) experience low levels of competition and believe other subgroups are complementary within the superordinate group (for example, American), then bias toward the other subgroups can decrease, and the superordinate group may cohere.[38] In a study of the recategorization process, two three-person teams were brought into a laboratory under conditions that varied their sense of the number of groups within the teams. When a team began to cooperate, bias within the team decreased, as the sense of separate groups decreased and the sense of a single group increased. In addition, groups that cohered into a single group experienced less intergroup bias even without cooperation among team members. These improved attitudes toward out-group members ex-tended to the out-group generally as well.[39]

Surveys of students in real life also support this finding. For example, a survey was conducted of 1,357 racially diverse students in a high school in the Northeast to test how contact among racially diverse groups affected bias. The survey asked students how they perceived the student body: as one group, as different groups on the same team, or as separate groups. The results indicated that racial or ethnic groups that had positive perceptions of intergroup contact also saw the student body as either one group or one team with different components. These groups also reported less bias.[40]

But if the subgroups are more independent or antagonistic, then recategorization will not reduce bias as effectively. Some of the problems that can arise include competition and comparison among the subgroups as to which group's values might predominate in the superordinate group; loyalty to the subgroup interfering with intergroup relations and the functioning of the superordinate group; and power differentials among the subgroups that affect the perspectives of the subgroups as to the success of the superordinate group.[41]

Thus, studies have shown that a threat to one's personal identity, if race is a powerful component, can hurt intergroup relations. In addition, surveys of people's perspectives on race relations typically show that black Americans are more likely than white Americans to see racism as an ongoing problem and to be more pessimistic about improvement.[42]

Given these problems, a model with more potential for reducing bias is mutual differentiation, in which people recognize and respect each individual's multiple subgroup identifications while developing cross-category commonalities.[43] This process might diminish intergroup comparison and competition in a number of ways: making social categorization more complex and reducing the magnitude of group distinctions; reducing the salience of racial categories as a basis for comparison; reducing the importance of any one social identity for satisfying an individual's need for belonging and self-definition; and encouraging greater accuracy in individual interactions to resolve inconsistencies between stereotypes and reality, the process for which can lead to more positive attitudes toward members of an outgroup and, by extension, to the out-group itself.[44]

The mutual differentiation hypothesis has been tested in and out of the laboratory. Marilynn B. Brewer describes a study she and several colleagues conducted that manipulated group membership and role assignment. The study created two arbitrary same-sex groups, the overestimators and the underestimators. Then members were reassigned into two groups with a cooperative task to reach consensus about the key traits for NASA astronauts. Within these task groups, two members were assigned to focus on cognitive and skill traits and two to focus on emotional and social traits. Within these expertise-based groups, members might come from the same original categories or from different categories. When the larger work groups reconvened, they determined the list of key traits and then evaluated each member's contributions to the work. When original group and expertise membership converged, bias about which team member contributed more was apparent. When original group and expertise fell into different categories, no such bias was apparent. Similar results have been replicated in studies using political party affiliation and college status groups.[45]

Outside the laboratory, a survey of college students' satisfaction with their schools also indicated the utility of mutual differen-

tiation in bias reduction. The survey questioned students about their level of satisfaction with their colleges, in terms of their willingness to stay at that school, their willingness to recruit for the school, and the strength of their group identification. Responses demonstrated that white students with a higher perception of the student body as either one superordinate group or one team with many different groups had a more positive perception of interracial contact and satisfaction. Students of color were most likely to be satisfied with their school if they perceived the student body to be one team with many different groups than if they perceived the student body to be one superordinate group.[46]

Perceptions of one superordinate group or of one team with many different groups are more likely to occur if the crossover among different in-group and out-group categories has functional significance for the larger community. Functional significance occurs when individuals "must confront the fact that their different in-group and out-group categories have overlapping memberships" that matter to the larger group. For example, in the mutual differentiation study conducted by Brewer, the categories of estimators were salient because the purpose of the study was to consider the effect of difference and the categories of experts were significant to the task of determining the key traits for astronauts.[47]

A study by Robin Ely and David Thomas provides real-world evidence of the importance of functional significance of cross-group memberships in achieving positive work and diversity outcomes. Ely and Thomas set out to develop a theory about how diversity conditions affect work group functioning. They studied three organizations that had achieved substantial numerical racial and ethnic diversity in both staff and management positions to see which conditions led to more successful work outcomes that were related to cultural composition. They concluded that the two firms that had brought in racial and ethnic minority employees for work-related purposes were more successful at performing their core tasks and at achieving racial harmony than was the firm that had brought in racial and ethnic minority employees out of a generalized sense of fairness and justice.[48]

The work-related purposes, or perspectives, were (1) integration and learning, in which employees of different backgrounds were seen as "valuable resources that the work group can use to rethink its primary tasks and redefine its markets, products, strategies, and business practices in ways that will advance its mission," and (2) access and legitimacy, in which employees of different racial and ethnic backgrounds were necessary to penetrate and sustain markets and constituencies that shared in-group membership with the new employees.

In both these instances, it was the category difference (race and ethnicity) itself that was functionally significant to the firms, and therefore the in-group/out-group crossover was essential to the success of the firms. With the integration and learning firm (a small, gender-discrimination, public-interest law firm) the firm itself was transformed into an integrated superordinate group. With the access and legitimacy firm (a bank with a local black client base), clearer group and power differences remained, but black and white employees recognized a symbiotic role for each group.[49]

The challenge, of course, lies in creating a successful environment that fosters the sense of either one superordinate group or one team with multiple subgroups. Ideally, in the latter situation, the subgroups would be equal, for if one subgroup dominates, then cross-category commonalities and differences might be lost. A successful cooperative environment would enable

people "to confront the fact that their different ingroup-outgroup categories have overlapping memberships . . . with functional significance within the same social context." This self-confrontation is more likely to occur where there is tolerance for complexity and uncertainty, promotion of inclusion, and a salient superordinate category that encompasses all the subgroups.[50]

IV. CREATING AN EGALITARIAN LAWYERING ENVIRONMENT

David W. Johnson and Roger T. Johnson identify three hallmarks of an egalitarian community: cooperation, constructive conflict resolution, and internalized civic values.[51] I will focus on how these hallmarks can be integrated in a law school clinic, as that is the milieu in which I work. In so doing, I will consider classroom and fieldwork settings. However, the suggestions here would have application in other lawyering settings as well.

As a preliminary matter, I note that the racial diversity of clinical lawyering settings will vary greatly. Although the Supreme Court has upheld the use of racial categories in law school admissions, law schools and their clinics differ in how they admit students and therefore in each clinic's racial composition among students.[52] Some clinics admit students by application in part to obtain racial diversity; others target race-based student organizations for recruitment; still others follow first-come, first-served registration. In addition, the client population served by a clinic will vary as well, depending on the racial composition of the area the clinic serves and the method of accepting clients for representation.

A. Cooperation

A cooperative community is characterized by common goals and culture and requires social interdependence, in which each member's outcomes are influenced by the behavior of other members. To be effective, the members of the community must share a sense of positive interdependence—"mutual goals, joint rewards, divided resources, complementary roles, or a shared identity." Such positive interdependence is more likely to occur when each member is individually accountable for her work and seen as doing her fair share, when each member has the opportunity to give input to others' work and promote others' successes, when each member can develop interpersonal and small group skills such as leadership, decision-making, trust-building, communication, and conflict-resolution skills, and when the community allows open and honest discussions about work and working relationships.[53]

The creation of such a cooperative community in the classroom is not easy. Traditional lecture classes and seminars can allow students to opt out of participating instead of sharing in and taking responsibility for the class's learning. Shin Imai describes a circle-based technique he uses in his clinic classes for developing a sense of group and to allow students to experience the creation of a collaborative structure: "After setting out a bare-bones fact situation, I ask each student in turn to ask me a factual question which will help the group understand the dimensions of the problem. A student is allowed to pass, but no one is allowed to go out of turn. The exercise makes structural room for students who are quieter, and it helps give the more talkative students the discipline to remain silent."[54] By using the circle, everyone in the class can learn to communicate and to listen and can contribute to the group's overall learning.

Law clinicians also long have incorporated small-group work into their classrooms to facilitate cooperative learning. The smaller groups allow the lawyers to get to know each other and their supervisors better cognitively and emotionally. Specifically, frequent, accurate, and open contact allows us to see each other as multidimensional, adaptable (to each other) people and to learn each other's perspectives, thought processes, and behaviors.[55] Examples of common small-group exercises that facilitate cooperation include introductory exercises that allow students to talk and get to know each other informally, breakout sessions that allow subgroups of students to work on a problem and then present their ideas to the larger group for review, simulation work, and student teams to lead classes.

On the fieldwork side, cooperation should be established among the legal professionals and with the client. First, student lawyers can be paired to work on client cases so that they can benefit from the synergy of different perspectives, skills, resources, and areas of expertise. For example, collaboration among students of different racial and ethnic backgrounds can teach them "to look at their work through someone else's eyes and, in the process of doing that, to identify their own biases and assumptions." Clinics also should not assume that students know how to cooperate but should teach cooperation skills, such as listening, giving feedback, analysis of projects and tasks, delegation of responsibility, and constructive conflict resolution. This learning would help to ensure that diverse voices are not silenced within the lawyering team and larger community.[56]

Second, collaboration with the client should be developed. Currently, the dominant theory of lawyer-client relationships is the client-centered model.[57] The model's focus on client decision making[58]—that the client should control the lawyering, to maximize client satisfaction with the lawyering—requires the lawyer to learn the client's priorities and values.[59] It therefore has the potential to encourage a more cooperative relationship between lawyer and client.[60] But as various critiques of this model have indicated, the model lends itself to maintaining a hierarchical divide that maintains lawyer dominance, to the particular detriment of clients of color because the lawyer controls the fact-finding and counseling structures by using models that favor the dominant white discourse.[61]

Refinements to the client-centered lawyering model make it more cooperative, although without the explicit motivation of reducing racial discrimination. For example, one of the basic lawyering textbooks, *The Counselor-at-Law: A Collaborative Approach to Client Interviewing and Counseling*, proposes a cooperative model in which the lawyer explicitly uses his expertise to "structure the process and provide advice in a manner that is likely to yield wise decisions" by the client. At the same time, the book cautions lawyers about ways that enable lawyer dominance and suggests two basic principles to avoid such dominance. The first is that lawyers see their role as translators of the client's situation so that a lawyer must strive to translate the client's original meaning accurately. This perspective addresses issues of power imbalance that might skew an interdependent relationship. The second is that lawyers and clients collaboratively negotiate their relationship, including goals, strategies, division of responsibility, and level of client participation in the relationship.[62] This approach incorporates the tenets of cooperation not only in specific lawyering tasks such as interviewing and counseling but in the very formation of the relationship. It thereby can set the basis for shared decision making throughout the lawyer-client relationship.

B. Constructive Conflict Resolution

Constructive conflict resolution helps to reinforce cooperation and respect by fostering motivation, achievement, and problem solving among the community's members.[63] Johnson and Johnson provide two models for resolving conflict in this manner.

In conflicts concerning the clash of substantive ideas (what the case theory is, how to understand the client's or an opposing party's interests or motivations, which option best resolves the legal issue), each person will prepare her position, presenting and advocating for it, and offering refutations to opposition. She also should undertake opposing perspectives to better understand them. Then the team members should synthesize the positions to determine which to adopt.[64]

In conflicts of interest among team members, in which the actions of one member may interfere with the desires of another, negotiating to achieve an integrative solution may be preferred. Here, each side lays out what he wants, how he feels, and his reasons for his wants and emotions. Then each side attempts to understand the other's wants, feelings, and reasons. The team can then brainstorm how best to maximize each member's position, with an eye on the benefits to the team, and pick an option.[65]

One of the difficulties about either type of conflict resolution is addressing racial and other cultural issues that infuse the conflict. Many of us tend to shy away from raising these issues because they can be sensitive issues to discuss and because we worry about making a conflict worse. However, if the team members bring to their conflict a perspective that values diversity for its positive influence on the team's work and a willingness to explore cultural differences in this light, then problems might be handled constructively.[66] Valuing process—"time spent exploring their different points of view and deliberating about whether and how they should inform the work"—can help team members to learn not to fear

TABLE **5.1.**

CORE VALUE	COMPONENT VALUES
Cooperation	Commitment to one's own and other's success and well-being; responsibility; respect; integrity; compassion; belief in each member's worth and contributions; motivation; inclusion
Constructive conflict resolution	Respect for the right to differ; accepting one's own fallibility; valuing reasoned positions; believing that discourse can lead to resolution; multiple perspectives; synthesis of differences
Integrative negotiation	Open and honest communication; empathy for other's wants and feelings; concern for other's outcomes; maximizing outcomes for all disputants; maintaining effective and caring long-term relationships

racial difference and to take risks in talking about and learning from conflict that involves racial difference.[67]

Constructive conflict resolution between lawyer and client must occur within the parameters of the rules of professional conduct. Under the model rules, the client retains ultimate decision-making authority over "the objectives of representation."[68] Nonetheless, when a lawyer disagrees with a client's decision she might attempt to counsel the client to choose the "right" option in a manner that seems patronizing and authoritarian.[69] If the lawyer employs constructive conflict resolution principles, with lawyer and client each owning and explaining her position, and with due respect for the values and emotions that might infuse the position, then perhaps the decision-making process would be more inclusive for the client and issues of power and bias might be resolved more satisfactorily.

C. Civic Values

The glue that holds a diverse cooperative community together is shared civic values. Indeed, "the more diverse that individuals are, the more essential is a set of common values that bind them together and pro-

vide guidelines for appropriate behavior." In Johnson and Johnson's blueprint, the key common values are cooperation, constructive conflict resolution, and integrative negotiation. Johnson and Johnson break down these core areas above.[70]

In a clinic setting, the faculty is responsible for instilling these values among the students. This can be done by explicit discussion of the goals of the clinic, including reducing bias, and of the contributions these values make to the students' lawyering and learning.[71] In addition, faculty can model adherence to these values in class, in supervision, and in lawyering. Finally, faculty can evaluate students on their implementation of these values, for such an evaluation would make clearer the importance of the values to the student's work and provide more incentive for students to learn and lawyer in a cooperative, egalitarian manner.

CONCLUSION

So, what now for our criminal defense lawyer? Assuming that she wants to lawyer in an egalitarian manner, we can help her to recognize when she might act unconsciously with bias toward clients and others and work with her to bring her behavior up to her standards. If she is not motivated to lawyer in an egalitarian manner, we can demonstrate ways in which egalitarian lawyering will benefit her work performance. In addition, we can try to organize her workplace to reinforce egalitarian values by increasing the number of racially diverse managers, lawyers, and staff and developing cooperative, integrative work structures that allow all employees to see each other as individuals, not as stereotypes; to learn from each other about different cultural perspectives; and to develop multicultural skills that they all can use to further their collective work.[72]

6

Race and Juries: An Experimental Psychology Perspective

Samuel R. Sommers and Omoniyi O. Adekanmbi

INTRODUCTION

With increasing regularity, the influence of race on jury decision making finds itself at the center of discussion and debate in contemporary America. Every year seems to bring with it a new "trial of the century," and a remarkable number of these cases provoke questions among the media and general public about the relationship between race and the legal system. Consider, as just a few examples, the Duke lacrosse rape case, Michael Jackson's trial, Kobe Bryant's sexual assault investigation, the shooting of Amadou Diallo, and, of course, the trials of O.J. Simpson. These cases are each very different, yet they have all captured public attention. For a variety of reasons—whether through the intentional efforts of the attorneys involved, the nature of media coverage, or by simple virtue of the fact that one of the principals in the case was black—this attention has often turned to questions about race. Many, though not all, of these questions

involve juries: To what extent does a defendant's race influence a jury's verdict? Do jurors of different races perceive the same trial differently? How influential is the racial composition of a jury in determining the outcome of a trial?

While the public and media are drawn to these high-profile examples and other anecdotal analyses, researchers continue to examine these questions empirically. There are numerous strategies for such investigations, each of which possesses unique strengths and limitations.[1] Some researchers conduct archival analyses using multiple regression to identify the variables that predict outcomes in a subset of actual trials. As one example, Baldus and colleagues examined more than 2,000 capital murder cases in Georgia during the 1970s and found that defendants charged with killing a white victim were significantly more likely to be sentenced to death than were defendants accused of killing a black victim; to a lesser extent, effects for defendant race also emerged.[2] Another strategy is to conduct posttrial interviews with actual jurors. For instance, as part of the Capital Jury Project, Bowers and colleagues interviewed more than 1,000 jurors and concluded that in trials with black defendants, white jurors were more likely than their black counterparts to view their jury as open-minded, thorough, and tolerant of disagreement.[3] Studies such as these are high in external validity because they examine actual trial outcomes and use former jurors. However, these studies can be difficult to do well, as they require researchers to identify and statistically control for a wide range of potentially confounding variables. The conclusions generated by such studies are by definition correlational, and in the case of juror interviews, the limitations of relying on self-report data to assess the influence of race poses additional concerns.

An entirely different strategy for examining the relationship between race and jury decision making is to make use of the research design of experimental psychology. In such experiments, participants are recruited to play the role of mock jurors and researchers systematically manipulate variables of interest. For example, to determine the influence of a defendant's race on individual jurors' perceptions, a researcher would present participants with the same written or video trial summary, but for half of the participants the defendant would be portrayed as white and for the other half the defendant would be black. In this manner, the researcher is able to hold all other factors constant and to isolate the causal effects of a defendant's race on jurors' judgments. Using more sophisticated designs, an investigator can also begin to address *why* race is influential. Perhaps the race of a defendant influences jurors' perceptions of the strength of the evidence; perhaps discrepancies in the judgments of white and black mock jurors are attributable to differential beliefs about the credibility of police testimony. By enabling conclusions regarding causality and process, experimental research design offers advantages over archival analysis and juror interviews. Of course, these gains of experimental control (or internal validity) come at the expense of generalizability of findings (or external validity), reinforcing the importance of utilizing multiple methodologies in any investigation of legal decision making.

Despite challenges of external validity, experimental research design clearly has a great deal to offer the investigation of race and jury decision making. In fact, the experimental method is essential to determining the circumstances under which race is particularly likely to influence jury decision making, as well as to answering the questions of why and through what psychological processes such effects occur. As such, the present chapter focuses on this experimental psychology approach to studying race and legal decision making. Specifically, we will address three major topics that have been examined by previous researchers: (1) the influence of a defendant's race on individual jurors' judgments, (2) between-race differences in individual jurors' judgments, and (3) the effects of racial composition on the group decision making of juries. For each topic we will review the published literature as well as identify questions that remain unanswered. Finally, we will conclude by considering the underexplored domain of civil trials—in particular, the nature of juror decision making in discrimination lawsuits.

I. INFLUENCE OF DEFENDANT RACE

The most frequent question posed by previous experimental research concerning race and legal decision making has been: To what extent does a defendant's race influence the judgments of individual jurors? Twenty-five years ago, Dane and Wrightsman described the nature of the research regarding this question as relatively inconsistent.[4] An updated review of this literature reveals an increase in the number of studies devoted to this topic, but the basic conclusion of Dane and Wrightsman arguably still applies. In large part, this is because studies concerning the influence of a defendant's race are often idiosyncratic and not grounded in any particular theoretical framework.[5] The inconsistencies in this literature also reflect the complexity and nuance of criminal trials, especially when compared to the pared-down stimuli often used in more general experiments regarding social judgment.

Just what are these inconsistent findings? As reviewed in detail by Sommers and Ellsworth, most experiments have focused on the influence of a defendant's race on the judgments of white mock jurors.[6] Of these studies, some have indicated that a defendant's race has no consistent effect on white jurors, a larger body of studies finds that white mock jurors are harsher in the judgments of nonwhite versus white defendants, and still other investigations suggest that white jurors are harsher toward white defendants (perhaps, in part, due to "black sheep" effects).[7] Complicating matters further is that meta-analytic reviews of this literature have utilized different inclusion criteria and have focused on different outcome variables, thereby producing inconsistent conclusions. In 1992, Sweeney and Haney examined fourteen studies with more than 2,800 participants and determined that white mock jurors were indeed harsher in their sentencing recommendations for black versus white defendants.[8] Two years later, Mazzella and Feingold analyzed studies examining verdict decisions as well as sentencing, but unlike Sweeney and Haney, they included data from partici-

pants of all races (though juror race was not a separate variable used in the meta-analysis). Their conclusion, based on data from more than 6,700 participants, was that there was no significant evidence of racial bias in verdict or sentencing decisions, though they cautioned that this finding was potentially "misleading because race apparently interacted complexly with other factors influencing jurors' judgments of guilt."[9] More recently, Mitchell and colleagues analyzed data from more than 7,000 participants in studies considering verdict decisions and 3,000 participants in studies examining sentencing decisions. They reported that a small yet significant effect of racial bias emerged for both outcome measures across studies.[10]

At least three strategies have emerged in the effort to reconcile the findings in this literature. One technique has been to look to individual difference measures that account for some of the variability in the effects of defendant race on whites. Using their responses to a pretrial questionnaire, McGowen and King classified undergraduate mock jurors into three categories: authoritarian, anti-authoritarian, and egalitarian.[11] Authoritarian mock jurors rendered harsher judgments when the defendant in the trial was the same race as they were, a pattern not obtained for the two other groups. More recently, Kemmelmeier identified social dominance orientation—the extent to which an individual prefers a rigid hierarchy in the social system in which she lives—as a critical determinant of the influence of defendant race on white jurors.[12] He found that white mock jurors high in social dominance orientation were harsher in their judgments of black versus white defendants in an assault case, but that this pattern was reversed for low-dominance-orientation jurors, potentially explaining the null findings of some previous studies of defendant race.

What we would suggest are the most critical individual difference measures to this investigation remain largely unexamined, however. Few studies have examined the relationship between whites' explicit racial attitudes and their judgments in cases with black defendants.[13] Also, researchers have failed to examine the predictive ability of self-reported motivations to respond without prejudice when it comes to juror decision making.[14] Much contemporary research on social perception and judgment goes beyond self-report assessment of explicit racial attitudes by considering links between social judgment/behavior and people's implicit associations and thoughts, but these relationships have also not been systematically examined in the legal domain.[15]

A second tactic researchers have adopted has been to identify situational moderators that exaggerate or attenuate the influence of a defendant's race on white jurors. Specific factors identified by studies as increasing the influence of defendant race include the presence of inadmissible incriminating evidence[16] and inflammatory pretrial publicity,[17] the absence of racially charged issues at trial[18] or judicial instructions regarding avoiding "sympathy or prejudice,"[19] when the crime is "blue-collar" as opposed to "white-collar,"[20] and when the evidence at trial is ambiguous enough to render the probability of the defendant's guilt uncertain.[21] These findings have led some researchers to conclude that the aversive (or modern) racism framework used by many social psychologists in the study of general social judgment[22] is also useful for reconciling the findings of the literature on defendant race.[23]

This theoretical perspective suggests that many if not most white jurors are motivated to avoid the appearance of racial bias (once again, illustrating the importance of future studies in which this individual-difference variable is included).

Therefore, when thoughts about race are made salient during their review of a trial (such as, for example, when the incident in question is racially charged) or when strong normative cues against the expression of racial bias are present (for example, when judicial instructions emphasize the importance of avoiding prejudice), white jurors will be motivated to correct for the perceived influence of a defendant's race and to render an objective, "color-blind" decision. However, in the absence of normative cues regarding race, even subtle racial biases are likely to make their way to the surface and to influence judgments. Furthermore, aversive racism theory suggests that when ample race-neutral justification is available for a decision—such as the presence of incriminating pretrial publicity or an ambiguous case that could reasonably be interpreted in different ways—white jurors are more likely to be influenced by a taboo factor such as the defendant's race because they have a ready-made, legitimate explanation for their decision.[24]

This application of social psychological theory to the investigation of defendant race is a noteworthy step toward building a more cohesive literature on this topic. Still, too little is known regarding the psychological processes underlying the influence of a defendant's race on white jurors. This gap in the literature prevents conclusions from being drawn regarding, for example, whether prejudicial attitudes account for the tendency of white jurors to be influenced at times by the race of a defendant, or whether simple awareness of cultural stereotypes regarding race and crime is sufficient to color perceptions.

Such exploration of the processes through which a defendant's race influences jurors is the third strategy some researchers have adopted in the effort to make sense of this literature. However, as alluded to above, these process questions are still in the early stages of investigation. One mechanism that has been explored, with inconsistent conclusions, is level of processing. To the extent that stereotypical thought processes are responsible for some of the effects of defendant race on white juror judgments, one might predict that jurors process information at trial more heuristically when a defendant is black. Interestingly, Sargent and Bradfield observed precisely the opposite pattern of results, as white mock jurors in their study were more sensitive to evidence strength (either alibi quality or effectiveness of cross-examination) when the defendant was black than when he was white.[25] The authors interpreted these findings as evidence that white mock jurors were motivated to avoid prejudice, and therefore scrutinized the trial information more carefully when the defendant was black. Other studies have arrived at the conclusions that mock jurors engage in more systematic processing when crimes are interracial[26] or when the defendant's race is incongruent with a crime stereotype (such as when a black defendant is charged with bank fraud).[27]

Though these initial examinations of level of processing have yet to produce consensus conclusions, they represent a necessary new direction in this investigation. This literature has successfully moved beyond the simple conclusion that a defendant's race sometimes influences juror judgments to the more interesting and important focus on the circumstances under which such effects occur, but questions of process persist. One potential consideration is the role played by prejudicial attitudes in the influence of defendant race. If an in-group/out-group framework is to be applied to this investigation, how exactly are prejudicial attitudes manifested in the legal context? Do jurors set a lower threshold for reasonable doubt when a de-

fendant is an out-group member as opposed to an in-group member? Would such effects represent leniency toward the in-group, harshness toward the out-group, or some combination thereof? These are questions with clear policy implications, yet they are more often raised in discussion sections of published articles than they are addressed with empirical data.

Another important—and also provocative—future direction is to fully explore the likelihood that the influence of a defendant's race can, at least in part, be explained by unintentional and even nonconscious processes. One reason for the dearth of research examining the link between explicit racial attitudes and juror judgments may be that such a relationship would hardly be surprising. Less intuitive, and perhaps more powerful as a result, are findings that even jurors who seek to be fair-minded can be biased by race. Consider the parallel investigation of suspect race and police perceptions. Several studies have demonstrated that participants (including actual police officers) in a police judgment task are biased by a suspect's race.[28] In one study, Correll and colleagues found that participants in a computer simulation task were quicker to "shoot" unarmed suspects when they were black, a tendency not predicted by individuals' personal endorsement of racial attitudes but rather by their awareness of cultural stereotypes regarding African Americans and crime.[29] The significance of this finding lies in its demonstration that one need not endorse overtly biased thoughts or attitudes in order for judgment and behavior to be biased. Similar tendencies may be observable in the juror context: Does a defendant's race change the way in which jurors interpret ambiguous evidence? Do jurors bring to the courtroom different implicit beliefs about crime base rates and racial group membership? If such tendencies exist, precisely how, then, are mock jurors able to accurately correct for the influence of race when motivated to do so in some cases?

Yet another way to approach these questions of process is to address some of the methodological oversimplifications and oversights found in previous research. For example, the vast majority of studies have compared white jurors' judgments of white versus black defendants. This focus on the white/black dichotomy mirrors the myopia found in the more general social psychological literature on prejudice, but for practical purposes it would be useful to know whether such effects generalize to whites' judgments of other racial groups as well. This is also an important issue from a theoretical perspective; previous research has indicated that laypeople's stereotypical beliefs about race and crime vary by the particular racial group in question, and it is reasonable to expect that race-related normative pressures also differ depending on the category membership of the defendant.[30] Many white jurors may be worried about the appearance of prejudice when a defendant is black, but such concerns may not be as strong or consistent when a defendant is a member of another racial category about which crime-related stereotypes exist, such as Latinos. Perhaps white jurors would have little or no reservations about exhibiting bias against an Arab American defendant in the wake of September 11, 2001. These possibilities remain largely unexamined, but they may shed light on the relationship between stereotypic thoughts, prejudicial attitudes, normative concerns, and juror decision making.

Even keeping within the traditional white/black dichotomy, there are gaps in the literature that merit attention. For one, despite the real-life relationship between socioeconomic status (SES) and imprisonment, too few of the studies reviewed herein have attempted to tease apart the effects of defendant race and SES. The use of the word *dichotomy* above is also problematic given that the perception of race is not always an either/or, cut-and-dried proposition. A great deal of variability exists within racial groups when it comes to skin tone and other physical features, and only recently have researchers begun to acknowledge this fact in psycholegal research. Dixon and Maddox, for example, presented participants with a crime-related newscast in which the skin tone of a black perpetrator was varied. Results indicated that personal television viewing habits predicted reactions to the perpetrator, but all participants tended to find the perpetrator most memorable when he was a dark-skinned black man.[31]

Even more disturbingly, Eberhardt and colleagues recently completed an analysis of forty-four capital murder cases from Philadelphia since 1979 in which a black defendant was charged with the murder of a white victim.[32] They asked naive participants to rate a photograph of each defendant and found that those with faces rated as most "stereotypically black" by participants were the defendants more likely to have been sentenced to death by their actual jury. In other words, the more prototypically black these men appeared to be, the more likely it was that their jury had sentenced them to be executed, implying a pernicious cultural association between "blackness," perceptions of dangerousness, and—as Eberhardt and colleagues refer to it—"deathworthiness."

Finally, yet another issue to be considered is the question of the differential effects of defendant race and victim race on juror decision making. Some studies of actual jury outcomes suggest that victim race not only is influential but can be more influential than the race of a defendant. Baldus and colleagues' review of capital trials in Georgia indicated that the race of the victim was almost four times as strong a predictor of trial outcome as defendant's race;[33] the Eberhardt study of capital murder defendants from Philadelphia revealed a significant relationship between prototypicality of appearance and sentencing when the victim was white, but no such relationship for same-race crimes.[34] Clearly, victim race is an important consideration for this literature, but some studies omit this variable, while others confound victim and defendant race. That said, this lack of consistent attention to victim race in the experimental literature does not preclude the conclusion that a defendant's race is often influential in juror decision making. Some studies of capital trial decision making have found a significant effect for defendant race but not victim race,[35] and the most recent meta-analysis of the literature indicated a significantly reliable effect of defendant race without even considering the variable of victim race.[36]

Where does that leave matters when it comes to the relative effects of race of victim and race of defendant? Certainly, there are enough published studies to permit the conclusion that both factors can exert an independent influence on jurors in a given case, though theoretically speaking, ingroup/out-group biases seem most likely when a juror and victim are of the same race and the defendant is not. Perhaps such a tendency would result from the additive effects of victim and defendant race, or perhaps different psychological tendencies emerge in evaluating interracial versus intraracial crimes. More generally, the precise mechanisms by which a victim's race is influential are also not well understood. When a victim is of the same race as jurors, does this elicit greater sympathy and therefore greater outrage directed toward a defendant? Does a same-race victim increase jurors' motivation to hold someone responsible, thereby lowering the certainty threshold necessary for conviction? On the other hand, in some cases a juror's own be-

lief in a just world could be threatened by a same-race victim, as the juror may worry that a similar fate could befall him one day. Such a reaction would likely lead jurors to hold the same-race victim responsible for his fate or to otherwise distance themselves from him. These are possibilities worthy of future consideration.

II. EFFECTS BY JUROR RACE

Many readers will have noticed that our review of the literature on defendant race typically referred to the effects on the judgments of *white* jurors. Of course, this is not to suggest that the influence of a defendant's race on nonwhite jurors is not important; rather, it reflects the unfortunate fact that the vast majority of legal decision making experiments continue to use entirely or predominantly white participant samples. Myriad justifications for this tendency have been offered. First, from a historical standpoint, racial bias on the part of white legislators, judges, attorneys, and jurors is well documented, suggesting the importance of understanding the influence of race on white decision-makers.[37] Second, from a demographic perspective, most courthouses in the United States continue to call jury pools that are predominantly white, thus underscoring the practical utility of examining this population. Third, this tendency to focus almost exclusively on white decision makers is hardly unique to legal researchers, but rather mirrors the tendencies of more general social science investigations of racial bias.[38] Finally, for many years, the consensus among mock jury researchers has been that little if any reliable relationship exists between a juror's race and her decision making tendencies.[39]

We would suggest that none of these justifications—alone or in combination with one another—is particularly compelling. They may be reasonable explanations for the decision to focus on white jurors in any one experiment, but they do not render any less problematic the dearth of data from nonwhite jurors in the broader literature. The final proposition above—that there is no meaningful relationship between juror race and decision making—is particularly unconvincing. This relationship may indeed be complicated and nuanced, but there hardly exists a substantial body of empirical data on which to base such a conclusion. The studies upon which this assertion was based were never intended to identify racial differences to begin with—typically, they were designed as investigations of nonracial issues including evidence comprehension, case complexity, and jury size, with participant race assessed for purely demographic purposes. Only a handful of studies have directly and explicitly addressed the extent to which decisions in a case vary by juror race.

Of this small number of studies, most have compared the influence of a defendant's race on white versus black jurors, and several of these studies have methodological limitations that prevent definitive conclusions. Foley and Chamblin presented both white and black mock jurors with the audiotape of a rape trial in which the defendant's race was manipulated.[40] Analyses indicated that white jurors were more likely to vote to convict when the defendant was black than when he was white; no such statistically significant results were found for black mock jurors. It is tempting to interpret these findings to indicate that a defendant's race influences white jurors but not black jurors, but of the 191 participants in this study, only 20 were black, a number too small to allow for meaningful between-race comparisons in juror performance.

In another article, Ugwuegbu manipulated the defendant's race and the strength of the prosecution's evidence in a rape trial summary presented to white and black

mock jurors.[41] He reported that the race of the defendant had little effect on white or black jurors when the evidence at trial was very weak or very strong, but in a more ambiguous case, jurors of both races were harsher toward an other-race defendant than toward a same-race defendant. These data lend support to an in-group/out-group explanation for the influence of a defendant's race, though their interpretation is complicated by the fact that white and black mock jurors participated in separate experiments.

Other studies have indicated that the race of a defendant has a greater influence on black mock jurors than whites. In a 1997 experiment conducted by Skolnick and Shaw, white mock jurors rendered comparable decisions for white and black defendants, but black mock jurors were harsher in their judgments when the defendant was white as opposed to black.[42] However, the authors note the unique context in which these results were obtained, as the experiment was conducted for a themed special issue of the *Journal of Social Issues* devoted to the O.J. Simpson trial. The materials Skolnick and Shaw used—a trial transcript in which the defendant was accused of fatally stabbing his white ex-wife—were intended to resemble the Simpson case, and the study was conducted in southern California while Simpson's civil trial was still ongoing. The generalizability of these results is therefore questionable.

More recently, Abwender and Hough obtained a similar result after varying the race of the defendant in a vehicular manslaughter case summary presented to white and black mock jurors.[43] White participants were not influenced by the defendant's race, whereas black mock jurors were more punitive in their judgments of the white defendant versus the black defendant. One potential explanation for the former finding is that—unlike most experiments with white mock jurors—this study described the trial of a female defendant charged with a nonviolent crime. To the extent that the influence of defendant race on white jurors is attributable to stereotypic thoughts about race and crime, this study may not have used a trial likely to activate such associations. Interestingly, this study is one of few to also include Latino participants (though no Latino defendant condition was included). Unlike white participants, Latino mock jurors rendered harsher decisions when the defendant was black than when she was white.

Another study paints a more complicated picture regarding between-race differences. Sommers and Ellsworth presented white and black mock jurors with the summary of an assault trial.[44] Though the incident in question was always interracial, in one version of the case the altercation was racially charged and in the other it was race-neutral (i.e., the alleged assailant and the victim were of different races, but race played no role in the incident, nor were racial issues made salient during the trial). As described above, white mock jurors were not influenced by the defendant's race when the incident was racially charged, presumably because such salient racial issues activated concerns about avoiding prejudice; in the race-neutral condition, white jurors were harsher in their judgments of a black defendant versus a white defendant. Black mock jurors, on the other hand, were not influenced by this situational variable, as they exhibited harsher judgments of the white defendant in both versions of the trial. This study also provides a rare glimpse at one potential reason *why* such between-race differences in juror tendencies emerge. When asked whether they believed that a defendant's race affects the treatment he or she receives in the legal system in general, black mock jurors expressed much greater skepticism about the

system's color blindness than did whites—in fact, blacks' average response to this question was a whopping 6.9 on a 7-point rating scale, suggesting the possibility that blacks' concerns regarding system fairness may account for some of the observed between-race differences in juror tendencies.

The scarcity of studies examining nonwhite jurors renders conclusions regarding juror race difficult. It is unclear, for example, whether the findings reviewed above indicate that black jurors are biased against white defendants or biased in favor of black defendants. Indeed, some researchers have described the observed effects of defendant race on black mock jurors as "black racism,"[45] whereas others refer to the same pattern as "same-race leniency."[46] The former terminology would be consistent with a straightforward ingroup/out-group explanation that black jurors are harsher in their judgments of nonblack defendants, particularly when the victim in question is an in-group member. Such a conclusion would suggest that the effects of a defendant's race on white and black jurors are similar in magnitude and occur through similar psychological processes.

However, it also seems plausible that the decision tendencies of white and black mock jurors are not simply mirror images of each other. One extrapolation of the "same-race leniency" terminology is that this pattern of results implies race-based jury nullification among blacks.[47] Even absent a nullification hypothesis, one might reasonably conclude that black and white individuals have different race-related motivations when they serve as jurors: "It therefore appears as if white and black jurors bring to the courtroom different concerns. . . . Many whites, according to theories of modern racism, are motivated to avoid prejudice. . . . Black jurors, on the other hand, appear to be concerned about institutional bias in the legal system."[48] It remains unclear precisely how such race-related concerns manifest themselves in terms of juror judgments. In cases with a black defendant, do black jurors raise the certainty threshold necessary for a guilty vote? Do black jurors interpret the same incriminating evidence as less persuasive when a defendant is black, and are such effects particularly likely for specific types of evidence (such as the testimony of police or forensic analyses conducted by police labs)?[49] To the extent that such tendencies occur, are they intentional and conscious?

All of the studies reviewed above examined the relative influence of a defendant's race on white versus black mock jurors, leaving unanswered additional questions concerning between-race differences in juror tendencies. For example, are differences between white and black juror judgments confined to cases involving black defendants? Even within one multi-study paper, the answer to this question varies. In a first study collapsing five different trials, Sommers and Ellsworth found that black mock jurors were harsher toward a white defendant than were white mock jurors, but in a second study the only differences by juror race were in the black defendant condition.[50] One might speculate that more general differences exist in the decision tendencies of white and black jurors. The controversy surrounding the use of race-based peremptories during jury selection, for example, arises in large part because of stereotypes and "juror folklore"[51] that suggest that black jurors are more lenient than white jurors in most cases.[52] These intuitions and assumptions remain largely untested; the individual differences—in terms of personal experiences, political ideology, and other attitudes—underlying such potential between-race differences in juror judgment tendencies are also poorly understood. And, of course, even though the relationship between race and legal decision making is often written about in strictly white/black terms, the increasingly multicultural nature of American society renders it all the more important for future studies to consider the judgments of jurors from other racial groups as well.

III. JURY RACIAL COMPOSITION

Despite the title of this chapter, we have to this point focused on the judgments of individual jurors as opposed to the performance of juries. However, the most practically important—and, we would suggest, psychologically interesting—issue regarding juror race is not simple comparison of individual jurors, but rather the question of how a jury's racial composition affects its decision making. Archival analyses of actual cases focus on this group-level question. In a study described above, Bowers and colleagues examined 340 capital trials and concluded that the greater the proportion of whites to blacks on a jury, the more likely a black defendant was to be sentenced to death (especially when the victim was white).[53] Daudistel and colleagues examined 317 nonfelony juries in Texas consisting of whites and Latinos, and reported a parallel finding.[54] These studies suggest that a relationship exists between a jury's racial composition and its decision making, but they do not identify the processes by which these effects occur. Experimental investigations of jury racial composition have been relatively infrequent, presumably in large part because of the logistical challenges posed by group-based experiments.

One experiment to examine jury racial composition was conducted by Bernard in 1979.[55] In this study, college-student mock juries were presented with the video of a simulated assault and battery trial in which the defendant was depicted as either white or black. Ten twelve-person juries of differing racial compositions viewed one version of the trial and then deliberated on the case. Across both versions of the trial, white jurors were more likely to vote guilty than were black jurors, but this was especially the case when the defendant was black; in fact, the only jury to reach a unanimous guilty verdict in the study was also the only all-white jury to view the trial of a black defendant. With such a small sample size—one of the aforementioned logistical challenges of mock jury studies is that the *n* for analysis is the number of groups, not the number of individual participants in a study—this effect is not statistically significant.

Other experiments have produced similar results that generalize these findings beyond the white/black dichotomy. Perez and colleagues presented the videotaped trial of a white or Latino defendant to six-person college student mock juries that were either majority white or majority Latino.[56] Overall, the more whites on a jury, the more conviction-prone the jury was, but this tendency was particularly pronounced when the defendant was Latino. Lipton also examined six-person college student juries and found that white mock jurors expressed a more negative affective reaction to the Latino defendant than did Latino jurors, a tendency that was exacerbated by the deliberation process.[57] Chadee examined jury decision making in Trinidad, where a racial division exists between residents of African and Indian descent, and found the similar result that Indian-dominated juries were more likely to convict an African defendant than were African-dominated juries.[58]

Again, these experiments demonstrate a causal link between a jury's racial composition and its final decision, but they do not illuminate the processes by which such influence occurs. At least three different—though not mutually exclusive—explanations exist for these effects. First,

the relationship between racial composition and jury verdicts may simply result from the effects of composition on a jury's predeliberation vote split. As reviewed in the previous section, there is evidence for generalized differences in the judgments of, for example, white and black jurors in some cases. To the extent that such differences emerge, the racial makeup of the jury is likely to determine the preliminary vote split heading into deliberations—and as Kalven and Zeisel famously noted, this vote split is the best predictor of jury verdicts.[59]

But the effects of a jury's racial composition likely manifest themselves in ways other than mere vote split variability. A second explanation for the influence of racial composition involves information exchange. That is, a diverse jury demographic is expected to lead to a diversity of perspectives, experiences, and attitudes during deliberations. This information exchange hypothesis is often offered by legal scholars and judges,[60] and it is captured eloquently by Thurgood Marshall in his opinion in *Peters v. Kiff*: "When any large and identifiable segment of the community is excluded from jury service, the effect is to remove from the jury room qualities of human nature and varieties of human experience, the range of which is unknown and perhaps unknowable."[61] Consistent with this sentiment, information exchange is also the most common process explanation postulated by psychologists who study the effects of diversity on group decision making more generally.[62]

The traditional take on information exchange and juries assumes that black (and other nonwhite) jurors are responsible for the effects of diversity on a jury's performance. Because black jurors are expected to bring different perspectives and experiences to the jury room, a racially diverse jury should consider a wider range of information during deliberations than a homogeneous jury. But one need only look to the next sentence in Justice Marshall's *Peters v. Kiff* opinion to realize that such an assumption is not required in order for jury racial composition to be influential: "It is not necessary to assume that the excluded group will consistently vote as a class in order to conclude, as we do, that its exclusion deprives the jury of a perspective on human events that may have unsuspected importance in any case that may be presented."[63] One reading of this passage is to conclude that the effects of a racially diverse jury composition are not simply attributable to black jurors introducing the "black perspective" to deliberations, implying that the traditional information exchange explanation does not fully account for the effects of a racially diverse jury composition.

Building on these ideas, a third explanation is that racial composition potentially influences jury decision making through noninformational processes. In the more general psychological literature on diversity and group performance, researchers have suggested that two types of diversity are influential: deep-level diversity (the expertise, attitudes, or values of individual group members) and surface-level diversity (the visible social category membership of individual members).[64] In the jury context, most information exchange explanations assume that surface-level diversity maps onto deep-level diversity. But perhaps simple surface-level diversity also exerts noninformational influences on jury decision making. Consider, for example, Hans and Vidmar's hypothesis that the presence of nonwhite jurors on a jury "may inhibit majority group members from expressing prejudice, especially if the defendant is from the same group as the minority group jurors."[65] Indeed, an experiment by Kerr and colleagues demonstrated that the mere expectation of deliberating on a racially diverse jury was

influential, in this instance by leading both white and black mock jurors to be more punitive toward a same-race defendant when they expected to be in the racial minority on their jury.[66]

Only one published experiment to date has tested these various explanations for the potential influence of a jury's racial composition on its decision-making processes. In this study, Sommers recruited jury-eligible community members (many of whom were actual jurors in the midst of jury duty) to serve on six-person mock juries.[67] Half of these juries were all-white and the other half racially diverse (composed of four white and two black jurors). All mock juries were shown the same video summary of a sexual assault trial with a black defendant and read pattern jury instructions before deliberating on the case. Indeed, the racial composition of the juries influenced predeliberation vote split, as jurors on racially diverse juries were less conviction prone than those on all-white juries. However, this tendency was due to more than just demographic differences by jury composition, as white jurors on diverse juries were less likely to privately lean toward guilty than were whites on all-white juries. That this effect emerged before deliberations even began demonstrates that the influence of a diverse jury racial composition is not wholly attributable to the performance of black jurors, and also that some of this influence occurs through noninformational means—perhaps as described by Hans and Vidmar.[68]

The Sommers study also provides evidence of informational differences in the deliberations of diverse versus homogeneous juries.[69] Racially diverse juries deliberated longer on the case, discussed more trial evidence, and made fewer factually inaccurate statements in discussing the evidence than did all-white juries. Interestingly, these effects also were not wholly attributable to the performance of black jurors, as white jurors were more thorough and accurate when discussing the trial as part of a diverse jury than when on an all-white jury. These results suggest that one of the processes through which racial composition exerts its effects may be that membership on a diverse jury leads white jurors to process evidence more systematically. In general, this experiment leads to the conclusion that jury representativeness is more than a constitutional ideal or a means to increase the perceived legitimacy of the system, but also may be an ingredient for improved jury performance.

Of course, one experiment hardly provides sufficient data on which to base definitive conclusions regarding the influence of jury racial composition. The Sommers study demonstrates that the processes through which racial composition is influential need not be solely informational, yet the study raises as many important questions as it answers: Why would membership on a diverse jury lead white mock jurors to demonstrate more systematic processing of the trial evidence, and would such effects occur in actual cases as well? Are the observed effects of jury diversity limited to cases in which the defendant is black and charged with a violent crime? What situational or personality characteristics might lead a diverse jury composition to engender conflict and polarization during deliberations as opposed to the positive effects observed in this study?

Clearly, much remains to be learned about the influence of a jury's racial composition on its deliberations and decision making, and we would suggest that mock jury experiments will play the leading role in this investigation. Archival analyses focus on trial outcomes; as such, they can demonstrate a statistical link between jury composition and final verdict, but they shed no light on the processes through which these effects emerge. Juror inter-

view studies offer more insight into the role of race in the deliberation room, but their reliance on retrospective self-report data typically means that their most reliable conclusions focus on participants' satisfaction with the jury experience as opposed to the processes by which race is influential.[70] Unfortunately, experimental psychologists have too infrequently examined the influence of race on legal decision making at the group or jury level. Until more researchers heed this call—and agree to wrestle with the practical obstacles inherent to such data collection—intuition and speculation will guide discourse regarding jury racial composition, and the extant experimental literature on the judgments of individual jurors will continue to suffer criticisms based on external validity.

FUTURE DIRECTIONS: DISCRIMINATION LAWSUITS

Throughout this chapter, we have attempted to identify future directions and unanswered questions in the race and juries literature. As such, we will focus our final section on a topic that we have not addressed at all thus far: race and the civil jury. Many research questions concerning juries—such as those of jury size, jury instructions, and inadmissible evidence—are equally applicable to criminal and civil juries, and indeed, researchers have investigated these topics using both trial contexts. But psycholegal investigation of race has focused almost exclusively on the criminal context, as reflected by our present review. From a practical as well as theoretical standpoint, it will be important for future researchers to consider the role of race in civil trials; to almost every paragraph above we could add the question of whether these effects for race are comparable for civil juries.

We have decided to conclude by focusing on one particular type of civil trial in which race is likely to play an important yet complicated role: discrimination lawsuits. The standards for successfully proving (or refuting) claims of employment discrimination have continued to evolve over the past forty years. Title VII of the Civil Rights Act of 1964 outlawed purposeful employment discrimination based on an individual's race, ethnicity, gender, or religion, but the practical implementation of this law has proven challenging.[71] In a 1973 ruling the U.S. Supreme Court established the first procedure for proving discrimination.[72] By the *McDonnell Douglas* standard, a plaintiff first had to be able to make out a prima facie case of bias, and then had to prove that the defendant's neutral explanation for the job action was false or was mere pretext for discrimination. In 1989 the Court's ruling in *Price Waterhouse v. Hopkins* recognized the possibility of mixed motives—when both legitimate and illegitimate factors are influential in a job action—but continued to require plaintiffs to provide direct evidence of discriminatory practice.[73] Then in 2003 the Court clarified this previous ruling, unanimously holding that discrimination could occur whenever membership in a protected group is one of the motivating factors for an employment decision, even if other, legitimate factors also contribute to the practice.[74] This ruling effectively opened the door to claims of discrimination based on more ambiguous and indirect evidence.

Clearly, the judiciary continues to wrestle with the definition of discrimination and how it can be proven at trial. But another important question is how laypeople (i.e., prospective jurors) evaluate claims of discrimination. Few, if any, studies have examined the decision making of mock jurors in this type of case, despite the potential methodological and theoretical contributions of experimental psychology to such an investigation. There are three

bodies of literature that offer some guidance in thinking about future research on decision making in discrimination cases: (1) a handful of social psychological experiments concerning more general appraisals of claims of discrimination, (2) mock juror investigations of age and gender discrimination suits, and (3) comparative studies investigating perceptions of race- and gender-based prejudice.

Research regarding the experiences of targets of prejudice suggests that there are social costs to claiming discrimination. Minority group members who make attributions to discrimination often report feeling "backlash" from co-workers and acquaintances.[75] This backlash is far from imagined. Studies have shown that individuals who attribute negative outcomes to discrimination are liked less by others than those who do not. Kaiser and Miller, for example, found that participants rated a black student who attributed a failing grade to racism as more of a complainer than a student who attributed the grade to other external or internal factors.[76] Similarly, when participants were asked to evaluate a black male who attributed being denied a position to racial discrimination, they rated the target as significantly more likely to be a troublemaker.[77] These findings have clear implications for the legal system. They suggest that some jurors may be predisposed to forming negative impressions about a plaintiff who alleges discrimination, as they harbor biased attitudes that could undermine support for the plaintiff's case. Indeed, research suggests that observers' evaluations of a discrimination target's personality influence their judgments regarding the likelihood that discrimination actually occurred.[78]

Few studies have directly examined perceptions of allegations of discrimination in a legal context. In one such study, Greene and colleagues found that presenting testimony from expert witnesses influences the award judgments jurors make in a case involving age discrimination.[79] A few studies have focused on juror decision making in gender discrimination cases. Elkins and colleagues found that female jurors were more likely than male jurors to believe a female plaintiff had been the victim of gender discrimination, and this tendency was strongest when the evidence of the company's discrimination was ambiguous. Women were also more likely than men to make negative character attributions about the company under ambiguous evidence conditions, but no gender differences were found for perceptions of a male plaintiff claiming discrimination.[80] Elkins and colleagues explain this tendency for female jurors to exhibit a gender-similarity bias to be a result of women's ability to identify with female plaintiffs; they suggest that women may connect the discrimination case to their own concerns about gender discrimination. Since male jurors are less likely to have personal experiences as targets of discrimination, they may require more evidence to be convinced as to the veracity of such a claim.

One interpretation of these results would be that individuals who are members of marginalized groups are more receptive to claims of discrimination than members of the demographic majority. However, additional studies suggest that the picture is more complicated, as majority group members can be led to show similar biases in favor of their in-group when the discrimination situation is made personally relevant. With regard to gender, Elkins and colleagues found that when males and females judged a mock child custody case—a situation in which men are more often the targets of gender discrimination—male jurors exhibited a gender-similarity bias in favor of male plaintiffs.[81] Interestingly, female jurors did not exhibit a gender bias for these cases. It

may therefore be the case that a perceived threat to one's own group is a critical determinant of observers' attitudes in discrimination cases. Regardless of the precise situational factors that exaggerate and attenuate juror biases in gender discrimination cases, these studies provide unambiguous evidence of the potential importance of jury composition for cases involving allegations of discrimination.

Attempting to replicate these findings with regard to race will be important because previous comparative studies have found that individuals evaluate race and gender discrimination differently. For example, individuals tend to perceive prejudicial actions as more severe when they involve race than when they involve gender.[82] Furthermore, individuals report feeling more guilt when accused of racism than sexism; racism accusations also appear to generate more irritation than allegations of sexism.[83] These different reactions to race indicate that individuals are highly sensitized to issues involving racism, such that they are particularly concerned about appearing racist, but simultaneously angered by charges of racism. Previous research also indicates that white and nonwhite individuals often have very different ideas regarding what constitutes racism, with whites demonstrating greater resistance to identifying subtle and ambiguous behaviors as indicative of bias.[84]

These and other findings in social psychology suggest that race (and racism) may be a unique social construct compared to other social identities, and imply that observers' judgments about a case involving racial discrimination likely differ from tendencies in cases involving other forms of discrimination. Previous research suggests that plaintiffs in discrimination cases often face an uphill battle, but they likely face an extra barrier to overcome when their allegation involves race. What psychological processes account for this difference? Is this hypothesized bias against plaintiffs in racial discrimination cases confined to trials with black plaintiffs or with ambiguous evidence? Is such a tendency exhibited only by white jurors? What about white female jurors, who are presumably more likely than white males to have had personal experiences with discrimination, even if their experiences involve a different type of bias? Would black jurors demonstrate a similarity bias in favor of black plaintiffs similar to that observed among females in gender cases? These are all empirical questions worthy of future investigation.

How jurors make decisions in discrimination lawsuits is obviously an issue of practical importance, but such investigations also raise more general questions regarding the psychological processes underlying jury decision making. For example, consider the differences in the relevant racial stereotypes in a criminal trial versus a discrimination lawsuit. In the criminal context, racial stereotypes are marked by an association between violent crime and racial groups such as blacks and Latinos. These stereotypes, in theory, would bias a juror against certain defendants. In the civil domain, one relevant stereotype is the general belief that the most common form of racial bias is discrimination perpetrated by whites against blacks.[85] One might expect such a stereotype to render jurors more receptive to allegations of racism brought by nonwhite plaintiffs, but our review above suggests that just the opposite is likely. Perhaps a competing stereotype of blacks as prone to unsubstantiated allegations of racism exists, or perhaps race-related stereotypes play a greater role in decision making in a criminal setting versus a civil one. As this analysis demonstrates, the benefit of extending psycholegal research on race from

the criminal context to the civil context involves more than mere generalization—such studies also have the potential to contribute to a fuller understanding of processes of legal decision making.

In sum, research on race and juries has infrequently considered civil trials, and we propose that judgments in discrimination lawsuits would be a logical place to begin such an investigation. If lessons are to be learned from the still-developing literature on criminal juror decision making, we believe that first and foremost is the importance of focusing research on questions of process as well as on simple outcomes. The influence of race on social judgment is complex and nuanced; some studies will produce evidence of racial bias, while others will not. Failure to ground new predictions in psychological theory (and failure to assess the mechanisms by which race is influential) is likely to produce a literature with findings that are difficult to reconcile as well as dependent on the idiosyncrasies of the trial materials used in a given study. More generally, it is important to bear in mind that the advantages of applying the methodology of experimental psychology to the study of the legal system are not limited to the ability to control independent variables or to draw causal conclusions. Rather, these benefits also include the potential to address what remains largely inaccessible for archival analysis: questions of why and through what process these effects occur. It is not on its own that psychological investigation of race and juries is likely to have practical effects on legal practice and policy, but through its convergence with research methodologies with greater levels of realism and external validity. It is therefore important for psychologists to make full use of the research tools available to them, and to maximize the unique contributions that the field has to offer.

7

African Americans on the Witness Stand:
Race and Expert Witness Testimony

Veronica S. Tetterton and Stanley L. Brodsky

INTRODUCTION

For centuries, expert witnesses have proffered specialized knowledge to laypeople in courts of law.[1] The function of expert witnesses in legal proceedings is to serve as "educators, supplying the information and opinions necessary to help the jury evaluate evidence that they would otherwise not be able to comprehend."[2] Early critics debated issues related to whether expert witness testimony prejudicially influenced jurors.[3] Since these early debates, the utilization of mental health experts has increasingly become accepted as a viable means of imparting specialized psychological knowledge, with the intent of aiding jurors in their decision-making process.

Expert witnesses are inherently placed in a position to persuade others. Testimony provided by experts has the potential to sway the attitudes of jurors and influence judgments about the case. Research evidence suggests that individual jurors often arrive at a verdict long before engaging in posttrial deliberation, a process sometimes credited in part to the influential impact of expert witnesses.[4] The outcomes of civil and criminal trials can pivot on the persuasive appeal of competing experts.

A substantial literature has emerged that addresses the manner in which mental health experts can be effective advocates of their own findings. In his books addressing court testimony, Brodsky argued that substantive knowledge is the basic foundation of good testimony, but that mastery of personal anxiety and of cross-examination queries are essential related skills for the expert.[5] From this perspective, the well-prepared expert is able to draw on good knowledge, to speak with confidence, to maintain a general sense of likability, and to be perceived as trustworthy and honest. During intense cross-examination, attorneys use various tactics to undermine the credibility of the expert witness, such as demanding arbitrary yes-or-no answers to complex questions and asking about reliability or validity studies for psychometric measures. Brodsky described this process as a struggle for power and control between the testifying expert and cross-examining attorney, the outcome of which depends in part on use of nonverbal tactics, nondefensiveness, and careful listening by the expert.[6]

In spite of the common demands on experts, once they are on the witness stand, expert witnesses are not homogeneous, nor are they uniformly persuasive. One can divide the persuasive role issues into contextual, tactical, and personal traits, the last of which is our focus here. Each psychological expert possesses personality, behavioral and physical attributes that help determine the degree to which jurors are influenced by the testimony. To begin with, jurors attend to the personal characteristics of the witness. These source cues are not limited to demographic characteristics such as race and gender, but also include perceptions of attractiveness and mastery of the topics discussed. The likelihood that jurors are persuaded by the testimony of the expert may be influenced by these and other variables. Previous research has convincingly demonstrated that the persuasive appeal of information from experts varies according to the expert's perceived credibility, expertise, attractiveness, speech patterns, confidence, eye contact, and ability to communicate effectively to jurors.[7] In this chapter we address the specific effects and nature of race as a sentencing, credibility, and witness variable.

I. RACE AND JUSTICE

Considerable research has reported racial influences on legal and criminal justice outcomes. In their review of the literature, Mitchell and others observed that African American drug offenders are up to thirteen times more likely to be sentenced to jail than their Caucasian counterparts, and that in death penalty sentencing, African Americans were sentenced to death four times as often as Caucasians.[8] These researchers conducted a meta-analysis of sixteen research studies that had twenty effect sizes. The sixteen studies involved a total of 3,141 participants who served as mock jurors deciding guilt or sentencing in designs in which the race of the defendant was experimentally manipulated. Small but consistent disparities were found in the sentencing of African American defendants compared to Caucasian defendants. The authors reported that mock jurors convict with greater frequency and recommend longer sentences for African American defendants in comparison to Caucasians. Mitchell and others additionally noted that "racial bias was more pronounced in the following conditions: for Black participants; when a continuous measure of guilt was utilized; when jury instructions were not provided; and in studies conducted or published in the 1970's."[9]

Juror stereotypic decision making appears to be rooted in generalized attributes about individuals of a specific racial or ethnic background. Some posit that culturally biased sentencing is derived from notions of increased dangerousness of certain racial backgrounds.[10] In essence, harsher sentencing of African American defendants stems from notions that they are perceived as more threatening and culpable than Caucasians. Racial stereotypes may also impact judges' attributions of responsibility and perceptions of danger. Albonetti posited that judges develop "patterned responses," that is, they use stereotypes linking individual characteristics to expectations about criminal responsibility.[11] For example, young African American males are perceived to be associated with increased culpability. These individual characteristics, in combination, may lead judges to pattern their responses in a manner consistent with the stereotypical view, resulting in harsher sentencing for minority offenders.

II. RACE, GENDER, AND CREDIBILITY

Few studies have examined the link between the race of an expert witness and the influence it has on perceptions of credibility. Evidence suggests that in the legal setting, the presentation of an African American individual evokes racial stereotypes that impact juror perceptions. However, little is known about the cognitive processes involved when the African American is presented in a capacity outside of the normative view or stereotypical social role of an African American (i.e., expert psychological witness). Memon and Shuman are among the few scholars who have investigated both race and gender effects on jurors' perceptions of expert witness credibility.[12] Using a slide presentation of a civil case, prospective jurors were exposed to photographs of one of four experts (black female, black male, white female, white male) while simultaneously listening to audiotaped testimony. The participants were asked to rate the expert on variables including qualifications, persuasion, and believability. The researchers found that the white jurors rated the black female expert most persuasive. In addition, there was a nonsignificant but interesting trend in which the black male was rated as the expert with the best reasoning ability. There were no overall significant differences in the ratings for male and female experts.

The fact that white jurors rated the black female expert as most persuasive is consistent with the flexible correction model. The flexible correction model explicates the manner in which individuals attempt to remove or reduce bias from

their judgments. The correction process is explored within the context of courtroom judgments, as triers of fact are subject to being influenced by stereotypes. Wegener and Petty posited that when individuals are presented with a message source, they evaluate their initial reaction to determine if it warrants an adjustment.[13] When a potentially biasing cue is detected, individuals "correct" for the probable effect of the bias on their judgment. This often leads to a judgment in the opposite direction of the uncorrected bias. In the Memon and Shuman study, when white jurors detected the potentially biasing cue of race, they apparently attempted to correct for the perceived negative influence that it had on their judgments.[14] This correction manifested in higher ratings of persuasiveness and reasoning ability for the black experts compared to the white experts. Although the flexible correction model provides a framework for understanding the mechanism through which perceived bias is corrected, the theory does not contend that the self-regulated correction aptly diminishes the effects of the bias. Instead, it is a distinct possibility that one may overcorrect for the racial bias, as described by Memon and Shuman.[15]

In light of the limited empirical evidence related to the influence of race on expert witness persuasion, researchers are compelled to draw heavily from social psychological research conducted on the impact of the race of a message source on persuasion, information processing, and attitude change.

III. INFORMATION PROCESSING

Petty and Cacioppo posited, in their *elaboration likelihood model*, that there are two routes to persuasion, or ways in which individuals develop and bring about change in attitudes.[16] The central route is a process by which the recipient of the message attends to the argument, makes a concerted effort to understand the argument, and carefully evaluates the message content.[17] The central route of information processing necessitates effortful thinking. The likelihood of individuals engaging in such effortful thinking largely rests on factors such as the perceived relevance of the argument topic and the recipient's need for cognition.[18]

The peripheral route of persuasion is one in which attitude change results from less effortful strategies such as "examining early but not late arguments, counting arguments, or relying on one's liking for the source."[19] In the absence of motivation to utilize effortful thinking strategies, individuals often rely on salient attributes of the message source (e.g., attractiveness, race, likability). Individuals who employ the peripheral route of persuasion avail themselves of contextual cues, in preference to meticulously processing the content of the message.[20] Considering the manner in which attitude change is brought about via the peripheral route, that is, with little attention to the substance of the message itself, this route has decided potential to lead to biased decisions.

Jurors, particularly those serving on criminal cases, are faced with the consequences of attending carelessly to information proffered by experts (e.g., innocent defendant found guilty). Kassin, Reddy, and Tulloch hypothesized that the nature of legal trials is extraordinarily engaging, such that jurors do actively consider the evidence being presented, despite typical low motivational tendencies.[21] Schul and Manzury found evidence in support of this hypothesis, suggesting that jurors recognize the value of their ultimate judgments.[22] These researchers presented mock jurors with witness testimony that was later discounted due to the lack of supportive evidence. The findings indicate

that mock jurors were successful in discounting the invalidated testimony. This evidence suggests that decision makers demonstrated the potential to disregard unsupported biasing information in an effort to render just verdicts.

A. Persuasion and Race

We turn now to the effect of race on persuasiveness. The literature has yielded mixed findings. According to White and Harkins, for white message receivers, a minority speaker has been found at varying times to be less persuasive, more persuasive, and equally as persuasive as white speakers.[23] White and Harkins attributed these divergent findings to the fact that past researchers did not have modern information processing models that explain when, if, and how a message source affects attitude change.[24]

Looking through the lens of the information processing models, with race serving as a peripheral cue, White and Harkins sought in a series of investigations to assess whether race impacted persuasion.[25] The first study involved seventy-eight Caucasian male and female participants. These participants were presented with the opinions of other students (one white and one black) regarding whether college students should be required to pass a comprehensive exam prior to graduation. These researchers found that, when exposed to a black or white message source, white participants were not differentially persuaded. In a second experiment, involving 160 Caucasian male and female participants, the researchers tested the hypothesis that white participants are more motivated to process the message of a black source in comparison to a white source. This was assessed in light of a widely accepted notion of elaboration likelihood, which suggests that when a message lacks personal relevance, individuals are not as invested in processing the message, thereby decreasing elaboration likelihood. The student participants were presented with information regarding a potential academic policy change at their university (high personal relevance) or at another university (low personal relevance). White and Harkins found that even under conditions lacking personal relevance, white participants were motivated to process the message of the black source.[26] In contrast, the participants were motivated to process the message of the white source only when it pertained to a policy change that could personally impact them. These findings suggest that in the presence of a black message source, irrespective of the personal relevance, the white participants' elaboration likelihood increased.

White and Harkins speculated that this pattern of results is attributable to aversive racism.[27] The *theory of aversive racism* posits that whites are not ordinarily aware of the negative attitudes they possess about minority group members. However, when a situation arises in which these negative attitudes become salient and threaten their egalitarian view of themselves, whites react by espousing convictions that reaffirm a nonracist status.[28] Accordingly, the white participants endeavored to present themselves as nonracist by attending to the message of a black source even when it lacked personal relevance and significance. Though informative, these studies provided a limited perspective on how race impacts persuasion and elaboration likelihood.

IV. RECEIVER VARIABLES

A. In-Group Bias

It is not enough to consider only the influence of the race of the expert. Characteristics of the message receiver also influence

the persuasive appeal of expert testimony. Evidence suggests that "receiver variables" can moderate receptivity to a persuasive message.[29] Individual characteristics of the jurors, such as their race and ethnic identity, can influence the degree to which the message of an expert is viewed favorably.

Attitudes and beliefs about members of a group with which one identifies generally differ from attitudes held about those perceived outside of the self-identified group. The *social categorization theory* posits that individuals "assign objects to groups and apply cognitions and affect associated with the group to an individual object."[30] The categorization of objects and people accentuates the difference between identified groups and provides a platform on which the groups are appraised. For instance, when jurors evaluate African American and Caucasian experts, social categorization theory posits that these jurors engage in a cognitive process that results in assigning these experts to a heuristic group. If all other variables are constant, jurors assign the experts to racial groups. Once the expert's race is identified, jurors consider their race and assess whether the expert is an in-group or out-group member. One consequence of social categorization is in-group favoritism. In-group favoritism is defined as a tendency to evaluate members of one's own group more favorably than members of another group.[31] Based on this theory, again assuming all other variables are equal, one might speculate that jurors would be more persuaded by expert witnesses with whom they share a common racial or cultural background.

B. Ethnic Identity

Ethnic identity is an additional and related receiver variable. Ethnic identity may be described as the part of an individual's self-concept that comes from personal knowledge of membership in a social group.[32] Individuals with high ethnic identity exhibit "behaviors and attitudes reflective of ethnic identity exploration, a sense of positive affiliation to one's ethnic group, and the expression of ethnic practices indigenous to one's ethnic origins."[33] Using an African American sample, Whittler and Spira investigated the effects of ethnic identity on favorability ratings of an advertising model.[34] The study involved 160 adults (66 percent females, 34 percent males) recruited from various social and civic organizations. Participants were randomly assigned to view one of four storyboard advertisements, which varied according to model's race (black or white) and argument quality. Overall, the participants expressed greater liking for the black model compared to the white model. In addition, those with a high ethnic identification rated the black model more favorably than the white model. Those with a low ethnic identification did not differentially rate the black and white models. Providing further evidence of in-group favoritism, black participants reported a stronger intention to purchase the advertised product when the model was black compared to when the model was white.

V. OUR RESEARCH

Our own research has addressed the effects of race on perceptions of expert witness credibility. Although a comprehensive report of this study has been provided elsewhere, the following summarizes our major findings.[35] Our work drew on a study of 257 undergraduate students of Caucasian or African American descent who were enrolled at a large state university in the southern region of the United States. Mock jurors were presented case information relating to a first-degree assault and exposed to videotaped testimony of one of four female expert witnesses (two African American and two Caucasian). The participants were later asked a series of questions regarding their perception of credibility of the expert witness. A manipulation check revealed that the participants attended to the race of the expert and later recalled the experts' race with remarkable accuracy. However, the data also suggested the mock jurors were successful in diminishing the effect of this peripheral cue. There was no significant effect of race on ratings of perceived credibility of the expert witness. This finding is divergent from our pilot data and from that of Memon and Shuman, which found that the African American female expert was rated most persuasive.[36] The pattern of racial minority individuals being proffered a more favorable rating has been explained by the flexible correction model, as described earlier. However, in our study, there was no indication that participants overcorrected for a bias, as evidenced by the fact that the African American experts were not provided significantly higher ratings of credibility.

A tentative explanation is offered for the lack of evidence for a corrective process in favor of the black experts. According to Wegener and Petty the greater a perceived bias, the more likely that participants will invoke a corrective process.[37] Thus, participants may have perceived little or no bias that they deemed worthy of correction in their initial assessments of the African American experts. Race may have been viewed as irrelevant to the overall goal of providing judgments concerning the case at hand. If contextual factors had been manipulated such that stereotypes and discrimination associated with the target race became more salient—for example, if the first-degree assault was racially motivated—perhaps the correction for perceived bias would have been observed.

Though Whittler and Spira found evidence of an in-group favoritism among

African American receivers, we found no such bias in our study.[38] The results revealed that African American participants were no more likely to provide favorable ratings for black experts than they were for whites. Similarly, Caucasian participants did not provide higher ratings of credibility for the expert witnesses with whom they shared a racial background. Furthermore, those with a high level of ethnic identification did not differentially rate the experts. This objectivity may in part be attributed to the motivational instructions that were provided to participants prior to the start of the study, in which they were encouraged to put themselves in the place of a juror and pay close attention to the testimony. These instructions were implemented based on Louis and Sutton's *switching gears model*, which argues that there are three situations likely to inspire the need to abandon automaticity and evoke effortful cognitive processes.[39] According to this theory, individuals "switch gears" in conditions that are novel or unusual, those in which a discrepancy exists, or conditions in which there is a "deliberate initiative, usually in response to an internal or external request for an increased level of conscious attention—as when people are asked to think."[40] The last of the three conditions was implemented in the current study. Evidence suggests that unmotivated participants were persuaded to switch gears with a direct request for increased levels of consciousness. Furthermore, findings suggest the manipulation was effective in activating central route processing and diminishing the influence of race as a peripheral cue on mock juror judgments of expert witness credibility.

CONCLUSION

From the body of literature contributing to the understanding of information processing, we infer that the influence of ex-

pert witness race on persuasion and attitude change is uncertain, and often secondary to probative and contextual factors. Unequivocal conclusions are unattainable regarding how jurors are persuaded by the testimony of a Caucasian expert in comparison to an African American expert, for example. Previous literature suggests that there are several moderating factors that should be considered. These factors include context-specific characteristics, characteristics of the expert, and those of the individual juror.

Nevertheless, responsible scholars should be attentive to the specific times at which racism does appear. One path toward addressing possible racial discrimination in capital trial sentencing has been presented by Schroeder, Chaisson, and Pogue.[41] They begin with the common assumption that discriminatory judgments by juries arise either from individual racist attitudes or from patterns of institutionalized racism. Their proposed method of intervention is to employ narrative in testimony in order to make the lives and experiences of the defendants meaningful to the jury. The specific mechanisms of change are stated to include increasing the self-awareness of the jurors about racial beliefs, which in turn would reduce bias and promote therapeutic jurisprudence. In the same sense, Brodsky has argued that in all trials, whether or not race is a factor, meaningful presentation of narrative testimony is important.[42] He has asserted that it promotes cognitive processing of emotional and sometimes murky and equivocal evidence, and serves the expert as well as the jury.

Good narrative presentation attends to contextual factors, that is, the specific and salient facts of each case. Depending on the actual crime, race may or may not become a salient feature. Cases involving racially salient issues, such as workplace discrimination, might cue jurors to attend to race variables and thereby be more sensitive to the race of the expert. This sensitization could result in differential perceptions of credibility of experts based on race alone.

In a justice system in which race is so compelling in many ways, it is worthwhile to note that the race of an expert witness does not have a uniform impact on perceptions of jurors. Other expert characteristics impact the degree to which race plays a role in persuasion. For instance, if presented with an expert whose speech is marked by verbal hesitancies, poor posture, and minimal eye contact, the overwhelming influence of these characteristics will likely overshadow the influence of the race of the expert. In light of these variables, race is less significant and likely has little or no impact on the development of juror attitude changes.

When attempting to assess how the race of an expert may impact juror perceptions, one must not overlook the importance of the characteristic of the message receiver. When evaluating the persuasive appeal of a message source, an exploration of the characteristics of the jurors and how they interact with that of the race of the expert commands attention. The race of individual jurors may impact perceptions of experts from different cultural backgrounds. However, one must not make assumptions that jurors of minority descent uniformly engage in in-group favoritism. One must first consider the individual juror's level of identification with his or her ethnic background. Even then, as indicated by the findings from our study, participants have the potential to remain objective.

In sum, does the race of an expert witness influence juror perceptions and decisions? Based on our examination of the existing literature and our own research, this question is yet to be answered clearly and is contingent upon many competing variables. The limited research in this area only modestly furthers our understanding of this complex process. Although there is a wealth of research on the influence of race on social perceptions and attitude change, specific examinations of expert witness testimony have been understudied. Until recently, there has been little relevance for this research, for historically those serving as expert witnesses have been predominately Caucasian. However, with recent efforts to increase racial minorities in the health professions, there is promise that the next generation of psychologists will be culturally diverse. As the cultural landscape of the profession changes, a burgeoning need exists to understand other effects of the expert witness's race on witness credibility and juror decision making.

8

Does Race Matter?

Exploring the Cross-Race Effect in Eyewitness Identification

Steven M. Smith and Veronica Stinson

INTRODUCTION

In June 1982, a woman in the Florida Keys had her home broken into by two men she described as "Latino," one of whom she described as shirtless and hairless. She claimed that the shirtless man forced her into her bedroom, fondled her, and ejaculated on her. Once the men left, the woman called police, who promptly stopped Orlando Bosquete (a Cuban American who happened to be shirtless and who had little hair) and several other Cuban men at a local convenience store. The victim later identified Bosquete as the man who had assaulted her. Although a semen sample was collected from the scene, it was not tested because the requisite DNA technology was not yet available. In January 1983 Bosquete was convicted of one count of burglary and one count of sexual battery. Bosquete's conviction was based exclusively on the testimony of the victim. He was sentenced to sixty-five years in prison. In 2003 Bosquete requested that the semen be subjected to DNA testing to determine if he was the criminal. DNA tests revealed that he could not have been the woman's assailant. On May 23, 2006, the charges against Bosquete were dismissed, twenty-three years after his conviction.

This is not the only case where race may have affected the testimony of a key witness and probably played a role in a defendant's conviction. Increasingly, courts are being asked to deal with this *cross-race effect* (i.e., the fact that other-race identifications are more error-prone than same-race identifications), and have even acknowledged the results of the psychological literature in their decisions. Nevertheless, courts continue to show reluctance in giving jurors access to scientific knowledge in this area. For example, in *Smith & Mack v. Maryland*, two black men were convicted of attempting to rob a white woman.[1] During the trial, the victim testified that she had a good memory for faces. The defense attempted to raise a cross-race identification issue and asked the trial judge to provide a cautionary instruction to the jury regarding this matter. The judge declined and the defendant was convicted. On appeal, the defense argued that the trial judge erred in his decision to exclude special jury instructions dealing with cross-racial identifications. The Maryland appellate court disagreed with this argument, but it did overturn the verdict on the grounds that the trial judge erred in barring the defendants from commenting on cross-racial identifications during their closing arguments. Interestingly, the appellate court acknowledged the converging data from both laboratory and field studies on cross-race facial memory and the strong consensus among social scientists on the existence of the cross-race effect.

I. THE PROBLEM OF LINEUP IDENTIFICATION ERRORS

Despite recent developments in forensic evidence collection and use, eyewitness testimony often plays an important role at trial. Across Canada, the United States, and Great Britain, eyewitnesses select hundreds of individuals from lineups every day. Eyewitness identification evidence is often the strongest or the only evidence prosecutors have against defendants in several types of criminal trials (e.g., assault). During criminal investigations and the trial process, police officers, prosecutors, judges, and jurors place a great deal of faith in eyewitness identification evidence.[2] It is estimated that in a typical year, eyewitness evidence plays a significant role in more than 75,000 criminal cases in Canada and the United States alone.[3]

False identification rates in eyewitness experiments can vary dramatically, from as low as a few percent to well over 90 percent, depending on the study conducted.[4]

Although actual rates of eyewitness errors in the real world are unknown, there is some evidence showing that false identifications happen and may indeed be fairly common. For example, of 8,000 suspects arrested for sexual assault who had DNA samples tested by the U.S. Federal Bureau of Investigation laboratory, more than 2,000 (or about 25 percent) were excluded as the perpetrator. Typically these arrests were made based (at least in part) on eyewitness identification.[5] Were it not for DNA testing, a large percentage of these individuals might have been convicted. The Innocence Project, led by Barry Scheck and Peter Neufeld, has to date overseen the exoneration of 180 defendants (many on death row in the United States) through the analysis of DNA evidence that was available but untested (or not testable) at the time of trial.[6] In more than 75 percent of the Innocence Project cases, erroneous identifications by eyewitnesses were a key factor in the conviction. This is consistent with the results of a study of more than 1,000 false convictions, where the majority of cases were primarily the result of mistaken identification.[7]

Often, eyewitness accounts are the primary evidence used by prosecutors at trial and are the most sought-after form of evidence during the investigative process.[8] Jurors often regard eyewitness testimony as the most useful evidence in a trial,[9] and combined with an eyewitness's confidence in his or her identification (which itself is highly malleable), it can be perceived as powerful evidence against any defendant.[10]

II. THE CROSS-RACE EFFECT AS A FACTOR IN FALSE IDENTIFICATIONS

One factor that has been explored as contributing to false identifications is cross-race situations. When the eyewitness is of a different race or ethnic background than the suspect, accuracy rates are lower than in same-race identifications.[11] Before we get into the evidence for the cross-race effect, it is worth noting that some researchers refer to this effect as the cross-race or own-race *bias*.[12] However, we choose to use the term *effect* because of its more neutral connotation with regard to the intentionality of the effect. Specifically, *cross-race bias* may suggest to some that the decreased accuracy rates for cross-race identifications are the result of anti-ethnic bias by the person making the identification. Generally, the research suggests that this is not the case.[13]

Although statistics are not collected concerning the frequency of cross-race lineups, some inferences can be made. The 2004 National Crime Victimization Survey results show that of 3,382,920 white violent crime victims, 52.7 percent perceived their offender to be of the same race, and 9.6 percent perceived the race of their offender to be black. Of the 559,130 black violent crime victims, 73.6 percent perceived their offender to be of the same race, and 10.8 percent perceived the race of their offender to be white. Moreover, the U.S. Justice Department states that 22 percent of sexual assaults involve black perpetrators and white victims.[14] Furthermore, an analysis of seventy-seven cases of people who had been falsely convicted of a crime due primarily to mistaken eyewitness identification found that 35 percent of those cases involved a white person misidentifying a black person, whereas only 27 percent were white-white misidentifications.[15]

However, the impact of the cross-race effect on real-world false convictions is not clear. The extent of the impact of cross-race errors, independent of eyewitness errors in general, requires additional research. Of course, it is impossible to know in real-world settings if errors are made solely because of race, or if other factors may have an impact. One very interesting set of results has come from a survey of factors that affect the likelihood that a witness will make a selection from a police lineup. Valentine, Pickering, and Darling conducted a study of 640 eyewitness attempts to identify suspects from 314 London Metropolitan Police lineups.[16] Characteristics of the witness, the suspect, the lineup, and the witness's opportunity to view the criminal were all recorded. Next, the authors used these factors to predict the likelihood that the suspect (who, of course, may or may not be the criminal) would be picked out of the lineup. These researchers found that although the age (under thirty) and race (white European) of the suspect as well as the level of detail of the description and length of time the witness viewed the criminal (over a minute) all predicted an increased likelihood of making a choice from the lineup, factors such as the presence of a weapon, cross-race identifications, or delay between the crime and the identification did not predict choice. These data are valuable and help us understand identifications in a real-world context, but because we do not know true error rates in the real world, it is not clear whether any of these factors predict the *accuracy* of that choice. Thus further investigation is clearly still warranted.

III. EVIDENCE FOR THE CROSS-RACE EFFECT

A. Evidence from the Eyewitness Literature

It has been almost forty years since Malpass and Kravitz published their first empirical study on the cross-race effect.[17] Their pioneering research has led to numerous studies in years since. Typically, facial recognition studies involve exposing research participants to a series of photographs of same-race and other-race people. After a delay, participants take part in a face recognition task. From a more applied perspective, eyewitness memory experiments in this area usually expose research participants to a simulated crime and then elicit a lineup identification decision from them. Most of these studies have used white and black faces as stimuli (i.e., photographs or perpetrators in the simulated crimes), and usually white participants (although some studies have included subjects of various races). Most of these studies have produced fairly consistent results, generally showing that white eyewitnesses who attempt to identify a black perpetrator from a lineup tend to be less accurate than white eyewitnesses who attempt to identify a same-race perpetrator. To a lesser extent, the opposite is true (i.e., black eyewitnesses tend to be more error-prone when they identify white perpetrators than black eyewitnesses making a same-race identification). More recently, Smith, Lindsay, Pryke, and Dysart[18] showed that the cross-race effect also occurred for Asian-white eyewitness situations, a finding replicated by Smith, Stinson, and Prosser.[19]

To date, there have been three meta-analyses exploring the existence and nature of the cross-race effect.[20] Most recently, Meissner and Brigham analyzed data from thirty-nine research articles that encompassed ninety-one independent groups and more than 5,000 witnesses.[21] Their meta-analysis revealed an overall "mirror effect" pattern such that people were consistently and significantly better able to identify people of their own racial group than those of other racial groups. The authors calculated likelihood ratios in order to assess the extent to which cross-race identifications were more likely to be error-prone. They found that witnesses in these studies were 1.56 times more likely to falsely identify someone of another race than someone of their own race. This

rather large effect translates to an estimate that a "black innocent suspect has a 56% greater chance of being misidentified by a white eyewitness than by a black eyewitness."[22]

In general, all three of these meta-analyses demonstrate that people are better at identifying individuals from their own race rather than at identifying those from another race.[23] Additionally, the cross-race effect is not specific to the two groups who have been most studied (i.e., blacks and whites) but is consistent across a number of ethnic and racial groups (e.g., blacks, whites, Hispanics, Asians). Before turning to potential explanations for these effects, we place these findings in context by discussing some of the potential shortcomings of this body of knowledge.

B. Potential Limitations of These Studies

It is worth noting that many eyewitness studies (and not just those dealing with the cross-race effect) have been criticized because of their perceived lack of generalizability to real-world settings. Some have argued that the lab does not capture the rich nature of actual crimes and the subsequent lineup identification process, that identification decisions are not done in realistic settings, and that (the mostly university-age) eyewitnesses understand that their decisions are inconsequential for the "perpetrator" and therefore may make hastier decisions. A number of studies have been explicitly designed to address these general issues.[24] For example, Smith and colleagues found that when asked how they made their decision, eyewitnesses reported that they were reluctant to make a choice because they did not want to make a mistake and they were afraid of the consequences if they chose the wrong person.[25] Other studies have explored a range of age groups[26] in a wide variety of settings[27] and have reported similar findings.

Naturalistic field studies, such as the cleverly conducted Platz and Hosch field experiment, also point to a similar conclusion.[28] In this field experiment, experimental confederates (white, black, or Mexican American) approached convenience store clerks and engaged them in an unusual interaction (e.g., paid for cigarettes with pennies only). Two hours later, "law clerks" dressed in business suits told the clerks that they were looking for a person of interest and presented them with a photo lineup. As with other studies in this area, Platz and Hosch's data support a cross-race effect, with their study contributing valuable data on Mexican Americans.[29]

There are other important caveats to consider when interpreting the results of cross-race eyewitness studies as well. First, as Wells and Olson point out, the cross-race effect is unlikely to be omnipresent or equally powerful across all situations.[30] There are a number of other variables that might moderate or mediate the effect, for example, police interviewing techniques or lineup instructions. Moreover, the magnitude of the cross-race effect is probably affected by variations across faces of people of different races. This raises the question of whether the faces used in these experiments to represent people of different races actually represent the full range of facial feature variations that actually exist. Another factor that may qualify the findings described above stems from a methodological paradigm often used in these studies that asks research participants to identify which faces shown are new versus old. Some studies use a lineup paradigm whereby participants are shown an array of photographs and asked to determine whether or not the "perpetrator" is in the lineup. Wells and Olson suggest that a lineup paradigm that includes a manipulation of presence of target is impor-

tant for understanding this effect; few studies include this variable, however.[31] Finally, as both Sporer[32] and Wells and Olson[33] point out, operationally defining race is very difficult in this context, and it may be more useful to consider perceived facial variability instead.

IV. POTENTIAL CAUSES OF THE CROSS-RACE EFFECT

With the cross-race effect literature placed in this context, we now turn to an examination of some possible roots behind this effect. Until recently, relatively little attention has been paid to the cause of the cross-race effect.[34] Nonetheless, there have been a number of propositions as to why the cross-race effect occurs. In this section, we will explore those explanations that have received the most attention, namely, the contact hypothesis, facial features and categorization, social cognitive factors, and finally a recent exploration of a dual-process explanation for the effect.

A. Perceptual Expertise

People may have more difficulty identifying members of other races because they do not distinguish among the numerous and subtle features that differentiate people in races other than their own. Along a similar vein, O'Toole, Abdi, Deffenbacher, and Valentin propose that people who are unfamiliar with other-race faces are oblivious to the variability in these faces and thus struggle to differentiate unique facial characteristics.[35] However, if perceptual expertise is the root of the cross-race effect, then increasing people's understanding of facial features that distinguish individuals of different races should eliminate this effect. The research that has explored this question provides inconclusive results, however.[36]

B. The Contact Hypothesis

A related explanation involves the extent to which we have contact with other-race individuals. The contact hypothesis predicts that the amount of cross-race contact an individual has had will be a strong predictor of that person's cross-race facial recognition ability.[37] An important factor in the hypothesized relationship between contact and recognition is the quality of the cross-race interactions; recognition ability should improve as the number of quality interactions increases. Although several studies have attempted to examine the viability of this explanation, the pattern of findings is somewhat mixed.[38] Byatt and Rhodes propose that measurement problems may obscure this relationship.[39] Indeed, they found that people's ratings of their experience with other-race faces were unrelated to cross-race recognition accuracy, but a more concrete measure of other-race contact (number of known individuals) significantly correlated with recognition performance. In their recent meta-analysis described above, Meissner and Brigham found that contact played a statistically significant but small role in cross-race identification errors, accounting for only 2 percent of the variance.[40]

A variation of the contact hypothesis was examined by Brigham and Malpass, who explored whether racially prejudiced attitudes could have a negative influence on the contact-recognition relationship.[41] Individuals high in prejudice may, upon recognition of an individual from another race, refuse to process further the individual's facial features. This simple categorization eliminates any chance that contact can increase recognition ability. Meissner and Brigham's meta-analysis reported that across studies, racial attitudes did not predict the cross-race effect.[42] Nonetheless, Brigham and Malpass suggest that a simplistic understanding of the contact hypothesis may be at the root of failure to find support for the hypothesis.[43] Moreover, they contend that mere contact is mediated by attitude as well as social orientation, difficulty of the identification task, and past experience with members of the other race. Consistent with this, Meissner and Brigham found a relationship between racial attitudes and self-reported contact.[44] Future research with implicit measures of racism may also help shed some light on this issue.[45] However, to date there is no evidence that the weak direct effect of contact on cross-race errors is mediated by racial attitudes (hence our use of the term *effect* instead of *bias*).

C. Utilitarian Hypothesis

As Malpass proposes, simply having contact with other-race members is not enough to reduce a cross-race effect.[46] His utilitarian perspective posits that people must have a reason or motivation to recognize distinctions among individuals of other races. Dunning and colleagues' interesting study of basketball fans supports this hypothesis.[47] They hypothesized that basketball fans probably like to identify players (who are predominately black) and thus would need to individuate players. Avid fans should therefore not display the cross-race effect compared to novice basketball viewers. Indeed, their data support this notion. They found that expert fans were better able to discriminate among black faces than nonexpert fans and that the facial recognition performance of expert fans was comparable to that of blacks. However, some more recent research[48] attempted to replicate Dunning and colleagues' research[49] and found that people who were experts with other-race faces (in terms of being basketball fans, having knowledge of basketball trivia, and recognizing of famous black names) were no better at recognizing cross-race faces than nonexperts. However, this research suggested that experts and nonexperts may process cross-race faces differently.[50] Thus, the utilitarian hypothesis is yet to be fully supported.

D. Facial Features and Facial Categorization

Inherent difficulty is one potential reason for the cross-race effect.[51] This explanation posits that it is simply more difficult to differentiate members of different races (i.e., Asians look alike to whites). Indeed, research examining in-group/out-group biases revealed that in-group members tend to assume that the facial features of in-group members are more idiosyncratic than those of out-group members.[52] This hypothesis is difficult to test because it would be very difficult to determine whether the cross-race effect is due to homogeneity of facial features or inappropriate use of facial cues.[53] In any event, analysis of anthropometric data reveals that the common assumption that members of some races "all look alike" is erroneous. Asian, black, and white faces are equally heterogeneous.[54] Even if there were greater homogeneity of facial features in one race compared to other races, it would not explain the relative ease with which individuals make same-race identifications.[55]

E. Social-Cognitive Factors

One approach that has been used to try to understand the cross-race effect has been to assess how people make their identification judgments and determine how characteristics of those judgments differ across situations.

1. RELATIVE VERSUS ABSOLUTE JUDGMENT STRATEGIES

Evidence that judgment strategy can be used to estimate errors has been demonstrated in a number of studies.[56] Judgment strategy is a "postdictor" variable because it is used to "predict" error after it has occurred. Wells has suggested that when presented with a lineup, eyewitnesses tend to compare the pictures to each other and select the photo that looks the most similar to the perpetrator (a relative judgment).[57] An alternative decision-making strategy is absolute judgments. Eyewitnesses make absolute judgments when they consider each lineup photograph individually and determine whether the photograph corresponds to the perpetrator. Only after making this yes/no decision do they move on to consider the next picture.

Lindsay and Bellinger provided descriptions of relative and absolute judgment strategies to participants and asked them to select which strategy was most like the strategy they had used in making their lineup identifications.[58] Eyewitnesses who reported using a relative judgment strategy accounted for a disproportionate number of false positive choices when compared to those indicating they had used an absolute judgment strategy. This effect is robust and has been replicated in subsequent studies.[59] Despite the success of judgment strategy as a postdictor of errors in same-race situations, its utility in cross-race situations has not been demonstrated. In recent work out of our lab, we have shown that relative versus absolute judgment strategy does not predict accuracy in cross-race situations. Specifically, in two separate studies we asked participants in same- and cross-race situations to indicate which judgment strategy they had used in coming to their decision.[60] In one, judgment strategy predicted accuracy only in the same-race conditions.[61] In the other, eyewitnesses tended to be more likely to indicate they had used a relative judgment strategy in the cross-race conditions than in the same-race conditions, but judgment strategy did not significantly predict accuracy.[62] Thus, at this point, relative versus absolute judgment strategy does not seem to explain the cross-race effect.

2. SUBJECTIVE EASE OF DECISION MAKING

Sporer demonstrated that quick responses are accurate responses.[63] This effect has been replicated in a number of studies.[64] Although some researchers[65] have tried to argue that a decision in ten to twelve seconds is most likely to be accurate, defining a specific time frame is both premature and problematic.[66] Nonetheless, the relative speed with which people make eyewitness decisions has been shown to be an effective way to postdict eyewitness accuracy in same-race conditions.[67] However, the ability of response time to identify accurate and inaccurate cross-race eyewitness identifications is questionable at best.[68]

Dunning and Stern attempted to distinguish accurate from inaccurate identifications using self-reports of the decision processes eyewitnesses used.[69] They hypothesized that quick responses are likely to be easy. Consistent with this logic, people who agreed with items designed to represent more time-consuming judgment strategies (e.g., "I compared the photos to each other to narrow the choices") were less likely to be accurate than eyewitnesses who endorsed absolute judgment strategies (e.g., "I just recognized him, I cannot explain why"). In one recent study we simply asked participants about how they made their decisions in both same- and cross-race situations.[70] Interestingly, although race had an impact on accuracy, participants did not seem aware of this effect. Perhaps it is not surprising that people were unaware of how they processed the information and made their decisions. Indeed, other research has found that in many circumstances, people are unaware of the cognitive processes in-

volved in their judgments.[71] Interestingly, the primary difference between same- and cross-race identifications is that participants indicated they had a less clear memory of the criminal in the cross-race conditions, and they were less confident they would be able to select the criminal out of the lineup (which they were less able to do). Poor clarity of memory may provide further evidence that encoding of cross-race facial features may be different from same-race encoding.

3. DEPTH OF PROCESSING

A third possible explanation is related to the extent to which people process information about the criminal. As described earlier, participants may use the race of the criminal as a cue for how much to process the relevant information. The result could be biased encoding, where the eyewitness may be less inclined to process the information carefully. Chance and Goldstein proposed that people may process own-race faces holistically and other-race faces more superficially.[72] Devine and Malpass provide some support for this contention,[73] but it is not clear why this might be the case.[74]

4. A DUAL-PROCESS EXPLANATION

Meissner, Brigham, and Butz examined the cross-race effect within the context of a dual-process theory of memory.[75] Differentiating memory processes that involve recall versus those based on familiarity, this theoretical approach appears to be useful for understanding the social cognitive processes involved in same- and cross-race facial recognition. Specifically, in a pair of studies Meissner and colleagues found that eyewitnesses tended to encode more information about same-race faces than about cross-race faces.[76] In the subsequent identification tasks, people in a same-race situation had a more diagnostic representation of the criminal's face in memory and were better able to make a correct identification than people in cross-race situations. Thus their data support an encoding-based explanation for the cross-race effect rather than a contact- or prejudice-based explanation.

V. WHAT CAN WE DO ABOUT THE CROSS-RACE EFFECT?

A. Legal Remedies

As we mentioned at the beginning of the chapter, the courts are dealing with cross-race identifications in a variety of ways. Although there are a number of approaches that could be taken (e.g., cross-examination of the witness regarding the nature of the identification, cautionary instructions to jurors, expert testimony), it is probably fair to say that in most cases, little attention is paid to the cross-race nature of the identification.[77] Even if action is taken, some would argue that enough racial bias currently exists throughout the legal system to sway the courts against a minority group member in any case.[78] Nonetheless, as described in our introduction above, some legal decisions have been made that open avenues for those seeking to introduce eyewitness issues in general, and the cross-race effect specifically, into court proceedings.[79]

Jury instructions are perhaps the most plausible manner in which to deal with cross-race issues. However, what is contained in those instructions will be a key determinant of their effectiveness. Understanding the nature of any bias is important to understanding exactly how to prepare a jury instruction.[80] Research has demonstrated that biases can be corrected, but appropriate correction depends in large part upon awareness of the bias and a person's motivation to make corrections for that bias. Thus we can over- or under-

compensate for biases if we inaccurately assess their nature or magnitude, or if we are more or less motivated to compensate. Wegener and colleagues argue that in the context of jury instructions, a key factor in developing an effective bias correction mechanism is to have a clear understanding of the nature of the existing bias.[81] In research exploring cautionary jury instructions, such instructions have been found to be effective if they contain easy-to-understand and accurate information.[82] Unfortunately, jury instructions are typically prepared by a judge or legal scholar who may have little knowledge or understanding of empirical findings.

Relatively recently, in *State v. Cromedy*, the New Jersey Supreme Court determined that defendants are entitled to a jury instruction that warns of the cross-race nature of the identification.[83] As noted in our introduction, Maryland courts are also taking the issue seriously. However, the instruction used in these courts is nondirectional, in that juries can be instructed that they should consider the cross-race issue but are not instructed on the nature of the cross-race effect. Instructions such as these are unlikely to be helpful to jurors. We propose that jury instructions on this issue should contain an overview of the factors eyewitness experts agree influence the likelihood of errors in the system.[84] Specifically, such testimony should discuss the nature of eyewitness errors, including factors that lead to mistakes (e.g., poor lineups, stress, short exposure time, and cross-race situations) and a discussion of the nature of the relationship between eyewitness confidence and accuracy.[85] Although all of these issues could be addressed in court by an expert witness, judges across Canada and the United States often (erroneously) deem this subject area as common knowledge (i.e., jurors already know these things). Thus, expert testimony on eyewitness issues is rarely admissible.

I. CATCHING ERRORS: SYSTEM VARIABLES VERSUS ESTIMATOR VARIABLES

Perhaps the most promising approach to dealing with cross-race false identifications is first to understand why errors occur, and then to construct police investigation and identification tasks designed to minimize the likelihood of errors in the first place. A substantial amount of research has been conducted to understand factors that enhance and distort eyewitness memory. Variables that play a role in eyewitness testimony can typically be categorized as either system or estimator variables.[86] Lineup presentation and lineup fairness typify "system" variables, as they can be controlled by the legal system.[87] Estimator variables are measured after the identification to determine the likelihood of eyewitness error (such as the relationship between confidence and accuracy).[88] These "postdictor" variables may be important to the legal process because they may be used at trial to assess the veracity of eyewitness testimony (although the variables used are not always the most appropriate ones).[89]

It is important to note, however, that variables that allow researchers to postdict accuracy in same-race paradigms, such as decision time and confidence, are not always predictive in cross-race situations.[90] Furthermore, the ability to postdict errors is based on group rather than individual data. Although these factors can be used to determine the *likelihood* of error, they cannot determine the ultimate issue—whether or not a specific witness identified an innocent person. Because diagnosing mistaken cross-race (or even same-race) identifications after the fact is difficult and problematic in its own right, research has increasingly focused on changing police investigation practices to reduce errors in the first place.

2. CHANGES IN POLICE PRACTICE: A GUIDE FOR LAW ENFORCEMENT

Scientifically rigorous research on eyewitness memory during the last forty years has substantially increased our understanding of human memory and decision making in this context. However, it is only recently that the legal system has begun to embrace these findings and change procedures in order to minimize errors. In 1999, the U.S. Department of Justice published a landmark set of recommendations on the treatment of eyewitness evidence, entitled *Eyewitness Evidence: A Guide for Law Enforcement* (which was updated in 2003). The guide provides step-by-step procedures for law enforcement for dealing with eyewitnesses, from the initial response to the emergency call to follow-up with the eyewitnesses after the investigation. The recommendations were based on scientific research on eyewitness memory that revealed practical modifications to lineup procedures that reduce eyewitness errors.[91]

Specifically, the *Guide* recommended the use of single-suspect lineups (i.e., one suspect with all others being known innocent fillers), ensuring the use of unbiased lineup instructions, and avoiding postidentification suggestions and feedback to witnesses. Lineups should also employ double-blind procedures (where the suspect is unknown to both the witness and the person conducting the lineup) to avoid any cues in the situation that might suggest the identity of the suspect to the witness. Such procedures have been found to reduce errors when compared to a standard simultaneous lineup procedure.[92] A final important factor (which was not included in the original guide but is validated by empirical research) is the use of a

properly conducted sequential lineup procedure (photos are shown one at a time) as
preferable to show-up (one photo) and simultaneous (all photos are shown at the
same time) lineups. The use of sequential
lineups has been convincingly shown to
dramatically reduce error rates compared
to other types of lineups.[93] However, the
sequential lineup procedure may not resolve the cross-race dilemma, as some research has found that the sequential lineup
does not solve this problem—errors are
still more likely in cross-race conditions.[94]
Nonetheless, although cross-race errors
still occur, fewer errors will occur overall
using properly conducted sequential lineups than with simultaneous lineups.

CONCLUSION

Although many questions remain about
the causes of the cross-race effect and
what we can do about it, it is clear that the
cross-race effect exists. We know that
eyewitness errors happen, although the
frequency of those errors in the real world
is unknown. We also know that once an
error occurs, it is very difficult to identify
it as an error; generally, eyewitnesses who
make such identifications honestly believe their decisions are accurate. At this
point, the solution to the cross-race effect
probably does not lie in the eradication of
racism (a rather ambitious and challenging goal) or in educating eyewitnesses. In
our opinion, the most practical recommendation we would make is to ensure
that the testimony of an eyewitness (including any lineup identifications) is
treated with the same care as forensic
evidence and that great efforts are made to
ensure that this evidence is gathered
properly and that it remains free from
contamination.[95]

Part Two
CIVIL LAW

9

The Search for Racial Justice in Tort Law

W. Jonathan Cardi

INTRODUCTION

In recent decades, tort scholarship has gravitated around a few broad topics: the efficacy of tort reform, the multifaceted puzzle of product liability, and the debate—waged between instrumentalists and corrective justice theorists—over the theoretical substance of tort law. Social science has played a role in each of these discussions, especially that unique brand of social science known as law and economics. Questions such as whether and how to limit damage awards, whether juries are capable of parsing complex litigation involving dangerous products, and whether tort law in fact deters risky behavior are all usefully informed by social scientific inquiry.[1]

During this same period of time, scholars of many stripes have begun to focus the lens of social science on the effects of racial bias on participants in the legal system and on the law itself. This anthology is evidence of this growing body of scholarship.

Although interest has increased, the doctrinal terrain covered by the movement remains limited. Topics in criminal law, antidiscrimination law, Fourteenth Amendment jurisprudence, and the persistence of bias in lawyers, witnesses, judges, and juries have thus far all but filled the agenda.

This chapter explores the applicability of critical race realism to a subject of less obvious relevance—tort law. A relatively small number of academics have begun to think about how racial bias might make its way into tort law and how tort law might disparately affect participants depending on their race. This chapter surveys existing literature in this area and in so doing charts a course for more robust future study.

At the outset, one might reasonably ask why this project is important. Why ought people concerned with the nature and function of tort law investigate its intersection with race? After all, aside from a few narrow pockets of tort cases—race-related defamation claims, racially motivated intentional torts, and claims brought pursuant to tort-like antidiscrimination statutes—tort law is primarily about accidents, in which plaintiff and defendant were not acquainted and did not know the other's race ex ante. The relevance of race to tort, however, lies not primarily in the facts of the cases themselves but in the process of their legal resolution. Three general categories of this process-relevance come to mind. First, race-related social policy or outright racial bias might have had historical significance in the doctrinal development of tort law. Second, to the extent that tort law aims to influence future behavior, the race of future actors might factor into courts' tort-related decisions (properly or improperly). Third, and most important, because each participant in a tort action—whether party, witness, juror, attorney, or judge—may be identified by other participants according to her or his race, race might in some manner influence the resolution of the case.

If race is indeed relevant to tort law in these ways, it should be clear why tort scholars and social scientists should study its effects. If a particular tort outcome is altered due to institutionalized or participant-specific racial bias, then the process, if not the judgment itself, has been tainted. This is true regardless of one's views as to the substance and purpose of tort law. If tort law is a means of enforcing an individual's moral obligation to repair a loss wrongfully inflicted on another (a corrective justice view), then the notion that one's obligation and courts' enforcement of it does not (or should not) vary according to the influence of race seems self-evident. If instead tort law is an instrument to reduce the cost of accidents to an efficient level (a law-and-economics view), a system infused with racial bias seems likely to reach inefficient results inefficiently. In any case, understanding the

role of race is an important step in the search for justice in tort cases.

I. A SURVEY OF RACE-RELATED SOCIAL SCIENCE RESEARCH IN TORT LAW

A. Participant Studies

A considerable body of literature examines the presence and effect of racial bias in jurors, judges, witnesses, and attorneys. The chapters in Part I of this volume are exemplary. Although aimed at legal participants generally, much of this research is readily applicable to torts. For example, articles on the effect of racial bias in jurors' reception of expert witness testimony,[2] bias in attorneys' jury selection,[3] the presence of and appropriate response to bias in judges,[4] and the effects of bias on interattorney communications[5] address issues potentially arising in any tort case. Research on participants in tort cases specifically, however, is less common.

Three studies to date have explored the relationship between juror race and the likely direction of tort verdicts and the size of damages awards. In one, Brian Bornstein and Michelle Rajki presented study participants with one of three versions of a product liability case in which the plaintiff suffered from cancer allegedly caused either by birth control pills, calligraphy ink, or a chemical toxin in the water supply.[6] Bornstein and Rajki found that minority participants were more likely than whites to hold the defendant liable, but that the race of the participant had no impact on the assessment of damages.

In a similar study, using five fact patterns representing a variety of tortious conduct, Chris Denove and Edward Imwinkelried found that race was "the single most important factor in predicting juror orientation."[7] Not only were African American participants 50 percent more likely than nonminority participants to find for the plaintiff, they also awarded more than five times the amount of emotional damages and twice the compensation for physical disability. Although Hispanic participants were no more likely than whites to hold the defendant liable, Hispanics also awarded higher compensatory damages than did white participants. Moreover, controlling for factors often associated with race, such as income and education, Denove and Imwinkelried concluded that juror orientation varied according to cultural rather than socioeconomic differences.

Most recently, Eric Helland and Alexander Tabarrok investigated the correlation between the race and income of jury pools and the size of trial awards in tort cases. Helland and Tabarrok examined thousands of cases decided from 1988 to 1997 and found that "[t]he average tort award increases as black and Hispanic county population rates increase and especially as black and Hispanic county poverty rates increase."[8] Although this study probed population trends rather than individual juror decision making, its results appear to track the damages-related findings of Denove and Imwinkelried.

None of the foregoing studies evidence racial bias in jurors; rather, they reveal a difference in perspective, along racial lines, with regard to jurors' normative judgments about culpability and the corresponding duty to compensate. At the most obvious level, the studies' significance lies in the information they provide to attorneys engaged in jury selection in tort cases.[9] Their significance also extends to broader tort issues, such as the legitimacy of damage caps and the general usefulness of juries as balanced and representative arbiters of community norms.[10] Although useful and important, however, the foregoing research is limited in one significant respect—it does not explain *why* a jury's

racial composition might lead to a particular verdict. Are juror proclivities explained best by socioeconomic factors, with race acting merely as proxy? As judged by the foregoing studies, the evidence is mixed on this question. If instead differences are due to cultural phenomena, which ones are involved, and what exactly is the connection?

Several behavioral law-and-economics scholars, led by Kip Viscusi, have begun such an investigation into the influence of juror demographics on assessments of punitive damages. In one study, Viscusi and Richard Zeckhauser tested the accuracy of jurors' understanding of risk.[11] Race of the juror served as one of the variables. Starting from the premise that risk consists of frequency of harm as a fraction of exposure to potentially harmful conditions, Viscusi and Zeckhauser found that although participants readily took note of the frequency numerator, they were much less capable of accounting for the exposure denominator. In light of this finding, the researchers concluded that participants overestimated the risk created by a defendant's conduct. Because the significance of risk is the basis of a jury's assessment of recklessness and because recklessness is often a prerequisite for punitive damages, Viscusi and Zeckhauser inferred that juries are likely overzealous in assigning punitive damages. Furthermore, the researchers found that African American and Hispanic participants were even more likely than whites to overestimate risk and were therefore more likely to award punitive damages. In related research, Viscusi also found that African American and Hispanic participants were either less able or less willing to adhere to specific numerical instructions in assessing punitive damages.[12]

Viscusi's work represents a useful first step in explaining the mechanism by which race might affect the assignment of tort damages. Still, Viscusi's studies did not attempt to explain the ultimate source of racial distinctions in risk assessment or the application of damages formulas—that is, what led minority participants to discount risk exposure and ignore damages instructions more than nonminorities? Without an investigation of this next step in the causal chain, it would be premature to judge the legitimacy of interracial differences and, if illegitimate, to determine the best course of correction. If, for example, Viscusi's results stem merely from relative educational disadvantage, then perhaps the differences can and should be ameliorated (e.g., by pattern jury instructions). On the other hand, if the differences arise from philosophical or cultural considerations that lie within the traditional purview of jury discretion, then perhaps the differences should stand.

Justin Levinson and Kaiping Peng have attempted to answer this "ultimate source" question in the context of jurors' assessment of factual causation and foreseeability in common-law negligence cases.[13] Levinson and Peng found cultural differences between people of European and Asian descent in three common psychological phenomena—the fundamental attribution error, the principle of culpable causation, and the illusion of control—and proposed that these cognitive differences translate into culturally divergent analyses of causation and foreseeability.[14] Unfortunately, Levinson and Peng's revealing method and focus of inquiry are exceedingly rare in the field of torts.

Levinson has also recently turned his attention to the presence and effect of racial bias in jurors and witnesses. Levinson presented study participants with two tort-based hypotheticals, one involving battery and the other wrongful termination.[15] The race of the hypotheticals' actors was varied randomly among study participants in order to test for implicit bias in the participants' memories of the events. Levinson found that participants systematically misremembered and even generated false memories in racially biased ways. For example, participants were significantly more likely to recall aggressive conduct in a story featuring African Americans than in the same story featuring Caucasians.[16] This was true whether or not such conduct in fact occurred. Consistent with many other studies of implicit racial bias, the degree to which participants demonstrated implicit bias did not correspond with their levels of explicit bias. The significance of Levinson's study should be clear—if the implicit racial bias of witnesses and jurors causes them to recall events or testimony in racially biased ways, the jury's determination of tort liability will reflect this bias. Moreover, because implicit bias does not manifest in explicit views, a juror's tendency toward racial bias is not likely to be revealed during voir dire.

The results of Levinson's study track similar research on participants' implicit bias in the context of criminal law and in nontort civil cases. If this homogeneity is true of participant studies generally (and this author is not asserting that it is), one might question why tort-specific participant studies are useful. Put differently, in what ways might the study of tort participants reveal unique aspects of racial bias, and what unique issues might bias in tort participants specifically pose for the law?

One answer lies in the difference between the standards of proof utilized in tort and criminal law. In the context of criminal proceedings, the jury decides the defendant's guilt or innocence pursuant to a standard of "beyond a reasonable doubt." When this standard is applied in a difficult case, the effect of racial bias might be too subtle to lead an otherwise ambivalent jury to a "guilty" verdict (or to lead a jury otherwise certain of guilt to doubt). By contrast, a jury determines tort liability according to the preponderance standard—that is, the jury decides whether the defendant "more likely than not" committed the tort. Because a tort plaintiff wins by convincing the jury to a mere 51 percent degree of certainty, implicit racial bias might serve to push the jury's collective mind past equipoise. Thus, the implications of tort-related racial bias are of particular import.

A second answer lies in the fact that as compared with other areas of the civil law, tort judgments more clearly embody a dimension of moral condemnation. They communicate that a defendant has acted unreasonably, aberrantly, in a way that offends society and the rights of the defendant. This moral judgment is not inherent, or at least not as potent, in cases involving breach of contract or property disputes. A juror's racial bias—which often includes a moral element—might affect the juror's determination of a tort defendant's wrongdoing or the degree to which a plaintiff is worthy of compensation.[17] Racial bias is thus of special concern to tort law. Social science research that seeks to correlate moral judgments made in the context of race with the types of moral judgments made in determining tort liability would be particularly probative.

Finally, racial biases are often behavior-specific and might correspondingly be cause-of-action-specific. Racial bias does not exist merely as a simple metric of superiority. Bias also often takes the form of a generalized association of a race with a particular behavior or characteristic. Two common (and obviously crass) examples are that African Americans are thought to be athletic but lazy or criminal, and Jews to be smart but miserly. Such behavior-specific racial biases no doubt manifest differently in different causes of action. One might hypothesize, for example, that African American defendants fare better

in contract actions than they do in the criminal or tort context. Jewish defendants, on the other hand, might have more success in tort than in contract. Behavior-specific biases must therefore be studied and accounted for with regard to each distinct area of the law.

In light of the importance of this line of inquiry, where might research regarding the psychology and behavior of tort participants turn from here? As an initial observation, most existing tort-specific participant studies focus on the jury. Research on the behavior of counsel, witnesses, and judges in tort cases is virtually nonexistent. Furthermore, because even jury-related research is still in its infant stages, the potential for research is quite broad. Some attractive questions (in addition to those mentioned above) include: Do cultural differences influence the manner by which jurors render tort-related moral judgments?[18] Do cultural differences affect the crediting and utilization of eyewitness and expert witness testimony in the context of various tort claims? Are judges or juries more likely to be affected by tort-related racial bias?[19] Does racial bias lead jurors to blame out-group plaintiffs, whether or not contributory negligence has been asserted? How does bias affect the dynamics of mixed-raced juries in tort cases?[20]

B. Rate of Success and Quantum of Recovery

Central to our system of jurisprudence, and indeed to American society in general, is our dedication to the "rule of law." As it relates to the intersection of race and tort law, the rule of law encompasses the following goals: neutrality—that cases should be decided by laws, not by judicial preference or prejudice;[21] consistency in law's interpretation and application—that like cases should be decided alike and different cases differently;[22] generality—that laws should be applied generally, without regard to the qualities of a particular person or group of persons;[23] and procedural fairness—that all persons subject to a tort action should have the opportunity fairly to be heard.[24] Consistent with these goals, plaintiffs' rate of success in tort cases ought to be unaffected by the race of the plaintiff or the defendant. Existing research suggests that this may not be the case.[25]

Several state court systems have taken up the study of the effects of race on jury awards in tort cases. Although none adhered to rigorous empirical methodology, task forces in Connecticut, Iowa, New York, Oregon, and Washington throughout the mid-1990s found a popular perception in the legal community that African American plaintiffs and defendants lost more frequently than did Caucasians.[26] These studies also revealed a perception that African American plaintiffs recovered less in damages than did Caucasian plaintiffs under similar factual circumstances.[27] Although the validity of such perceptions has not been tested in those states, the results of a Rand Corporation study in Cook County, Illinois (Chicago), from 1959 to 1979 tend to confirm the perceptions' accuracy.[28] In this empirical study of 9,000 trials, researchers found that "blacks lost more often than whites, both as plaintiffs and defendants, and black plaintiffs received smaller awards."[29]

A complete understanding of racial distinctions in the resolution of tort cases must include a study of settlements. This is so for three reasons: first, because a vast majority of tort cases do not result in jury verdicts, but rather are settled; second, because settlements serve as a window to expected verdicts; and third, because racial bias and cultural distinctions might manifest differently in settlement negotiations than at trial. Frank McClellan has illustrated this last point in qualitative fashion by recounting a number of settlement discussions in which racial bias affected attorneys' interpretation of the actions and ability of opposing counsel, the legitimacy of the opposing party's claim, and the perceived likelihood of success before a jury.[30] Similarly, several state task force studies have reported the perception that minorities' claims are settled for less than those of similarly situated nonminorities.[31] And on the quantitative front, at least one study of asbestos cases in the 1980s found substantial disparities between the settlements reached by minority and nonminority plaintiffs.[32]

Limitations inherent in all of the foregoing studies' methodology and geographical restrictions and their growing datedness indicate the need for further study of racial disparities in tort verdicts and settlements. Indeed, existing scholarship only scratches the surface of this important topic. Rigorous state-by-state empirical work is needed to determine the true extent of the gap in treatment between minority and nonminority parties in tort cases. Moreover, little social science research exists regarding the source of such disparities. Is it possible that minorities commit more unreasonable acts than nonminorities? Are minorities more litigious under circumstances in which the case for tort liability is less compelling? Are there differences among particular torts with regard to the success of minority litigants? Might disparities in damage awards be explained entirely by socioeconomic differences?[33] Or might the better part of racial disparities in tort verdicts be explained simply by demonstrated racial bias in jurors?

In addition to assessments of settlements and jury verdicts, other pieces of the puzzle remain unexplored. For example, might racial bias influence judges' rulings on the admissibility of expert witnesses, rulings that are often outcome-determinative in tort actions? Does racial bias affect the rate at which judges decide as a matter of law issues typically left to the jury—issues such as negligence, causation, proximate causation, or, in some jurisdictions, the existence of a defect? How do interracial differences in the ability to obtain adequate counsel affect outcomes? Does the race of potential parties affect the likelihood that legal action will be brought in the first place, and if so, what does this reflect about the tort system's efficacy? Few scholars have begun the difficult process of answering these questions, despite their importance to the rule of law in tort cases.

C. Racial Bias Incorporated by Tort Doctrine

1. RACIAL BIAS IN THE HISTORICAL DEVELOPMENT OF TORT LAW

Through the decades, tort law has been shaped by many factors—contemporary social conditions, intellectual and political movements, the insights and inclinations of particular judges, even the peculiar facts of watershed cases. Many of tort law's catalysts have, in turn, been influenced by the dynamics of race. At times, this influence has been overt and constructive. The political and social climate surrounding the passage of Title VII of the Civil Rights Act and the creation of a statutory tort for employment discrimination is an obvious example. More often, however, the influence of race has likely been veiled and counterproductive. To the extent that this is so, the manner in which race has shaped tort doctrine must be scrutinized for indications of bias. Tort doctrine exists today as a set of moral, practical, and policy judgments made by judges and frozen (in various degrees) by the force of precedent.

If those judgments were shaped in part by racial bias, then application of tort doctrine today—even in cases in which race is not a factor—remains flawed.

Martha Chamallas has pursued this subject in the context of gender, exposing male hierarchies embedded within contemporary tort damages doctrine.[34] Others have examined aspects of the development of criminal and property law for embedded racial meaning.[35] Unfortunately, tort scholars have yet to take up this inquiry in any serious way.[36] Although this subject seems primarily to call for traditional historical and legal analysis, social science might also play a useful role both in measuring the race-based social and psychological factors at work in landmark tort decisions, and in unmasking their influence on the jurisprudential choices that underlie contemporary doctrine.

2. THE OPERATION OF RACIAL BIAS THROUGH FACIALLY NEUTRAL TORT STANDARDS

Tort law has the potential to interact with racial bias in yet another way. Facially neutral tort standards often inherently incorporate community bias and racial disparities, thereby having a disparate impact on parties according to their race. Academic study of this issue represents the quintessential marriage of traditional legal analysis and social science. It requires a sophisticated understanding of applicable legal doctrine but also calls for empirical study of the psychological and social factors co-opted (if inadvertently) by the law.

The most generalized research on this phenomenon focuses on the basic elements of negligence: duty, breach, causation, proximate cause, and injury. Because each element draws in some way upon purposely imprecise community norms—reasonableness and foreseeability, for example—their resolution is prone to the preexisting biases of the community itself and of those charged with applying community norms to the facts of a particular case. Amy Kastely has studied this effect and offers, as a qualitative example, a case in which a white rape victim's negligent-failure-to-warn claim turned upon the jury's assessment of whether rape was foreseeable to the defendant motel owner and to the victim, a guest and stranger to the neighborhood.[37] The motel was located near a naval base and next to a primarily low-income African American neighborhood. Upon concluding (apparently without any real evidence) that the motel was located next to a "high-crime area: murder, prostitution, robbery, drugs—the works," the Seventh Circuit held as a matter of law that the plaintiff should have foreseen the possibility of being raped upon opening her motel room door.[38] As Kastely reasons, because the victim would have no reason to know the actual crime rate of the surrounding neighborhood, this holding makes sense only in light of an assumption that any white woman would foresee the possibility of rape when in relative proximity to low-income African Americans. Thus, according to Kastely, the racial bias of the decision maker was able to invade the otherwise neutral test of foreseeability.[39]

Another example of tort law's inherent incorporation of racial bias may be found in the context of lead-paint litigation—claims brought on behalf of children who have suffered cognitive injuries from the ingestion of lead paint. Although children of all walks of life suffer from lead-paint-related injuries, low-income families and African Americans are disproportionately affected. An assemblage of racial stereotypes has thus burdened public perception of the problem and the resulting litigation. The legal incorporation of racial bias in

these cases stems from the fact that because the victims are typically very young, courts often allow damages calculations for lost future income to rely on exceedingly speculative indicia, such as the victim's preinjury IQ (or even that of family members), life expectancy, familial employment history, and projected education levels. A number of scholars have argued that the consideration of race-based economic and education projections produces an unjustified disparate impact on minority plaintiffs.[40] Others have asserted that the consideration of IQ testing likely reduces plaintiffs' damages in a way directly traceable to racial bias often associated with IQ test results.[41] In short, although courts in lead-paint cases seem merely to be relying on the most specific (and therefore accurate) data available regarding a particular plaintiff's future earning capacity, researchers have shown that racial disparities inherent in the underlying data result in racially biased damages verdicts.[42]

The legal doctrine governing intentional torts is subject to racial bias in a rather different way. Where a plaintiff bases an allegation of intent on claims of racial bias, the law's standard for intent is often incapable of accounting for implicit bias, or even at times explicit bias.[43] As ably explained by Linda Hamilton Krieger and Susan Fiske in Chapter 12 of this text, the courts' approach to so-called mixed-motives claims in Title VII cases serves as a clear illustration.

If facially neutral tort standards unwittingly lead to racially biased results, the next step is to ask whether the law might counteract this effect. As it stands, juries generally are provided with little guidance in assessing damages. This lack of guidance alone allows for the influence of implicit bias.[44] A few scholars have addressed the possibility that counsel be allowed to address potential racial bias during voir dire or closing statements, or that courts might instruct the jury to search out and cognitively correct any existing bias.[45] Social scientists have measured the success of attempts at conscious correction of implicit bias and found mixed results.[46]

D. Race-Related Effects of Tort Law

From an instrumentalist perspective, tort law serves as a tool to achieve certain social goals. In addition to concrete ends such as compensating victims and punishing wrongdoers, the goals of an instrumentalist approach also typically encompass some aspiration to influence social behavior. The desired mix of behavior depends upon the instrumentalist; however, common examples include a reduction in risk taking, the maximization of efficient commercial exchange, the elimination of vigilantism, and the encouragement of an industry to internalize and spread its social costs. Indeed, whether or not instrumentalism accurately describes the substance of tort law, it is difficult to deny that such goals play a frequent and express role in courts' resolution of tort cases.

To the extent that tort law hopes to be successful as a social instrument, courts must have a complete understanding of how their rulings will be received by the people whose behavior they seek to influence. Legal stimuli (like any stimuli) seem likely to have varying effects depending upon the characteristics of the person affected. As this topic relates to race, two general subquestions arise.

First, how does tort law affect race-related behavior? Specifically, for example, does the application of tort law as a means of curbing manifestations of racial bias have the desired effect? A number of legal scholars have addressed this question within the context of Title VII and common-law claims for infliction of emotional distress.[47] The question is ripe for investigation by social scientists, yet none to this author's knowledge have taken up its study.

A second, broader sub-question is whether tort law influences people's behavior differently according to race. For example, cultural variations in the perceived fairness or availability of the tort process might influence tort's deterrent effect. Differences in the stigma associated with litigiousness might also limit tort's instrumental reach. And particular doctrinal rules might have distinct social impact depending on the race of those affected. For instance, the tort of nuisance is often subject to a defense known as the "coming-to-the-nuisance doctrine," which limits or bars a plaintiff's nuisance claim where the nuisance preexisted the plaintiff's purchase of neighboring property. Although this defense might discourage many potential buyers from purchasing a lot located next to a pig farm or an all-night bus station, minorities may be forced by financial means or unfavorable zoning restrictions to purchase such a lot. Thus, although the coming-to-the-nuisance defense rightly deters many potential nuisance plaintiffs, it might not deter (although it may, perhaps wrongfully, bar) minority plaintiffs.

Despite the seeming importance of this topic, existing research is again scarce.[48] A growing cadre of behavioral law and economics scholars has begun to apply cognitive science to the effects of tort rules on public behavior.[49] Few, however, have focused on racial distinctions within those effects.

E. Race and Related Institutions

The use of social science to study the intersection of race and tort law might extend to one final area—the role of race in large, loss-shifting institutions such as the liability insurance industry, workers' compensation, and specialized instruments such as the 9/11 Fund. Unfortunately, like so many topics discussed in this chapter, few such studies exist. Legal scholars have investigated the practice of insurance redlining, by which insurers categorically deny access or coverage to low-income and minority applicants.[50] The role of implicit bias in this practice has not been extensively studied, however. The dearth of scholarship with regard to tort-related institutions is conspicuous, for such institutions are of significant import to the operation of tort law. Questions to be addressed by future research include: Does implicit racial bias affect the success of workers' compensation claims? Does the degree of access to liability insurance alter the intended effects of substantive tort rules? In addition to intentional insurance practices that disparately impact minorities, does implicit bias influence liability insurance coverage? Do cultural differences result in variations in the rate and manner by which people avail themselves of the benefits of workers' compensation and insurance? Does implicit bias affect the dispensation of benefits by special compensation funds?

CONCLUSION

The prospect of intensive study of implicit racial attitudes and the law is not without its skeptics. Some wonder whether "[i]f the full myriad of psychological shortcomings were introduced into the legal world, they could potentially become so prolific that any behavioral analysis would inevitably omit a contradictory phenomenon."[51] Others question the usefulness of revelations regarding racial bias in light of the Sisyphean task of overcoming its effects. Revelation in the absence of solution might even have the unjustified and counterproductive effect of undermining public perceptions of the system's legitimacy. These concerns are valid and serious. They are, however, merely additions to the growing list of questions in need of research, not reasons to end the inquiry altogether.

In many respects, this chapter has been more about what has not been studied than what has regarding the intersection of social science, race, and tort law. Given the import of the subject, this should be rather unsettling. It is this author's hope that the academy's recognition of this relatively open field will serve to bring together more collaborations between legal and social science scholars in an attempt to fill the research void.

10

Trojan Horses of Race

Jerry Kang

There is no immaculate perception.

—Commonly attributed to Nietzsche[1]

You are what you eat.

—Nutritional maxim

In all fighting, the direct method may be used for joining battle, but indirect methods will be needed in order to secure victory.

—Sun Tzu[2]

INTRODUCTION

Consider the following studies, with an open mind.

Computer Crash. Social cognitionist John Bargh asked participants to count whether an even or odd number of circles appeared on a computer screen.[3] After the 130th iteration, the computer was designed to crash, and the participants were told to start over. A hidden videocamera recorded their reactions. Third-party observers then evaluated those recordings to measure participants' frustration and hostility. What neither participants nor observers knew was that for half the participants, a young Black male face was flashed subliminally before each counting iteration; for the other half, the face was White. As rated by the observers, those who had been shown the black faces responded with greater hostility to the computer crash.

Mug Shot. Political scientists Frank Gilliam and Shanto Iyengar created variations of a local newscast: a control version with no crime story, a crime story with no mug shot, a crime story with a Black-suspect mug shot, and a crime story with a White-suspect mug shot.[4] The Black and White suspects were represented by the same morphed photograph, with the only difference being skin hue—thus controlling for facial expression and features. The suspect appeared for only five seconds in a ten-minute newscast; nonetheless, the suspect's race produced statistically significant differences in a criminal law survey completed after the viewing. Having seen the Black suspect, White participants showed 6 percent more support for punitive remedies than did the control group, which saw no crime story. When participants were instead exposed to the White suspect, their support for

Editors' Note: This chapter is an abridged version of Jerry Kang, *Trojan Horses of Race*, 118 HARV L. REV 1489 (2006), reprinted by permission of the author.

punitive remedies increased by only 1 percent, which was not statistically significant.

Math Test. Social psychologist Margaret Shih asked Asian American women at Harvard University to take a hard math test.[5] Before taking the exam, each participant answered a questionnaire designed to prime subtly different social identities: female (with questions relating, for example, to coed dormitory policy) or Asian (with questions relating, for example, to language spoken at home). A control group answered questions related to neutral topics, such as telecommunications usage. As measured by an exit survey, these questions had no conscious impact on self-reports of test difficulty, self-confidence in math ability, the number of questions attempted, or how well participants thought they did. Yet something happened implicitly. The group that had its Asian identity triggered performed best in accuracy (54 percent); the group that had no identity triggered came in second (49 percent); and the group that had its female identity triggered ranked last (43 percent). "Being" Asian boosted, while "being" female depressed, math performance. Of course, these students were both.

Shooter Bias. Social cognitionist Joshua Correll created a video game that placed photographs of a White or Black individual holding either a gun or another object (wallet, soda can, or cell phone) into diverse photographic backgrounds.[6] Participants were instructed to decide as quickly as possible whether to shoot the target. Severe time pressure designed into, the game forced errors. Consistent with earlier findings,[7] participants were more likely to mistake a Black target as armed when he in fact was unarmed (false alarms); conversely, they were more likely to mistake a White target as unarmed when he in fact was armed (misses). Even more striking is that Black participants showed similar amounts of "shooter bias" as Whites.

What is going on here? Quite simply, a revolution. These studies are the tip of the iceberg of recent social cognition research elaborating what I call "racial mechanics" — the ways in which race alters intrapersonal, interpersonal, and intergroup interactions. The results are stunning, reproducible, and valid by traditional scientific metrics. They seriously challenge current understandings of our "rational" selves and our interrelations.

In [section] I, I import crucial findings from the field of social cognition with emphasis on the recent "implicit bias" literature. This research demonstrates that most of us have implicit biases in the form of negative beliefs (stereotypes) and attitudes (prejudice) against racial minorities. These implicit biases, however, are not well reflected in explicit self-reported measures. This dissociation arises not solely because we try to sound more politically correct. Even when we are honest, we simply lack introspective insight. Finally, and most importantly, these implicit biases have real-world consequences—not only in the extraordinary case of shooting a gun, but also in the more mundane, everyday realm of social interactions.

A vast intellectual agenda opens when we start probing what this new knowledge might mean for law. [Section] I, which is necessarily long and detailed, establishes the foundation for that scholarship in the law reviews. In [section] II, I focus on a single application of the racial mechanics model to a timely question of communications policy. I start by asking a fundamental question: Where does bias come from? One important source is vicarious experience with the racial other, transmitted through the media. If these experiences are somehow skewed, we should not be surprised by the presence of pervasive implicit bias. What, then, might we do about such media programming given the rigid constraints of the First Amendment? To be sure, private actors of good faith can voluntarily adopt best practices that decrease implicit bias and its manifestations. But can the state, through law, do anything?

If there is any room for intervention, it would be in the communications realm of broadcast, which enjoys doctrinal exceptionalism. In broadcast, notwithstanding the First Amendment, we tolerate the licensing of speakers. In broadcast, we tolerate suppression of speech we dislike, such as indecency and violence. In broadcast, we tolerate encouragement of speech we like, such as educational television and locally oriented programming. All this is in the name of the "public interest," the vague standard that Congress has charged the Federal Communications Commission with pursuing.

That "public interest" standard was recently reshaped in the controversial June 2003 Media Ownership Order.[8] There, the FCC repeatedly justified relaxing ownership rules by explaining how such changes would increase, of all things, local news. Since local news was viewed as advancing "diversity" and "localism," two of the three core elements of the "public interest,"[9] any structural deregulation that would increase local news was lauded.

Troubling is what's on the local news. Sensationalistic crime stories are disproportionately shown: "If it bleeds, it leads." Racial minorities are repeatedly featured as violent criminals. Consumption of these images, the social cognition research suggests, exacerbates our implicit biases against racial minorities. Here, then, is the link between [sections] I and II: since implicit bias is fueled in part by what we see, the FCC has recently redefined the public interest so as to encourage the production of programming that makes us more biased. Unwittingly, the FCC linked the

public interest to racism. No one spotted the issue for the commission.

For a race paper, my using social cognition and applying it to communications law are unorthodox, but purposely so. Race talk in legal literature feels like it is at a dead end. No new philosophical argument or constitutional theory seems to persuade those sitting on one side of the fence to jump to the other. One way to break current deadlocks is to turn to new bodies of knowledge uncovered by social science, specifically the remarkable findings of social cognition.[10] Not only do they provide a more precise, particularized, and empirically grounded picture of how race functions in our minds and thus in our societies, they also rattle us out of a complacency enjoyed after the demise of de jure discrimination. Further calls for equality are often derogated as whining by those who cannot compete in a modern meritocracy. Social cognition discoveries dispute that resentful characterization and make us reexamine our individual and collective responsibilities for persistent racial inequality. The inquiry is not, however, a simple witch hunt by those "pure" for those "tainted": as Charles Lawrence observed long ago, albeit drawing on a very different psychology, we may all be infected in ways we cannot admit, even to ourselves.[11]

My point is not that "hard science" is the only way to engage in critical thinking about the relationship between law and race. This would respark an unhelpful methodology war we endured in the 1980s and 1990s about the essential role of narrative in critical race theory. Like most scholars, I believe that multiple methodologies produce the deepest insight. I am also aware of the limits of the scientific method and of the ignominious history of pseudoscience's complicity in brutally subordinating entire peoples. That said, I am confident that the language, methodologies, and findings of social cognition provide trenchant additions to the philosophical, anthropological, sociological, literary, and political science modes of argument that have so far dominated critical race studies. For better and worse, law has turned sharply in favor of quantified and empirical analyses. Social cognition allows a phalanx of those who study race to take that same turn, instrumentally to fight fire with fire, and substantively to profit from a body of science that supports, particularizes, and checks what we intuit as the truth of our lived experiences. The potential reward in insight and persuasion is substantial, as I hope to demonstrate.

Another way to generate new insights is to view old topics through new lenses. That explains my invocation of the metaphor of "Trojan horses," which is more familiar to cyberlaw than to critical race studies. This strategy further explains why I apply my social cognitive model of racial mechanics to FCC regulations. I start with the theory and evidence of racial mechanics.

I. RACIAL MECHANICS

I have coined the term "racial mechanics" to describe how race alters interpersonal interactions. My model draws heavily from the field of social cognition, with emphasis on the recent implicit bias literature. For most lawyers and legal academics, this science will be jaw-dropping. For social cognitionists, what will be eye-opening is the theoretical translation of social cognitive findings to themes in critical race studies and the practical translation to potential legal and policy reforms.

A. Racial Schemas

1. SCHEMAS GENERALLY

A schema is a "cognitive structure that represents knowledge about a concept or type of stimulus, including its attributes and the relations among those attributes."[12] These knowledge structures can be modeled as prototypes or exemplars for a class of objects, providing rules that map objects into the class, as well as general information about members of the class. For instance, when we see something that has four legs, a horizontal plane, and a back, we immediately classify that object into the category "chair." We then understand how to use the object, for example, by sitting on it. This schematic thinking operates automatically, nearly instantaneously.

We employ schemas out of necessity. Our senses are constantly bombarded by environmental stimuli, which must be processed, then encoded into memories (short- and/or long-term) in some internal representation. Based on that representation of reality, we must respond. But we drown in information. Perforce we simplify the datastream at every stage of information processing through the use of schemas.

Different schema types exist for different types of entities, such as objects, other people, the self, roles, and events. To be clear, this most basic process operates not only on inanimate objects, such as chairs or bananas, but also on human beings. When we encounter a person, we classify that person into numerous social categories, such as gender, (dis)ability, age, race, and role. My focus is on race.

2. RACIAL SCHEMAS

Through law and culture, society provides us (the perceivers) with a set of racial *categories* into which we map an individual human being (the target) according to prevailing rules of racial *mapping*. Once a person is assigned to a racial category, implicit and explicit racial meanings associated with that category are triggered. These activated racial *meanings* then influence our interpersonal interaction. All

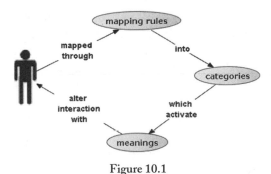

Figure 10.1

three elements (presented as ovals in Figure 10.1)—racial categories, racial mapping rules, and racial meanings—constitute components of the racial schema.

I include in the term "racial meanings" both cognitive and affective components. The *cognitive* component includes thoughts or beliefs about the category, such as generalizations about their intelligence or criminality. The *affective* component reflects emotions, feelings, and evaluations that range on the scales of positive/negative, good/bad, approach/avoid. Social psychologists often call cognitive beliefs about social groups "stereotypes" and (negative) affective feelings about such groups "prejudice." The racial meanings triggered upon schema activation include both thoughts and feelings, rational and emotional, that can independently and jointly drive the perceiver's reactions.

This social cognitive framing of racial mechanics provides new, concrete translations of various themes central to critical race studies. For example, critical race scholars repeat the mantra that "race is a social construction." My social cognitive account provides a particularized understanding of that general claim: all three components—racial categories, mapping rules, and racial meanings—are contingent, constructed, and contestable. Not one of these elements is biologically inevitable.

This framing also helps translate the critical race theme "race (almost always)

matters." In interpersonal encounters, multiple schemas may be activated. For example, when one first meets a young Asian male law professor, multiple schemas could come into play, including age, race, gender, and role (profession). Which schemas actively influence the interaction depend on numerous variables, such as primacy (what gets activated first),[13] salience (which schema cues catch attention),[14] accessibility (which schemas can be retrieved in memory easily, perhaps because of recent priming),[15] and individuating information.[16]

Notwithstanding such complexity and the variance among perceivers and environments, the scientific consensus is that racial schemas are not of minor significance. Instead, racial schemas are "chronically accessible" and can be triggered by our mere appearance, since we are especially sensitive to visual and physical cues. As the Computer Crash study demonstrated, the visual information can be so fleeting as to be subliminal, yet it can still activate the racial schema. We may not be color-blind even when we cannot see.

Once activated, the racial meanings embedded within the racial schema influence interaction. The apocryphal quotation attributed to Nietzsche, that "there is no immaculate perception," nicely captures how schemas guide what we see, encode into memory, and subsequently recall. At the attentional stage, schemas influence what we notice and immediately reduce information complexity. At the encoding and recall phases, schemas are again influential, although the memory literature is conflicted and qualified. There is now evidence that schemas influence not only interpretation (that is, "social perception") but also what we actually see and remember seeing ("visual perception").[17]

In sum, schemas automatically, efficiently, and adaptively parse the raw data pushed to our senses. These templates of categorical knowledge are applied to all entities, including human targets. Racial schemas, because they are chronically accessible, regularly influence social interactions. The obvious ways in which this might happen need little elaboration. To take an extreme example, the hate criminal will map an African American into the racial category "Black" (or some other term) by visual inspection, at which point both emotional hatred and the cognitive beliefs that fuel that hatred (for example, scapegoating) can catalyze racial violence. No fancy psychological model is necessary to make sense of such vulgar acts. The payoff of this social cognitive model comes in parsing subtler cases. For instance, what if we don't even see the Black man?

3. AUTOMATICITY

The Computer Crash experiment reveals that we do not have to consciously "see" the Black male face for it to influence our behavior. The researchers in that study concluded that the Black face automatically activated schema-consistent behavior through the principle of "ideomotor action."[18] Prior research by Patricia Devine had revealed that subliminal priming with words stereotypically associated with African Americans could lead participants to interpret ambiguous behavior as more aggressive.[19] But scientists wondered whether the result stemmed partly from using words with negative affect, such as *lazy*. The Computer Crash study answered this question by demonstrating that the mere image of a Black face—and a subliminal one at that—could activate a Black racial schema.

Further research has demonstrated the connection between subliminal priming (through words or pictures) and subsequent tasks, such as evaluations, interpretations, and speed tasks.[20] These findings indicate that schemas operate not only as part of a conscious, rational deliberation

that, for example, draws on racial meanings to provide base rates for Bayesian calculations (what social cognitionists might call a "controlled process"). Rather, they also operate automatically—*without conscious intention and outside of our awareness* (an "automatic process"). Here we see translation of yet another critical race studies theme, that the "power of race is invisible."

To summarize: we think through schemas generally, and through racial schemas specifically, which operate automatically when primed, sometimes even by subliminal stimuli. The existence of such automatic processes disturbs us because it questions our self-understanding as entirely rational, freely choosing, self-legislating actors. We are obviously not robots that mechanically respond to stimuli in precisely programmed ways. We do respond to individuating information when we are motivated and able to do so. Nevertheless, we ignore the best scientific evidence if we deny that our behavior is produced by complex superpositions of mental processes that range from the controlled, calculated, and rational to the automatic, unintended, and unnoticed. Finally, we must recognize that these biases are not random errors; rather, they have a tilt. After all, the participants in the Computer Crash experiment got more hostile, not more friendly, after being flashed Black faces. Why?

B. Implicit Bias

I. THE PROBLEM: OPACITY

Social psychologists have long sought to measure the nature and content of the racial meanings contained within our racial schemas. One way to measure is simply to ask people directly, and on such surveys, we see a substantial decline in racial stereotypes and prejudice in the past fifty years.[21] But are such self-reports trustworthy? Given prevailing social norms in favor of racial equality, an individual may feel awkward showing her ambivalence, anxiety, or resentment toward specific racial categories.[22]

In order to fly under the political correctness radar, social psychologists and political scientists have asked indirect questions about race. Prominent examples, developed since the 1970s, include scales that measure symbolic and modern racism.[23] Unfortunately, this indirect questioning risks confounding political conservatism with racism.[24]

More troubling, we may honestly lack introspective access to the racial meanings embedded within our racial schemas.[25] Ignorance, not deception, may be the problem. Relatedly, our explicit normative and political commitments may poorly predict the cognitive processes running beneath the surface. While connected to the automaticity point, this disconnect between explicit and implicit bias raises a different issue: dissociation. The point here is not merely that certain mental processes will execute automatically; rather, it is that those implicit mental processes may draw on racial meanings that, upon conscious consideration, we would expressly disavow. It is as if some "Trojan horse" virus had hijacked a portion of our brain.

2. THE SOLUTION: MEASURING SPEED

How have social cognitionists measured the bias in racial meanings if it is so opaque? One method has been to use sequential priming procedures that take advantage of the automaticity of schemas. Such procedures begin by priming a participant with a particular stimulus, such as a word or a face, which activates a particular racial schema. Then, the racial meanings associated with that schema should alter performance on some subsequent linguistic,[26] interpretive,[27] or physical task.[28] If the prime and the task are schema-consistent, one expects a faster response; by contrast, if they are inconsistent, one expects a slower response.

The first such study was by Samuel Gaertner and John McLaughlin, who primed participants subliminally with the word *White* or *Black*, then immediately replaced the word with a string of letters that were sometimes words and sometimes gibberish.[29] Participants had to identify as quickly as possible whether the string of letters was indeed a word. The words chosen were associated with stereotypes of either Whites or Blacks. Participants were faster at recognizing a positive word such as *smart* if they had just been primed with the word *White* instead of *Black*.[30] The time differential in task execution was deemed a measure of "implicit bias."

A flurry of studies adopted and varied this reaction-time paradigm by priming participants with some social category, subliminally or consciously (supraliminally), and then measuring whether their ability to execute some task was facilitated or hindered.[31] The Implicit Association Test (IAT) has become the state-of-the-art measurement tool.[32] The IAT examines how tightly any two concepts are associated with each other. In a typical experiment, two racial categories are compared, say "Black" and "White." Next, two sets of stimuli (words or images) that correspond to the racial meanings (stereotypes or attitudes) associated with those categories are selected. For example, words such as *violent* and *lazy* are chosen for Blacks, and *smart* and *kind* for Whites.

Participants are shown a Black or White face and told to hit as fast as possible a key on the left or right side of the keyboard. They are also shown words stereotypically associated with Blacks or Whites and again told to hit a key on the left or right side of the keyboard. In half the runs, the Black face and Black-associated word are assigned to the *same* side of the keyboard (schema-consistent arrangement). In the other half, they are assigned *opposite* sides (schema-inconsistent arrangement). The same goes for the White face/White-associated stimulus combination.

Tasks in the schema-consistent arrangement should be easier, and so it is for most of us.[33] How much easier—as measured by the time differential between the two arrangements—provides a measure of implicit bias. The obvious confounds—such as overall speed of participant's reactions, right- or left-handedness, and familiarity with test stimuli—have been examined and shown not to undermine the IAT's validity.

Amygdala. Millisecond measurements in front of computers may seem far removed from our commonsense understanding of "prejudice." But consider what functional magnetic resonance imaging (fMRI) of the brain has recently shown. The amygdala is an almond-sized subcortical structure within our brains, involved in emotional learning, perceiving novel or threatening stimuli, and fear conditioning. Neuroscientists, collaborating with social cognitionists, have recently demonstrated that the amygdalas of White participants "light up" far more when they are *subliminally* shown Black faces as compared to White faces.[34] Moreover, the degree of amygdala activation is significantly correlated with participants' IAT scores. There is, however, no correlation with explicit measures of bias, which again demonstrates dissociation between explicit self-reports and implicit measures revealed by reaction-time differentials.[35]

The fact that some observable behavior (differences in reaction time as measured by the IAT) maps to some neural activity (as measured by fMRI) says little: all human behavior must map to some neural activity. What is significant is that implicit bias seems connected to a particular area

of the brain, the amygdala. We know that the amygdala becomes active when a person is exposed to stimuli with emotional significance, such as emotional faces, especially fearful ones. While hardly definitive, such neural imaging gives us greater reason to think that the IAT is measuring something real and significantly connected to emotion-laden racial mechanics.

3. THE RESULTS: PERVASIVE IMPLICIT BIAS
Using the IAT and similar tools, social cognitionists have documented the existence of implicit bias against numerous social categories. According to Nilanjana Dasgupta, the "first wave" of research demonstrated that socially dominant groups have implicit bias against subordinate groups (White over non-White, for example). By her count "almost a hundred studies have documented people's tendency to automatically associate positive characteristics with their ingroups more easily than outgroups (i.e. ingroup favoritism) as well as their tendency to associate negative characteristics with outgroups more easily than ingroups (i.e. outgroup derogation)."[36] These studies address not only automatic attitudes (prejudice) but also automatic beliefs (stereotypes). In the United States, bias has been found against Blacks, Latinos, Jews, Asians, non-Americans, women, gays, and the elderly.[37] Implicit bias against out-groups has also been found in other countries.[38]

Fascinating is the overwhelming evidence that implicit bias measures are dissociated from explicit bias measures.[39] Put another way, on a survey I may honestly self-report positive attitudes toward some social category, such as Latinos. After all, some of my best friends are Latino. However, implicit bias tests may show that I hold negative attitudes toward that very group. This is dissociation—a discrepancy between our explicit and implicit meanings. This dissociation appears most vividly when "the group averages for conscious and unconscious measures [are] placed side-by-side using a common metric," which reveals "wide divergences" between the means.[40]

Web Harvest. For example, recent research by Brian Nosek, Mahzarin Banaji, and Anthony Greenwald, based on extraordinarily large data sets harvested from the Web, revealed such dissociation beautifully.[41] Whites exhibited some *explicit* preference for themselves over Blacks, but that explicit preference paled in comparison to their *implicit* preference. This dissociation does not necessarily indicate lack of covariation. The same research revealed a positive (although often weak) relationship between an individual's implicit and explicit attitudes. Those of us with the greatest explicit bias (as measured by self-reported answers to indirect survey questions) against a racial minority tend also to have the greatest implicit bias against them, and vice versa.[42] To recap, although explicit and implicit biases can register at quite different levels (including entire changes in valence, from positive to negative), there is often weak covariation.

C. Behavioral Consequences

By now, even patient readers demand a payoff: Do racial schemas alter behavior? More particularly, does implicit bias represent anything besides millisecond latencies in stylized laboratory experiments? What is the evidence, for instance, that the IAT predicts any real-world behavior, much less anything that is legally actionable?

Research addressing behavioral consequences has been called the "second wave" of implicit bias research. There is now persuasive evidence that implicit bias against a social category, as measured by instruments such as the IAT, predicts disparate

behavior toward individuals mapped to that category. This occurs notwithstanding contrary explicit commitments in favor of racial equality. In other words, even if our sincere self-reports of bias score zero, we would still engage in disparate treatment of individuals on the basis of race, consistent with our racial schemas. Controlled, deliberative, rational processes are not the only forces guiding our behavior. That we are not even aware of, much less intending, such race-contingent behavior does not magically erase the harm.

I. INTERPRETING

Even before the rise of reaction-time measurements, social psychologists demonstrated convincingly that schemas influence interpretation.[43] We have already discussed how activated schemas influence which stimuli we give attention to, how we encode representations of those stimuli, and how easily we retrieve information thus stored. To a first approximation, we see what we expect to see. Like well-accepted theories that guide our interpretation of data, schemas incline us to interpret data consistent with our biases.[44]

Emily or Lakisha? A recent experiment provides powerful evidence that our racial schemas, triggered simply by names, can alter how we interpret resumes. Behavioral economists Marianne Bertrand and Sendhil Mullainathan responded to more than 1,300 help-wanted ads in Boston and Chicago with fictitious resumes that were crafted to be comparably qualified.[45] The sole difference was that half of the resumes were randomly assigned African American–signaling names (for example, Lakisha Washington), while the other half were assigned "White" names (for example, Emily Walsh). The White resumes received 50 percent more callbacks.

To study the impact of differences in resume quality, the researchers sent both standard and higher-quality resume pairs to employers. A White higher-quality resume enjoyed a statistically significant 30 percent greater callback rate than the White standard resume. By contrast, a black higher-quality resume received a statistically insignificant 9 percent greater callback rate than the black standard resume.

To explain these results, the researchers tentatively suggest "lexicographic search by employers." Given the surfeit of resumes passing their desks, employers quickly scan them, and many stop reading after seeing a Black name. This phenomena also explains why higher-quality resumes do not produce much return for African Americans—the employer never actually gets to the details. Rearticulated in terms of racial schemas, the employer applies verbal rules of racial mapping to categorize applicants by name into certain racial categories. Once the names are mapped, some set of negative racial meanings (stereotypes and prejudices) are automatically activated that produce fewer callbacks for African Americans.

To be sure, this study did not measure the bias of those who reviewed the resumes either through explicit self-reports or reaction-time measurements. Instead, it simply reported behavioral consequences. Accordingly, we cannot know specifically whether the employers were conscious of or endorsed the schematic thinking that produced these results. I am, however, confident that an explicit survey given to these firms would reveal a total commitment to equal opportunity—and not entirely for impression-management reasons. In sum, although the Emily or Lakisha study suffers from some potential confounds,[46] it speaks volumes about the continuing race discrimination in the labor market.

Agentic Backlash. So far, I have described how schemas generally influence our in-

terpretations, but this claim is neither controversial nor novel for social psychologists. What's new is that interpretive biases have recently been correlated to reaction-time measures of implicit bias. The best experiment is in the context of gender, not race. Laurie Rudman and Peter Glick examined the relationship between implicit bias against women and their job interview evaluations.[47] Four tester candidates were created for the position of a computer lab manager: agentic man, androgynous man, agentic woman, and androgynous woman. In the "agentic" profile (for both genders), the videotaped interview and "life philosophy" essay of the job candidates emphasized self-promotion and competence. In the "androgynous" profile (again, for both genders), the written essay added qualities of interdependence and cooperation. Half the study participants were told that they had to evaluate the candidates for a job that required masculine qualities; the other half were told that it also required some feminine qualities. After reviewing the interview tapes and the essays, participants rated the candidates on three measures: competence, social skills, and hireability.

The participants evaluated women differently than men in only one setting. In the feminized job condition (in which the job explicitly called for the ability to cooperate with others), the agentic female was rated less hireable than the identical agentic male. The researchers isolated the mediating variable to be differences in evaluation of "social skills," not "competence." In other words, if the job required cooperative behavior, women who showed agentic qualities were penalized more than their identical male counterparts.

In addition to rating the job applicants, the participants completed a gender IAT and explicit gender stereotype questionnaires. Not surprisingly, explicit bias measures did not correlate with how participants evaluated the social skills of agentic females. What did correlate were their IAT scores: the higher the implicit bias against women, the lower the social skills rating.

Biased interpretation can have substantial real-world consequences. Consider a teacher whose schema inclines her to set lower expectations for some students, creating a self-fulfilling prophecy.[48] Or a grade school teacher who must decide who started the fight during recess. Or a jury who must decide a similar question, including the reasonableness of force and self-defense. Or students who must evaluate an out-group teacher, especially if she has been critical of their performance. The Agentic Backlash study provides support for a more specific version of our tendency toward schema-consistent interpretation by demonstrating behavioral consequences of implicit bias.

Of course, schemas do not blind us entirely to individual qualities signaled by the object of interest. Students in my class, for instance, do not treat me the same as a busboy in a Korean restaurant who speaks limited English simply because we are both mapped to the category "Asian." Even if race is a central schema, it is simple enough to activate the subtype of "model minority" versus the "FOB" (fresh off the boat). Moreover, my students have much higher motivation to be accurate since I am in a position of power over them. And motivation for accuracy can prevent use of heuristics or other cognitive shortcuts when adequate cognitive resources are available. Similarly, in a night-time encounter, a Black man dressed as a police officer is not treated the same as one in a jogging suit: role schemas often dominate the field. Nonetheless, in some situations, especially in stranger-to-stranger interactions, little additional individuating information besides what we look like and how we dress is available. In such circum-stances, ambiguous actions produce schema-consistent interpretations. As Susan Fiske succinctly notes, "People are hardly equal opportunity perceivers."[49]

2. PERFORMING

Differential assessments may not be caused entirely by subjective interpretations. Rather, racial meanings transmitted through the culture, coupled with implicit cognitive processes, may alter how we actually perform on objectively measured tests. Evidence comes from the remarkable "stereotype threat" literature launched by psychologist Claude Steele.[50] In a seminal experiment, Claude Steele and Joshua Aronson gave a difficult verbal test to White and Black Stanford undergraduate students. One group was informed that the test was *ability diagnostic*—testing how smart they were. Another, comparable group given the same test was told that the test was *ability nondiagnostic*—simply a laboratory problem-solving task. In the latter condition, the Black students performed comparably to equally skilled White students. But in the former condition, Black students greatly underperformed equally skilled White students.

The apparent explanation for this odd result is that somehow the stereotype that Blacks are intellectually inferior got activated in the former group. According to Steele, this "stereotype threat" may have raised the group's fear that by doing poorly, they would reinforce a negative stereotype of the group they belong to. Thus, doing poorly had a "double consequence": not only individual failure but also confirmation of the negative stereotype. This anxiety somehow disrupted their performance. In the stereotype threat model, this "threat" does not operate by way of explicit internalization of negative self-concept; in other words, these Black students would not self-report that they are intellectually inferior to their White peers because they are Black. In my view, the precise mechanism of performance disruption has not yet been specified. Nonetheless, the general empirical findings of stereotype threat have been duplicated across various social categories, including women, Latinos, and poor White students.[51]

What is amazing is that not only can test scores be depressed, they can also be boosted. That was the finding of the Math Test study described in the introduction. By unconsciously activating a particular identity, performance on difficult tests by the very same category of people could be boosted upward (Asian) or depressed downward (woman), notwithstanding the fact that the participants were already two standard deviations above the mean in SAT math scores. Margaret Shih performed the same experiment in Vancouver, British Columbia, where the stereotype that Asians are good at math is less robust, as measured by surveys. In that iteration, which involved nineteen female high school students, the control group scored highest (accuracy 59 percent), followed by the Asian identity group (44 percent), and then the female identity group (28 percent). These results suggest that it is not Asian identity alone as much as the local stereotype of Asian mathematical ability that drives the differences in performance.

A later, more comprehensive study by Shih revealed further fascinating results. First, the priming cannot be blatant. When Asian Americans were asked explicit questions about Asian stereotypes and told that the test examined whether "Asian Americans are good at mathematics," the boost disappeared. Second, the activated stereotypes do not have to be self-relevant. In other words, you may not have to be Asian to get the boost, as long as you simply *think* Asian. Shih primed Asian and non-Asian students either subliminally or supraliminally with words as-

sociated with Asians or with a control list. In the supraliminal runs, Asian American performance was depressed, which is consistent with the blatant priming findings. But non-Asian-participant performance was actually boosted. The researchers interpreted this boost according to a "perception-behavior expressway" in which activation of a trait catalyzes trait-consistent behavior. This explanation comports with the larger theory of ideomotor action. The results changed with subliminal primes: non-Asians failed to perform differently when the words were flashed subliminally, which suggests that they were not even sensitive to the prime, at least in the test performance context. By contrast, Asians were sensitive to the subliminal primes, perhaps because of the self-relevance of the stimuli, and they received a boost in test performance.

I want to be up front about the limited state of our knowledge. We have no deep understanding of such bizarre testing phenomena. But even without any clear explanation, we can safely say that racial stereotypes, both negative and positive, can be activated implicitly and explicitly to alter test performance in striking ways. We should remember stereotype threat each time we judge someone, including ourselves, on the basis of a test score.

3. INTERACTING

Nonverbal Leakage. Recent research demonstrates that implicit bias, as measured by reaction time studies, also predicts behavior in stranger-to-stranger social interactions, such as interviews and face-to-face meetings. Researchers have termed this phenomenon behavioral "leakage." Allen McConnell and Jill Leibold were the first to demonstrate the linkage between IAT results and intergroup behavior.[52] In this study, White participants completed an explicit bias survey and took the IAT. They were guided through the first part of the experiment by a White female experimenter but the last part of the experiment by a Black female experimenter. Both experimenters asked questions of participants according to a prepared script. Participants' interactions with both experimenters were videotaped.

Trained judges blind to the participants' bias scores coded the videotaped interactions, focusing on nonverbal behaviors such as friendliness, eye contact, and number of speech errors. In addition, the experimenters were asked to evaluate their interactions with each participant. A strong correlation was found between the IAT scores and the ratings of both the judges as well as the experimenters. "[L]arger IAT effect scores predicted greater speaking time, more smiling, more extemporaneous social comments, fewer speech errors, and fewer speech hesitations in interactions with the White (vs Black) experimenter."[53]

These nonverbal behaviors that leak out from our implicit bias influence the quality of our social interactions. In classic experiments by Carl Word, Mark Zanna, and Joel Cooper, White interviewers were trained to display less friendly nonverbal behavior—the sort that has now been correlated with higher implicit bias against racial minorities.[54] When such behavior was performed in front of naive *White* interviewees, those interviewees gave objectively worse interviews, as measured by third parties blind to the purpose of the experiment. In addition, the perceiver's (interviewer's) unfriendly nonverbal behavior can instigate retaliatory responses from the target (interviewee), causing a positive feedback loop. This creates a vicious circle that reinforces the racial schema. Worse, the perceiver's decision not to hire the target based on that social interaction is understood as legitimately on "the merits."[55]

This phenomenon was demonstrated nicely in an experiment by Mark Chen and John Bargh.[56] Participants played a "password" game, in which one player (guesser) had to guess a word based on clues provided by a partner (clue giver). All participants were White. The clue givers were subliminally primed with either a White or Black face. No guesser in either group received a racial prime.

As frustration increased throughout the game, different levels of hostility and aggression were expected. Those clue givers primed with Black faces were expected to show greater hostility. If there was a self-fulfilling prophecy, in which the clue giver's hostility catalyzed the guesser's hostility, then we would expect to see greater hostility on both sides (not just on the part of the clue giver). The audio of the game was recorded and responses by clue giver and guesser were randomly shuffled, then evaluated by third parties unaware of who received what prime. The Black-face-primed clue givers *and their partner guessers* were evaluated as more hostile—providing evidence of the vicious circle.

4. SHOOTING

But for some of us, things get much, much worse. Recall the Shooter Bias study. Under threat conditions that police officers face, our racial schemas incline us to shoot Black men faster. Keith Payne performed the first gun study in 2001.[57] He subliminally primed non-Black participants with a Black or White face and subsequently asked them to identify as fast as possible whether the object displayed was a tool or gun. Those who had been primed with the black face were quicker to identify guns correctly. By contrast, those primed with the white face more quickly identified tools correctly. When participants were time-pressured to force more errors, those primed with a Black face erred more in mistaking a tool for a gun (false alarm). In this study, various forms of dissociation appeared again.

Joshua Correll and his colleagues performed a second gun study in 2002.[58] They created a simple video game that placed White or Black targets holding either guns or other objects (such as wallets, soft drinks, or cell phones) into realistic background settings. There was no prior priming with a face; the target's face would act as a simultaneous prime. The researchers directed participants to decide as soon as possible whether to shoot or not shoot. In the main study, which employed almost all White participants, the experiment revealed that participants more quickly came to the correct decision to shoot armed targets when the target was Black. Conversely, participants more quickly came to the correct decision not to shoot unarmed targets when the target was White. In a variation of this study, again with nearly all White participants, the researchers forced errors by decreasing the amount of time available to respond. Consistent with Payne's earlier results, participants were more likely to trigger "false alarms" against a Black target (that is, shoot when no gun was present); conversely, they were more likely to "miss" against a White target (that is, not shoot when a gun was present).

The researchers next tested whether "shooter bias" (as measured by the difference in response times to White and Black targets) was correlated with other bias measures. In the next experimental iteration, in addition to playing the video game, participants answered a battery of questions that included numerous indirect tests for racism. They were also asked about their personal views of the violence, dangerousness, and aggressiveness of African Americans (an explicit measure of a *personal stereotype*, reflecting actual endorsement of the stereotype). Finally, they were asked how most White Americans would answer the same question (an explicit measure of a *cultural stereotype*, reflecting mere knowledge of the stereotype). The personal stereotype measure, reflecting endorsement, showed no correlation with shooter bias—again, demonstrating dissociation. Interestingly, what did correlate was the measure of the cultural stereotype. The more stereotypes that participants thought that *other* Whites had against Blacks, the greater their shooter bias. Finally, experimenters recruited Black participants to play the game. They obtained similar results: the race of the player, surprisingly, had no impact on shooter bias.[59]

Charles Judd and his colleagues performed a follow-up study in 2004 to identify what types of racial meanings generate the shooter bias[60]—negative emotional affect (negatively valenced evaluations of Blacks), cognitive stereotype (linking Blacks to guns), or some combination (stereotyping associated with a particular evaluative valence). Participants were primed with a Black or White face. The subsequent task involved categorizing a photograph as a handgun or insect. While both categories are negatively valenced, only the first category is stereotypically associated with Blacks. Researchers next asked participants to categorize objects as either sports equipment or fruits. Both categories are positively valenced, but only the first category is stereotypically associated with Blacks. If (negative) prejudice were the sole source of the shooter bias, then we would expect to see no facilitation in categorizing sports equipment after a Black prime. By contrast, if stereotypes were the sole cause, then we would expect to see facilitation with both guns and sports equipment and no facilitation with insects or fruit.

Consistent with both Payne and Correll, the experimenters discovered that participants categorized guns faster when primed with a Black face. They also found, however, faster categorization of sports equipment when primed with a Black face. The effect was slightly larger with the gun, but not in a statistically significant way. Accordingly, the researchers concluded that stereotypes, rather than prejudice, best explain the shooter bias results. If borne out in further studies, there would be practical consequences in terms of solution strategies. For example, to decrease racially disparate shooting outcomes, the task would not be to look for cops who have positive as opposed to negative evaluations of Blacks; rather, the goal would be to sever somehow the widely shared stereotypical linkage between the Black male body and guns.

Recall Amadou Diallo, the young West African immigrant standing in the doorway to his apartment, who was shot at forty-one times by New York police who "saw" a gun that did not exist. It should haunt us to read social science that suggests that if Diallo had been White, he might still be alive. For those who doubt race played any such role, the shooter bias studies cannot be pooh-poohed as another tiresome play of the "race card." For those who always knew race mattered, here is cold quantification. And more chilling is the fact that Whites and Blacks both exhibited shooter bias—a contention that would be hard to make politically without the test results.

D. *Objections*

1. CORRECTION IS EASY

Can't individuals of goodwill compensate for so-called implicit biases by force of will? In other words, if my interpretations might be biased, I can will myself to be more accurate and seek out individuating information. If my performance might be altered by stereotype threat, I can will myself to concentrate and not be "psyched

out." If I might treat a racial minority differently in an interview, I can will myself to ask friendly questions, to smile, and not to cross my arms during the interaction. If I might shoot minorities more quickly, I can simply will myself not to do so; that is the moral thing to do. In neurobiological terms, if my amygdala gets excited, my prefrontal cortex can be commanded to compensate moments later. This is the "correction is easy" objection.

On the one hand, this challenge raises an important point: just because behavior is automatic does not mean that it is immutable. On the other hand, this challenge underappreciates how difficult such behavior may be to avoid: simply "willing" a more correct or unbiased result may produce little benefit.

First, in order to counter otherwise automatic behavior, one must accept the existence of the problem in the first place. In other words, we must be both aware of the bias and motivated to counter it. If we instead trust our own explicit self-reports about bias—namely, that we have none—we will have no motivation to self-correct. One point of this article is to alert readers of a dissociated implicit bias and its automatic consequences.

Second, even if such will (predicated on awareness of the potential problem) exists, success is not guaranteed because compensation may require cognitive resources that are unavailable.[61] For example, when a police officer must decide to shoot or not shoot under extraordinary pressure, the time necessary to compute the correct response does not exist. One might think that a high motivation to be unbiased, especially in life-and-death situations, could compensate notwithstanding time pressures. But another sobering study by Keith Payne demonstrated that participants explicitly instructed to *avoid using race* ironically performed worse (although not in a statistically significant way) than participants told nothing at all.[62] These limitations are consistent with findings that even when we are told what the IAT measures, we cannot through simple conscious "will" erase the time differentials:[63] we cannot be politically correct even when it is embarrassing not to be. Also, certain behaviors, such as eye blinking and nervousness, are simply less controllable through conscious will. There is no evidence, for instance, that the test-disrupting anxiety identified as "stereotype threat" can be mitigated by repeating the mantra "I will not be psyched out."

By no means am I suggesting that self-correction is impossible. An accuracy motivation—fueled by the carrot of financial reward or the stick of accountability—coupled with adequate cognitive resources will correct against many automatic biases. For instance, if all employers in the Emily or Lakisha study were told that an independent third party would judge their screening interview decisions for fairness and that a finding of any racial preference toward Whites (or Blacks) would lead to the death penalty, we would likely have found no statistically significant bias against (or for) African Americans. In fact, in some cases, we might find individuals overcompensating for what they fear to be the behavioral consequences of their implicit bias.

My point is not that self-correction of bias is impossible. Rather, it is that such compensation may be difficult and, in quotidian situations, unlikely.[64] In addition, if we are to compensate for these implicit cognitive processes, conscious, post hoc, effortful attempts at correction may not be the most effective tactic; implicit techniques that decrease implicit bias, for example, may be superior.

2. CORRECTION IS IMPOSSIBLE

Another objection raises the opposite concern: resistance is futile. Drawing on sociobiology and/or evolutionary psychol-

ogy,[65] one could argue that schematic thinking simply cannot be avoided. Just as we may be hardwired to be averse to rattlesnakes and to be fond of our parents' smiles, we may simply be hardwired through hundreds of thousands of years of natural selection to dread other races and to love our own. In other words, the objection goes, race is not a social construction. It is a biological reality, to which we have inborn reactions, and almost nothing can be done about it. This is the "correction is impossible" objection.

One can accept schematic thinking as inevitable, and even concede arguendo that affective reactions to certain stimuli are hardwired, without abandoning the position that race is socially constructed. Recall the racial mechanics model, which specified that the racial categories, mapping rules, and meanings associated with the categories are socially constructed. First, even if there are some basic hardwired mapping rules that use gross morphology to classify human beings into affective clumps, it is a logical leap to say that race—as legally and culturally experienced in the United States in the twenty-first century—is hardwired. According to current racial categories and mapping rules, fair-skinned northern Chinese are put into the same racial category as Filipinos and Asian Indians; *blancos* and *morenos* are both "Latinos"; visually similar American Indians and Koreans are not in the same racial category. There is no evidence, however, that our brains are hardwired precisely in this manner.

Second, even if we are hardwired to clump people by some phenotype (regardless of whether they align identically with current racial categories and their mapping rules), the meanings associated with those categories are not immutably set. As evidence, consider how racial meanings can change radically within a lifetime. At the end of the nineteenth century, the illegal immigration problem in America had a Chinese face. The Chinese were viewed as inscrutable, subhuman, incapable of higher learning; useful laborers but otherwise despicable; vectors for disease, filth, and immorality. And now, the racial meaning ascribed to the very same body is often "model minority."[66] To be sure, some meanings—such as unfair competitor and forever foreign—have persisted over time. But it would be disingenuous to deny substantial transformations in both the cognitive and affective content toward Asian people. While explicit and implicit biases against that category have by no means disappeared, they have transformed within one lifetime. Natural selection simply does not work this quickly.

Finally, the "correction is impossible" objection could suggest that because implicit bias in favor of one's in-group is inevitable, it should not be morally chastised. But as an empirical matter, all groups do not show such in-group bias. Recall the Web Harvest study, which provided evidence of pervasive implicit bias among whites, dissociated from their explicit self-reports of racial equality. In that study, the researchers also examined racial minorities and their schematic baggage. They inquired, for instance, whether belonging to a minority category somehow immunized members against implicit bias against their own category. On the one hand, according to theories such as social identity theory (SIT),[67] we would expect to see the same in-group favoritism and out-group derogation seen in Whites. This prediction would also be consistent with an evolutionary psychology story that speculates that in-group bias is adaptive. On the other hand, we might see an opposite impulse. John Jost and Mahzarin Banaji's System Justification Theory (SJT),[68] for instance, recognizes our need to feel

that the world is fair and just. Therefore, large disparities in wealth, power, and social success as accreted through history are interpreted as "warranted" on the merits. Racial categories low on the hierarchy are thus seen as deserving their lowly status—even if one belongs to such a group.

The data reveal that racial minorities show both impulses: to favor not only their in-group (consistent with SIT) but also those on top of the racial hierarchy—Whites (consistent with SJT). According to Nosek, Banaji, and Greenwald's processing of more than 17,000 runs of the IAT, African Americans on average exhibited no implicit in-group favoritism; in fact, depending on how the data set was circumscribed, they showed a slight bias in favor of Whites or no bias either way. This is the mean; the distribution around the mean looks like a bell curve. By contrast, as already stated, Whites show substantial implicit in-group favoritism on the IAT. If we expected only in-group favoritism to be in play, then African Americans should have shown substantial favoritism for Blacks (at the expense of Whites); after all, on explicit measures, Blacks showed even greater in-group favoritism for themselves than whites did for themselves. But on implicit measures, on average, African Americans exhibited no favoritism. These results have been replicated for other racial groups as well, suggesting that implicit in-group bias is not inevitable.[69]

Also, as a normative matter, we must not conflate "is" and "ought." Even if it is descriptively true that we are hardwired to have implicit bias in favor of our "race" (or clumps of people loosely affiliated with today's social construction of race), that says nothing about what we should do about it normatively. If resistance were truly futile, one could question moral disapprobation of what is genetically determined. But we know that this is not the case.

E. A Research Agenda

My model of racial mechanics is a simple application of schematic thinking. We map individuals to racial categories according to the prevailing racial mapping rules, which in turn activates racial meanings that alter our interaction with those individuals. The mapping and activation are automatic, and the racial meanings that influence our interaction may be stereotypes and prejudice we explicitly disavow. But disavowal does not mean disappearance, and it turns out that reaction time measures, such as the IAT, can measure the latent persistence of these implicit racial meanings. And implicit bias has behavioral consequences, which can be deadly.

Shooter bias, while most graphic, should not overshadow the cumulative effects of more banal encounters. Because of background stereotypes, you may do worse than you would have otherwise. (See Math Test.) Those objective scores may put you on par with another applicant, but because of the racial schemas triggered by your name, you may never get the interview. (See Emily or Lakisha.) And even when you do get the interview, agentic backlash suggests that you may be interpreted as having worse skills because of the social category to which you are mapped. In addition, the interview may go badly because of nonverbal leakage. The total impact of these interactional phenomena on education (admissions, mentoring), employment (hiring, promotion), social networking (friendship, marriage, collegiality), and market transactions (auto purchases, mortgages) cannot be underestimated.

As future research confirms, constrains, and elaborates these results, a vast research agenda will open for those who explore the nexus of law and racial mechanics. Topics on that agenda include:

- The role of intent in all bodies of law[70]
- Criminal law (for example, racial profiling, self-defense, community policing, jury selection,[71] penalty setting[72])
- Antidiscrimination law (for example, disparate treatment,[73] disparate impact, unconscious discrimination, hostile environments, mortgage lending)
- Civil rights law and policy (for example, affirmative action's contact hypothesis, role model justifications, merit definitions, advocacy strategies, housing segregation)
- Lawyering and evidence (for example, strategies and rules with which to engage jurors' implicit biases)[74]
- Education law and policy (for example, teaching strategies, interpretation of tests, debiasing programs and environments)
- Privacy law (for example, comparing measures of implicit bias, such as the IAT, with polygraph results; widespread use of fMRI brain scans; IATs for Article III confirmations or legislators[75])
- Labor law (for example, comparing IATs to other psychological tests, such as the Myers-Briggs test, given before hiring or promotion; employment discrimination; new compliance intermediaries; evidentiary privileges for voluntary debiasing programs[76])
- Constitutional law (for example, equal protection intent versus impact, autonomy as a constitutional value, paternalism)
- Cultural policy (for example, spectrum regulation, campus speech codes, subsidization of production and distribution of debiasing content, media ownership policy)
- Remedies, both voluntary and court-ordered (for example, requiring debiasing screensavers as part of a settlement in a discrimination suit; providing debiasing booths in lobbies where jurors wait to be picked; providing debiasing software installed on computers)

If we move beyond law and consider markets, social norms, and architecture, the research possibilities become myriad. This paper serves as an explicit call for legal scholars to join the investigation. We can follow the lead of Linda Hamilton Krieger, Gary Blasi, and Jody Armour, who have already blazed significant paths.

Some might say that I am calling for an overeager extension of a premature science, embraced for political reasons. And one must concede that science has been and will always be exploited for political purposes. Just as the right might jump on *Bell Curve*[77] findings, the left might jump on stereotype threat findings. There will always be those who out of convenience declare faith in some set of scientific explanations without due diligence. Accordingly, the goal has to be honest, public, and transparent engagement on the merits.

This requires, for instance, highlighting scientific findings that cut against one's political orthodoxy. The most vivid example this article points out is the fact that even African Americans seem to suffer from shooter bias. I also point out that Asian Americans generally have implicit biases against African Americans that are almost as strong as those held by Whites. Neither finding is convenient to progressive politics, but that does not mean they should be swept under the rug. And in this article, they are not.

Finally, in demanding due diligence of scientific models and explanations, we must not privilege the status quo's conventional wisdom as somehow apolitical and uncontroversial. For example, right now the dominant scientific description of human behavior within legal discourse is rational choice theory.[78] Even though there is compelling evidence that this model thoroughly misdescribes human behavior, it is still deployed as the dominant model, from which a laundry list of minor deviations are conceded. For those who complain that acceptance of the implicit bias science is "politically" motivated, one can make the same claim of the status quo.

Recognizing our self-understandings to be provisional, we must still confront the difficult choices to come. As social cognitionists further demonstrate the possibility of altering levels of implicit bias—and explore the mechanisms to do so most efficiently—we will encounter difficult philosophical and legal questions about our autonomy, our normative commitments to racial equality, and the proper role of explicit collective action by private and public actors to decrease implicit bias.

II. TROJAN HORSES

A. Tuning In to Broadcast

In the second half of this article, I pursue a concrete application of the racial mechanics model. This [section] concerns, of all things, recent FCC decisions about the local news. To understand my choice of topic, we must start with a fundamental question: "Where do racial meanings come from?" Racial meanings that accrete in our schemas can, on the one hand, come from direct experiences with individuals mapped into those categories. On the other hand, the racial meanings can arise from what I call "vicarious experiences," which are stories of or simulated engagements with racial others provided through various forms of the media or narrated by parents and our peers. Given persistent racial segregation, we should not underestimate the significance of vicarious experiences. Even if direct experience with racial minorities more powerfully shapes our schemas, vicarious experiences may well dominate in terms of sheer quantity and frequency.

The next question becomes "Why are racial meanings biased against racial minorities?" One hypothesis is that people encounter skewed data sets—or as the computer scientists say, "garbage in, garbage out." If these principally vicarious experiences, transmitted through electronic media, are somehow "skewed," then the racial meanings associated with certain racial categories should also be skewed. This analysis invites further study of culture and mass media policy, topics that social cognitionists have largely avoided.

Suppose that social cognitionists identify which types of vicarious experiences trigger and exacerbate bias and which ameliorate it. Private parties will obviously be free to act on the basis of such discoveries. Voluntary attempts to create a "diversity" of role models on television reflect some such impulse (in addition to financial self-interest, since "diversity" is sometimes good for business). But what about collective action, mediated through the state and implemented through law?

Maybe the state can do nothing [given our First Amendment rights]. [. . .] But there is one communications medium that has always tolerated substantial state intervention: broadcast.[. . .]

In its history, the FCC has promulgated (and the courts have enforced) regulations that restrict the broadcast of content deemed "bad," such as obscenity,[79] indecency, and excessive commercialization.[80] Specific to anti-racism, the FCC, at the specific instruction of the courts, has revoked the broadcast licenses of stations that favored segregation and aired anti-Black racial epithets.[81] Conversely, the FCC has also promulgated regulations that promote content deemed "good" through informational programming guidelines,[82] the fairness doctrine, community needs and interests ascertainment requirements,[83] and children's educational television guidelines.[84] Specific to questions of race, the FCC has also tried to promote "good" and diverse content by increasing minority ownership of stations

through affirmative action. Finally, the FCC has regulated market structure at each stage of production, distribution, and consumption.

* * *

B. Redefining the Public Interest

The touchstone for governmental management of broadcast is the "public interest" standard. That standard has recently been explicated [in the 2003 Mass Media Ownership Order] in an unusual way. At least in the context of ownership policy, the public interest has been functionally equated with the local news.

[. . .] But what in fact is on the local news?

C. Local News

I. CRIME AND PUNISHMENT

Violent crime occupies a heavy share of broadcast news programming. This is true for national news. It is also true for local news, which is "the most widely used source of information about crime."[85] The Project for Excellence in Journalism's annual study of local news programming consistently finds that local newscasts spend about a quarter of their time on crime stories.[86]

Political scientists Frank Gilliam and Shanto Iyengar examined local news of a Los Angeles network affiliate for thirteen months, randomly selecting a thirty-minute newscast two days per week.[87] The absolute number of minutes dedicated to crime stories was high. On average, there were three crime stories per day, accounting for 25 percent of the total minutes aired. In 51 percent of the newscasts, crime was the lead story. For comparison, the researchers obtained actual crime statistics during the corresponding time period. Although the ratio of violent crime arrests compared to all crime arrests in Los Angeles was 30 percent, violent crime news stories accounted for 78 percent of crime stories broadcast. Although the ratio of murder arrests compared to all arrests in Los Angeles was 2 percent, murder news stories accounted for 27 percent of all crime stories broadcast.

These figures do not in themselves demonstrate disproportionality because any such claim must provide a normative account of newsworthiness. We should not presume that a one-to-one correspondence is "proportional." For example, even if murders happen quite infrequently as compared to tax evasion, under what theory of newsworthiness should broadcasters have to provide thousands of minutes covering tax evasion for a single minute of murder? Still, the disparities suggest a lurid fascination with violent crime. They are also consistent with findings that the time allocated to crime stories does not correlate with changes in crime rates.[88] These findings should not surprise us, given the strong financial incentives to focus on sensationalistic stories such as violent crimes. Financial success of broadcast stations requires high ratings, in order to sell more advertisements at higher rates. In turn, this strategy requires stations' pulling in more viewers any way they can.

Violent crime news stories frequently involve racial minorities, especially African Americans. One reason is that racial minorities are arrested for violent crimes more frequently on a per capita basis than Whites.[89] Given our social cognition review, we can predict what watching local news might do to us. If subliminal flashes of Black male faces can raise our frustration, as shown by the Computer Crash study, would it be surprising that consciously received messages couched in violent visual context have impact, too? In fact, we have already seen in the Mug Shot study, described in the introduction, that even ephemeral exposure to race can alter our opinions about crime and punishment. That study, also conducted by Gilliam and Iyengar, is one of the more sophisticated studies in a line of newscast experiments finding similar results.

For example, using a similar experimental design,[90] Gilliam had earlier found that exposure to a Black-perpetrator mug shot produced statistically significant increases in two variables, defined as "concern for violent crime" and "causal attributions for rising crime." Another study has concluded that "judgments of the suspect's guilt are significantly affected by the visual image of the race of the suspect, respondents' stereotypes of blacks, and the interaction between these two variables."[91] A political scientist has even demonstrated how exposure to crime stories, depending on the race of the suspect, can alter self-reports of which presidential candidate participants will vote for.[92]

In the Mug Shot study, Gilliam and Iyengar also used survey data to corroborate their experimental findings. In a large survey conducted at approximately the same time and location as the experiments, participants answered questions about their political opinions and media consumption habits.[93] Three statistically significant correlations emerged: greater viewing of local news led to greater support for punitive remedies, more old-fashioned racism, and more "new racism."[94] Such results, confirmed in various contexts,[95] should give us all pause. On the basis of this evidence alone, one could challenge the FCC's unmindful adoration of local news as furthering the public interest—at least as local news is currently constituted. But the social science described in [section] I suggests that far more might be at stake.

2. TROJAN HORSE VIRUSES

I now make explicit what I have so far left implicit: local news programs, dense with images of racial minorities committing violent crimes in one's own community, can be analogized to Trojan horse viruses. A type of computer virus, a Trojan horse installs itself on a user's computer without her awareness. That small program then runs in the background, without the user's knowledge, and silently waits to take action—whether by corrupting files, e-mailing pornographic spam, or launching a "denial of service" attack—that the user, if conscious of it, would disavow.

Typically, a Trojan horse comes attached secretly to a program or information we actively seek. For instance, we might download a new program for a trial run, and embedded inside may be a Trojan horse that installs itself without our knowledge. Or we might browse some Web site in search of information, and a small JavaScript bug may be embedded in the page we view. Here is the translation to the news context: we turn on the television in search of local news, and with that information comes a Trojan horse that alters our racial schemas. The images we see are more powerful than mere words.[96] As local news, they speak of threats nearby, not in some abstract, distant land. The stories are not fiction but a brutal reality. They come from the most popular and trusted source.

Two clarifications are warranted. First, in the computer world, Trojan horse viruses are written by programmers and unleashed into the wild to do the authors' bidding. That is not my account of race and racism. For example, I do not believe that broadcast licensees or local news producers are purposely designing visceral images of minority-perpetrated crimes to implant viruses in the audience's brains that harm racial minorities. One could plausibly accuse political advertisers of doing precisely this when they launch Willie Horton–like ads[97] or their more sophisticated equivalents.[98] But no such case can be made against local news producers generally, who are merely trying, on a charitable view, to provide satisfactory news while maintaining top ratings in increasingly competitive media environments.

Second, viruses are executable code, programs that take inputs and generate outputs. Isn't news, or any other media input, something different—just data? Doesn't my account blur the data/program distinction? Yes, it does, but that distinction may not be tenable if our minds function partly like neural networks, which they seem to do. As suggested earlier, my racial schemas model can be seen as a higher-level metaphor for a lower-level description that models the brain as a neural network, a massively distributed mesh of nodes with varied strengths in linkages among them. Neural nets are not programmed by writing a linear, flowchart-like order of instructions for execution. Rather, they are trained through exposure to countless cases. Through some learning rule, such as back propagation, those connections that produce a correct answer are subtly strengthened, and those that produce a wrong answer are subtly weakened. After sufficient numbers of exposures, the neural network is deemed "trained," and its knowledge/programming is reflected in the relative strengths of the links among the various nodes. When the brain is modeled this way, much of the data/program distinction dissolves: a part of us is in fact programmed by what we see.

How do we know violent crime stories can, like Trojan horses, exacerbate implicit bias? The Mug Shot study and other work by political scientists using the newscast paradigm are suggestive. Further evidence comes from studies that demonstrate media primings of racial schemas. For example, we now know that exposure to violent rap music can increase implicit bias against African Americans[99] and that playing the video game Doom can increase one's implicit self-concept of aggressiveness[100]—all the while having no statistically significant impact on one's explicit, self-reported views. Still further evidence comes indirectly from research Nilanjana Dasgupta calls the "third wave" of implicit bias research, which examines the malleability of implicit bias. This research demonstrates that implicit bias can be exacerbated or mitigated by the information environments we inhabit.

Positive Role Models. Consider, for example, how exposure to positive exemplars of subordinated categories can decrease implicit bias. Nilanjana Dasgupta and Anthony Greenwald found that implicit attitudes could be changed without conscious effort simply by exposing people to particular types of content.[101] Participants were first given a "general knowledge" questionnaire. For the pro-Black condition group, the researchers used names and images of positive Black exemplars, such as Martin Luther King Jr., and negative White exemplars, such as Jeffrey Dahmer. For the pro-White condition group, the valences of the images were reversed (Louis Farrakhan and John F. Kennedy, for example). Finally, for a control group, the questionnaire required correct identification of insects and flowers. After finishing the questionnaire, participants took an IAT and then completed a survey of racial bias.

The type of questionnaire had no impact on participants' explicit bias as measured by the self-reports. By contrast, the researchers found that the questionnaires had a surprisingly significant effect on implicit bias as measured by the IAT: those participants who had experienced the pro-Black condition reduced their implicit bias by more than half. These results persisted for over twenty-four hours, as measured by a follow-up test.

The authors explained the results in terms of exemplar accessibility. When we evaluate social groups, we do so by calling on particular exemplars of that group retrieved from memory. The cache of racial meanings associated with a racial category may have internally inconsistent content, which may be maintained through the use of subcategories, subtypes, or different exemplars; which exemplar gets activated depends partly on which exemplar is most accessible. Thus, recent priming through visual images (such as the pictures presented in the "general knowledge" questionnaire) can alter the accessibility of one exemplar over another (Martin Luther King Jr. over Louis Farrakhan, Michael Jordan over Mike Tyson). The control group, which answered a questionnaire about flowers and insects, produced results that were indistinguishable from the pro-White condition, which suggests that the default "exemplar" or racial meaning for Whites is favorable.

The dissociation between explicit and implicit bias deserves highlighting. Again, the researchers found a discrepancy between explicit and implicit attitude measures. For the explicit surveys, participants could discount the set of images provided as atypically favorable or unfavorable and consciously correct their attitudes before answering. By contrast, the more automatic processes, as measured by the IAT, seemed not to be subject to conscious compensation or discounting. Such dissociation recommends a dual-pronged approach to addressing problematic racial schemas: those strategies that correct for explicit bias may not be particularly useful as a solution to implicit bias, and vice versa.

Mental Imagery. A study by Irene Blair, Jennifer Ma, and Alison Lenton focusing on counterstereotypic mental imagery is also telling. Motivated by evidence that visualization shares many characteristics with real experiences and thus can influence learning and behavior, they tested whether mental imagery could moderate implicit stereotypes.[102] Individuals instructed to visualize a counterstereotypic image would, in effect, be priming themselves in a way that would make counterstereotypic actions easier.

In the first experiment, one group of participants was instructed to spend a few minutes imagining a strong woman, her attributes and abilities, and the hobbies she enjoys; another group was asked to imagine a Caribbean vacation. Those who imagined the strong woman registered a significantly lower level of implicit stereotype in the IAT. In subsequent experiments, additional groups were added for comparison, including a group asked to imagine stereotypic "feminine women, such as storybook princesses or Victorian women," and a group that engaged in no imagery whatsoever. There were statistically significant differences in the IATs among the counterstereotypic, no imagery/neutral imagery, and stereotypic groups, with reaction time differences increasing in that order. In further experiments, Blair and colleagues employed different measures of implicit stereotypes, including the more recently invented Go/No-go Association Test (GNAT)[103] and a false memory measure.[104] Based on the results of these experiments, the researchers concluded that there is "little doubt that the [counterstereotypic] mental imagery per se was responsible for diminishing implicit stereotypes."[105]

These studies suggest that the images that are consumed matter.[106] Specifically, consuming positive images can decrease individuals' implicit bias, although they may register no difference on measures of explicit bias. Conversely, it seems reasonable to suppose that consuming negative images can exacerbate implicit bias. Recall the group in the Blair study instructed to

imagine stereotypic women. And if mental imagery can produce such effects, watching direct portrayals in electronic media may well have an even stronger impact.

Coed Education. For those who are rightly skeptical about external validity—translating laboratory findings into real-world results—there is now some evidence that exposure to counterstereotypic exemplars decreases implicit bias in real-world situations. Nilanjana Dasgupta and Shaki Asgari performed a longitudinal study of female students before and after their first year of college.[107] Half the participants were recruited from a coeducational college, whereas the other half attended a women's college. Both groups took tests measuring explicit and implicit bias and completed campus experience questionnaires. The two groups started with statistically indistinguishable levels of *implicit* bias: both groups viewed women stereotypically, as more "supportive" than "agentic." What happened after one year of college? On average, the implicit bias of those who had attended women's colleges disappeared. By contrast, the implicit bias of those who had attended coeducational colleges increased. Providing further evidence of dissociation, the groups' *explicit* self-reported endorsements of stereotypes did not change regardless of the college attended or time of measurement.

But what was the mediating variable? On the basis of the campus experience questionnaire, the researchers ran regressions to see which, if any, campus environmental factors correlated with the change in implicit bias. Of the variables measured, the only statistically significant correlation was to "exposure of female faculty" (and not, for example, number of courses taken with gender-related content, say in the women's studies department). Although this longitudinal field study explored the social schema of gender, we should not be surprised to find similar results soon on race. In the end, although we may not be able to directly command ourselves to show less implicit bias on the IAT, we may be able to do so indirectly by altering our informational and interactional environment. This solves the riddle of how automatic processes may resist direct conscious control but nevertheless be mutable.[108]

To summarize: Local news provides data that we use consciously in a rational analysis to produce informed opinions on, say, criminal punishment. But these newscasts also activate and strengthen linkages among certain racial categories, violent crime, and the fear and loathing such crime invokes. In this sense, the local news functions precisely like a Trojan horse virus. We invite it into our homes, our dens, in through the gates of our minds, and accept it at face value, as an accurate representation of newsworthy events. But something lurks within those newscasts that programs our racial schemas in ways we cannot notice but can, through scientific measurements, detect. And the viruses they harbor deliver a payload with consequences, affecting how we vote for "three strikes and you're out" laws, how awkwardly we interact with folks, and even how quickly we pull the trigger.

3. THE ACCURACY OBJECTION

A predictable objection is that the violent content, including crime committed by racial minorities, is a feature, not a bug. In other words, the data presented are not skewed and instead faithfully reflect a reality that the local news did not create. I have three responses to this "accuracy objection": the data are likely not fairly presented, our memories and abilities to see patterns are selective, and we interpret the data in self-serving ways.

First, the information broadcast is prob-ably not fair and balanced. There is a prima facie case that the local media give dispro-portionate attention to violent crime, in which Black suspects feature prominently. Furthermore, ample evidence shows that the media treats Black-perpetrator stories differently, representing and portraying suspects in a more threatening manner than comparable White perpetrators.[109] Specifically, Robert Entman explains that because of production biases in local news-casts, Black suspects are more likely to re-main unnamed and in physical custody, and less likely to speak for themselves.[110] As a result, while there is evidence that the statistical prominence of Blacks portrayed in crime news is "not that much out of line with the actual Black arrest rate,"[111] the emphasis on violent crime appears to skew public perceptions.[112]

Second, even if local news accurately re-flected reality, we see "illusory correla-tions."[113] Whenever two salient events are noticed together, that combination leaves a deep impression in our memories and leads us to overestimate its frequency.[114] Because racial minorities are numerical minorities (and therefore often salient) and because bad acts (for example, crimes) are also un-usual and salient, when racial minorities commit bad acts, the information gets more deeply imprinted and weighted than is statistically warranted. In other words, even if the exact same percentage of Whites and Blacks commit a bad act, and the data are provided objectively, we will (mis)remember Blacks committing a dis-proportionately higher number of bad acts. These findings have been confirmed in nu-merous experiments. This bias can couple with even more dramatic memory errors. For instance, Gilliam and Iyengar have demonstrated that even when a crime news story does not show any perpetrator and provides no information about race, people nevertheless recall seeing schema-consistent minority perpetrators.[115] We are not color-blind even when there is nothing to see.

Third, even if our recollections are accurate, our interpretations may be biased. Consider, for example, the "out-group homogenization" effect. Outgroups are viewed as more homogeneous and monolithic than the in-group,[116] and the in-group is viewed as more heterogeneous than the average.[117] Therefore, even if the news conveys descriptively accurate information about the *mean* criminality of racial minority groups, the public still may seriously underestimate the *variance*. This would contribute to the fallacy of thinking that simply because 50 percent of crimes are committed by a group X, 50 percent of group X commit crimes. Consider how this tendency to view members of outgroups as monolithic could affect Arab Americans during our indefinite war on terror.

Another concern is the "fundamental attribution error" (FAE). The FAE is a general tendency to attribute the causes of behavior to dispositional, instead of situational, factors.[118] In other words, we tend to underweight contingent, environmental factors that cause a particular action and to highlight putatively stable factors such as personality traits instead. This type of error is made more often about others and less often about ourselves. In other words, we each individually have the tendency to describe the causes of other people's behavior as dispositional but to explain our own behavior as highly situational, since we naturally view ourselves as complicated, richly textured, and multidimensional.

The same disparity exists across social-category boundaries. Thomas Pettigrew calls this the "ultimate attribution error" (UAE)—"the tendency to accept the good for the in-group and the bad for the out-group as personal and dispositional, but

more important, to explain away the bad for the in-group and the good for the out-group with situational attributions."[119] Accordingly, when we see a Brown terrorist, we are inclined toward "out-group essentialism" and interpret the violence as part of their way; by contrast, when we see John Walker Lindh or Timothy McVeigh, we see only wayward souls, saying nothing larger about our White selves. In addition to being found in social cognition research, the FAE has been demonstrated in political science experiments employing the newscast paradigm.[120] After a White-perpetrator mug shot, for example, participants emphasize societal variables in explaining the causes of crime; after a Black-perpetrator mug shot, participants emphasize individual nature.[121]

Finally, our attitudinal interpretation of descriptively accurate information may vary tremendously and may not be especially amenable to "accurate" versus "inaccurate" classifications. Suppose the news reports that the average Jewish household savings rate is higher than the national average. Does this support the stereotype that Jews are stingy, or does it show that they are frugal? Could one successfully persuade the anti-Semite that the "stinginess" interpretation is somehow inaccurate, when he points to the accurate data as evidence? Or suppose the local news shows Korean store owners defending their shops with guns during looting and rioting. Does this support the stereotype that Koreans are self-reliant, or does it show that they are vigilantes?

The accuracy objection has lost much of its force. The data are likely unrepresentative. Even when they are not, the biases of illusory correlation, out-group essentialism, and out-group homogenization—each of which maps nicely to themes in critical race theory—conspire to produce inaccurate assessments. They incline us to see more minority-committed crimes than actually exist, to attribute those bad acts to stable, fixed dispositions (either bad genes or stable pathological culture), and to think that racial minorities are monolithically "this" way. Of course, our cognitive biases cannot be attributed to the local news itself. However, only formalism would allow us to bank on the "accuracy" of the local news and to refuse to take into account the empirical findings of our cognitive limitations.

D. Virus Protection

*   *   *

[Editors' Note: In this deleted section, Professor Kang offers a specific recommendation: decouple the presumption that more local news furthers the "public interest": "First, we should reject the strong linkage the FCC made between the public interest and the number of hours of local news aired. [. . .] Second, the FCC should reconsider its decision to limit viewpoint diversity analysis to news and public affairs programming. [. . .] Third, further study through a Notice of Inquiry is warranted. [. . .] Fourth, the FCC in conjunction with media elites should publicly explore how the news exacerbates implicit bias, with an eye toward voluntary development and adoption of 'best journalistic practices.'" Professor Kang also explores two thought experiments, based on the ideas of firewalls and disinfection, which draw on the comptuer virus metaphor. Although a soft cap (or firewall) on the amount of crime-related news is unlikely to be constitutionally permissible, our nonchalant acceptance of similar indecency regulation raises provocative questions. By contrast, a disinfection approach that encourages debiasing public service announcements could be easily designed to withstand legal challenge. Finally, Professor Kang addresses anxieties that such strategies threaten individual autonomy.]

CONCLUSION

Indulge me in some science fiction.

*   *   *

It is the year 2200. Extraordinary advances in neural network computing and nanotechnologies have allowed us to implant "augmented intelligence," called <augI>, into our brains. IntelliDyne Corp. has patented this and related technologies. For example, standard retina upgrades allow us to see ultraviolet and infrared rays, zoom into fine detail, and "see" radio-frequency identification (RFID) signals that radiate from nearly all objects. These data are recorded 24/7 in digital memory, with processors engaged in real-time pattern recognition and self-initiated, intelligent queries to massively interlinked, ubiquitously available databases. All this in a carbon-wrapped piece of silicon circuitry weighing three grams and implanted in the limbic system, next to the amygdala. These days, no one forgets anyone's name, face, marital status, or even sexual orientation; <augI> presents that information to us inside of 200 milliseconds.

IntelliDyne's creative breakthrough was in user interface. It recognized that users would quickly be overwhelmed by information if it were provided explicitly, in semantic form. Therefore, calculation results had to be provided implicitly, through sight, sound, smell, touch, and taste, as well as mood. For example, first responders equipped with public safety <augI> can actually smell radiation. Law enforcement <augI> not only enables officers to run identity checks from a distance but also biochemically quickens physiological responses whenever officers are in "threat mode." When <augI> senses danger, for example, by recognizing a face and associating it with an outstanding felony warrant, officers see increasingly deeper hues of red as a function of estimated threat, and they experience rushes of adrenaline.

IntelliDyne's profits are immense. Demand for the academic <augI> is insatiable as parents of all economic classes struggle to implant their children before high-stakes testing. Managers have become accustomed to using <augI> to assist financial, employment, and strategic decision making. Productivity is bounding for those nation-states that have widely adopted these technologies. Society seems to be on the edge of a new cyberassisted, rational, hyperefficient utopia.

Except for rumors that simply refuse to die. In the blogosphere, many rant that there are bugs in the IntelliDyne system. Some worry whether <augI> has been hacked and whether Trojan horse viruses have unexpectedly entered our brains. Critics say that <augI> has a systematic bias, that it makes reproducible errors. The rumors are growing, especially among the Browns. Just last month, law enforcement shot another Brown who was not armed and lacked a criminal record. Digital audit trails revealed that the officers were operating under extreme threat mode.

After receiving special congressional authorization, university scientists are permitted to decrypt, reverse-engineer, then examine IntelliDyne's <augI> neural network modules. Initial research suggests that these modules produce different results among what should be arbitrary differences in visual stimulus. For example, in a stunning finding, scientists revealed that "threat mode" is quicker to identify guns when they are held by Browns than when they are held by Whites. Under the highest "threat" level, these modules make it easier to shoot Browns than to shoot Whites. Scientists repeatedly confirm these and other troubling results. For instance, the academic <augI> modules seem to malfunction under particular circum-

stances, especially when implanted in Browns.

When Congress subpoenas the IntelliDyne engineers for an inquiry, they explain that neural networks are not "programmed" to execute specific lines of code that instruct mechanically what should be done if certain conditions are satisfied. Rather, they are "programmed" through millions of exposures to exemplar cases, which over countless iterations set the appropriate strength of linkages between neural network nodes. The engineers are confident that the programming exposures are appropriate and representative.

There is growing pressure to stop the implants of <augI> or to fix <augI> somehow to remove these biases. At the same time, many strongly resist, saying that the evidence of bias is equivocal at best and that conspiracy theorists should not be heeded. Anyway, as IntelliDyne repeats, <augI> merely "assists" decisions that are made under the conscious control of human beings exercising independent, fully human judgment. As their advertisements go, "Assisted Autonomy: It's Your Choice." The most vociferous supporters assert that it is their fundamental human right to implant <augI> if they so choose, and Big Brother must not interfere with private choices. A catastrophic showdown looms.

*   *   *

It is only the year 2005, and thankfully there is no IntelliDyne and there is no <augI>. But the social cognition research I have introduced demonstrates that we may not need anything foreign stuck in our brains for disturbing biases to be present. If man-made neural implants were demonstrably faulty because of bad programming or virus infection, would we not aggressively demand governmental intervention? Regulatory approvals would be revoked; lawsuits would be filed; legislation would be passed. But of course, we are talking instead about our brains and not some external implant, which changes our response, perhaps radically. Maybe this is entirely appropriate. I am asking why.

The arc of this article has been long, and given its multiple goals, it has been more evocative than comprehensive. A primary goal is to make the case for using social cognition in critical race studies. In the 1980s and 1990s, debates raged about the best or most appropriate methodology with which to engage in "criticism" of law and legal institutions on matters of racial equality. Countless articles explored, for example, whether narrative defended through postmodernism would be the best or only way. Countless articles explored whether minority scholars did or should have preferred standing to make these inquiries. We have learned from those debates, and the time has come to move on and add things new. One valuable addition is the substance and method of social cognition. This article has been an attempt to demonstrate how and why that should be done.

The benefits will not flow only in one direction, from science into law. Instead, legal analysts who are subject to different craft norms can apply and extend the science into the policy realm in ways that social cognitionists cannot. Less instrumentally, as outsiders, we can identify scientific blind spots. For example, the lack of exchange between psychologists who study stereotype threat and those who study implicit bias is perplexing when the same or related cognitive processes are likely to be at the heart of both phenomena. The lack of exchange between political scientists and social cognitionists is also odd; for instance, why do political scientists still measure only explicit bias after exposing participants to differently edited news stories? Adding one round of the IAT would be enormously illuminating.

The upshot is a call for a new school of thought called "behavioral realism," in which legal analysts, social cognitionists (with emphases in implicit bias and stereotype threat literatures), evolutionary psychologists, neurobiologists, computer scientists, political scientists, and behavioral (law and) economists cooperate to deepen our understanding of human behavior generally and racial mechanics specifically, with an eye toward practical solutions. The next generation of critical race scholars should be at the forefront of this endeavor and not in some rearguard action. Sitting at the back of this bus is not an option.

A more modest goal of this article is to bridge divides with the law itself. As in "Cyber-race,"[122] I am trying to cajole legal scholars working in cyberlaw and communications to engage with race as well as other social categories of subordination. At the same time, I am trying to persuade race scholars to select unconventional points of entry by adopting unorthodox subjects, metaphors, and analytic tools. The cross-fertilization should help us think things anew. The crucible for this article has been the FCC's recent mass media ownership deregulation—specifically the commission's fixation on local news. Local news explicitly furthers the public interest, but its fetish for violent crime makes it a Trojan horse, a "thing that undermines from within."[123]

I have made a solid case for recoding the FCC's definition of the public interest to decrease its reliance on local news. I recognize that counting hours of local news is simple, but something can be both simple and wrong. My ideas about capping crime stories and broadcasting debiasing PSAs are purposely labeled "thought experiments." The value of these inquiries is that they prepare us for actual conversations that will come soon. Moreover, they hint at another sort of implicit bias running beneath the surface of our law. The difference between our complacency about modulating indecency and our anxiety about modulating bias speaks volumes about our culture, politics, and law. Not everything it says is about our explicit commitments. Rather, much of our doctrine might be best explained by our implicit beliefs, which have remained shielded from critical examination.

I close with a caution and a call. The caution is that the remarkable science of implicit bias could draw all of our interest and attention. But implicit bias is not the only source of pervasive and persistent inequalities among social groups. Explicit bias still thrives in many circles.[124] Durable inequality may also be maintained by structural arrangements that are no longer tightly connected to bias, implicit or explicit. Implicit bias should not circumscribe the content of our concerns.

Mahzarin Banaji, a leading scientist in the field of implicit bias, has suggested that "one measure of the evolution of a society may indeed be the degree of separation between conscious and unconscious attitudes—that is, the degree to which primitive implicit evaluations that disfavor certain social groups or out-groups are explicitly corrected at the conscious level at which control is possible."[125] Although my response to the autonomy objection was framed at the individual level, Banaji's insight restates that response at the level of entire societies. Maybe this alignment between the explicit and implicit cannot be reached, at least not perfectly. Evolutionary psychology will surely have its say. Still, achieving this convergence is our challenge. It is our call.

11

Affirmative Action: Images and Realities

Kristina R. Schmukler,

Elisabeth Morgan Thompson,

and Faye J. Crosby

INTRODUCTION

Since affirmative action became a federally mandated program in 1965, it has been controversial. Despite a large amount of research in many academic disciplines on people's reactions to affirmative action, many people have little understanding of it as a policy or in practice. This chapter aims both to give the reader a clear understanding of what affirmative action is and how it functions in employment and education as well as to serve as an entry into people's reactions to affirmative action. Our goal is to present the realities and then to probe why the images diverge from the realities.

The first section of this chapter explains the policy and practice of affirmative action. The second section reviews the major findings in psychological research regarding attitudes toward affirmative action. We conclude with a brief review of psychological theories that have been used to explain how people perceive affirma-

tive action and suggest areas of promising research.

I. WHAT IS AFFIRMATIVE ACTION IN BOTH EMPLOYMENT AND EDUCATION?

Affirmative action policy has often been discussed without a clear definition of what the policy is, especially in newspapers, a source of information for many people.[1] In order to more thoroughly understand such a policy and its implications it is necessary to define what affirmative action actually entails. Affirmative action can be defined as any focused, active effort by an institution to ensure that it is not discriminating against any ethnic, racial, or gender group.[2] The American Psychological Association defines affirmative action as "both voluntary and mandatory efforts undertaken by federal, state, and local governments; private employers; and schools to combat discrimination and to promote equal opportunity in education and employment for all."[3]

Although affirmative action attempts to guarantee equal opportunity, it is conceptually distinct from the concept of equal opportunity.[4] Equal opportunity promotes the ideal—a color-blind society where all are treated according to their merit without prejudice. Equal opportunity policy also assumes that, by and large, the ideal is already a reality. In contrast, affirmative action policies accept the existence of institutionalized discrimination due to both conscious and unconscious prejudice. Therefore, affirmative action policies are developed to proactively prevent and discover discrimination, while equal opportunity policies are more passive and dependent on organizations to act in good-faith, color-blind ways. While affirmative action policies promote proactive monitoring, equal opportunity policies are reactive in that they rely on victims of discrimination to not only recognize the discrimination but be responsible for bringing the situation to the correct authority.[5]

The reactive nature of equal opportunity policies is problematic for two main reasons. First, decades of psychological research have documented that members of oppressed groups often recognize that discrimination exists for their "group" but have a much harder time recognizing their own personal disadvantage.[6] This psychological occurrence has been studied by various researchers and has been called "denial of personal discrimination" or "denial of personal disadvantage" as well as "personal/group discrimination discrepancy."[7] Regardless of what we call it, it is clear that denial of personal discrimination suggests that placing the burden of recognition on the shoulders of the oppressed is a questionable practice.

Second, researchers have found that recognition of systematic discrimination is hard to detect from individualized or isolated information. In experiments with both undergraduate and graduate business school students, researchers found that awareness of discrimination was significantly higher when the information was presented in a table with the relevant information listed clearly than when the information was given seriatim.[8] In one study, for example, half of the participants were placed in the "aggregate" condition. They were presented with a table that brought together all the information on salaries and on the different factors such as education and years of employment that were supposed to determine salary. The other half of the participants received the same information split up by individuals in a nonaggregate manner. Those in the aggregate condition were more able than others to see that women were, on average, making 80 percent less than men with equivalent qualifications. Without the proactive collection of information, discrimination can remain undetected, even by those with little prejudice. Even well-meaning people will have trouble correcting discrimination if they do not see the discrimination as existing in the first place.

While affirmative action is easily differentiated from equal opportunity policies, it is also quite distinct from any quota system. In terms of college admission, a quota system would require a number of slots to be filled by members of oppressed groups. This is not the way that affirmative action programs have functioned in the last thirty years. Instead, admissions officers scan the data on high school graduates and the data on their own applicant pools and pools of admitted students. When a discontinuity is found, the university usually investigates the discrepancy and devises remedial action, including targeted outreach and special scholarships. Similarly, in employment, quotas are nowhere to be found.

A. Affirmative Action in Employment

In 1965 Lyndon B. Johnson signed Executive Order 11246, requiring that all federal government contracting agencies employ affirmative action strategies in their hiring processes.[9] Executive Order 11246 is enforced by the Office of Federal Contract Compliance Programs (OFCCP), which monitors workplace statistics such as hiring, promotions, and salary of firms that have contracts with the federal government. There are four main racial groups of concern to the OFCCP: African Americans, Native Americans, Latinos/as, and Asian Americans. On the dimension of gender, women are considered to be a targeted class.[10] When the OFCCP performs an audit and finds a federal contractor, they look, in all job titles, for a match between incumbency or utilization of people from designated groups and the availability of people from designated groups, keeping in mind needed job qualifications. When incumbency is not aligned with availability, the organization is responsible for formatting and implementing plans to address the inequity. As long as the organization makes a good-faith effort to get the numbers aligned, no ill effect occurs. But if there is not a good-faith effort, debarment as a federal contractor may, theoretically, occur. Debarment is rare.[11]

An example may illustrate. Imagine a government health care agency or a medical organization that does at least $50,000 worth of business a year with the federal government and that has at least fifty employees. Imagine that the organization calculates that 25 percent of their M.D.'s should be women, but only 5 percent are. Such an organization would need to spend energy to purposely increase the amount of qualified female M.D. employees without firing any current employees or refusing to hire future qualified male M.D. applicants. An example could be spending more money on advertising the position to qualified female applicants or investing time devising other ways to get more qualified female applicants.

In an interesting case study of affirmative action in the workplace, Thomas found that the affirmative action policies enacted in the electronics industry changed the ways that employers consider applicants.[12] Racial stereotypes were less likely to be used by employers than before. The use of objective measures of qualification eroded the importance of stereotypes. Economists have found that those firms with active affirmative action programs were just as profitable as those without.[13]

B. Affirmative Action in Education

Much of the heated debate regarding affirmative action has occurred within the context of higher education. Despite serious misconceptions among groups of average Americans, affirmative action in education operates in much the same way as it does in employment. Within the realm of education, the spotlight for affirmative action falls mostly on college and university admissions. An effort is made by college and university admissions boards to determine the total availability of qualified applicants. Of total available qualified applicants, the percentage of these applicants that come from minority groups is measured. Each group must be represented in proportion to the percentage of qualified high school graduates. If any group is not proportionally represented, then active steps must be taken by the school to represent all groups equally.

In 2003, the Supreme Court made clear its opinions on affirmative action in education in the cases of *Gratz v. Bollinger* and *Grutter v. Bollinger*. *Gratz* concerned an undergraduate admissions policy in which a numeric system assigned extra points for minority status and in which admission to the university depended on the total points of any applicant. *Grutter* concerned the law school, where no quantitative system was used. Both cases were filed against the University of Michigan by white applicants who had not been granted admission and whose "on-paper" qualifications looked better than the qualifications of some blacks who had gained entry.[14] The applicants answered newspaper advertisements from the Center for Individual Rights, a conservative organization that was developing a case against the university's admission polices.

In the *Gratz v. Bollinger* case the Supreme Court ruled the university's system for awarding points to individuals from minority groups was unconstitutional, but noted that diversity did indeed serve as a "compelling state interest" and therefore ruled in favor of the university in the *Grutter v. Bollinger* case.[15] Writing the majority opinion in the case of *Grutter*, Associate Justice Sandra Day O' Connor outlined the necessity of diversity and appropriate representation of minorities within a population of students.[16] For the most part, both decisions in the Michigan cases supported the *Bakke v. Regents of the University of California* decision, which they interpreted as affirming the state's compelling interest in ensuring diverse student bodies in state-supported universities.

That the Court interpreted *Bakke* in a manner favorable to affirmative action was a relief for many well-informed supporters of the policy. In a decision concerning the law school of the University of Texas, the Fifth Circuit Court of Appeals had earlier explicitly interpreted those parts of the *Bakke* decision that referred to the state's compelling need for diversity as being the private opinions of Justice Powell and as not, therefore, having the force of law.[17] The Supreme Court could have made the same interpretation of *Bakke* as the Fifth

Circuit did. Indeed, the present Court, now more conservative than just a few years ago, may undo the 2003 rulings.

The majority of the Supreme Court justices in the Michigan case, including Justice O'Connor, appeared to have been influenced by the amicus briefs submitted by former generals in the military, by business leaders, and by associations such as the American Psychological Association. Some of the brief writers were, in turn, influenced by the work of social scientists. Especially important was the work of Patricia Gurin and her colleagues on the positive effects of racial diversity for the learning of whites as well as for minority students.[18] Gurin's work documented that diverse classrooms tend to enhance the ability of whites and others to think in complex and good ways about issues that face an engaged citizenry.

Other researchers have supported Gurin's conclusions. An experimental study placed participants in small groups with different mixes of black and white students to complete an essay task.[19] Diverse groups showed signs of complex thinking not present in other groups.[20] Another study, using archival data of student freshman GPA at the University of Illinois at Chicago, found that those students who came from more diverse high schools, controlling for other factors, had on average a GPA that was one-fourth to one-half point higher than those who did not have experience with people from different groups.[21] The effects were greater for students on the lower side of the average GPA, and among women there was a stronger relationship between diversity and GPA than among men.[22]

One point that was not addressed by the Court was the supposed deleterious effect of the policy on the attitudes and behaviors of its intended beneficiaries.[23] For three decades outspoken critics have leveled three charges against affirmative action. First, they claim that the policy undermines the self-esteem of those whom it seeks to help by implying that the beneficiaries are not capable of success without help.[24] Second, claim the critics, affirmative action causes others to stigmatize its beneficiaries. Third, affirmative action sets its intended beneficiaries up for failure by putting them in situations where they are not capable of success.

Researchers have systematically examined the putative self-diminishing or degrading effects of affirmative action, attempting to see how widespread are the feelings of being undermined that are so eloquently described by a few vocal men of color. Reviews of the literature show it is possible to re-create a feeling of inadequacy experimentally and also that these effects can be reversed as long as beneficiaries are reminded of their own qualifications.[25] The reviews also reveal little survey-based support for the assertion that ordinary beneficiaries of affirmative action experience the sort of self-doubt articulated by some high-profile beneficiaries such as Shelby Steele.[26]

Nor does the research literature fully support the claim that the existence of affirmative action programs causes men or whites to stigmatize women or people of color. Experimental researchers who tell observers little about the attitude target and who manipulate whether or not the target is associated with affirmative action do find that their research participants derogate the targets of affirmative action.[27] Survey researchers, looking at actual interactions in the real world, are unable to detect any stigmatizing effect.[28] On the contrary, and in accordance with the contact hypothesis, which predicts decreased prejudice with increased contact with outgroup members,[29] in nonlaboratory situations affirmative action may be a positive force against the tendency to stigmatize out-group others.[30]

Still unsettled is the claim that affirmative action harms its intended beneficiaries, especially in educational settings, by thrusting them into situations where they are, in fact, incapable of doing the required work. For years, the argument turned on anecdote (e.g., Shelby Steele's 1991 article "The Content of Our Character"). When William Bowen and Derek Bok published their massive study of race-conscious admissions policies, showing that those admitted through affirmative action graduated at the same rate as other students and went on through professional and graduate school at the same rate, the matter seemed settled.[31] Other empirical evidence showed that black students at the University of Michigan Law School were unharmed by very active outreach programs.[32] Recently, however, Richard Sander has complicated matters. From his study of 27,000 women and men who entered American law schools in 1991, Sander concludes that black applicants have been given access to law schools that are more competitive than is justified on the basis of admission criteria, only to drop disproportionately to the bottom of their law school classes, and to then disproportionately drop out of law school and fail to pass the bar exam. Sander's treatment of the data has been criticized by a number of scholars.[33] Some, although not all, aspects of his rebuttal to the critics are convincing.[34]

II. ATTITUDES TOWARD AFFIRMATIVE ACTION

Most Americans do not know the realities of affirmative action.[35] Instead, they react to some vague image that they have of the policy and the practice. Such reactions are usually measured as explicit attitudes, and researchers have been examining people's attitudes toward and perceptions of affirmative action for almost three decades.

They have used a variety of methodologies including survey, social-cognition tasks, experiments, and interviews.[36] Reviews of the research literature shows that attitudes toward affirmative action tend to fluctuate.[37] Attitudes vary as a function of perceptions of the policy, as a function of the characteristics of the attitude holders, and as a function of interactions between aspects of the policy and aspects of the individual.[38]

A. Attitudes as a Function of Affirmative Action Plans

Vague descriptions of affirmative action and general lack of knowledge of the policy have resulted in fluctuating attitudes toward the policy of affirmative action. Opinion polls show a lack of predictability in the general level of support for or opposition to affirmative action. The ways in which affirmative action is framed or described, furthermore, strongly influence how the policy is received.[39]

Across the fluctuations in attitudes, one pattern is quite clear. Americans favor "soft" affirmative action polices such as outreach and disfavor "hard" types of affirmative action such as the practice of tie-breaking, whereby the woman or the ethnic minority candidate is selected rather than the male or the white candidate whenever the two candidates have equivalent qualifications.[40] Americans dislike quotas.[41] The opposition to strong affirmative action practices is evident both in surveys and in experiments, and both in situations where the research participant generates his or her own definition of affirmative action and in situations where the participant is presented with a definition or description by the researcher.[42]

An example of a study in which participants generated their own definitions of affirmative action is a survey conducted in 1993 of a random selection of Chicago residents.[43] Over the telephone, participants were asked: "Which of the following two statements come closer to defining the policy of affirmative action for you? The first definition is: 'Affirmative action occurs when an organization monitors itself to make sure that it employs and promotes qualified minorities and white women in proportion to their numbers.' The second definition is: 'Affirmative action occurs when the government forces organizations to meet quotas for minorities and white women." On a 0 to 10 rating scale of endorsement, an average of 6.8 was given by those participants who equated affirmative action with a monitoring system. Those participants who equated affirmative action with a quota system endorsed the policy much less vigorously than others. The differential levels of endorsement persisted even when one took into account demographic characteristics, such as a person's ethnicity or gender, that have been found to predict attitudes.

It is not only when researchers look at a person's existing definition of affirmative action that they find a preference for "soft" over "hard" practices. In 1991, researchers presented approximately 1,800 randomly selected whites in California with a question about affirmative action. Half of the participants were asked to react to the practice of giving qualified blacks preferential treatment for college admittance; the other half were asked to react to the practice of making an extra effort to ensure that qualified blacks were regarded for college admittance. Forty percent of the participants strongly opposed preferential treatment, while 34 percent weakly opposed it. In contrast, 13 percent strongly opposed making an extra effort and 22 percent weakly opposed it. In a meritocratic society, people are less likely to endorse a policy equated with preferential treatment than they are to endorse a policy that consists of simply making an extra effort.[44]

Support for affirmative action also varies according to the targeted beneficiaries. Kravitz and Platania found that people were less inclined to support affirmative action programs for minorities than they were to support those programs aimed at helping disabled people.[45] Also, women seem to be deemed more deserving of help than blacks, as another study found 60 percent of participants approved of women receiving government help and only 20 percent approved of blacks receiving government help.[46]

Recently researchers have begun to examine the effect of justification on attitudes toward affirmative action.[47] In a survey of 387 undergraduate and graduate students from northern California, Aberson found that support for affirmative action increased when participants were told that the policy is intended to compensate for past discrimination than when no justification was given. Knight and Hebl found that while some types of justification did increase support for affirmative action, justifications did not increase the perceived fairness of the policy.[48]

B. Attitudes as a Function of the Attitude Holder

Many individual characteristics have been found to affect the way people react to affirmative action.[49] Characteristics that have been studied include both those that are acquired at birth (gender and ethnicity) and those that are attained later in life (e.g., prejudices, personal experiences). In some cases the individual variables, such as gender or experience with discrimination, interact with each other.

Numerous studies have shown that women tend to support affirmative action more than men.[50] In comprehensive reviews of the literature, only a tiny minority of the studies show men to be as supportive as or more supportive than women.[51] Similarly, virtually all studies that include ethnic comparisons show that racial minorities are more likely to support affirmative action than are whites. Comprehensive reviews of the research literature documents the persistence over many years of ethnic differences in support for affirmative action.[52] The difference has also been found in studies that were not included in the prior reviews.[53]

Demographic characteristics are not the only aspects of attitude holders that matter. Experiences also matter. Researchers found that while women who had personal experience with workplace affirmative action policies were more likely to support them than women who did not have such experiences, for men the opposite was true—those who had experience with affirmative action for women had more negative attitudes toward affirmative action.[54] Tougas and colleagues found that beneficiaries of affirmative action who were most dissatisfied with their experiences with discrimination were more likely to have higher ratings of themselves as a beneficiary.[55]

One variable that has received much attention is racial prejudice.[56] Generally, those who are prejudiced dislike affirmative action and those who are nonprejudiced like affirmative action. Again, both the comprehensive reviews and the studies published subsequent to the reviews present the same pattern of results.[57]

Some studies examine attitudes toward affirmative action as a function of two other attitudes. Researchers in Canada found that participants who expressed anti-affirmative-action attitudes noted *merit violations* and those who support affirmative action cite the *merit-upholding* values of affirmative action.[58] Recalling a classic study that showed support for affirmative action to depend on the belief that discrimination is a problem, the researchers divided their sample into two groups: those who believed that society treated minorities and whites equally and those who thought discrimination persisted.[59] In the former group, the more strongly a person endorsed the principles of meritocracy, the more the person opposed affirmative action. In the latter group, the opposite was found; thus, among those who admitted the existence of discrimination, the more one cared about fairness the more one supported affirmative action. Similar patterns of findings have been found elsewhere.[60]

C. Attitudes as a Function of Characteristics of the Policy and Characteristics of the Attitude Holder

As Harrison and colleagues point out, much may be learned by looking simultaneously at how aspects of the policy and aspects of the research participants interact.[61] Kravitz and Klineberg surveyed whites, blacks, and Latino/as born in the United States and other countries regarding their attitudes toward affirmative action.[62] The researchers created four categories of affirmative action ranging from "soft" to "hard." The softest program described a company's dedication to removing discrimination, and the hardest option described a policy that would hire minorities and women with fewer qualifications than white men. The results showed that among whites, attitudes toward affirmative action grew more negative as the policy grew stronger. Among Latino/a participants a similar pattern with slightly less variation was visible. Blacks, meanwhile, showed equally strong support for the first three types of affirmative action and significantly less support for the fourth (hardest) option.

III. UNDERSTANDING ATTITUDES TOWARD AFFIRMATIVE ACTION

Psychologists and other social scientists have used attitudes toward affirmative action as a lens into both interpersonal and intrapersonal processes. In other words, by understanding the dynamics of people's attitudes toward affirmative action, researchers can gain insights into fundamental interpersonal and intergroup processes. Social scientists have used four different theories to explain the observed variations in support for affirmative action. Sometimes the theoretical differences are a matter of emphasis, but on some points the theories clash.

First, some researchers conclude from their studies of attitudes toward affirmative action that racist and sexist attitudes in the United States today are still alive but have now gone underground. The modern racist is thought to differ from the classic racist in being unwilling to declare in a straightforward fashion a simple antipathy to people of color or a conviction that people of color are somehow inferior to white people. Yet, despite his or her reluctance to make open declarations, the modern racist believes in covert ways that whites are superior to other people or subtly experiences a dislike or distrust of people of color.

One group of researchers who see in Americans' reactions to affirmative action the operation of modern racism and sexism are social scientists who have posited the existence of what is called "symbolic racism."[63] According to symbolic politics, white Americans' reactions to racially relevant public policies are determined less by how the policies might affect people in some tangible way than by what the policies are thought to symbolize. Thus, white opposition or support for school desegregation has not been linked to whether respondents have children who might be bused but has, instead, varied according to deeply held ideas about blacks and whites. Symbolic racists envision people of color as violators of foundational American values such as individualism and hard work. Thus programs that help people of color are seen to constitute threats to the principles of meritocracy.

Closely linked to the concept of symbolic racism is the concept of aversive racism.[64] An aversive racist is someone who holds negative views of people of color but for whom it would be aversive to recognize the extent of prejudice. Aversive racists do not treat people of color any different than they treat white people when the differential treatment would be obvious and would obviously be linked to skin color. But when given a convenient excuse for differential reactions, the aversive racist acts more positively toward whites than toward other people. Similarly, the aversive sexist does not have conscious awareness of responding differentially to women and men. Yet, when there is a good rationale for treating men well or for treating women ill, the aversive sexist may do so with a clear conscience. The aversive racist is likely to see affirmative action as a policy that gives preferential treatment to people of color and may thus feel justified in opposing the policy. Similarly, the aversive sexist is prone to see affirmative action as giving preferential treatment to women.[65]

The second explanation for patterns of findings concerning people's reactions to affirmative action suggests that Americans are principled, not racist. Sniderman and colleagues argue that people can appear to be racists, but really they are not.[66] Instead, those who oppose affirmative action do so using principles of hard work and individualism. For example, Sniderman and colleagues found no differences between conservatives and liberals in allotment of governmental assistance to blacks who did not meet traditional American values. Yet when asked about blacks who did fulfill the traditional American values of hard work, conservatives allotted significantly more governmental help to struggling blacks than liberals did. These researchers argue that these results support the idea that judgments about assistance, such as affirmative action programs, are made based on principle and on ideals of merit and value rather than on contemporary forms of racism.

It is important, in thinking about affirmative action, to note that people can be both principled and prejudiced. That is, they may believe in hard work and assume (in a prejudging way) that blacks do not work hard. A prejudiced person may oppose affirmative action because he or she genuinely believes it is important to reward merit and also sincerely believes that people of color lack merit. If there are no objective data to show that people of color lack merit, then the belief is based simply on prejudice.

The first two theories agree that, in the service of some high-minded principles or some low-minded preconceptions, people often act in ways that do not promote their own material self-interest.[67] A third explanation for observed patterns of data challenges such a view and asserts that, instead, people's attitudes and actions are governed by self-interest, broadly construed. Bobo says that individual self-interests are less predictive of attitudes and behaviors than are group self-interests.[68] Bobo proposes that negative attitudes toward affirmative action arise when one's group is perceived as not benefiting from the policy. Thus, for example, when working-class whites are surveyed, they cite job competition with nondeserving blacks as reason for their negative attitudes toward affirmative action.[69]

The development of social dominance theory gives us a new, expanded frame with which to consider attitudes toward affirmative action. Social dominance theory posits that the driver of attitudes is less how whites feel about people of color per se (and how people of color feel about whites) than it is about how whites and people of color feel about social hierarchy.[70] Some people are high in "social dominance orientation," while others are low. Because affirmative action perturbs social hierarchy at its most fundamental level, those who are high in social dominance orientation dislike the policy.

As Crosby notes, different individuals may like or dislike affirmative action for different reasons.[71] What motivates one person's reactions may not motivate another person's reactions, especially because affirmative action means many different things to different people. Perhaps some opponents of affirmative action are racist while others are entirely nonracist and base their opposition on principle or on self-interest.

CONCLUSION

In reality, the basis of affirmative action is quite simple: monitor the degree of unfairness in any given situation and then make the proper adjustments. The images of affirmative action presented by the media are vague and often inaccurate.[72] As a result, affirmative action has not been strongly endorsed by most Americans. Perhaps the time has come to supplant the old and negative images of affirmative action with new, more accurate ones. In such a way America might best become the nondiscriminatory nation that it genuinely aspires to be.

12

Behavioral Realism in Employment Discrimination Law: Implicit Bias and Disparate Treatment

Linda Hamilton Krieger and Susan T. Fiske

The first call of a theory of law is that it should fit the facts.
—Oliver Wendell Holmes[1]

INTRODUCING BEHAVIORAL REALISM

Although they serve different social functions and employ different methods and tools, both law and the empirical social sciences need, use, and produce theories of human behavior. But their respective relationships to these theories differ in significant ways, and for this reason, law and social science often stand in tension with each other when they meet in the courtroom or the case reporter.

For its part, law needs, uses, and produces theories of human behavior when judges elaborate constitutional or common law doctrines or interpret ambiguous statutory provisions that implicate human motivation, subjective experience, or choice.

Editors' Note: This chapter is an abridged version of Linda Hamilton Krieger & Susan T. Fiske, *Behavioral Realism in Employment Discrimination Law: Implicit Bias and Disparate Treatment*, 94 CAL. L. REV. 997 (2006), reprinted by permission of the California Law Review, Inc.

Legal actors (judges, jurors, administrative fact finders, dispute handlers, and disputants) also use behavioral theories when they evaluate, litigate, or adjudicate specific disputes, as they attempt, for example, to attribute causation, assess witness credibility, or determine whether particular evidentiary facts constitute persuasive circumstantial evidence of some ultimate fact at issue in a particular case.

Acceptance of judicial authority depends heavily on jurisprudential stability, continuity, and adherence to precedent. As a result, judges are understandably hesitant to endorse proposed changes to the unstated psychological models underpinning legal doctrine, particularly if this would require modifying the doctrine itself. Consequently, as this article discusses, behavioral theory change comes slowly to law, when it comes at all.

In contrast to law, the empirical social sciences construct and use theories of human behavior with a more accepting eye toward their possible emendation, supplementation, or even outright replacement. While change in the behavioral theories embedded in law is viewed, most sympathetically, as a periodic necessary evil fraught with institutional peril, theoretical revision in the empirical social sciences codes as progress. To be sure, scientific communities resist fundamental theory change, as historians of science have vividly described. Nonetheless, the point remains: empirical social scientists expect that as empirical investigation continues and progress is made, the behavioral theories structuring their fields will evolve. In short, empirical psychology progressively refines its descriptive theories of human behavior because it is the goal of empirical psychology to do just that.

It is not the goal of law, however, to refine behavioral theories—even the behavioral theories embedded within legal doctrines. It is the goal of law to structure public and private ordering, to provide mechanisms for efficacious dispute resolution, and, in the process, to safeguard popular perceptions of judicial legitimacy. While the enterprise we call empirical social science is fundamentally descriptive, law is fundamentally normative. So, as we will describe, when law uses behavioral theories, it does so not in the interests of the theories themselves, but in pursuit of other goals.

For these and other reasons, the behavioral theories embedded in legal doctrines often go unstated. Even when stated, they are often unexamined, and they are almost never empirically tested, except perhaps by a small cadre of empirical "law and" scholars whose articles judges seldom read. Sometimes, behavioral theories enter case law as mere rhetorical flourishes, used to justify legal decisions made for reasons having nothing to do with the empirical validity of the theories themselves. However, once embedded in published decisions, a behavioral theory can develop

precedential legitimacy, and for that reason be difficult to modify, even if it is empirically unsound.

When litigants attempt to use social scientific theories in factual adjudication, rules of evidence provide at least some institutionalized gatekeeping role in scrutinizing those theories' validity. But there is no systematic method through which the validity of behavioral theories used in legal reasoning is tested. Behavioral theories can thus enter and remain embedded in legal doctrine long after they have been disconfirmed or superseded by advances in the empirical social sciences.

*   *   *

As Oliver Wendell Holmes Jr. wrote in 1881, "The first call of a theory of law is that it should fit the facts."[2] In context, of course, Holmes was referring to descriptive theories of law; he was not constructing, at least at that point, a prescriptive theory of judicial decision making. More recently, however, as typified by Justice Souter's dissent in *United States v. Morrison*,[3] Holmes's "first call" principle has emerged as a rallying cry against the premising of legal doctrines on inaccurate conceptions of real world conditions. Used in this way, Holmes's "first call" principle points to a prescriptive principle of adjudication, related to but distinct from the legal realism Holmes presaged.

This new principle, which the contributers to this Symposium call "behavioral realism," holds that as judges develop and elaborate substantive legal theories, they should guard against basing their analyses on inaccurate conceptions of relevant, real world phenomena. [. . .]

*   *   *

In the context of antidiscrimination law, behavioral realism stands for the proposition that judicial models—of what discrimination is, what causes it to occur, how it can be prevented, and how its presence or absence can best be discerned in particular cases—should be periodically revisited and adjusted so as to remain continuous with progress in psychological science.

[...] First, antidiscrimination law should be behaviorally realistic because a normative theory of nondiscrimination based on faulty premises about how and why decision makers treat people differently because of their social group status cannot realistically perform much normative work. Even if people *want* to conform their behavior to the norms underlying antidiscrimination law, full compliance with the law's prescriptions is unlikely if the relevant legal doctrines fail to capture accurately how and why discrimination occurs, how targets respond to it, and what can be done to prevent it from occurring. Furthermore, antidiscrimination doctrine should be naturalizing, or behaviorally realistic, because a legal model of discrimination that fails to reflect accurately its real world counterpart will prove inefficient and ineffective from a forensic standpoint. Ironically, one might criticize such legal theories as lacking field validity.

*   *   *

Of course, in many situations, empirically testable claims play no role in the legal analysis grounding judicial interpretation of statutes or constitutional provisions, or in the elaboration of common-law rules. But in interpreting and applying ambiguous statutory provisions, in crafting legal rules to incentivize behavior consistent with a statute's purpose, or in adjudicating individual cases, judges necessarily draw on models of real world phenomena and incorporate those models into their legal reasoning. When these models represent empirically testable—or even tested—claims, behavioral realism maintains that judges should take reasonable steps, whether through the solicitation of expert testimony, amicus participation, or otherwise, to make sure they have the science right.

Stated in this way, the core principle underlying behavioral realism seems obviously correct. But where psychological theories are involved, judicial compliance with this principle is harder than one might suppose. This is because judges, like most people, take for granted certain assumptions about how people behave and what motivates them. These assumptions seem self-evidently correct, even when they are wrong. For this reason, judges sometimes incorporate empirically testable social science claims into their legal reasoning without even noticing that they are doing so. As we discuss in [section] I, judges, no less than litigants, are quick to recite and hesitant to question the behavioral theories that underpin established legal doctrines.

Slowly, however, this may be changing. [...]

*   *   *

[... T]here has emerged in the past ten years a school of legal scholarship exploring the implications of insights emerging from psychological science for antidiscrimination law and policy. Taken as a whole, this scholarship chronicles the many ways in which established civil rights jurisprudence is premised on models of social perception and judgment that have been significantly discredited by empirical work in social and cognitive psychology.

Reflecting this behavioral realist turn in civil rights scholarship, many scholars have drawn on advances in the empirical social sciences to demonstrate that what the law refers to as "intentional discrimination" can just as easily result from the uncontrolled application of implicit, unconscious, or automatic stereotypes and other subtle ingroup preferences as from the operation of conscious discriminatory designs. These scholars, who include both lawyers and social psychologists, endeavor to identify this broader set of mental processes that results in disparate treatment of members of negatively stereotyped or otherwise marginalized groups. In doing so, they generally advocate a causation-based, rather than an intent-based, understanding of the antidiscrimination principle. They also support an expansive application of disparate impact theory in cases involving subjective decision-making systems or other processes or criteria that tend to systematically deprive historically marginalized groups of employment opportunities.

*   *   *

Those who criticize the use of social science in shaping legal doctrine have long argued that normative legal principles and traditional tools of statutory and constitutional interpretation—not social science theories—should guide substantive lawmaking. Judges, these critics demand, "should abandon the practice of basing their decisions on the basis of empirical propositions."[4]

Identifying the proper role of social science in substantive lawmaking is an enormously complex theoretical undertaking, and it is not our purpose to resolve here the many vexing questions that undertaking represents. Our aim is far more modest. Using Title VII jurisprudence as a reference point, we argue here that those who criticize the use of insights from empirical social psychology in shaping or applying antidiscrimination doctrines are overlooking one extremely important point—social psychology is already there. In discrimination cases, as elsewhere, judges are constantly using "intuitive" or "common sense" psychological theories in the construction and justification of legal doctrines and in their application to specific legal disputes. A psychologically trained eye can spot these intuitive psychological theories all across Title VII's doctrinal landscape. Behavioral realism is not a jurisprudential innovation; it is a ju-risprudential corrective. In discrimination law, there already is, and there has long been, an "intuitive psychologist behind the bench."[5]

The problem is, as Stanford social psychologist Lee Ross observed many years ago, the "intuitive psychologist" has significant shortcomings.[6] When subjected to empirical scrutiny, "common sense" theories of how people perceive and judge themselves and others in their social environment often turn out to be wrong. Behavioral realism, understood as a prescriptive theory of judicial decision making, addresses this problem by proposing that, before judges use lay or "common sense" psychological theories in their legal analysis, they should take reasonable steps to ensure that those theories are valid.

*   *   *

Even conceding that normative legal analysis, and not empiricism, must supply the fundamental principles with which judges work, once the law's normative goals have been specified, they must be operationalized through particular legal doctrines and policies. When those doctrines and policies are based on faulty models of relevant social phenomena, the law's ability to advance its normative agenda will be compromised. In short, when the doctrines and policies designed to operationalize normative legal principles are premised on empirically testable assumptions about human social thought or behavior, it is hard to argue with the proposition that insights from the empirical social sciences have an important role to play in ensuring that those assumptions are sound.

In this article, we seek to illustrate and advance behavioral realism in law by applying its methods to the problem of defining and identifying discriminatory motivation in Title VII individual disparate treatment cases. [. . .]

*   *   *

I. THEORIES OF HUMAN BEHAVIOR IN LAW AND EMPIRICAL PSYCHOLOGY

*   *   *

A. Behavioral Theories in Law

Law uses theories of human behavior for a number of distinct purposes. Judges use such theories when they interpret the meaning of ambiguous statutory provisions that implicate human perception, judgment, or choice. Behavioral theories also figure prominently in the development of common law theories of liability, as judges identify and elaborate the essential elements of proof and defense that constitute the various common law crimes and civil causes of action. Behavioral theories work their way into constitutional law, as well, most notably as judges attempt to justify established or novel constitutional doctrines. Trial and administrative judges, litigants, jurors, and dispute handlers also use behavioral theories when they evaluate or adjudicate specific disputes, as they attempt, for example, to attribute causation, assess witness credibility, or determine whether particular evidentiary facts constitute persuasive circumstantial evidence of some ultimate fact at issue. And finally, judges, legislators, and administrative regulators use behavioral theories when they formulate legal rules in an attempt to structure behavior through individual or organizational incentives. In the discussion that follows, we elaborate on each of these uses of behavioral theories in the judicial process.

I. THE USE OF BEHAVIORAL THEORIES IN STATUTORY INTERPRETATION

When judges are called upon to interpret and apply statutes that bear on social perception, judgment, and choice, they need theories of human behavior in order to interpret ambiguous statutory terms and apply them to particular fact patterns. Judicial explication of terms that connote phenomena implicating cognition, affect, incentives, and choice necessarily rely upon psychological models of how people go about making sense of themselves and others in the social world. Because judges need psychological theories to interpret statutes, it should come as no great surprise that judges produce and use those theories, and that the theories either directly or indirectly influence how the law develops over time.

For example, when enacted in 1964, Title VII made discrimination based on race, color, sex, national origin, or religion unlawful.[7] But the statute nowhere defined what "discrimination" meant. Then, when Congress passed the Civil Rights Act of 1991, it amended Title VII to provide that actionable discrimination occurred whenever someone's race, color, sex, national origin, or religion was a "motivating factor" in an employment decision.[8] Here again, Congress did not explain what it meant by a "motivating factor."

As a result, the courts turned to how they themselves had previously defined the term. In *Price Waterhouse v. Hopkins*,[9] a 1989 Supreme Court decision endorsing the use of "mixed motive" analysis in Title VII disparate treatment cases, the plurality relied on a "motivating factor" analysis. In describing for the plurality what it means for gender bias to "motivate" a challenged employment decision, Justice Brennan wrote:

> In saying that gender played a motivating part in an employment decision, we mean that, if we asked the employer at the moment of the decision what its reasons were and if we received a truthful response, one of those reasons would be that the applicant or employee was a woman.[10]

This description reflects two "common sense" theories about the nature of discriminatory motivation. In speaking of the decision maker providing a "truthful" (as opposed to an "accurate") response, this description reflects an unstated assumption that, when disparate treatment discrimination occurs, the discriminator is consciously aware, "at the moment of decision,"[11] that he or she is discriminating. As Professor Krieger described in earlier work, the implications of which will be extended later in this article, these two lay psychological theories—the belief in transparent mental processing, and the modeling of perception and decision making as two discrete processes—have not withstood empirical scrutiny. Decision makers are often *not* aware of the impact of a target's social group membership on their judgments, and those biased judgments are often formed quite early in the social perception process, long before the moment that a decision about the target person is made.

As this illustration suggests, it is not possible for judges to interpret what Congress meant when it used the term "discrimination" or the phrase "motivating factor" in Title VII without applying psychological theories about how human social perception, motivation, and judgment work—that is, psychological theories about when people are discriminating and when they are not.

2. THE USE OF PSYCHOLOGICAL THEORIES IN CIVIL ADJUDICATION

In civil adjudication, judges and other legal actors employ models of human behavior in the production and justification of abstract legal doctrines, and in the application of those doctrines to concrete cases. In either situation, judicial reliance on psychological models may be expressed directly, or it may function as an unstated, taken-for-granted conception of the various social and psychological phenomena implicated by a particular area of law.

At least in the Anglo-American system, law seeks to regulate individual and organizational behavior through the elaboration and application of doctrinal structures variously referred to as "causes of action," "remedial theories," or "claims for relief." If a person feels wronged, and desires legal redress for that wrong, she must fit the facts of her case into at least one legally cognizable claim for relief.

A claim for relief can usefully be understood as a type of schema, which we might call a "claim schema." Every claim schema comprises a particular set of narrative and analytical elements. On the narrative side, each claim schema is associated with a script—a prototypic narrative in which prototypic characters, acting from prototypic motivations, behave in prototypic ways with prototypic consequences for a prototypic victim, who becomes a prototypic claimant. From an advocacy perspective, the narrative resonance of one's case is key to its success. As Anthony Amsterdam and Jerome Bruner observe, "Law lives on narrative, for reasons both banal and deep."[12]

But narrative flow is not all that matters; law has a formal analytical side as well. In this regard, any claim schema can be parsed into a set of "essential elements," legal analytic components that must be discernable in the narrative to form a legally cognizable claim. To establish entitlement to legal relief, a claimant must introduce admissible evidence sufficient to establish the existence of each essential element of one or more legally recognized causes of action.

For example, to establish a right to recover for fraud, a plaintiff must establish five essential elements constituting the fraud cause of action: 1) the making of a false or misleading representation to the victim; 2) with actual or constructive knowledge of its falsity or misleading nature; 3) intent to defraud; and 4) actual reliance on the victim's part, which reliance; 5) redounds to the victim's detriment. To establish a claim for individual disparate treatment discrimination under Title VII, a plaintiff must establish through the introduction of admissible evidence: 1) that he or she is a member of a protected group; 2) that he or she was subjected to some negative employment decision; and 3) that his or her protected-group status was a motivating factor in that decision.[13] In either of these examples, and indeed in any legal case, a failure of proof on any one of the claim's essential elements results in a judgment for the defendant.[14]

Lay psychological theories necessarily find their way into law at the level of doctrinal construction as courts define and describe the essential elements of proof and defense constituting legally cognizable crimes or civil claims for relief. For example, theories of intentionality figure centrally in the substantive criminal law, where crimes are defined largely by the subjective state of mind with which a particular act was performed. In this regard, for example, recklessness is distinguished from intent, and mere intent from intent with malice aforethought. Criminal adjudication requires the trier of fact to discern, usually through the drawing of inferences from circumstantial evidence, the subjective state of mind with which the crime's *actus reus* was performed. For this reason, criminal legal doctrine necessarily reflects and reifies a particular theory of the mind. So, too, with respect to the law of torts, where the same act and resulting harm is accorded profoundly different legal significance according to the state of mind with which an ultimately harmful act is performed, from mere thoughtlessness to malicious injurious purpose.

The incorporation of a particular essential element into a crime or civil cause of action may in and of itself reflect an implicit psychological theory. For example,

we assume (and we do not mean to suggest that this assumption is incorrect), that intent to kill is practically as well as theoretically distinguishable from malice aforethought. The substantive law of fraud implicitly assumes that "knowledge of falsity" is psychologically distinct and empirically distinguishable from the spontaneous, subjective construal of ambiguous information in a self-serving manner, a well-documented cognitive process that often occurs outside of conscious awareness.

Of course, this pattern also holds for civil claims derived from statutes or constitutional provisions. For example, in both statutory and constitutional antidiscrimination law, the distinction between disparate treatment theory and disparate impact theory inherently relies on the assumption that the "intent to discriminate" required to establish a disparate treatment claim is psychologically distinct and practically distinguishable from the mindless indifference to harms inflicted on an outgroup by facially neutral policies.

In most cases, it is not merely the evidence placed into the record that establishes or disestablishes an essential element of the particular claim for relief for which it was offered. Rather, in most situations, the essential elements of a litigant's case are proven (or not) through the presentation of numerous evidentiary facts, which, combined with inferences reasonably drawn from those evidentiary facts, either do or do not establish the existence of each essential element by a preponderance of the evidence.

In the adjudication of summary judgment motions, judges use implicit theories of human behavior to determine, among other things, what inferences would be "reasonable" or "unreasonable" to draw from a particular factual pattern, since only "reasonable" inferences need be drawn in favor of the non-moving party (usually the plaintiff) and against the moving party (usually the defendant).[15]

Assuming that a case survives summary judgment and gets to trial, jurors then need theories of human behavior to know which of various competing "reasonable" inferences should be drawn from the facts adduced in evidence. In most cases, proof is circumstantial; inferences form a kind of logical bridge between the evidentiary facts adduced in evidence and the ultimate facts that must be established or disestablished for one or the other litigant to prevail.

Obviously, in cases involving social interaction, one's implicit or explicit theories of human and organizational behavior will play a central role in drawing inferences from facts, and in determining whether those inferences are reasonable. Generally speaking, people view particular inferences as relatively more reasonable, and are more likely to draw them, if such inferences comport with their subjective understanding of the common nature of things in the world. For this reason, in any lawsuit involving human social interaction, judgment, or choice, both judge and jury act as "intuitive psychologists," bringing to bear on the unfolding case narrative their implicitly held theories of human behavior.

3. BEHAVIORAL THEORIES AND MORAL AUTHORITY IN CONSTITUTIONAL INTERPRETATION

In constitutional lawmaking, judges sometimes use psychological theories to justify decisions based on independent normative grounds. In this regard, consider the "separate but equal" principle pronounced in *Plessy v. Ferguson*[16] and repudiated fifty-six years later in *Brown v. Board of Education*.[17] As described in this article's introduction, many commentators criticized the Warren Court's use of social science evidence in its decision in *Brown*. But for the most part, these critics fail to acknowledge that *Plessy* used social science, too.

The *Plessy* Court's interpretation of the equal-protection mandate was analytically based on and rhetorically justified by the essentially psychological claim that laws relegating Blacks to separate public accommodations could effectuate equality, not simply as a legal conclusion, but also in terms of the lived experience of the Black citizens whose lives these laws affected. Specifically, Justice Brown wrote for the *Plessy* majority that state enforced separation of the races stamps Blacks with a badge of inferiority only "because the colored race chooses to put that construction upon it."[18] This statement asserted an essentially empirical claim—that the social and personal meaning of Jim Crow, and hence its effect on an individual Black person's psyche, was simply a product of subjective interpretation that could easily be transformed into something psychologically benign through the exercise of individual or collective cognitive free will.

Fifty-six years later, in *Brown*, the Court reversed course on both the law and the psychology of state-sanctioned segregation. Relying in part on empirical research by Dr. Kenneth Clark and other social scientists, the *Brown* Court concluded, "To separate [Black children] from others of similar age and qualifications solely because of their race generates a feeling of inferiority as to their status in the community that may affect their hearts and minds in a way unlikely ever to be undone."[19]

As this passage suggests, the *Brown* Court's interpretation of the equal protection mandate was based on and justified by an empirically testable claim about the psychological effects of segregation on Black children. The social science research described in *Brown*'s footnote eleven functioned to justify not only the Court's decision on the merits but also its departure from the principle of *stare decisis*, as Justice Sandra Day O'Connor noted in *Planned Parenthood of Southeastern Pennsylvania v. Casey*.[20] The logic of *Brown* suggests that advances in empirical social psychology not only allowed but even compelled the Court to repudiate the separate but equal doctrine, on the grounds that the psychology relied upon by the *Plessy* majority had been not only publicly repudiated but also empirically invalidated.

Brown v. Board of Education is, of course, not the only Fourteenth Amendment case in which the Supreme Court invoked social science theories to justify its decision. Almost fifty years earlier, in *Muller v. Oregon*,[21] the Court upheld an Oregon law restricting the daily number of hours women could work, basing its decision in part on the contents of the original "Brandeis brief," which surveyed medical and social science theories about the effect of long working hours on women's physical and mental health. More recently, social science theories reported in the amicus contributions of organizations such as the American Psychological Association and the American Sociological Association were used by the Supreme Court majorities and minorities in the Michigan affirmative action cases of *Gratz v. Bollinger*[22] and *Grutter v. Bollinger*.[23]

In each of these three instances, social science was arguably used to justify the Court's choice of a legal rule based on independent normative grounds. In *Muller*, insights from the medical and social sciences were used to bolster the Court's decision that the Oregon law restricting women's, but not men's, working hours was rational. In *Brown*, social science findings relating to the psychological effects of segregation on Black children were used to legitimate the Court's repudiation of *Plessy v. Ferguson* and the "separate but equal"

doctrine it embraced. And, in *Gratz* and *Grutter*, the Court's minority and majority opinions, respectively, based their qualified defense of preferential forms of affirmative action on a set of essentially empirical claims about the effect of student body diversity on educational quality. Reading any of three of these cases, one could easily be left with the troubling sense that the Court had used the normalizing power of science to airbrush away the sharp edges of a difficult and divisive normative choice.

We return in our conclusion to problems stemming from the misuse of social science in substantive lawmaking. For present purposes, however, this counterpoint is key: those who criticize the use of insights from the empirical social sciences in constitutional lawmaking often fail to recognize that the alternative to empiricism is often bare judicial surmise, posing as common sense, and having a lesser claim to validity than the imperfect science such critics would exclude from the legal analytical process.

4. THE USE OF BEHAVIORAL THEORIES IN THE SHAPING OF LEGAL INCENTIVES

Two of the core insights of the law and economics movement are that people respond to incentives and that law can serve as a powerful tool for structuring those incentives in socially beneficial ways. It is testimony to the enormous success of this movement that legal rules are increasingly crafted with an eye toward structuring incentives so as to encourage people and organizations to act in particular ways and forbear from acting in others. Indeed, one finds all across the legal landscape the shaping of statutes, regulations, and judicial interpretations of statutes and regulations in ways explicitly designed to encourage desirable behaviors and discourage undesirable ones within a particular compliance community.

When judges craft legal rules to shape incentives and thereby further the law's normative goals, they necessarily draw upon theoretical models of individual and organizational motivation and behavior. Sometimes the models on which judges draw are simply assumed to be accurate, even though they represent testable theories that have been subjected to scrutiny in the empirical social sciences.

In the antidiscrimination law context, the legal doctrine governing employer liability for sexual harassment by supervisors illustrates how judges sometimes use unexamined, often even unstated, behavioral theories when they craft legal rules with an eye toward structuring individual and organizational incentives. For example, in two cases decided in 1998, *Faragher v. City of Boca Raton*[24] and *Burlington Industries v. Ellerth*,[25] the Supreme Court established an affirmative defense to Title VII claims of hostile work environment harassment by supervisors. The defense permits an employer to defeat an otherwise meritorious hostile environment harassment claim if it can show that it had promulgated antiharassment policies and instituted antiharassment education and grievance procedures, and that the plaintiff had failed to use those procedures early in an escalating sequence of harassing events.[26]

Writing for the *Faragher* majority, Justice Souter acknowledged that the Court's decision to establish the affirmative defense deviated from a long line of cases applying agency principles to hold employers responsible for tortious conduct by their supervisory employees.[27] Justice Souter justified this departure, however, on utilitarian grounds. By providing employers with incentives to institute antiharassment policies, education programs, and grievance procedures, and by encouraging employees to complain early in an escalating sequence of harassing events, the new affirmative defense would serve Title VII's "primary objective," which Justice Souter described as "not to provide redress but to avoid harm."[28] As various commentators have noted, the Court's reasoning in *Faragher* reflects and relies upon a particular set of unstated and unexamined, but empirically testable, assumptions. First, the Court assumes that by promulgating policies against harassment and by establishing antiharassment education and grievance procedures, employers will prevent harassment from occurring, or will, at the very least, significantly decrease its incidence. Second, the Court's analysis rests on the premise that employees who are subjected to unwelcome sexualized workplace conduct will use an employer-run grievance procedure if one is provided, and that they will do so before the conduct becomes egregious.

However, as numerous commentators have documented, virtually no empirical support exists for the proposition that antiharassment policies, training programs, or internal grievance procedures actually reduce the amount of unwanted sexualized conduct in the workplace.[29] Moreover, a large amount of empirical evidence indicates that reporting through existing internal grievance mechanisms is an extremely rare response to unwanted sexualized workplace conduct, and that women generally have quite reasonable justifications for their decision not to report. In other words, in their efforts to use the *Faragher/Ellerth* affirmative defense to structure incentives and ultimately prevent harassment from occurring, the justices appear to have presumed a behavioral world that does not in fact exist.

If sexual harassment doctrine is premised on the essentially empirical claim that antiharassment policies, training, and grievance procedures reduce harassment, or that "reasonable" women will use those procedures early in an escalating sequence of harassing events, and if these claims are empirically false, the justices' attempt to deploy the *Faragher/Ellerth* affirmative defense to prevent harassment from occurring will fail to achieve its policy objectives. Rather than preventing harassment from occurring, the affirmative defense will simply operate to defeat otherwise meritorious harassment claims.

*   *   *

Of course, apart from judicial attempts to engineer incentives, legal rules can be devised to serve other functions about which empiricism has little if anything to say. So, for example, the Court could have premised the *Faragher/Ellerth* defense on the notion that it would be unfair to impose liability on a corporation that is trying, however imperfectly, to ensure that its employees comply with the ambiguous and often conflicting set of legal and practical considerations that sexual-harassment law implicates. Alternately, the Court might have based the defense on the grounds that, as a matter of judicial economy, if an employer provides an internal grievance mechanism for redressing harassment claims and if an allegedly aggrieved employee has failed to use it, she should not be allowed to seek redress from the already overburdened federal court system. In other words, legal doctrines can be, and often are, premised on normative principles about which, in the final analysis, empirical research has little to say.

For example, were it empirically established that state-sanctioned segregation does *not* injure Black children's self-esteem, would we want to reverse *Brown*? How many supporters of preferential forms of affirmative action would change their views as to its constitutionality if it were established that student body diversity had no discernable effects on educational outcomes? As these questions illustrate, empiricism is no substitute for normative analysis.

However, empiricism is indispensable to sound consequential analysis. Obviously, a legal rule can effectively shape conduct through the structuring of individual or organizational incentives only if that rule is built upon accurate models of individual and organizational behavior and choice. When judges premise legal doctrines on the notion that a particular legal rule will structure individual and organizational incentives and thereby shape behavior in a particular way, they need to get the social science right. Although far from infallible, psychological science often serves as a better source of such models than "common sense" or other forms of *a priori* theorizing.

B. Behavioral Theories in Cognitive Social Psychology

What then does it mean to "get the science right"? How do social-scientific communities go about evaluating the theories that structure their investigations, and what, if anything, can jurisprudence learn from science about its own relationship to the psychological theories it generates and employs?

When creating or updating behavioral theories, psychological science employs a wholly empirical standard of proof. Normative analysis has no role to play in determining whether a behavioral theory is sound. In psychological science, investigations proceed from hypotheses, which state the expected relationship between two or more variables. Usually, causality is stated (A increases B) or strongly implied (A and B go together, and A is temporally prior). Hypotheses most often derive from theories supported by basic research (i.e., research concerned with fundamental principles rather than with the application of those fundamental principles to a specific applied problem). Scientists share criteria for what makes good theory. These criteria include causality, coherence, parsimony, and falsifiability.

Questions about causation occupy most scientific research, and social science is no exception. Well-established empirical standards for causal inference require that: (a) two variables be associated (co-vary; change together over time, occasions, or persons); (b) the proposed cause temporally precede the proposed effect; (c) the relationship is not spurious (i.e., in reality jointly caused by a third variable); and (d) a rationale be argued. The following discussion will briefly elaborate on each one of these requirements.

To meet these standards, an individual conducting an experiment—the gold standard for inferring causality—would first show temporal priority by manipulating experimental conditions and measuring the result. Next, she would establish association by measuring the result at different values of the putative cause. She would also demonstrate nonspuriousness by having randomly assigned subjects to different conditions and having controlled for extraneous variables. Finally, theory would provide the rationale by explaining mechanisms linked to a network of other theories and observations. Without theory, empirical observations would merely collect a series of isolated facts without larger meaning.

In addition to inferring causality, a good theory possesses coherence. It must not contradict itself. It must reflect internal logic, and it must tell a plausible story.

Good theories are also parsimonious. So long as accuracy is not compromised, explaining a phenomenon with a few measurable variables is preferable to explaining it with many. Unfortunately, nature does not always cooperate. Elegance makes theories more esthetically pleasing, and more testable, but it may not make them more accurate. Neoclassical economics provides a salient example. Economic theories based on the rational-actor assumption are elegant and parsimonious,

but as research in behavioral economics has shown, they do not accurately predict much of human economic behavior.[30]

Finally, and perhaps most importantly, to be legitimate a social scientific theory must be falsifiable. The central criterion for falsification is that observations, made under suitably controlled conditions, can contradict the theory being tested. Enough of these observations, replicated over time and investigator, topple the theory, and new contenders emerge.

The evidence for and against any previously accepted social-scientific theory is subject to rigorous peer review. As a rule, scientists are conservative and resist new approaches, holding their colleagues to very high standards. New theoretical models that survive this process are then themselves subjected to attempts at falsification.

Thus, theories in psychological science are inherently destined to evolve. Current theories explain the body of observations to date, and new variants incorporate the older observations as well as new ones. The body of data remains constant, though its interpretation shifts as it is viewed through the lenses of evolving theories. That psychological theories change does not make them arbitrary; they must withstand scrutiny under the best methods and data available at the time.

C. Quality Control: Incorporating Psychological Theories into Legal Doctrines

Given the relative impermanence of psychological theories, what standards should govern their incorporation into law? This question, or at least one much like it, occupies an entire field of law and scholarship on the admissibility of expert testimony, and we do not intend to review or add directly to that literature here. A set of basic principles, however, bears mention.

At a minimum, as suggested by the

Supreme Court's decision in *Daubert v. Merrell Dow Pharmaceuticals*,[31] the law should not incorporate a psychological theory into one of its many doctrines unless it has been empirically tested, has been subject to peer review and publication, has garnered widespread acceptance within the relevant scientific community, and, where applicable, has a known and acceptable error rate.[32] In connection with factual adjudication, a trial court, applying *Daubert*, plays a gatekeeping role; it screens proffered scientific evidence to determine whether it satisfies applicable scientific standards, and whether it would be useful to the trier of fact.

Social science models must clear an additional hurdle before use in adjudication. Psychological science is basic research, often conducted in the laboratory. Meanwhile, legal disputes concern events in the real world. As such, questions of "external" or "field" validity inevitably arise. The challenge often takes this form: does the experimental result pertain only to the rarefied, highly controlled, artificial context of the laboratory, or does it also accurately represent how things work in the real world?

A theory might have laboratory but not field validity for a number of reasons. First, by controlling for extraneous factors, a well-designed experiment might amplify an effect that outside the laboratory is dominated by the very factors being controlled. Second, a laboratory finding may be statistically significant at the 0.01 or 0.05 level even when the actual effect size is relatively small. Third, the dependent variable measured in a laboratory demonstration of a particular effect may differ from the actual real world behavior it was designed to simulate.

Using primary research in psychological science implicates all of these issues, but tools exist to reckon with them. Effect sizes can be measured and expressed as a standardized statistical unit. Researchers can use representative-sample survey and field observations to assess the field validity of a theory validated in the laboratory environment.

Individuals who question the field validity of laboratory demonstrations often base their criticisms on a questionable assumption. These individuals assume that by removing most sources of noise, the laboratory setting increases rather than decreases the strength of the studied phenomenon's signal. This assumption flatters social science by likening it to the field of pure physics, comparing a reduced-noise psychology experiment with a frictionless vacuum. But people are not particles, and the noise in a social system tends to conform to other noise in the system. Fortunately, through the use of meta-analysis, which allows the quantitative summary of results across multiple studies, social scientists can sometimes identify field effects that are *larger* than their laboratory-bound counterparts.

Several such meta-analyses have been done on phenomena pertaining to prejudice and discrimination. Stronger field than laboratory effects have demonstrated the real world generality of favoring members of one's ingroup,[33] remembering stereotypic more than counterstereotypic information,[34] judging the outgroup as more homogeneous than the ingroup,[35] and liking people one sees frequently.[36]

In short, psychological science provides effective mechanisms not only for testing the laboratory validity of psychological theories, but also for determining whether those theories accurately represent effects that occur with meaningful frequency in the real world. And even where only a few studies demonstrating field validity exist, it is hard to understand why judges' *a priori* psychological intuitions, which have no demonstrated validity at all, should be preferred to psychological theories validated by solid, laboratory-based science. As we noted above, *Daubert* stands for the proposition that adjudicative facts should not be based on a psychological theory unless that theory has been empirically tested, has been subjected to peer review and publication, has garnered widespread acceptance within the relevant scientific community, and, where applicable, has a known and acceptable error rate. But, as we have shown and will demonstrate in greater detail in [section] II, in elaborating legal doctrines and in applying them in legal reasoning, judges routinely articulate and apply intuitive psychological theories that satisfy none of these normative criteria. And once incorporated into legal doctrine, these lay psychological theories can be quite difficult to modify or uproot.

D. Modifying Behavioral Theories in Law: When Is Theory Change Needed, and Why Is It So Hard to Effect?

As we have shown, as judges develop, interpret, explain, and apply legal rules, they necessarily construct and draw upon models of human behavior they assume to be empirically sound. They do this in a number of ways: by incorporating certain essential elements of proof into the claims for relief they recognize as legally cognizable; by the language they use to explain why, in any particular case, those elements have or have not been established; by their crafting of jury instructions; and through their definition of ambiguous statutory terms. Judges make assumptions about human behavior in their evidentiary rulings and in their written opinions granting or denying summary judgment or judgment as a matter of law. Sometimes records of judicial reasoning explicitly posit these theories of human behavior, and sometimes they do not. Either way, because law's legitimacy is based on the appearance of stability, continuity, and fi-

delity to precedent, the judiciary faces high costs when it questions or changes the implicit psychology behind established legal doctrines. The kind of course correction taken in *Brown v. Board of Education* can happen only so often if the judiciary is to preserve rule-of-law notions and popular legitimacy.

Litigants, like judges, have little incentive to question the inferential architecture undergirding the substantive legal theories on which their claims or defenses are premised. Although civil litigation is in many ways highly technical, at the end of the day, lawsuits tell stories. Because judicial opinions incorporate popular, taken-for-granted assumptions about the common nature of things, they function as a society's core stories; they offer an interpretation of experience and provide the participants of future lawsuits a narrative comprising a set of easily recognized plots, symbols, themes, and characters.

Future litigators fall hostage to these narratives. As the narratives become paradigms—as they become entrenched in legal doctrine—litigators have an irresistible incentive to construct from the facts of their client's particular case a story that closely resembles them. Challenging the law's implicit, phenomenological metatheories is a good way for a lawyer to lose her client's case. In short, whether one is a judge or a litigant, legal institutions structure incentives in ways that protect the implicit theories of human behavior underpinning established legal doctrines from challenge or change.

On the other hand, as the last section described, empirical psychology has a very different relationship to its theories of human behavior. Empirical social science progresses by testing, problematizing, refining, supplementing, and sometimes disconfirming, established theories of human perception, judgment, behavior, and choice. Social psychology is interesting because it produces vivid, replicable demonstrations of how human beings tend to behave in particular contexts. These demonstrations are useful because they often sharply contradict our "common sense" theories of human behavior, including those embedded in law.

Empirical social psychologists, unlike judges and litigants, have powerful incentives to challenge the established theoretical models that constitute their discipline. In a very real sense, empirical psychology develops theories of human behavior as scaffolding for further investigation, which, if successful, conduces over time to the theory's modification. In empirical psychology, as in all science, theory emendation represents success. In jurisprudence, on the other hand, theory change, unaccompanied by legislation or constitutional amendment, threatens subjective conceptions of judicial legitimacy. For this reason, once a particular model of human behavior becomes embedded in legal doctrine, judges may go to great lengths to avoid having to modify it. As a result, in terms of their accuracy and comprehensiveness, empirically tested psychological theories tend to get ahead of their judicial counterparts.

Numerous examples of this lag between psychological and jurisprudential theories of the same phenomenon come readily to mind. Together, they reveal the critical need for the law to find more effective mechanisms for examining, and where indicated, changing, the behavioral theories it employees. Eyewitness identification testimony, for example, has retained its judicial imprimatur of singular probative value long after empirical social scientists vividly demonstrated its frightful unreliability.[37] Cases involving repressed memories continue to circumvent otherwise applicable statutes of limitations, despite research by Elizabeth Loftus and others casting the syndrome's very existence as a genuine phenomenon into serious doubt.[38] And courts continue to admit as evidence expert testimony purporting to predict future violence in convicted murderers[39] in death penalty cases, despite the work of psychologists like John Monahan, Robert Menzies, and others, who have demonstrated that in most contexts such predictions have little, if any, validity.[40]

Where social science does influence legal doctrine, the lag-time between scientific and legal acceptance appears to be at least five years. In one respect this lag serves a useful purpose; it allows scientific consensus to solidify, and it inhibits the overeager adoption of fads and flukes. In another respect, however, the five-year lag poses a problem if the alternative is not older science but flawed common sense theories of behavior. Unvalidated intuitions are often a poor substitute for science, even five-year-old science.

Nowhere, we suggest, have the intuitive psychological theories employed by judges in the elaboration of legal doctrine and the adjudication of individual cases fallen further behind their empirically vetted social science counterparts than in the context of antidiscrimination law. In virtually every way that judges presiding over civil rights cases employ implicit psychological theories—in the construction of legally cognizable claims for relief; the schematic abstraction and description of those claims' constituent elements in judicial opinions; the analysis of factual records in connection with summary adjudication motions; the analysis of motions for judgment as a matter of law; the crafting of jury instruction; and substantial-evidence review on appeal—antidiscrimination doctrine lags far behind the psychological science of intergroup bias.

In other words, current judicial models of what discrimination is, what causes it to occur, and how one should go about determining whether it happened in any given case, now diverge in significant ways from the models of intergroup bias validated through empirical inquiry in the social sciences. Furthermore, although from time to time apparent doctrinal inroads have been made, antidiscrimination jurisprudence has in many respects proven stubbornly refractory to the conceptual adjustments the science of implicit bias suggests it needs. We now turn our attention to that subject.

II. A BEHAVIORAL REALIST CRITIQUE OF DISPARATE TREATMENT DOCTRINE

The past thirty years of empirical research in social psychology have yielded four fundamental insights of central importance to antidiscrimination law and to theories of proof in discrimination cases. The first concerns the relative roles of controlled and automatic processes in human judgment and choice. Far more appears to go on in the cognitive background, beyond the perceiver's conscious attentional focus, than naïve theories of human behavior suggest. In other words, much of what we do is "mindless," proceeding on automatic pilot.[41]

The second principle concerns the importance of subjective construal in shaping human judgment and behavior. Recent research has shown that raw perceptual input does not, on its own, shape impression formation, memory, or eventual choice. Rather, perceptual input is rendered meaningful only through a process of subjective construal.[42] Construal is subject to a variety of distortions stemming from implicit schematic expectancies, including but not limited to social stereotypes. This biased construal is not unique to intergroup perception. Social perception and judgment more generally are subject to numerous biases, which often impair people's ability to accurately predict the

future, attribute causation, and otherwise understand the social world in which they act, judge, and choose. Frequently, as the first principle suggests, these biases may operate outside of the perceiver's conscious, attentional focus. Often, they can be controlled only through the application of effortful, deliberate, cognitive "correction."[43]

Social psychology's third important principle taps into the importance of belonging[44] to one's primary social groups. People demonstrably conform to their social surroundings far more than they think they would.[45] This finding holds across cultures and over time.[46] The importance of understanding people as social beings permeates all of social psychology. This follows from the fact that people have never survived well outside of primary groups. Due to this core social motive to get along with and feel accepted by one's group, most people attune their behavior to the thinking and feelings of those around them more than introspection would admit. Social context has an enormous impact on individual behavior.

This leads into the fourth key principle emerging from empirical social psychology—the surprising power of situations, as opposed to assumedly stable, dispositional traits or tastes, in shaping judgment, behavior, and choice. Empirical investigations in social psychology have shown that by varying even minor aspects of the situation in which people are asked to judge, act, or choose, one can elicit completely different patterns of behavior, even if nothing about the actor's self-interest has been changed. Situational variables, as contrasted with stable dispositional traits or "tastes," have far more power in shaping preferences and in driving social behavior than most people assume.[47]

These four principles—the important role played by the cognitive unconscious in social perception and judgment; the centrality of subjective construal; the motivational power of belonging; and the power of situations—function together as the weight-bearing pillars of modern social psychology. Significantly, they all directly challenge the "intuitive psychology" underpinning much of currently accepted federal antidiscrimination doctrine. In numerous ways, antidiscrimination law reflects and reifies a common sense theory of social perception and judgment that attributes disparate treatment discrimination to the deliberate, conscious, and intentional actions of invidiously motivated actors. These actors purportedly know when they act in a discriminatory manner, do so consistently across situations, and then dissemble about the real reasons for their decisions when challenged.

In the remainder of this [section], we map the four pillars of modern social psychology onto two nettlesome issues concerning the Title VII disparate treatment doctrine. [First] we examine a principle known as the honest belief rule and demonstrate that it derives from an intuitive model of social perception and judgment that has been significantly discredited by empirical social science research. This research, which implicates the above-described principles of automaticity and subjective construal, undermines many of the descriptive assumptions on which the honest belief rule is premised. Next [. . .] we scrutinize a doctrine known as the same-actor inference, and argue that it is based on a naïve psychology of cross-situational consistency disconfirmed by research reflecting the principle of behavioral situationism and the need for social belonging. Through these analyses, we illustrate both the aims and the methods of behavioral realism in employment discrimination law.

A. Discriminatory Motivation, Implicit Cognition, and the Honest Belief Rule

Section 703(a)(1) of Title VII of the Civil Rights Act of 1964, the statute under which most federal employment discrimination cases arise, provides in pertinent part that it is an unlawful employment practice "to fail or refuse to hire or to discharge any individual, or otherwise to discriminate against any individual with respect to his compensation, terms, conditions, or privileges of employment, because of such individual's race, color, sex, national origin, or religion. . . ."[48]

This statute makes it unlawful to discriminate, yet it never defines exactly what discrimination is. Congress, in essence, left to the courts the task of assigning meaning to the term "discrimination" through a process of judicial elaboration in case law. Given that race, sex, national origin and other forms of discrimination implicate social perception, judgment, and choice, this process of judicial elaboration necessarily relies on descriptive models of how people go about making sense of themselves and others in the social world. For this reason, judicial understandings of the nature of the psychological processes involved in discrimination play a legally constitutive role—that is, they determine the ultimate legal meaning of discrimination.

Despite years of judicial elaboration, the meaning of discrimination is still a work in progress. Following the Supreme Court's 2003 decision in *Desert Palace, Inc. v. Costa*,[49] an individual seeking to prove a discrimination case under Title VII's disparate treatment theory must establish three things: 1) that s/he is a member of a Title VII protected class; 2) that s/he was subjected to some negative employment action (e.g., a failure to hire or promote, or a discharge from employment); and 3) that her/his protected group status was a "motivating factor" in the challenged decision. The critical question of course, left for the courts' future explication, is what it means for one's protected-group status to be a "motivating factor" in an employment decision. In [section] III, below, we offer a constructive account, informed both by behavioral realism and traditional methods of statutory interpretation, of how, in our view, the phrase "motivating factor" should be understood for Title VII purposes. In this [section], on the other hand, we seek to show that many federal courts are according the phrase "motivating factor" an unduly crabbed meaning, in part because they are basing their legal analysis on faulty psychological models of intergroup perception and judgment. This, we will argue, leaves many instances of disparate treatment discrimination doctrinally unintelligible and therefore judicially irremediable.

The doctrinal roots of this problem are reflected, ironically, in the plurality opinion in *Price Waterhouse v. Hopkins*,[50] a case we discussed in [section] I and in which one of the authors of this article testified as an expert witness on the psychological science of cognitive bias,[51] and which was widely considered a major civil rights victory. Consider again how Justice Brennan, writing for the *Price Waterhouse* plurality, described what it means for gender bias to "motivate" a challenged employment decision:

> In saying that gender played a motivating part in an employment decision, we mean that, if we asked the employer at the moment of the decision what its reasons were and if we received a truthful response, one of those reasons would be that the applicant or employee was a woman.[52]

This statement reflects an assumption that, when disparate treatment discrimination occurs, the discriminator is, at the moment a decision is made, consciously aware that he or she is discriminating. Gilbert Ryle refers to this assumption as "the official theory" of transparent mental process and describes it as follows:

> [A] person has direct knowledge of the best imaginable kind of the workings of his own mind. Mental states and processes are (or are normally) conscious states and processes, and the consciousness which irradiates them can engender no illusions and leaves the door open for no doubts. A person's present thinkings, feelings and willings, his perceivings, rememberings and imaginings are intrinsically "phosphorescent"; their existence and their nature are inevitably betrayed to their owner.[53]

Research on implicit social cognition has substantially discredited the "official theory" Ryle described. Much of human mental process, including those processes mediating interpersonal perception and judgment, occur in "the cognitive unconscious," outside the perceiver's mindful attentional focus.[54] In other words, actors often do not realize that they have formed biased judgments of others. If you ask an employer at the moment of the decision what his reasons for making a decision were, he might well not be aware that one of the reasons was that the applicant or employee was a woman, even if her sex did, in fact, influence his judgment.

*   *   *

At a very early age, young Americans learn the stereotypes associated with the various major social groups.[55] These stereotypes generally have a long history of repeated activation, and are apt to be highly accessible, whether or not they are believed. In other words, one can be "nonprejudiced" as a matter of conscious belief and yet remain vulnerable to the subtle cognitive and behavioral effects of implicit stereotypes. Indeed, recent neurological research using functional magnetic resonance imaging (fMRI) technology reveals that subjects who score low on measures of explicit prejudice, but whose performance on the Implicit Association Test (IAT) reveals negative implicit attitudes toward Black targets, exhibited both a heightened startle response (measured by [electromyograph] eye blink potentiation) and elevated amygdala[56] activation when viewing photographs of unfamiliar Black faces.[57]

Left uncorrected through motivated, effortful mental processing, implicit stereotypes can exercise a powerful effect on social perception and judgment. As social psychologists John Bargh and James Uleman, among others, have demonstrated, merely encountering a member of a stereotyped group primes the trait constructs associated with and, in a sense, constituting, the stereotype. Once activated, these constructs can function as implicit expectancies, spontaneously shaping the perceiver's perception, characterization, memory, and judgment of the stereotyped target.[58] The science of implicit bias demonstrates that disparate treatment can result not only from the deliberate application of consciously endorsed prejudiced beliefs, but also from the unwitting and uncorrected influence of implicit attitudes and associations in the social-perception process.

*   *   *

As we will argue in [section] III, Title VII's operative text prohibits these subtle forms of discrimination, but the science of implicit stereotyping has barely begun to influence federal disparate treatment jurisprudence. Indeed, from a behavioral realist standpoint, in many circuits, judicial conceptions of intergroup bias have actually regressed over the past two decades, even as psychological science has surged toward an increasingly refined understanding of the ways in which implicit prejudices bias the social judgments and choices of even well-meaning people.

One stark example of this arguably widening disconnect between the legal de-sign of discrimination and the science of everyday prejudice can be found in a now decade-old doctrine known as the honest belief rule, which posits that to rebut an employer's nondiscriminatory explanation of a challenged employment decision, a discrimination plaintiff must prove not only that the employer's proffered reason is unworthy of credence, but also that the employer *did not honestly believe* the reason it gave.

*   *   *

This approach is plainly inconsistent with what empirical social psychologists have learned over the past twenty years about the manner in which stereotypes, functioning not as consciously held beliefs but as implicit expectancies, can cause a decision maker to discriminate against members of a stereotyped group. [...] Spontaneous biased construal, often occurring outside of the decision maker's conscious attentional focus, can easily result in the differential treatment of members of a negatively stereotyped group.

In societies or groups in which antidiscrimination norms are strong, people are highly motivated to be seen by others, and to see themselves, as nonprejudiced. Thus, when faced with making a choice between members of different social groups, people whose preferences are implicitly shaped by group membership spontaneously search for independent decision criteria consistent with their preference, and use those criteria to justify their choices to themselves and others. In a powerful series of experiments, MIT business-management professor Michael Norton and his colleagues demonstrated this effect in simulated hiring and higher-education admissions decisions. They showed that subjects consistently altered the qualifications they deemed most relevant to the selection of a high-level construction manager, a stereotypically male job. When the male candidate had more education and less relevant job experience, subjects—who overwhelmingly preferred the male candidate—reported that they viewed education as more important than job experience. When the male candidate had more job experience and less education than the female candidate, subjects ranked job experience as more important than education. Either way, subjects tended to rank the criteria in a way that would justify selection of the male candidate on the grounds that he was "better qualified" than the female candidate they were rejecting. However, when subjects were forced to rank the selection criteria before seeing the candidates' resumes, gender bias in selection largely disappeared.[59] Other studies demonstrate a similar "elasticity effect" through which decision makers' judgments of the importance of various decision criteria shift in ways that justify implicit *ex ante* preferences.[60]

*   *   *

Why should it matter that the intuitive psychology underlying the honest belief rule is unsound? The answer, of course, is that it may or may not matter, depending on the purposes being served by a court's decision whether or not to adopt it. In elaborating what it means for group status to be a motivating factor within the meaning of Title VII, courts necessarily balance a variety of competing considerations. Such considerations might include a recognition of the significant stigma associated with labeling an employer as a "discriminator" or a desire to focus scarce judicial resources on the potentially most meritorious cases. But none of the honest belief rule cases cite any such rationale in support of the rule. Rather, the logic of the honest belief rule decisions points to the operation of an unstated and unexamined judicial theory about the nature of discriminatory motivation itself—that when people discriminate they know that they are doing so. The honest belief rule as-

sumes that a reason proffered by an employer to explain its action is either, in the words of *Price Waterhouse*, an "honest answer," or a deliberate lie.

But as we have seen, empirical cognitive social psychology has demonstrated that the lay psychological theory that underlies the honest belief rule is woefully incomplete. Stereotypes can influence social decision making through processes of subjective construal that occur outside of conscious, attentional focus. A well-meaning but implicitly biased decision maker can believe that he is basing a judgment about a member of a stereotyped group on legitimate nondiscriminatory reasons when, in fact, the target's group membership "caused" the decision maker to view the target in an unjustifiably negative light. For this reason, the honest belief rule would have little place in a behaviorally realistic disparate treatment doctrine.

B. Dispositionism, Situationism, and the Same Actor Doctrine

One of the most important insights emerging from social psychology in the past fifty years is the principle that situations, along with one's subjective construal of those situations and one's attempt to negotiate the conflicting pressures they impose, exert a far more powerful effect on people's behavior than the "intuitive psychologist" generally assumes. This principle is often referred to as "situationism," and it contrasts with the "dispositionism" that often characterizes common sense psychological theories about what makes people act the way they do.

*   *   *

Dispositionism has profoundly influenced the way people think about discrimination. People tend to view intergroup bias as though it were a kind of stable disposition, analogous to a personality trait, which expresses itself consistently across time and situation. Indeed, following the lead of Nobel Laureate Gary Becker, economists often describe this bias as a "taste for discrimination."[61] Under this view, if a person is going to discriminate against members of a particular group, we expect him to do so *consistently*. We view tastes as relatively stable phenomena.

Of course, there is some merit to this view. Under certain circumstances, past behavior is a reasonably good predictor of future behavior. As recent research in social-personality psychology has shown, in some circumstances, clusters of personality traits can interact with a particular situation to predict behavior pretty reliably—*in that situation*.[62] And, at least with respect to the more extreme forms of bigotry, prejudices do tend to run in "packs."

That said, people, including judges, have a tendency to overestimate the role of stable traits or tastes and to underestimate the role of situational variables in shaping social perception and behavior. As social psychologists Lee Ross and Richard Nisbett have observed, unexpected behavioral inconsistencies result from the fact that people operate in a state of tension.[63] Some perceptions, thoughts, incentives, and concerns pull a person in one direction; others pull him in another. Under such conditions, small changes in a situation, or in a person's subjective interpretation of that situation, can lead to surprising changes in the person's behavior.

*   *   *

[. . .] Thus, while old-fashioned dominative racism might function like a stable trait or taste, there is significant reason to believe that the expression of implicit bias is far less consistent across situations. Why would this be so?

As noted earlier, people learn at a very early age the stereotypes associated with different social groups in their society. As a person gets older and is exposed to more egalitarian ideals, however, she may consciously reject the proposition expressed by a stereotype she has learned. However, when this occurs, neither the associations the stereotype comprises nor the emotional states that accompany them are necessarily replaced by a new enlightened attitude. Rather, the cognitive and emotional associations that formed the earlier biased attitude often continue to exist alongside the stereotype-holder's new, more enlightened conscious belief.[64] This leaves the social perceiver with "dual attitudes" toward members of the stereotyped group, one implicit and the other explicit.

According to social psychologist Timothy Wilson and his associates, "[w]hen dual attitudes exist, the implicit attitude is activated automatically, whereas the explicit one requires more capacity and motivation to retrieve from memory."[65] A person who holds a dual attitude will react to a stereotyped target in dramatically different ways, depending on whether implicit or explicit attitudes dominate the perceiver's judgmental process while he or she is forming an impression of the stereotyped target. [. . .]

*   *   *

These principles, now widely accepted in the psychological sciences, have been almost completely overlooked in the judicial elaboration of Title VII's disparate treatment doctrine. As we have already observed in our discussion of the honest belief rule, disparate treatment doctrine expects biased decision makers to discriminate *consistently*.

Another judicial manifestation of this expectation can be found in a doctrine known as the "same actor inference," which emerged in 1991 in the Fourth Circuit's decision in *Proud v. Stone*,[66] an age discrimination case. [. . .]

*   *   *

In affirming the district court's decision to grant the defendant judgment as a matter of law, the Fourth Circuit stated that it did not even need to consider the plaintiff's evidence of discriminatory motivation because one fact overwhelmed all others: the person who made the decision to fire Mr. Proud had, only five months earlier, made the decision to hire him. [. . .]

* * *

Most circuits [. . .] justify the same actor rule on grounds of adjudicative accuracy and efficiency. An employer decision maker who has participated in a decision to hire a member of a protected group, the argument goes, is so unlikely to express bias against him at a later date that a "strong inference" or presumption of nondiscrimination is justified on forensic grounds. Why does such an inference seem so commonsensical? Because it coheres with dispositionism, a strong belief in the cross-situational consistency of expressions of bias in discriminatory behavior. However, a great deal of empirical research suggests that dispositionism, the common sense model of behavioral consistency on which the same actor inference is based, is deeply flawed, and that human behavior is far less consistent across situations than lay people tend to believe.

* * *

[. . . W]hether attitudes predict behavior depends on the attitude, the context, and the person. Some attitudes (e.g., strong, unambivalent ones), some contexts (e.g., those emphasizing acting on one's values), and some people (those for whom values are especially important) show higher attitude-behavior correlations than others (e.g., weak attitudes in norm-driven contexts for socially oriented people). The relevant point here is that even professional psychological scientists have to jump through many measurement hoops to detect stability in the expression of a person's underlying attitudes. Just as the law cannot take for granted that past behavior will predict future behavior in a different context, so it cannot take for granted that attitudes, even strongly held ones, will be consistently expressed across different situational contexts.

For present purposes, the important point is that bias, understood as an attitude toward members of a particular group, only predicts overt discrimination under certain circumstances. Whether biased decision makers will act in a way that expresses their bias varies as a function of many different variables, including the influence of social norms, the extent to which particular social norms are made salient in particular situations, decision makers' perceptions of control, their motivation to avoid biased decision making, and the apparently relevant information they have at their disposal.[67]

In general, people will judge others only when they feel entitled to do so, either on the basis of their position or on the basis of having sufficient information.[68] Thus, people tend to refrain from using their stereotypes, or making any judgment at all, when they lack what they perceive to be decision-relevant information. However, possessing even the illusion of information is sufficient to free people to make judgments. For example, Belgian researcher Vincent Yzerbyt and colleagues showed that people made more extreme and confident stereotypic judgments when they were told that a flash of light represented subliminal individuating information about the decision target—even though it was indeed merely a flash of light.[69]

* * *

There are well-founded reasons for believing that implicit bias will express itself less readily in the hiring context than later in the employment relationship. In particular, the hiring context tends to make equal employment opportunity (EEO) norms and goals salient. As such, managers may be more vigilant about inhibiting responses based on stereotypes or other implicit attitudes. Moreover, during the hiring process, human resources specialists or EEO managers may play a role in selecting applicants for a "short list," may be present at interviews, or may review decisions for compliance with the employer's EEO policies and goals. Where this occurs, the person who actually makes the hiring decision may be influenced in ways that blunt the effects of any implicit stereotypes he holds. However, this influence may wane as time goes on and equal opportunity goals become less prominent.

Accurate prediction of an applicant's future performance is often difficult because the hiring decision is based on the minimal information contained in a resume or gleaned from a brief interview. In these circumstances, employment decision makers [...] may forbear from making decisions based on stereotypes. However, once the selected employee begins performing, the decision maker, now a performance evaluator, may be influenced by implicit stereotypes [...]. In the context of the information rich day-to-day evaluation of often ambiguous employee behaviors, equal opportunity goals are generally not salient, and decision makers are likely to be operating under conditions of relatively greater cognitive busyness. They can often believe they are basing tepid or outright negative evaluations of stereotyped employees exclusively on "legitimate nondiscriminatory reasons," rather than on perceptions and judgments biased by implicit stereotypes.

There is, in short, little reason to believe that an implicitly biased employment decision maker who has hired a stereotyped person will necessarily succeed in keeping his or her subsequent evaluations of that person's performance free from the influence of implicit stereotypes. Implicit stereotypes are latent infiltrators of social perception and judgment. Decision makers who hold egalitarian beliefs but are affected by implicit bias operate in the very type of tension system that Ross and Nisbett describe. Subtle differences in the social, physical, or organizational environment can be expected to introduce a great deal of inconsistency into such decision makers' perceptions, judgments, and decisions about the stereotyped target. Under these conditions, cross-situational consistency in intergroup perception and judgment simply cannot be expected to rise to the level required to support a presumption, or even a "strong inference," like the same actor rule. As is the case with so much of federal disparate treatment jurisprudence, the same actor inference is based on an intuitive psychological model that has been disconfirmed by advances in cognitive social psychology.

III. A BEHAVIORAL REALIST RECONSTRUCTION OF INDIVIDUAL DISPARATE TREATMENT THEORY: DEFINING AND (DIS)PROVING DISCRIMINATORY MOTIVATION

What exactly would it mean to use insights from the science of implicit bias to reconstruct Title VII disparate treatment theory from a behavioral realist perspective? [...]

In this section, we pursue two goals. First, we seek to demonstrate that a behavioral realist interpretation of Title VII's anti–disparate treatment principle is fully consistent with the statute's plain text, with Supreme Court precedent, and with accepted, even conservative, methods of statutory interpretation. Second, we will show that a behavioral realist reading of Title VII's operative provisions would change relatively little about how disparate treatment discrimination claims are proven or defended, either in terms of the burden of proof borne by the plaintiff or in the types of evidence a plaintiff would need to adduce to prove a claim. Far from representing a radical innovation in civil rights law, a behavioral realist interpretation of the anti–disparate treatment principle would actually serve to correct the truly radical innovations represented by doctrines like the same actor inference and the honest belief rule, which are based neither in the statute's text nor on Supreme Court precedent, and which have unjustifiably narrowed Title VII's remedial reach.

A. A Textualist Reading of Section 703(a)(1)

*   *   *

There is nothing in either the text of Title VII nor the dictionary definition of the verb "discriminate" that limits the statutory text to differences in treatment resulting from an employer's conscious intention to subordinate (or favor) an individual because of his or her protected-group membership. Moreover, the Supreme Court has repeatedly acknowledged that the statute's remedial reach is broader than this crabbed interpretation. For example, the Court has repeatedly stated that, in enacting Title VII, "Congress intended to prohibit all practices in whatever form which create inequality in employment opportunity due to discrimination on the basis of race, religion, sex, or national origin."[70] On other occasions, the Court has observed, "Title VII tolerates no racial discrimination, subtle or otherwise."[71]

Given conditions prevailing in the early 1960s, it is of course reasonable to assume that conscious, purposeful disparate treatment was the most salient evil against which Title VII was directed, at least as far as race discrimination was concerned. But there is nothing in either the text of the statute or the legislative history accompanying it that would foreclose other meanings, as the Court's above-cited observations reflect. Thus, the notion that Section 703(a)(1)'s anti–disparate treatment principle proscribes only the deliberate, willful use of an employee or applicant's protected-group status in an employment decision is a judicial innovation, not a legislative one. What the plain language of Section 703 requires is that an employer not allow an applicant or employee's group status to play a causal role in any employment decision.

*   *   *

B. Discriminatory Motivation, Congressional Intent, and the 1991 Amendment of Section 703

The argument that Section 703(a)(1)'s use of the term "to discriminate" refers only to intentional action in its narrowest sense suffers from a second and perhaps even more damning flaw. Specifically, in a portion of the Civil Rights Act of 1991 codified as Title VII's Section 703(m), Congress amended Section 703's operative language, providing that "an unlawful employment practice is established when the complaining party demonstrates that race, color, religion, sex, or national origin was a motivating factor for any employment practice, even though other factors also motivated the practice."[72]

*   *   *

The *Webster's Third New International Dictionary of the English Language, Unabridged* defines the word "motive" as "something within a person (as need, idea, organic state, or emotion) that incites him to action."[73] In other words, a "motivating factor" is an internal mental state, a category that includes cognitive structures like implicit stereotypes or other social schema that influence social perception, judgment, and action. For race, color, sex, national origin, or other protected characteristics to "motivate" an employment decision means that the characteristic served as a stimulus which, interacting with the decision maker's internal biased mental state, led the decision maker to behave toward the person differently than he otherwise would.

C. Behavioral Realism, Legal Normativity, and the Nature of Discriminatory Motivation

* * *

D. Proving and Disproving Discriminatory Motivation

At this point, an astute reader might well be asking, "What about proof? What kind of evidentiary showing would be required to establish motivation if we were to adopt the theory of intergroup bias toward which behavioral realism points?" [. . .]

[. . .] Under the framework we propose, the evidence would remain much the same, but the inferences reasonably drawn from that evidence, and the nature of the ultimate fact the evidence would be offered to prove, would expand to accommodate the insight that disparate treatment can result from the uncorrected influence of implicit stereotypes as well as from their deliberate, fully conscious use.

* * *

Over the past thirty-three years, the Supreme Court has described the types of evidentiary facts a trier of fact may consider in a disparate treatment case in deciding whether the plaintiff's protected group status was a motivating factor in a challenged employment decision. These include:

- Comparative evidence showing whether similarly situated persons not in the plaintiff's protected group were treated more favorably than the plaintiff or other members of the plaintiff's group;[74]
- Statements or expressive conduct by decision makers evincing negative stereotypes or attitudes toward the plaintiff or others in his or her protected group;[75]
- The employer's willingness to tolerate harassment of the plaintiff or other members of the plaintiff's protected group;[76]
- The employer's general pattern of treatment of members of the plaintiff's group, including statistical evidence;[77]
- The specific decision maker's treatment of plaintiff and other members of the plaintiff's protected group;[78]
- Whether the defendant has come forward with evidence of a legitimate, nondiscriminatory reason for its action;[79]
- Whether the nondiscriminatory reasons proffered by the defendant fail to rationally explain the decision it made or are otherwise unworthy of credence;[80]
- Whether the nature or operation of the employer's decision-making process left room for the operation of bias;[81] and
- Whether the employer had in place and applied effective mechanisms for detecting the possible influence of bias and for preventing such biases from influencing the ultimate decision made.[82]

Under the behaviorally realistic approach to defining discriminatory motivation described earlier, these species of evidence are as probative as they have always been. What changes under a behavioral realist interpretation of Section 703(m) is the set of inferences that can reasonably be drawn from these species of evidence and what exactly "discriminatory motivation" means, as an essential element of the plaintiff's disparate treatment claim. For example, comparative evidence showing that an African American plaintiff was treated more harshly than a similarly situated White employee in a disciplinary situation could be offered to show that implicit stereotypes had caused the decision maker to perceive the plaintiff's misconduct to have been more serious, reprehensible, or likely to recur than the similar misconduct of the White comparator. Statements made by the decision maker that suggest that the decision maker harbored stereotype-infused attitudes or beliefs could bolster such an inference, whether such statements were directed toward the plaintiff or not. On the other hand, the decision maker's record of hiring or promoting other African Americans might tip the balance the other way.

The point is that in any given case, particular pieces of evidence may not be legally sufficient to *compel* a finding of discriminatory motivation, but legal doctrine should not be so constrictive as to deprive the trier of fact of its proper role in determining whether, taken together, they are. The trier of fact's proper role is to consider all the evidence and combine it with inferences it deems reasonable in order to determine whether the challenged conduct violates the operative terms of the statute as interpreted by existing legal doctrine.

In determining in disparate treatment cases what inferences would be reasonably drawn from particular evidentiary facts, or in describing the meaning of discriminatory motivation or intent, judges are constantly using psychological theories. As we have shown, disparate treatment doctrine has been premised on numerous factual suppositions about the nature, causes, and characteristics of intergroup bias. These suppositions are neither indicated nor justified by sound principles of statutory interpretation, and in many respects, they are descriptively inaccurate. In the Title VII context, naïve psychological theories like those underlying the same actor and honest belief rules function primarily to obscure an ideologically premised and jurisprudentially unjustifiable constriction of the statute's remedial reach.

13

African American Families, Child Maltreatment, and Parental Rights Termination Litigation

Matthew B. Johnson, Kideste M. Wilder, and Misha S. Lars

INTRODUCTION

Parental rights termination (PRT) is an end point of several processes that results in a permanent severing of the legal ties between a parent and his or her child. The process begins with allegations of child maltreatment (abuse and/or neglect), can proceed to child removal and foster care placement, and may eventually result in a court-ordered termination of parental rights. The termination order legally voids the parent-child relationship. Thus the parent has no enforceable rights to care for, or have contact with, his or her child. The child becomes eligible for adoption. The state's authority to legally terminate a parent-child relationship stems from the recognized parens patriae doctrine, which holds the state responsible to protect children and other dependent persons.[1] As a result of the stakes in PRT—that is, the dismembering of the parent-child relationship—the litigation can be highly contentious. Among African Americans,

given our particular history and relationship with the state, characterized by multiple generations of state-supported slavery, segregation, and discrimination leading to the current era with disproportionate incarceration and concentrated poverty, a state-imposed order permanently separating a child from her parent warrants, at the very least, critical review.[2] Though these issues have received scholarly attention and analysis recently, for example Roberts's comprehensive review and critique, *Shattered Bonds: The Color of Child Welfare*, there remains a need for further critical review and vigilant advocacy for African American children and families facing parental rights termination complaints in the family courts.[3]

The current contribution will present legal and psychological aspects of PRT among African Americans. There will be a discussion of child maltreatment, the child protective system, and the sequence of legal events that lead to PRT litigation. The impact of child removal and PRT for individual children and families will be considered as well as the "group harm" to the black community at large.[4] Various models that are useful in illustrating the problem of child maltreatment and "child protection," such as the stress-resiliency model, the public health model, the human rights model, and others, will be described. Suggestions for solutions on the individual case level as well as broader policy-level intervention and prevention efforts also will be offered.

I. CHILD PROTECTION, FOSTER CARE, AND PARENTAL RIGHTS TERMINATION

The modern history of the child protection system (CPS) is often dated as beginning with the 1962 landmark paper by Kempe and colleagues, "The Battered Child Syndrome."[5] In the aftermath of its publication, all states passed laws mandating designated professionals, such as physicians, teachers, nurses, police, psychologists, and social workers, to report "suspected" child maltreatment. Thus was born the child protective agencies known by various initials and acronyms in different states. A brief outline of the relevant federal legislation provides context.

The 1974 Child Abuse Prevention and Treatment Act (CAPTA) was the first federal legislation to address child abuse and neglect.[6] CAPTA provided funding to states for child protection services.[7] Through the 1970s the foster care population grew dramatically and there was concern that large numbers of children were languishing in foster care without being returned to their homes nor adopted into other permanent homes. In an effort to address the expanding foster care population, the 1980 Adoption Assistance and Child Welfare Act (AACWA) required states to make "reasonable efforts" to prevent or eliminate the need for removal of

children from their homes and to make possible their return to their homes.[8] However, as discussed in greater detail below, the foster care population grew even more rapidly through the 1980s. In the 1970s, and accelerating into the 1980s, there was an increasing concentration of impoverished African Americans in U.S. urban centers.[9] Critics of the AACWA argued that the "reasonable efforts" requirement led to children remaining in unsafe homes, prolonged periods of foster care while deficient parents were receiving services, and delays in achieving permanent placement through PRT and adoption.[10]

Ideally foster care provides a temporary placement in a family environment for children exposed to abuse or neglect. The parents (or other caregivers) facing allegations receive remedial services during the period of foster placement designed to eliminate the risks of abuse or neglect. The goal of the family court in overseeing the CPS, and the use of foster care placements, is to ensure permanent placements for children. That is, if it is determined that the children cannot be returned to their families ("reunification") then an alternative permanent home is to be sought through PRT and adoption.

In response to the alleged deficiencies of the AACWA, the Adoption and Safe Families Act of 1997 (ASFA) seeks to address the problems plaguing the CPS by promoting the adoption of children in foster care, primarily through expediting termination of parental rights and allocating financial incentives to the states for arranging adoptions.[11] Thus ASFA provisions, such as requiring states to file a petition to terminate parental rights when a child has been in foster care for fifteen of the most recent twenty-two months, adoption incentive payments, and cross-jurisdictional placement options, amount to a retreat from reasonable efforts to prevent foster care and facilitate reunification. In effect, as the foster care system came to service a more heavily African American population, the service provision became more punitive and coercive.[12]

II. AFRICAN AMERICAN FAMILIES AND THE CHILD PROTECTIVE SYSTEM

Many investigators have noted the overrepresentation of African American children in the child protection and foster care systems.[13] However, data indicate that the rates of child maltreatment among blacks are no higher than the rates among whites.[14] There are multiple decision points in the CPS that may be contributing to the overrepresentation of blacks. In addressing this question Roberts cites several relevant sources.[15] The overrepresentation of African Americans among the poor contributes to blacks' overrepresentation in the CPS. With poverty there are increased levels of stress, parental poverty can be mistaken for neglect, and the poor are subject to greater surveillance by authorities. In addition, and especially relevant, the black poor are more likely to live in neighborhoods with high concentrations of poverty as compared with the white poor.[16] A U.S. Department of Health and Human Services report indicates that African American children, when compared to white children, are more likely to be placed in foster care than to receive in-home services, even when controlling for characteristics of the children and types of problems.[17] Neighborhoods with concentrated poverty are associated with greater stressors and limited resources as compared to family poverty among communities of means (discussed further below). Further, substantiation of abuse is associated with neighborhoods characterized by high concentrations of poverty.[18] Roberts also notes that blacks may be more vulnerable to CPS sanctions because African Americans are less likely to defend themselves with attorneys. In addition, Roberts cites data[19] noting that the magnitude of overrepresentation, more than 100 percent in Illinois and New Jersey and approaching 700 percent in Minnesota, indicates racial bias in decision making.[20] Further, child protective service decision making invites racial and other types of bias because of the common ambiguity and discretion in identifying neglect and risks of abuse.[21]

Along with the overrepresentation of African American children in the CPS, data indicate that black children's course through the CPS is typically quite different from that of white children. While PRT is an end point, it is not the only one. Some children are returned to their families after a period of foster care placement, some children are adopted, and still other children languish in the foster care system until they reach the age of majority. Examination of child maltreatment, foster care, and adoption rates helps to clarify processes involved in PRT among African American families. Over the last two decades, changes in child protection legislation have achieved little with respect to reducing the number of children in foster care nationwide. Estimates suggest the number of children in foster care recently declined from 581,000 in 1999 to 517,000 in 2004.[22] When examined within the context of the past two decades, the decline is not very significant. Following the passage of AACWA,[23] the foster care population decreased from 303,443 in 1980 to 276,266 by 1985.[24] However, as noted above, the late 1980s witnessed a dramatic growth in the foster care population. National estimates of the foster care population from 1980 to 1994 reveal a 65 percent increase, beginning with 300,428 children in 1987 and rising to 405,473 in 1990 and 465,820 by 1994.

FIGURE **13.1 Trends in Foster Care and Adoption by Race/Ethnicity, FY 2004**

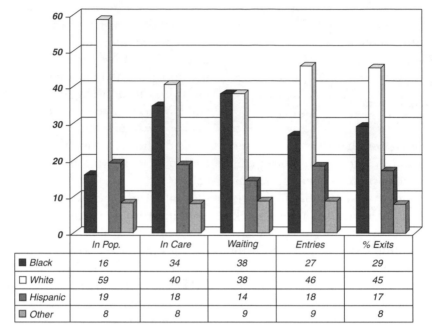

	In Pop.	In Care	Waiting	Entries	% Exits
■ Black	16	34	38	27	29
□ White	59	40	38	46	45
■ Hispanic	19	18	14	18	17
■ Other	8	8	9	9	8

Source: Adoption and Foster Care Analysis and Reporting System (AFCARS) data submitted for FY 2004, 10/01/03 through 9/30/04. "In Pop." represents the percentage of youth by race/ethnicity in population based on U.S. Census data for 2000. "In Care" reflects an estimated percentage of children in foster care on the last day of the year. "Waiting" reflects an estimated percentage of children who were waiting to be adopted on the last day of the year. Children waiting to be adopted include children with the goal of adoption and/or whose parents' parental rights have been terminated. "Entries" reflects the estimated percentage of children who entered foster care during the year. "Exits" represents the estimated percentage of children who exited foster care during the year.

Figure 13.1 presents data describing the current foster care population, indicating the percentage of children (by ethnic group) in the total population, in foster care, and awaiting adoption (those whose legal ties to their parents have been severed along with those children for whom adoption is the designated case goal), as well as entries and exits from foster care. black children consistently represent between 35 and 40 percent of the foster care population despite constituting only 12 to 17 percent of the nation's youth.[25] Conversely, white youth are 59 percent of the youth population but 34 to 39 percent of the foster care population. Hispanic youth representation in the foster care popula-

tion is consistent with Hispanics' proportion in the population at large (about 18 percent). Similarly, all other children, including those identified as Asian, Hawaiian, American Indian, Alaskan Native, or mixed race, represent 8 percent of American youth and between 3 and 9 percent of children in foster care.[26]

Among foster care children awaiting adoption, the overrepresentation of black children is more evident.[27] Though data indicate the number of children awaiting adoption has declined from 127,000 in 1999 to 118,000 in 2004,[28] for black male children over the age of six adoption prospects are quite limited.[29] In 2004, black and white children each accounted for 38 percent of those awaiting adoption, compared to Hispanic children, who were 14 percent of those awaiting adoption. Children described as "other" represented 9 percent of those awaiting adoption.[30] Thus when viewing the proportion of children by ethnic group in the population versus in foster care versus awaiting adoption, the proportion of black children increases dramatically while the proportion of white children decreases. The proportions for Hispanic and "other" children are consistent with their representation in the population. This pattern suggests that at various decision points, black children become more deeply involved in the CPS while the proportional involvement of white children is reduced.

The number of children exiting foster care increased from roughly 240,000 in 1999 to 283,000 in 2004.[31] However, these data fail to indicate how many of the children exited for adoption as opposed to reunification, nor how many later reenter foster care. Guggenheim and others have found that the number of children exiting foster care has not increased at the same rate of those entering the system.[32] The most common method of foster care exodus, reunification with parents or principal caregiver, witnessed a decline over the last decade from 66.2 percent of exits in 1994 to 55 percent in 2004. While adoption rates have remained fairly consistent, reflecting 16 to 19 percent of foster care exits over the last five years (1999–2004), this is a significant increase from national estimates throughout the early 1990s, where only 8 to 9 percent of foster care exits were attributable to adoptions. Emancipation rates have remained constant over the last decade, representing roughly 7 percent of all foster care exits.[33] Of the 52,000 children adopted from the public foster care system in 2004, white children accounted for 42 percent, while black children were 32 percent, Hispanic children 17 percent,

and all other youth 7 percent. Thus available data indicate that roughly 48 to 50 percent of children awaiting adoption still have not been adopted after three years in continuous care.[34]

While it has been reported that Asian American, American Indian/Alaska Native, and African American children have higher rates of victimization than white and Hispanic youth,[35] many researchers indicate there is little difference in the actual incidence of child abuse or neglect among ethnic groups.[36] Thus some combination of socioeconomic factors, disparate reporting and service delivery, and racial bias contributes to the over-representation of African Americans.[37] Additional studies suggest that race influences which harms to children are labeled as child abuse or neglect, as doctors often grant white parents greater latitude when determining symptoms that indicate abuse.[38] Still others identify how American law and legal processes have been consistent in singling out minorities, particularly people of African descent, as the primary group to be subjected to continual control.[39]

From 1995 to 2004, between 15 and 21 percent of designated child victims were placed in foster care.[40] Sixty to 66 percent of children placed in foster care are victims of neglect, 15 to 17 percent are multiple maltreatment victims (see the next section), and 10 to 13 percent are victims of physical abuse. Children with certain characteristics—prior victimization, being under four years of age, reported disabilities, being a victim of multiple maltreatment, and being nonwhite—were more likely to be placed in foster care than children without these characteristics.[41] Thus, cumulatively, data indicate that while black children are more likely to be placed in foster care, they are also subject to longer stays in foster care and are less likely to exit with permanent placements.

III. MODELS OF CHILD MALTREATMENT

Child maltreatment (CM) covers a wide array of behaviors and concerns. Most immediately, there is the concern of physical abuse and neglect, but also there are sexual abuse and emotional abuse as well as various other types of neglect, such as medical and educational.[42] In many cases of CM there is evidence of the co-occurrence of several types of maltreatment. CM has psychological, social, medical, and legal aspects. Most professionals in the field recognize that maltreatment is multidetermined. Different investigators and commentators have offered various models of CM. Models are useful in illustrating certain cases of CM and also in providing direction for further research and policy initiatives. Melton and colleagues identified the psychodynamic, social-learning, and sociological models.[43] The psychodynamic model views child maltreatment as a consequence of psychological disturbance or pathology on the part of the perpetrator. Thus there is a focus on the history, traits (anger, rigidity, impulsivity), substance abuse, or psychiatric impairment (diagnosis, intellectual deficit) of the abuser. The psychodynamic model suggests individual mental health treatment as an intervention. The social-learning model portrays CM as stemming from a lack of knowledge of child development and child rearing. In this model the offending adult is regarded as being inadequately prepared rather than disturbed. The social-learning model focuses on the parent's inappropriate expectations given the child's developmental level (such as expectations related to bowel and bladder control, or care of a younger sibling), or the caregiver's overreliance on corporal punishments for discipline and ignorance of alternatives (such as reward, monitoring, routine, and modeling). Thus the social-

learning model suggests parent training and skill enhancement interventions. The sociological model sees CM as a social problem reflective of differential stress exposure, unequal distribution of resources, and the low status of children (and women) in our society. Adherents to the sociological model point out that the poor have more stress in their lives and fewer resources to cope with that stress, which results in increased likelihood of abuse to low-status members among the poor (children and women). The sociological model suggests community-based interventions and primary prevention efforts.

A fourth model is the two-variable stress-resiliency model. This model suggests that increased stress requires adaptations and accommodations by individuals, families, and communities. A combination of high stress and low resiliency will result in increased vulnerability. CM occurs when those who are more vulnerable fail to adapt, and break under the burden of increased stress. CM is only one type of break; there could also be disabling substance abuse, psychiatric or health impairment, domestic violence, or family abandonment, which can in turn compound and exacerbate the stress. Apparently certain individuals have increased vulnerability and others have more resilience. One advantage of this model is that it can recognize racial and socioeconomic stress while acknowledging that everyone so exposed does not succumb.[44]

Garrison, in a recent discussion of foster care and PRT, advocates for a public health model of CM.[45] Garrison reviews the two waves of child protection reform that occurred in the past generation and argues that they were flawed in their conception of the CM problem. According to her analysis, the early impetus for reform leading to the 1980 AACWA was based on an anti-authoritarian stance toward the CPS. The ideal was that readily available, limited services (such as child care, housing, and financial support), typically provided without child removal, could resolve CM complaints. Garrison characterized this as based on an "acute care" model of CM. However, the CM problem grew tremendously during the 1980s, as noted above. According to Garrison, the subsequent and less optimistic reform wave that followed culminated with the 1997 ASFA. ASFA relied on private "market" mechanisms (that is, a demand for adoptable children) to remedy the problem of children needing permanent homes.[46] According to Garrison, assumptions underlying ASFA are also reliant on the "acute care" concept of CM, erroneously suggesting that the residual effects of maltreatment and child removal will be remedied by adoption placement.[47]

Garrison asserts that the public health model clarifies the nature and gravity of CM. It fosters a "fact-based," nonpolitical view of CM that defines it as a disease to be controlled and combated. Also, Garrison argues that a public health perspective offers robust empirical methods to be utilized in analysis, research, and intervention planning. Garrison suggests that the public health model brings into focus the enormous human and economic costs associated with CM, which are typically underestimated in the "acute care" concept of CM.[48] Garrison points out that clarification of these costs (and the requisite cost-benefit analysis) is essential for a persuasive argument for the type of investment necessary for effective reform.

Garrison presents a comprehensive public health view of CM, citing data from U.S. and international sources. She also recognizes the lack of evidence-based data to guide placement decisions and treatment interventions, and she underlines the need for further rigorous research efforts. However, Garrison states that much is known about CM from a public health perspective, noting that the "environmental conditions that promote CM have been charted in detail. . . ."[49] Citing multiple data sources, Garrison explains that all forms of CM, and especially neglect, are strongly associated with poverty. Further, extreme poverty is associated with extreme abuse and neglect. Garrison elaborates on the public health epidemiology of CM, detailing the other relevant risk factors identified in the research literature, such as substance abuse, mental illness, domestic violence, single and adolescent parenthood, and neighborhood characteristics. Garrison notes that while there are obstacles, targeting these risk factors—which commonly cluster together—can result not only in reductions in CM but also in reductions in a host of associated adverse residual effects. Garrison cites well-designed early childhood education programs and cost-effective substance abuse interventions for mothers as examples of effective public health initiatives that reduced child maltreatment and associated harm.

Twenty years ago in *The Truly Disadvantaged*, Wilson described and documented the emerging demographic configurations that came to characterize urban life for many African Americans. In so doing he argued that the changes were attributable neither to deficient family structure and values (as alleged by conservatives) nor simply to current racism (as charged by some critics).[50] Rather, Wilson explained that it was African Americans' concentration in certain industrial sectors such as automobile production, steel, and rubber, rather than racist social policy, that led to substantial increases in (male) unemployment into the 1980s. Further, Wilson detailed the exodus of the black middle-class and stable working-class elements from inner-city "ghetto" neighborhoods. An increasing proportion of those left behind came to constitute an "underclass," disadvantaged and socially disconnected from the larger U.S. economy and society. These demographic changes resulted in neighborhoods with concentrated poverty, increased joblessness, increased female-headed households, decreased academic achievement, increased violent crime including homicides, and associated social problems. The resulting "social dislocations" and "pathologies," to use Wilson's terms, are largely consistent with the public health risk factors for CM delineated above.[51]

An additional model of child maltreatment is the human rights model. This model is seen in the work of Penn and Coverdale, who offer a human rights perspective on the transracial adoption controversy.[52] Penn and Coverdale cite the 1989 United Nations Convention on the Rights of the Child as a document that provides clarity regarding states' obligations with regard to child protection and placement. They point out that the human rights perspective clarifies that concerns about African American children being separated from their families is not an appeal for race-based preferences but rather consistent with internationally recognized rights. Article 20, clause 3 of the convention, holds: ". . . when considering solutions [when children have been removed from their family environment], due regard should be paid to the desirability of continuity in the child's upbringing and to the child's ethnic, religious, cultural and linguistic background."[53] In addition, Penn and Coverdale suggest that the government policy that fosters and/or neglects increasing incarceration, joblessness, and educational failure, which disproportionately and adversely impact African American families, is contrary to the convention's mandate that nations provide the means whereby all parents may fulfill their responsibilities.[54] The human rights model is also informed by other sources.

The 1978 U.S. Indian Child Welfare Act embraced a human rights focus in its emphasis on the preservation of native tribes' unique culture, heritage, and traditions. The act included several provisions designed to maintain cultural continuity for native children as well as the recognition of tribal jurisdiction regarding child custody. Some scholars have argued that the act's provisions have practical value for African Americans.[55] Implicit in the human rights model is the recognition that child placement policy involves not only "best interest" considerations for individual children but also the potential for domination of minority ethnic, religious, or cultural groups by larger or more powerful groups. Thus the human rights model emphasizes the role of government responsibility and liability in CM policy.

Perry also is critical of a narrow reading of the child's "best interest" in the context of child placement decisions. Perry contrasts "liberal colorblind individualism" with "color and community consciousness" as opposing views regarding the role of race in the analysis of child placement (and other legal) considerations.[56] According to Perry, the ideal of color blindness actually converges, in many respects, with the racially conservative politics that emerged in the 1980s and 1990s. That is, opponents of affirmative action remedies have invoked the ideal of color blindness in their opposition to government programs to protect and enhance opportunities for blacks as minorities. Similarly, the ideal of individualism, while heralded as integral to America's vision of itself, is contrary to the fact that group membership determines much about our fate. Historically and currently, African Americans suffer discrimination based on their group identity rather than their individual characteristics. Thus Perry clarifies that African Americans experience racial discrimination as individuals and concurrently are subject to adverse circumstances secondary to the subjugation of blacks as a group.

IV. PARENTAL RIGHTS TERMINATION LITIGATION AND BLACK FAMILIES: THE PSYCHOLEGAL INTERFACE

As noted above, PRT is a potential end point of a process that typically begins with an allegation of child abuse or neglect. However, the vast majority of child maltreatment allegations do not proceed to PRT litigation. As reported above, most allegations are not substantiated. Even where there is substantiation, the child may remain in the home while the family is provided services, or the child may be placed with another family member. In other cases a period of foster care will be followed by a return to the family. Generally, states are obliged to provide services to remedy the circumstances that led to the child removal. However, ASFA directs the states to file PRT complaints when children have been in foster care for fifteen of the past twenty-two months.[57] Psychological findings are often central in PRT litigation. Both the counsel for the state child protective agency and the counsel for the respondent parent commonly engage psychologists and other experts to conduct examinations and present testimony relevant to the legal considerations in PRT proceedings. What follows is a presentation of several commonly encountered psychological issues in PRT litigation involving black families. The focus of the presentation is on the psychologist's findings in response to the allegations in the PRT complaint. In addition, the presentation illustrates how the concepts of abuse, neglect, and psychological impairment are so ambiguous that the CPS can

easily find psychologists to argue that each charged parent is impaired in some way. Yet in many cases the allegations against the parent in the PRT complaint lack merit and/or ignore other important psychological considerations related to the child's well-being. There is no claim that the issues presented here are representative of PRT cases; rather, the material illustrates common disputes.

The legal criteria for a PRT ruling are state-specific; that is, there are jurisdiction-specific statutes and/or case law rulings that outline the standards to apply. While variation among the states exists, there are typically two main elements. One is a finding that the parental relationship exposes the child to harm ("parental unfitness" and abandonment) and the other is that termination of parental rights is in the best interest of the child. The cases presented below are from New Jersey, where the following four-point standard has been established:[58]

1. The child's safety, health, and development have been or will continue to be endangered by the parental relationship;
2. The parent is unwilling or unable to eliminate the harm facing the child or is unwilling or unable to provide a safe and stable home for the child and the delay of permanent placement will add to the harm. Such harm may include evidence that separating the child from his foster parents would cause serious and enduring emotional or psychological harm to the child;
3. The [child protective agency] has made diligent efforts to provide services to help the parent correct the circumstances which led to the child's placement outside the home and the court has considered alternatives to termination of parental rights; and
4. Termination will not do more harm than good.

Three frequently contested psychological issues (mental state or psychiatric condition, parenting competence, and attachment and "bonding") are presented and illustrated. While the following presentation focuses on single issues, typically within each case there are disputes involving several psychological issues.

A. Mental State or Psychiatric Condition

Psychiatric symptoms may impair a parent's ability to provide a safe and stable home for a child. However, such determination warrants careful consideration of the alleged impairment. In one instance, a state psychologist presented testimony that the psychological test scores of an eighteen-year-old black mother of a two-year-old child indicated she had a narcissistic personality disorder. This was based on the results of the MCMI-III test.[59] However, the opposing expert (Matthew B. Johnson) pointed out that the respondent's score elevations were on "personality pattern" scales rather than the more severe "pathology or syndrome" scales; thus the results, if valid, were descriptive of her personality rather than a diagnosis. Also, the mother had been tested when she was seventeen and the test was normed on a population age eighteen and above. The PRT complaint was eventually dismissed and the child was placed in the mother's custody. In this case the use of the test instrument was questionable in and of itself, and its use with this particular client given her age was inappropriate. In addition, the relevance of the findings was inflated by the state psychologist to convey the impression of a serious pathological condition.

In another case, an infant was removed from a black mother at birth due largely to the mother's diagnosis of schizophrenia, paranoid type. She had older children being cared for by others or in institutions. There were no family members willing to care for the child in question, nor was the child's father prepared to raise the child. While her psychiatric condition was stable enough that she could live independently, she had residual symptoms that interfered with her having a viable social support system to assist in the care of the child. Given her lack of social support coupled with her psychiatric condition, it was Johnson's opinion that she did not present a viable permanent placement option for the child. The diagnosis of schizophrenia, paranoid type, in and of itself was not sufficient to rule out the parent as a placement option. However, the lack of a viable system of social support, when considered in the context of her diagnosis, indicated a high-risk placement option.

B. Parenting Competence

In some cases it is alleged that the parent exhibits parenting skill deficits that are relevant to "best interests" considerations in determining whether to terminate parental rights. In one case, the state filed a PRT complaint against a father alleging he had "failed . . . to maintain contact with and plan for the future [of twin infants]." The twins were the product of an extramarital affair of the father's. The twins were removed from their mother at birth secondary to her history of chronic mental illness and failure to maintain a stable home that had resulted in the prior removal of other children. However, the father's plan was to raise the twins in his home with his wife and his other child. Contrary to the state's allegation, the father had visited regularly with the twins. At trial the state psychologist presented his findings from the Child Abuse Potential (CAP) Inventory, noting the father's elevated score on one of the six individual factor scores.[60] However, the manual for the CAP Inventory states explicitly that "only the total 77 item abuse scale score, not individual factor scores, should be employed for the screening of physical child abusers."[61] In addition, the CAP Inventory manual also points out that the test discriminates best when the rate of abuse (base rate) in the subject population is 50 percent. Since there were no allegations that the father had ever been a child abuser, the use of the test in his examination was suspect and likely to yield a false positive result. The attorney for the father brought out these points when cross-examining the state psychologist. However, the father's parental rights to the twins were terminated. In this instance there was inappropriate use of a test as well as inappropriate interpretation of findings. The father had a plan to raise the children, and his wife appeared and testified that she was willing to raise the twins in her home. The father was a fit and capable parent currently raising another child in his home with his wife.

In another case, the state counsel asserted, while cross-examining Johnson, that a toddler had speech and language deficits and the mother was not capable of ensuring that the child would receive adequate services. However, it turned out that the speech and language consultant had been unaware that the child had been in foster care with a Haitian family that spoke patois. The child was actually developing bilingual skills. The child was eventually returned to the care of his mother. In this circumstance, the state attorney was either being deceptive or ignorant of the relevant facts of the child's case by asserting that the child had developmental language delays when actually the child's English-language exposure had been limited. That is, there was an exaggeration of the child's needs to suggest that the mother was not capable of attending to those needs.

C. "Bonding" and Attachment

In some cases the state will argue that the child has developed an attachment or "bond" to a foster parent such that removing the child from the foster parent will result in serious emotional harm to the child, as noted in the second of New Jersey's four criteria for parental rights termination. There is some controversy regarding the use of attachment and bonding theories in this context, and it requires careful clinical assessment.[62] In one case, PRT complaints were filed against a West African immigrant father and the child's African American mother. The parents were raising the child together in their home. A local hospital reported the family to the child protection authorities following a series of injuries to the child, which medical professionals determined was "possible child abuse." Johnson made it clear to the father's attorney that he could not offer an opinion on the cause or nature of the injuries in question.[63] However, part of the state's case involved the allegation that the child had no "bond" or substantial relationship with either parent after the prolonged period of foster placement that preceded the parental rights termination trial. At trial Johnson testified, based on his examination, observation, and review of records, that the child was attached primarily to the father. It was pointed out that the agency's own records for the prior year included multiple notations describing the child's affection for and expressed desire to see his father, as reported by the foster mother. Just four months prior to the termination hearing, the records stated, the child "wakes up [at night] crying for his father and when he does she [the foster mother] goes to his room and pick [sic] him up and cuddle him and tell him that he will see his father soon." The examiner also testified that the state psychologist's characterization of the father as "tall, angry and edgy" was distorted. If the father appeared angry and edgy, it was likely due to the issues at stake in the examination. The judge terminated the father's parental ties to his son.[64] In this case the psychologist for the state (and the court) ignored the compelling evidence in the state's own records that the child was attached to his father and suffering emotional pain from the separation from his father. Also, the state psychologist's characterization of the father as "angry" and "edgy," without consideration of the context of the examination, lent itself to a racial stereotype of the angry black man for this African immigrant father with a thick accent.

In another case, the appellate court reversed a trial court termination ruling and ordered further examinations focused on three preadolescent, African American children and their attachment to their father. The appellate court ruled that the state had failed to prove that termination would not result in more harm than good, the fourth point of the standard. The father and his wife had more than a dozen children and, in addition to the three children named in the complaint, there were other minor children in long-term foster care. The father was employed full time and the family had a six-bedroom apartment in a public housing project. The mother had a chronic, recurrent psychiatric disturbance that frequently required hospitalization. The allegations against the father were limited to neglect; that is, one of the children was falling asleep in school, which triggered an investigation. It was determined that the children were sleeping on mattresses on the floor. The father initially refused to cooperate with the agency, and when threatened with child removal, he signed a "voluntary" placement agreement. Thereafter he found it impossible to have the children

returned to his care. At an initial examination of the father with the three children, the older two children stated explicitly that they wanted to return to their parents' home. The youngest child, who was female, stated that she wanted to be able to visit with her father, though she was apparently happy and adjusting well in her proposed adoptive home. Subsequently, a joint interview was conducted with both parents at their home. The mother's psychiatric symptoms were in remission; however, the parents argued with each other and could not agree on a plan to monitor and care for the three children whose placement was in question. It was reported by Johnson that as a result of the parents' lack of coordinated planning and cooperation with each other, coupled with the mother's psychiatric condition, returning the three children to the care of the parents was not recommended at that point. Testimony from Johnson was requested at trial to counter a state psychologist who recommended "adoption by an African American family with similar skin coloring to [the two male children]," in spite of both children explicitly stating to the state psychologist that they did not want to be adopted and they wanted to return to their parents' care. Johnson testified that the state psychologist's recommendation lacked credibility and demonstrated a lack of sensitivity and knowledge of African American family life. It was recommended that the father's parental rights be maintained so that he could resume regular visits with the two older children. It was also recommended that the female child be provided visits with her father pending further examination of the proposed adoptive home. The judge terminated the father's parental rights to the youngest (female) child. The case regarding the father's parental ties to the two older (male) children was dismissed and they were to remain in foster care with regular visits with their parents. In this case the state psychologist dismissed and/or ignored the clear evidence of the boys' enduring attachment to their father and recommended adoption. The prospects for successful adoptive placement for these boys was remote given their age, ethnic group, gender, and expressed desire to return to their parents' care. As children approach adolescence, their desires with regard to placement warrant substantial consideration to prevent running away. In addition, the state psychologist harbored some uninformed notion that black children's identification with caregivers was dependent upon skin color matching. Another element in this case involved the father's reluctance to comply with the child protective agency and the agency's effort to coerce his compliance by removing the children.

Given the stakes in PRT proceedings—that is, the permanent loss of the parent-child relationship—each parent facing parental rights termination complaints deserves a rigorous defense of the allegations. Parents' custody of and companionship with their children is a fundamental, cherished right that is recognized universally. While it has been argued that parental rights should not infringe upon children's rights, foremost among children's rights is that their parents' rights are not violated. Vigilant protection of parents' rights in parental rights termination proceedings is an essential first step in protecting children's interests. Without such strict attention to parents' rights, children's interests are left to the whim of state attorneys and caseworkers. There is no question that child maltreatment is a serious matter that has devastating effects for black children and families. However, the child protection system often uses fears and sentiment generated by the highly publicized, rare cases of severe abuse to justify aggressive action in the more common neglect cases where there has been negligible harm.[65]

V. INTERVENTIONS AND INNOVATIONS

The ASFA adoption incentive payments, described as one of the "problematic aspects" of the federal legislation, are an appropriate starting point for the discussion of necessary reforms.[66] Once a child enters the child protective system the state has a financial interest in pursuing parental rights termination rather than family preservation or reunification. Thus decisions regarding the child's best interest are tainted by financial considerations.[67] In contrast, in child custody matters involving children whose parents are not poor, a prevailing principle is that money is not supposed to influence child placement decisions.

Even prior to the ASFA adoption incentive payments, the entire economic structure of the foster care system was based on monies paid for children placed in foster care without comparable investment in preventing child removals. Eichner pointed out, "In 2002, the federal government spent at least nine dollars on foster care and three more on adoption for every dollar spent to prevent foster care or speed reunification."[68] Fundamental reform in the financing of child protection efforts can provide the opportunity for advances in service delivery. The public health focus described above maps out the epidemiological landscape of child maltreatment. Substance abuse, mental illness, and domestic violence are major contributors. Eliminating barriers to effective, gender-specific, and culturally relevant interventions needs to be a priority of child protection policy. Research and development funding of treatment outcome studies, focused on harm reduction and prevention, can produce further effective innovations in mental health and social work practice.

Further, child maltreatment shares an epidemiological landscape with substance abuse, many forms of juvenile and adult offending, increased risk of incarceration, inadequate housing, limited educational achievement, high unemployment, poor health outcomes, impaired family functioning, and other social dislocations. Poverty in general, and concentrated neighborhood poverty especially, are highly correlated with these adverse environmental conditions for children and families. This recognition is spelled out in the work of Roberts, Garrison, Wilson, and others.[69] It is apparent that poverty is a cause and/or contributor to a host of social ills and adverse risk factors. Further, a public health cost-benefit analysis demonstrates that poverty adversely affects those living in poverty as well as the society at large. Social policy directed toward eradicating poverty and its adverse consequences, along with promoting the human commonwealth, is in order. With this recognition, genuine child protection advocacy can reduce harm to children. The fact that so many of these risk factors are concentrated among the poor presents a challenge and an opportunity to provide multitargeted interventions.[70]

VI. RACISM AND INCREASED RISK EXPOSURE

As noted above, Roberts described the racially discriminatory impact of the common punitive approach to child protection experienced by black families. She noted the increased risk exposure of black children and families associated with poverty and its correlates, as well as the damaging effects of racist influence in child welfare decision making. It is important to view child maltreatment and PRT in the context of broader forces adversely affecting African Americans. That is, as suggested above, racial discrimination in the child protection system is supported and abetted by racial discrimination in education, the criminal justice system, employment, and the allocation of resources in a range of areas. The deterioration of the social landscape of so many black urban communities, delineated by Wilson, facilitates the aggressive prosecutorial approach to child protection described by Roberts. Racism is not likely to go away, and people of African descent are faced with the continuing challenge of creating methods and structures to combat racism, protect ourselves and our children, and thrive. Among Roberts's contributions is articulating how child welfare intrusions in black families not only can be damaging to particular children and families but also have harmful effects on the black community at large, through perpetuating negative stereotypes, undermining parent-child bonds, and contributing (along with mass incarceration) to the depletion of social capital and the potential for enclaves of progressive opposition.

Unfortunately, in the context of the multiple critical issues facing the African American community, child welfare intrusion is not a high priority. Within the black community there is inadequate attention paid to child poverty and even less attention paid to the parents of poor children. As Roberts linked the harm to individual families to harm to the black community at large, black scholars and activists can link child protection reform to the agenda of critical issues facing the black community. African American families that are disrupted by the CPS are largely a neglected population. More often than not, parents in litigation with the CPS feel stigmatized and have few allies. They are typically poor and lack advocacy skills to negotiate the complex legal and social service bureaucracy in which they are caught. They are reliant on appointed counsel with overwhelming workloads. It is critical that these families no longer be marginalized but instead be organized into groups where they can support and advocate for one another. These parents, better than others, can identify their needs and lobby family courts and legislators. They can investigate the number and ethnic composition of the children in foster care locally and follow the outcomes of children following PRT. They can develop lists of competent legal and mental health professionals to provide services and expert testimony. They can build alliances with professional, civil rights, religious, and activist groups to advance an agenda for meaningful child protection reform.

VII. REFORM AND DEVELOPMENT

Program reform to reduce child maltreatment and aggressive child protection policy need to go beyond palliative services to support adaptation to adverse conditions.

That is, we do not advocate merely supporting the poor in their impoverished state. In combating child maltreatment it is valuable to envision conditions that facilitate optimal child development. The human rights model focuses attention on government responsibility to protect children, not only from their parents' failings but also from broader harmful social conditions. As Eichner points out, the care that children receive from their parents is intimately linked to state policies other than child protection.[71] Minimum-wage laws, union rights, protection from compulsory overtime, family leave, child care and after-school care subsidies, and early childhood education, as well as access to health care and adequate low-income housing, are all indicators of government support (or lack of) for children and families. We believe in and advocate combating CM through supporting and thus strengthening families. This will nurture networks of social support and community ties that will sustain stable, healthy environments for children.

14

The Law of Implicit Bias

Christine Jolls and Cass R. Sunstein

INTRODUCTION

Consider two pairs of problems:

1A. A regulatory agency is deciding whether to impose new restrictions on cloning mammals for use as food. Most people within the agency believe that the issue is an exceedingly difficult one, but in the end they support the restrictions on the basis of a study suggesting that cloned mammals are likely to prove unhealthy for human consumption. The study turns out to be based on palpable errors.

1B. A regulatory agency is deciding whether to impose new restrictions on cloning mammals for use as food. Most people within the agency believe that the issue is an exceedingly difficult one, but in the end they support the restrictions on the basis of a "gut feeling" that cloned

mammals are likely to be unhealthy to eat. It turns out that the "gut feeling," spurred by a widely publicized event appearing to establish serious risk, is impossible to support by reference to evidence.

2A. An employer is deciding whether to promote Jones or Smith to a supervisory position at its firm. Jones is white; Smith is African-American. The employer thinks that both employees are excellent, but it chooses Jones on the ground that employees and customers will be "more comfortable" with a white employee in the supervisory position.

2B. An employer is deciding whether to promote Jones or Smith to a supervisory position at its firm. Jones is white; Smith is African-American. The employer thinks that both employees are excellent, but it chooses Jones on the basis of a "gut feeling" that Jones would be better for the job. The employer is not able to explain the basis for this gut feeling; it simply thinks that "Jones is a better fit." The employer did not consciously think about racial is-

Editors' Note: This chapter first appeared in a symposium on behaviorial realism as Christine Jolls & Cass R. Sunstein, *The Law of Implicit Bias*, 94 CAL. L. REV. 969 (2006), reprinted by permission of the California Law Review, Inc.

sues in making this decision; but, in fact, Smith would have been chosen if both candidates had been white.

In case 1A, the agency is violating standard principles of administrative law. Its decision lacks a "rational connection between facts and judgment"[1] and, thus, is most unlikely to survive judicial review. In case 1B, the agency is in at least equal difficulty; administrative choices must receive support from relevant scientific evidence.[2]

The second pair of cases is analytically parallel. Case 2A involves a conscious and deliberative judgment that clearly runs afoul of antidiscrimination law.[3] Case 2B might well seem equally troublesome. But in fact it is not at all clear that Smith would be able to prevail in case 2B, at least if there is no general pattern of race-based decisionmaking by the employer. Smith will face a burden of proof that will be hard to surmount on the facts as stated.[4] And note that these conclusions apply even if the employer is (parallel to cases 1A and 1B) a government rather than a private actor; the administrative law and antidiscrimination law regimes treat "gut feelings" in quite different ways.

Case 2B is far from unrealistic in today's world, as the present Symposium makes clear. A growing body of evidence, summarized by Anthony Greenwald and Linda Hamilton Krieger,[5] suggests that the real world is probably full of such cases of "implicit," or unconscious, bias. This is likely to be true not only with respect to race, but also with respect to many other traits.[6]

Much evidence of these forms of implicit bias comes from the Implicit Association Test (IAT), which has been taken by large and diverse populations on the Internet and elsewhere.[7] The IAT asks individuals to perform the seemingly straightforward task of categorizing a series of words or pictures into groups. Two of the groups are racial or other categories, such as "black" and "white," and two of the groups are the categories "pleasant" and "unpleasant." In the version of the IAT designed to test for implicit racial bias, respondents are asked to press one key on the computer for either "black" or "unpleasant" words or pictures and a different key for either "white" or "pleasant" words or pictures (a stereotype-consistent pairing); in a separate round of the test, respondents are asked to press one key on the computer for either "black" or "pleasant" words or pictures and a different key for either "white" or "unpleasant" words or pictures (a stereotype-inconsistent pairing). Implicit bias against African-Americans is defined as faster responses when the "black" and "unpleasant" categories are paired than when the "black" and "pleasant" categories are paired. The IAT is rooted in the very simple hypothesis that people will find it easier to associate pleasant words with white faces and names than with African-American faces and names—and that the same pattern will be found for other traditionally disadvantaged groups.

In fact, implicit bias as measured by the IAT has proven to be extremely widespread. Most people tend to prefer white to African-American, young to old, and heterosexual to gay.[8] Strikingly, members of traditionally disadvantaged groups tend to show the same set of preferences. The only major exception is that African-Americans themselves are divided in their preferences; about equal proportions show an implicit preference for African-Americans and whites.[9] Note, however, that unlike whites, African-Americans taken as a whole do not show an implicit preference for members of their own group.[10]

It might not be so disturbing to find implicit bias in experimental settings if the results did not predict actual behavior, and in fact the relationship between IAT scores and behavior remains an active area of research.[11] But we know enough to know that some of the time, those who demonstrate implicit bias also manifest this bias in various forms of actual behavior. For example, there is strong evidence that scores on the IAT and similar tests are correlated with third parties' ratings of the degree of general friendliness individuals show to members of another race.[12] More particularly, "larger IAT effect scores predicted greater speaking time, more smiling, [and] more extemporaneous social comments" in interactions with whites as compared to African-Americans.[13] And it is reasonable to speculate that such uneasy interactions are associated with biased behavior. In the employment context in particular, even informal differences in treatment may have significant effects on employment outcomes, particularly in today's fluid workplaces.[14] If this is so, then the importance to legal policy is clear. If people are treated differently, and worse, because of their race or another protected trait, then the principle of antidiscrimination has been violated, even if the source of the differential treatment is implicit rather than conscious bias.[15]

It should not be controversial to suggest that in formulating and interpreting legal rules, legislatures and courts should pay close attention to the best available evidence about people's actual behavior—an approach this Symposium terms "behavioral realism."[16] Indeed, the influence of economic analysis of law stems largely from its careful emphasis on the behavioral effects of legal rules. The need to attend to good evidence, applied to the domain of civil rights, animates the work in this Symposium. In much the same spirit, work in behavioral law and economics has argued in favor of incorporating psychological insights about people's actual behavior across a range of domains.[17] We believe that there are productive links among all behavioral approaches to law,

and one of the goals of our discussion below is to call attention to some of those links. We devote special attention to the promise of "debiasing" actors through legal strategies that are designed to counteract biases of various sorts across a variety of domains.

Our discussion below comes in three parts. Part I explores two systems of cognitive operations—roughly, "intuitive" and "deliberative"—with the suggestion that the distinction between the two helps to illuminate legal responses to a wide range of behavioral problems, including those raised by the IAT. Part II investigates the possibility of using the law to "debias" people in order to reduce implicit bias; we develop several illustrations of such debiasing, as well as relating the general approach of debiasing both to work that follows in this Symposium and to work elsewhere in the legal literature. Part III investigates some of the normative issues that are raised when regulators attempt to respond, through "debiasing" or otherwise, to implicit bias.

I. SYSTEM I AND SYSTEM II

Implicit bias of the sort manifested on the IAT has not generally been grouped with the "heuristics and biases" uncovered by research in cognitive psychology and behavioral economics.[18] Thus far, the reception within law of the two areas of research has been largely independent. But we believe that legal responses to implicit bias are illuminatingly analyzed in terms that bring such bias in direct contact with cognitive psychology and behavioral economics. Most important, implicit bias—like many of the heuristics and biases emphasized elsewhere—tends to have an automatic character, in a way that bears importantly on its relationship to legal prohibitions.

In cognitive psychology and behavioral

economics, much attention has been devoted to heuristics, which are mental shortcuts or rules of thumb that function well in many settings but lead to systematic errors in others.[19] Consider, for instance, the well-known study involving people's judgments about a thirty-one-year-old woman, Linda, who was concerned with issues of social justice and discrimination in college. People tend to say that Linda was more likely to be a "feminist bank teller" than to be a "bank teller."[20] This judgment is patently illogical, for a superset cannot be smaller than a set within it. The source of the mistake is the representativeness heuristic, by which events are seen to be more likely if they "look like" certain causes.[21] In the case of Linda, the use of the representativeness heuristic leads to a mistake of elementary logic— the conclusion that characteristics X and Y are more likely to be present than characteristic X.

Research in cognitive psychology emphasizes that heuristics of this kind frequently work through a process of "attribute substitution," in which people answer a hard question by substituting an easier one.[22] For instance, people might resolve a question of probability not by investigating statistics but by asking whether a relevant incident comes easily to mind.[23] The same process is familiar in many contexts. Confronted with a difficult problem in constitutional law, people might respond by asking about the views of trusted specialists—as, for example, through the use of (say) the "Justice Scalia heuristic," by which some people might answer the difficult problem by following the views of Justice Scalia.

Often, of course, people deliberately choose to use a heuristic, believing that it will enable them to reach accurate results. But some of the most important heuristics have been connected to "dual process" approaches, which have recently received considerable attention in the psychology literature.[24] According to such approaches, people employ two cognitive systems. System I is rapid, intuitive, and error-prone; System II is more deliberative, calculative, slower, and often more likely to be error-free.[25] Much heuristic-based thinking is rooted in System I, but it may be overridden, under certain conditions, by System II.[26] Thus, for example, some people might make a rapid, intuitive judgment that a large German shepherd is likely to be vicious, but this judgment might be overcome after the dog's owner assures them that the dog is actually quite friendly. Most people would be reluctant to drink from a glass recently occupied by a cockroach; but it is possible (though far from certain) that they would be willing to do so after considering a reliable assurance that, because the cockroach had been sterilized by heat, the glass was not contaminated.[27] In a context of greater relevance to law, heuristic-driven fears about eating cloned animals or genetically modified food might be overcome on the basis of careful studies suggesting that the risk of harm is quite low.[28] Judgments about potentially harmful events are often founded in System I,[29] and System II sometimes supplies a corrective. In other cases, however, responses within the System I domain itself may supply correctives, as discussed at some length in Parts II and III below.

We believe that the problem of implicit bias is best understood in light of existing analyses of System I processes. Implicit bias is largely automatic; the characteristic in question (skin color, age, sexual orientation) operates so quickly, in the relevant tests, that people have no time to deliberate. It is for this reason that people are often surprised to find that they show implicit bias. Indeed, many people say in good faith that they are fully committed to an antidiscrimination principle with respect to the very trait against which they show a bias.[30] When people exhibit bias toward African-Americans, System II may of course be involved, as in case 2A above, but in a great many cases System I is the culprit. In case 2B above, the employer has no conscious awareness of the role race played in its decision to hire Jones over Smith; in fact, the employer might regard its decision as a "mistake," either factually or morally, if it were aware of the role race played.

In responding to implicit bias understood in this way, the legal system could emphasize System II; perhaps the law could produce or encourage a System II override of the System I impulse. But it is also possible that interventions within the domain of System I itself would be more efficacious—although also more normatively charged. We explore these possibilities in the next two Parts.[31]

II. ANTIDISCRIMINATION LAW AND "DEBIASING"

From the standpoint of a legal system that seeks to forbid differential treatment based on race and other protected traits, implicit bias presents obvious difficulties. In many cases entirely unaware of their bias and how it shapes their behavior, people will frequently fail to override their System I inclinations. Ordinary antidiscrimination law will often face grave difficulties in ferreting out implicit bias even when this bias produces unequal treatment.[32]

Of course, antidiscrimination law has long forbidden various forms of differential treatment on the basis of race and other protected traits. If, for example, a state official treats someone worse because of race, there might well be a violation of the Constitution as well as antidiscrimination statutes. Some of the hardest

cases present problems of proof: if there is no "smoking gun," how can bias be established? There are also vexing conceptual questions—explored below by Richard Banks, Jennifer Eberhardt, and Lee Ross.[33] What, exactly, does the category of unlawful "discrimination" include?[34] However the hardest questions are resolved, it seems clear that when System I is producing differential treatment, the legal system will often encounter unusually serious difficulties.

The parallels described above between implicit bias and the heuristics and biases emphasized by cognitive psychology and behavioral economics help to illuminate the primary approaches the law can adopt in response to unequal treatment stemming from implicit bias. In the domain of heuristics and biases, the law has now-familiar methods with which to respond.[35] In the context of "hindsight bias," for example, the law protects against error by broadly restricting adjudicators' ability to reconsider decisions from the perspective of hindsight.[36] Likewise, in the area of consumer behavior, many people believe that consumers show unrealistic optimism in evaluating potential product dangers, and the law may respond by imposing a range of restrictions on their choices.[37] These approaches attempt to *insulate* outcomes from the problems created by heuristics and biases, which themselves are taken as a given. Such insulating strategies are readily imaginable in the antidiscrimination law domain, as explored in Part II.A below.

Social scientists have also focused substantial attention on the possibility of *debiasing* in response to heuristics and biases.[38] The law might engage in such debiasing as well, seeking to reduce people's level of bias rather than to insulate outcomes from its effects.[39] If, for instance, consumers suffer from unrealistic optimism, then regulators might respond not by banning certain transactions or otherwise restricting consumer choice but instead by working directly on the underlying mistake.[40] They might, for example, enlist the availability heuristic, according to which people estimate the likelihood of events based on how easily they can imagine or recall examples of such events. Drawing on availability, regulators might then offer concrete examples of harm in order to help consumers understand risks more accurately. In the domain of smoking, an emphasis on specific instances of harm does appear to increase people's estimates of the likelihood of harm.[41] Attention to strategies for what we have elsewhere termed "debiasing through law" can help both to understand and to improve the legal system.[42] Note that many of these strategies—including the example just given of harnessing the availability heuristic—reflect System I rather than System II responses to System I problems. Debiasing strategies may also be applied in the domain of antidiscrimination law. We offer a series of illustrations—as well as relating the general approach of debiasing to work in this Symposium and elsewhere in the legal literature—in Parts II.B. and II.C below.

A. Insulation

When people show bias on the basis of race or another protected trait, the most conventional legal response is to attempt to insulate outcomes from the effects of such bias. Because, for instance, certain forms of employment behavior are unlawful under Title VII of the Civil Rights Act of 1964,[43] people will face monetary and other liability for engaging in such behavior. The desire to avoid such liability should, on the traditional view, deter the prohibited behavior. The point is particularly obvious with respect to consciously biased behavior of the sort at issue in case 2A above. There is no question that such behavior is squarely prohibited by antidiscrimination law, and—because the behavior is conscious—actors can be expected to respond to legal incentives not to engage in it, at least if people care enough about complying with the law (or at least if the penalties are stiff enough for those who are deterred only by actual sanctions). With respect to conscious bias, existing law attempts not to "debias" people—by reducing their conscious bias on the basis of race or another protected trait (although this may be a longer-term effect of the law)—but to insulate outcomes from the effects of such bias.[44]

A central problem in today's world, however, is the possibility that many people act on the basis of implicit bias. In response, legal rules might seek to reduce the likelihood that implicit bias will produce differential outcomes; but it would be quite difficult to conclude that current antidiscrimination law adequately achieves this goal.[45] As Linda Hamilton Krieger and Susan Fiske illustrate in their contribution to this Symposium, recent trends in antidiscrimination law seem to leave much implicitly biased behavior unpoliced in the employment context.[46] Krieger and Fiske suggest, for instance, that most courts have now made explicit that any facially neutral basis for an employer's decision will, if honestly although mistakenly or foolishly held, suffice to defeat a claim of intentional discrimination under Title VII.[47] As Krieger and Fiske powerfully demonstrate, an "honest" concern about an employee may very often be both "honest" and (unbeknownst to the decisionmaker) entirely a product of the employee's status as an African-American worker.[48]

It is important not to overstate the point. In discrete corners of existing antidiscrimination law and policy, it is possible to find promising attempts to insulate outcomes from the effects of implicit bias. Consider, for example, the affirmative action plans seen at all levels of government.[49] Such plans can illuminatingly be understood—in light of the analysis of Jerry Kang and Mahzarin Banaji in this Symposium[50]—as attempts by the state to correct for implicit bias, and thus to break the connection between such bias and outcomes.[51] If assessments of merit are inappropriately clouded by implicit bias, then a preference for those harmed by the biased assessments can help prevent the implicit bias from being translated into final outcomes.[52] If implicit bias typically leads an African-American employee to be incorrectly evaluated as worse than a white counterpart, an appropriately tailored affirmative action plan can counteract this mistake. And, likewise, antidiscrimination law's framework for assessing the legality of affirmative action plans[53] can be understood as enabling employers, educational institutions, and other organizations to use such plans to break the connection between implicit bias and outcomes.

B. "Direct Debiasing"

In addition to the "insulating" strategies discussed in Part II.A, it is often possible for government to target implicit bias more directly. If decisionmakers, wholly without their intent and indeed to their great chagrin, are acting on the basis of race or another protected trait, the law may be able to help them to correct their unintended actions. Debiasing solutions reflect this approach, and we now turn to those solutions. Below we develop several illustrations of debiasing through antidiscrimination law, as well as relating the general approach of debiasing through this body of law to work by others in this

Symposium and elsewhere in the legal literature.

In the most obvious form of debiasing, antidiscrimination law or policy either does or could act *directly* to reduce the level of people's implicit bias. Consider four examples of such "direct debiasing."

I. PROHIBITING CONSCIOUSLY BIASED DECISIONMAKING

The central focus of existing antidiscrimination law is on prohibiting consciously biased decisionmaking—a focus that has produced intense criticism from those interested in implicit bias.[54] Thus, it is easy to overlook the way in which existing antidiscrimination law, despite its focus on conscious bias, nonetheless has some effect on the level of implicit bias. A key causal path here is that the prohibition on consciously biased decisionmaking in workplaces, educational institutions, and membership organizations naturally tends to increase population diversity in these entities, and population diversity in turn has a significant effect on the level of implicit bias.[55] Put differently, while the prohibition on consciously biased behavior prompts a System II response to the System II phenomenon of conscious bias, it *also* yields a System I response to the System I phenomenon of implicit bias.

A significant body of social science evidence supports the conclusion that the presence of population diversity in an environment tends to reduce the level of implicit bias.[56] In one particularly striking study, the simple fact of administration of an in-person IAT by an African-American rather than a white experimenter significantly reduced the measured level of implicit bias.[57] Put differently, people's speed in characterizing black-unpleasant and white-pleasant pairs was closer to their speed in characterizing black-pleasant and white-unpleasant pairs when the African-American experimenter was present. Another study found that white test subjects paired with an African-American partner exhibited less implicit bias as measured by the IAT than white test subjects paired with a white partner; the same study found that within pairs involving an African-American partner, participants who were told they were to evaluate the African-American partner exhibited more implicit racial bias on the IAT than participants who were told they would be evaluated by the African-American partner.[58]

The effects of population diversity in the environment on the level of implicit bias may stem from the availability heuristic discussed in Part I; people often tend to assess probabilities based on whether a relevant incidence comes easily to mind. The effects of diversity may also reflect a more general role for the "affect heuristic," by which decisions are formed by reference to rapid, intuitive, affective judgments.[59]

It follows from these findings that simply by increasing the level of population diversity in workplaces, educational institutions, and other organizations, existing antidiscrimination law tends to reduce the level of implicit bias in these environments.[60] It bears emphasis in this connection that antidiscrimination law's clear rejection of explicit quotas counters the risk that this law might paradoxically *increase* implicit bias by means of overly heavy-handed diversity initiatives.[61] A closely related point is important: existing antidiscrimination law's effects on implicit bias through increased population diversity may be greatest in cases in which people's initial levels of implicit bias represent errors in judgment as opposed to statistically accurate perceptions. As discussed in Part I above, implicit bias, like the heuristics and biases emphasized in cognitive psychology and behavioral economics, may often reflect a genuine factual error; but of course this may not always be the case. If implicit bias corresponds to statistically accurate perceptions about the group in question, then the effects of population diversity may be muted by conflicting signals corresponding to the statistical reality.

2. PROHIBITING HOSTILE ENVIRONMENTS
Existing antidiscrimination law's prohibition on "hostile environments" is also likely to reduce the level of implicit bias in workplaces, educational institutions, and other organizations, here through its effect on the physical and sensory environment.[62] Again, what is generally viewed as a System II response to a System II problem is also a System I response to a System I problem.

Both evidence and common sense suggest that the presence of stereotypic images of a particular group tends to increase implicit bias.[63] A particularly striking study, outside the direct context of measures of implicit bias, found that men who had viewed a pornographic film just before being interviewed by a woman remembered little about the interviewer other than her physical characteristics—while men who had watched a regular film before the interview had meaningful recall of the content of the interview.[64] Mechanisms such as the availability and affect heuristics may again be in play.[65]

Under current antidiscrimination law, hostile environments featuring negative or demeaning depictions of protected groups (including, but not limited to, depictions in posters and other visual media) are generally unlawful in workplaces, educational institutions, and membership organizations.[66] In this way, current law governing sexual and racial harassment almost certainly produces some effect on the level of implicit bias in these institutions.[67] Compared to an environment in which such demeaning depictions were not unlawful, the current framework is likely to have a debiasing effect.

The prohibition on hostile environments may be felt throughout the organization, not merely by those directly targeted by the behavior. The law does not simply protect an immediate victim or set of victims from behavior deemed to be unlawful; instead the law tends to shape and affect the level of implicit bias of all those present. Of course, the law does not target people's beliefs as such; the point is that in proscribing certain conduct it undoubtedly has an *effect* on the level of implicit bias.[68]

3. THE REQUIREMENTS FOR EMPLOYERS SEEKING TO AVOID VICARIOUS LIABILITY

A third example of a direct debiasing mechanism involves potential reforms of the existing doctrine governing employers' vicarious liability for Title VII violations. At present that doctrine allows employers to defend against such liability on the basis of actions such as policy manuals or training videos disseminated in the workplace.[69]

Just as there are biasing effects (described just above) from negative imagery in the physical environment, there is strong evidence of debiasing effects from favorable portraiture or imagery—for instance, photographs of Tiger Woods—in the physical environment.[70] People show significantly less bias on the IAT directly after being exposed to Woods's picture—and also when tested again twenty-four hours after exposure to the picture.[71] Thus, in the real world, if portraiture in the workplace or elsewhere consistently reflects positive exemplars, it is likely—though certainly not guaranteed[72]—that those present will show less implicit bias, with likely mechanisms once more being the availability and affect heuristics.[73]

Note that in contrast to the experimental setting, positive exemplars in the workplace or elsewhere would be a recurrent rather than fleeting aspect of the individual's environment. And, parallel to the point above, the manner in which the display of positive exemplars occurs is important; if it is too heavy-handed, implicit bias may not decrease at all (and could even increase).[74]

In light of the available evidence, it may make a good deal of sense to treat an employer's positive effort to portray diversity as an express factor weighing against vicarious employer liability under Title VII. This approach would be parallel to the way that, under current Title VII doctrine, employers regularly defend against such liability on the basis of actions such as manuals or training videos disseminated in the workplace.[75] Our basic suggestion is that the existing Title VII approach to employers' vicarious liability might be extended beyond the discrete mechanisms (manuals, handbooks, videos, internet instructional programs) contemplated by present law—at least if doing so is consistent with the First Amendment (a question beyond the scope of the present discussion). While many of the mechanisms contemplated by present law governing vicarious liability are distinctly System II in character, the evidence suggests the important role of System I mechanisms in reducing implicit bias. The display of positive exemplars in the workplace may do far more to reduce implicit bias than yet another mandatory training session on workplace diversity.

4. AFFIRMATIVE ACTION POLICY

Existing affirmative action policy can also be understood as a form of direct debiasing. We have already noted that at all levels of government, officials have chosen to adopt affirmative action plans.[76] Because population diversity helps to reduce implicit bias through mechanisms including availability and affect (as described above), these government affirmative action plans may operate as a form of direct debiasing.[77]

To be sure, government affirmative action may fail to debias people—and might even increase implicit bias depending on a given plan's specific contours. Krieger, while noting how affirmative action may reduce bias,[78] has explored the possible negative effects of affirmative action on the level of bias with reference to the existing social science literature,[79] and the question of whether and when such negative effects will occur is obviously a crucial one. From the standpoint of reducing implicit bias, the good news is that the empirical studies discussed above highlight the potential of increased diversity to reduce implicit bias, while the evidence discussed by Krieger provides many insights on the specific types of affirmative action plans that do and do not appear to have negative effects on the level of bias.[80]

Our analysis of affirmative action here differs from the insulating analysis of affirmative action discussed in Part II.A above. In the conception here, government affirmative action does not act to insulate outcomes from the effects of implicit bias but, instead, acts directly to reduce such bias.[81] Of course, a government affirmative action plan may have both types of effects simultaneously.

*   *   *

Let us offer a concluding comment about all of the methods of direct debiasing explored in this section. Uniting all of these methods is the general idea that government does or might act against implicit bias using System I rather than System II mechanisms. The direct debiasing approaches described here thus mark a substantial departure from alternative efforts focused on "deliberate 'mental correction' that takes group status squarely into account."[82] We discuss normative issues arising out of this System I–System II difference in Part III below.

C. *"Indirect Debiasing"*

We now turn to mechanisms for what we call "indirect debiasing"—mechanisms

that receive sustained and insightful treatment in this Symposium in the work by Linda Hamilton Krieger and Susan Fiske and the work by Jerry Kang and Mahzarin Banaji.[83] Under indirect debiasing mechanisms, law prohibits or permits certain behavior and, as an indirect result of the prohibition or permission, creates incentives (or avoids disincentives) for regulated actors to adopt a debiasing approach. Indirect measures differ from direct measures in that it is no longer *necessarily* the case that in conforming to the specific dictates of law or policy, an actor will take steps that tend to reduce implicit bias. We consider two examples of indirect debiasing mechanisms below.

I. A PROHIBITION ON IMPLICITLY BIASED BEHAVIOR

Many scholars suggest that existing antidiscrimination law does little to police implicitly biased behavior.[84] A variety of proposed reforms, including those proposed by Krieger and Fiske in this Symposium, would broaden the reach of antidiscrimination law in addressing that behavior.[85]

It is obvious that if antidiscrimination law were to proscribe implicitly biased behavior in an effective manner, the law would encourage employers to adopt mechanisms to reduce implicit bias. (Obviously, the greater the translation of implicit bias to implicitly biased behavior, the greater the incentive for employers.) Following the discussion above, such mechanisms could include population diversity in the organization (Parts II.B.1 and II.B.4) and careful attention to depictions of protected groups in the physical environment (Parts II.B.2 and II.B.3). The discussion above described how those steps tend to reduce the level of implicit bias.

Alternatively, effective prohibition of implicitly biased behavior could encourage employers to adopt general decisionmaking structures or processes that reduce the intensity and frequency of implicit bias, implicitly biased behavior, or both. In the words of one commentator, steps may include "creating interdependence among in-group and out-group members, providing structure and guidance for appraisal and evaluation, and making decisionmakers accountable for their decisions."[86] It is unclear whether the mechanisms in play here will be predominantly System I or System II in nature. In a related vein, Susan Sturm has recounted how major accounting firm offices came to recognize and address sex-based disparities in assignments through the simple step of having the office managing partners list the nature and quantity of assignments to employees by sex.[87] (They were very surprised by the simple fact that there were significant disparities in assignments by sex.)

It is reasonable to suppose that steps such as these would reduce the underlying level of implicit bias as well as implicitly biased behavior; if so, then the law's inducement of employers to adopt such steps is an illustration of indirect debiasing. But such steps may in some cases simply insulate outcomes from the effects of an underlying level of implicit bias, in which case they are insulating rather than debiasing approaches within our framework.

We do not take a position here on the relative effectiveness of the many diverse means by which decisionmakers might seek to reduce implicit bias, implicitly biased behavior, or both in response to effective prohibition of implicitly biased behavior. It is uncertain whether approaches centered in System II would do much to reduce the phenomena; so too the potential limits on some of the System I approaches were explored in Part II.B above. Here we simply highlight the likelihood that much-discussed reform efforts with respect to policing implicitly biased

behavior would produce responses that, in turn, would tend to reduce the level of implicit bias.

2. THE LEGAL TREATMENT OF AFFIRMATIVE ACTION PLANS

A second example of an indirect debiasing mechanism is the legal treatment of affirmative action plans. We have emphasized that government might engage in direct debiasing through the adoption of such plans. It follows that in tolerating such plans (whether imposed by public or by private actors), the law is engaging in a form of indirect debiasing; that is, regulated actors are permitted to take steps that, in turn, tend to reduce implicit bias.

Kang and Banaji argue in this Symposium that a proper interpretation of the Equal Protection Clause and Title VII would allow employers to engage in affirmative action in order to produce a diverse workforce and thereby reduce implicit bias.[88] Importantly, Kang and Banaji explain that these forms of affirmative action are distinct from the "role model" arguments that have met with very mixed reception in the courts; in the debiasing approach, the emphasis is on the attitudes and behavior of those *outside*, rather than within, the traditionally underrepresented group.[89]

To clarify, the emphasis in the present discussion is on creating legal structures within which actors may choose to adopt debiasing mechanisms; by contrast, our discussion in Part II.B.4 above involved the affirmative choice by the state to adopt such mechanisms itself. In our terminology, the state engages in direct debiasing when it chooses to adopt an affirmative action plan that directly reduces implicit bias. By contrast, the state can be said to engage in indirect debiasing when it enables actors (including government itself) to adopt such affirmative action plans. In one case, the legal policy itself debiases, while in the other case the legal policy provides a space in which regulated actors may adopt debiasing mechanisms. Of course, insofar as government affirmative action plans are concerned, both types of debiasing will be in play.

D. Summary

In a variety of ways, existing law and policy seek to respond to the problem of implicit bias; imaginable reforms could do far more. Some strategies focus on insulating outcomes from the effects of implicit bias, which itself is taken largely as a given. But many actual and imaginable legal approaches instead act to reduce implicit bias. Such effects occur directly when the law requires steps that tend to reduce implicit bias (Part II.B). They occur indirectly when the law encourages or enables regulated actors to craft steps that, in turn, reduce implicit bias (Part II.C). Table [14.1] provides a summary of these alternative approaches.

Note that while our focus throughout is on the law's role in debiasing in response to implicit bias, private individuals may act, apart from law, in an effort to debias themselves.[90] Such steps represent non-legal alternatives to the problem of implicit bias. For purposes of legal scholarship, however, the central question, and the question emphasized in Table [14.1], is the role of law in combating implicit bias.

E. Debiasing of Whom?

In the various debiasing interventions discussed above, the presumed targets of the debiasing were actors at risk of displaying implicit bias or implicitly biased behavior toward members of a protected group. But the contribution of Gary Blasi and John Jost to this Symposium illustrates that such behavior is only one part of a complete analysis. As Blasi and Jost describe, those who are *victims* of implicitly biased behavior may often accept and even justify, rather than object to, such behavior—a manifestation of the broader phenomenon of "system justification."[91] In our view, Blasi and Jost should be understood to be supplementing a great deal of work that explores the general possibility of "adaptive preferences"—preferences that have adapted to existing injustice.[92]

In the employment context, for example, George Akerlof and Robert Dickens argue that employees may fail to confront the real magnitude of occupational risks, simply because it is so distressing to do so.[93] Speaking in broader terms, Amartya Sen has long emphasized that "deprived people . . . may even adjust their desires and expectations to what they unambitiously see as feasible."[94] Describing the hierarchical nature of pre-Revolutionary America, historian Gordon Wood writes that those "in lowly stations . . . developed what was called a 'down look,'" and "knew their place and willingly walked while gentlefolk rode; and as yet they seldom expressed any burning desire to change places with their betters."[95] In Wood's account, it is impossible to "comprehend the distinctiveness of that premodern world until we appreciate the extent to which many ordinary people still accepted their own lowliness."[96] If Blasi and Jost are right, then the modern world is not entirely different from its premodern counterpart.

In addition to the general evidence that they muster, the results of the IAT itself provide some support for system justification. As we noted above, a significant number of African-Americans show the same implicit racial bias on the IAT as whites.[97]

In this light, an important potential benefit of the debiasing approaches described above is that they may reduce levels of implicit bias in victims as well as perpetrators of implicitly biased behavior.

TABLE 14.1. Debiasing and Other Legal Responses to Implicit Bias

Type of Law		
Insulating Mechanisms: *Law or policy insulates outcomes from the effects of implicit bias*	Direct Debiasing Mechanisms: *Specific legal or policy dictates directly reduce implicit bias*	Indirect Debiasing Mechanisms: *Law encourages or enables regulated actors to take steps that reduce implicit bias*
1. Existing government affirmative action policies' overriding of "merit" evaluations that will tend to be implicitly biased (Part II.A)	1. Existing antidiscrimination law's prohibition on consciously biased behavior and resulting positive effect on workplace, educational, or other diversity (Part II.B.1)	1. Existing antidiscrimination law's prohibition on implicitly biased behavior (to the extent such a prohibition exists) or extension of existing antidiscrimination law's prohibitions to cover implicitly biased behavior (Part II.C.1)
2. Antidiscrimination law's framework for assessing the legality of affirmative action policies; these policies may override "merit" evaluations that will tend to be implicitly biased (Part II.A)	2. Existing antidiscrimination law's prohibition on hostile workplace, educational, or other environments (Part II.B.2)	2. Antidiscrimination law's framework for assessing the legality of affirmative action policies; these policies may encourage employers to adopt diversity-oriented hiring practices that reduce implicit bias (Part II.C.2)
	3. Extension of existing antidiscrimination law to require employers seeking to avoid vicarious liability to foster diversity in the physical environment (Part II.B.3)	
	4. Existing state affirmative action policies' positive effect on workplace, educational, or other diversity (Part II.B.4)	

If, for example, population diversity reduces implicit bias among those present—whatever their particular group—then such diversity should not only reduce implicitly biased behavior by perpetrators, but also increase resistance to such behavior by victims. Likewise, if avoiding sexually explicit visual displays in the workplace reduces levels of implicit sex stereotyping among women as well as men, then avoiding such displays may affect women's, as well as men's, behavior. Debiasing victims is undoubtedly a massive issue for law and policy. Our suggestion here is that many efforts to debias perpetrators help simultaneously to counteract the problem that Blasi and Jost explore in this Symposium.

III. NORMATIVE QUESTIONS

The central emphasis of Part II was the way in which antidiscrimination law and policy either does or could act to reduce implicit bias. While the analysis thus far has been purely descriptive, these sorts of debiasing strategies raise important normative questions. Consideration of those questions turns out to be importantly assisted by the parallels from Part I between implicit bias and the heuristics and biases emphasized in cognitive psychology and behavioral economics.

A. Thought Control?

No doubt the most obvious normative question raised by legal attempts to reduce people's implicit bias is whether such debiasing strategies amount to objectionable government "thought control." Like the other contributors to this Symposium, we believe that implicit bias is a serious problem and that it is exceedingly important for the law to attempt to address implicitly biased behavior. Often, as noted above, the most plausible responses to the problem of implicit bias will be legal steps that reduce such bias. But any use of the law to this end raises immediate normative questions. Is it appropriate for government to seek to shape how people think about their coworkers, fellow students, or other colleagues?

In many domains, some government control over what people think is simply unavoidable. Illustrations from current law, outside of the antidiscrimination context, are easily imagined. Whenever the government is so much as presenting information to people in response to factual misjudgments, government is making decisions about the manner of presentation, and these choices inevitably will affect how its citizens perceive the world around them.[98] But in the domain of civil rights addressed in this Symposium, it may be difficult to disentangle factual mistakes in judgment—where changing what people think is common and frequently unobjectionable in a wide range of domains[99]—from genuine preferences and values with which government may have no business

engaging. While government, on this view, may be entitled to discourage *conduct* based on such preferences and values, it might well seem illegitimate for it to seek to alter the preferences and values themselves.

We emphasize two main points here. *First*, it is plainly unobjectionable for government to act in response to factual errors; if people are simply mistaken as a matter of fact in associating a particular trait or attribute with members of one race, attempts at government correction do not raise especially profound issues. Information campaigns, either for risk regulation or for antidiscrimination law, are not objectionable in principle.[100] Public defenses of such campaigns may readily be made without affront to the "publicity condition," under which government must be able to make full disclosure of its actions to the citizenry.[101] And, our discussion in Part I suggested how implicit bias may sometimes be akin to a factual error. If implicit bias leads people to make such errors in assessing others, then government may legitimately seek to correct those errors.

Second, it is equally unobjectionable for government to ban biased *behavior*—whether consciously biased or implicitly biased—even if one effect of the ban is to alter people's values and preferences. Of course, this suggestion does not mean that government may use the force of law to target beliefs rather than behavior—even if the beliefs are targeted as a way of preventing behavior. Suppose, for example, that a workplace features demeaning pictures and jokes that are likely to increase both implicit bias and implicitly biased behavior against female employees or students. Suppose then that regulators attempt to eliminate those pictures and jokes because of their likely negative effects; perhaps regulators are aware that relevant conditions will likely activate

System I in a way that has concrete effects on women in the workplace. It is not unreasonable to see a problem with regulating speech (posters and jokes) on the ground that it is likely to lead to biased behavior.

There is, however, another possibility, rooted most obviously in our discussion of hostile environment liability in Part II.B.2 above. In some circumstances, workplace practices (such as posters and jokes) that are likely to produce biased behavior are themselves independently a form of unlawful discrimination. Suppose, for example, that demeaning pictures and jokes are pervasive in a certain workplace, in a way that creates a hostile environment for women. As described above, the pictures and jokes are then directly targeted as unlawful under existing antidiscrimination law. If there were a compelling concern with government "thought control" under this law, one would naturally expect successful challenges to it under the First Amendment, but in fact the standard view is that the legal prohibition here is consistent with First Amendment principles.[102] As this example illustrates, the law tolerates some government prohibitions on discriminatory behavior, even when they relate directly to speech, despite their potential effects on people's values and preferences.

We do not mean in this space to settle all of the dimensions of the "thought control" objection to government efforts to reduce implicit bias. But this much is clear. The normative problems are least severe when government is counteracting either factual mistakes or forms of discriminatory behavior such as hostile work environments; and if efforts to combat such forms of biased behavior also reduce implicit bias, no one should complain in light of existing law.

One final point. Many people are both surprised and embarrassed to find that they show implicit bias, and their bias conflicts with their explicit judgments and their moral commitments.[103] As we have suggested, it is likely to be the case that some people engage in biased behavior inadvertently or despite their own ideals. Such people want, in a sense, to be debiased, but their own conscious efforts are at most a partial help. Many normative objections to debiasing strategies, as forms of objectionable government meddling, are weakened to the extent that such strategies help people to remove implicit bias that they themselves reject on principle.

B. Heterogeneous Actors

Without more, the "thought control" concerns discussed above might, for some, argue in favor of insulating over debiasing strategies when insulating approaches—which do not seek to alter people's underlying level of bias—are feasible. However, insulating approaches lack a key advantage of debiasing strategies; debiasing often has the virtue of avoiding significant effects on those who do not exhibit bias in the first place.[104]

Recall our earlier illustration of consumer optimism bias; government, believing that consumers often underestimate the likelihood of injury from risky products, restricts consumer choice in a variety of ways.[105] Such restrictions introduce new distortions in outcomes for those who did not err in the first instance, as products are banned, more expensive, or otherwise less available to them. By contrast, debiasing techniques may affect those who are biased without much affecting those who are not.[106] So too in the context of antidiscrimination law: debiasing approaches target implicit bias for reduction and thus are unlikely to affect those who initially do not show implicit bias.[107]

To illustrate the basic point here, return to the alternative analyses of government affirmative action plans in Part II above. One analysis emphasizes insulation. On this account, affirmative action plans may protect outcomes from the effects of implicit bias—itself taken as a given—by granting discrete preferences to members of a particular group.[108] Here, as applied to a particular decisionmaker who in fact harbors no implicit bias, the government's action will introduce a distortion in, rather than a corrective to, decisionmaking; depending on the nature of the affirmative action plan the alteration may be significant.[109] If a given decisionmaker evaluates an African-American in a wholly unbiased fashion but the candidate nonetheless receives a thumb on the scale under an affirmative action plan, then the plan causes, rather than insulates against, race-based decisionmaking.

The analysis differs with respect to the debiasing account of affirmative action. On this account, affirmative action, by increasing population diversity, may reduce implicit bias—but there is no reason to think the increased population diversity will significantly alter the views of those who did not show implicit bias in the first place. The perceptions of a decisionmaker who already has no trouble envisioning African-Americans in authority roles are unlikely to move substantially in response to increased population diversity in the organization. Of course empirical testing would be important to verify this conjecture, but debiasing solutions at least hold out the possibility of leaving unaffected or less affected the decisionmaking of those who were not biased in the first instance. The use of a System I response to a System I problem may be able to leave relatively untouched those not exhibiting the System I problem in the first instance.[110]

The system justification notion discussed above provides another example of the potential advantage of debiasing approaches. Consider the suggestion of Blasi and Jost that, as a result of system justification tendencies, victims of biased behavior will often not mount legal challenges to such behavior.[111] If so, one could imagine responding with policies greatly lowering the legal barriers to bringing such challenges. But such steps would naturally tend to affect the frequency of legal challenges even outside the set of cases in which system justification was depressing legal challenges in the first instance. Again, debiasing strategies may avoid such distortions in the behavior of those not exhibiting bias in the first instance.

CONCLUSION

Antidiscrimination law, no less than any other area of law, should be based on a realistic understanding of human behavior. If consumers underreact to certain risks, the law should take their underreactions into account. And if individuals act on the basis of implicit bias against African-Americans or other groups, without awareness that they are doing so, the law should respond, if only because similarly situated people are not being treated similarly. As in risk-related behavior, so too with implicitly biased behavior: System I, involving rapid, intuitive responses, is often responsible for people's behavior, and it can lead them badly astray.

We have suggested the importance of distinguishing between two responses to implicit bias. Sometimes the legal system does and should pursue a strategy of insulation—for example, by protecting consumers against their own mistakes or by banning or otherwise limiting the effects of implicitly biased behavior. But sometimes the legal system does and should attempt to debias those who suffer from consumer error—or who might treat people in a biased manner. In many domains, debiasing strategies provide a preferable and less intrusive solution. In the context of antidiscrimination law, implicit bias presents a particularly severe challenge; we have suggested that several existing doctrines now operate to reduce that bias, either directly or indirectly, and that these existing doctrines do not on that account run into convincing normative objections.

It is now clear that implicit bias is wide-spread, and it is increasingly apparent that actual behavior is often affected by it, in violation of the principles that underlie antidiscrimination law. The question for the future, illuminatingly explored by the contributors to this Symposium, is how the law might better deal with that problem.

Part Three
CRIMINAL LAW

15

Toward a Radical Psychology:
Psychology, Race, Environment, and Crime

Shayne Jones and Michael J. Lynch

INTRODUCTION

Despite their early influence,[1] psychological perspectives have been noticeably absent from mainstream criminology throughout much of the latter half of the twentieth century.[2] Nevertheless, in recent years psychological criminology has been garnering increased attention, and a number of psychological factors (e.g., personality, neuropsychological deficits) have been advanced as causes or correlates of antisocial behavior.

Because criminology, broadly defined, is the interdisciplinary study of crime, criminal behavior, and the processes employed to control crime, the inclusion of psychological perspectives enriches the field. However, there are at least two problems with current conceptualizations of psychological criminology. First, many of the purported etiological mechanisms of psychological factors related to criminal behavior identify individual-level features

(e.g., genes).[3] While these may, in fact, serve as the basis for many psychological factors related to criminal behavior, they are almost assuredly not the sole sources. In fact, there are likely environmental sources that precede and exacerbate these individual-level characteristics that have not been examined in depth within psychological criminology. Second, the vast majority of psychological criminology, much like criminology in general, has focused on traditional conceptualizations of crime. That is, factors such as neuropsychological deficits, cognitive processing models, and personality have been investigated as causes of homicide, rape, assault, theft, substance use, and juvenile delinquency. While these actions are certainly important to study, they represent only one facet of criminal behavior, ignoring a class of more prevalent and detrimental offenses—white-collar crimes. Yet little research exists that explores white-collar offending from a psychological perspective.

In this chapter, we address these two key issues confronting psychological criminology. First, we examine the links between environmental exposure to toxins, psychological factors, and criminal behavior. Through this discussion it will be argued that a more nuanced psychological criminology that incorporates environmental factors has the potential of yielding more accurate etiological explanations of criminal behavior. Second, we review the extant literature that has identified psychological factors related to white-collar offending. Because this literature is relatively scant, we also provide additional avenues of psychological research that should be explored to better understand white-collar crime. Last, throughout this chapter we explore these issues from a radical criminological perspective, which emphasizes the roles of race and class. Because of the relative obscurity of radical criminology, the following section briefly familiarizes readers with what this perspective offers and how it can be used to better understand psychological criminology.

I. RADICAL CRIMINOLOGY

What is radical criminology? A complete answer to this question is complex and beyond the scope of the current chapter.[4] What is pertinent to the context of the current chapter is the radical suggestion that links social structure to explanations of crime and justice. This leads to the observation that constructs such as race, class, and gender (among others), represent core structural features of a society that impact the lives of individuals. For radical criminologists, consideration of these structural characteristics cannot be divorced from discussions of crime and justice.

A central tenet of radical criminology is that the root causes of crime are to be found in the social structure. How can this observation be connected to those offered by psychological criminology? We would argue that some of the causes of criminal behavior advanced in psychological criminology (e.g., neuropsychological deficits) may very well stem from social forces.

Another crucial component of the radical perspective is that crime is socially constructed, which is to say that what is considered a crime has more to do with social factors than any inherent behavioral feature.[5] Stated differently, definitions of crime, whether proffered by the government, researchers, or even laypeople, are created from a complex exchange and interplay of social forces and actors. Thus, the concept of crime is not contingent upon any universal law or truth. Radicals employ the idea that crime is a social construction to why some socially injurious actions are defined as crime, while other equally harmful behaviors are not. Take, for instance, criminal homicide. Few individuals would argue against the idea that a man who shoots another man in cold blood is guilty of homicide. In contrast, deaths that result from explicit safety violations are much less likely to be classified as homicides even though, as Reiman argues, the offender knows his or her behavior will cause the death of someone.[6] The difference between these acts isn't the intention of the actor to cause harm but the selection of a specific target. Yet many (even the criminal justice system) are reluctant to define deaths resulting from workplace safety violations as criminal homicide. This suggests that perceptions of what constitutes a criminal homicide do not simply exist as truths but are (socially) created.

How does the social construction of crime relate to psychological criminology? Much psychological criminology research has focused on traditional street crimes—rape, robbery, assault. However, we believe that psychological perspectives can provide valuable insights into nontraditional crimes such as white-collar crime. To do so, researchers would need to move beyond standard definitions of crime to include a wider array of harmful behaviors.

Thus, our use of radical criminology in this chapter is relatively circumscribed in the sense that we draw on this perspective as a means of supplementing psychological criminology. We do this in two ways: first, by linking social structural factors to some of the central constructs used in psychological criminology, and second, by extending the dependent variable in psychological criminology to include white collar offenses.

II. THE ENVIRONMENT AND BEHAVIOR

A. The Potential Mediating Capacity of Psychological Factors

As mentioned above, psychological criminology has become more widely accepted within mainstream criminology. Factors such as decision-making processes,[7] personality,[8] psychopathology,[9] and neuropsychological functioning[10] have been identified as causes or correlates of criminal behavior. Many of these psychological factors are discussed as individual differences present early in the life course, some of which are theorized to have a genetic basis.[11] These etiological explanations have received empirical support, and we offer no counterclaim to these contentions. Instead, we suggest that the causes of these psychological phenomena are complex, and environmental factors play an influential role in their etiology and course.

Studies by medical researchers, epidemiologists, and environmental scientists illustrate the variety of ways in which the physical environment can impact behavior. For example, studies indicate that en-vironmental exposure to heavy metals can produce numerous adverse behavioral affects. For instance, exposure to heavy metals, in particular lead, has been associated with increased crime, juvenile delinquency, aggression, and violence.[12] While studies have demonstrated a connection between lead exposure and negative behavioral outcomes at both the individual and ecological levels, the exact processes involved are still unclear. It is clear, for instance, that lead exposure causes adverse behavioral outcomes by altering biological processes and promoting brain dysfunction.[13] These processes may impact behavior directly by disturbing impulse controls, or by impacting functions that promote psychological dysfunction.

To be sure, heavy metal exposure has been associated with a variety of psychological states criminologists have correlated with crime, including attention-deficit/hyperactivity disorders, conduct disorder, neuropsychological deficits, impulsivity, disruption of the central nervous system, and various cognitive and learning disorders.[14] Interestingly, these outcomes include several of the most widely researched psychological causes of criminal behavior. This evidence should not be taken as a suggestion that psychological factors are irrelevant to the causes of crime; rather, it suggests that exposure to toxic environments aids in producing the psychological deficits that have been associated with crime, and thus may be precursors to and causes of them. Stated differently, the findings from the medical literature can be used to suggest that psychological factors may sometimes be mediating factors of the relationship between exposure to toxins and criminal behavior.

The idea that environmental toxins may modify behavior has not been widely examined within criminological literature.[15] It should be kept in mind that the probability and degree of exposure to environmental toxins that modify behavior is socially structured.[16] Specifically, not all individuals or communities are at equal risk for exposure to toxic environments. Indeed, extant research indicates that the probability of exposure to environmental toxins varies with community racial and class characteristics.[17] These communities are targeted as areas where waste can be dumped, or where polluting industries exist, because they do not possess the requisite political, economic, and social capital to resist.[18]

In sum, exposure to environmental toxins has important behavioral impacts. Moreover, some of the most widely studied and supported psychological causes of criminal behavior—neuropsychological deficits, psychopathology—are caused, in part, by exposure to environmental toxins. In addition, the likelihood of exposure to environmental toxins has social structural correlates, and exposure varies with community racial and class characteristics. This chain of evidence suggests that social structure has important impacts on the composition of human psychology.[19] This observation has not been employed in discussions of criminal behavior.

B. The Potential Moderating Influence of the Environment

In addition to being a precursor to psychological factors, the environment plays a role in the course of criminal behavior. One of the most active areas of research within psychological criminology is the role of personality.[20] Traits such as impulsivity,[21] antagonism,[22] sensation seeking,[23] and negative emotionality,[24] to name a few, have been consistently related to involvement in crime. Yet these effects appear to be moderated, or conditioned, as a function of social context. At the neighborhood level, it has been found that impulsive individuals are at an elevated risk of engaging in delinquency when they also

reside in poorer (and often disproportionately minority) neighborhoods.[25] Other studies have found that the relationship between personality and criminal behavior varies as a function of social factors such as education, parenting, employment, and peer affiliations.[26] Some of these social factors (e.g., education and employment) are systematically related to race such that minorities are less likely to be provided with an equitable education or quality job than whites.[27]

Another important tenet of the radical perspective is that choices in life are related to one's position in the social structure. That is, wealthy white individuals have a greater variety of choices than economically deprived minorities. This places some of the decision-making literature on aggression in a new context. For example, Dodge and colleagues have found that aggressive individuals demonstrate patterned models of decision making such that they are most attuned to aggressive cues in the environment, as well as more likely to positively value and employ aggressive responses.[28] At least one source of this characteristic pattern of decision making may be the environment. Anderson has documented in great detail how predominantly minority and impoverished urban areas are often plagued by violence and aggression.[29] Furthermore, Anderson suggests that many individuals (even those he refers to as being from "good" families) adopt a behavioral style of toughness, bravado, and a willingness to use violence if necessary. In the context of Dodge's social information processing model, it would seem to be an adaptive skill to be cognizant of aggressive cues in the environment in the sorts of neighborhoods identified by Anderson. One can easily see how positive evaluations and engagement in aggression in such neighborhoods are an adaptive feature. We are aware of no study exploring the interrelationship between social location and cognitive decision making, yet there are compelling reasons to believe such a link exists.

We have touched on only a few of the psychological factors that have been studied and offered as explanations of criminal behavior. Again, our contention is not that these psychological phenomena are irrelevant or spurious, but rather that social structural factors are inevitably related to their etiology and course. Furthermore, one's position in the social structure is dependent, in part, on one's race. In an effort to better understand the purported causes of crime, we suggest researchers embrace multiple perspectives that cross (or even ignore) disciplinary boundaries. To this end, radical criminological perspectives can provide valuable insights.

III. OMITTED CRIMES: WHITE-COLLAR CRIME AND VICTIMIZATION

To this point, we have described radical criminology and the way it can further advance psychological criminology in terms of etiology and course, and specifically how this is linked to race. In this section, we explore how psychological criminology can facilitate our understanding of another major focus in radical criminology—white-collar crime. This topic is also related to issues of race (and class) in that white-collar offenses are typically perpetrated by members of the majority (i.e., whites). However, unlike street crimes, which are perceived to be committed more often by racial minorities, white-collar crimes are relatively neglected. This aspect of white-collar crime itself suggests racial dynamics influence the social construction of crime. We begin this section by first providing a brief overview of white-collar crime, focusing specifically on its definition and prevalence. Then we explore how psychological factors and processes might

provide insights into the phenomenon of white-collar crime.

As discussed above, crime is socially constructed. Thus, when thinking about crime, the image conjured up by many Americans is that of traditional street crime. Street crime, as defined here, refers to Part I and II offenses included in the Uniform Crime Reports (UCR): homicide, rape, robbery, aggravated assault, stolen property, and vandalism, among others. Certainly these crimes are harmful to individuals and society, and particularly minorities, as they are disproportionately more likely to be victims of such crimes.[30] Yet the extant evidence indicates that street crimes pose a far lesser threat to individuals and society than white-collar crimes.[31] Sutherland was the first to coin the term "white-collar crime," which he defined "as a crime committed by a person of respectability and high social status in the course of his occupation."[32] While the precise definition and scope of what constitutes white-collar crime is continually debated, there is little doubt as to its deleterious effects.[33]

Behavioral science scholars have suggested that white-collar crime is widespread and costly, although precise estimates are lacking. This is due, in part, to the relative absence of white-collar crime research,[34] but it is also a result of the inherent difficulty in studying this phenomenon.[35] Nonetheless, estimates have been provided. In terms of financial costs, estimates range from $40 billion to $1 trillion per year. These figures are ten to fifty times greater than the direct costs of street crime and do not include indirect costs (increased insurance premiums, physical pain, psychological trauma, etc.). As Friedrichs explains, regardless of whether the lowest or highest estimate is used, the financial costs of street crime pale in comparison to white-collar crime.

While pecuniary factors are important,

they are of little import when compared to the health and well-being of individuals and communities. In this regard, the costs of white-collar crime are mind-boggling. One of the most illustrative examples comes from Reiman's analysis comparing workplace and street crime.[36] He defines workplace crime as a violation of laws (e.g., safety laws) that result in death, severe bodily injury, and disease (e.g., exposure to toxic chemicals). Street crimes are defined as Part I and II offenses listed in the UCR. His analysis indicates that there are nearly six times as many workers killed as there are victims of street homicides. More than five and a half times as many workers are severely injured as there are assaults committed on the streets. Based on 2000 estimates (UCR), there were 12,943 homicides recorded. Yet, after including deaths resulting from occupational hazards and disease (30,238), the number of Americans killed climbs to 43,181. Reiman also suggests that many "medical errors" constitute crime because they are easily preventable. For example, he notes that 16,000 deaths occur annually from unnecessary surgeries, and 100,000 from faulty prescription labels. It is important to note that these statistics consider only deaths, not injuries, which themselves are estimated to directly affect millions of individuals. As this evidence indicates, our nation's workplaces (and the toxins they produce) and hospitals are much more dangerous than the streets.

While some might argue that the deaths stemming from corporate activity and the medical field should not be classified as murder, it should be kept in mind that many of these deaths were preventable.[37] Furthermore, these actions are often undertaken despite the fact that the perpetrators know they are violating the law or are simply indifferent to the readily apparent lethal consequences. Even in those instances where mens rea is absent, this does not negate that a crime has occurred. For instance, there are several criminal violations that do not require intent, including strict liability laws, transferred intent, and negligence. Thus, what differentiates one killing from another is less contingent upon specific legal standards than upon the social construction of what constitutes homicide.

Despite the staggering social problem created by white-collar crimes, there is a relative dearth of empirical research on white-collar crime generated in criminology. Lynch and colleagues examined the representation of white-collar crime research in mainstream criminology journals and textbooks as well as white-collar crime courses offered at the doctoral level in criminology programs in the United States.[38] Despite the enormous costs of white-collar crime and the extent to which it is much more prevalent than street crime, they found its presence in publications (journal articles and textbooks) sorely underrepresented. Specifically, there was a ten-to-one ratio of publications on street crime to those on white-collar crime. Additionally, less than half of criminology doctoral programs offered any white-collar crime courses, and none required such a course.

This scarcity of research and attention is even more pronounced in the psychological literature. As discussed above, several studies have linked personality and street crime. However, much less research exists that explores the link between personality and white-collar offending. Some of the few studies that do exist suggest it is important. For example, white-collar offending appears to be linked to higher levels of narcissistic and manipulative traits,[39] as well as an antagonistic orientation.[40] Others have noted white-collar offending is related to approaching business decisions in a Machiavellian manner (i.e., from an amoral standpoint, whereby the ends justify the means).[41] Thus, there exists some empirical evidence to support the notion that personality and white-collar offending are related.

Other lines of research in this area provide more conceptually coherent frameworks. For instance, there has been an interest among researchers in identifying the "successful" psychopath.[42] These individuals are hypothesized to possess the interpersonal traits characteristic of psychopathy (e.g., callousness, manipulativeness, deceitfulness, etc.) but do not engage in explicitly criminal behavior. Further, to the extent successful psychopaths do exist, they may very well be present in business settings.[43] Babiak has provided some preliminary evidence of the successful psychopath.[44] Specifically, he notes that psychopathic individuals within business settings demonstrate more of the interpersonally antagonistic and emotionally deficient characteristics of this personality disorder than the impulsive, anti-social, and criminal components.

Despite the relatively nonexistent research focusing on personality and white-collar offending in general, and that incorporating psychopathy in particular, there are compelling reasons to believe such relationships exists. It is not difficult to see how individuals who are callous and lacking in emotion are probably less likely to be concerned with stealing from pension funds, polluting the environment, and placing workers in harm's way. Individuals who are antagonistic and aggressive might be more easily persuaded to bend the rules in order to increase profits, and less affected when their actions could result in harm to others. Traits such as risk taking or sensation seeking might even be considered a valued trait in the business world.[45] Other traits that have been consistently linked to street crime (e.g., impulsivity) are probably less relevant when examining white-collar crime.[46] Nonethe-

less, our knowledge in this regard is relatively weak and requires more attention from researchers.

Beyond personality psychology, theory and research from social psychology might yield insights into white-collar crime. For instance, many corporate decisions are made in group contexts. Furthermore, the composition of these groups is relatively homogeneous, meaning that they are composed of like-minded individuals who share common educational and social backgrounds. Social psychological research involving group decision making would suggest that these factors are fertile ground for potentially negative decisions. Studies have found that initial attitudes are strengthened after discussion in a group, a process referred to as group polarization.[47] Thus, to the extent that corporate board members espouse relatively homogeneous attitudes, those attitudes will be exacerbated after discussion. For example, corporate boards are charged with increasing profit margins for their stockholders (among other things). Corporate meetings, then, may potentially result in a greater emphasis on increasing profit margins and on taking more substantial risks to achieve those gains. Furthermore, to the extent that there is little disagreement on substantive issues and future plans, the social psychological phenomenon of groupthink may come into play.[48] This occurs when members of a group who hold similar attitudes, experiences, and outlooks become overly focused on singular outcomes, ignoring or deemphasizing potentially negative consequences. Together, these group processes might lead to decisions that are unethical or illegal, thus resulting in white-collar crime.

Another social psychological phenomenon that likely exists in the context of corporate decision making is the diffusion of responsibility, or deindividuation.[49] That is, the degree of individual responsibility for a decision or action is inversely proportional to the number of individuals making that decision. For instance, when a corporate board of executives makes a decision to reduce the company's workforce, no single member must take responsibility for that action. Instead, each individual member assumes only some of the responsibility. Other factors, such as market forces, may be used as additional rationalization to absolve individuals of responsibility. When deindividuation occurs, individuals feel less restrained, are less likely to engage in behavior that is consistent with their own values, and are more likely to allow situational factors to dominate decision making.[50]

These social psychological processes might help to explain some actions that have been defined as white-collar crimes. For example, in 1985 the space shuttle *Challenger* exploded shortly after takeoff. Subsequent investigations found that NASA management did not sufficiently heed the warnings expressed by some of the engineers, who cautioned that the ambient temperature made the launch unsafe. Despite these concerns, and in light of economic and political influences, the decision was made to launch, which resulted in a devastating tragedy. Myers suggests that the phenomenon of groupthink (discussed above) may have played a role in the *Challenger* explosion.[51] Even though there may have been no specific intent to place the astronauts in harm's way, Vaughan has argued that social and political forces created a context in which amoral decision making was normative.[52] Some scholars have suggested this represents a specific form of white-collar crime—state-corporate crime.[53]

Another example can be gleaned from the Ford Pinto case.[54] Ford executives made a conscious decision not to recall one of their popular vehicles, the Pinto, despite explicit knowledge of a serious safety concern. Specifically, the Pinto stood a relatively high likelihood of explosion during rear-end collisions. While the civil case cost Ford Motor Company an estimated $100 million, the executives were acquitted on the criminal charges.[55] Although it remains uncertain, it seems reasonable to conclude that group decision-making processes influenced Ford's actions in such a manner as to minimize the negative, and ultimately deadly, consequences while maximizing the gains.

Janis has offered a variety of strategies that may disrupt the process of groupthink.[56] One tactic is assigning a member of the group to play the role of devil's advocate, underscoring the risks and potential negative consequences of the group's decisions. In response to the recent wave of corporate scandals, and consistent with this policy, some corporations have designated an ethics officer. These individuals are charged with the responsibility of ensuring ethical behavior. To the extent that these individuals successfully implement strategies designed to avoid groupthink, it seems possible that some unethical and/or illegal behavior will be avoided. However, the use of ethics officers is too new to know what effect, if any, it will have on white-collar crime.

These examples provide only a glimpse into the possibilities of incorporating psychological concepts in the studying of white-collar crimes. Given the enormous costs of white-collar crime, both in lives taken and dollars stolen, relying on multiple disciplinary perspectives and methodologies can only yield greater understanding. It is also important to once again point out that race is almost certainly linked to white-collar crime in at least two ways. First, racial majorities are more likely to be engaged in white-collar crime. Second, the fact that white-collar crimes typically receive much less attention than street crimes, despite being substantially more harmful, suggests that race (and class) is a factor affecting the social construction of crime. This latter issue is even more egregious when considering the differences between how white-collar and street crimes are addressed (or not) by the justice system.

IV. WHITE-COLLAR CRIME AND JUSTICE

In addition to the relative lack of focus on empirical investigations of white-collar crime, there are also notable differences in how white-collar and street crimes are handled. Street crimes are processed by the criminal justice system, and while some white-collar crimes fall under the purview of the criminal law (e.g., antitrust violations, insider trading, etc.), most are not addressed as criminal violations. Instead, white-collar offenses are investigated and dealt with by administrative or regulatory agencies. Thus, the "policing" of white-collar crimes is often the responsibility of agencies such as the Environmental Protection Agency (EPA), Occupational Safety and Health Administration (OSHA), Securities and Exchange Commission (SEC), and Food and Drug Administration (FDA), among others. While policy initiatives to increase the number of police officers are enacted to combat street crime (despite the fact that crime rates are already declining),[57] administrative regulatory agencies have been facing dramatic budget cuts, hampering their ability to adequately police corporations.[58] In some instances, "internal policing" standards are heavily utilized. For instance, unethical and illegal behaviors committed by lawyers and physicians are addressed by "internal" agencies such as the American Bar Association and American Medical Association, respectively. Regardless of which type of agency is charged with enforcement of regulations and laws, the most typical response to white-collar crimes (that is, when any response exists) is a consent decree, which simply requests that the unethical/illegal behavior cease. In rarer instances, a fine is imposed, which translates into a business cost that is passed on to consumers.

This discussion demonstrates that there are really two separate systems that we rely upon to protect us from harm. One system—the criminal justice system—focuses primarily on the crimes of poor minorities and responds with (increasingly) harsh punishments. The other system—comprising various, nonintegrated regulatory agencies—concentrates on the crimes of the wealthy and responds with comparatively exculpatory actions. This notable discrepancy begs the question of the true purpose of criminal law. Mainstream responses to this question highlight that its purpose is to protect individuals and society, and that it is based on consensus. Radical responses underscore that the purpose of law, at least as it is practiced, is to maintain the status quo of controlling the behaviors of the poor and promoting the interests of the powerful.[59] Furthermore, radical criminology suggests that legal architecture is based more on a conflict model than a consensus model. Given the history of law enforcement used to curb labor unrest, the lack of enforcement of white-collar crimes, the differential definitions of what constitutes a "real" crime, the marked disparities in punishments for street and white-collar crimes, and the racial inequalities inherent in these actions, the radical perspective offers a sobering critique and legitimate interpretation of the nature and purpose of the law.[60]

CONCLUSION

Our goal in this chapter was to demonstrate how the study of crime, criminal behavior, and crime control can benefit from an interdisciplinary exchange of ideas drawn from psychological and radical perspectives. To this end, we argued that many of the psychological correlates of street crimes are all too often decontextualized. That is, they are considered separate from the social structure in which they occur. The evidence we put forth suggests that some of the psychological correlates most often studied may stem, in part, from exposure to toxic environments. This toxicity refers not only to the chemicals and pollutants that are most heavily concentrated in poor, minority neighborhoods but also to the "socially toxic" environments in such neighborhoods. In addition, we reviewed the evidence that indicates the relationship between psychological factors and criminal behavior is conditioned upon social factors. Thus, psychological factors appear to serve as more proximal mediators of the link between the environment and criminal behavior, while the social and physical context also acts as a moderator of psychological factors. We hope future psychological research on criminal behavior places more emphasis on the environment.

In addition, we implore researchers in psychological criminology to broaden the scope of behaviors examined by investigating white-collar offending. Much of the research on this topic has explored social factors. However, as we articulated above, a richer explanatory framework should include notions derived from personality and social psychology. Given the devastating toll white-collar crime has on society and its members, it is imperative that it be given greater attention by criminologists and behavioral scientists.

On a broader level, throughout this chapter we have shown how these issues are related to race. As a final connection, it is also important to point out that one of the most devastating forms of white-collar crime is environmental pollution. As delineated above, exposure to environmental toxins is much more pronounced in poorer, minority neighborhoods. Thus, the crimes of the powerful are themselves linked to the crimes of the poor. This vicious cycle, we argue, is most readily understood and appreciated by exploring the radical criminological perspective. We hope that our efforts here can be expanded upon by scholars in a variety of fields, as we have only touched on some of the most important issues found at the intersection of psychology, race, and law.

16

The Psychology of Hate Crime Law, Victims, and Offenders

Megan Sullaway

INTRODUCTION

"A hate crime is a traditional offense like murder, arson, or vandalism with an added element of bias."[1] The victim of a hate crime is selected because of "actual or perceived race, color, religion, disability, sexual orientation, or national origin."[2] Hate crime laws typically enhance penalties of existing categories of crimes. The Supreme Court ruled in favor of penalty enhancement in *Wisconsin v. Mitchell*.[3] "Although the government can't punish abstract beliefs, it can punish a vast array of depraved motives. . . . [Hate crime statutes do not] prohibit people from expressing their views, nor punish them for doing so. . . ."

In 2004, the most recent year for which the FBI has national hate crime statistics, race was the motivating bias for 53.8 percent of reported hate crimes, followed by religion (16.4 percent), sexual orientation (15.6 percent), ethnicity (13.3 percent), disability (0.8 percent), and multiple bias (0.2

percent). Of all reported hate crimes, 62.4 percent were crimes against persons (simple and aggravated assaults, intimidation) and 36.9 percent were against property (destruction, damage, vandalism).[4] Compared to overall crime base rates, hate crimes are significantly more likely to be against persons (versus property).[5] If one analyzes data based not on absolute numbers but rather on a per capita basis, gay people report the greatest number of hate crimes, followed by Jewish people and blacks.[6]

A recent development in legal scholarship[7] is the study of the "intersection of emotion and law" which "proceeds . . . from the belief that the legal relevance of emotion is both significant and deserving of (and amenable to) close scrutiny".[8] While a large literature exists about the constitutionality of hate crime laws, focusing particularly on First Amendment and equal protection clause issues,[9] the emotional and psychological aspects of hate crime law have been less systematically addressed.[10] Yet virtually any discussion or critique of hate crime law invokes psychological constructs: Are hate crime laws unique in considering perpetrators' emotions? How can we detect motives without "mind reading"? Do hate crime laws criminalize emotions and prejudicial attitudes? Are victims of hate crimes more injured than victims of comparable but non-bias-motivated crimes?

The psychological literature may offer insights to these questions. The goal of this chapter is to (1) enumerate the psychological constructs invoked in discussions of hate crime law, including motive, intent, emotion, attitude, and behavior; (2) describe applications of psychological research methodology to the study of these elements of hate crimes; and (3) summarize some of the psychological research on hate crime victims and perpetrators.

I. PSYCHOLOGICAL CONSTRUCTS

A. Motivation and Intent

Criminal law traditionally concerns itself with mens rea (the reason for which one acts, the conscious intent) in assessing culpability. For example, the conscious *intent* of a person who breaks into a bank is to steal money; his underlying *motivation* might be to buy drugs or buy food for a hungry family.[11] The intent of the perpetrator matters in determining if a crime has occurred; the motive is irrelevant (although it could be taken into account at sentencing). Intent has, as its object, a perceived good. Hurd, in congressional testimony, noted, "To act so as to get money or so as to kill someone is not (necessarily or intrinsically) to act on an emotion—it is rather to act so as to obtain what one perceives as a future good."[12] Morsch argues that hate crime laws are untenable because they require a determination of motive,

which is "inherently subjective, entirely within the contents of an individual's mind."[13] Hurd suggests that hate crime laws incorrectly criminalize vicious character traits, "a dangerous and illiberal role for the State to take."[14]

In hate crime cases, intent and motivation have a much closer correspondence than acknowledged by Hurd or Morsch. Lawrence, in congressional testimony, suggests that in a hate crime, the two concepts, intent and motivation, are virtually the same. A bias-motivated perpetrator who assaults an African American may possess "a *mens rea* of purpose with respect to the assault along with a motivation of racial bias" or may possess "a first-tier *mens rea* of purpose with respect to the parallel crime of assault and a second tier *mens rea* of purpose with respect to assaulting *this* victim because of his race."[15]

B. Emotion, Attitude, and Behavior

"Inasmuch as hatred is an *emotion* and bias is a *disposition* to make false judgments, both hatred and bias are quite different from the motivations with which defendants act when committing specific intent crimes."[16] This implies, first, that a particular emotional state is necessary in order to define a crime as hate-based. Second, it implies that biased intent is no more than a "disposition to make false judgments." Third, it implies that hate crime laws are unique in consideration of the emotional state of the perpetrator. These issues are discussed below.

The presence of the emotion of hate is a poor criterion by which to define hate crimes. Many other types of crime involve hatred for the victim (although many do not, such as the murder of a stranger in the course of a robbery to escape identification). In a hate (or bias-motivated) crime, the *emotion* of hate may not be prominent relative to the more deliberative process of victim selection based on the latter's membership in a despised group. The term "bias-motivated crime" is more accurate. Laws defining hate crimes typically refer to bias in victim selection and are silent on the topic of perpetrators' subjective experiences of "hate."[17]

Whether bias is nothing more than "a disposition to make false judgments" is debatable. Using Hurd's language, hate crimes are sometimes committed to achieve a particular "future good," to "send a message," or to discourage in-migration of a particular group. For example, German xenophobes have as their goal the expulsion of foreigners from Germany. "When the government reacted by moving foreigners or changing laws, [the xenophobes] felt they had achieved part of their desired future good."[18]

Discussions of hate crime laws sometime seem to confuse the punishment of criminal *behavior* with punishment of prejudicial *attitudes*. This distinction can be made clearer. Prejudice may be inevitable given ordinary categorization processes in cognition, yet the individual with measurably high prejudicial attitudes may have no history of criminal prejudicial behavior and extremely low probability of future engagement in such.[19] This is not surprising, as the psychological literature that concerns itself with the study and measurement of attitudes suggests that associations between attitudes and behaviors are frequently weak.[20] Individuals with prejudicial attitudes are more likely to want to withdraw from and avoid any contact with members of the perceived out-group.[21] For example, studies have found that once the proportion of blacks in predominantly white neighborhoods reaches 25 percent, "white flight" accelerates.[22]

In contrast, evidence from the Los Angeles County Human Relations Commission suggests that many convicted perpetrators of hate crimes are career criminals who seek to engage with the object of their hate in an aggressive manner rather then avoid the objects of their disdain.[23] Anecdotal observation by police and community-based organizations suggest that "gay-bashing" that occurs in West Hollywood (a predominately gay area of Los Angeles County) is frequently perpetrated by individuals who do not live there and who must drive significant distances from their homes to carry out their desire to hurt gays.

Long before hate crimes were defined in law, "provocation doctrine" considered the emotional state of the perpetrator, and was applied in the following circumstances: "(1) There must have been adequate provocation. (2) The killing must have been in the heat of passion. (3) It must have been a sudden heat of passion—that is, the killing must have followed the provocation before there had been a reasonable opportunity for the passion to cool. (4) There must have been a causal connection between the provocation, the passion, and the fatal act."[24] These distinctions are reflected in contemporary law, in which first-degree murder includes malice aforethought, and manslaughter includes provocation or extreme emotional disturbance—the latter defined as a loss of control that might be experienced by a "reasonable person" in that situation.[25] Emotional state is even more central to the definition of a crime under the "rule of provocation" than it is to the definition of a hate crime.

II. PSYCHOLOGICAL METHODOLOGY APPLIED TO THE STUDY OF HATE CRIMES

A. Validity and Reliability Issues

The Hate Crime Statistics Act directs the establishment of "guidelines for the collection of such data including the necessary evidence and criteria that must be present for a finding of manifest prejudice and procedures for carrying out the purposes of this section."[26] How does one reliably measure intent and motivation in a criminal population? Little research exists that examines this question. Questions about measurement can be framed as questions about the validity and reliability of assessment for (or evidence of) bias motivation in the commission of a crime. A valid assessment is one that measures what it is intended to measure; a reliable assessment is one that has consistency, for example, across situations or observers, as in the case of a rating scale used by different raters of the same phenomenon.

The difficulty of establishing valid and reliable methods to determine the types of forensic evidence consistent with hate based motivation was recognized by FBI data collection guidelines.[27] "Because of the difficulty of ascertaining the offender's subjective motivation, bias is to be reported only if investigation reveals sufficient objective facts to lead a reasonable and prudent person to conclude that the offender's actions were motivated, in whole or in part, by bias."[28] The utility of hate crime statutes depends, in part, on the ability of law enforcement agencies to operationalize hate-based motives such that bias/hate-motivated criminal behavior can be described in specific and measurable ways.

B. Measuring Prejudice, Measuring Biased Intent

In the behavioral sciences, the issue of accurate measurement is a fundamental domain of study, particularly measurements of abstract constructs such as intelligence—or prejudice. Such constructs are not directly observable. Rather, they must be inferred based on valid and reliable methods. There are various ways to do so. Prejudice as a psy-chological construct has been measured, predominantly, via psychological tests. Tests have been designed to measure anti-Semitism,[29] homosexual bias,[30] anti-black racism,[31] blatant and subtle prejudice,[32] and subtle racism against blacks.[33]

There are more unobtrusive approaches to measuring prejudice. The prejudice (Pr) scale of the Minnesota Multiphasic Personality Inventory (MMPI) and MMPI-2 is significantly associated with anti-Semitism[34] and intolerance.[35] Recent research strongly supports the construct and criterion validity of this scale.[36] The Implicit Association Test (IAT) was developed to tap automatic, learned, hidden stereotypes that may bypass conscious awareness.[37] The degree of relationship between IAT-measured attitudes and behavior is, however, disputed.[38]

These psychological methods of testing are not useful in a criminal situation, as they assess attitudes, feelings, and traits, not criminal behavior. Behaviorally oriented psychologists offer a different set of measurement techniques. Since "the concept of personality represents a high level abstraction, which is nothing more than the sum total of the individual's behavior," the focus of a behavioral psychologist is to operationalize the construct of interest in terms of observable events, rather than attempting to infer unobservable constructs or traits.[39]

Behavioral methods of measurement may include verbal report (in which participants report on their own and peers' behavior), behavioral observation (including ratings by trained observers of observable and definable behaviors captured live or on video- or audiotape), and archival records and behavioral traces that were not generated for the benefit of the investigator.[40] This approach is consistent with the recommendations of the International Association of Chiefs of Police,[41] which advises officers to "collect and photograph physical evidence such as hate literature, spray paint cans, threatening letters, and symbolic objects used by hate groups." Police officers consider these pieces of evidence "unambiguous cues" of hate crimes.[42]

Dunbar has developed methodology to assess bias motivation using several criteria. The Bias Motivation Profile–Revised (BMP-R) uses reports by victims and eyewitnesses, police and detective reports, and offenders' criminal records to assess behavioral and historical evidence of bias motivation.[43] This methodology is similar to that used in the Historical, Clinical, and Risk Management (HCR)-20, a widely used technique to assess risk for future violent behavior in criminal and psychiatric populations.[44] Signifiers of bias intent include, for example, articulated beliefs about superiority, hate speech during the crime, use of hate symbols, and memberships or affiliation with like-minded others. This measure appears to have acceptable specificity (distinguishing between hate-motivated and non-hate-motivated crimes) and sensitivity (distinguishing between hate crimes and hate incidents).

Adding to the difficulty of determining biased intent is the question of whether a victim was selected for his or her "symbolic" versus "actuarial" status.[45] For example, is a gay man targeted because of his sexual orientation per se, or because gay men are assumed to be easy targets, who may be reluctant to report the crime?[46] In the former case, sexual orientation is the raison d'être for the crime. In the latter case, sexual orientation is nothing more than a marker for an easy robbery victim, and the selection of the victim is seemingly more motivated by greed than by bias per se.

The BMP-R allows examination of both "positive indicators" of bias (presence of hate iconography, hate symbols, etc.) and "negative indicators" (absence of a ma-

terial reward or other competing motivation for the offense). In a case-by-case analysis of hate crime reports between 1994 and 1997 in Los Angeles County, more than 80 percent of reported hate crimes were not related to material gain. In 74 percent there was no provocation by the victim, and the victim was usually (76 percent of the time) a stranger to the perpetrator. These factors, in addition to the presence of "positive" signs of bias motivation, help to determine the presence of bias intent.[47]

C. Speech as Evidence

Hate crime statutes penalize the criminal behavioral enactment of hate-based attitudes and feelings. Such statutes do not penalize hateful beliefs, emotions, or speech per se. The courts have allowed expression of prejudiced and hateful beliefs in public settings, whether a Nazi march, Internet hate sites, or books advocating racial violence.[48] According to a Supreme Court ruling, "offensiveness is insufficient basis to punish speech."[49] On the other hand, courts have recognized the validity of using speech as evidence. In *People v. Superior Court*, defendants were convicted of assaulting a trio of Mexican men.[50] One defendant's statement that he was "hitting home runs with Mexicans" and another defendant's tattoos (including a swastika and the phrase "Thank God I'm White") were used as evidence to support hate crime charges. The defendants alleged that their constitutional rights of free speech were thereby violated. The Superior Court accepted the state's construction that this evidence helped demonstrate that the attack was "because of" the ethnicity of the victims. In this case, speech was used as evidence. Speech was not itself prosecuted under criminal statutes. However, using hate speech as the only indicator of bias intent is likely to produce many false positives. Hate speech alone does not reliably differentiate hate crimes, hate incidents, and biased speech used in non-criminal acts.[51]

III. PSYCHOLOGY OF VICTIMS AND OFFENDERS

Hate crimes appear to differ from other crimes in the degree and type of violence manifested. Psychological, criminological, and sociological research suggests that hate crimes may create greater harm for both the victim and the community at large compared to other types of crime. Data from Los Angeles County indicated that hate crimes were more likely to be physically violent and were less likely to include crimes of material gain.[52] Offenders who targeted sexual minorities showed greater instrumentality and greater violence against their victims.[53] Instrumental violence is goal-directed, is relatively purposeful, and frequently targets strangers and acquaintances as opposed to intimates. Reactive violence occurs in response to frustration and hostility, and may be triggered, for example, by a perceived threat or provocation.[54]

According to some researchers, hate crimes are more likely than crimes in general to involve multiple offenders, to cause injury, and to require hospitalization.[55] In a mail survey of 2,657 law enforcement agencies administered as part of a larger study, police officers overwhelmingly agreed that "[g]iven similar assault/vandalism cases, bias assault/vandalism is generally more serious than non-bias assault/vandalism."[56]

A. Hate Crime Victims

Victims of hate crimes may suffer greater physical trauma relative to other crime victims. Previously described FBI data suggested that hate crimes are more likely (relative to non-hate-related crimes) to be crimes against persons than property, and that hate crimes against persons are much more likely to be assaults.[57] In congressional testimony McDevitt reports that his research in the Boston area showed that victims of hate crime assaults were three times more likely to require hospitalization than victims of non-hate-crime assaults.[58]

Victims of violent hate crimes may also be more severely traumatized than victims of comparably violent non-hate-based crimes. Herek, Gillis, and Cogan compared psychological distress suffered by gay men and lesbians after a bias crime to distress suffered by gay men and lesbians after a non-bias-related crime of comparable violence.[59] Recent victims of hate crimes suffered greater psychological distress than victims of non-bias-motivated crimes, and after five years they reported significantly greater levels of depression, traumatic stress, anxiety, and anger than did subjects who experienced non-bias-motivated assaults. Victims of bias crime were more likely to "regard the world as unsafe, to view people as malevolent, to experience a relatively low sense of personal mastery" compared to other subjects.[60] According to Herek and colleagues, there is some evidence that it may take longer to recover from a hate crime than a comparable non-hate-related crime. Weiss, Ehrlich, and Larcom found that hate crime victims reported, among other behaviors, "trying to be less visible" and moving to another neighborhood.[61] McDevitt cites data in which victims of assault (bias- and non-bias-motivated) were assessed one year after the crime was committed against them.[62] Victims of bias assault reported significantly greater nervousness, anger, intrusions ("thinking about it when [they] didn't want to"), and difficulty concentrating at work compared to victims of non-bias-motivated assaults.

Attributing an event to discrimination is associated with greater psychological distress and a sense of less control and mastery.[63]

Psychology offers possible theoretical models to account for the apparent increased psychological impact of hate crimes. Janoff-Bulman has distinguished between behavioral self-blame and characterological self-blame.[64] Crime victims in general suffer psychological distress because the comforting illusion of personal invulnerability, of the world as a reasonable and somewhat predictable place, is shattered. Behavioral self-blame is a means to reestablish a sense of control by attributing the event (correctly or incorrectly) in some degree to one's own behavior, which implies the ability to prevent a recurrence of the event. A rape victim engaged in behavioral self-blame concludes, "I knew I needed to have better security for my home." In contrast, in characterological self-blame the cause of the event is attributed to one's own character. As this is not easily modified, an uncontrollable risk of future victimization is implied. A rape victim engaged in characterological self-blame concludes, "This happened to me because I am a bad or weak person." Behavioral self-blame has been associated with higher self-esteem and perceived future avoidability of victimization in rape victims,[65] whereas characterological self-blaming has been a predictor of depression[66] and poorer adjustment after rape.[67]

This model offers a framework to understand why victims of hate crime assaults may experience greater distress relative to victims of assaults in general. The latter may be able to make some behavioral changes to minimize perceived future risk. They may even attribute the crime to bad luck, and assume that future risk for assault is correspondingly low: "I was just in the wrong place at the wrong time." But if victimization is attributable

to such attributes as race, ethnicity, or sexual orientation, these are as immutable as character. "The realization that one's 'community' may be targeted because of its immutable or prominent characteristics slowly erodes feelings of safety and security."[68] Perhaps victims of hate crimes, who are targeted specifically because of their membership in a particular group, are less able to preserve an illusion of control, for they cannot change their race, ethnicity, sexual orientation, and so on even if they desired to.

B. Reporting Problems

Many victims of bias-related crimes do not report those crimes to law enforcement; 2005 statistics suggest that of lesbian, gay, bisexual, and transsexual (LGBT) victims, only 31 percent made reports to law enforcement in addition to reports made to nongovernmental community groups.[69] Dunbar finds that in Los Angeles County, hate crimes motivated by sexual orientation were reported to the police at a lower rate than other types of hate crimes (72 percent versus greater than 95 percent).[70] Unfortunately, more severe attacks—physical assault, assault with a deadly weapon, and verbal threat of harm—were unlikely to be reported to the police.

C. The Psychology of the Perpetrators

The previously noted distinction between instrumental and reactive violence may be useful in considering different types of hate crime offenders. Instrumental offenders are reliably distinguishable from reactive offenders on the basis of violent crime behavior and level of psychopathy, independent of the extent of prior criminal record, age, race, or length of incarceration.[71] If in fact the mens rea in hate crimes is the intent to select particular victims because of group membership, evidence of instrumentality would reinforce this point. At least two studies found associations between instrumentality and bias. In 813 reported hate crimes in Los Angeles County, a positive relationship was found between bias indicators and instrumental aggression; furthermore, instrumentally aggressive bias offenders appeared to be solely in pursuit of social dominance rather then monetary or other material gain. There was increased instrumentality in attacks against sexual minorities and increased reactivity in crimes based on victim racial/ethnic makeup.[72] Dunbar, Sullaway, and Krop examined forty-six convicted murderers who had shown bias motivation.[73] Seventy-nine percent of these murders were instrumental in nature. The greater the bias component to the homicide, the more likely there was to have been planning of the crime before the offense.

Various classification schemes have been proposed to describe perpetrators. McDevitt and colleagues identified four types of offenders, including "thrill-motivated" offenders, who are motivated by excitement, bragging rights, and peer acceptance; "defensive" offenders, who perceive a threat by outsiders to their way of life, their community, and privileges; "mission offenders," defined as those committed to a supremacist ideology; and "retaliatory" offenders, inspired to avenge perceived assaults on the group.[74] Ezekial took a qualitative approach to the study of hate group members and noted a variety of "types" of members, including those who simply seek group membership and belonging, those who were more interested in crime opportunities than ideology, and those who were "true believers."[75]

Associated with questions of classification are questions of cause. The majority of hate crime offenders are adults over

eighteen years of age; in Los Angeles County the average perpetrator was thirty years old.[76] What creates an offender? The causes seem to have less to do with family inculcation of biased beliefs and more to do with an alienated, often violent family of origin and parental (especially paternal) absence and neglect. Ezekial makes several fascinating observations about "recruits" into a small hate group in Detroit.[77] The majority of these young men had lost a parent (usually the father) to divorce or separation and grew up with frail or nonexistent interpersonal connections; many, if not most, had dropped out of high school. Hightower studied the role of childhood background in the development of racist attitudes.[78] Racists reported disturbances in their parental relationships as well as in their ties with peers and had poorer interpersonal skills, poorer internal controls, and reduced cognitive resourcefulness.

Turpin-Petrosino[79] describes hate group members "as youth who are academically unsuccessful, have poor family relationships . . . and are insecure, alienated, impotent, and angry . . . backgrounds of family violence and child and substance abuse are not uncommon."[80] Prior participation in lawbreaking is common. Deprivation theory suggests that hate ideology fulfills needs for social affiliation and group membership in youths who are emotionally and economically vulnerable. Interpersonal bonds theory suggests that recruitment into hate ideology occurs through social networks. Once social ties are established, the new member is introduced into group ideology, which maintains the social tie.

Discomfort with social change may be involved in formation of hate attitudes.[81] An intriguing study by McGregor, Zanna, Holmes, and Spencer found that under some circumstances "the threat of personal uncertainty appears to cause a kind of situational authoritarianism involving exaggerated intergroup bias and attitude hardening" toward social issues and groups.[82] Whether this phenomenon helps to explain hate crimes remains to be seen, although it is consistent with the surge in hate crimes found when there is rapid in-migration of a minority group[83] and consistent with the finding that white supremacists and hate crime perpetrators are more obsessed with diversity, race mixing, immigration, and gender role changes than the general public.[84] In tracking anti-LGBT violence over several years, the National Coalition of Anti-Violence Programs (NCAVP) attributes the increase in violence between 2003 and 2004, the decrease in 2005, and an upward trend in 2006 to the national political and cultural climate.[85]

Various crises may contribute to or exacerbate hate crime occurrence. In the four months after the September 11, 2001, attacks, more than 1,450 bias crimes and incidents against Muslims (and perceived Muslims) were reported to law enforcement and community groups not associated with law enforcement, a dramatic increase from the prior 240 to 366 reported per year between 1997 and 2000.[86] In the FBI hate crime database, between 1996 and 2000, reported hate crimes against Muslims ranged between 21 and 32; in the final months of 2001 there was an eighteen-fold increase to 481.[87] The relative contribution made by such news events compared to other factors predicting bias crime needs further examination.

In some perpetrators' cases, genuine mental illness may play a contributory role. Unfortunately, defense strategies have occasionally been attempted in which particular kinds of "mental illness" are blamed, including racial-paranoia-induced delusional disorder, homosexual panic, and homosexual advance. Racial-paranoia-induced delusional disorder (RPIDD) is a "disorder" proposed by Tesner in which the perpetrator has a "delusion" that members of the victim's group are immediately dangerous to the offender.[88] RPIDD or similar arguments have been made in a limited number of cases. For example, in *Commonwealth v. Gilchrist*, a black stockbroker fired by his white employer returned the next day and killed the employer.[89] Mental health professionals testified that the defendant suffered from "a longstanding personality disorder that led him to harbor irrational beliefs that he was being persecuted because he is black," and that the "stress of being fired, combined with his irrational beliefs . . . triggered a temporary psychosis."[90] This defense failed. The RPIDD "diagnosis" has no basis in the medical or psychological literature. Neither a Medline/Medscape search from 1990 to 2006 nor a search of the PsycINFO database revealed any references to the "disorder."

A similar strategy, used in gay-bashing cases, is the "homosexual panic"[91] or "gay panic"[92] defense. The origins of the notion of "homosexual panic" appear to be clinical studies from the 1920s[93] that referred to "*both* the patient's terror of her or his attraction to homosexuality *and* her or his fear of heterosexuality."[94] According to Glick, the term "homosexual panic" "should be used to refer to an acute episodic schizophrenic reaction accompanied by intense terror based on the patient's unconscious wish to present himself as a homosexual object with the expectation of dire consequences."[95] The notion of homosexual panic depends on psychoanalytic theories such as latent homosexuality, repression, unconscious conflict, projection, and displacement. In a 1988 review of the concept of "homosexual panic"

Chuang and Addington conclude that the term "should be permanently assigned to the junkyard of obsolete psychiatric terminology."[96] It is not a mental disorder, and a Medline/Medscape search from 1996 to 2006 did not find any articles containing the term. Forensic psychiatrists have been cautioned against providing "unjustified clinical support" for the concept of the gay panic defense, as it is inadequate for a diminished-capacity defense.[97] While 28 percent of the fifty states have reported court opinions discussing gay or transsexual panic arguments, no state has codified gay and transsexual panic defenses in its penal code.[98]

Another defense that references the psychological state of the offender is the concept of "homosexual threat" or "homosexual advance." This defense proposes that a sexual proposition (not a threat) by a homosexual provokes "understandable" reactions of fear and rage. "As the law now stands . . . only a homosexual advance can mitigate murder to manslaughter," as such an advance "in and of itself constitutes sufficient provocation to incite a reasonable man to lose his self control and kill in the heat of passion."[99] This defense has been used with occasional success, as in *Schick v. State*, in which a man voluntarily walked into a park with a gay man to participate in a mutually agreed-upon sexual act, then killed him.[100] A "homosexual advance" provocation was argued, and the judge instructed the jury on voluntary manslaughter—which was the verdict returned by the jury.

The psychological defense strategies outlined above appear to be variations on insanity, diminished competence, extreme emotional disturbance, or provocation defense strategies. The situations in which perpetrators' psychological state mitigates murder change inevitably with societal mores. The existence of hate crime laws reflects social and political values that are incompatible with the justifications required for these defense strategies.

IV. IMPACT OF HATE CRIME LAWS

Concerns have been expressed that hate crime laws may actually increase intergroup tension in the United States.[101] Existing data fail to confirm that hypotheses. At a national level, there have not been convincing statistical analyses that show an association between the enactment of hate crime laws such as the Hate Crime Statistics Act,[102] the Hate Crime Sentencing Act,[103] and the Church Arson Prevention Act[104] and increased intergroup tension. It is unclear if the laws have a deterrent effect. Yet if one considers hate crime laws to be an "authority sanction" of peaceful coexistence, it could be argued that hate crime laws ultimately work toward reduction of intergroup tension. And, to the degree that discriminative behavior, including bias-motivated violence, is codetermined by individual prejudice and situational factors, hate crime laws may inhibit at least some individuals from violent manifestations of their beliefs.[105] For example, McDevitt and colleagues suggest that thrill-seeking offenders may be deterred from repeating the crime if there is a strong societal response.[106]

Yet even if hate crime laws have little deterrence effect, they nevertheless have a powerful symbolic role in communicating social and political values to individuals. Hate crime laws make a symbolic statement that, for example, the negative evaluation of homosexuality implicit in a gay-bashing attack is unreasonable and neither normative nor proper in our society. "At issue is whom we should regard as low and contaminating—the persons singled out for attacks on the basis of their identities, or the persons who attack them for that reason."[107]

Bias-motivated violence occurs in a context of environmental contingencies, ranging from the officially sanctioned discrimination of the segregated South in the United States to unofficially condoned and accepted discrimination and, finally, to state discouragement or punishment of bias-motivated discrimination and violence.[108] The legal and political environment may thus augment, inhibit, or be neutral toward bias-motivated violence. Forty-two states have hate crime laws that cover at least race, religion, and national origin.[109] Not surprisingly, there are inconsistencies between states in terms of which categories are covered. For example, despite preliminary data indicating that crimes against homosexuals may be particularly vicious, several states' hate crime laws do not include sexual orientation in their protected categories. Hate crime statutes should accurately reflect our state of knowledge about the groups commonly targeted.

Group position theory[110] suggests that "prejudice involves more than negative stereotypes and negative feelings, that it involves most centrally a commitment to a relative status positioning of groups in a racialized social order,"[111] and that "change in a racial order would spring . . . not . . . from inner considerations of industrial efficiency. Instead they arise from outside pressure, chiefly political pressures."[112] Hate crime laws might be considered an example of the political pressure mentioned by Blumer.

Critical race theory suggests that hate speech and hate-based violence not only are crimes against individuals but also can be viewed as terrorist acts against the entire group to which the individual belongs. Hate crimes that terrorize and subordinate entire groups deprive them of their civil liberties, and hate crime laws reflect the state's recognition of and protection of the civil rights of all groups.[113]

CONCLUSION

The Supreme Court ruled in favor of penalty enhancements for hate-based crimes in 1993. Some individual states have enacted their own hate crime legislation. Psychology has much to contribute to the definition and measurement of hate intent and motivation and to the study and treatment of perpetrators and victims. While the state of research as it now exists is quite incomplete, evidence that we have thus far suggests that hate-motivated crimes may be particularly severe in nature and in impact, and that hate-based crimes may be qualitatively different from other crimes. Clearly, the greatest weakness of the research cited is the preliminary nature of the area of inquiry, and, consequently, the lack of replication and the number of unanswered questions. Furthermore, one cannot have faith that statistics collected nationally by law enforcement truly capture the extent of the problem, as many cases go unreported. One hopes these problems will be addressed in the future, as data collection by law enforcement improves and research studies find their way into the literature.

17

Prejudice and Police Profiling

Roger G. Dunham and George Wilson

INTRODUCTION

One of the most intriguing concerns facing all societies, and American society in particular, is the use of race as a criterion in official or governmental decision making. There are many examples of the consequences of race-based discrimination, but one situation dramatically sets the scene for our study. If police officers use race inappropriately as a criterion in professional decision making, it is often called *racial profiling* or *racially biased policing*. In this chapter, we identify the general issues and concepts that frame concerns and claims about racial profiling, and tie in relevant theories and research on racial prejudice.

In any discussion of racial profiling, it is important to discuss the various conceptualizations of racial profiling and provide a working definition of it and its various forms.

I. WHAT IS RACIAL PROFILING?

In 1986, a racially based drug courier profile was introduced to law enforcement by the Drug Enforcement Agency. Based on that profile, Operation Pipeline was developed as a drug interdiction program using pretext stops in order to locate contraband in vehicles. The strategies and techniques used in Operation Pipeline were influential in making popular the use of pretext stops, which are at the heart of the racial profiling debate. In many law enforcement circles, Operation Pipeline and the three specific profiles developed by state agencies were considered a proper method of enforcement that produced results: specifically, the arrest of individuals in possession of various quantities of drugs. The argument made by the law enforcement community was one of efficiency: that police on the nation's highways should stop disproportionate numbers of those who fit the circulated profile in an effort to reduce drug trafficking. The profile was developed using crime and arrest statistics and described those likely to possess drugs or commit other crimes. Because those crime statistics showed that blacks were significantly overrepresented among those arrested, it was justified to stop and interrogate black citizens, as there was a greater likelihood that they might be guilty of something.

Of course, this argument centers on the problematic assumption that criminal profiling and racial profiling are effectively one and the same, an argument that transfers to terrorism in contemporary America: profiling specific groups at our airports and seaports has become commonplace. In today's world, Arabs or those who resemble Arabs are actively profiled because of potential terrorist activities. Stopping a disproportionate number of Arab Americans on the highways is just as tendentious as stopping a disproportionate number of Arab Americans at our airports. Those on this side of the argument maintain that while Arabs may be responsible for some terrorist acts, just as blacks may be arrested more often than whites, it is neither appropriate nor logical nor fair to assume that all Arabs or blacks should be stopped and investigated. Leaving terrorist issues for another day, it seems clear that while blacks may be arrested more often than whites, there is no tangible evidence that they violate traffic laws at a different rate; consequently, members of this group should not be stopped at a greater rate. Nonetheless, the "ecological fallacy" persists. When a police officer makes an inference about an individual, it is perceived as legitimate because it is based on aggregate data for a group. However, most opponents of racial profiling would further argue that while there is racial disparity in crime rates generally, the social costs of racial profiling outweigh the potential or arguable efficiency that is gained from the practice. For example, an officer might recognize that blacks are arrested as a group more than whites and then infer that all blacks are likely to be criminals. Based on this information, which passes for "knowledge," the officer can make a conscious (or unconscious) effort to stop more black citizens, thinking he or she will uncover more crime. Since most members of minority groups who are stopped are not carrying illegal drugs or other contraband, they are highly likely to resent being stopped, questioned, or searched. The practice of stopping blacks and other minorities in turn promotes contempt for or distrust of police officers, and accordingly can create negative attitudes toward law enforcement and undermine their efforts by creating an atmosphere of mistrust.

"Definitions of racial profiling pose complex questions both in law and social science, and definitions will shape estimates of its extent, nature, and consequences."[1] For example, the manner in which we define racial profiling will directly affect how we set out to estimate its incidence and prevalence. The following are examples given by Jeffrey Fagan of how professionals define racial profiling:[2]

1. The International Association of Chiefs of Police: "proactive traffic enforcement that is race or ethnic-based . . . stops and searches made simply because of race"
2. U.S. General Accounting Office: "highway stops that use race as a key factor in deciding whether to stop a motorist"
3. Skolnick and Caplovitz (2001): "police targeting people solely or primarily because of their skin color"
4. Gross and Livingston (2002): "when a police officer stops, arrests, questions, searches or otherwise investigates a person because the officer believes that

members of that person's racial or ethnic group are more likely than the population at large to commit the sort of crime that the officer is investigating"

Fagan points out that in all of these definitions, there is an implicit assumption that the police make an a priori probabilistic assessment that members of some group are more likely than others to be engaged in criminal activity. This leads us to one of the many difficult issues surrounding the practice of racial profiling: even if it is true that members of one group have a greater likelihood of offending than others, does that justify targeting members of that group for intense crime control measures, such as stops and searches? It is true that officers are called upon as part of their duty to determine suspicious behavior and to act to protect the public from crime or victimization. Often they have to form suspicions based upon incomplete information, which is fertile ground for prejudice to exert some influence. Further, it is true that the use of informal profiles has always been a part of policing as a type of shorthand to help identify suspicious individuals worthy of attention. Officers develop schemas or mental images or sets of clues that help ferret out the abnormal from the normal, the suspicious from the innocuous. Also, it is customary for the officers to form working rules with respect to these mental images that direct their work. Racial profiling is the use of race as *one of the factors* in any profile that affects police discretionary action.

"The term 'racial profiling' emerged only in the late 1990s, but concerns about whether some police are racially biased in their decision making dates back decades, arguably even centuries, in U.S. history."[3] Organizational profiles began with the "war" on drugs as a means of detecting drug traffickers. Law enforcement agencies including the Border Patrol, Drug Enforcement Agency, and U.S. Customs issued profiles of drug traffickers to help officers identify potential drug dealers. These profiles were overtly race-based, listing certain racial/ethnic groups as being typical of drug traffickers. The motivation for the profiling was to stop the flow of drugs from Miami to the cities of the Northeast via Interstate 95. In 1985, the Florida Department of Highway Safety and Motor Vehicles issued guidelines for police on "the common characteristics of drug couriers," in which race/ethnicity was mentioned as one of the characteristics. The police used this information to make stops in order to produce more efficient crime control as opposed to the less efficient practice of making random stops. Since then, other law enforcement agencies began using formal profiles. More recently, however, overt racial profiling has come under attack and in most jurisdictions is either illegal or strongly discouraged.

There are a number of important distinctions that are useful when defining and discussing racial profiling. They allow us to specify more clearly the wide variety of behaviors that are all lumped under the rubric of "racial profiling." For example, some examples of racial profiling directly involve racial animus, while others clearly are unintentional, entailing no malice or ill will.

II. DIRECT VERSUS INDIRECT RACIAL PROFILING

Direct racial profiling involves using race or ethnic group identification as the only criterion, the major criterion, or one of many criteria for determining suspicion. Race is directly used as a factor in the decision making. Direct racial profiling is one of the more troubling types because, at the individual level, it often involves racial prejudice and/or bigotry and has a definite discriminatory nature to it.

Indirect racial profiling entails using presumptively race-neutral criteria but nonetheless focuses on behaviors or characteristics that may be more typical of certain racial or ethnic groups than others. An example would be targeting people wearing certain clothing or jewelry that is typical of specific groups, such as gold chains, indirectly targeting the racial group. Geographical racial profiling or deploying police officers and/or enforcement so that certain groups are more likely than others to be present (e.g., an officer going to a known minority area to give out tickets) is another example of indirect racial profiling. In this case, there seems to be no police bias within each neighborhood with respect to who is stopped or arrested, but overall disparities exists because of the policies for deploying the police. Although indirect profiling typically does not involve racial animus or bigotry, it nevertheless results in racial disparity in enforcement.

III. INDIVIDUAL VERSUS ORGANIZATIONAL RACIAL PROFILING

Organizational racial profiling is when there are organizational rules or policies specifying racial profiles or encouraging officers to use race as a criterion in their decision making. The organization, through practice, training, or policy, generates a profile meant to describe a typical offender, and that profile includes race as a criterion. Individual racial profiling is when an individual officer uses racial profiles in the *absence* of institutional policy or encouragement to do so.

IV. MAJOR TYPES OF RACIAL PROFILING

Drawing upon these two broad domains of racial profiling, more specific types can be delineated by focusing on their intersection. We define four major types of racial profiling in Figure 17.1. Bigoted profiling is when an individual officer constructs and uses racial profiles that directly incorporate race as the only or major criterion for decision making. This type is distinguished from stereotypical profiling, which takes place when an individual uses criteria other than race as the basis for suspicion. However, the other criteria that are used may be more typical of certain racial or ethnic groups than others, resulting in a racial disparity in enforcement. Characteristics typical of the racial minority are constructed as part of a general stereotype of the typical offender, so that the general stereotype results in racial disparities in enforcement, hence the name "general stereotypical profiling." Institutionalized racial profiling occurs when there are organizational rules or policies specifying racial profiles or encouraging officers to use race as a criterion in their decision making. This type of racial profiling is distinguished from latent policy profiling by its directness in using race as a criterion for decision making. Latent policy profiling involves organizational policies and practices that do not use race directly as a criterion for decisions but do use criteria that are correlated with race so as to effectively cause disparate impacts upon certain racial groups.

FIGURE 17.1. Types of Racial Profiling		
	Indirect Profiling	Direct Profiling
Individual Profiling	General stereotypical profiling	Bigoted profiling
Organizational Profiling	Latent policy profiling	Institutionalized racial profiling

V. RACIAL ANIMUS VERSUS OTHER MOTIVATIONS

Beyond the typologies listed above, another key element to consider is racial animus. This suggests that sometimes the act of using racial profiles is motivated by active racism, prejudice, or dislike of members in a particular group. This is a much different and more serious motivation than using racial profiles because one believes or has information that members of one group are much more likely to engage in specific types of criminal behavior than others. That is, the motivation here is more sinister.

It is also important to recognize that not all types of racial profiling are equally serious or reprehensible. Perhaps the more direct racial profiling is, the more serious it would be considered to be. Likewise, the more racial animus is involved in the decision making, the more reprehensible it will be judged to be. And the more disparities between groups it engenders, the more serious the problem becomes. These evaluations form a continuum from the most serious forms of racial profiling to the least serious, some of which even may be condoned under some unique circumstances.

Perhaps the most serious types of racial profiling involve direct racial profiling with racial animus: motivated by active racism and prejudice. In comparison, perhaps the least serious types are those characterized by indirect racial profiling without any racial animus (e.g., motivated by data showing a particular group, such as a specific group of terrorists, to be more likely to commit specific offenses). While we do not make this distinction, some scholars have argued that there is a distinction between legitimate racial profiling and discriminatory racial profiling—between responsible profiling and profiling that is based on bigotry and that has the same effect as bigotry.

VI. PREJUDICE AS AN UNDERPINNING OF PROFILING

Despite varying levels of racial animus or overt/intentional discrimination directed at racial/ethnic minorities in profiling, there is a growing body of evidence that can be distilled from social science research that prejudice, in a relatively benign form, constitutes an underpinning of profiling in a majority of its forms. To back up this stance, it is necessary to review several aspects of sociological and social psychological research—namely, the nature of prejudice and its distribution across individuals who occupy decision making roles within police organizations.

A. Nature of Prejudice

A sizable literature in sociology and social psychology has traced the structure and evolution of racial prejudice in the United States.[4] In this vein, evidence indicates that the form it has taken has changed drastically in recent decades. Specifically, traditional "Jim Crow" prejudice, which is characterized by its foundation in stereotypes regarding the biological bases of racial differences in perceived psychological attributes/dispositions and behavioral differences as well as support for segregation across institutional spheres, has given way to a more "subtle" and "benign"[5] form of prejudice grounded in stereotypes about cultural and motivational differences between racial groups.[6] Stereotypes underlying the more contemporary form of prejudice—which has variously been labeled "laissez-faire racism,"[7] "symbolic racism,"[8] and "contemporary prejudice"[9]—are characterized by notions that equality, at least in principle, should govern relations between racial groups and support for integration across institutional spheres.[10] Overall, the contemporary form of racial prejudice is based on widespread but relatively benign stereotypes rather than the ill will and overt hostility of the classic "bigoted" personality that more closely captures the nature of the Jim Crow form of prejudice.[11]

Racial prejudice is "an antipathy [directed toward an out-group] based upon a faulty and inflexible generalization."[12] Significantly, racial prejudice is rooted in stereotypes, "a set of beliefs about the perceived attributes of members of a particular social category."[13] Stereotypes are not in a statistical sense aberrant, but rather are the product of a basic cognitive function—the need to classify, categorize, and form judgments about objects in our environment.[14] Overall, stereotypes serve the function of "racializing"[15] the most minute phenomena of everyday life: stereotypes ranging in content about groups' temperament, intelligence, athletic ability, and aesthetic preferences, as well as dispositions toward wealth/poverty and criminality, ensure that race constitutes a primary cleavage in representing the social world.[16]

Significantly, the gap created by the physical impossibility of acquiring direct information, as well as processing and forming evaluative judgments about objects in our environment, is filled by the readily available judgments of external sources and social-psychology-based needs related to such issues as esteem and status maintenance.[17] Accordingly, stereotypes are acquired through several analytically distinct but often overlapping sources. Specifically, they may have a cognitive underpinning—social-learning—that encompasses patterns of socialization/interaction[18] and exposure to media-disseminated messages.[19] Also noteworthy is an affective base to stereotypes—self interest—which encompasses both "individual" and "cooperative" variants.[20] These variants capture the importance of direct (i.e., having to do with oneself) and indirect (i.e., having to do with significant others in one's life such as family, friends, and co-ethnics with whom one identifies) symbolic and material advantages that accrue from stereotyping.[21]

Stereotypes—irrespective of their source—make social categories (e.g., racial groups) salient and activate an existing bundle of preexisting perceptions and information about them. This existing cognitive structure or schema about "African Americans," "Hispanics," "Asians," and "whites" organizes and directs information taken in by individuals in any specific situation. That is, stereotypes bias perceptions and the meaning assigned to objects and events in the immediate situation. Further, as Bobo and Massagli have recently noted, stereotypes are not neutral.[22] They are not merely a shortcut in which order is substituted for the great confusion of reality. Stereotypes serve critical functions: they play a pivotal role in guaranteeing self-respect, and they are a basis for projecting upon the world a justification for specific values and rights and for defending positional differences and/or justifying the unequal distribution of material and symbolic rewards. In short, stereotypes are the fortress of tradition, and from behind its defenses those who benefit from the status quo feel safe in the positions they occupy and justified in the rewards they receive.[23] Finally, additional social psychological research establishes that stereotypes are acted upon when there is both opportunity and motivation to do so.[24] Opportunity refers to power to exert formal or informal control over the objects of stereotypes.[25] Motivation encompasses having an incentive to act, or deriving a benefit from acting, on one's stereotypes—such as gaining legitimacy in one's position or socioeconomic gain.[26]

B. Operation of Prejudice Across Key Decision Makers

The basis in social science for maintaining that prejudice is operating subtly in police profiling derives from existing research regarding its operation for other key decision makers across other institutional spheres in daily life, namely, employers in the workplace and realtors/brokers in the real estate market. It is to this analogy that we now turn in building a case that prejudice, in its modern iteration, underlies police profiling.

Social science research has established that stereotypes forming the basis of "contemporary prejudice" are underpinnings of decision making among key actors in the domains of work and the housing market. In this regard, emerging from a distillation of recent research spanning multiple methods is that discriminatory practices denying blacks with equivalent human capital credentials as whites similar access to the labor market and blacks with equivalent financial resources as whites similar residential options are undergirded by a range of stereotypes that depict blacks as unsuitable workers and neighbors.[27] In particular, two kinds of negative stereotypes about blacks can be identified. The first is interpersonal traits that constitute variants of "dirtiness/uncleanliness"[28] and "laziness."[29] The second is behavioral dispositions that capture variants of "disinterest in keeping up property"[30] and preferences for "living off welfare and disinterest in work."[31]

In fact, no existing social science research has systematically assessed stereotypes in the context of profiling. However, a plausible case that stereotypes are a crucial source of profiling derives from findings regarding how deep-rooted and widely held domain-specific stereotypes relating to crime—which one researcher characterized as forming the "hallmark" of contemporary prejudice—are among the American population.[32] In this vein, results from several recent survey-based analyses indicate that stereotypes regarding both interpersonal traits and behavioral dispositions associated with

criminality—namely, items that constitute themes related to "violence," as well as those that capture engaging in antisocial activity such as associations with "drugs" and "gangs"—obtain higher levels of support than parallel negative stereotypes associated with suitability as workers and neighbors among both genders, across age groups and categories of social class, and among nonblack racial groups.[33] Accordingly, it should not be surprising that in the last half dozen or so years several criminologists have maintained that the pervasive, stereotypically rooted "color coding" of crime has permeated the criminal justice system and is driving the decision making of key actors such as judges, parole officers, and criminal lawyers.[34]

In addition, a series of experimentally based studies,[35] survey-based analyses,[36] and ethnographic case studies[37] that examine prejudicial dynamics have identified several critical social-psychology-based cognitive processes—namely, "statistical discrimination" and "attribution bias"—utilized by decision makers analogous to the police when exercising discretion in the performance of job functions. Significantly, these cognitive processes tend to be pronounced in specific contexts and serve to "activate" the stereotypes that comprise contemporary racial prejudice.[38] In particular, they operate among those who render decisions regarding social control over racial minorities—for example, employers and real estate brokers/landlords—but lack complete information for doing so.[39] Accordingly, decision making is often predicated on minimal information, such as the identification of one's race at, for example, the outset of a job interview[40] or pursuant to completing a racial status question on a job or rental application.[41] Statistical discrimination operates when key—primarily white—decision makers such as employers, real estate brokers, or landlords assign the perceived average characteristics (i.e., stereotypes) of that group to any one of its members, adversely impacting prospects for being hired in the workplace or for being able to rent or purchase real property.[42]

Confirmatory attribution bias refers to the tendency of employers, real estate brokers, and landlords to selectively accentuate negative aspects of the physical appearance, characteristics/traits, credentials, or behavior of racial minorities.[43] In this regard, information that disconfirms preexisting stereotypes is dismissed as an aberration, while information that reinforces stereotypes is highlighted and viewed as normative.[44]

No research has explicitly examined the extent to which cognitive processes resembling statistical discrimination and attribution bias operate in the context of profiling by the police. Nevertheless, there are bases in social science research for maintaining they should be at least as pronounced in the sphere of profiling as in hiring among employers and in the selling/renting of real estate by brokers and landlords. Specifically, experimentally based research and case studies have found that both cognitive processes function in inverse relation to the amount of predecision contact with minority groups.[45] In this regard, contact provides information that can help to overcome cognitively based forms of bias. However, the context of profiling is distinct from the workplace or the real estate market: police have no opportunity to have contact with specific citizens prior to reaching decisions regarding whether to engage in suspicion-based stops of their automobiles. In addition, these same studies also indicate that statistical discrimination and attribution bias function in direct relation to the severity of domain-specific stereotypes. Accordingly, the relatively pronounced nature of stereotypes regarding blacks' penchant for criminality should serve to render cognitive

processes such as statistical discrimination and attribution bias integral to profiling.

Finally, social science research offers an additional basis for concluding that the behavior of police in racial profiling—just as is the case for employers in hiring and brokers/landlords in selling and renting real property—is based on contemporary racial prejudice: namely, actors in all three domains derive legitimacy from acting upon prejudicial attitudes. In the context of hiring, employers derive legitimacy from, most notably, superiors in the form of professional esteem, status, and standing based on their ability to manage an efficient business operation.[46] Accordingly, adhering to existing racial norms of exclusion in the workplace that are rooted in racial stereotypes are perceived as advantageous for at least two reasons: (1) it ensures that new workers have the requisite personal characteristics,[47] and (2) it prevents dominant-group workers from becoming disgruntled pursuant to the changing racial composition in the workplace.[48] In the realm of selling or renting real property, landlords and brokers are evaluated as competent and successful to the extent they are responsive to community and neighborhood concerns regarding such issues as maintaining existing real estate values and the quality of existing residential life.[49] Accordingly, the premium put on fulfilling these professional obligations militates toward making decisions based on stereotypes regarding blacks' suitability as real estate owners and renters.[50]

C. Arguments for and Against Racial Profiling

Key information for deciding whether or not to permit any types of racial profiling is to weigh the benefits against the burdens. Even for instances of racial profiling that are viewed as legitimate by some, there is a trade-off between liberty and public safety. The benefits may be more efficient crime control and enhanced public safety. The burdens are personal inconvenience and infringement on privacy.

There are not many arguments for racial profiling since nationally we have decided it is an undesirable practice, and local jurisdictions are beginning to make it illegal (e.g., Miami-Dade County, Florida). However, one could argue that, based on crime statistics, one group or another is disproportionately involved in a specific type of crime, or in a crime specific locale. Therefore, racial profiles could be justified on that basis. For example, if it was the case that a community had experienced a high level of juvenile violence over a period of time, and the police had credible information that the high level of violence was due to disputes between two rival Latino gangs, it wouldn't make much sense to begin surveillance on African American gangs in the community to address this violence problem. The terrorist threats since 9/11, coming from fundamentalist Islamic groups, were almost exclusively Middle Eastern men, so it makes sense for the profiles concerning terrorist activities to include these characteristics.

The argument could be made that racial profiles are used all the time for individual cases. One example would be a BOLO (be on the lookout) announcement that comes out describing two black males who have robbed a convenience store and driven off in a blue Ford Taurus. Obviously we should not pull over white minivans with Latina women simply to be fair. It is justified in these types of cases to use race as a criterion in deciding who is suspicious.

Actually, age and gender profiles are much more commonplace than racial profiles, yet we seldom question them. These profiles are justified by the fact that young males commit more crime than others. However, all the arguments against racial profiling can be applied to age and gender

profiles. Should these types of profiling be outlawed?

Historically, the courts have allowed restrictions of liberty (e.g., Japanese internment camps during World War II) on the grounds that they protected public safety, and have been willing to accept the trade-off of some loss of rights for increased efficiency in providing public safety (e.g., airport searches after 9/11). In fact, most of the public seems willing to make the trade-off as well, especially when the burdens are minor (time and inconvenience) and the benefit is to save lives and prevent criminal victimization. While there are only a few general arguments for racial profiling, as you may expect, there are lots of specific arguments against the practice.

1. *Creates a disproportionate burden*. Even if crime figures show that certain racial or ethnic groups are disproportionately involved in certain types of crime, usually only a very small proportion of that group will be involved in the crime (e.g., 1 percent, 2 percent, 5 percent). So even if we assume that the profile is 100 percent correct, 99 percent of the stops may be unjust. This is a lot of burden for very little benefit.

2. *Leads to racial tension and police illegitimacy*. Racial profiling and its accompanying burdens on some groups damage the credibility and legitimacy of policing. The "tax" it levies on the few, for the benefit of the many, damages police credibility among the affected group and among others who see that justice is not being administered fairly. It is well documented that African Americans trust the police considerably less than non-minorities do. Therefore, racial profiling can have a negative impact on social cohesion and governmental legitimacy.

3. *Propagates prejudice*. Profiling legitimizes or makes acceptable prejudicial motivation in making important deci-

sions (e.g., major enforcement decisions by the state). Often negative and unflattering stereotypes form the basis of composites, sketches, or profiles of likely suspects, which propagates stereotypes and prejudice.

4. *Violates the value of racial egalitarianism.* The practice of racial profiling violates the ideal that existing patterns of social disparity between racial groups should, as an ethical goal, be reduced. Specifically, this ideal holds that disproportionate burdens on groups that live with a legacy of past discrimination and consistently suffer from a disproportionate share of social burdens in other areas are an evil to be avoided.

Certainly most people believe that the burdens outweigh the benefits when it comes to racial profiling, but it is difficult to agree on an equity norm for law enforcement practices to distribute the burdens of crime control fairly across all groups. What would be a fair distribution of stops and searches? Many possible standards of equity exist, and it may be difficult to obtain a consensus on one of them.

David Thacher outlined and evaluated several norms of equity with respect to police stops and searches.[51] Should the police strive for a pattern in which individuals from all racial groups face equal risk of being stopped and searched, so there would be no racial disparities? Thatcher called this equity norm pure racial equality. Another possible equity norm, according to Thatcher, would be procedural equality. The pattern of stops and searches across groups is not important in itself if the patterns can be explained by factors other than explicit racial profiling (offending, police presence, etc.). Under this equity norm, racial disparities may be produced, but they must be explained by legitimate reasons. A more stringent equity norm, according to Thatcher, places equal burdens on the innocent.[52] In other words, the risk that an innocent person will be stopped or searched by the police should be equal across all groups. We all agree that there should be equal burdens on the guilty. This equity norm extends that value to the innocent as well. Any police procedure that places a greater burden on any group of innocent people would violate this equity norm.

D. Racial Profiling and the Law

The term "racial profiling" generally describes the inappropriate use of race by the police during traffic stops. Unfortunately, there is no uniform agreement on the activities that constitute racial profiling or that explain when and how race can be used properly by the police. In recent years, many police departments have formulated policies that define the proper use of race in law enforcement, but the courts have neither condoned nor condemned, nor even ruled uniformly on, the various definitions and levels of tolerance that have been set in place. In their traditional manner, the courts have applied existing legal doctrines to law enforcement practices that involve race and have reached a number of varied conclusions. As each state has different statutes and case law, it is not practicable to comprehensively discuss claims of discrimination. We will therefore limit our discussion at this point to federal claims of discrimination or unequal treatment of citizens by the police in order to provide context both for the litigation undertaken and for the type of research that would be helpful in this field.

E. Legal Standards in Racial Profiling Cases

If citizens believe they have been discriminated against because of their race, the United States Constitution provides some relief. The Fifth and Fourteenth amendments prohibit governmental agents, including law enforcement officers, from discriminating against citizens based upon their race, ethnicity, or national origin. Additionally, other federal statutes have been passed that address directly the actions of law enforcement officers. These statutes prohibit the discrimination of citizens based on race, religion, sex, color, or national origin.

Generally speaking, the Constitution and federal statutes prohibit the police from purposely discriminating against persons *because* of their race. The current standard requires that a successful claim show that the police action had a discriminatory effect that was created by a discriminatory purpose. While this standard does not require proof of racial animus, it does require proof that the officer acted deliberately to create or cause an adverse impact on an identifiable group. This standard is a particularly difficult one for plaintiffs to meet, as it requires them to convince the court that the police officers discriminated against them in order to create a harmful outcome. Clearly, research of any relevance will have to identify police officer and agency patterns and practices and the impact of those actions and patterns on identifiable groups. Research on this type of issue is complex and difficult to conduct.

While the use of race as the sole criterion for a discretionary traffic stop is clearly illegal under existing federal laws and in accordance with court decisions, the use of race as one of several factors used in the decision to make a stop is neither condemned nor condoned. Historically, the courts have generally allowed the police to consider race as a physical descriptor when looking for a suspect whose race is known to them. This said, there is no established rule that states explicitly how race can or cannot be used. Consequently, different courts may allow the use

of race in a variety of ways. In contrast to the laws and policies, what happens in real-world situations is an empirical question that requires extensive investigation.

Another response to claims of racial profiling has emerged through the intervention of the United States Department of Justice. In 1998, a Justice Department investigation of activities of the New Jersey State Police raised public awareness of racial profiling and surprised the law enforcement community when it published its finding of a pattern of conduct violations wherein members of minority groups were singled out by the police for what amounted to relatively minor traffic stops. Even more surprising to the law enforcement community was the consent decree that the New Jersey State Police entered into with the U.S. Department of Justice in order to correct the problems. The investigation and consent decree influenced the explosion of media coverage of the problems associated with racial profiling. This media feeding frenzy heightened public awareness of racial profiling and thrust it into the public spotlight along with other social issues that divided society along the lines mentioned above. The media coverage helped create a social and political environment in which claims of profiling were rife. Law enforcement responded to these claims with explanations of the discrepancies in their treatment of black and white citizens that were at least partially legitimate but were ignored.

F. The Importance of Race

General sociological theory[53] as well as research on policing[54] clearly show the importance of race in police-citizen contacts. For example, Rawls notes that minority citizens and the police have different underlying expectations regarding such basic concepts as conversation. Barlow and Barlow suggest that police research must be multicultural and not forget the "views of the communities that are policed."[55] The importance of race in policing cannot be overlooked; rather, it must be seen as an integral part of any research scheme.

Typically, race has been used as a control variable in research on police behavior. As noted above, research findings have not provided authoritative results concerning the influence of race on police decision making. Research also shows mixed results regarding the influence of suspect race on police response and on the influence of officer race on the suspect's reaction. For example, some studies indicate that African American suspects are more likely to be arrested and/or to be treated more harshly by police than white suspects,[56] while other studies report no effect.[57] The research findings are also mixed concerning the importance of race with regard to both the use of deadly force[58] and nondeadly force.[59] After an exhaustive review of the literature, the National Research Council concluded:

> This research finds that the impact of legally relevant factors is strong. Taking these into account, the class and gender of suspects play a small role. However, more research is needed on the complex interplay of race, ethnicity, and other social factors in police-citizen interactions.
>
> Among officer characteristics, neither race, nor gender has a direct influence on the outcome of routine police-citizen encounters, and there is no clear effect of officer's attitudes, job satisfaction, or personality.[60]

To look at all situations in which police officers use discretion and make decisions is manifestly unrealistic, and researchers have therefore focused on areas that are either controversial or convenient to study. Discretionary traffic stops are one police activity that has generated complaints by black citizens. We can investigate claims of racial profiling by examining traffic stops and behavior after the stop to char-

acterize patterns of practice that can either affirm or refute accusations of racial profiling. At the center of the racial profiling debate is the premise that police officers target minorities, particularly black citizens, during their routine activities because of the belief that they are more likely to be guilty of having committed a crime than are whites. According to Russell, "blackness has become an acceptable 'risk factor' for criminal behavior."[61] Empirical evidence shows that blacks are overrepresented in official and self-reported records regarding criminal activity, and especially regarding violent crime.[62] However, if police officers are making decisions based on the race of the suspect, then there are clearly serious implications for due process and equal protection under the law.[63] Indeed, the American Civil Liberties Union argues that racial profiling causes "tens of thousands of motorists each year" to be stopped and treated unfairly, an accusation that, if accurate, threatens the core principles of American society.[64]

Based on these and other claims, it is manifestly critical that social science researchers thoroughly investigate the patterns and practices of police officers; specifically, it is vital that researchers determine the bases upon which police officers are making their decisions to invoke their discretionary power to stop and detain motorists. Additionally, while research in this field may or may not reveal that officers are acting within the letter of the law when undertaking their duty, there are certain ethical issues that must be considered and implemented for the law to maintain legitimacy and fairness in the eyes of citizens. Clearly, just because a certain practice or specific behavior is legal does not make it de facto fair. While stops may ultimately prove to be legal, because they reveal criminal activity of some sort, they may nonetheless be inappropriate, unethical, or just plain wrong; that is, they may be the result of racial profiling, which is plainly in breach of an individual's constitutional rights. It is imperative that such improper decisions be halted. A combination of more stringent policies, proactive training, ongoing supervision, and increased officer and management accountability would seem to offer an appropriate set of solutions, all of which could aid an officer in his or her decision making, although none would be effective in isolation. The courts can also play a role in curtailing unacceptable behavior by police officers by censoring police departments' problematic policies. If an officer does not apply his or her training and adhere to departmental policy, or if a department's policy systematically promotes racial pro-

filing, then legal action becomes a real possibility. Of course, there remains the proviso that many of the actions undertaken by police officers are not de facto illegal, as they fall under the auspices of police discretion and are therefore difficult to prosecute in the absence of a clear departmental policy that promotes profiling. Establishing whether these patterns of profiling do or do not exist, therefore, becomes critical if the system of law enforcement is to become truly equitable. The results of this process would be twofold: first, it would expose problematic departmental policies, and second, it would prompt change within that department, ideally out of a desire to ensure social justice.

18

The Influence of Criminal Defendants'
Afrocentric Features on Their Sentences
William T. Pizzi, Irene V. Blair, and Charles M. Judd

INTRODUCTION

One of the authors of this chapter tells the story of the time he and two academic colleagues were ticketed by the Boulder, Colorado, police for hiking in a mountain location that was off-limits to hikers. On the day indicated on the summons, the three showed up at the municipal court, each wearing a blue blazer, dress shirt, and tie. The courtroom was crowded with defendants charged with the usual mix of minor crimes that clog municipal courts everywhere—petty thefts, public urination offenses, minor traffic offenses, and the like. When the judge came onto the bench and surveyed the courtroom, he saw the three well-dressed defendants and blurted out, "What are you guys doing here?" When they explained why they were in court, the judge imposed a minimal fine on each of them and quickly disposed of their case.

We suggest that this example illustrates how the appearances of defendants can cue immediate responses to them. In this case the dress of these defendants immediately suggested to the judge that they were different from the other defendants in the courtroom. Their dress perhaps suggested that they came from a better socioeconomic class than typical municipal court defendants and deserved preferential treatment, which might mean an expedited hearing of their matter or even a more favorable disposition than for other defendants charged with similar crimes.

Many of our opinions about others are often triggered by simple appearance cues. Some of these appearance cues may be consciously thought about and may guide our reactions in very deliberate ways. Other such cues, however, may influence our opinions and actions in a much more subtle fashion, without conscious thought or reflection. Consider a college professor scanning the class of students in front of her. She may actively look for the most attentive face in the class, hoping to ask that person a question that will be readily answered. In this case, the professor deliberately finds a face with the right appearance cues, hoping to elicit a correct response. At the same time, that professor may also be subconsciously influenced by other appearance cues, passing over, perhaps, faces that are clearly African American, even though the professor is not aware, and even would deny, that racial cues influenced her judgment of whom to call on.

As this hypothetical example illustrates, race can be a powerful psychological cue. Racial bias can be conscious and intentional, but it can also be subconscious. In almost every aspect of government interaction with citizens, we worry about racial bias, conscious or unconscious, by government officials. The reasons are fairly obvious, starting with the long history of racism that we have struggled to overcome.

The criminal justice system impacts a very high percentage of our citizens through the effects on those who are incarcerated in the system and on their families and friends. Our prisons and jails hold more than two million of our citizens, and the racial breakdown of those incarcerated is a special cause for concern. Although African Americans constitute only 13 percent of the general population, approximately 48 percent of those incarcerated are African American.[1] Not surprisingly, practically a cottage industry has arisen to examine our prison population from many different angles in an attempt to explain why African Americans exhibit a rate of incarceration that is six or seven times greater than it is for whites. One area that has come under scrutiny has been judicial sentencing discretion. Just as the example at the start of this chapter suggested possible discretion based on appearance, it is natural to wonder if some of the racial disparity among those incarcerated might be due to racial discrimination by judges in their sentencing decisions. It is possible,

for example, that in sentencing defendants, judges might consciously or subconsciously see those who are black as less repentant or more likely to reoffend than those who are white.

But the empirical studies fail to show strong evidence of racial discrimination in sentencing. Summing up the literature, Michael Tonry, a leading criminologist on the subject of sentencing, states, "Most modern empirical analyses of sentencing conclude that when legitimate differences among individual cases are taken into account, comparatively little systematic difference in contemporary sentencing outcomes appears to be attributable to race."[2]

Unable to find strong evidence of racial discrimination in sentencing when directly comparing the sentences of white and African American defendants, studies have begun to look at more subtle factors associated with race. For example, in death penalty cases, it has been suggested that what triggers discrimination is not the race of the defendant but rather the race of the defendant in conjunction with the race of the victim, so African American defendants who killed white victims are much more likely to receive a death sentence than African American defendants who killed African American victims or white defendants who killed white or African American victims.

Our research also suggests that a more subtle form of discrimination is taking place at sentencing that is missed by research focused exclusively on discrimination between racial groups (i.e., differences between whites and African Americans). What we have found is that when one looks not at a person's race per se but rather at the strength of a person's Afrocentric features, there is discrimination taking place. By Afrocentric features, we mean those features that are perceived as typical of African Americans—for example, darker skin, fuller lips, or a broader nose. What our research found was that when one examines sentencing from this perspective, those inmates who have more pronounced Afrocentric features tend to receive longer sentences than others *of the same race* who have less pronounced Afrocentric features.[3]

That there may be little discrimination in sentencing between African Americans and whites and yet there is discrimination against those with more pronounced Afrocentric features within a racial group may seem puzzling. But it is our thesis that while judges have learned to be careful to avoid sentencing differences between racial groups, they have not been similarly sensitized to the possibility of discrimination based on Afrocentric features for individuals of the same race. This chapter's purpose is to make the legal community aware of the potency that a person's Afrocentric features may have in biasing judgment within racial categories.

Section I of this chapter describes a series of experiments—classic social science studies using primarily undergraduate students—in which the willingness of people to affix positive and negative stereotypical descriptions to another person was shown to be related to the strength of that person's Afrocentric features, for African Americans and, somewhat surprisingly, for whites as well. Section I is important because it provides the framework for the research described in section II, in which we studied the influence of Afrocentric features on sentencing in Florida. The consistent results in section I, showing the strong biasing of a person's Afrocentric features on judgment, shows why we were not surprised that a person's Afrocentric features might have a biasing effect when it comes to sentencing decisions.

Section II describes the study we did on sentencing among inmates in the Florida prison system. Using photographs and other information about inmates, including their conviction offense (or offenses) and their prior criminal record, we found that if one compares the sentences given to defendants who committed similar crimes and who had similar criminal histories, inmates who had stronger Afrocentric features tended to receive longer sentences than others of the same race who had less pronounced Afrocentric features.

I. LABORATORY RESEARCH ON THE INFLUENCE OF AFROCENTRIC FEATURES ON JUDGMENT

A. Perceptions of Afrocentric Features

Our research is related to scholarship on what is referred to as "colorism," which deals with prejudice and discrimination directed against African Americans with darker skin so that, for example, benefits are more likely to be given to those African Americans with lighter skin.[4] Colorism has been traced even as far back as the colonial period, where those slaves who had lighter skin coloring were more likely to be assigned to work in the homes of slave owners, while those with darker skin were relegated to working in the fields. But our research is also very different from colorism, because colorism focuses primarily on skin color and our research is broader and includes all facial features associated with African Americans, including, for example, hair texture, nose width, and the fullness of one's lips. But even more important for understanding our research is the fact that our research is not limited to bias solely toward or among African Americans. Our research finds a biasing effect among whites that mirrors the biasing effect of Afrocentric features among African Americans. The bottom line is the same for the two racial categories: African American and white inmates who are perceived as having stronger Afrocentric features within their racial category receive longer sentences than those who have less pronounced Afrocentric features.

Our initial research aimed to see if, as we expected, people could perceive differences in Afrocentric features among African American faces and among white faces, and furthermore, the degree to which there is consensus in those perceptions. We started this research by creating an initial pool of head-and-shoulders photographs of eighty-four young males, forty-six of whom were African American and thirty-eight of whom were white

People in the study were asked to judge the degree to which each face manifested Afrocentric features using a 1-to-9 point rating scale (with 1 meaning "not at all" and 9 meaning "very strongly"). They did this in two blocks, either judging the block with all the African American photographs first and then in a second block all the white photographs, or reversing the order of the two blocks.

Not surprisingly, the African American faces were on average given a higher rating than the white faces on the Afrocentric features scale. But what was most important was the fact that this study showed that people saw differences in Afrocentric features within each of the two racial groups and they displayed a very high degree of consensus in their perceptions. These results suggest that the degree to which a person has Afrocentric features is something that is recognized at a broad level, perhaps even a culturally known phenomenon.

B. Demonstrating the Influence of Afrocentric Features on Judgment

Having shown that people can easily and reliably judge faces for the degree to which they manifest Afrocentric features, we undertook studies to demonstrate the influence of such features on judgment. Three different studies were conducted, all using the same research paradigm. In this paradigm, people were then given short, two-paragraph descriptions of different individuals. After reading each description, they were shown a series of facial photographs and told that one of the individuals was the person described. Their job was to judge the probability (on a 0-to-100 scale) that each photograph showed the person who matched the description.

Each participant in the study repeated this process for four different types of descriptions that varied along two dimensions: how stereotypic they were of whites or African Americans and whether they described someone who was generally sympathetic and likable or someone who was not.[5] We expected that the probability ratings would show that faces with more Afrocentric features would be judged as more probable in the descriptions that were stereotypically African American and as less probable in the descriptions that were stereotypic of whites, compared to faces with less Afrocentric features.

We varied the race grouping shown to subjects—sometimes subjects were shown only photos of African Americans, sometimes only those of whites, and sometimes a set from both races. Our studies showed that those faces possessing stronger Afrocentric features—be they African American or white—were given significantly higher probability ratings when the descriptions were stereotypic of African Americans and significantly lower probability ratings when the descriptions were stereotypic of whites, compared to faces of the same race with less strong manifestations of those features. Thus, even whites were stereotypically judged according to the degree to which they manifested Afrocentric features.

When the subjects were shown photos

from both races, the study demonstrated that the participants clearly used the race of the individual to guide their probability judgments, in that African American faces were assigned higher probabilities in the African-American-stereotypic descriptions than white faces, while this was reversed in the white-stereotypic descriptions (what we call race-based stereotyping). However, even though they could have relied exclusively on race, the participants continued to assign higher probabilities to faces with more Afrocentric features in the African American–stereotypic descriptions and lower probabilities to them in the white-stereotypic descriptions, compared to faces of the same race with less Afrocentric features (what we call feature-based stereotyping). And again, this occurred for both the African American faces and the white faces.

In sum, within both racial categories, Afrocentric features seemed to be guiding the stereotypic inferences that were made about the individuals. Moreover, close questioning of the participants at the end of the studies suggested that they were not aware of the influence that Afrocentric features had on their judgments.

The question that we turned to in our next studies was whether the biasing effects of Afrocentric features would continue to be observed under conditions that one might expect would limit such bias.

C. Exploring Some Limiting Conditions

One subject of obvious interest after the initial studies had demonstrated the biasing influence of Afrocentric features was the question of how pervasive this influence is on judgment. It is our hypothesis that citizens in the United States have been conditioned and sensitized to be aware of possible racial bias and are "on guard," so to speak, against direct racial bias. But when forms of racial bias are more indirect, we will often not be aware of those sources of bias and thus there will be no counterweight to avoid bias. Thus, we wished to examine what would happen to the biasing effect of Afrocentric features if we gave the study participants what lawyers would call a "cautionary instruction" about the influence of Afrocentric features on judgment. We wanted to see if the instruction would lessen the impact of such features and, if so, by how much.[6]

In a final laboratory study, we took a different approach and gave the study participants additional information, obviously relevant to the task at hand, about the individuals in the photos.[7] We wanted to see whether the biasing effect of Afrocentric features would be lessened or eliminated if people had more knowledge about the individuals in the photos.

I. THE EFFECT OF CAUTIONARY INSTRUCTIONS

To explore the influence that cautionary instructions might have on the use of Afrocentric features in stereotyping, we used the research paradigm described above in which people were asked to make probability judgments about a set of faces, some African American and some white, that varied within each racial category in Afrocentric features. In this study some of the study participants, again mostly undergraduate students, were asked to perform the task exactly as described in the previous studies, that is, without any cautionary instructions. But other participants were given one of two different cautionary instructions aimed at decreasing stereotyping. One set of instructions told participants that impressions of others are often based on racial stereotypes and, because the goal of the study was to measure the accuracy of their impressions, they should avoid using any racial stereotypes they might have in judging the probability that each face presented was the person described. The other set of instructions given to other participants specifically targeted stereotyping based on Afrocentric features, informing them that often people are particularly likely to stereotype those with stronger Afrocentric features and asking them to avoid doing so.

The probability ratings for the participants not given the cautionary instructions revealed results much like those reported previously—namely, African American faces were assigned higher probabilities for those descriptions stereotypically associated with African Americans (race-based stereotyping) and, within each racial category, faces with more pronounced Afrocentric features were also rated as more probable with respect to these stereotypic descriptions (feature-based stereotyping). Of greater interest, however, were the ratings made by the participants given cautionary instructions. We found that with regard to race-based stereotyping, the participants who were told to avoid stereotyping—either race-based or feature-based—were in fact much less likely to give ratings that indicated race-based stereotyping. However, neither type of cautionary instruction had any impact on feature-based stereotyping: these participants continued to use Afrocentric features in making their judgments of individuals of both races. This is an important result because it suggests that even when made aware of the possibility of feature-based stereotyping and told that they should avoid this bias, people seem unable to control it.

We worried that the inability of the participants to control feature-based stereotyping might derive from the fact that they were unfamiliar with such features and unaware of how they might be used. Accordingly, we conducted another study, involving these same cautionary instructions, in which the study participants were

first asked to judge faces for the degree to which each one manifested Afrocentric features, exactly as the participants had done in the first study reported above. These participants, just like those in that study, manifested both reliable and consensual judgments of Afrocentric facial features. However, when they subsequently were given cautionary instructions to avoid feature-based stereotyping in the probability judgment task, they were unable to do so. In other words, even though they knew what such features are, the participants were unable to control their influence.

This work suggests biases due to racial category can in fact be largely reduced if people are sensitized to their use and consciously try to avoid them. On the other hand, people seem unable to reduce the biases associated with Afrocentric features, even when explicitly asked to do so and even when they demonstrate that they knew what such features are. We would suggest that the ability to control the influence of race per se comes from a long history of sensitization and training received by most people in our culture, training that has resulted in substantial reductions in overt racial biases. Perhaps such extensive training could also reduce feature-based stereotyping, but at present few people are sensitized to the issue and we suspect that even fewer have engaged in prolonged efforts to avoid it.

2. FEATURE-BASED STEREOTYPING IN THE PRESENCE OF ADDITIONAL RELEVANT INFORMATION

The studies described thus far demonstrate the effect that Afrocentric features may have on judgment, but they do so in a relatively impoverished situation where the only information that is available is the facial photograph. It is important to ask whether Afrocentric features bias judgment even when relevant factual information is available about the individuals who are being judged. To explore this question, we conducted a final laboratory study in which study participants were shown photographs of sixty-four African Americans who varied in their Afrocentric features. In addition to the photograph, for each individual, the participants were told whether or not the person had acted aggressively in four prior situations. Some individuals were portrayed as acting aggressively in all four situations, others in three of the four, others in two of the four, others in only one of the four, and still others in none of the four. The participants' task was to judge the probability that each individual would act aggressively in a fifth situation based on the information they were given.[8]

Unsurprisingly, the participants' judgments about the probability of aggression in the fifth situation were heavily influenced by the individuals' level of aggression in the four prior situations. However, the Afrocentric facial features of the individuals continued to impact the probability judgments: over and above the very large impact of information about prior levels of aggression, those individuals with more pronounced Afrocentric facial features were judged as more likely to engage in aggression in the fifth situation, compared to those with less strong Afrocentric features.

To put this last result together with the earlier studies, the series of laboratory studies shows that a person's Afrocentric facial features have a powerful effect on judgment, for both African Americans and whites. People seem unable to control the use of such features even when explicitly asked to do so and even after Afrocentric features have been described to them and they demonstrate their ability to identify the relevant features within each racial category. Additionally, even when diagnostic and obviously relevant information

is abundantly available, people continue to be influenced by a person's Afrocentric features in making stereotypic judgments.

II. THE INFLUENCE OF AFROCENTRIC FEATURES ON SENTENCING DECISIONS

Stereotypes are commonly defined as widely shared beliefs about the attributes of particular social groups. Stereotypes are believed to influence judgments through categorization, meaning that people are judged to have stereotypic attributes if they are categorized as members of the relevant social group. Thus, stereotypes associated with African Americans or Asian Americans will be applied to a person once that person is determined to be a member of the particular racial category. What makes the laboratory research in section I important is that it shows that facial features have the power to affect judgment by triggering the application of racial stereotypes *within* as well as between racial groups. Moreover, stereotypes associated with one group (e.g., African Americans) may be applied to members of a different group (e.g., whites) who have some of the relevant facial features.

The research showed that attributes stereotypically associated with African Americans (e.g., criminal, athletic) were judged to be more true of individuals who possessed stronger Afrocentric features, and this occurred independently of any stereotyping due to racial category. That is, feature-based stereotyping was found when all of the individuals were clearly members of the same racial category, African American or white. Additionally, when judgments were made of both African American and white individuals, racial category and (within race) Afrocentric features were shown to have independent effects on judgment.

Having demonstrated in laboratory research the way that Afrocentric features can affect judgment, we wanted to see if similar effects could be observed outside of structured experiments. One area that suggested possible research was that of sentencing in criminal cases. This was a natural follow-up to the lab research for two reasons.

The first reason is the sheer importance of criminal sentencing to our country and our society. At a time when our country has so many citizens in our prisons, we need to make sure at a minimum that those in prison have been treated fairly, at least as fairly as others similarly situated.

Another reason for looking at the possible influence of Afrocentric features on sentencing decisions has to do with the worries over racism in our criminal justice system, and especially in sentencing decisions. Obviously, racism can influence the criminal justice system in many ways, but sentencing has been a particular worry for many years because judges typically have considerable sentencing discretion when the crime is serious. As the introduction explains, there have been many studies of sentencing that have focused on the race of the offender. But the effect of a person's Afrocentric features on sentencing has never been studied. The laboratory research suggested that a judge's assessment of a defendant might be susceptible to the same sort of biasing effect from a defendant's Afrocentric features as was found in the laboratory. If such a biasing effect were found, it might help explain at least to some extent the feeling many have that something seems "not right" about sentencing, even though studies seem to show no significant racial discrimination when looking at racial categories. Our study showed that indeed something is "not right" about sentencing—there is bias related to racial features, but it is not visible when one looks only at the race of the defendant.

A. The Decision to Study Sentencing in Florida

We chose Florida for our study for one initial reason: there is a wealth of information about inmates in the Florida prison system on the Internet, which means that sentencing decisions can be studied efficiently and inexpensively. For each inmate in the Florida prison system—and it is a large prison system, with approximately 80,000 inmates—there is available on the Internet identification information about the offender (including aliases, tattoos or scars, height, weight, age, and racial category), information about the conviction offense or offenses, information about the sentence imposed, and information on the prior criminal record of the inmate. Importantly, for this research, the information about each inmate also includes a picture of the inmate. These pictures are typical mug shots showing the full face of the inmate from the shoulders up. While the decision to look at sentencing in Florida was driven by the fact that the study could be done efficiently, Florida turns out to be an excellent state to study if one has to choose a single state jurisdiction. In the first place, it is an important jurisdiction because it is the country's fourth most populous state, containing slightly less than 6 percent of the U.S. population. Second, it is a very diverse state with a large African American population. Almost 16 percent of Florida's population is African American (compared to about 13 percent of the U.S. population), and Hispanics are more than 18 percent of Florida's population (but only 13 percent of the U.S. population). Thus, the impact of discrimination, whether based on race or Afrocentric features, will affect a significant number of inmates.

Finally, Florida is a good state to study because, as is true in the overwhelming majority of states throughout the country, trial judges have very broad sentencing discretion, so it is not unusual for a defendant who has committed even a moderately serious crime to face a judge at sentencing who has the discretion to impose a prison sentence on the offender ranging from only a year or two in prison up to ten or even twenty years in prison.

There is thus nothing about the sentencing procedures in Florida that makes it different from almost all other states. This is important because it suggests to us that one would expect very similar results to those we found in Florida were studies of discrimination in sentencing on the basis of Afrocentric features to be conducted in other states.

B. The Methodology of the Study

I. THE INMATES IN THE STUDY, THEIR BACKGROUND, AND THE ASSESSMENT OF THEIR FACIAL FEATURES

Individual inmates were randomly selected from the Florida Department of Corrections database.[9] Within the population of all young (eighteen to twenty-four years of age) male inmates, a sample of 216 was randomly selected, stratified by race, as designated on their court records.[10] There were 100 African American inmates and 116 white inmates.

We researched the Florida criminal statutes to help code each case for a number of different variables: the amount of time the inmate had been sentenced to serve in prison, the seriousness of the primary offense, the number of any additional offenses and their average seriousness, and the number of prior offenses and their average seriousness.[11] In this sample inmate population, a total of 138 different types of offenses had been committed. The seriousness of each was determined by consulting the Florida state statutes, which categorizes felonies using a series of ten different levels, each higher level ex-

posing a defendant to a longer possible sentence. Thus, for example, supplying an unauthorized driver's license is a Level 1 offense, possessing child pornography or selling cocaine is a Level 5 offense, and murder is a Level 10 offense.

We then assessed the degree to which the facial photograph of each inmate manifested Afrocentric facial features. To accomplish this, the 216 photographs were randomly divided into two sets, with approximately equal numbers of African American and white inmates in each set. Each set was given to a group of undergraduate students to rate in terms of the strength of the Afrocentric features, using the same procedure followed in the studies describer earlier in this chapter.

As anticipated, the students were very consistent in their ratings of the photographs for Afrocentric features, and while the African American inmates were found to possess significantly more pronounced Afrocentric features than the white inmates, there was considerable variability within each group.

2. LEGITIMATE INFLUENCES ON THE LENGTH OF SENTENCES IN FLORIDA

Before examining the degree to which race and, within race, the strength of inmates' Afrocentric features predicted length of prison sentence, we looked at the way in which the seriousness of the primary crime committed, the number and average seriousness of additional concurrent crimes, and the number and average seriousness of the offender's prior offenses (what we will henceforth refer to as the criminal record) influenced sentences. Our analysis showed, as one might expect, that an inmate's criminal record was a major factor in determining the length of the sentence given the offender. Also not surprising was the fact that our analysis showed that the seriousness of the primary offense and both the seriousness and number of additional offenses the offender might have committed (along with the offense for which he was being sentenced) were significant predictors of sentence length.

3. SENTENCES AS INFLUENCED BY RACIAL CATEGORY AND AFROCENTRIC FEATURES

We then looked at the race of the inmate to see if a defendant's race influenced the sentencing decision. Our analysis (referred to by social scientists as "regression analysis") showed that the race of the offender did not account for a significant amount of variance in sentence length over and above the inmates' criminal record. This is consistent with the studies of the influence of race on sentencing that were mentioned at the start of this chapter that fail to show that discrimination by racial category is a significant factor in sentencing outcomes.

But when we analyzed sentencing adding as a factor the degree to which the inmates manifested Afrocentric features (as judged from their photographs), the results were quite different. This analysis showed that an inmate's Afrocentric features significantly predicted sentence length over and above the other factors.

How large are the impacts of Afrocentric features on sentences? We tried to estimate the impact by looking at those inmates within each racial category who are one standard deviation above the mean level of Afrocentric features for their racial group. When this is done, it appears that individuals one standard deviation above their group mean on Afrocentric features are receiving sentences about seven to eight months longer than individuals one standard deviation below their group mean (assuming also the same criminal record). This is clearly a meaningful difference.

4. EVALUATING THE RESULTS

The results when we compared the sentences of African American and white in-

mates by racial category were consistent with research into racial discrimination in sentencing. We observed no adverse effect on sentencing when we looked only at the race of the inmate: African American and white offenders in the state of Florida, given equivalent criminal records, are given roughly equivalent sentences.

But when one looks more closely at features associated with race, the sentencing inmates receive is not unbiased—offenders with equivalent criminal records within the same racial category (African American or white) receive longer sentences if they have stronger Afrocentric features.

That Afrocentric features might distort criminal sentences when judges have the most relevant information about offenders at their disposal may seem surprising as well as disheartening. Before accusations of unbridled bias begin to fly, we remind readers that this result is consistent with our laboratory studies that show the difficulty of eliminating the influence of Afrocentric features on judgment. Even when people were given very clear and diagnostic information upon which to base their judgments, and even when they were told explicitly about the influence of Afrocentric features and told to avoid it, such features continued to influence their judgments. Although one might argue that judges have the most pertinent information, they must still rely on their subjective perceptions to some extent, with the consequence that stereotypes may lead to the conclusion that some individuals (i.e., those with more Afrocentric features) are more threatening, more dangerous, less remorseful, and more culpable, and thus more deserving of longer sentences.

We must acknowledge of course that the effects we have shown may be attributable to a series of stages or decisions taken during the criminal sentencing process. For instance, the inmate records to which we had access contained no indication of whether plea bargaining had taken place, either to determine the primary offense or to affect the resulting sentence length. It may well be the case that the biases due to Afrocentric facial features that we have shown are attributable not only to judges but also to district attorneys and many others involved in the plea bargaining and sentencing process. Thus, throughout our discussion we have referred to *judges* being influenced by Afrocentric features, but the more appropriate characterization is that there may be biases in the whole process, of which sentencing is the final outcome.

Taking the results as a whole, some might be tempted to say that the picture is fairly positive. Race is not being used in sentencing decisions. But such a conclusion is a serious misinterpretation of the study's results. Racial stereotyping in sentencing decisions is still going on, but it is more subtle because it is not a function of the racial category of the individual. Racial stereotyping in sentencing is still occurring based on the facial appearance of the offender. Be they white or African American, those offenders who possess stronger Afrocentric features are receiving harsher sentences for the same crimes. This is an indirect form of racial discrimination, but equally pernicious in the way it impacts defendants.

CONCLUSION

Our laboratory research described in section I of this chapter shows that people use Afrocentric features to infer traits that are stereotypic of African Americans and, importantly, this form of stereotyping appears to occur without people's awareness and outside of their immediate control. Given the laboratory findings, it is not surprising to have found similar results, as described in section II, when we looked at the influence of Afrocentric features on sentencing decisions. Judges appear to be-

have like the laboratory participants in the studies, and this suggests that they were unaware of the fact that Afrocentric features were influencing their decisions.

What is causing this bias based on Afrocentric features is unclear, but we theorize that a person's facial features lead to stereotyping in two ways. First, one can use a person's facial features to infer that a person is a member of a racial category and racial stereotyping can then ensue on that basis. But we believe that something else is going on at this point in time and that a person's Afrocentric features can trigger stereotypic inferences about that person even within a racial category. In short, Afrocentric features have come to have potency on their own to influence judgment and trigger stereotypic inferences.

Obviously, race-based stereotypes have the potential to lead judges to perceive African American offenders more negatively than white offenders and for that reason our criminal justice system continues to monitor sentencing from that perspective. However, judges have been well sensitized to this form of possible bias and it seems that they are able to avoid it for that reason. But judges have not been sensitized to the discrimination that has been described in this chapter, namely, discrimination on the basis of a person's Afrocentric features. The perception that a particular offender appears more dangerous or culpable than other offenders within the same racial group is unlikely to raise the red flag of racial bias, as it is customarily understood, and thus no steps are taken to ensure that sentencing is not biased by the mere fact that the offender has more pronounced Afrocentric features.

Our study helps understand the continued perception that many African Americans have that our sentencing system discriminates against them with the result that they are treated more harshly than whites within the system. There is definitely discrimination taking place, but it is more subtle because it is based on the strength of one's Afrocentric features. This form of discrimination is particularly pernicious as we move to a society in which a growing percentage of citizens find that they identify themselves as members of more than one racial category. What our research shows is that one's racial category per se does not influence sentencing. But if one has strong Afrocentric features—perhaps has darker skin or coarser hair—that person will pay a price for those features at sentencing whether that person is considered or considers himself to be African American or white.

Thus those who have long maintained that something is unfair and wrong in our sentencing system, despite studies showing no racial discrimination, are correct. Something is very wrong, but it is not racial discrimination per se; rather, it is discrimination against those who have more pronounced Afrocentric features. It is as if racial discrimination has gone underground—it still exists, but in a form that is harder to detect.

One wonders whether judges can learn not to manifest sentencing biases based on such features, much as they have been sensitized to and have learned to avoid biases in sentencing due to racial categories. We would optimistically suggest that they can. On the other hand, these sorts of biases may be inherently harder to overcome than racial category biases. Our society categorizes individuals by their race: someone is consensually seen as either African American or not, white or not, Asian or not, and so on. And when such categorization is agreed upon, it may be relatively easy to avoid treating people on the basis of their race. On the other hand, Afrocentric features are harder to define in yes-or-no terms, since they vary more or less continuously within each racial group and since many different individual facial features are relevant. So we would suggest that it might be much more difficult to learn how to avoid feature-based stereotyping than category-based stereotyping, simply as a function of the nature of the cues that underlie the former.

All this remains speculation at this point. What is not speculation, we believe, is the nature of our evidence and the basic phenomenon we have demonstrated, that is, that while sentencing decisions may no longer manifest significant racial bias, there is evidence of a more subtle form of bias, due to Afrocentric features, and this bias influences sentencing decisions. We hope our work will begin the process of sensitizing judges and the lay public to this bias. And just perhaps, that might be the first of many steps that eventually lead to its elimination.

19

Fear and Fairness in the City:
Criminal Enforcement and Perceptions
of Fairness in Minority Communities
Richard R. W. Brooks

[I]n any context, such a standard—the community's attitude—is usually unknowable. It resembles a slithery shadow, since one can seldom learn, at all accurately, what the community, or a majority, actually feels.[1]

INTRODUCTION

Blacks in central city neighborhoods are more likely than any other group to perceive crime as a problem.[2] They have the highest rates of violent-crimes victimization[3] and they are seven times more likely to be murdered than whites.[4] Grim statistics such as these, along with impassioned personal accounts of violent encounters and heroic daily efforts to avoid such encounters, have led race and criminal law scholars, such as Randall Kennedy, to express a seemingly natural though unconventional claim: frustrated and overwhelmed by gangs, drugs, and crime, blacks in high-crime neighborhoods welcome disproportionately tough criminal sanctions and expanded police discretion.[5] This

claim, which I label the "urban frustration argument," remains unconventional because African Americans are broadly viewed to perceive law enforcement with suspicion and distrust.[6] This perception of distrust has been significantly bolstered by recent reports of extreme police misconduct in major urban areas such as Chicago, Los Angeles, New York City, and Philadelphia. In New York City, for example, community tension and distrust of police appear to be rising as residents struggle to reconcile a recent string of police killings of unarmed black men. These recent incidents notwithstanding, scholars have noted that the general sense of police distrust among African Americans is giving way to "a demand . . . for higher levels of law-enforcement"[7]—a demand that is supported by a new sense of equity and partnership achieved through growing minority political power in urban areas and new problem-oriented law enforcement approaches. These new approaches promise to give high-crime urban communities

Editors' Note: This chapter is an abridged version of Richard R. W. Brooks, *Fear and Fairness in the City: Criminal Enforcement and Perceptions of Fairness in Minority Communities*, 73 S. Cal. L. Rev. 1219 (2000), reprinted by permission of the University of Southern California and the author.

greater protection from criminal activity by vesting enforcement agencies with increased discretion. Proponents of this approach contend that law-abiding minorities in urban communities are willing to yield more discretionary powers to law enforcement because "the continued victimization of minorities at hands of criminals poses a much more significant threat to the well-being of minorities than does the risk of arbitrary mistreatment at the hands of the police."[8]

The urban frustration argument, however, has been challenged on several fronts, most notably for lacking empirical support.[9] There is no broad-based evidence showing that African Americans in higher-crime neighborhoods are willing to support increased police discretion and harsher sanctions, as the urban frustration argument maintains. In fact, a significant amount of survey data reveals little or no association between citizen support for the police and fear of victimization. With limited confirming evidence, the urban frustration argument remains largely anecdotal, for while urban minorities clearly seek protection from criminals, they (largely the victims of police harassment and abuse) are also wary of the police.[10] The tension between controlling crime and police discretion is well expressed by one community member in the Bronx neighborhood where Amadou Diallo was shot:

> We're grateful for a lot of what the police have done to bring down crime, and we realize most officers, like most residents of our community, are honest, hardworking citizens, . . . [b]ut people are being stopped for no reason, thrown against a fence and searched. Their cars are stopped without probable cause. . . . What some of the officers are doing is just creating an atmosphere of fear.[11]

This article presents results from survey data of perceptions concerning the police and the legal system in order to make inferences about the desire for differential and discretionary legal enforcement among African Americans.[12] Analysis of the data indicates, unsurprisingly, that the majority of African Americans believe that the American legal system treats blacks unfairly. However, compared to their wealthier counterparts, poor blacks are more likely to view the American legal system as fair. In particular, African American respondents in the lowest income brackets are twice as likely as those in the highest income brackets to state that the legal system is fair. This "endorsement" of the American legal system by poor blacks does not necessarily imply a desire for disparate criminal enforcement in their communities; still, it is not inconsistent with that claim. The data also reveal a strong countervailing consideration: poor blacks are more inclined to respond that the police behave "like just another gang." That poor blacks are inclined to view the police as gang-like, and yet are more likely to believe in the fairness of the legal system, suggests that they may welcome heightened enforcement but not by means of expanding police discretion. This interpretation of the data is consistent with the fact that urban minorities are the likely victims of criminal behavior and police misconduct. Taken together, these findings hint at an understanding of African Americans' desire for safety and fairness that balances increased police presence with limited discretion. In particular, expanded service-oriented patrols and heightened community involvement are plausibly more consistent with the desires of minorities in high-crime neighborhoods than a policy of unleashing special tactical units (e.g., gangs, guns, or drugs) with limited guidance. For example, Herbert Williams and Anthony Pate discuss several promising community-based policing mechanisms in their evaluation of various policing strategies in Newark, New Jersey.[13] They found that increased quality of contact between citizens and police (such as door-to-door police visits in the neighborhood and other nonconfrontational interactions with community members) gave the police more opportunities to feel connected to the communities, learn about their desires, and better serve them. "There is ample evidence among the data analyzed to suggest that this approach had significant, positive effects on the attitudes of residents exposed to it."[14]

To explore further the implications of African Americans' views of the criminal justice system, arrest rates and reported crime figures were determined for each respondent's county using the Uniform Crime Reports (UCR).[15] These data suggest that favorable perceptions of the police are negatively correlated with arrest rates for the low-level offenses of vandalism and vagrancy. That is, respondents are more likely to view the police as "gang-like" in communities with higher arrest rates for these offenses. On the other hand, the data show that favorable perceptions of the police are positively correlated with arrest rates for more serious offenses, such as violent crimes. These findings point to a possible cost of increased police attention to low-level offenses that promote community disorganization and invite more serious crimes—the so-called order-maintenance policy.[16] Though largely recognized as an effective crime-fighting tool, this policy has been criticized for intensifying community conflict with the police. As Wesley Skogan notes, "Enthusiasm for closer police attention is not universally shared."[17] Minorities in urban neighborhoods are often ambivalent about the police. While needing protection from crime, many distrust the police and see their order-maintenance efforts as bullying and fear-producing.

How much of an impact should all of these findings have in the debate on asymmetric criminal enforcement in urban communities? Conspicuous findings, such as these, tend to carry a misleading amount of weight in popular debates, as is often the case with glaring, acontextually offered statistics and emotionally ladened anecdotal accounts. One aim of this article is to highlight the need for more research and investigation of an empirical nature. Ultimately, there are many stories that are consistent with the data presented here—some more plausible than others. The benefit of this type of examination is not simply that it offers answers, but rather that it informs our questions. No causal claims are made in this analysis; this analysis highlights significant correlations only. With this qualification in mind, several important implications can be drawn from the data. First, the data do not suggest that poor urban blacks are prepared to waive their constitutional rights in order to reduce crime. Second, the skepticism and distrust expressed by blacks may signal a more general wave of lack of faith in the legal system by all citizens. In recent years, for instance, prosecutors have reported a trend among grand jurors of increasing their scrutiny of police testimony.[18] Understanding the source of distrust and skepticism among blacks—especially among middle-class blacks who are most distrustful of the legal system—may provide insight into how to prevent a crisis of confidence in the police and the legal system. Third, if poor blacks have more confidence in the legal system than wealthier blacks have, then prosecutorial efforts to prevent jury nullification by removing poor blacks may actually increase jury bias. Fourth, by merging crime figures with attitudinal data regarding police, this work depicts an important though often dismissed cost of order-maintenance policing. Community tension with and distrust of police may rise with more aggressive policing of low-level offenses. Section I presents a brief review of the literature assessing African American desire for criminal enforcement. Section II places this work in the broader context of the debate over differential enforcement in urban minority communities. Section III describes a simple model of individual willingness to trade away constitutional protections for increased safety. This model is explored empirically in section IV. That [section] begins with a discussion of the methodology and data used and closes with a presentation of the results, which are discussed in section V. The conclusion offers a brief summary and a discussion of future research directions.

I. AFRICAN AMERICAN PERCEPTIONS OF RACIAL INJUSTICE IN THE AMERICAN LEGAL SYSTEM

Public opinion and attitudes on injustice and criminal law enforcement have been extensively studied. Researchers have sought to identify significant correlates of public opinion toward the police,[19] the courts,[20] various legal sanctions,[21] and the legal system.[22] Surveys have consistently found that a nontrivial portion of the general population believes that the legal system treats minorities unfairly.[23] Researchers have also consistently found a significantly greater level of perceived bias in the legal system among minorities.[24] In particular, African American perception of racial discrimination in criminal law enforcement has been consistently identified in empirical research and opinion polls.[25] To clarify the salient factors behind this perception, recent studies of African American crime concerns have noted that while blacks are more likely than the general population to view police brutality and harassment as a problem, they are also

much more likely to perceive crime as a serious problem.[26] Thus blacks suffer from a "dual frustration"—being fearful of both the police and criminals.[27] Additionally, Regina Austin identified cultural ambivalence when it comes to "black criminal behavior and the debates that it engenders."[28] Tracey Meares also identified a complex set of issues underlying African American desire for tough criminal enforcement.[29] While these works highlight the complexity of assessing African American attitudes on criminal justice, other research provides insight into interpreting results. For example, rather than treating the fairness finding as an "endorsement" of the American legal system by poor blacks, it may be appropriate to interpret this finding as black middle-class disenchantment with the system. Heightened disenchantment among better-off blacks has been identified in many institutional settings.[30] Evidence of black middle-class distrust of the legal system has been documented by scholars for some time.[31] The research presented here extends these works by introducing new theories and data to explain the phenomenon of black middle-class disenchantment.

II. COMMUNITY PREFERENCE FOR DIFFERENTIAL ENFORCEMENT

Lowering standards for arrests and convictions may lower crime rates, but at what cost? Amy Farmer and Dek Terrell argue that reduced standards in high-crime neighborhoods and the resulting inequality in arrest and conviction rates may be optimal for a society that cares about both controlling crime and ensuring fairness.[32] Farmer and Terrell further claim that urban minorities who are concerned with crime and victimization "might even prefer more inequality in the justice system."[33] This claim is simply a restatement of the urban frustration argument—an argument that is currently being used to promote heightened sanctions and expanded police discretion in urban minority communities. Roughly, the argument maintains that the majority of law-abiding residents in these communities welcome (or should welcome) disparate enforcement policies even at the expense of certain civil liberties: poor high-crime communities are willing to trade away civil liberties in order to ensure the provision of more basic needs, such as decent housing, fewer gangs and incidents of gang-related violence, better education for their children, drug-free neighborhoods, and so forth.

Federal drug enforcement policies provide an apposite application of the argument. Consider the sentencing disparity between crack cocaine (crack) and powder cocaine, the so-called 100-to-1 rule.[34] Under this rule, someone charged with the offense of possession with intent to distribute 50 grams of crack faces the same mandatory prison sentence as someone charged with possession with intent to distribute a hundred times more powder cocaine (i.e., 5,000 grams). Since crack distribution is concentrated in urban communities, the 100-to-1 rule has resulted in higher incarceration rates and significantly longer prison terms for African American drug law offenders.[35] Thus, some opponents of the rule have labeled it racist—if not in design, then in implementation. However, Kate Stith has argued that rather than working against the interest of African Americans, the 100-to-1 rule disproportionately benefits black communities. Stith claims that these communities benefit from stringent enforcement of crack cocaine laws because such enforcement removes criminal offenders from the neighborhood for longer periods of time and provides greater deterrence for prospective dealers.[36] Stith and others argue that poor blacks living in urban drug-

devastated communities should welcome the heightened enforcement. Proponents of this view, such as Kennedy, further assert that judges, scholars and casual observers who condemn the consequential race-based disparity for criminal defendants are missing the big picture: "In [their] zeal to protect that mainly black pool of persons convicted of crack offenses, [they] almost completely ignore[ ] those, also mainly black, who must share space on streets and in buildings with crack traffickers."[37]

Another application of the urban frustration argument can be found among the commentaries in favor of the Chicago Housing Authority's (CHA) former building search policy. The search policy, which allowed for mass searches of public housing units without probable cause, was reported to have the support of the overwhelming majority of the public housing residents. Supporters of the policy viewed it as an appropriate and necessary response to rampant shootings and lawlessness in the housing projects. To highlight this view, Meares and [Dan M.] Kahan note that "in one four-day period near [the time the policy was put in place], the police recorded more than 300 gun-fire incidents in the Robert Taylor Homes and Stateway Gardens projects."[38] Thus, when the American Civil Liberties Union (ACLU) challenged the CHA's building search policy on the grounds that it violated the constitutional rights of the residents, "an overwhelming majority of the residents opposed the ACLU's effort to block the building searches."[39]

Residents of urban communities have also resisted efforts to promote "their" constitutional rights over their desire to establish exclusively black male public schools. Confronted with the failure of current models used to educate young black males, some proponents of gender- and race-segregated public schools are willing to trade away the constitutional rights that many of them fought for decades earlier in order to achieve better educational results.

Debates over urban youth curfews have also triggered application of the urban frustration argument. Perhaps the most compelling recent contribution to the contentious debate over the desirability and constitutionality of discretionary legal enforcement in high-crime minority communities involves so-called gang-loitering laws and the use of civil injunctions to restrict gang members from congregating in public spaces. Consider, for example, Chicago's controversial "gang congregation ordinance," which allowed the police to disperse any loitering group of people in the presence of a suspected gang member. According to the Illinois Supreme Court in *City of Chicago v. Morales*, the ordinance gave the police unconstitutionally broad enforcement discretion.[40] Meares and Kahan assert that discretionary enforcement should be allowed because the local community, overwhelmed by gangs and drug-related crimes, sponsored and broadly supported the ordinance.[41] In addition to local sponsorship and support, Meares and Kahan maintain that the "[courts] should have upheld the gang-loitering ordinance" because adequate safeguards were in place, and because incentive alignment between the supporters of the ordinance and those likely to be burdened by it operated to prevent misuse of discretion.[42] They and other scholars, such as Debra Livingston, distinguish current discretionary law enforcement approaches from those of the 1960s and 1970s that the U.S. Supreme Court deemed as failing to meet constitutional standards.[43] Meares and Kahan suggest that courts should respect a (high-crime) community's desire to strike an appropriate balance between broadened police powers and safety when that community internalizes the burden of ex-

panded police discretion, and when the community's interests are sufficiently represented through political and legal institutions. They cite the increase in African American political participation and the fact that "African-Americans today make up a significant percentage of all urban police departments" as evidence that safeguards were in place to protect against abuse of discretion under the ordinance.[44] Supporting this position, Justice Thomas, in his dissenting opinion in *Morales*, issued the same criticism to opponents of the gang-loitering ordinance that Randall Kennedy delivered to opponents of the 100-to-1 rule:

> Today, the Court focuses extensively on the "rights" of gang members and their companions. It can safely do so—the people who will have to live with the consequences of today's opinion do not live in our neighborhoods. Rather, the people who will suffer from our lofty pronouncements are people . . . who have seen their neighborhoods literally destroyed by gangs and violence and drugs.[45]

To be sure, disparately harsh punishments for crack cocaine offenses, discretionary police enforcement of gang ordinances, curfews, and mass building searches all differ in meaningful ways—there are probably more differences than similarities among these law enforcement policies. Still, all of these policies have been promoted with the claim that black communities support expanded enforcement in order to combat the rampant crime in central city neighborhoods. However, the claim of overwhelming black support for (and benefit from) differential legal enforcement has been contested.[46] For example, Meares and Kahan's claims of strong community support for Chicago's gang-loitering ordinance have been challenged by Albert Alschuler and Stephen Schulhofer: "The truth is that the anti-loitering ordinance was intensely controversial, . . . and that to the extent one can identify any predominant view, Chicago's anti-loitering ordinance was opposed by the very groups that Meares and Kahan identify as its principal supporters."[47]

The remainder of this work focuses on the issue of community support for differential policies and expanded police discretion to combat gangs and neighborhood crime. Results from this research may be interpreted as providing some empirical evidence for the urban frustration argument. This evidence, however, does not by itself support an expansion of discretionary and differentially harsh legal enforcement in poor urban communities. First, it must be noted that a large majority of African Americans across most surveys tend to view the American criminal justice system as unfair to African Americans. It is among the minority of respondents, who believe that the legal system is fair, where disproportionately strong support is identified among the poor. Second, survey data show that poor blacks are more likely to view the police as gang-like themselves, rather than as an important solution to gang violence. Taken together, this evidence reveals the difficulty in identifying broad-based support for differential enforcement in poor urban communities. The data suggest that there is disproportionate support for, or at least belief in, legal institutions among poor blacks. However, the data do not support (even inferentially) the notion that the majority of poor urban blacks support expanded police powers to reduce gang violence and crime.

Furthermore, this work does not maintain that high-crime urban communities should or should not receive differential enforcement. There are, arguably, many reasons to support broadened criminal enforcement in high-crime urban communities. For example, the social harm from underenforcement may be greater because crime in these communities affects more people or because there is more violence associated with it; or the police may find enforcement easier in poor urban communities; or a long history of underenforcement and police neglect might mandate greater attention to these communities. There are also, arguably, many reasons not to support harsher criminal enforcement in high-crime urban communities. For example, the criminal justice system may already be too biased against black criminal defendants to tolerate any more discretion at their expense; or differential enforcement, no matter how sensible or well intended, might substantially weaken the normative force of our criminal laws; or a more nuanced equal protection doctrine based on effect as well as purpose is required. These competing arguments, in addition to rival constitutional interpretations, may continue to frame this important debate. Yet the argument for expansion of differential enforcement based on the claim that these "communities" desire such a policy (i.e., the urban frustration argument) is not supported by the data presented here.

III. MODEL OF INDIVIDUAL'S WILLINGNESS TO TRADE RIGHTS

This section describes a simple model of a community resident's willingness to trade constitutional protections for aggressive policing. Assume that more aggressive policing reduces crime and increases the resident's perceived and actual level of safety, the first commodity of interest. Assume further that more aggressive policing requires that the resident sacrifice some portion of her bundle of constitutional protections and rights, the second commodity of interest. Let $U(r, s)$ represent the resident's utility from rights (r) and safety (*s*). Figure 19.1 depicts an indifference curve for this resident, U_A. At the point A, the resident enjoys a high level of safety, *s*, and the current level of constitutional protections and rights, r^*.

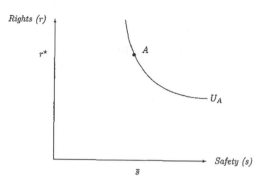

Figure 19.1

The slope of U_A at point A captures the individual's marginal willingness to trade rights for safety. Now consider the individual's preferences at a lower level of safety, *s*, and the same level of rights. This bundle is represented by point B in Figure 19.2.

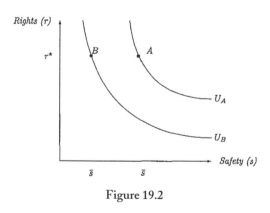

Figure 19.2

The claim that a resident in a high-crime area is more willing to sacrifice constitutional protections can be interpreted as a higher marginal willingness to trade rights for safety at point B than at point A. However, the two parallel lines in Figure 19.3 (one tangent to U_A at A and the other

tangent to U_B at B) graphically show that the marginal willingness to trade at B need not be greater than at A.

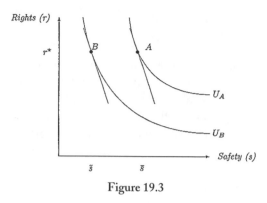

Figure 19.3

Of course, individuals make choices based on prices as well as preferences. Introducing differential prices for ensuring rights and providing safety in high-crime and low-crime communities may lead the resident to make very different choices. Indeed, the price of aggressive policing may be lower in a poor high-crime community or the price of ensuring rights may be greater in these communities. Under these circumstances, the resident may choose a weaker bundle of rights for increased safety. However, as discussed in section II above, arguments in favor of expanded enforcement in high-crime neighborhoods based on price and cost considerations are not the same as arguments in favor of increased enforcement based on preferences and marginal willingness to substitute rights for safety. Whether residents in high-crime communities have a greater willingness to trade away certain rights to ensure their safety is an empirical question, not a theoretical one. Unfortunately, these are communities for which there has traditionally been little data. When included in surveys, their numbers are often too few to make reliable statistical inferences. Using what data are available, the following parts seek to explore the relationship between African American preferences to feel safe from crime and their willingness to expand police discretion, thereby limiting their individual rights. It should be acknowledged at this point that the data do not allow direct investigation of minority stated preferences to trade rights for safety. The data and analysis merely provide a window into these preferences by looking at trends among responses to questions about the legal system and the police. The results that follow do not settle the empirical question; they only lay out some important considerations and suggest certain plausible interpretations.

IV. METHODOLOGY AND RESULTS

*   *   *

V. DISCUSSION OF DATA

In *The Rage of a Privileged Class*, Ellis Cose presents a narrative description of a phenomenon broadly supported by more quantitative sources: the black middle and upper-middle class (who, by almost all accounts, have made tremendous gains under the American economic, legal, and political system) express greater discontent about "the system" than do poor blacks, who increasingly find themselves more impoverished, less represented, and less protected from crime. Numerous analyses of survey data point to the same conclusion. [Jennifer L.] Hochschild observes that well-off blacks are more likely than poor blacks to agree that "American society is racist" and are less likely to believe in the "American dream."[48] Michael Dawson finds that affluent blacks are more likely than poor blacks to view the economic condition of blacks as "much worse than whites."[49] [Howard] Schuman, [Char-

lotte] Steeh, [Lawrence] Bobo, and [Maria] Krysan note that "it is middle-class blacks who express the most impatience with the pace of civil rights activity."[50] With respect to perceptions of criminal injustice, [John] Hagan and [Celesta] Albonetti find that blacks in professional positions are more likely to believe that the American legal system is unfair to blacks.[51] [Scot] Wortley, [John] Hagan, and [Ross] Macmillan find a similar result for well-educated blacks in Canada.[52] Finally, [Ronald] Weitzer and [Steven A.] Tuch have recently reported that better-educated blacks are more critical of the criminal justice system.[53] This catalogue of black middle-class discontent directs attention to the question of why better-off blacks express more dissatisfaction with the legal system. The discussion below addresses this question by presenting several possible explanations under two broad categories: differences in perception and differences in treatment and experiences.

A. Differences in Perception

Individuals witnessing the same event often reach different conclusions or focus on different aspects of the event. This phenomenon may underlie the observed differences between the better-off and poor respondents in this study. The source of this phenomenon might be understood as being driven by relative deprivation, heightened sensitivity, or both.

I. RELATIVE DEPRIVATION

A century ago, Alexis de Tocqueville observed that successful Americans are "restless in the midst of abundance."[54] This observation may aptly be made about successful African Americans today, and perhaps the cause of the discontent is the same. Tocqueville conjectured that professional access promotes discontent:

When all the privileges of birth and fortune are abolished, when all professions are accessible to all, . . . [a man] will readily persuade himself that he is born to no vulgar destinies.

. . .

. . . [M]en easily attain a certain equality of conditions [but] they can never attain the equality they desire.

. . .

. . . [This causes] that strange melancholy which oftentimes will haunt [them] in the midst of their abundance. . . .[55]

Hochschild advances a notably similar conjecture to explain the present discontent among successful blacks: "[O]nce the formal barriers of racial discrimination are mostly dismantled[,] then one is tempted to anticipate more and more success, even if less and less reasonably. . . . [People] run the risk of becoming more dissatisfied as they become more successful."[56] That is, because of their history of success, middle-class and upper-class blacks maintain higher expectations both of themselves and of their environment than do poor blacks. Additionally, well-off blacks expect more class privilege. Given these high expectations, better-off blacks experience greater levels of personal disappointment when the legal, economic, or political system fails to support their expectations. Sociologists refer to this phenomenon as relative deprivation—that is, successful blacks perceive their individual outcomes adversely relative to their high personal expectations. Ellis Cose frequently encountered this phenomenon in his survey of the black professional class:

"Here I am, a black man who has done all the things I was supposed to do," he said and proceeded to tick off precisely what he had done: gone to Harvard, labored for years to make his mark in an elite law firm, married a highly motivated woman who herself had an advanced degree and a lucrative career. He and his wife were in the process of raising three exemplary children. . . . Yet he was far from fulfilled.[57]

[W.G.] Runciman provides a useful dichotomy in the theory of relative deprivation: egoistical (or personal) deprivation and fraternal (or group) deprivation. Personal relative deprivation refers to the perception that one's outcome is viewed negatively compared to one's reference group. When one's reference group as a whole is perceived as deprived compared to other groups, that phenomenon is referred to as group relative deprivation. This dichotomy helps to explain why better-off and poor blacks differ in their assessment of the legal system. First, low-income African Americans may be more inclined to restrict their frame of reference to their immediate community when evaluating their outcomes. Their restricted frame results from having fewer reference groups against which to compare their outcomes. Therefore, poor blacks in homogeneous communities may be more likely to focus on personal relative deprivation with a narrowly defined reference group of other blacks in their community. Scholars have highlighted this point in discussing why poor people appear more tolerant of injustice.

Middle-class blacks, however, are more focused on group relative deprivation. Scholars speculate that better-off blacks are more concerned about the status of blacks compared to other groups as opposed to maintaining a strictly black reference group. As middle-class African Americans achieve more success at home, in schools, and in the workplace, situations involving a strictly black reference group become less available. These successful blacks develop multiple reference groups, which allow them to compare more easily their outcomes to those of whites and other racial groups. Thus, despite achieving good individual outcomes, they continue to feel deprived as long as blacks as a whole fare poorly.

2. HEIGHTENED SENSITIVITY

In addition to a greater propensity to make adverse assessments based on comparisons to similarly situated whites, successful blacks may be more sensitive to race-based differential treatment due to environmental factors. This sensitivity might develop from discrimination and other negative experiences in integrated workplace settings. For example, Erik Wright observed that income discrimination may be greatest among the black professional-managerial class.[58] Using this observation, Hagan and Albonetti speculate that the members of this class "who perceive income discrimination may be sensitive to the perception of injustice elsewhere as well."[59] African Americans in integrated (or mostly white) residential or workplace settings may have more occasions to observe racial bias. Such experiences place middle-class and upper-class blacks in a constant state of alert with respect to differential treatment. Often this bias is not obvious to casual observers. Scholars and lay commentators have noted that race-based differential treatment is often quite subtle—petty indignities or the so-called micro-inequities—but not unobservable to blacks attuned to it.

On the other hand, poor African Americans living and working in racially homogeneous environments may view the American legal system as harsh, but believe it is that way for everyone. In this sense the narrow frame of reference of their immediate neighborhood isn't chosen by the individuals so much as it is determined by their experiences. One might thus conclude that blacks living in high-minority-concentrated central city neighborhoods are less able to identify racial bias given their environmental constraints. Nancy Apple and David O'Brien, however, provide evidence indicating a significant negative correlation between the concentration of blacks in a neighborhood and black individuals' attitudes toward the police.[60] In other words, as the number of blacks in a neighborhood increases, blacks in that neighborhood are less likely to view the police favorably. Apple and O'Brien speculate that increasing the number of blacks in a neighborhood allows for more opportunities "for blacks to associate with others who have negative attitudes toward the police, [resulting] in an overall increase in the negative sentiment toward the police."[61] Of course, police behavior itself may be affected by increased concentration of blacks in a given neighborhood—or at least affected by factors correlated with increased black concentration in a neighborhood. That is, the police may behave less well when the number of blacks in a neighborhood increases. This issue notwithstanding, the findings of Apple and O'Brien are not entirely inconsistent with the heightened-sensitivity model, since the respondents in their study commented on the "quality of police protection" and not necessarily racial bias by the police or the legal system generally. Apple and O'Brien may have captured the sentiment that the police are tough or unfair to all individuals in the neighborhood. Indeed, as the concentration of blacks in the neighborhood increases, there are fewer opportunities to witness differential treatment to others. Therefore blacks in high-concentration black neighborhoods may be less able to identify racially biased treatment.

B. Experienced Differences

While the section above focused on differences in perceptions of racial bias in the legal system between better-off and poor blacks, the discussion now turns to actual differences in the treatment that these two groups receive. A separate discussion of actual differences is not intended to suggest that it is mutually exclusive of differences in perceptions of racial bias. In fact, there is every reason to expect that these phenomena are inextricably connected.

1. LINKED-FATE/DIRE-FATE

The "linked-fate/dire-fate" argument maintains that better-off blacks bear the costs of racially biased legal enforcement in urban areas but experience none of the benefits. Experiencing few or no benefits from differentially harsh enforcement, better-off blacks may be more willing to critique the American legal system as unfair. This argument begins with the observation that well-off, more-educated blacks tend to exhibit greater race consciousness than other groups and are likely to maintain a connection and sense of responsibility to urban black culture.[62] Additionally, better-off blacks have a strong sense that their fate is linked to the black community. Furthermore, some studies suggest that ethnic groups are more aligned in their view of criminal justice than class groups. Thus the views of injustice held by the black middle and upper classes may be largely informed by the perceived experiences of poor blacks in "the black community." However, since middle- and upper-class blacks do not live in neighborhoods where they face the same dire fate as poor urban blacks, they do not directly appreciate the benefit of reduced crime rates due to racially uneven, perhaps unfair law enforcement policies. Therefore, these African Americans may maintain a more negative view of criminal enforcement and American justice. On the other hand, since harsh policies directed at black criminal defendants may reduce crime in their neighborhoods, poor urban blacks tend to discount any procedural unfairness when evaluating tough criminal enforcement. Therefore, this group of African Americans may maintain a more positive view of the American legal system. This claim is supported by the study of Robert Boeckmann and Tom Tyler, which found that "instrumental fears about the dangers that people pose" were a primary factor underlying willingness to deny procedural protections to potential lawbreakers.[63] Other cognitive research has highlighted instances where perceptions of injustice collide with pragmatic self-serving choices. Daryl Bem found that individuals in these instances may adjust their notions of justice, "rather than live with stressful inconsistency between their beliefs and their behaviors."[64] Finally, William Julius Wilson's thesis concerning the declining significance of race for poor African Americans also supports the claim: concerns about poverty, crime, and social disorder have superseded matters of race for poor blacks.[65] Thus, fairness to black criminal defendants becomes a second-order consideration.

2. EXPRESSIVE ALIGNMENT

Better-off blacks may be more likely to condemn the legal system as racist in order to maintain their commitment to the broader black community and their own self-image. Successful blacks who have moved out of poor, mostly black neighborhoods may voice a lack of confidence in the legal system's treatment of blacks as a means of expressing their continued connection with the old neighborhood. These well-to-do, well-educated blacks may ignore hard-to-swallow facts, such as the level of black-on-black crime and community devastation by gangs, in order to express their alignment with the poor black community (and especially those members of the community who are perceived as victims of the white dominant culture) and against the economic, legal, and political establishment.

[Phoebe C.] Ellsworth and [Lee] Ross, as well as [Austin] Sarat and [Neil] Vidmar, provide evidence indicating that individuals often discount countervailing facts (which they themselves state are important) when reaching decisions about the fairness of legal rules.[66] Ellsworth and Ross label this behavior "irrational consistency" in beliefs and documented it in the context of opinions concerning the death penalty. When respondents in these studies were confronted with evidence that directly contradicted arguments they used to support their beliefs concerning capital punishment, the respondents stated that new evidence (even if factual) would not alter their death penalty views. This led Ellsworth and Ross to conclude that these views do not reflect informed, reasoned consideration of facts, but rather an "undifferentiated, emotional reflection of one's ideological self-image."[67] Donald Kinder and David Sears provide a similar argument in the context of suburban racism, noting that beliefs appear to be expressive or symbolic rather than instrumental.[68] Also, [Francis T.] Cullen, [James] Frank, and [Robert H.] Langworthy, in their empirical study of the perception of the police's use of deadly force, found that the views of African Americans on the topic were less a distinctive set of attitudes than a reflection "of a more global liberal crime ideology."[69]

3. DIFFERENTIAL BIAS

It is widely known that blacks are arrested and imprisoned at rates that are significantly disproportionate to their numbers in the general population. Recent studies show that racial bias does not account for much of this disproportionality at the formal stages of arrest, conviction, and sentencing in criminal enforcement. However, these studies have not been able to dismiss claims of bias as a principal force in less formal enforcement decisions, such as the decision to stop black motorists. Stories of black judges, lawyers, professors, doctors, and other professionals being stopped, de-

tained, and sometimes wrongfully arrested are well reported in the popular press. Popular press coverage and acknowledgment of the practice of stopping black motorists who happened to be driving an expensive car or driving in an expensive neighborhood (or who appeared to be otherwise out of place) was so broad that the term "driving while black" quickly became common parlance. If members of the black middle and upper classes enter and exit the criminal justice system at this stage—replete with racial bias—then one might argue that they experience more discrimination than poor blacks, who either participate in the more formal stages of the criminal justice system or who seldom venture out of their neighborhoods or "place." Consider Ronald Weitzer's survey of African Americans' and whites' perceptions of misconduct. He found that in some respects, middle-class blacks share more common experiences and views of the police with middle-class whites than they do with poor blacks.[70] For example, the middle-class blacks in his study reported experiencing little police suspicion and mistreatment in their own neighborhoods. However, outside of their middle-class black community, they experienced greater levels of suspicion and mistreatment. Weitzer argues that greater mobility among the middle class in conjunction with being African American makes better-off blacks more vulnerable to stops outside their neighborhoods.

Of course, opportunities for informal legal discrimination against blacks in poor communities exist, and poor African Americans do venture out of their neighborhoods, too. However, it may be that better-off blacks are more susceptible to discretionary bias because they have more opportunities to "appear out of place." The contention that better-off blacks experience more racial bias than do poor blacks is an empirical issue. If this contention is true, even in part, then it could explain why wealthier African Americans have less faith in the American legal system.

*   *   *

CONCLUSION

The claim that blacks in urban communities desire differentially tough legal enforcement and greater police discretion to combat rampant crime is not obvious. While it is true that blacks in these communities perceive crime as a significant problem, they also view police brutality and harassment as a nontrivial concern. Therefore, identifying African American desire for differential and discretionary enforcement is a difficult task—but a task that, nonetheless, must be undertaken before advancing claims based on such a desire. To shed some light on the desire of the "black community" for differential and discretionary legal penalties, this research used survey data on African Americans' perceptions of the legal system. Most of the results in this work confirm commonly held views, such as the belief that younger respondents tend to find the legal system unfair to African Americans, while respondents who characterize themselves as conservative tend to find the legal system fair to all groups. However, the finding that African American perception of fairness is inversely related to income is somewhat unexpected. That is, one might predict that African Americans who have achieved greater material success in American society would view the legal system as more fair than those who experience greater poverty, crime, and social disorder. Just the opposite was found—that is, poor blacks are more likely to view the American legal system as fair. One might infer that poor blacks view the legal system as fair despite (or perhaps because of) the differentially tough legal enforcement in their communities. This inference is consistent with the argument that poor African Americans desire disproportionately tough legal enforcement in their communities. However, data also indicate that poor blacks have little confidence in the police. Poor blacks are more inclined to report that the police behave too much like a gang to be an effective response to gang-related crimes. In the context of the urban frustration argument, these findings suggest that aggressive enforcement with limited police discretion may be consistent with high-crime black communities' desire for safety and fairness. On the other hand, one may question whether it is sufficient that individuals in these communities "choose" (from a truncated set of alternatives) to have harsher penalties. That is, the basis of these choices must be considered when informing legal policy. The analysis of black perceptions of fairness presented in this work does not lend strong support for the policy of differential enforcement based on the claim that these "communities" desire such a policy.

ABOUT THE CONTRIBUTORS

Omoniyi O. Adekanmbi, B.S.—Ph.D. Candidate, Psychology Department, Tufts University

Jody Armour, J.D.—Roy P. Coker Professor of Law, University of Southern California

Irene V. Blair, Ph.D.—Associate Professor, Department of Psychology, University of Colorado at Boulder

Gary Blasi, M.A.—Professor of Law, University of California at Los Angeles

Stanley L. Brodsky, Ph.D.—Professor, Department of Psychology, University of Alabama

Richard R. W. Brooks, J.D., Ph.D.—Associate Professor, Yale Law School

W. Jonathan Cardi, J.D.—Associate Professor, University of Kentucky College of Law

Faye J. Crosby, Ph.D.—Professor, Psychology Department, University of California at Santa Cruz

Richard Delgado—University Distinguished Professor of Law and Derrick Bell Fellow, University of Pittsburgh Law School

Roger G. Dunham, Ph.D.—Professor, Department of Sociology, University of Miami

Theodore Eisenberg, J.D.—Henry Allen Mark Professor of Law, Cornell Law School

Susan T. Fiske, Ph.D.—Professor, Department of Psychology, Princeton University

Matthew B. Johnson, Ph.D.—Associate Professor, Psychology Department, John Jay College, City University of New York

Sheri Lynn Johnson, J.D.—Professor of Law, Cornell Law School

Christine Jolls, J.D., Ph.D.—Gordon Bradford Tweedy Professor of Law and Organization, Yale Law School

Shayne Jones, Ph.D.—Assistant Professor, Department of Criminology, University of South Florida

Charles M. Judd, Ph.D.—Professor, Department of Psychology, University of Colorado at Boulder

Jerry Kang, J.D.—Professor, University of California at Los Angeles Law School

Linda Hamilton Krieger, J.D.—Professor, University of California at Berkeley School of Law

Misha S. Lars, B.S.—Ph.D. Candidate, Psychology Department, John Jay College, City University of New York

Michael J. Lynch, Ph.D.—Professor, Department of Criminology, University of South Florida

Gregory S. Parks, Ph.D.—J.D. Candidate, Cornell Law School

William T. Pizzi, J.D.—Professor, University of Colorado Law School

Kristina R. Schmukler, M.S.—Ph.D. Candidate, Psychology Department, University of California at Santa Cruz

Steven M. Smith, Ph.D.—Associate Professor, Psychology Department, St. Mary's University

Samuel R. Sommers, Ph.D.—Assistant Professor, Psychology Department, Tufts University

Veronica Stinson, Ph.D.—Associate Professor, Department of Psychology, St. Mary's University

Megan Sullaway, Ph.D.—Clinical Psychologist, Pacific Psychological Associates

Cass R. Sunstein, J.D.—Karl N. Llewellyn Distinguished Service Professor of Jurisprudence, University of Chicago Law School, and Department of Political Science, University of Chicago

Veronica S. Tetterton, Ph.D.—Associate Psychologist, Denton State School

Elisabeth Morgan Thompson, M.S.—Ph.D. Candidate, Psychology Department, University of California at Santa Cruz

Carwina Weng, J.D.—Clinical Associate Professor of Law, Indiana Law School

Kideste M. Wilder, M.A.—Ph.D. Candidate, Psychology Department, John Jay College, City University of New York

George Wilson, Ph.D.—Associate Professor, Department of Sociology, University of Miami

NOTES

1. Toward a Critical Race Realism

Gregory S. Parks

Author's Note: This chapter is dedicated to the memory of Fletcher James Campbell. The author thanks the University of Kentucky's Office of the Vice President for Research for the Lyman T. Johnson Post-doctoral Fellowship, which funded my research for this chapter and early work on this book. The author also thanks the University of Kentucky's Department of Psychology and College of Law for providing me with needed resources to get this chapter and book under way. Finally, the author thanks Professor Sherri Lynn Johnson for her early comments on this chapter and Dr. Valarie Hans for her considerable feedback on this chapter.

1. *See* JOHN P. JACKSON JR., SOCIAL SCIENTIST FOR SOCIAL JUSTICE: MAKING THE CASE AGAINST SEGREGATION 84 (2001).

2. *See generally* JOHN P. JACKSON JR., SCIENCE FOR SEGREGATION: RACE, LAW, AND THE CASE AGAINST BROWN V. BOARD OF EDUCATION (2005).

3. Michael Heise, *Brown v. Board of Education, Footnote 11, and Multidisciplinarity*, 90 CORNELL L. REV. 279, 280, 307 (2005).

4. *Id.* at 312–14.

5. Gregory Mitchell, *Empirical Legal Scholarship as Scientific Dialogue*, 83 N.C. L. REV. 167, 180–82 (2004).

6. *See* Theodore Eisenberg, *Why Do Empirical Legal Scholarship?*, 41 SAN DIEGO L. REV. 1741, 1742–46 (2004). *See also* Elizabeth Warren, *The Market for Data: The Changing Role of Social Sciences in Shaping the Law*, 2002 WIS. L. REV. 1, 7 (2002).

7. http://www.aals.org/am2006/theme.html (last visited October 26, 2006).

8. Michael Heise, *The Past, Present, and Future of Empirical Legal Scholarship: Judicial Decision Making and the New Empiricism*, 2002 U. ILL. L. REV. 819, 828 (2002).

9. Robert C. Ellickson, *Trends in Legal Scholarship: A Statistical Study*, 29 J. LEGAL STUD. 517, 527–29 (2000); Tracey E. George, *An Empirical Study of Empirical Legal Scholarship: The Top Law Schools*, 81 IND. L.J. 141, 141 (2006).

10. Yale offers Empirical Law and Economics. Stanford offers Bayesian Statistics and Econometrics, Empirical Analysis: Mathematical Methods, Quantitative Methods: Finance, Quantitative Methods: Statistical Inference, and Statistical Inference and Empirical Research. Harvard offers Empirical Studies of Economic Transformations, while Northwestern offers Social Science Research Methods. Cornell offers Empirical Studies in Leading Civil Rights Issues, and the University of Texas at

Austin offers an empirical methods course called Social Science and Law.

11. Eisenberg, *supra* note 6, at 1742.

12. Colleen M. Cullen & S. Randall Kalberg, *Chicago-Kent Law Review Faculty Scholarship Survey*, 70 Chi.-Kent L. Rev. 1445, 1453 (1995) (noting that the Journal of Legal Studies is one of the most cited and prestigious journals among law faculty); Eisenberg, *supra* note 6, at 1742; Heise, *supra* note 8, at 825.

13. *See* http://www.elsblog.org/the_empirical_legal_studi/2006/06/my_take_on_new_.html (last visited Nov. 10, 2006), where a number of members of the Empirical Legal Studies blog indicate that they cannot readily discern how new legal realism differs from the law and society movement.

14. Howard Erlanger, Bryant Garth, Jane Larson, Elizabeth Mertz, Victoria Nourse & David Wilkins, *Foreword: Is It Time for a New Legal Realism?*, 2005 Wis. L. Rev. 335, 336 n.7 (2005).

15. *Id.* at 337.

16. *New Legal Realism Symposium: Is It Time for a New Legal Realism?*, 2005 Wis. L. Rev. 335 (2005); Symposium, *New Legal Realism*, 31 Law & Soc. Inquiry 797 (2006).

17. Erlanger et al., *supra* note 14, at 339.

18. *Id.* at 340.

19. *Id.* at 336, 341–42.

20. *Id.* at 342–43.

21. *Id.* at 336, 343–44.

22. *Id.* at 345.

23. *See generally* Thomas W. Mitchell, *Destabilizing the Normalization of Rural Black Land Loss: A Critical Role for Legal Empiricism*, 2005 Wis. L. Rev. 557 (2005); Laura Beth Nielsen & Robert L. Nelson, *Rights Realized? An Empirical Analysis of Employment Discrimination Litigation as a Claiming System*, 2005 Wis. L. Rev. 663 (2005); Devah Pager, *Double Jeopardy: Race, Crime, and Getting a Job*, 2005 Wis. L. Rev. 617 (2005).

24. *See* John M. Conley, *Tales of Diversity: Lawyers' Narratives of Racial Equity in Private Firms*, 31 Law & Soc. Inquiry 831 (2006); *see generally* Mitu Gulati & Laura Beth Nielsen, *Introduction: A New Legal Realist Perspective on Employment Discrimination*, 31 Law & Soc. Inquiry 797 (2006); Cheryl R. Kaiser & Brenda Major, *A Social Psychological Perspective on Perceiving and Reporting Discrimination*, 31 Law & Soc. Inquiry 801 (2006); Alexandra Kalev & Frank Dobbin, *Enforcement of Civil Rights Law in Private Workplaces: The Effects of Compliance Reviews and Lawsuits Over Time*, 31 Law & Soc. Inquiry 855 (2006).

25. Jerry Kang, Behavioral Realism: Future History of Implicit Bias and the Law, Lecture at Ohio State University (Nov. 2006), *available at* http://www.law.ucla.edu/kang/Talks/talks.html.

26. *See generally* Jerry Kang, *Trojan Horses of Race*, 118 Harv. L. Rev. 1489 (2005).

27. *See generally* Gary Blasi & John T. Jost, *System Justification Theory and Research: Implications for Law, Legal Advocacy, and Social Justice*, 94 Cal. L. Rev. 1119 (2006); R. Richard Banks, Jennifer L. Eberhardt & Lee Ross, *Discrimination and Implicit Racial Bias in a Racially Unequal Society*, 94 Cal. L. Rev. 1169 (2006); Anthony G. Greenwald & Linda Hamilton Krieger, *Implicit Bias: Scientific Foundations*, 94 Cal. L. Rev. 945 (2006); Linda Hamilton Krieger & Susan T. Fiske, *Behavioral Realism in Employment Discrimination Law: Implicit Bias and Disparate Treatment*, 94 Cal. L. Rev. 997 (2006); Christine Jolls & Cass Sunstein, *The Law of Implicit Bias*, 94 Cal. L. Rev. 969 (2006); Kang, *supra* note 25; Jerry Kang & Mahzarin R. Banaji, *Fair Measures: A Behavioral Realist Revision of Affirmative Action*, 94 Cal. L. Rev. 1063 (2006).

28. *See* Peter H. Schuck, *Why Don't Law Professors Do More Empirical Research?*, 39 J. Legal Educ. 323, 331–33 (1989).

29. *Id.* at 326.

30. Dorothy A. Brown, *Fighting Racism in the Twenty-First Century*, 61 Wash. & Lee L. Rev. 1485, 1488–89 (2004).

31. Richard Delgado, *Storytelling for Oppositionists and Others: A Plea for Narrative*, 87 Mich. L. Rev. 2411, 2413 (1988).

32. *Id.* at 2437–38.

33. Toni M. Massaro, *Empathy, Legal Storytelling, and the Rule of Law: New Words, Old Wounds?*, 87 Mich. L. Rev. 2099, 2105 (1989).

34. Daniel A. Farber & Suzanna Sherry, *Telling Stories Out of School: An Essay on Legal Narratives*, 45 Stan. L. Rev. 807, 830–40 (1993).

35. *Id.* at 831–32.

36. *Id.* at 832–40.

37. *See generally* David M. Trubek and John Esser, *"Critical Empiricism" in American Legal Studies: Paradox, Program, or Pandora's Box?*, 14 Law & Soc. Inquiry 3 (1989).

38. Thomas S. Ulen, *The Unexpected Guest: Law and Economics, Law and Other Cognate Disciplines, and the Future of Legal Scholarship*, 79 Chi.-Kent L. Rev. 403, 428 (2004).

39. Gregory Mitchell, *Empirical Legal Scholarship as Scientific Dialogue*, 83 N.C. L. Rev. 167, 180–82 (2004).

40. Schuck, *supra* note 28, at 335.

41. Stewart Macaulay, *The New Versus the Old Legal Realism: "Things Ain't What They Used to Be,"* 2005 Wis. L. Rev. 365, 397 (2005).

42. Schuck, *supra* note 28, at 335.

43. *See generally* Derrick Bell, *Racial Realism*, 24 CONN. L. REV. 365 (1992).

44. Tanya Kateri Hernandez, *A Critical Race Feminism Empirical Research Project: Sexual Harassment & the Internal Complaints Black Box*, 39 U.C. DAVIS L. REV. 1235, 1239 (2006).

45. Dorothy A. Brown, *Fighting Racism in the Twenty-First Century*, 61 WASH. & LEE L. REV. 1485, 1489–91 (2004).

46. Karl N. Llewellyn, *Some Realism About Realism: Responding to Dean Pound*, 44 HARV. L. REV. 1222, 1254 (1931).

47. Farber & Sherry, *supra* note 34, at 838.

48. ROBERT SAMUEL SUMMERS, INSTRUMENTALISM AND AMERICAN LEGAL THEORY 20, 22–37 (1982).

49. Lee Epstein & Gary King, *The Rules of Inference*, 69 U. CHI. L. REV. 1, 8 (2002).

50. Richard Lempert, *"Between Cup and Lip": Social Science Influences on Law and Policy*, 10 LAW & POL. 167, 170–75 (1988); *see also* Warren, *supra* note 6, at 7.

51. Gary B. Melton, John Monahan & Michael J. Saks, *Psychologists as Law Professors*, 42 AM. PSYCHOLOGIST 502, 502 (1987).

52. *Id.*

53. *See generally* WILLIAM C. LOUTHAN, THE POLITICS OF JUSTICE: A STUDY IN LAW, SOCIAL SCIENCE, AND PUBLIC POLICY (1979).

54. JEROLD L. AUERBACH, UNEQUAL JUSTICE: LAWYERS AND SOCIAL CHANGE IN MODERN AMERICA 212 (1976).

55. Gerald Lawrence Fetner, Counsel to the Situation: The Lawyer as Social Engineer, 1900–1945 at 42–82, 83–126 (1973) (unpublished Ph.D. dissertation, Brown University) (on file with author).

56. STUART NAGEL & LISA BIEVENUE, SOCIAL SCIENCE, LAW, AND PUBLIC POLICY 5–6 (1992).

57. *Id.* at 35, 38–39, 40–41.

58. *Id.* at 35–36.

59. Abner J. Mikva, *Bringing the Behavioral Sciences to the Law: Tell it to the Judge or Talk to Your Legislator?*, 8 BEHAV. SCI. & LAW 285, 285–89 (1990).

60. Schuck, *supra* note 28, at 325.

61. Epstein & King, *supra* note 49, at 8.

62. *Id.* at 45–48.

63. Richard L. Revesz, *A Defense of Empirical Scholarship*, 69 U. CHI. L. REV. 1, 169, 188 (2002).

64. *See* Lee Epstein and Gary King, *Building an Infrastructure for Empirical Research in the Law*, 53 J. LEGAL EDUC. 311, 313 (2003).

65. Theodore Eisenberg offers a course at Cornell Law School entitled Empirical Studies in Leading Civil Rights Issues.

66. Epstein & King, *supra* note 49, at 315.

67. *Id.*; George, *supra* note 9, at 150.

68. Heise, *supra* note 8, at 829; *see generally* Gary B. Melton, John Monahan & Michael J. Saks, *Psychologists as Law Professors*, 42 AM. PSYCHOLOGIST 502 (1987).

69. RICHARD DELGADO & JEAN STEFANCIC, CRITICAL RACE THEORY xix (2001).

70. Rachel F. Moran, *The Elusive Nature of Discrimination*, 55 STAN. L. REV. 2365, 2365–2367 (2003).

2. Stereotypes and Prejudice: Helping Legal Decisionmakers Break the Prejudice Habit

Jody Armour

1. 273 N.E.2d 748 (Ill. App. Ct. 1971).

2. JAMES HENDERSON ET AL., THE TORTS PROCESS (1994).

3. *Id.* at 75. ***

4. Wolfgang Stroebe & Chester A. Insko, *Stereotype, Prejudice, and Discrimination: Changing Conceptions in Theory and Research*, in STEREOTYPING AND PREJUDICE: CHANGING CONCEPTIONS 3, 5 (Daniel Bar-Tal et al. eds., 1989).

5. HOWARD J. EHRLICH, THE SOCIAL PSYCHOLOGY OF PREJUDICE 110 (1973) (emphasis added).

6. Charles R. Lawrence III, *The Id, the Ego, and Equal Protection: Reckoning with Unconscious Racism*, 39 STAN. L. REV. 322 (1987) (emphasis added) (footnote omitted).

7. Charles E. Case & Andrew M. Greeley, *Attitudes Toward Racial Equality*, 16 HUMBOLDT J. SOC. REL. 67, 68 (1990).

8. Charlotte Steeh & Howard Schuman, *Young White Adults: Did Racial Attitudes Change in the 1980s?*, 98 AM. J. SOC. 340, 361 (1992).

9. Sheri Lynn Johnson, *Black Innocence and the White Jury*, 83 MICH. L. REV. 1611, 1648–49 (1985). ***

10. *Id.* at 1648.

11. *Id.* at 1650.

12. Harold Sigall & Richard Page, *Current Stereotypes: A Little Fading, A Little Faking*, 18 J. PERSONALITY & SOC. PSYCHOL. 247, 248 (1971).

13. Johnson, *supra* note 9, at 1649.

14. *Id.* at 1649–50. ***

15. Patricia G. Devine, *Stereotypes and Prejudice: Their Automatic and Controlled Components*, 56 J. PERSONALITY & SOC. PSYCHOL. 5, 6 (1989).

16. Phyllis A. Katz, *The Acquisition of Racial Attitudes in Children*, in TOWARDS THE ELIMINATION OF RACISM 125, 147 (Phyllis A. Katz ed., 1976).

17. Anthony R. Pratkanis, *The Cognitive Representation of Attitudes*, in ATTITUDE STRUCTURE AND

290

Notes to Pages 16–29

FUNCTION 71, 91 (Anthony R. Pratkanis et al. eds., 1989).

18. Margo J. Monteith et al., *Prejudice and Prejudice Reduction: Classic Challenges, Contemporary Approaches, in* SOCIAL COGNITION: IMPACT ON SOCIAL PSYCHOLOGY 323, 333–34 (Patricia G. Devine et al. eds., 1994).

19. Devine, *supra* note 15, at 5.

20. *See, e.g.,* Patricia G. Devine et al., *Prejudice With and Without Compunction,* 60 J. PERSONALITY & SOC. PSYCHOL. 817, 817–19 (1991).

21. *Quoted in* Daniel Coleman, *"Useful" Modes of Thinking Contribute to the Power of Prejudice,* N.Y. TIMES, May 12, 1987, at C1, C10. ***

22. Devine et al., *supra* note 20, at 819.

23. *See, e.g.,* Margo J. Monteith et al., *Self-Directed Versus Other-Directed Affect as a Consequence of Prejudice-Related Discrepancies,* 64 J. PERSONALITY & SOC. PSYCHOL. 198, 200–208 (1993); Margo J. Monteith, *Self-Regulation of Prejudiced Responses: Implications for Progress in Prejudice-Reduction Efforts,* 65 J. PERSONALITY & SOC. PSYCHOL. 469, 471–78 (1993).

24. Devine, *supra* note 15, at 12–13.

25. Peggy C. Davis, *Law as Microaggression,* 98 YALE L.J. 1559, 1564–65 (1989); Samuel L. Gaertner & John F. Dovidio, *The Aversive Form of Racism, in* PREJUDICE, DISCRIMINATION, AND RACISM 61, 84 (John F. Dovidio & Samuel L. Gaertner eds., 1986).

26. Lawrence, *supra* note 6, at 335.

27. Johnson, *supra* note 9, at 1649.

28. Lawrence, *supra* note 6, at 335.

29. *Id.* at 339.

30. Davis, *supra* note 25, at 1565 (quoting Gaertner & Dovidio, *infra* note 61, at 85–86).

31. Gaertner & Dovidio, *supra* note 25, at 77. In fact, white rescuers helped blacks more often than whites (94 percent to 81 percent). *Id.*

32. *Id.* ***

33. Jerome S. Bruner, *On Perceptual Readiness,* 64 PSYCHOL. REV. 123, 132 (1957).

34. Lawrence, *supra* note 6, at 337.

35. E. Tory Higgins & Gillian King, *Accessibility of Social Constructs: Information-Processing Consequences of Individual and Contextual Variability, in* PERSONALITY, COGNITION, AND SOCIAL INTERACTION 69, 71–72 (Nancy Cantor & John F. Kihlstrom eds., 1981).

36. Steven L. Neuberg, *Behavioral Implications of Information Presented Outside of Conscious Awareness: The Effect of Subliminal Presentation of Trait Information on Behavior in the Prisoner's Dilemma Game, in* 6 SOCIAL COGNITION 207, 208 (1988).

37. E. Tory Higgins et al., *Category Accessibility and Impression Formation,* 13 J. EXPERIMENTAL SOC. PSYCHOL. 141, 141–45 (1977).

38. Birt L. Duncan, *Differential Social Perception and Attribution of Intergroup Violence: Testing the Lower Limits of Stereotyping of Blacks,* 34 J. PERSONALITY & SOC. PSYCHOL. 590, 595–97 (1976). ***

39. H. Andrew Sager & Janet Ward Schofield, *Racial and Behavioral Cues in Black and White Children's Perceptions of Ambiguously Aggressive Acts,* 39 J. PERSONALITY & SOC. PSYCHOL. 590, 594–97 (1980).

40. David L. Ronis et al., *Attitudes, Decisions, and Habits as Determinants of Repeated Behavior, in* ATTITUDE STRUCTURE AND FUNCTION 213, 218 (Anthony R. Pratkanis et al. eds., 1989).

41. WILLIAM JAMES, 1 PRINCIPLES OF PSYCHOLOGY 112 (1890) (*quoting* WILLIAM B. CARPENTER, PRINCIPLES OF MENTAL PHYSIOLOGY 339–45 (1874)).

42. Ronis et al., *supra* note 40, at 219.

43. Devine, *supra* note 15, at 6.

44. *Id.*

45. *Id.*

46. *Id.* at 16.

47. Gaertner & Dovidio, *supra* note 25, at 77.

48. Arthur Weinberg, *You Can't Live There!, in* ATTORNEY FOR THE DAMNED 229, 229 (Arthur Weinberg ed., 1957).

49. *Id.* at 234–35, 252, 257 (quoting Clarence Darrow's closing argument).

50. 497 N.E.2d 41 (N.Y. 1986).

51. GEORGE P. FLETCHER, A CRIME OF SELF-DEFENSE: BERNHARD GOETZ AND THE LAW ON TRIAL 206 (1988). ***

52. *Id.* at 208.

53. *See* Lawrence, *supra* note 6, at 355 (arguing that the prevalence of unconscious discrimination thwarts intent analysis). Lawrence argues for a "cultural meaning test," by which governmental conduct would be evaluated "to see if it conveys a symbolic message to which the culture attaches racial significance." *Id.* at 356. ***

54. Johnson, *supra* note 9, at 1799–800. Employing the term "racial imagery" to refer to any racial reference, whether blatant or subtle, Johnson proposes the following test for racial imagery:

"Racial imagery" is any word, metaphor, argument, comment, action, gesture, or intonation that suggests, either explicitly or through commonly understood allusion, that

(1) a person's race or ethnicity affects his or her standing as a full, capable, and decent human being; or

(2) a person's race or ethnicity in any way affects the credibility of that person's assertions; or

(3) a person's race or ethnicity in any way affects the likelihood that he or she would choose a particular course of conduct whether criminal or noncriminal; or

(4) a person's race or ethnicity in any way affects the appropriate sanctions for a crime committed by or against him or her; or

(5) a person's race or ethnicity sets him or her apart from members of the jury, or makes him or her allied with members of the jury or, more generally, that a person's race or ethnicity allies him or her with other persons of the same race or ethnic group or separates him or her from persons of another race or ethnic group.

Racial imagery will be conclusively presumed from the unnecessary use of a racially descriptive word.

Where a metaphor or simile uses the words "white," "black," "brown," "yellow," or "red"; where any comparisons to animals of any kind are made; or where characters, real or fictional, who are strongly identified with a racial or ethnic group are referred to, racial imagery will be presumed, subject only to rebuttal through proof that the term in question could not have racial connotations with respect to any witness, defendant, attorney, or judge involved in the case.

That a speaker disclaims racial intent, either contemporaneously or at a later date, shall have no bearing upon the determination of whether his or her remarks or actions constitute a use of racial imagery. *Id.*

55. ANDREW HACKER, TWO NATIONS 32 (1992).

56. Stanton by Brooks v. Astra Phramaceutical Products, Inc., 718 F.2d 553 (3d Cir. 1983). ***

57. *Id.* at 578 (quoting from the trial transcript).

58. *Id.* at 578–79 (quoting from the trial transcript).

59. *Id.* at 579.

60. *Id.* ***

61. *See, e.g.,* Douglas L. Colbert, *Challenging the Challenge: Thirteenth Amendment as a Prohibition Against the Racial Use of Preemptory Challenges,* 76 CORNELL L. REV. 1, 110–15 (1990) (discussing empirical findings that all-white juries are not always impartial); Johnson, *supra* note 9, at 1616–51 (discussing data on the influence of racial bias on a determination of guilt).

62. W.E.B. DU BOIS, THE SOULS OF BLACK FOLK 10 (Bantam Books 1989).

3. Implicit Racial Attitudes of Death Penalty Lawyers

Theodore Eisenberg and Sheri Lynn Johnson

1. A race-of-victim effect is widely supported by empirical studies. The existence of a broad race-of-defendant effect has been much more difficult to detect. David Baldus et al., *Racial Discrimination and the Death Penalty in the Post-Furman Era: An Empirical and Legal Overview, with Recent Findings from Philadelphia,* 83 CORNELL L. REV. 1638, 1658–59 n.61, 1662, app. B (1998) ***. For recent evidence of such an effect, see John H. Blume et al., *Explaining Death Row's Population and Racial Composition,* 1 J. EMPIRICAL LEGAL STUD. 165, 167, 200 (2004).

2. *See generally* Furman v. Georgia, 408 U.S. 238 (1972).

3. *See, e.g.,* DAVID BALDUS ET AL., EQUAL JUSTICE AND THE DEATH PENALTY: A LEGAL AND EMPIRICAL ANALYSIS (1990); Baldus et al., *supra* note 1; SAMUEL R. GROSS & ROBERT MAURO, DEATH AND DISCRIMINATION: RACIAL DISPARITIES IN CAPITAL SENTENCING (1989); John H. Blume et al., *Post-McCleskey Racial Discrimination Claims in Capital Cases,* 83 CORNELL L. REV. 1771, 1790 (1988); RICHARD C. DIETER, THE DEATH PENALTY IN BLACK AND WHITE: WHO LIVES, WHO DIES, WHO DECIDES 17 fig. 7 (1998).

4. For a particularly egregious example, *see* Andrews v. Shulsen, 485 U.S. 919, 920 (1988) (Marshall, J., dissenting) (A juror handed the bailiff a napkin with a drawing of a man on a gallows above the inscription "Hang the Niggers.").

5. U.S. GEN. ACCOUNTING OFFICE, DEATH PENALTY SENTENCING: RESEARCH INDICATES PATTERN OF RACIAL DISPARITIES 1–6 (1990).

6. 481 U.S. 279 (1987).

7. *See* Tom Moranthau & Peter Annin, *Should McVeigh Die?,* NEWSWEEK, June 16, 1997, at 20. Nonwhite respondents overwhelmingly agreed.

8. *See, e.g.,* BALDUS ET AL., *supra* note 3; Baldus et al., *supra* note 1; GROSS & MAURO, *supra* note 3; Blume et al., *supra* note 3; Jeffrey J. Pokorak, *Probing the Capital Prosecutor's Perspective: Race of the Discretionary Actors,* 83 CORNELL L. REV. 1811 (1998).

9. *See* Sheri Lynn Johnson, *Racial Imagery in Criminal Cases,* 67 TUL. L. REV. 1739, 1760–66 (1993).

10. *See, e.g.,* HOWARD SCHUMAN ET AL., RACIAL ATTITUDES IN AMERICA: TREND AND INTERPRETATIONS (1997); T. Alexander Aleinikoff, *The Constitution in Context: The Continuing Significance of Race,* 63 COLO. L. REV. 325 (1992).

11. *See, e.g.,* Harold Sigall & Richard Page, *Current*

Stereotypes: A Little Fading, a Little Faking, 18 J. PER-SONALITY & SOC. PSYCHOL. 247, 252 (1971).

12. *See, e.g.*, Sheri Lynn Johnson, *Unconscious Racism and the Criminal Law*, 73 CORNELL L. REV. 1016, 1027–28 (1988).

13. We do not refer to our subjects as "African American" because, although virtually all of the black subjects in the two lawyer groups were African American, in the constitutional law class, Caribbean and African students are a significant part of the total.

14. ALAN AGRESTI, CATEGORICAL DATA ANALYSIS 559 (2d ed. 2002). To ensure positive values of the dependent variable in the negative binomial analyses, a positive integer was added to the values of the dependent variable for all observations. *Id.*

15. This preference is not the result of greater familiarity with white faces. Researchers have eliminated the familiarity hypothesis by using familiar black faces (or names) and unfamiliar white faces (or names), and find that the automatic preference of whites subjects for white survives unchanged. *See generally* Nilanjan Dasgupta et al., *Automatic Preference for White Americans: Eliminating the Familiarity Explanation*, 36 J. EXPERIMENTAL. SOC. PSYCHOL. 316 (2000), *available at* http://faculty.washington .edu/agg/pdf/DasguptaEtAl.JESP2000.pdf (last visited Apr. 13, 2004).

16. We were, however, able to compare the strength of automatic preferences in our law student and defense lawyer groups with the strength of the automatic preferences of *undergraduates* who attended the Race to Execution Symposium, and found no significant differences. We do not report the symposium data because it reflects such a hodgepodge of respondents that we were uncertain as to the meaning of any results, but the undergraduate component of the symposium was large enough to analyze, and gives us some reason to believe that our sample does not differ in strength of the automatic-race preference from lay populations, just as the Web data give us confidence that the direction of our sample's preferences is indistinguishable from that of the general population.

17. *See* Brian A. Nosek et al., *Harvesting Implicit Group Attitudes and Beliefs from a Demonstration Web Site*, 6 GROUP DYNAMICS: THEORY RES. PRAC. 101, 102–3 (2002), *available at* http://projectimplicit .net/nosek//papers/harvesting.GroupDynamics.pdf (last visited Apr. 13, 2004).

18. *See, e.g.*, Theodore Eisenberg et al., *Juries, Judges, and Punitive Damages: An Empirical Study*, 87 CORNELL L. REV. 743 (2002) [. . .] ; Neil Vidmar & Jeffrey J. Rice, *Assessments of Noneconomic Damage Awards in Medical Negligence: A Comparison of Jurors*

with Legal Professionals, 78 IOWA L. REV. 883, 896 (1993); Roselle L. Wissler et al., *Decisionmaking About General Damages: A Comparison of Jurors, Judges and Lawyers*, 98 MICH. L. REV. 751, 812 (1999).

19. Chris Guthrie et al., *Inside the Judicial Mind*, 86 CORNELL L. REV. 777, 816 (2001). Judges also fall prey to framing effects and the representative heuristic, though they are less susceptible than others.

20. Richard Revesz, *Environmental Regulation, Ideology, and the D.C. Circuit*, 83 VA. L. REV. 1717 (1997).

21. Fred C. Zacharias, *The Humanization of Lawyers*, 2002 PROF. LAW. 9, 10 (2002).

22. GORDON W. ALLPORT, THE NATURE OF PREJUDICE 56–57 (1954).

23. *Id.* at 56–57.

24. Thus, for example, mock jury studies of race and guilt attribution find race-of-defendant effects in the "marginal evidence" cases; when proof of guilt is either weak or strong, these effects do not appear. *See* Sheri Lynn Johnson, *Black Innocence and the White Jury*, 83 MICH. L. REV. 1611, 1626–34 (1985) [. . .]. The same pattern is reflected in the Baldus data on capital cases in Georgia; race-of-victim effects are found in the cases that are in the middle range of aggravating factors. *See* McCleskey v. Kemp, 481 U.S. 279, 364 (1987) (Stevens, J., dissenting).

25. *See, e.g.*, HOWARD EHRLICH, THE SOCIAL PSYCHOLOGY OF PREJUDICE 40 (1973).

26. Annie Murphy Paul, *Where Bias Begins: The Truth About Stereotypes*, PSYCHOL. TODAY, May–June 1998, at 52 (quoting researcher Margo Monteith). However, attempts to suppress stereotypes may also sometimes backfire, causing them to return in a stronger form. *Id.*

4. Advocacy Against the Stereotype: Lessons from Cognitive Social Psychology

Gary Blasi

1. W.E. BURGHARDT DU BOIS, THE SOULS OF BLACK FOLK, at vii (1903). Now mostly remembered as a founder of the movement for civil rights and, later, of pan-Africanism, W.E.B. DuBois would probably now also be recognized as the first American social scientist, but for the intense racism of the time. His book *The Philadelphia Negro: A Social Study* preceded the work of the "Chicago School" sociologists by two decades. W.E.B. DU BOIS, THE PHILADELPHIA NEGRO: A SOCIAL STUDY (1967).

2. 347 U.S. 483 (1954).

3. *Id.* at 493.

4. *See* Williams v. California, No. 312236 (S.F. Super. Ct., May 17, 2000). [. . .]

5. *See* Gary Blasi, *Reforming Educational Accountability, in* CALIFORNIA POLICY OPTIONS 2002 53–55 (Daniel J.B. Mitchell ed., 2002).

6. 163 U.S. 537 (1896). [. . .]

7. *See* Linda Hamilton Krieger, *The Content of Our Categories: A Cognitive Bias Approach to Discrimination and Equal Employment Opportunity*, 47 STAN. L. REV. 1161 (1995); Charles R. Lawrence III, *The Id, the Ego, and Equal Protection: Reckoning with Unconscious Racism*, 39 STAN. L. REV. 317 (1987). [. . .]

8. *See* Allen J. Hart et al., *Differential Response in the Human Amygdala to Racial Outgroup vs. Ingroup Face Stimuli*, 11 NEUROREPORT 2351 (2000); Kevin N. Ochsner & Matthew D. Lieberman, *The Emergence of Social Cognitive Neuroscience*, 56 AM. PSYCHOLOGIST 717 (2001); Elizabeth A. Phelps et al., *Performance on Indirect Measures of Race Evaluation Predicts Amygdala Activation*, 12 J. COGNITIVE NEUROSCIENCE 729 (2000).

9. *See* Samuel R. Sommers & Phoebe C. Ellsworth, *White Juror Bias: An Investigation of Prejudice Against Black Defendants in the American Courtroom*, 7 PSYCHOL. PUB. POL'Y & L. 201, 216–21 (2001); *see also* Samuel R. Sommers & Phoebe C. Ellsworth, *Race in the Courtroom: Perceptions of Guilt and Dispositional Attributions*, 26 PERSONALITY & SOC. PSYCHOL. BULL. 1367–79 (2000).

10. Sommers & Ellsworth, *supra* note 9, at 220.

11. *See* John A. Bargh et al., *Automaticity of Social Behavior: Direct Effects of Trait Construct and Stereotype Activation on Action*, 71 J. PERSONALITY & SOC. PSYCHOL. 230, 236–38 (1996).

12. *See* ZIVA KUNDA, SOCIAL COGNITION 334 (1999).

13. Ziva Kunda & Lisa Sinclair, *Motivated Reasoning with Stereotypes: Activation, Application, and Inhibition*, 10 PSYCHOL. INQUIRY 12, 16 (1999).

14. [. . .] *See* http://buster.cs.yale.edu/implicit/ (last visited May 12, 2002). [. . .]

15. *See* Claude M. Steele & Thomas J. Liu, *Dissonance Processes as Self-Affirmation*, 45 J. PERSONALITY & SOC. PSYCHOL. 5 (1983).

16. *See* Steven Fein & Steven J. Spencer, *Prejudice as Self-Image Maintenance: Affirming the Self Through Derogating Others*, 73 J. PERSONALITY & SOC. PSYCHOL. 31, 32–34 (1997).

17. *See* Steven J. Spencer et al., *Automatic Activation of Stereotypes: The Role of Self-Image Threat*, 24 PERSONALITY & SOC. PSYCHOL. BULL. 1139 (1998).

18. *See* John A. Bargh, *The Automaticity of Everyday Life*, 10 ADVANCES IN SOC. COGNITION 1 (1997).

19. *See* Patricia G. Devine & Margo J. Monteith, *Automaticity and Control in Stereotyping, in* DUAL-PROCESS THEORIES IN SOCIAL PSYCHOLOGY 339 (Shelly Chaiken & Yaacov Trope eds., 1999).

20. John A. Bargh, *The Cognitive Monster: The Case Against the Controllability of Automatic Stereotype Effects, in* DUAL-PROCESS THEORIES IN SOCIAL PSYCHOLOGY 361, 376 (Shelly Chaiken & Yaacov Trope eds., 1999).

21. [. . .] STEREOTYPE ACTIVATION AND INHIBITION (Robert S. Wyer Jr. ed., 1998).

22. *See* C. Neil Macrae et al., *The Dissection of Selection in Person Perception: Inhibitory Processes in Social Stereotyping*, 69 J. PERSONALITY & SOC. PSYCHOL. 397 (1995).

23. *See* C. Neil Macrae et al., *Out of Mind but Back in Sight: Stereotypes on the Rebound*, 67 J. PERSONALITY & SOC. PSYCHOL. 808 (1994).

24. *See* Janiel M. Wegner & Ralph Erber, *The Hyperaccessibility of Suppressed Thoughts*, 63 J. PERSONALITY & SOC. PSYCHOL. 903 (1992). [. . .]

25. *See* Devine & Monteith, *supra* note 19, at 339, 355; Gordon B. Moskowitz et al., *Preconscious Control of Stereotype Activation Through Chronic Egalitarian Goals*, 77 J. PERSONALITY & SOC. PSYCHOL. 167 (1999).

26. *See* John A. Bargh et al., *The Automatic Will: Nonconscious Activation and the Pursuit of Behavioral Goals*, 81 J. PERSONALITY & SOC. PSYCHOL. 1014, 1017 (2001).

27. John A. Bargh, Presentation at the UCLA Department of Psychology (Jan. 25, 2002).

28. *See* Barbara C. Malt & Edward E. Smith, *Correlated Properties in Natural Categories*, 23 J. VERBAL LEARNING & BEHAVIOR 250, 250–69 (1984).

29. [. . .] GEORGE LAKOFF, WOMEN, FIRE, AND DANGEROUS THINGS: WHAT CATEGORIES REVEAL ABOUT THE MIND (1987). [. . .]

30. *See* Eliot R. Smith & Michael A. Zárate, *Exemplar-Based Model of Social Judgment*, 99 PSYCHOL. REV. 3 *passim* (1992).

31. Devon W. Carbado, *Black Rights, Gay Rights, Civil Rights*, 47 UCLA L. REV. 1467, 1469 (2000).

32. For a comprehensive overview, *see* KUNDA, *supra* note 12, at 211–63.

33. *See* Galen V. Bodenhausen et al., *Happiness and Stereotypic Thinking in Social Judgment*, 66 J. PERSONALITY & SOC. PSYCHOL. 621 *passim* (1994).

34. *See* Lisa Sinclair & Ziva Kunda, *Reactions to a Black Professional: Motivated Inhibition and Activation of Conflicting Stereotypes*, 77 J. SOC. PSYCHOL. 885 *passim* (1999).

35. *See* LEON FESTINGER, A THEORY OF COGNITIVE DISSONANCE *passim* (1957).

36. Joshua Aronson et al., *Self-Affirmation Theory: An Update and Appraisal, in* COGNITIVE DISSONANCE:

PROGRESS ON A PIVOTAL THEORY IN SOCIAL PSYCHOLOGY 127, 128 (Eddie Harmon-Jones & Judson Mills eds., 1999).

37. Dan Simon, *A Psychological Model of Judicial Decision Making*, 30 RUTGERS L.J. 1, 53–54 (1998). [. . .]

38. *See* Ziva Kunda et al., *Combining Social Concepts: The Role of Causal Reasoning*, 14 COG. SCI. 551, 551–52 (1990). There is an extensive literature on the phenomena entailed in conceptual combination more generally. *See, e.g.*, Fintan J. Costello & Mark T. Keane, *Efficient Creativity: Constraint-Guided Conceptual Combination*, 24 COGNITIVE SCI. 299 (2000).

39. *See* BRENT STAPLES, PARALLEL TIME: GROWING UP IN BLACK AND WHITE 202–3 (1994).

40. *See* Gary Blasi, *Advocacy and Attribution: Shaping and Responding to Perceptions of the Causes of Homelessness*, 19 ST. LOUIS U. PUB. L. REV. 207, 213–16 (2000).

41. *Id.* at 228.

42. *See* ALBERT J. MOORE ET AL., TRIAL ADVOCACY: INFERENCES, ARGUMENTS AND TECHNIQUES 85–86 (1996).

43. *See* Ziva Kunda & Kathryn C. Oleson, *Maintaining Stereotypes in the Face of Disconfirmation: Constructing Grounds for Subtyping Deviants*, 68 J. PERSONALITY & SOC. PSYCHOL. 565 (1995).

44. *See* Nilanjana Dasgupta & Anthony Greenwald, *On the Malleability of Automatic Attitudes: Combating Automatic Prejudice with Images of Admired and Disliked Individuals*, 82 J. PERSONALITY & SOC. PSYCHOL. 800 (2001).

45. *Id.* at 800 (citations omitted).

46. *See* Martin Gilens, *"Race Coding" and White Opposition to Welfare*, 90 AM. POL. SCI. REV. 593, 594–95 (1996).

47. *See* Lucy A. Williams, *Race, Rat Bites and Unfit Mothers: How Media Discourse Informs Welfare Legislation Debate*, 22 FORDHAM URB. L.J. 1159 (1995).

48. *See* Naomi R. Cahn, *Representing Race Outside Explicitly Racialized Contexts*, 95 MICH. L. REV. 965 (1997).

49. *See* Linda L. Ammons, *Mules, Madonnas, Babies, Bathwater, Racial Imagery and Stereotypes: The African-American Woman and the Battered Woman Syndrome*, 1995 WIS. L. REV. 1003 (1995).

50. *See, e.g.*, Mark Peffley & Jon Hurwitz, *The Racial Components of "Race-Neutral" Crime Policy Attitudes*, J. POL. PSYCHOL. (forthcoming), *available at* http://www.uky.edu/AS/PoliSci/Peffley/pdf/ RacGenCrimeAttPolPsy_2-12-01_.pdf (last visited May 12, 2002).

51. Mark Peffley & Jon Hurwitz, *Whites' Stereotypes of Blacks: Sources and Political Consequences, in*

PERCEPTION AND PREJUDICE (Mark Peffley & Jon Hurwitz eds., 1998).

52. *See* Samuel R. Sommers & Phoebe C. Ellsworth, *White Juror Bias: An Investigation of Prejudice Against Black Defendants in the American Courtroom*, 7 PSYCHOL. PUB. POL'Y & L. 220 (2001).

53. John M. Conley et al., *The Racial Ecology of the Courtroom: An Experimental Study of Juror Response to the Race of Criminal Defendants*, 2000 WIS. L. REV. 1185, 1213–14 (2000).

54. *See* C. Neil Macrae et al., *Saying No to Unwanted Thoughts: Self-Focus and the Regulation of Mental Life*, 74 J. PERSONALITY & SOC. PSYCHOL. 578 (1998).

55. *See* Bargh et al., *supra* note 26.

56. At least in the larger courts of Los Angeles, jurors have ample free time to be exposed to such treatments, as I have attested from personal experience. *See* Gary Blasi, *Let Jurors Complain and Courts Listen*, L.A. TIMES, July 22, 2001, at M5.

57. *See* Brian Mullen et al., *Crossed Categorization Versus Simple Categorization and Intergroup Evaluations: A Meta-Analysis*, 31 EUR. J. SOC. PSYCH. 721 (2001).

58. For a short overview, *see* ZIVA KUNDA, SOCIAL COGNITION 381–84 (1999).

59. *Id.* at 390.

60. No. 312236 (S.F. Super. Ct. filed May 17, 2000) [. . .].

5. Individual and Intergroup Processes to Address Racial Discrimination in Lawyering Relationships

Carwina Weng

1. Jerry Kang, *Trojan Horses of Race*, 118 HARV. L. REV. 1489, 1549–51 (2005).

2. Kim Taylor-Thompson, *Empty Voices in Jury Deliberations*, 113 HARV. L. REV. 1261, 1293 (2000); Gary Blasi, *Advocacy Against the Stereotype: Lessons from Cognitive Social Psychology*, 49 UCLA L. REV. 1241, 1246–47 (2002).

3. *See generally* Clark D. Cunningham, *The Lawyer as Translator, Representation as Text: Towards an Ethnography of Legal Discourse*, 77 CORNELL L. REV. 1298–387 (1992).

4. For reviews of current social cognition research, written for the legal audience, *see* Jody Armour, *Stereotypes and Prejudice: Helping Legal Decisionmakers Break the Prejudice Habit*, 83 CAL. L. REV. 733, 739–59 (1995); Ronald Chen & Jon Hanson, *Categorically Biased: The Influence of Knowledge Structures on Law and Legal Theory*, 77 S. CAL. L. REV. 1106, 1131–218 (2004).

5. American Psychological Association, *Guidelines on Multicultural Education, Training, Research, Practice, and Organizational Change for Psychologists*, available at http://www.apa.org/pi/multicultural guidelines/formats.html (last visited Sept. 27, 2006); Chen & Hanson, *supra* note 4, at 1131–33; *see generally* John F. Dovidio, Kerry Kawakami & Samuel L. Gaertner, *Reducing Contemporary Prejudice: Combating Explicit and Implicit Bias at the Individual and Interpersonal Level, in* REDUCING PREJUDICE AND DISCRIMINATION 137–63 (Stuart Oskamp ed., 2000) [hereinafter REDUCING PREJUDICE]; Lorelle Lepore & Rupert Brown, *Category and Stereotype Activation: Is Prejudice Inevitable?*, 72 J. PERSONALITY & SOC. PSYCH. 275–87 (1997).

6. Kang, *supra* note 1, at 1500.

7. Prejudice occurs when the perceiver accepts or endorses unfair, inaccurate, or negative racial or cultural stereotypes. Armour, *supra* note 4, at 742.

8. *Id.* at 746; Dovidio, Kawakami & Gaertner, *supra* note 5, at 137–63; Susan T. Fiske, *Interdependence & the Reduction of Prejudice, in* REDUCING PREJUDICE 115–35; Kang, *supra* note 1, at 1514–15.

9. Ziva Kunda & Steven J. Spencer, *When Do Stereotypes Come to Mind & When Do they Color Judgment? A Goal-Based Theoretical Framework for Stereotype Activation & Application*, 129 PSYCH. BULL. 522–44 (2003).

10. Fiske, *supra* note 8.

11. Dovidio, Kawakami & Gaertner, *supra* note 5, at 137–63.

12. *See, e.g.*, DAVID A. BINDER ET AL., LAWYERS AS COUNSELORS: A CLIENT-CENTERED APPROACH 32–40 (2d ed. 2004); *see generally* Susan Bryant, *The Five Habits: Building Cross-Cultural Competence in Lawyering*, 8 CLINICAL L. REV. 33–107 (2001); ROBERT F. COCHRAN JR., JOHN M.A. DiPIPPA & MARTHA M. PETERS, THE COUNSELOR-AT-LAW: A COLLABORATIVE APPROACH TO CLIENT INTERVIEWING AND COUNSELING 203–21 (1999); STEFAN KRIEGER & RICHARD NEUMANN, ESSENTIAL LAWYERING SKILLS: INTERVIEWING, COUNSELING, NEGOTIATION, AND PERSUASIVE FACT ANALYSIS 49–57 (2d ed. 2003); Marjorie A. Silver, *Emotional Competence, Multicultural Lawyering and Race*, 3 FLA. COASTAL L.J. 219–44 (2002), Paul R. Tremblay, *Interviewing and Counseling Across Cultures: Heuristics and Biases*, 9 CLINICAL L. REV. 373–416 (2002); and Carwina Weng, *Multicultural Lawyering: Teaching Psychology to Develop Cultural Self-Awareness*, 11 CLINICAL L. REV. 369–403 (2005).

13. *See generally* Patricia G. Devine et al., *The Regulation of Explicit and Implicit Race Bias: The Role of Motivation to Respond Without Prejudice*, 82 J. PERSONALITY & SOC. PSYCH. 835–48 (2002).

14. Dovidio, Kawakami & Gaertner, *supra* note 5, at 137–63; *see generally* Kerry Kawakami et al., *Just Say No (To Stereotyping): Effects of Training in the Negation of Stereotypic Associations on Stereotype Activation*, 78 J. PERSONALITY & SOC. PSYCHOL. 871–88 (2000); Lepore & Brown, *supra* note 5.

15. Kerry Kawakami et al., *supra* note 14.

16. *Id.* at 880.

17. *Id.* at 874–84.

18. Devine et al., *supra* note 13.

19. Dovidio, Kawakami & Gaertner, *supra* note 5.

20. Patricia G. Devine, E. Ashby Plant & Brenda N. Buswell, *Breaking the Prejudice Habit: Progress and Obstacles, in* REDUCING PREJUDICE, *supra* note 5, at 185–208.

21. Dovidio, Kawakami & Gaertner, *supra* note 5.

22. Project Implicit, "Background Information," and "FAQ," Project Implicit, *available at* https://implicit.harvard.edu/implicit/backgroundinformation .html and https://implicit.harvard.edu/implicit/demo/faqs.html (accessed June 29, 2006).

23. Dovidio, Kawakami & Gaertner, *supra* note 5; Devine, Plant, & Buswell, *supra* note 20.

24. Devine, Plant & Buswell, *supra* note 20.

25. *Id.* at 197–201.

26. *Id.* at 203.

27. Dovidio, Kawakami & Gaertner, *supra* note 5.

28. Marilynn B. Brewer, *Reducing Prejudice Through Cross-Categorization: Effects of Multiple Social Identities, in* REDUCING PREJUDICE at 165–83; Dovidio, Kawakami & Gaertner, *supra* note 5.

29. Brewer, *supra* note 28.

30. Thomas F. Pettigrew & Linda R. Tropp, *Does Intergroup Contact Reduce Prejudice? Recent Meta-Analytic Findings, in* REDUCING PREJUDICE, at 93–114.

31. Dovidio, Kawakami & Gaertner, *supra* note 5.

32. Fiske, *supra* note 8.

33. *Id.* at 131.

34. Dovidio, Kawakami & Gaertner, *supra* note 5; David W. Johnson & Roger T. Johnson, *The Three Cs of Reducing Prejudice & Discrimination, in* REDUCING PREJUDICE, at 239–68.

35. Dovidio, Kawakami & Gaertner, *supra* note 5.

36. Brewer, *supra* note 28; Dovidio, Kawakami & Gaertner, *supra* note 5.

37. Brewer, *supra* note 28; Dovidio, Kawakami & Gaertner, *supra* note 5.

38. Brewer, *supra* note 28.

39. Dovidio, Kawakami & Gaertner, *supra* note 5.

40. *Id.* at 151–52.

41. Brewer, *supra* note 28.

42. Dovidio, Kawakami & Gaertner, *supra* note 5.

43. Brewer, *supra* note 28; Dovidio, Kawakami & Gaertner, *supra* note 5.

44. Brewer, *supra* note 28; Dovidio, Kawakami & Gaertner, *supra* note 5.

45. Brewer, *supra* note 28.

46. Dovidio, Kawakami & Gaertner, *supra* note 5.

47. Brewer, *supra* note 28.

48. Robin J. Ely & David A. Thomas, *Cultural Diversity at Work: The Effects of Diversity Perspectives on Work Group Processes and Outcomes*, 46 ADMIN. SCI. Q. 229–73 (2001).

49. *Id.* at 240–45.

50. Brewer, *supra* note 28.

51. Johnson & Johnson, *supra* note 34.

52. Grutter v. Bollinger, 539 U.S. 306 (2003).

53. Johnson & Johnson, *supra* note 34.

54. Shin Imai, *A Counter-Pedagogy for Social Justice: Core Skills for Community-Based Lawyering*, 9 CLINICAL L. REV. 195, 203–5, 220–25 (2002).

55. Johnson & Johnson, *supra* note 34.

56. *See generally* Susan Bryant, *Collaboration in Law Practice: A Satisfying and Productive Process for a Diverse Profession*, 17 VT. L. REV. 459–531 (1993). Indeed, the law firm studied by Ely & Thomas, *supra* note 48, switched to staffing all cases with two attorneys to take advantage of cross-cultural learning and exposure.

57. KRIEGER & NEUMANN, *supra* note 12, at 15–18.

58. *See generally* Katherine Kruse, *Fortress in the Sand: The Plural Values of Client-Centered Representation*, 12 CLINICAL L. REV. 369 (2006); Robert D. Dinerstein, *Client-Centered Counseling: Reappraisal and Refinement*, 32 ARIZ L. REV. 501 (1990) discussing the different rationales underlying client-centeredness.

59. DAVID BINDER & SUSAN PRICE, LEGAL INTERVIEWING & COUNSELING: A CLIENT-CENTERED APPROACH 148–49 (1977).

60. KRIEGER & NEUMANN, *supra* note 12, at 16, for example, enumerate as core elements of client-centered lawyering a focus on the client's hopes, not needs, and treating the client as "an effective collaborator."

61. *See, e.g.*, Michelle Jacobs, *People from the Footnotes: The Missing Element in Client-Centered Counseling*, 27 GOLDEN GATE U. L. REV. 345 (1997); *see generally* Anne Shalleck, *Constructions of the Client within Legal Education*, 45 STAN. L. REV. 1731 (1993).

62. COCHRAN, DIPIPPA & PETERS, *supra* note 12, at 6–7, 11–30.

63. Johnson & Johnson, *supra* note 34.

64. *Id.* at 256–57.

65. *Id.* at 258–59.

66. Bryant, *supra* note 12, at 471; Ely & Thomas, *supra* note 48.

67. Ely & Thomas, *supra* note 48 (quoting study participant at the "integration and learning" perspective law firm).

68. MODEL RULES OF PROF'L CONDUCT 1.2(a) (2002), *available at* http://www.abanet.org/cpr/mrpc/mrpc_toc.html (last visited September 25, 2006) (hereinafter MRPC).

69. Indeed, the MRPC enjoin lawyers to "exercise professional judgment and render candid advice" (MRPC 2.1), including an explanation of risks and alternatives, to allow clients informed consent (MRPC 1.0(e)).

70. Johnson & Johnson, *supra* note 34.

71. Lee Anne Bell, *Theoretical Foundations for Social Justice Education*, *in* TEACHING FOR DIVERSITY AND SOCIAL JUSTICE: A SOURCEBOOK 3–15 (Marianne Adams, Lee Anne Bell & Pat Griffin eds., 1997).

72. Ely & Thomas, *supra* note 48; Fiske, *supra* note 8.

6. Race and Juries: An Experimental Psychology Perspective

Samuel R. Sommers and Omoniyi O. Adekanmbi

Authors' Note: The first author was generously supported by the Russell Sage Foundation and the Tufts University Faculty Research Award Committee during the preparation of this chapter.

1. *See generally* Samuel R. Sommers & Phoebe C. Ellsworth, *How Much Do We Really Know About Race and Juries? A Review of Social Science Theory and Research*, 78 CHI.-KENT L. REV. 997 (2003).

2. *See generally* David C. Baldus et al., *Comparative Review of Death Sentences: An Empirical Study of the Georgia Experience*, 74 J. CRIM. L. & CRIMINOLOGY 661 (1983).

3. William J. Bowers et al., *Death Sentencing in Black and White: An Empirical Analysis of Jurors' Race and Jury Racial Composition*, 3 U. PA. J. CONST. L. 259 (2001).

4. Francis C. Dane & Lawrence S. Wrightsman, *Effects of Defendants' and Victims' Characteristics on Jurors' Verdicts*, *in* THE PSYCHOLOGY OF THE COURTROOM 104 (Norbert L. Kerr & Robert M. Bray eds., 1982).

5. For notable exceptions, see Galen V. Bodenhausen & Meryl Lichtenstein, *Social Stereotypes and Information-Processing Strategies: The Impact of Task Complexity*, 52 J. PERSONALITY & SOC. PSYCHOL. 871 (1987); Bernd Wittenbrink et al., *Structural Properties of Stereotypic Knowledge and Their Influences on*

the Construal of Social Situations, 72 J. PERSONALITY & SOC. PSYCHOL. 526 (1997).

6. Sommers & Ellsworth, *supra* note 1, at 1005.

7. Tanya S. Taylor & Harmon M. Hosch, *An Examination of Jury Verdicts for Evidence of a Similarity-Leniency Effect, an Out-Group Punitiveness Effect or a Black Sheep Effect*, 28 LAW & HUM. BEHAV. 587 (2004).

8. Laura T. Sweeney & Craig Haney, *The Influence of Race on Sentencing: A Meta-Analytic Review of Experimental Studies*, 10 BEHAV. SCI. & L. 179 (1992).

9. Ronald Mazzella & Alan Feingold, *The Effects of Physical Attractiveness, Race, Socioeconomic Status, and Gender of Defendants and Victims on Judgments of Mock Jurors: A Meta-Analysis*, 24 J. APPLIED SOC. PSYCHOL. 1315 (1994).

10. Tara L. Mitchell et al., *Racial Bias in Mock Juror Decision-Making: A Meta-Analytic Review of Defendant Treatment*, 29 LAW & HUM. BEHAV. 621 (2005).

11. Ramsey McGowen & Glen D. King, *Effects of Authoritarian, Anti-Authoritarian, and Egalitarian Legal Attitudes on Mock Juror and Jury Decisions*, 51 PSYCHOL. REPORTS 1067 (1982).

12. Markus Kemmelmeier, *The Effects of Race and Social Dominance Orientation in Simulated Juror Decision Making*, 35 J. APPLIED SOC. PSYCHOL. 1030 (2005).

13. *See* Bette L. Bottoms et al., *Effects of Victim and Defendant Race on Jurors' Decisions in Child Sexual Abuse Cases*, 34 J. APPLIED SOC. PSYCHOL. 1 (2004); John F. Dovidio et al., *Racial Attitudes and the Death Penalty*, 27 J. APPLIED SOC. PSYCHOL. 1468 (1997); Gordon Hodson et al., *Aversive Racism in Britain: The Use of Inadmissible Evidence in Legal Decisions*, 35 EUR. J. OF SOC. PSYCHOL. 437 (2005).

14. *See* Bridget C. Dunton & Russell H. Fazio, *An Individual Difference Measure of Motivation to Control Prejudiced Reactions*, 23 PERSONALITY & SOC. PSYCHOL. BULL. 316 (1997); E. Ashby Plant & Patricia G. Devine, *Internal and External Motivation to Respond Without Prejudice*, 75 J. PERSONALITY & SOC. PSYCHOL. 811 (1998).

15. *See* Anthony G. Greenwald & Mahzarin R. Banaji, *Implicit Social Cognition: Attitudes, Self-Esteem, and Stereotypes*, 102 PSYCHOL. REV. 4 (1995).

16. James D. Johnson et al., *Justice Is Still Not Colorblind: Differential Racial Effects of Exposure to Inadmissible Evidence*, 21 PERSONALITY & SOC. PSYCHOL. BULL. 893 (1995).

17. Steven Fein et al., *Hype and Suspicion: The Effects of Pretrial Publicity, Race, and Suspicion on Jurors' Verdicts*, 53 J. SOC. ISSUES 487 (1997).

18. Samuel R. Sommers & Phoebe C. Ellsworth, *Race in the Courtroom: Perceptions of Guilt and Dispositional Attributions*, 26 PERSONALITY & SOC. PSYCHOL. BULL. 1367 (2000).

19. Jeffrey E. Pfeifer & James R.P. Ogloff, *Ambiguity and Guilt Determinations: A Modern Racism Perspective*, 21 J. APPLIED SOC. PSYCHOL. 1713 (1991).

20. Randall A. Gordon et al., *Perceptions of Blue-Collar and White-Collar Crime: The Effect of Defendant Race on Simulated Juror Decisions*, 128 J. SOC. PSYCHOL. 191 (1988).

21. Jean-Willem van Prooijen, *Retributive Reactions to Suspected Offenders: The Importance of Social Categorizations and Guilt Probability*, 32 PERSONALITY & SOC. PSYCHOL. BULL. 715 (2006).

22. Samuel L. Gaertner & John F. Dovidio, *The Aversive Form of Racism*, in PREJUDICE, DISCRIMINATION, AND RACISM 61 (John F. Dovidio & Samuel L. Gaertner eds., 1986).

23. Samuel R. Sommers & Phoebe C. Ellsworth, *White Juror Bias: An Investigation of Racial Prejudice Against Black Defendants in the American Courtroom*, 7 PSYCHOL. PUB. POL'Y & LAW 201 (2001).

24. *See* Michael I. Norton et al., *Mixed Motives and Racial Bias: The Impact of Legitimate and Illegitimate Criteria on Decision Making*, 12 PSYCHOL. PUB. POL'Y & LAW 36 (2006).

25. Michael J. Sargent & Amy L. Bradfield, *Race and Information Processing in Criminal Trials: Does the Defendant's Race Affect How the Facts Are Evaluated?*, 30 PERSONALITY & SOC. PSYCHOL. BULL. 995 (2004).

26. Robert Forster Lee et al., *The Effects of Defendant Race, Victim Race, and Juror Gender on Evidence Processing in a Murder Trial*, 24 BEHAV. SCI. & L. 179 (2006).

27. Christopher F. Jones & Martin F. Kaplan, *The Effects of Racially Stereotypical Crimes on Juror Decision-Making and Information-Processing Strategies*, 25 BASIC & APPLIED SOC. PSYCHOL. 1 (2001).

28. Joshua Correll et al., *The Police Officer's Dilemma: Using Ethnicity to Disambiguate Potentially Threatening Individuals*, 83 J. PERSONALITY & SOC. PSYCHOL. 1314 (2002); Jennifer L. Eberhardt et al., *Seeing Black: Race, Crime, and Visual Processing*, 87 J. PERSONALITY & SOC. PSYCHOL. 876 (2004); B. Keith Payne, *Prejudice and Perception: The Role of Automatic and Controlled Processes in Misperceiving a Weapon*, 81 J. PERSONALITY & SOC. PSYCHOL. 181 (2001).

29. Correll, *supra* note 28.

30. Cynthia Willis Esqueda, *European American Students' Perceptions of Crimes Committed by Five Racial Groups*, 27 J. APPLIED SOC. PSYCHOL. 1406 (1997).

31. Travis L. Dixon & Keith B. Maddox, *Skin Tone, Crime News, and Social Reality Judgments: Priming the Stereotype of the Dark and Dangerous Black Criminal*, 35 J. APPLIED SOC. PSYCHOL. 1555 (2005).

32. Jennifer L. Eberhardt et al., *Looking Death-worthy: Perceived Stereotypicality of Black Defendants Predicts Capital-Sentencing Outcomes*, 17 PSYCHOL. SCI. 384 (2006).

33. Baldus et al., *supra* note 2.

34. Eberhardt et al., *supra* note 32.

35. Mona Lynch & Craig Haney, *Discrimination and Instructional Comprehension: Guided Discretion, Racial Bias, and the Death Penalty*, 24 LAW & HUM. BEHAV. 337 (2000); Thomas W. Brewer, *Race and Jurors' Receptivity to Mitigation in Capital Cases: The Effect of Jurors', Defendants', and Victims' Race in Combination*, 28 LAW & HUM. BEHAV. 529 (2004).

36. Mitchell et al., *supra* note 10.

37. Sommers & Ellsworth, *supra* note 23.

38. *See* J. Nicole Shelton, *A Reconceptualization of How We Study Issues of Racial Prejudice*, 4 PERSON-ALITY & SOC. PSYCHOL. REV. 374 (2000).

39. *See id.*

40. Linda A. Foley & Minor H. Chamblin, *The Effect of Race and Personality on Mock Jurors' Deci-sions*, 112 J. PSYCHOL. 47 (1982).

41. Denis C. Ugwuegbu, *Racial and Evidential Factors in Juror Attribution of Legal Responsibility*, 15 J. EXPERIMENTAL SOC. PSYCHOL. 133 (1979).

42. Paul Skolnick & Jerry I. Shaw, *The O.J. Simp-son Criminal Trial Verdict: Racism or Status Shield?*, 53 J. SOC. ISSUES 503 (1997).

43. David A. Abwender & Kenyatta Hough, *In-teractive Effects of Characteristics of Defendant and Mock Juror on U.S. Participants' Judgment and Sen-tencing Recommendations*, 141 J. SOC. PSYCHOL. 603 (2001).

44. Sommers & Ellsworth, *supra* note 18.

45. Skolnick and Shaw, *supra* note 42, at 503.

46. Sommers & Ellsworth, *supra* note 18, at 1367.

47. *See* Paul Butler, *Racially Based Jury Nullifica-tion: Black Power in the Criminal Justice System*, in AFRICAN AMERICAN CLASSICS IN CRIMINOLOGY AND CRIMINAL JUSTICE (Shaun L. Gabbidon & Helen T. Greene eds., 2002).

48. Sommers & Ellsworth, *supra* note 1, at 1021.

49. *See* Jordan Abshire & Brian H. Bernstein, *Ju-ror Sensitivity to the Cross-Race Effect*, 27 LAW AND HUM. BEHAV. 471 (2003).

50. Sommers & Ellsworth, *supra* note 18, at 1370.

51. Solomon M. Fulero & Steven D. Penrod, *The Myths and Realities of Attorney Jury Selection Folklore and Scientific Jury Selection: What Works?*, 17 OHIO N.U. L. REV. 229 (1990).

52. *See* Miller-El v. Dretke, 545 U.S. 231 (2005); Antony Page, *Batson's Blind-Spot: Unconscious Stereo-typing and the Peremptory Challenge*, 85 B.U. L. REV. 155 (2005); Mary R. Rose, *The Peremptory Challenge Accused of Race or Gender Discrimination? Some Data from One County*, 23 LAW AND HUM. BEHAV. 695 (1999).

53. Bowers et al., *supra* note 3.

54. Howard C. Daudistel et al., *Effects of Defen-dant Ethnicity on Juries' Dispositions of Felony Cases*, 29 J. APPLIED SOC. PSYCHOL. 317 (1999).

55. J.L. Bernard, *Interaction Between the Race of the Defendant and That of Jurors in Determining Verdicts*, 5 LAW & PSYCHOL. REV. 103 (1979).

56. Dolores A. Perez et al., *Ethnicity of Defendants and Jurors as Influences on Jury Decisions*, 23 J. AP-PLIED SOC. PSYCHOL. 1249 (1993).

57. Jack P. Lipton, *Racism in the Jury Box: The His-panic Defendant*, 5 HISP. J. BEHAV. SCI. 275 (1983).

58. Derek Chadee, *Race, Trial Evidence, and Jury Decision Making*, 1 CARIBBEAN J. CRIMINOLOGY & SOC. PSYCHOL. 59 (1996).

59. *See generally* HARRY KALVEN JR. & HANS ZEISEL, THE AMERICAN JURY (1966).

60. Nancy S. Marder, *Juries, Justice, and Multicul-turalism*, 75 U. S. CAL. L. REV. 678 (2002).

61. Peters v. Kiff, 407 U.S. 493, 503 (1972).

62. *See* Elizabeth Mannix & Margaret A. Neale, *What Differences Make a Difference? The Promise and Reality of Diverse Teams in Organizations*, 6 PSY-CHOL. SCI. PUB. INT. 31 (2005).

63. *Kiff*, 407 U.S. at 504.

64. *See* Katherine W. Phillips & Denise Loyd, *When Surface and Deep-Level Diversity Collide: The Effects on Dissenting Group Members*, 99 ORGANIZA-TIONAL BEHAV. & HUM. DECISION PROCESSES 143 (2006).

65. Valerie P. Hans & Neil Vidmar, *Jury Selection*, in THE PSYCHOLOGY OF THE COURTROOM (Norbert L. Kerr & Robert M. Bray eds., 1982).

66. Norbert L. Kerr et al., *Defendant-Juror Simi-larity and Mock Juror Judgments*, 19 LAW AND HUM. BEHAV. 545 (1995).

67. Samuel R. Sommers, *On Racial Diversity and Group Decision-Making: Identifying Multiple Effects of Racial Composition on Jury Deliberations*, 90 J. PERSONALITY SOC. PSYCHOL. 597 (2006).

68. Hans & Vidmar, *supra* note 65, at 42.

69. Sommers, *supra* note 67.

70. *See* Michael E. Antonio & Valerie P. Hans, *Race and the Civil Jury: How Does a Juror's Race Shape the Jury Experience?*, in PSYCHOLOGY IN THE COURTS: INTERNATIONAL ADVANCES IN KNOWL-EDGE 69 (Ronald Roesch et al. eds., 2001); Marder, *supra* note 60.

71. *See* Norton et al., *supra* note 24.

72. McDonnell Douglas Corp. v. Green, 411 U.S. 792 (1973).

73. Price Waterhouse v. Hopkins, 490 U.S. 228 (1989).

74. Desert Palace v. Costa, 539 U.S. 90 (2003).

75. *See generally* Joe Feagin & Melvin Sikes, Living with Racism: The Black Middle Class Experience (1994).

76. Cheryl R. Kaiser & Carol T. Miller, *Stop Complaining! The Social Costs of Making Attributions to Discrimination*, 27 Personality & Soc. Psychol. Bull. 254 (2001).

77. Cheryl R. Kaiser & Carol T. Miller, *Derogating the Victim: The Interpersonal Consequences of Blaming Events on Discrimination*, 6 Group Processes & Intergroup Rel. 227 (2003).

78. Teri Elkins & James Phillips, *Evaluating Sex Discrimination Claims: The Mediating Role of Attributions*, 84 J. Applied Psychol. 186 (1999).

79. Edith Greene et al., *Juror Decisions About Damages in Employment Discrimination Cases*, 17 Behav. Sci. & L. 107 (1999).

80. Teri Elkins et al., *Evaluating Gender Discrimination Claims: Is There a Gender Similarity Bias?* 44 Sex Roles 1 (2001).

81. *Id.*

82. Gloria Cowan & Cyndi Hodge, *Judgments of Hate Speech. The Effects of Target Group, Publicness, and Behavioral Responses of the Target*, 26 J. Applied Soc. Psychol. 355 (1996).

83. Alexander Czopp & Margo Monteith, *Confronting Prejudice (Literally): Reactions to Confrontations of Racial and Gender Bias*, 29 Personality & Soc. Psychol. Bull. 532 (2003).

84. Samuel R. Sommers & Michael I. Norton, *Lay Theories about White Racists: What Constitutes Racism (and What Doesn't)*, 9 Group Processes & Intergroup Rel. 117 (2006).

85. *Id.*

7. African Americans on the Witness Stand: Race and Expert Witness Testimony

Veronica S. Tetterton and Stanley L. Brodsky

1. *See generally* Steven C. Bank & Norman G. Poythress, *The Elements of Persuasion in Expert Testimony*, 10 J. Psychiatry & L. 173 (1982).

2. *See generally* Steven D. Hurwitz, Murray S. Miron & Blair T. Johnson, *Source Credibility and the Language of Expert Testimony*, 22 J. Applied Soc. Psychol. 1909 (1992).

3. *See generally* Harmon Hosch, E. Link Beck & Patricia McIntyre, *Influence of Expert Testimony Regarding Eyewitness Accuracy on Jury Decision*, 4 Law & Hum. Behav. 287 (1980); Michael McCloskey & Howard Egeth, *A Time to Speak, or Time to Keep Silence?*, 38 Am. Psychologist 573 (1983); Gary L. Wells, Roderick C.L. Lindsay & James P. Tousignant, *Effects of Expert Psychological Advice on Human Performance in Judging the Validity of Eyewitness Testimony*, 4 L. & Hum. Behav. 275 (1980).

4. *See generally* Harry Kalven & Hans Zeisel, The American Jury (1966).

5. *See generally* Stanley L. Brodsky, Testifying in Court: Guidelines and Maxims for the Expert Witness (1991); Stanley L. Brodsky, The Expert Expert Witness: More Maxims and Guidelines for Testifying in Court (1999); Stanley L. Brodsky, Coping with Cross-Examination and Other Pathways to Effective Testimony (2004).

6. Brodsky, *supra* note 5.

7. *See generally* Marcus T. Boccaccini & Stanley L. Brodsky, *Believability of Expert Lay Witnesses: Implications for Trial Consultation*, 33 Prof. Psychol.: Res. & Prac. 384 (2002); Shelly Chaiken, *Communication Physical Attractiveness and Persuasion*, 37 J. Personality & Soc. Psychol. 1387 (1979); Joel Cooper & Isaac M. Neuhass, *The "Hired Gun" Effect: Assessing the Effect of Pay, Frequency of Testifying, and Credentials on the Perceptions of Expert Testimony*, 24 L. & Hum. Behav. 149 (2000); Bonnie Erickson, Allan E. Lind, Bruce C. Johnson & William M. O'Barr, *Speech Style and Impression Formation in a Court Setting: The Effects of "Powerful" "Powerless" Speech*, 14 J. Experimental Soc. Psychol. 266 (1978).

8. *See generally* Tara L. Mitchell, Ryann M. Haw, Jeffrey E. Pfeifer & Christian A. Meissner, *Racial Bias in Juror Decision-Making: A Meta-Analytic Review of Defendant Treatment*, 29 Law & Hum. Behav. 621 (2005).

9. Mitchell, Haw, Pfeifer & Meissner, *supra* note 8, at 627.

10. *See generally* Sara S. Steen, Rodney L. Engen & Randy R. Gainey, *Images of Danger and Culpability: Racial Stereotyping, Case Processing, and Criminal Sentencing*, 43(2) J. Criminology 435 (2005).

11. *See generally* Celesta A. Albonetti, *An Integration of Theories to Explain Judicial Discretion*, 38 Soc. Probs. 247 (1991).

12. *See generally* Amina Memon & Daniel Shuman, *Juror Perception of Experts in Civil Disputes: The Role of Race and Gender*, 22 Law & Psychol. Rev. 179 (1998).

13. *See generally* Duane T. Wegener & Richard E. Petty, *The Flexible Correction Model: The Role of Naïve Theories of Bias in Bias Correction*, 29 J. Advances Experimental Soc. Psychol. 141 (1997).

14. Memon & Shuman, *supra* note 12.

15. *Id.*

16. *See generally* Richard E. Petty & John T. Cacioppo, *The Effects of Involvement on Responses to Arguments Quantity and Quality: Central and Peripheral Routes to Persuasion*, 46 J. Personality & Soc. Psychol. 69 (1984).

17. Richard E. Petty & John T. Cacioppo, *Epilog: A General Framework for Understanding Attitude Change Processes*, in Attitudes and Persuasion: Classic and Contemporary Approaches 255–69 (1996).

18. *Id.*

19. *See generally* Richard E. Petty, Monique A. Fleming & Paul H. White, *Stigmatized Sources and Persuasion: Prejudice as a Determinant of Argument Scrutiny*, 76 J. Personality & Soc. Psychol. 19 (1999).

20. Petty & Cacioppo, *supra* note 17.

21. *See generally* Saul M. Kassin, Maria E. Reddy & William F. Tulloch, *Juror Interpretations of Ambiguous Evidence: The Need for Cognition, Presentation Order, and Persuasion*, 14 Law & Hum. Behav. 43 (1990).

22. *See generally* Yaacov Schul & Frieda Manzury, *The Effects of Type of Encoding and Strength of Discounting Appeal on the Success of Ignoring an Invalid Testimony*, 20 Eur. J. Soc. Psychol. 337 (1990).

23. *See generally* Paul H. White & Stephen G. Harkins, *Race of Source Effects in the Elaboration Likelihood Model*, 67 J. Personality & Soc. Psychol. 790 (1994).

24. *Id.*

25. *Id.*

26. *Id.*

27. *Id.*

28. Samuel L. Gaertner & John F. Dovidio, *The Aversive Form of Racism*, in Prejudice, Discrimination, and Racism 61–89 (John F. Dovidio & Samuel L. Gaertner eds., 1986).

29. Bank & Poythress, *supra* note 1.

30. *See generally* Tommy E. Whittler & Joan S. Spira, *Model's Race: A Peripheral Cue in Advertising Messages?*, 12 J. Consumer Psychol. 293 (2002).

31. Susan T. Fiske & Shelley E. Taylor, Social Cognition 2 (1991).

32. *See generally* Jean S. Phinney, *The Multigroup Ethnic Identity Measure: A New Scale for Use with Diverse Groups*, 7 J. Adolescent Res. 156–76 (1992).

33. *See generally* Joseph G. Ponterotto, Denise Gretchen, Shawn O. Utsey, Thomas Stracuzzi & Robert Saya, *The Multigroup Ethnic Identity Measure (MEIM): Psychometric Review and Further Validity Testing*, 63 Educ. & Psychol. Measurement 504 (2003).

34. Whittler & Spira, *supra* note 30.

35. Veronica S. Tetterton, Female Expert Witnesses: The Influence of Race and Expertise on Expert Witness Credibility, Perceived Defendant Dangerousness and Sentencing Decisions (2006) (unpublished Ph.D. dissertation, Univ. of Alabama) (on file with author); Veronica S. Tetterton & Stanley L. Brodsky, When African-American Experts Are on the Witness Stand: A Study of Race, Expertise, and Credibility, Paper presented at the American Psychology-Law Society Conference, La Jolla (2005).

36. Memon & Shuman, *supra* note 12.

37. Wegener & Petty, *supra* note 13.

38. Whittler & Spira, *supra* note 30.

39. *See generally* Meryl R. Louis & Robert. I. Sutton, *Switching Cognitive Gears: From Habits of Mind to Active Thinking*, 44 Hum. Rel. 55 (1991).

40. *Id.*

41. *See generally* Julie Schroeder, Rebecca Chaisson & Rene Pogue, *Restoring the Defendant's Life: Using Narrative to Revise Juror Viewpoint in Capital Cases*, 14 J. Ethnic & Cultural Diversity Soc. Work 1 (2005).

42. Brodsky, *supra* note 5.

8. Does Race Matter? Exploring the Cross-Race Effect in Eyewitness Identification

Steven M. Smith and Veronica Stinson

Authors' Note: Support for this chapter was provided by SSHRC grants to both authors and a CIHR grant to the first author. The authors thank Stephanie Quigg for her help in the preparation of this chapter.

1. Smith & Mack v. Maryland, 388 Md. 468 (Md. 2005).

2. *See generally* John C. Brigham & Melissa P. Wolfskiel, *Opinions of Attorneys and Law Enforcement Personnel on the Accuracy of Eyewitness Identifications*, 7 Law & Hum. Behav. 337 (1983); Roderick C.L. Lindsay, Gary L. Wells & Carolyn M. Rumpel, *Can People Detect Eyewitness Identification Accuracy Within and Across Situations?*, 66 J. Applied Psychol. 79 (1981).

3. *See generally* Alvin G. Goldstein, June E. Chance & Gregory R. Schneller, *Frequency of Eyewitness Identification in Criminal Cases: A Survey of Prosecutors*, 27 Bull. Psychonomic Soc'y 71 (1989).

4. *See generally* Gary L. Wells, *What Do We Know About Eyewitness Identification*, 48 Am. Psychologist 553 (1993).

5. *See generally* Barry Scheck, Peter Neufeld & Jim Dwyer, Actual Innocence (2001).

6. The Innocence Project, *available at* www .innocenceproject.org (last visited Oct. 7, 2006).

7. *See generally* RUTH BRANDON & CHRISTIE DAVIES, WRONGFUL IMPRISONMENT (1973).

8. Brigham & Wolfskiel, *supra* note 2; Lindsay, Wells & Rumpel, *supra* note 2.

9. Brigham & Wolfskiel, *supra* note 2; Lindsay, Wells & Rumpel, *supra* note 2.

10. *See generally* Steven M. Smith, Roderick C.L. Lindsay & Sean Pryke, *Postdictors of eyewitness accuracy: Can False Identifications Be Diagnosed?*, 85 J. APPLIED PSYCHOL. 542 (2000); Siegfried L. Sporer, *Decision Times and Eyewitness Identification Accuracy in Simultaneous and Sequential Lineups*, in ADULT EYEWITNESS TESTIMONY 300–327 (David F. Ross, John D. Read & Michael P. Toglia eds., 1994).

11. *See generally* John C. Brigham, *Perspectives on the Impact of Lineup Composition, Race, and Witness Confidence on Identification Accuracy*, 4 LAW & HUM. BEHAV. 315 (1981).

12. *See generally* Robert K. Bothwell, John C. Brigham & Roy S. Malpass, *Cross-Racial Identification*, 15 PERSONALITY & SOC. PSYCHOL. BULL. 19 (1989); Christian A. Meissner & John C. Brigham, *Thirty Years of Investigating the Own-Race Bias in Memory for Faces: A Meta-Analytic Review*, 7 PSYCHOL. PUB. POL'Y & L. 3 (2001).

13. For an exception, see James M. Doyle, *Discounting the Error Costs: Cross-Racial False Alarms in the Culture of Contemporary Criminal Justice*, 7 PSYCHOL. PUB. POL'Y & L. 253 (2001).

14. SCHECK, NEUFELD & DWYER, *supra* note 5.

15. *Id.*

16. *See generally* Tim Valentine, Alan Pickering & Stephen Darling, *Characteristics of Eyewitness Identification That Predict the Outcome of Real Lineups*, 17 APPLIED COGNITIVE PSYCHOL. 969 (2003).

17. *See generally* Roy S. Malpass & Jerome Kravitz, *Recognition for Own- and Other-Race*, 13 J. PERSONALITY & SOC. PSYCHOL. 330 (1969).

18. *See generally* Steven M. Smith, Roderick C.L. Lindsay, Sean Pryke & Jennifer E. Dysart, *Postdictors of Eyewitness Errors: Can False Identifications Be Diagnosed in the Cross-Race Situation?*, 7 PSYCHOL. PUB. POL'Y & L. 153 (2001).

19. *See generally* Steven M. Smith, Veronica Stinson & Matthew A. Prosser, *Do They All Look Alike? An Exploration of Decision-Making Strategies in Cross-Race Facial Identifications*, 36 CANADIAN J. BEHAV. SCI. 146 (2004).

20. *See* Bothwell, Brigham & Malpass, *supra* note 12; Peter N. Shapiro & Steven Penrod, *Meta-Analysis of Facial Identification Studies*, 100 PSYCHOL. BULL. 139 (1986).

21. Meissner & Brigham, *supra* note 12.

22. Gary L. Wells & Elizabeth A. Olson, *The Other-Race Effect in Eyewitness Identification: What Do We Do About It?*, 7 PSYCHOL. PUB. POL'Y & L. 230, 231 (2001).

23. Bothwell, Brigham & Malpass, *supra* note 12; Meissner & Brigham, *supra* note 12; Shapiro & Penrod, *supra* note 20.

24. *See* Wells, *supra* note 4.

25. Smith, Stinson & Prosser, *supra* note 19.

26. *See generally* STEPHEN J. CECI, MICHAEL P. TOGLIA & DAVID F. ROSS, CHILDREN'S EYEWITNESS MEMORY (1987); Daniel Yarmey, *Age As a Factor in Eyewitness Memory*, in EYEWITNESS TESTIMONY: PSYCHOLOGICAL PERSPECTIVES 142–54 (Gary L. Wells & Elizabeth L. Loftus eds., 1984).

27. *See generally* Thomas E. O'Rourke, Steven D. Penrod, Brian L. Cutler & Thomas E. Stuve, *The External Validity of Eyewitness Identification Research: Generalizing Across Subject Populations*, 13 LAW & HUM. BEHAV. 385 (1989).

28. *See generally* Stephanie J. Platz & Harmon M. Hosch, *Cross-Racial/Ethnic Eyewitness Identification: A Field Study*, J. APPLIED SOC. PSYCHOL. 972 (1988).

29. Platz & Hosch, *supra* note 28.

30. Wells & Olson, *supra* note 22.

31. *Id.*

32. *See generally* Siegfried L. Sporer, *The Cross-Race Effect: Beyond Recognition of Faces in the Laboratory*, 7 PSYCHOL. PUB. POL'Y & L. 170 (2001).

33. Wells & Olson, *supra* note 22.

34. *See generally* Wei-Jen Ng & Roderick C.L. Lindsay, *Cross-Race Facial Recognition: Failure of the Contact Hypothesis*, 25 J. CROSS-CULTURAL PSYCHOL. 217 (1994); Smith, Lindsay & Pryke, *supra* note 10; Smith, Stinson & Prosser, *supra* note 19.

35. *See generally* Alice J. O'Toole, Kenneth A. Deffenbacher, Dominique Valentin & Herve Abdi, *Structural Aspects of Face Recognition and the Other-Race Effect*, 22 MEMORY & COGNITION 208 (1994).

36. *See generally* Alvin G. Goldstein & June E. Chance, *Effects of Training on Japanese Face Recognition: Reduction of the Other-Race Effect*, 23(3) BULL. PSYCHONOMIC SOC'Y 211 (1983); Roy S. Malpass, Henry Lavigueur & David E. Weldon, *Verbal and Visual Training in Face Recognition*, 14 PERCEPTION & PSYCHOPHYSICS 285 (1973); Roy S. Malpass, *Training in Face Recognition*, in PERCEIVING AND REMEMBERING FACES 271–85 (G. Davies, H. Ellis & J. Shepherd eds., 1981).

37. *See generally* John C. Brigham & Roy S. Malpass, *The Role of Experience and Contact in the Recognition of Faces of Own and Other-Race Faces*, 41 J. SOC. ISSUES 139 (1985); Ng & Lindsay, *supra* note 34.

38. *See generally* John C. Brigham & Paul Barkowitz, *Do "They All Look Alike?" The Influence Effect of Race, Sex, Experience, and Attitudes on the Ability to Recognize Faces*, 8 J. APPLIED SOC. PSYCHOL. 306 (1978); Patrick Chiroro & Tim Valentine, *An Investigation of the Contact Hypothesis of the Own-Race Bias in Face Recognition*, 48 Q. J. EXPERIMENTAL PSYCHOL. 879 (1995); J.F. Cross, J. Cross & J. Daly, *Sex, Race, Age, and Beauty as Factors in Recognition of Faces*, 10 PERCEPTION & PSYCHOPHYSICS 393 (1971); Paul J. Lavarkas, John R. Buri & Mark S. Mayzner, *A Perspective on the Recognition of Other-Race Faces*, 20 PERCEPTION & PSYCHOPHYSICS 475 (1976); Ashlyn E. Slone, John C. Brigham & Christian A. Meissner, *Social and Cognitive Factors Affecting the Own-Race Bias in Whites*, 22 BASIC & APPLIED SOC. PSYCHOL. 71 (2000); Daniel B. Wright, Catherine E. Boyd & Colin G. Tredoux, *Inter-Racial Contact and the Own-Race Bias for Face Recognition in South Africa and England.*, 17 APPLIED COGNITIVE PSYCHOL. 365 (2003); Platz & Hosch, *supra* note 28.

39. *See generally* Graham Byatt & Gillian Rhodes, *Recognition of Own-Race and Other-Race Caricatures: Implications for Models of Face Recognition*, 38 VISION RES. 2455 (1998).

40. Meissner & Brigham, *supra* note 12.

41. Brigham & Malpass, *supra* note 37.

42. Meissner & Brigham, *supra* note 12.

43. Brigham & Malpass, *supra* note 37.

44. Meissner & Brigham, *supra* note 12.

45. *But see also* Michael A. Olson & Russell H. Fazio, *Relations Between Implicit Measures of Prejudice: What Are We Measuring?*, 14(6) PSYCHOL. SCI. 636 (2003).

46. *See generally* Roy S. Malpass, *An Excursion Into Utilitarian Analysis*, 24 BEHAV. SCI. RES. 1–15 (1990).

47. D. Dunning, J. Li & R.S. Malpass, Basketball Fandom and Cross-Race Identification Among European-Americans: Another Look at the Contact Hypothesis, Paper presented at the conference of the American Psychology-Law Society, Redondo Beach, CA (March 1998).

48. *See generally* O.H. MacLin, B.R. Van Sickler, M.K. MacLin & A. Li, *A Re-Examination of the Cross-Race Effect: The Role of Race, Inversion, and Basketball Trivia*, 6 N. AM. J. PSYCHOL. 189 (2004).

49. Dunning, Li & Malpass, *supra* note 47.

50. MacLin, Van Sickler, MacLin & Li, *supra* note 48.

51. *See generally* R.E. Ayuk, *Cross-Racial Identification of Transformed, Untransformed, and Mixed Race Faces*, 25 INT'L J. PSYCHOL. 509 (1990).

52. Malpass & Kravitz, *supra* note 17; Cross, Cross & Daly, *supra* note 38.

53. John W. Shepherd, *Social Factors in Face Recognition*, in PERCEIVING AND REMEMBERING FACES 55–79 (Graham Davies, Hadyn Ellis & John Shepherd eds., 1981).

54. *See generally* A.G. Goldstein, *Race-Related Variation of Facial Features: Anthropometric Data I*, 13 BULL. PSYCHONOMIC SOC'Y 187 (1979); A.G. Goldstein, *Facial Feature Variation: Anthropometric Data II*, 13 BULL. PSYCHONOMIC SOC'Y 191 (1979).

55. Ng & Lindsay, *supra* note 34.

56. *See generally* Roderick C.L. Lindsay & Karen Bellinger, *Alternatives to Sequential Lineups: The Importance of Controlling the Pictures*, 84 J. APPLIED PSYCHOL. 315 (1999); Smith, Lindsay & Pryke, *supra* note 10; Smith, Lindsay, Pryke & Dysart, *supra* note 18.

57. *See generally* Gary L. Wells, *The Psychology of Lineup Identifications*, 14 J. APPLIED SOC. PSYCHOL. 89 (1984).

58. Lindsay & Bellinger, *supra* note 56.

59. Smith, Lindsay & Pryke, *supra* note 10; Smith, Lindsay, Pryke & Dysart, *supra* note 18.

60. Smith, Lindsay, Pryke & Dysart, *supra* note 18; Smith, Stinson & Prosser, *supra* note 19.

61. Smith, Lindsay, Pryke & Dysart, *supra* note 18.

62. Smith, Stinson & Prosser, *supra* note 19.

63. *See generally* Siegfried L. Sporer, *Eyewitness Identification Accuracy, Confidence, and Decision Times in Simultaneous and Sequential Lineups*, 78 J. APPLIED PSYCHOL. 22–33 (1993); Sporer, *supra* note 10.

64. Smith, Lindsay & Pryke, *supra* note 10; Smith, Lindsay, Pryke & Dysart, *supra* note 18.

65. *See generally* David Dunning & Scott Perretta, *Automaticity and Eyewitness Accuracy: A 10- to 12-Second Rule for Distinguishing Accurate from Inaccurate Positive Identifications*, 87 J. APPLIED PSYCHOL. 951 (2002).

66. Smith, Lindsay & Pryke, *supra* note 10; *see generally* Nathan Weber, Neil Brewer, Gary L. Wells, Carolyn Semmler & Amber Keast, *Eyewitness Identification Accuracy and Response Latency: The Unruly 10-12-Second Rule*, 10 J. EXPERIMENTAL PSYCHOL.: APPLIED 139 (2005).

67. Smith, Lindsay & Pryke, *supra* note 10.

68. Smith, Lindsay, Pryke & Dysart, *supra* note 18.

69. *See generally* David Dunning & Lisa Beth Stern, *Distinguishing Accurate from Inaccurate Eyewitness Identifications Via Enquiries About Decision Processes*, 67 J. PERSONALITY & SOC. PSYCHOL. 818 (1994); Lisa Stern & David Dunning, *Distinguishing Accurate from Inaccurate Eyewitness Identifica-*

tions: A Reality Monitoring Approach, in ADULT EYE-WITNESS TESTIMONY 273–99 (David F. Ross, Don Read & Michael P. Toglia eds., 1994).

70. Smith, Stinson & Prosser, *supra* note 19.

71. *See generally* Larry L. Jacoby, Colleen Kelley, Judith Brown & Jennifer Jasechko, *Becoming Famous Overnight: Limits on the Ability to Avoid Unconscious Influences of the Past*, 56 J. PERSONALITY & SOC. PSYCHOL. 326 (1989); Larry L. Jacoby, Stephen D. Lindsay & Jeffrey P. Toth, *Unconscious Influences Revealed: Attention, Awareness, and Control*, 47 AM. PSYCHOLOGIST 802 (1992).

72. *See generally* June E. Chance & Alvin G. Goldstein, *Depth of Processing in Response to Own- and Other-Race Faces*, 7 PERSONALITY & SOC. PSYCHOL. BULL. 475 (1981).

73. *See generally* Patricia Devine & Roy S. Malpass, *Orienting Strategies in Differential Face Recognition*, 11 PERSONALITY & SOC. PSYCHOL. BULL. 33 (1985).

74. *See also* MacLin, Van Sickler, MacLin & Li, *supra* note 48.

75. *See generally* Christian A. Meissner, John C. Brigham & David A. Butz, *Memory for Own- and Other-Race Faces: A Dual-Process Approach*. 19 APPLIED COGNITIVE PSYCHOL. 545 (2005).

76. Meissner, Brigham & Butz, *supra* note 75.

77. Meissner & Brigham, *supra* note 12; Wells & Olson, *supra* note 22.

78. Doyle, *supra* note 13.

79. *See also* State v. Cromedy, 158 N.J. 112 (N.J. 1999).

80. *See generally* Duane T. Wegener, Norbert L. Kerr, Monique A. Fleming & Richard E. Petty, *Flexible Correction of Juror Judgments*, 6 PSYCHOL. PUB. POL'Y & L. 629 (2000).

81. *Id.*

82. *See generally* Brian L. Cutler, Hedy R. Dexter & Steven D. Penrod, *Nonadversarial Methods for Sensitizing Jurors to Eyewitness Evidence*, 20 J. APPLIED SOC. PSYCHOL. 1197 (1990).

83. *Cromedy*, 158 N.J. 112 (1999).

84. *See generally* Saul M. Kassin, Phoebe C. Ellsworth & Vicki L. Smith, *The "General Acceptance" of Psychological Research on Eyewitness Testimony: A Survey of the Experts*, 44 AM. PSYCHOLOGIST 1089 (1989); Michael R. Lieppe, *The Case for Expert Testimony About Eyewitness Memory*, 1 PSYCHOL. PUB. POL'Y & L. 909 (1995).

85. Sporer, *supra* note 10; Meissner & Brigham, *supra* note 12.

86. *See generally* Gary L. Wells, *Applied Eyewitness-Testimony Research: System Variables and Estimator Variables*, 36 J. PERSONALITY & SOC. PSYCHOL. 1546 (1978).

87. *See generally* Roderick C.L. Lindsay, Steven M. Smith & Sean Pryke, *Measures of Lineup Fairness: Do They Work Cross-Race?*, 13 APPLIED COGNITIVE PSYCHOL. 109 (1999); Roy S. Malpass & Roderick C.L. Lindsay, *Measuring Lineup Fairness*, 13 APPLIED COGNITIVE PSYCHOL. 1 (1999); Wells & Olson, *supra* note 22.

88. *See generally* Saul M. Kassin, *Eyewitness Identification: Retrospective Self-Awareness and the Confidence-Accuracy Correlation*, 49 J. PERSONALITY & SOC. PSYCHOL. 878 (1985); Roderick C.L. Lindsay, *Confidence and Accuracy of Eyewitness Identifications from Lineups*, 10 LAW & HUM. BEHAV. 229 (1986); Siegfried L. Sporer, Steven D. Penrod, Don Read & Brian Cutler, *Choosing, Confidence and Accuracy: A Meta-Analysis of the Confidence-Accuracy Relation in Eyewitness Identification Studies*, 118 PSYCHOL. BULL. 315 (1995).

89. Meissner & Brigham, *supra* note 12.

90. Smith, Lindsay, Pryke & Dysart, *supra* note 18.

91. *See generally* Gary L. Wells, Roy S. Malpass, Roderick C.L. Lindsay, Ronald P. Fisher, John W. Turtle & Solomon M. Fulero, *From the Lab to the Police Station: A Successful Application of Eyewitness Research*, 55 AM. PSYCHOLOGIST 581 (2000).

92. Wells, *supra* note 4; Wells & Olson, *supra* note 22.

93. *See generally* Roderick C.L. Lindsay & Gary L. Wells, *Improving Eyewitness Identifications from Lineups: Simultaneous Versus Sequential Lineup Presentation*, 70 J. APPLIED PSYCHOL. 556 (1985); Nancy Steblay, Jennifer Dysart, Solomon M. Fulero & Roderick C.L. Linsday, *Eyewitness Accuracy Rate in Sequential and Simultaneous Lineup Presentations: A Meta-Analytic Review*, 25 LAW & HUM. BEHAV. 459 (2001); Wells & Olson, *supra* note 22.

94. Roderick C.L. Lindsay & Steven M. Smith, Race and Identification Procedure: Does the Sequential Lineup Effect Generalize?, Paper presented at the 4th Biennial Meeting of the Society for Applied Research in Memory and Cognition, Kingston, Ont. (June 2001).

95. *See generally* Gary L. Wells & C.A. Elizabeth Luus, *Police Lineups as Experiments: Social Methodology as a Framework for Properly Conducted Lineup*, 16(1) PERSONALITY & SOC. PSYCHOL. BULL. 106 (1990).

9. The Search for Racial Justice in Tort Law

W. Jonathan Cardi

1. *See, e.g.*, Philip G. Peters Jr., *Hindsight Bias and Tort Liability: Avoiding Premature Conclusions*, 31

Ariz. St. L.J. 1277 (1999); Neil Vidmar, *The Performance of the American Civil Jury: An Empirical Perspective*, 40 Ariz. L. Rev. 849 (1998); *see generally* Gary T. Schwartz, *Reality in the Economic Analysis of Tort Law: Does Tort Law Really Deter?*, 42 UCLA L. Rev. 377 (1994).

2. *See, e.g.*, Veronica S. Tetterton & Stanley L. Brodsky, *African-Americans on the Witness Stand: Race and Expert Witness Testimony*, *supra* Chapter 7.

3. *See, e.g.*, M. Juliet Bonazzoli, *Jury Selection and Bias: Debunking Invidious Stereotypes Through Science*, 18 Quinnipiac L. Rev. 247 (1998).

4. *See, e.g.*, Frank M. McClellan, *Judicial Impartiality & Recusal: Reflections on the Vexing Issue of Racial Bias*, 78 Temp. L. Rev. 351 (2005).

5. *See, e.g.*, Frank M. McClellan, *The Dark Side of Tort Reform: Searching for Racial Justice*, 48 Rutgers L. Rev. 761 (1996).

6. *See* Brian H. Bornstein & Michelle Rajki, *Extra-Legal Factors and Product Liability: The Influence of Mock Jurors' Demographic Characteristics and Intuitions About the Cause of an Injury*, 12 Behav. Sci. & L. 127 (1994).

7. Chris F. Denove & Edward J. Imwinkelried, *Jury Selection: An Empirical Investigation of Demographic Bias*, 19 Am. J. Trial Advoc. 285, 293 (1995).

8. Eric Helland & Alexander Tabarrok, *Race, Poverty, and American Tort Awards: Evidence from Three Data Sets*, 32 J. Legal Stud. 27, 27 (2003).

9. *See* Bonazzoli, *supra* note 3, at 270–71 (describing research regarding attorneys' preference of juror ethnicity).

10. For a useful summary of research on the value of culturally diverse juries, see Justin D. Levinson, *Suppressing the Expression of Community Values in Juries: How "Legal Priming" Systematically Alters the Way People Think*, 73 U. Cin. L. Rev. 1059, 1062–65 (2005).

11. *See* W. Kip Viscusi & Richard J. Zeckhauser, *The Denominator Blindness Effect: Accident Frequencies and the Misjudgment of Recklessness*, 6 Am. L. & Econ. Rev. 72 (2004).

12. *See* W. Kip Viscusi, *The Challenge of Punitive Damages Mathematics*, 30 J. Legal Stud. 313 (2001).

13. *See* Justin D. Levinson & Kaiping Peng, *Different Torts for Different Cohorts: A Cultural Psychological Critique of Tort Law's Actual Cause and Foreseeability Inquiries*, 13 S. Cal. Interdisc. L.J. 195 (2004).

14. The fundamental attribution error is "the tendency of observers to overestimate how much a person's behavior is determined by his or her internal stable dispositions." *Id.* at 206. Culpable causation refers to the effect by which people's perceptions regarding an actor's moral culpability influence their

assessment of whether the actor caused the plaintiff's injury. The illusion of control is the tendency to expect success that is "inappropriately higher than objective probability would warrant." *Id.* at 220.

15. *See, e.g.*, Justin D. Levinson, *Forgotten Racial Equality: Implicit Bias, Decision-Making and Misremembering*, 25 Duke L.J. (forthcoming 2007).

16. Others have reached analogous findings. *See* Birt L. Duncan, *Differential Social Perception and Attribution of Intergroup Violence: Testing the Lower Limits of the Stereotyping of Blacks*, 34 J. Personality & Soc. Psychol. 590, 595–97 (1976); H. Andrew Sagar & Janet Ward Schofield, *Racial and Behavioral Cues in Black and White Children's Perceptions of Ambiguously Aggressive Acts*, 39 J. Personality & Soc. Psychol. 590, 593–95 (1980).

17. One measure of explicit racial bias is the Social Dominance Orientation (SDO) scale, which, according to its creators, measures "the extent to which one desires that one's in-group dominate and be superior to out-groups." Felicia Pratto et al., *Social Dominance Orientation: A Personality Variable Predicting Social and Political Attitudes*, 67 J. Personality & Soc. Psychol. 741 (1994). Among other questions, the SDO asks subjects to make moral judgments about whether their in-group is better, more worthy, more deserving, and superior to others. *Id.*

18. Research on this general topic exists, although it is rare in the tort context. For example, attribution research has shown that Westerners tend to ascribe a person's criminal behavior to innate bad character, whereas Asians point more to the actor's situational context. *See, e.g.*, Michael W. Morris & Kaiping Peng, *Culture and Cause: American and Chinese Attributions for Social and Physical Events*, 67 J. Personality & Soc. Psychol. 949 (1994). On the whole, however, quality research regarding the role of race in juror decision making is lacking. Samuel R. Sommers & Phoebe C. Ellsworth, *How Much Do We Really Know About Race and Juries? A Review of Social Science Theory and Research*, 78 Chi.-Kent L. Rev. 997 (2003).

19. Frank McClellan suggests that having to justify one's position to other jury members acts as a potential curb on race bias. McClellan, *supra* note 4. It is possible that the threat of appellate review might not have the same influence. On the other hand, Jeffrey Rachlinski, Andrew Wistrich, Sherri Johnson, and Chris Guthrie have recently conducted a study of judges in which they found that although judges respond to the Implicit Association Test with levels of racial bias similar to that of the general public, judges' bias did not seem to manifest in their resolution of hypothetical legal questions.

Discussion with Chris Guthrie, Associate Dean and Professor of Law, Vanderbilt Law School, in Nashville, TN (Nov. 2006).

20. This question is addressed qualitatively by at least one scholar. *See, e.g.*, Peggy C. Davis, *Law as Microaggression*, 98 YALE L.J. 1559 (1989).

21. *See* Dan T. Coenen, *A Constitution of Collaboration: Protecting Fundamental Values with Second-Look Rules of Interbranch Dialogue*, 42 WM. & MARY L. REV. 1575, 1594 (2001).

22. *See* W. Bradley Wendel, *"Certain Fundamental Truths": A Dialectic on Negative and Positive Liberty in Hate Speech Cases*, 65 LAW & CONTEMP. PROBS. 33, 55 (2002).

23. *See id.*

24. *See* Richard H. Fallon Jr., *"The Rule of Law" as a Concept in Constitutional Discourse*, 97 COLUM. L. REV. 1, 15–18 (1997).

25. *See* Francis C. Dane & Lawrence S. Wrightsman, *Effects of Defendants' and Victims' Characteristics on Jurors' Verdicts*, in THE PSYCHOLOGY OF THE COURTROOM 84–88 (Norbert L. Kerr & Robert M. Bray eds., 1982); James K. Hammitt et al., *Tort Standards and Jury Decisions*, 14 J. LEGAL STUD. 751, 753–58 (1985). *But see* J. ALEXANDER TANFORD, THE TRIAL PROCESS: LAW, TACTICS AND ETHICS 14–15 (2d ed. 1993) (suggesting that jurors are not ordinarily swayed by racial prejudice).

26. STATE OF CONNECTICUT JUDICIAL BRANCH TASK FORCE ON MINORITY FAIRNESS 40 (Apr. 1996); IOWA EQUALITY IN THE COURTS TASK FORCE, FINAL REPORT (1993); NEW YORK STATE JUDICIAL COMMISSION ON MINORITIES, REPORT OF THE NEW YORK STATE JUDICIAL COMMISSION ON MINORITIES 186–87 (1991); WASHINGTON STATE MINORITY AND JUSTICE TASK FORCE, FINAL REPORT (1990); Edwin J. Peterson et al., *Report of the Oregon Supreme Court Task Force on Racial/Ethnic Issues in the Judicial System*, 73 OR. L. REV. 823, 897–98 (1994). Similar studies have also been conducted by the Florida Supreme Court in 1990, the Massachusetts Supreme Court in 1994, the Michigan Supreme Court in 1989, the Minnesota Supreme Court in 1993, and the New Jersey Supreme Court in 1992. Frank M. McClellan, *Confronting Racial, Ethnic, or Gender Bias in Product Liability Cases*, SB16 ALI-ABA 145, 149 n.3 (1996).

27. Interestingly, in a similar study in the District of Columbia—where the jury pool is primarily African American—minority attorneys thought minority litigants to be at a disadvantage in bench trials, a hurdle neutralized by the presence of a jury. Caucasian attorneys, however, concluded the opposite—that minority parties suffered from no disadvantage before a judge, and in fact enjoyed an advantage in front of the largely African American juries of the District. *See* 1 THE GENDER, RACE AND ETHNIC BIAS TASK FORCE PROJECT IN THE D.C. CIRCUIT IV-106 (1995).

28. *See* AUDREY CHIN & MARK A. PETERSON, DEEP POCKETS, EMPTY POCKETS: WHO WINS IN COOK COUNTY JURY TRIALS (1985). Jennifer Wriggins found similar results in a study of wrongful death and survival act claims in Louisiana from 1900 to 1949. *See* Jennifer B. Wriggins, *Torts, Race, and the Value of Injury, 1900–1949*, 49 HOW. L.J. 99 (2005).

29. CHIN & PETERSON, *supra* note 28, at v. African American defendants, however, paid lower levels of damages than Caucasians. *Id.*

30. *See* McClellan, *supra* note 5, at 768.

31. *See, e.g.*, Peterson et al., *supra* note 26, at 897–98.

32. *See* WASHINGTON STATE MINORITY AND JUSTICE TASK FORCE, *supra* note 26, at 123–25 (1990).

33. *See infra* section 3.b for a discussion of this possibility.

34. *See* Martha Chamallas, *The Disappearing Consumer, Cognitive Bias and Tort Law*, 6 ROGER WILLIAMS U. L. REV. 9 (2000); Martha Chamallas, *The Architecture of Bias: Deep Structures in Tort Law*, 146 U. PA. L. REV. 463 (1998).

35. *See, e.g.*, David E. Bernstein, *Lochner, Parity, and the Chinese Laundry Cases*, 41 WM. & MARY L. REV. 211 (1999).

36. In one near-exception, Mark Wolff explored the potential effects of implicit bias on a change in tax law, by which damages awards resulting from discrimination actions are now taxed as income, unlike tort damages awards for physical injury. *See* Mark J. Wolff, *Sex, Race, and Age: Double Discrimination in Torts and Taxes*, 78 WASH. U. L.Q. 1341 (2000).

37. *See* Amy H. Kastely, *Out of the Whiteness: On Raced Codes and White Race Consciousness in Some Tort, Criminal, and Contract Law*, 63 U. CIN. L. REV. 269 (1994).

38. Wassell v. Adams, 865 F.2d 849 (7th Cir. 1989).

39. Another example of the inherent incorporation of racial disparities by basic tort doctrine is the fact that "tort law values physical injuries and property damages more highly than emotional injuries or relational harms," a preference that Martha Chamallas argues favors whites over minorities and males over females. *See* Chamallas, *The Architecture of Bias*, *supra* note 34, at 468.

40. *See* Martha Chamallas, *Questioning the Use of Race-Specific and Gender-Specific Economic Data in Tort Litigation: A Constitutional Argument*, 63 FORDHAM L. REV 73 (1994); August McCarthy, *The

Lost Futures of Lead-Poisoned Children: Race-Based Damage Awards and the Limits of Constitutionality, 14 Geo. Mason U. Civ. Rts. L.J. 75 (2004); Laura Greenberg, Comment, *Compensating the Lead Poisoned Child: Proposals for Mitigating Discriminatory Damage Awards*, 28 B.C. Envtl. Aff. L. Rev. 429 (2001).

41. *See* Jennifer Wriggins, *Genetics, IQ, and Torts: The Example of Discovery in Lead Exposure Litigation*, 77 B.U. L. Rev. 1025 (1997).

42. For an analogous discussion of racial bias inherent in the rules governing taxation of employment discrimination damages, see Karen B. Brown, *Not Color- or Gender-Neutral: New Tax Treatment of Employment Discrimination Damages*, 7 S. Cal. Rev. L. & Women's Stud. 223 (1998).

43. *See* Mijha Butcher, *Using Mediation to Remedy Civil Rights Violations When the Defendant Is Not an Intentional Perpetrator: The Problems of Unconscious Disparate Treatment and Unjustified Disparate Impacts*, 24 Hamline J. Pub. L. & Pol'y 225, 238–40 (2003); Lu-in Wang, *Race as Proxy: Situational Racism and Self-Fulfilling Stereotypes*, 53 DePaul L. Rev. 1013, 1020 (2004).

44. *See generally* Roselle L. Wissler et al., *Instructing Jurors on General Damages in Personal Injury Cases*, 6 Psychol. Pub. Pol'y & L. 712 (2000).

45. *See, e.g.*, McClellan, *supra* note 5. Many courts forbid closing statements that explicitly seek to overcome racial bias. *Id.* at 761–62. More (but not all) courts allow questions regarding racial bias during voir dire. *Id.* at 778–79.

46. For a description of this research, see Jerry Kang's work in Chapter 10 of this text.

47. *See, e.g.*, Regina Austin, *Employer Abuse, Worker Resistance, and the Tort of Intentional Infliction of Emotional Distress*, 41 Stan. L. Rev. 1 (1988); Paulette M. Caldwell, *Reaffirming the Disproportionate Effects Standard of Liability in Title VII Litigation*, 46 U. Pitt. L. Rev. 555 (1985); Richard Delgado, *Words That Wound: A Tort Action for Racial Insults, Epithets, and Name-Calling*, 17 Harv. C.R.-C.L. L. Rev. 133 (1982).

48. Justin Levinson again provides a rare example in his consideration of whether certain cultural variations on the fundamental attribution error might over-deter desirable behavior. *See* Levinson, *supra* note 15, at 207–11.

49. *See* Donald C. Langevoort, *Behavioral Theories of Judgment and Decision Making in Legal Scholarship: A Literature Review*, 51 Vand. L. Rev. 1499, 1512–14 (1998).

50. *See, e.g.*, Willy E. Rice, *Race, Gender, "Redlining," and the Discriminatory Access to Loans, Credit,* *and Insurance: An Historical and Empirical Analysis of Consumers Who Sued Lenders and Insurers in Federal and State Courts, 1950–1995*, 33 San Diego L. Rev. 583 (1996); Jill Gaulding, Note, *Race, Sex, and Genetic Discrimination in Insurance: What's Fair?*, 80 Cornell L. Rev. 1646 (1995).

51. Levinson & Peng, *supra* note 13, at 197.

10. Trojan Horses of Race

Jerry Kang

1. Apparently Nietzsche never actually said this, although he used the term "immaculate perception" (*unbefleckten Erkenntniss*) in *Thus Spoke Zarathustra* to disparage traditional views of knowledge. *See* Friedrich Nietzsche, Thus Spoke Zarathustra, *reprinted in* The Portable Nietzsche 100, 233–36 (Walter Kaufmann ed. & trans., 1954).

2. Sun Tzu, The Art of War, *reprinted in* Roots of Strategy: A Collection of Military Classics 31 (Thomas R. Phillips ed., 1940).

3. John A. Bargh et al., *Automaticity of Social Behavior: Direct Effects of Trait Construct and Stereotype Activation on Action*, 71 J. Personality & Soc. Psychol. 230, 238–39 (1996) (describing experimental procedure).

4. Franklin D. Gilliam Jr. & Shanto Iyengar, *Prime Suspects: The Influence of Local Television News on the Viewing Public*, 44 Am. J. Pol. Sci. 560, 563–67 (2000). [. . .]

5. *See* Margaret Shih et al., *Stereotype Susceptibility: Identity Salience and Shifts in Quantitative Performance*, 10 Psychol. Sci. 80, 80–81 (1999).

6. Joshua Correll et al., *The Police Officer's Dilemma: Using Ethnicity to Disambiguate Potentially Threatening Individuals*, 83 J. Personality & Soc. Psychol. 1314, 1315–17 (2002). [. . .]

7. *See* B. Keith Payne, *Prejudice and Perception: The Role of Automatic and Controlled Processes in Misperceiving a Weapon*, 81 J. Personality & Soc. Psychol. 181, 185–86 (2001).

8. In the Matter of 2002 Biennial Regulatory Review, 18 F.C.C.R. 13, 620 (2003) [hereinafter Media Ownership Order]; Prometheus Radio Project v. FCC, 373 F.3d 372 (3d Cir. 2004).

9. The third element is "competition." Media Ownership Order, 18 F.C.C.R. at 13, 627.

10. An accessible introductory volume to social cognition is Susan T. Fiske & Shelley E. Taylor, Social Cognition (2d ed. 1991).

11. This recognition and reframing could help us get beyond "blaming" and toward "solving." *Cf.*

Charles R. Lawrence III, *The Id, the Ego, and Equal Protection: Reckoning with Unconscious Racism*, 39 STAN. L. REV. 317, 321 (1987). [. . .]

12. FISKE & TAYLOR, *supra* note 10, at 98.

13. *See, e.g., id.* at 145. *** Visual information tends to disclose age, gender, and race immediately and simultaneously. But one could have been told before meeting a person that he was a law professor, in which case the role schema would have been activated first.

14. *See id.* In a room full of law professors, role may not be as salient as race. At a social gathering of Asian Americans, on the other hand, race may not be as salient as role.

15. *See id.* Priming "refers to the incidental activation of knowledge structures, such as trait concepts and stereotypes, by the current situational context." Bargh et al., *supra* note 3, at 230. Also, there is the possibility of schemas canceling each other out on some relevant metric, for example, if the target is simultaneously a member of one ingroup and one outgroup. *See, e.g.,* RUPERT BROWN, PREJUDICE: ITS SOCIAL PSYCHOLOGY 49–54 (1995).

16. Other variables include mood, motivation (for example, for accuracy), hierarchy (for example, we tend to pay more careful, individuating attention to those who wield power over us), and cognitive busyness (or "load"). *See* FISKE & TAYLOR, *supra* note 10, at 145–467. [. . .]

17. *See* Jennifer L. Eberhardt et al., *Believing Is Seeing: The Effects of Racial Labels and Implicit Beliefs on Face Perception*, 29 PERSONALITY & SOC. PSYCHOL. BULL. 360 (2003). In this study, the researchers tested whether racial labels ("White" or "Black") would influence what participants "saw" and remembered, in terms of physical characteristics, when they encountered racially morphed faces on a computer screen. [. . .]

Those participants identified as "entity theorists," who view traits as largely immutable, showed an assimilation effect. In other words, depending on the demographic label they were given, they "saw" an image consistent with that label. By contrast, those participants identified as "incremental theorists," who see traits as tentative descriptors and are drawn more to individuating information, showed a contrast effect. By being surprised by the disconnect between the racial label and the morphed image, incremental theorists were predicted to examine the face more closely to see the deviation from the prototype member of that category. The researchers concluded that "racial labels operated as an invisible magnet, attracting entity theorists yet simultaneously repelling incremental theorists."

[. . .] *Cf.* Paul R. Wilson, *Perceptual Distortion of Height as a Function of Ascribed Academic Status*, 74 J. SOC. PSYCHOL. 97 (1968). In Wilson's study, students were introduced to a person, variously described as a student, demonstrator, lecturer, senior lecturer, or professor. Later, when asked to guess the person's height, the higher the social status, the taller the guessed height, ranging from 68.9 inches (student) to 72.3 inches (full professor).

18. Bargh et al., *supra* note 3, at 231; *see also id.* at 232. [. . .] This idea traces back to William James, who suggested that "every representation of a movement awakens in some degree the actual movement which is its object." *Id.* at 231 (quoting WILLIAM JAMES, 2 THE PRINCIPLES OF PSYCHOLOGY 526 (1890)). Bargh also notes a fascinating line of ironic control studies that suggest that people instructed not to move an object (such as a pendulum along a particular axis) or think in a particular way (sexist thoughts) did just that. *See id.* at 232. [. . .]

19. *See* Patricia G. Devine, *Stereotypes and Prejudice: Their Automatic and Controlled Components*, 56 J. PERSONALITY & SOC. PSYCHOL. 5 (1989). In that seminal study, participants were subliminally exposed to stereotypical words associated with African Americans such as *Negroes, lazy, Blacks, blues, rhythm, Africa, stereotype, ghetto, welfare, basketball, unemployed,* and *plantation*. None of these words directly mentioned aggressiveness, however. Next, participants read a passage about Donald, whose race was not identified, who engaged in the ambiguous behavior of refusing to pay rent. Those who received a heavy dose of priming (80 percent stereotypical words) interpreted Donald's actions as more hostile than those who received a milder dose (20 percent).

20. *See, e.g.,* John F. Dovidio et al., *On the Nature of Prejudice: Automatic and Controlled Processes*, 33 J. EXPERIMENTAL SOC. PSYCHOL. 510, 516–17 (1997) (demonstrating time differentials in classifying positive or negative words as a function of receiving subliminal flashes of Black or White faces). [. . .]

21. For example, in 1994, roughly 90 percent of White Americans said they would vote for a qualified Black man for president. In 1958, a majority answered no to the same question. Dolly Chugh, *Societal and Managerial Implications of Implicit Social Cognition: Why Milliseconds Matter*, 17 SOC. JUST. RES. 203, 206 (2004) (citing JAMES ALLEN DAVIS & TOM W. SMITH, GENERAL SOCIAL SURVEYS, 1972–1994: CUMULATIVE CODEBOOK 150 (1994)).

22. There is clear evidence of such impression management. For example, in the well-known "bogus pipeline" studies, Edward Jones and Harold

Sigall convinced participants that they were attached to a machine that would measure their true attitudes regardless of what they in fact said. The participants did not know that the machine was bogus. Their explicit self-reports changed significantly when they were hooked up to this bogus machine. *See* Edward E. Jones & Harold Sigall, *The Bogus Pipeline: A New Paradigm for Measuring Affect and Attitude*, 76 PSYCHOL. BULL. 349 (1971); *see also* Russell H. Fazio et al., *Variability in Automatic Activation as an Unobtrusive Measure of Racial Attitudes: A Bona Fide Pipeline?*, 69 J. PERSONALITY & SOC. PSYCHOL. 1013, 1014 (1995) (discussing possibility of a bona fide pipeline).

23. "Symbolic racism," a term introduced in the 1970s, is a belief system that combines the following ideas:

> that racial discrimination is no longer a serious obstacle to blacks' prospects for a good life; that blacks' continuing disadvantages are due to their own unwillingness to take responsibility for their lives; and that, as a result, blacks' continuing anger about their own treatment, their demands for better treatment, and the various kinds of special attention given to them are not truly justified.

P.J. Henry & David O. Sears, *The Symbolic Racism 2000 Scale*, 23 POL. PSYCHOL. 253, 254 (2002) (citation omitted); *see also* Donald R. Kinder & David O. Sears, *Prejudice and Politics: Symbolic Racism Versus Racial Threats to the Good Life*, 40 J. PERSONALITY & SOC. PSYCHOL. 414, 416 (1981).

Modern racism was introduced approximately one decade after "symbolic racism." Similar in substance, the new term was chosen "to emphasize that the new racism was not the only form of prejudice to be rooted in socialization and in abstract, symbolic beliefs; old-fashioned racism had been as well." Henry & Sears, *supra*, at 254–55; *see also* John B. McConahay, *Modern Racism, Ambivalence, and the Modern Racism Scale*, *in* PREJUDICE, DISCRIMINATION, AND RACISM 91, 92–93 (John F. Dovidio & Samuel L. Gaertner eds., 1986).

24. *See* Fazio et al., *supra* note 22, at 1021 (questioning the usefulness of the MRS based on both confounding and reactivity concerns); *see also* Paul M. Sniderman & Phillip E. Tetlock, *Symbolic Racism: Problems of Motive Attribution in Political Analysis*, J. SOC. ISSUES, Summer 1986, at 129, 145–47; Paul M. Sniderman & Phillip E. Tetlock, *Reflections on American Racism*, J. SOC. ISSUES, Summer 1986, at 173, 180–82.

25. *See, e.g.,* Allen R. McConnell & Jill M. Lei-

bold, *Relations Among the Implicit Association Test, Discriminatory Behavior, and Explicit Measures of Racial Attitudes*, 37 J. EXPERIMENTAL SOC. PSYCHOL. 435, 435–36 (2001). [. . .]

26. For example, researchers may task participants with deciding whether a string of letters is a word or not, selecting words that are schema-consistent or schema-inconsistent. *See, e.g.,* Bernd Wittenbrink et al., *Evidence for Racial Prejudice at the Implicit Level and Its Relationship with Questionnaire Measures*, 72 J. PERSONALITY & SOC. PSYCHOL. 262, 265 (1997).

27. For example, participants may be primed and then required to decide how "hostile" ambiguous behavior was. *See, e.g.,* Devine, *supra* note 19, at 8–12.

28. For examples of experiments containing physical tasks, see the shooter bias studies discussed *infra* section I.C.4.

29. Samuel L. Gaertner & John P. McLaughlin, *Racial Stereotypes: Associations and Ascriptions of Positive and Negative Characteristics*, 46 SOC. PSYCHOL. Q. 23, 23 (1983).

30. Although Gaertner and McLaughlin did not find the converse phenomenon, with participants responding faster to bad words when primed with the word "Black," subsequent studies did. *See, e.g.,* J.F. Dovidio et al., *Racial Stereotypes: The Contents of Their Cognitive Representations*, 22 J. EXPERIMENTAL SOC. PSYCHOL. 22 (1986).

31. *See, e.g.,* Dovidio et al., *supra* note 20, at 534 (finding "clear evidence" that the race of the face participants were primed with—Black or White—influenced how quickly they could identify positive versus negative words). [. . .]

32. [. . .] For the most current recommendations on how to conduct and read IATs, see Anthony G. Greenwald et al., *Understanding and Using the Implicit Association Test: I. An Improved Scoring Algorithm*, 85 J. PERSONALITY & SOC. PSYCHOL. 197 (2003). Readers are invited to take the test themselves online at the Project Implicit website. *See* Project Implicit, *IAT Home*, available at http://implicit.harvard .edu/implicit/demo (last visited Feb. 13, 2004). For a list of other implicit bias measurement tools, *see* Irene V. Blair, *The Malleability of Automatic Stereotypes and Prejudice*, 6 PERSONALITY & SOC. PSYCHOL. REV. 242, 260–61 (2002).

33. To date there is no agreed-upon cognitive theory of why the implicit effect exists. When the IAT was introduced in 1998, the creators intentionally decided to provide only a minimal theory—namely, that the more associated any two concepts were, the easier it would be to generate the same response. *See, e.g.,* Anthony G. Greenwald et al., *Measuring Individual Differences in Implicit Cognition: The Im-*

plicit Association Test, 74 J. PERSONALITY & SOC. PSY-CHOL. 1464, 1469 (1998). [. . .]

34. *See* William A. Cunningham et al., *Separable Neural Components in the Processing of Black and White Faces*, 15 PSYCHOL. SCI. 806, 811 (2004). [. . .]

35. *See* Elizabeth A. Phelps et al., *Performance on Indirect Measures of Race Evaluation Predicts Amygdala Activation*, 12 J. COGNITIVE NEUROSCIENCE 729, 732 (2000). [. . .]

36. Nilanjana Dasgupta, *Implicit Ingroup Favoritism, Outgroup Favoritism, and Their Behavioral Manifestations*, 17 SOC. JUST. RES. 143, 146 (2004). [. . .]

37. *Id*. at 147.

38. *Id*. at 147 (citing studies regarding aborigines in Australia and Turkish immigrants in Germany).

39. *See, e.g.*, Dovidio et al., *supra* note 20, at 517. [. . .]

40. *See* Mahzarin R. Banaji, *The Opposite of a Great Truth Is Also True: Homage to Koan #7, in* PERSPECTIVISM IN SOCIAL PSYCHOLOGY: THE YIN AND YANG OF SCIENTIFIC PROGRESS 127, 131 (John T. Jost et al. eds., 2003).

41. *See* Brian A. Nosek, Mahzarin R. Banaji & Anthony G. Greenwald, *Harvesting Implicit Group Attitudes and Beliefs from a Demonstration Web Site*, 6 GROUP DYNAMICS 101, 105 (2002). [. . .]

42. *Id*. at 106 (finding that self-identified liberals had slightly lower IAT bias scores than self-identified conservatives). [. . .]

43. For example, in 1976, B.L. Duncan demonstrated that automatic activation of negative stereotypes can influence the interpretation of ambiguous behavior, leading people to conclude that Blacks are more hostile than Whites. Duncan generated two videos involving one student pushing another; everything was held constant between the videos except for the race of the pusher. These videos were shown to participants, all of whom were White. When the pusher was Black, 90 percent characterized the action as violent or aggressive; by contrast, when the pusher was White, only 40 percent came to the same conclusion. *See* Birt L. Duncan, *Differential Social Perception and Attribution of Intergroup Violence: Testing the Lower Limits of Stereotyping of Blacks*, 34 J. PERSONALITY & SOC. PSYCHOL. 590 (1976); *see also* BROWN, *supra* note 15, at 100 [. . .]. Andrew Sagar and Janet Schofield confirmed these results in a study of sixth-grade boys' characterization of line drawings and accompanying verbal narratives. The "race" of the characters was set by shading in drawings that were otherwise identical. The darker the skin, the more that the ambiguous narrative, which described a bump in the hallway, was interpreted as aggressive and hostile. This bias

appeared in both White and Black youths. *See* H. Andrew Sagar & Janet Ward Schofield, *Racial and Behavioral Cues in Black and White Children's Perceptions of Ambiguously Aggressive Acts*, 39 J. PERSONALITY & SOC. PSYCHOL. 590, 593–95 (1980).

44. *See, e.g.*, EDWARD E. SAMPSON, DEALING WITH DIFFERENCES: AN INTRODUCTION TO THE SOCIAL PSYCHOLOGY OF PREJUDICE 121–22 (1999). [. . .]

45. [. . .] MARIANNE BERTRAND & SENDHIL MULLAINATHAN, ARE EMILY AND GREG MORE EMPLOYABLE THAN LAKISHA AND JAMAL? A FIELD EXPERIMENT ON LABOR MARKET DISCRIMINATION 2 (Nat'l Bureau of Econ. Research, Working Paper No. 9873, 2003). [. . .]

46. Using names that unambiguously signal Black or White raises vexing confounds. The unambiguously Black names could have provided negative proxy information about social background (class and mainstream cultural assimilation). Of course, such racial profiling itself could be morally and legally troubling unless one could somehow argue that the proxy information appropriately influenced the callback decision, notwithstanding more diagnostic information available on the face of the resume itself.

To explore this possibility, the researchers collected statistics about mothers' high school graduation rates for each of the names used in the study. They found that the Black names used in the study fell below the overall Black average (61.0 percent versus 70.2 percent), while the White names chosen were above the White overall average (91.7 percent versus 83.9 percent). These findings support the class-confound interpretation. That said, there was substantial heterogeneity of social backgrounds, as measured by mother's education, among the names within each race. If accurate proxy estimates were taking place, then we would expect correlations between callbacks and actual mother's education rates. In other words, "Aisha" (percentage of mothers with high school educations, 77.2 percent) should have received more callbacks than "Ebony" (65.6 percent). But all the correlations were negative, and none was statistically significant. In addition, if class were the principal driver, one would expect to see less of a callback difference between Whites and Blacks living in wealthier zip codes, but researchers saw no such results.

47. Laurie A. Rudman & Peter Glick, *Prescriptive Gender Stereotypes and Backlash Toward Agentic Women*, 57 J. SOC. ISSUES 743, 747–48 (2001).

48. In a classic but controversial demonstration, Robert Rosenthal and Lenore Jacobson went into an American elementary school and gave the

children intelligence tests. *See* Robert Rosenthal & Lenore Jacobson, Pygmalion in the Classroom: Teacher Expectation and Pupils' Intellectual Development 61, 68–69 (1968). They randomly selected 20 percent of the students and told only the teachers that these select children would excel in the near future. Eight months later, the psychologists revisited the school and retested the students. Amazingly, those who had been identified *randomly* as having high potential ended up in fact overperforming. [. . .] The explanation is that the "high potential" schema biased the teachers' interpretations, which in turn influenced their interactions with the students in ways that ended up genuinely raising their educational performance.

There have been various criticisms about the appropriateness of this experiment as well as its methodology. Moreover, these results have not been consistently replicated in higher grades. Nevertheless, in the educational literature, there is substantial consensus on the significant effect of teacher expectations on student performance. [. . .]

49. *See* Susan T. Fiske, *Stereotyping, Prejudice, and Discrimination*, *in* 2 The Handbook of Social Psychology 369 (Daniel T. Gilbert et al. eds., 4th ed. 1998).

50. *See generally* Claude M. Steele, *A Threat in the Air: How Stereotypes Shape Intellectual Identity and Performance*, 52 Am. Psychologist 613 (1997).

51. *See* Margaret Shih et al., *Stereotype Performance Boosts: The Impact of Self-Relevance and the Manner of Stereotype Activation*, 83 J. Personality & Soc. Psychol. 638, 638 (2002). [. . .]

52. The authors recognized that the behavior link had been demonstrated for other implicit bias measures. *See* McConnell & Leibold, *supra* note 25, at 436; *see also* Fazio et al., *supra* note 22, at 1018 (showing correlation between "facilitation" scores and subjective ratings of Black experimenter regarding friendliness and interest of participant).

53. *Id.* [. . .]

54. *See* Carl O. Word et al., *The Nonverbal Mediation of Self-Fulfilling Prophecies in Interracial Interaction*, 10 J. Experimental Soc. Psychol. 109 (1974).

55. *See* Ziva Kunda, Social Cognition: Making Sense of People 349 (1999). ("[W]e may often believe that our reactions to a stereotyped individual are free of prejudice because they are based on the individual's behavior and attributes rather than on the stereotype. What we may not realize is that the very meaning of these behaviors and attributes has been colored by the stereotype."); *see also* Dovidio et al., *supra* note 20. Dovidio points out that in an interracial interaction, a White person who is aware of only his controlled behavior may think he treated the Black person in a warm and friendly manner. However, the Black person experiences not only this controlled behavior but also the spontaneous behavior correlated with implicit bias, and the net behavioral phenomenon may be negative. This disjunction imparts a *Rashomon* quality to interactions in which participants exhibit high levels of dissociation.

56. *See* Mark Chen & John A. Bargh, *Nonconscious Behavioral Confirmation Processes: The Self-Fulfilling Consequences of Automatic Stereotype Activation*, 33 J. Experimental Soc. Psychol. 541, 554–55 (1997).

57. *See* Payne, *supra* note 7, at 183–86.

58. *See* Correll et al., *supra* note 6.

59. The only other variable with statistically significant correlation with shooter bias was, unbelievably, the amount of contact that the participants claimed to have with African Americans. *See id.* at 1325. Before rushing to the conclusion that interracial contact leads to increased implicit bias, we should note that the "contact hypothesis" requires interaction under specific conditions in order to decrease racial prejudice, as conventionally measured and defined. *See* Norman Miller & Marilynn B. Brewer, *The Social Psychology of Desegregation: An Introduction*, *in* Groups in Contact: The Psychology of Desegregation 1, 2 (Norman Miller & Marilynn B. Brewer eds., 1984). [. . .] For a recent study that finds correlations between interracial friendships and lower implicit bias, *see generally* Christopher L. Aberson et al., *Implicit Bias and Contact: The Role of Interethnic Friendships*, 144 J. Soc. Psychol. 335 (2004). Aberson asked White participants for self-reports of the number of close outgroup friends: African Americans in one experiment and Latinos in another. On the basis of these self-reports, he classified participants into two categories: "no friends" or "friends." Then he ran standard IATs. Those with outgroup friends had lower implicit bias scores. This finding reflects only correlation, not causation. Consistent with general dissociation findings, the friendship measure had no correlations with measures of explicit bias. One concern with this study is the use of self-reports of "close friends," apparently without much guidance or definition of the term.

60. Charles M. Judd et al., *Automatic Stereotypes vs. Automatic Prejudice: Sorting Out the Possibilities in the Payne (2001) Weapon Paradigm*, 40 J. Experimental Soc. Psychol. 75 (2004).

61. *See* Patricia G. Devine & Margo J. Monteith, *Automaticity and Control in Stereotyping*, *in* Dual-Process Theories in Social Psychology 339,

346–47 (Shelly Chaiken & Yaacov Trope eds., 1999) (identifying three requirements for overriding automatic response based on stereotype activation: awareness of stereotypes, cognitive capacity, and motivation to counter).

62. B. Keith Payne et al., *Best Laid Plans: Effects of Goals on Accessibility Bias and Cognitive Control in Race-Based Misperceptions of Weapons*, 38 J. Experimental Soc. Psychol. 384, 390–91 (2002). [. . .]

63. *See, e.g.*, McConnell & Leibold, *supra* note 25, at 436. [. . .]

64. For a powerful statement of this argument, see John A. Bargh, *The Cognitive Monster: The Case Against the Controllability of Automatic Stereotype Effects*, in Dual-Process Theories in Social Psychology, *supra* note 61, at 361.

65. In the law reviews, *see, e.g.*, Owen D. Jones, *Law and Biology: Toward an Integrated Model of Human Behavior*, 8 J. Contemp. Legal Issues 167 (1997); Owen D. Jones, *Time-Shifted Rationality and the Law of Law's Leverage: Behavioral Economics Meets Behavioral Biology*, 95 Nw. U. L. Rev. 1141 (2001). [. . .]

66. For a review of changing socioeconomics and demographics that led up to the "model minority" stereotype, see Eric K. Yamamoto, Margaret Chon, Carol L. Izumi, Jerry Kang & Frank H. Wu, Race, Rights, and Reparation: Law and the Japanese American Internment 258–71 (2001).

67. Crudely summarized, SIT contends that if we want to feel better about ourselves, we must feel better about the groups with which we identify and to which we belong. In the process, we must create a devalued outgroup. Meanings associated with both ingroup and outgroup are tilted accordingly. This phenomenon is well demonstrated, for example, by the work of Henri Tajfel and his "Minimal Group Paradigm." *See* Brown, *supra* note 15, at 45–47. [. . .]

68. *See* Jost et al., *supra* note 40, at 203–4 [SWAT]; *see also* John T. Jost et al., *Non-Conscious Forms of System Justification: Implicit and Behavioral Preferences for Higher Status Groups*, 38 J. Experimental Soc. Psychol. 586, 589–97 (2002) (providing evidence of outgroup favoritism by low-status groups—of Stanford University by San Jose State University students, of Whites by Latinos and Asian Americans, of men by women—through implicit measures, not explicit self-reports).

69. *See* Eric Uhlmann et al., *Subgroup Prejudice Based on Skin Color Among Hispanics in the United States and Latin America*, 20 Soc. Cognition 198, 202 (2002). [. . .] Uhlmann and his colleagues ran IATs comparing Latinos and Whites and found no ingroup favoritism among Latinos in the United States. This result obtained regardless of whether the face prime was light-skinned (Blanco) or dark-skinned (Moreno). [. . .]

To test the significance of place and cultural context, the experimenters conducted a similar study in Chile. Latinos in Chile responded similarly to Latinos in the United States. They too implicitly favored Whites, regardless of the use of a Blanco or Moreno prime. [. . .] What was different was that Chileans were comfortable displaying *explicit* preference for Blancos as well (thus not demonstrating dissociation). In Latin America, there appears to be less stigma attached to preferring Blancos over Morenos. An explanation may be an ideology of racial democracy that conceptualizes such preferences as merely aesthetic, not racial or status-related and not especially invidious.

Another study found that Asian Americans also had implicit bias against Asian Americans on the American/Foreign IAT, notwithstanding that participants were told that all pictures they saw in the test were of "Americans." *See* Thierry Devos & Mahzarin R. Banaji, *American = White?*, 88 J. Personality & Soc. Psychol. (forthcoming Mar. 2005) (manuscript at 29, on file with the Harvard Law School Library).

70. *See, e.g.*, Reshma M. Saujani, *"The Implicit Association Test": A Measure of Unconscious Racism in Legislative Decision-Making*, 8 Mich. J. Race & L. 395, 413–15 (2003) (suggesting IAT scores as an additional evidentiary factor for measuring racial intent under the rule of *Village of Arlington Heights v. Metropolitan History Development Corp.*, 429 U.S. 252, 267–68 (1977)).

71. *See, e.g.*, *id.* at 419–20 (discussing the use of IAT in jury selection process). [. . .]

72. *See, e.g.*, Irene V. Blair et al., *The Influence of Afrocentric Facial Features in Criminal Sentencing*, 15 Psychol. Sci. 674, 677 (2004) (finding no disparate sentencing on the basis of race in Florida data set, but finding that within each racial category, White or Black, those individuals with more Afrocentric facial features received harsher sentences). [. . .]

73. *See, e.g.*, Linda Hamilton Krieger, *The Content of Our Categories: A Cognitive Bias Approach to Discrimination and Equal Employment Opportunity*, 47 Stan. L. Rev. 1161, 1164–65 (1995); [. . .] Rebecca Hanner White & Linda Hamilton Krieger, *Whose Motive Matters?: Discrimination in Multi-Actor Employment Decision Making*, 61 La. L. Rev. 495, 499 (2001). [. . .]

74. *See, e.g.*, Jody Armour, *Stereotypes and Prejudice: Helping Legal Decisionmakers Break the Prejudice Habit*, 83 Cal. L. Rev. 766–72 (1995) (arguing in favor of allowing counsel to address issues of race directly in order to counteract potential bias among jurors).

75. *See, e.g.*, Saujani, *supra* note 70, at 414 (suggesting that legislators could be forced to take the IAT "on the stand"). [. . .]

76. *See, e.g.*, Deana A. Pollard, *Unconscious Bias and Self-Critical Analysis: The Case for a Qualified Evidentiary Equal Employment Opportunity Privilege*, 74 WASH. L. REV. 913, 916 (1999) (persuasively calling for "the recognition of a privilege for unconscious-bias testing to encourage its use in equal employment opportunity efforts").

77. RICHARD J. HERRNSTEIN & CHARLES MURRAY, THE BELL CURVE (1994).

78. *See* Russell Korobkin, *Problems with Heuristics for Law*, *in* HEURISTICS AND THE LAW (Gerd Gigerenzer & Christopher Engle eds., forthcoming 2005) (manuscript at 1–2) ("All versions of [rational choice theory] assume that actors will process information, make choices, and execute behaviors in a way calculated to maximize their expected utility—that is, maximize the differential between expected benefits and expected costs.").

79. *See, e.g.*, 18 U.S.C. § 1464 (2000) (criminalizing radio communication of "obscene, indecent, or profane" content); 47 C.F.R. § 73.3999(a) (prohibiting the broadcast of obscene material).

80. *See* The Revision of Programming and Commercialization Policies, Ascertainment Requirements, and Program Log Requirements for Commercial Television Stations, 98 F.C.C.2d 1076, 1101 (1984) [hereinafter TV Deregulation Order] (describing a 1973 order setting guidelines of sixteen minutes per hour for commercials). [. . .]

81. *See, e.g.*, Office of Communication of the United Church of Christ v. FCC, 425 F.2d 543, 547–50 (D.C. Cir. 1969); *see generally* JERRY KANG, COMMUNICATIONS LAW AND POLICY 334–36 (2001) (providing background on these cases).

82. [. . .] *See* TV Deregulation Order, *supra* note 80, at 1078. [. . .]

83. *Id.* at 1097. [. . .]

84. Congress passed the Children's Television Act (CTA) of 1990. *See* Pub. L. No. 101-437, 104 Stat. 996 (codified as amended at 47 U.S.C. §§ 303(a), 303(b), 394 (2000)). [. . .]

85. Franklin D. Gilliam Jr. et al., *Crime in Black and White: The Violent, Scary World of Local News*, 1 HARV. INT'L J. PRESS/POL. 6, 7 (1996).

86. Tom Rosenstiel et al., *Local TV News: What Works, What Flops, and Why*, COLUM. JOURNALISM REV., Jan.–Feb. 1999, at 65, *available at* http://archives.cjr.org/year/99/1/pej. The PEJ is an affiliate of the Columbia University Graduate School of Journalism.

87. [. . .] Gilliam et al., *supra* note 85, at 8.

88. *See* Barry C. Feld, *Race, Politics and Juvenile Justice: The Warren Court and the Conservative "Backlash"*, 87 MINN. L. REV. 1530 (2003) [. . .]; *see also* LORI DORFMAN & VINCENT SCHIRALDI, OFF BALANCE: YOUTH, RACE & CRIME IN THE NEWS 7 (2001), *available at* http://www.buildingblocksforyouth.org/media/media.pdf [. . .].

89. *See* FBI, U.S. DEP'T OF JUSTICE, CRIME IN THE UNITED STATES 2002: UNIFORM CRIME REPORTS 17 (2003) [. . .], *available at* http://www.fbi.gov/ucr/02cius.htm. [. . .] This disproportionality in arrest rates is likely exacerbated, however, by unfavorable portrayals of Black criminals by local news media and concentration of news stories featuring blacks in violent crime stories. *See* KATHLEEN HALL JAMIESON, DIRTY POLITICS: DECEPTION, DISTRACTION, AND DEMOCRACY (1992) [. . .].

90. The researchers randomly exposed participants to a fifteen-minute videotaped local newscast that reported either a violent or a nonviolent crime. The report was digitally edited so that some of the participants saw a mug shot of a Black perpetrator, while others saw a White perpetrator. Gilliam et al., *supra* note 85, at 15. Afterward, the participants filled out a survey on crime attitudes that inquired about their level of fear of violent crime, their theories of why crime was rising, and how society might remedy the problem.

91. Mark Peffley et al., *The Intersection of Race and Crime in Television News Stories: An Experimental Study*, 13 POL. COMM. 309, 315 (1996). In Peffley's experiment, participants viewed a newscast of a violent crime. Although race was not mentioned in the dialogue, the perpetrator was seen being taken away in handcuffs. Some of the participants saw a White perpetrator, while others saw a Black perpetrator. The participants were ninety-five White students in a political science class at a midwestern university. One week earlier the participants had been instructed to complete a survey, which was an explicit (self-reported) measure of racial bias against African Americans. After viewing the video, the students answered various questions, such as assessing the likelihood of guilt. Not surprisingly, those students who displayed the highest self-reported bias against Blacks were the most negative and punitive in their evaluations of the suspect in the Black perpetrator scenario.

92. In one experiment, Nicholas Valentino showed participants a twelve-minute newscast that featured one crime story. Nicholas A. Valentino, *Crime News and the Priming of Racial Attitudes During Evaluations of the President*, 63 PUB. OPINION Q. 293, 301–2 (1999). [. . . A] five-second mug shot of two suspects of the same race was edited in. The researchers showed some participants the mug shot,

altered to reflect various racial groups, including White, Black, Asian, and Hispanic, and showed some participants no mug shot. They showed a control group no crime story at all. After seeing this newscast, participants were asked to evaluate Bill Clinton and Bob Dole, who were the respective presidential nominees of the Democratic and Republican parties at the time of the study.

[. . .] For the control group (*n* = 31), who saw no crime story, there was an 84 percent lead for Clinton over Dole. However, for those participants who saw the crime story and saw either a White suspect or no suspect at all (*n* = 118), Clinton's lead fell to 60 percent. Finally, for those who saw a minority perpetrator (*n* = 137), Clinton's lead was reduced to 40 percent. All these results were statistically significant at *p* <0.01. These results are impressive, in part because nothing in the newscast directly mentioned the presidential race.

93. *See* Gilliam & Iyengar, *supra* note 4, at 570.

94. *See id.* at 571, tbl.5. [. . .] Gilliam and Iyengar characterize "new racism" as "symbolic, subtle, covert, hidden, or underground." [. . .]

95. [. . .] There is convincing data that people respond differently to news reports about welfare based on whether a Black or White person is depicted as the welfare recipient. *See, e.g.*, James M. Avery & Mark Peffley, *Race Matters: The Impact of News Coverage of Welfare Reform on Public Opinion*, *in* RACE AND THE POLITICS OF WELFARE REFORM 140–42 (Sanford F. Schram et al. eds., 2003) [. . .].

96. *See, e.g.*, BARRIE GUNTER, POOR RECEPTION: MISUNDERSTANDING AND FORGETTING BROADCAST NEWS 71–72 (1987) [. . .].

97. Tali Mendelberg has carefully demonstrated that exposure to this now infamous advertisement during the 1988 presidential campaign implicitly triggered racial resentment (what I would call "negative racial meanings"), which in turn influenced the election. *See* TALI MENDELBERG, THE RACE CARD: CAMPAIGN STRATEGY, IMPLICIT MESSAGES, AND THE NORM OF EQUALITY 134–68 (2001) [. . .].

98. *See* generally Nicholas A. Valentino et al., *Cues That Matter: How Political Ads Prime Racial Attitudes During Campaigns*, 96 AM. POL. SCI. REV. 75 (2002) (demonstrating that political advertisements that make no verbal mention of race but use racial images can activate racial attitudes that even influence viewers' opinions on subjects not especially connected to race, such as the federal budget and taxes).

99. Laurie Rudman and Matthew Lee found that a thirteen-minute audio-only exposure to violent, misogynistic rap music increased the implicit racial bias of participants, as measured by the IAT. *See*

Laurie A. Rudman & Matthew R. Lee, *Implicit and Explicit Consequences of Exposure to Violent and Misogynous Rap Music*, 5 GROUP PROCESSES & INTERGROUP REL. 133, 137–38, tbl.1 (2002); [. . .] *see also* James D. Johnson et al., *Converging Interracial Consequences of Exposure to Violent Rap Music on Stereotypical Attributions of Blacks*, 36 J. EXPERIMENTAL SOC. PSYCHOL. 233, 238 (2000).

In the study by Johnson et al., researchers exposed participants to a four minute audio-only rap song with extremely violent lyrics and sound effects, a four minute audio-only nonviolent rap song, or no music at all. Both songs were attributed to Black musicians. On subsequent interpretive tasks, participants who heard the violent music evaluated Black targets in schema-consistent ways: those who listened to the violent music were more likely than those in the other two groups to attribute Black male violence to disposition rather than situation. They were also more likely to view Blacks as less qualified for a job requiring intelligence. These effects were seen in both Black and White participants.

100. [. . .] *See generally* Eric Uhlmann & Jane Swanson, *Exposure to Violent Video Games Increases Automatic Aggressiveness*, 27 J. ADOLESCENCE 41 (2004). [. . .]

101. Nilanjana Dasgupta & Anthony G. Greenwald, *On the Malleability of Automatic Attitudes: Combating Automatic Prejudice with Images of Admired and Disliked Individuals*, 81 J. PERSONALITY & SOC. PSYCH. 800, 807 (2001).

102. Irene V. Blair et al., *Imagining Stereotypes Away: The Moderation of Implicit Stereotypes Through Mental Imagery*, 81 J. PERSONALITY & SOC. PSYCHOL. 828, 828–29 (2001).

103. The GNAT measures an attitude or stereotype for a single category. By contrast, the IAT requires pairs of categories, such as female/male (as mapped to supportive/agentic). This use of pairs sometimes raises questions regarding whether the reaction time differential is produced by the association that female is more supportive or less agentic. The GNAT avoids such confounds. *See id.* at 834; *see also* Devos & Banaji, *supra* note 69, at 15–16 [. . .].

104. The false memory test measured the rate at which participants incorrectly "remembered" being presented with words that are stereotypically associated with those that were actually presented. *See* Blair et al., *supra* note 102, at 835–36.

105. *Id.* at 837.

106. *See* Paul G. Davies et al., *Consuming Images: How Television Commercials That Elicit Stereotype Threat Can Restrain Women Academically and Professionally*, 28 PERSONALITY & SOC. PSYCHOL. BULL. 1615 (2002). [. . .]

107. *See generally* Nilanjana Dasgupta & Shaki Asgari, *Seeing Is Believing: Exposure to Counterstereotypic Women Leaders and Its Effect on the Malleability of Automatic Gender Stereotyping*, 40 J. EXPERIMENTAL SOC. PSYCHOL. 642 (2004).

108. [. . .] *See also* Jason P. Mitchell et al., *Contextual Variations in Implicit Evaluation*, 132 J. EXPERIMENTAL PYSCHOL.: GENERAL 455 (2003). In Mitchell's study, the researchers had each participant identify popular Black athletes and unpopular White politicians. IATs were run using images from these two categories. When the participants were asked to focus on profession, they predictably showed substantial bias in favor of Black athletes. By contrast—and this is what is surprising—when the participants were asked to focus on race, they showed a mild preference in favor of the White politicians notwithstanding the fact that they were chosen because they were unlikable. According to the authors, this was the "first such study to demonstrate a sharp, rapid attitude dissociation as a function of the attended category."

109. *See, e.g.*, JAMIESON, *supra* note 89, at 133–34 (concluding that national news from 1985 to 1989 was more likely to show Blacks restrained and in mug shots, as compared to Whites) [. . .].

110. *See* Robert M. Entman, *Blacks in the News: Television, Modern Racism and Cultural Change*, 69 JOURNALISM Q. 341, 349–53 (1992). [. . .] Although I have focused on racial meanings of violence and criminality, there are other meanings as well, such as poverty and welfare. Martin Gilens has done substantial work in this field, demonstrating that the news portrays poverty as a Black problem. *See* MARTIN GILENS, WHY AMERICANS HATE WELFARE: RACE, MEDIA, AND THE POLITICS OF ANTIPOVERTY POLICY 149 (1999). [. . .]

111. Gilliam & Iyengar, *supra* note 4, at 562 [. . .].

112. *See* ROBERT M. ENTMAN & ANDREW ROJECKI, THE BLACK IMAGE IN THE WHITE MIND 79 (2000) (reporting one study in which a plurality of White respondents guessed that Blacks constitute 60 percent of violent crime arrests, although the actual figure is closer to 40 percent).

113. *See* Diane M. Mackie et al., *Social Psychological Foundations of Stereotype Formation*, in STEREOTYPES AND STEREOTYPING 41, 50–51 (C. Neil Macrae et al. eds., 1996) [. . .].

114. *See* BROWN, *supra* note 15, at 86–88. The conventional wisdom explanation for this phenomenon is a general psychological bias in parsing rare events.

115. *See* Gilliam & Iyengar, *supra* note 4, at 564, 565 tbl.2 (reporting that in an experiment in which viewers saw no perpetrator, 63 percent recalled that they *had* seen one: 44 percent recalled a Black perpetrator, whereas only 19 percent recalled a White perpetrator).

116. *See* BROWN, *supra* note 15, at 55 [. . .]; FISKE & TAYLOR, *supra* note 10, at 123 [. . .].

117. *See, e.g.*, Fiske, *supra* note 49, at 367. [. . .]

118. *See, e.g.*, FISKE & TAYLOR, *supra* note 10, at 67.

119. Fiske, *supra* note 49, at 369 (citing Thomas F. Pettigrew, *The Ultimate Attribution Error: Extending Allport's Cognitive Analysis of Predjudice*, 5 PERSONALITY & SOC. PSYCHOL. BULL. 461 (1979)) [. . .].

120. *See* SHANTO IYENGAR, IS ANYONE RESPONSIBLE?: HOW TELEVISION FRAMES POLITICAL ISSUES 43–45 (1991) (finding that the race of the suspect in a crime story had more of an effect on viewers in assigning blame than the way the crime was framed).

121. *See id.*

122. *See* Jerry Kang, *Cyber-Race*, 113 HARV. L. REV. 1207 (2000) [. . .].

123. 18 THE OXFORD ENGLISH DICTIONARY 574 (2d ed. 1989) [. . .].

124. Consider, for example, the recent survey of 135 undergraduates from Yale—hardly a site of White supremacy. As Devos and Banaji report, even after being explicitly told to "consider individuals from each ethnic group who were born in the U.S., lived in the U.S., and were U.S. citizens," they rated Asian Americans as much less "American" than White and Black Americans. [. . .]

125. Banaji, *supra* note 40, at 134.

11. Affirmative Action: Images and Realities

Kristina R. Schmukler, Elisabeth Morgan Thompson, and Faye J. Crosby

1. Faye J. Crosby & Diana I. Cordova, *Words Worth of Wisdom: Toward an Understanding of Affirmative Action*, in SEX, RACE, AND MERIT: DEBATING AFFIRMATIVE ACTION IN EDUCATION AND EMPLOYMENT, 13–20 (Faye Crosby & Cheryl VanDeVeer eds., 2000).

2. *See generally* Faye J. Crosby, Aarti Iyer & Sirinda Sincharoen, *Understanding Affirmative Action*, 57 ANN. REV. PSYCHOL. 585–611 (2006).

3. *See generally* AMERICAN PSYCHOLOGICAL ASSOCIATION, AFFIRMATIVE ACTION: WHO BENEFITS? (1996).

4. Faye J. Crosby & Stacy Blake-Beard, *Affirmative Action: Diversity, Merit, and the Benefit of White People*, in OFF WHITE: READINGS ON POWER, PRIVILEGE, AND RESISTANCE 146–60 (Michelle Fine, Lois Weis, Linda Powell Pruitt & April Burns, eds., 2004).

5. *See generally* Faye J. Crosby, Aarti Iyer, Susan

Clayton & Roberta A. Downing, *Affirmative Action: Psychological Data and the Policy Debates*, 58 AM. PSYCHOLOGIST 93 (2003).

6. *See generally* June N. Branscombe, *Denial and More* (Amherst, MA: 13th Nag's Heart Conference, 1995); FAYE J. CROSBY, RELATIVE DEPRIVATION AND WORKING WOMEN (1982).

7. *See generally* Faye J. Crosby & Susan Clayton, *Affirmative Action: Psychological Contributions to Policy*, 1 ANNALS SOC. ISSUES & PUB. POL'Y 71 (2001).

8. *See generally* Faye J. Crosby, Susan Clayton, Olaf Alksnis & Kathryn Hemker, *Cognitive Biases in the Perception of Discrimination: The Importance of Format*, 14 SEX ROLES 637 (1986).

9. U.S. DEPARTMENT OF LABOR, FACTS ON EXECUTIVE ORDER 11246—AFFIRMATIVE ACTION (2002), *available at* http://www.dol.gov/esa/regs/compliance/ofccp.aa.htm (last visited Jan. 28, 2006).

10. Crosby, Iyer, Clayton & Downing, *supra* note 5; U.S. DEPARTMENT OF LABOR, *supra* note 9.

11. Crosby, Iyer, Clayton & Downing, *supra* note 5.

12. *See generally* Ward F. Thomas, *The Meaning of Race to Employers: A Dynamic Qualitative Perspective*, 44 SOC. Q. 227 (2003).

13. *See generally* FAYE J. CROSBY, AFFIRMATIVE ACTION IS DEAD, LONG LIVE AFFIRMATIVE ACTION (2004).

14. *See generally* GREG STOHR, A BLACK AND WHITE CASE: HOW AFFIRMATIVE ACTION SURVIVED ITS GREATEST LEGAL CHALLENGE (2004).

15. Gratz v. Bollinger, 539 U.S. 244 (2003); Grutter v. Bollinger, 539 U.S. 306 (2003); STOHR, *supra* note 14.

16. Grutter, 539 U.S. 306, *supra* note 15.

17. Amy E. Smith & Faye J. Crosby, *The Path from Desegregation to Diversity*, in THE SOCIAL PSYCHOLOGY OF RACISM AND OPPRESSION: SETBACK AND ADVANCES SINCE BROWN V. BOARD OF EDUCATION (G. Adams, M. Biernat, N. Branscome, C. Crandall & L. Wrightsman, eds., in press).

18. *See generally* Patricia Gurin, Eric L. Dey, Sylvia Hurtado & Gerald Gurin, *Diversity and Higher Education: Theory and Impact on Educational Outcomes*, 72 HARV. EDUC. REV. 330 (2002).

19. Anthony Lising Antonio, Mitchell J. Chang, Kenji Hakuta, David A. Kenny, Shana Levin & Jeffrey F. Milem, *Effects of Racial Diversity on Complex Thinking in College Students*, 15 AM. PSYCHOL. SOC. 507 (2004).

20. *Id.*

21. *See generally* Mo Yin S. Tam & Gilbert W. Bassett Jr., *Does Diversity Matter? Measuring the Impact of High School Diversity on Freshman GPA*, 32 POL'Y STUD. J. 129 (2004).

22. *Id.*

23. *See generally* TERRY EASTLAND, ENDING AFFIRMATIVE ACTION (1996); Stanley Rothman, S.M. Lipset & Neil Nevitte, *Diversity and Affirmative Action: The State of Campus Opinion*, 15 ACAD. QUESTIONS 52 (2002).

24. STEPHEN L. CARTER, REFLECTIONS OF AN AFFIRMATIVE ACTION BABY (1991); RICHARD RODRIQUEZ, HUNGER OF MEMORY (1981); Shelby Steele, *The Content of Our Character*, in SEX, RACE, AND MERIT: DEBATING AFFIRMATIVE ACTION IN EDUCATION AND EMPLOYMENT 144–50 (Faye J. Crosby & Cheryl VanDeVeer eds., 1990).

25. CROSBY, *supra* note 13; Joel Gills, Kristina Schmukler, Margarita Azmitia & Faye Crosby, *Affirmative Action and Ethnic Minority Student: Enlarging the Pipelines and Supporting Success at University*, in SOCIAL DEVELOPMENT, SOCIAL INEQUALITIES, AND SOCIAL JUSTICE (Cecilia Wainryb, Judith G. Smetana & Elliot Turiel eds., in press).

26. CROSBY, *supra* note 13.

27. Madeline E. Heilman, Caryn J. Block & Jonathan A. Lucas, *Presumed Incompetent? Stigmatization and Affirmative Action Efforts*, 77 J. APPLIED PSYCHOL. 536 (1992); Gregoary R. Maio & Victoria M. Esses, *The Social Consequences of Affirmative Action: Deleterious Effects on Perceptions of Groups*, 24 PERSONALITY & SOC. PSYCHOL. BULL. 65 (1998); Kimberly A. Quinn, Erin M. Ross & Victoria M. Esses, *Attribution of Responsibility and Reactions to Affirmative Action: Affirmative Action as Help*, 27 PERSONALITY & SOC. PSYCHOL. BULL. 321 (2001).

28. Jacqueline A. Gilbert & Bette Ann Stead, *Stigmatization Revisited: Does Diversity Management Make a Difference in Applicant Success?*, 24 GROUP & ORG. MGMT. 239 (1999); Alison M. Konrad & Frank Linnehan, *Race and Sex Differences in Line Managers' Reactions to Equal Employment Opportunity and Affirmative Action Interventions*, 20 GROUP & ORG. MGMT. 409 (1995); Christopher P. Parker, Boris B. Baltes & Neil D. Christiansen, *Support for Affirmative Action, Justice Perceptions and Work Attitudes: A Study of Gender and Racial-Ethnic Group Differences*, 82 J. APPLIED PSYCHOL. 376 (1997).

29. Thomas F. Pettigrew & Linda R. Tropp, *A Meta-Analytic Test of Intergroup Contract Theory*, 90 J. PERSONALITY & SOC. PSYCHOL. 751 (2006).

30. CROSBY, *supra* note 13.

31. WILLIAM G. BOWEN & DEREK C. BOK, THE SHAPE OF THE RIVER: LONG-TERM CONSEQUENCES OF CONSIDERING RACE IN COLLEGE AND UNIVERSITY ADMISSIONS (1998).

32. Richard O. Lempert, David L. Chambers & Terry K. Adams, *Michigan's Minority Graduates in*

Practice: The River Runs Through Law School, 25 Law & Soc. Inquiry 395 (2000).

33. Smith & Crosby, *supra* note 17.

34. Richard H. Sander, *Response and Reply: A Reply to Critics*, 57 Stan. L. Rev. 1963 (2005).

35. Crosby, *supra* note 13.

36. *Id.*

37. Crosby, Iyer & Sincharoen, *supra* note 2.

38. Crosby, *supra* note 13.

39. Rosalee A. Clawson, Elizabeth R. Kegler & Eric N. Waltenburg, *Supreme Court Legitimacy and Group-Centric Forces: Black Support for Capital Punishment and Affirmative Action*, 25 Pol. Behav. 289 (2003); Rosalee A. Clawson, Harry "Neil" C. Strine IV & Eric N. Waltenburg, *Framing Supreme Court Decisions: The Mainstream Versus the Black Press*, 33 J. Black Stud. 789 (2003); Rosalee A. Clawson & Eric N. Waltenburg, *Support for a Supreme Court Affirmative Action Decision: A Story in Black and White*, 31 Am. Pol. Research 251 (2003); Heather Golden, Steve Hinkle & Faye J. Crosby, *Reactions to Affirmative Action: Substance and Semantics*, 31 J. Applied Soc. Psychol. 73 (2001); Louis Harris, *Unequal Terms*, 30 Colum. Journalism Rev. 20 (1992); *see generally* David R. Kinder & Lynn M. Sanders, Divided by Color: Racial Politics and Democratic Ideals (1996); David A. Kravitz, *Attitudes Toward Affirmative Action Plans Directed at Blacks: Effects of Plan and Individual Differences*, 25 J. Applied Soc. Psychol. 2192 (1995); David A. Kravitz, Stephen L. Klineberg, Derek R. Avery, Ann Kim Nguyen, Christopher Lund & Emery J. Fu, *Attitudes Toward Affirmative Action: Correlations with Demographic Variables and with Beliefs about Targets, Actions and Economic Effects*, 30 J. Applied Soc. Psychol. 1109 (2000); David A. Kravitz & Judith Platania, *Attitudes and Beliefs about Affirmative Action: Effects of Target and of Respondent Sex and Ethnicity*, 78 J. Applied Psychol. 928 (1993); Dorothy P. Moore, Public: Only Merit Should Count in College Admissions (2003); Quinn, Ross & Esses, *supra* note 27; Paul M. Sniderman & Edward G. Carmines, Reaching Beyond Race (1997).

40. David A. Harrison, David A. Kravitz, David M. Mayer, Lisa M. Leslie & D. Lev-Arey, *Understanding Attitudes Toward Affirmative Action Programs in Employment: Addressing Reactions to Redressing Discrimination*, J. Applied Psychol. (forthcoming); David A. Kravitz & Stephen L. Klineberg, *Reactions to Two Versions of Affirmative Action Among Whites, Black and Hispanics*, 85 J. Applied Psychol. 597 (2000); David A. Kravitz & Stephen Klineberg, *Affirmative Action Attitudes: Effects of Respondent Ethnicity, AAP Strength and Anticipated Impacts*, in Academy of Management

Best Paper Proceedings (D. Nagao ed., 2002); Kravitz & Platania, *supra* note 39.

41. Crosby, *supra* note 13.

42. Harris, *supra* note 39; Kravitz, *supra* note 39; Kravitz, Klineberg, Avery, Nguyen, Lund & Fu, *supra* note 40; Kravitz & Platania, *supra* note 39; Moore, *supra* note 39; Quinn, Ross & Esses, *supra* note 27.

43. Golden, Hinkle & Crosby, *supra* note 39; *Gratz*, 539 U.S. 244.

44. Paul M. Sniderman and T. Piazza, The Scar of Race (1993).

45. Kravitz & Platania, *supra* note 39.

46. Susan D. Clayton, *Reactions to Social Categorizations: Evaluating One Argument Against Affirmative Action*, 26 J. Applied Soc. Psychol. 1472 (1996).

47. Christopher L. Aberson, *Support for Race Based Affirmative Action: Self-Interest and Procedural Justice*, 33 J. Applied Soc. Psychol. 1212 (2003); Christopher L. Aberson & Sarah C. Haag, *Beliefs About Affirmative Action and Adversity and Their Relationship to Support for Hiring Policies*, 3 Analysis Soc. Issues & Pol'y 121 (2003); Christine Reyna, Amanda Tucker, William Korfmacher & P.J. Henry, *Searching for Common Ground Between Supporters and Opponents of Affirmative Action*, 26 Pol. Psychol. 667 (2005); Leanne S. Son Hing, Ramona D. Bobocel & Mark P. Zanna, *Meritocracy and Opposition to Affirmative Action: Making Concessions in the Face of Discrimination*, 83 J. Personality & Soc. Psychol. 493 (2002).

48. Jennifer L. Knight & Michelle R. Hebl, *Affirmative Reaction: The Influence of Type of Justification on Nonbeneficiary Attitudes Toward Affirmative Action Plans in Higher Education*, 61 J. Soc. Issues 547 (2005).

49. Aberson & Haag, *supra* note 47; Ann M. Beaton & Francine Touges, *Reactions to Affirmative Action: Group Membership and Social Justice*, 14 Soc. Just. Research 61 (2001); Donna M. Garcia, Serge Desmarais, Nyla R. Branscombe & Stephanie S. Gee, *Opposition to Redistributive Employment Policies for Women: The Role of Policy Experience and Group Interest*, 44 The Brit. Psychol. Soc. 583 (2005); Golden, Hinkle & Crosby, *supra* note 39; Kravitz & Platania, *supra* note 45.

50. Crosby, Iyer & Sincharoen, *supra* note 2; Harrison, Kravitz, Mayer, Leslie & Lev-Arey, *supra* note 40.

51. Crosby, Iyer & Sincharoen, *supra* note 2; Harrison, Kravitz, Mayer, Leslie & Lev-Arey, *supra* note 40.

52. Crosby, Iyer & Sincharoen, *supra* note 2; Harrison, Kravitz, Mayer, Leslie & Lev-Arey, *supra* note 40.

53. Kwame Badu Antwi-Boasiako & Joseph O. Asagba, *A Preliminary Analysis of African American*

College Students Perceptions of Racial Preferences and Affirmative Action in Making Admissions Decisions at a Predominantly White University, 39 C. STUDENT J. 734 (2005).

54. Garcia, Desmarais, Branscombe & Gee, *supra* note 49.

55. Francine Touges, Stéphane Joly, Ann M. Beaton & Line St. Pierre, *Reaction of Beneficiaries to Preferential Treatment: A Reality Check*, 49 HUM. REL. 453 (1996).

56. Jerry Kang & Mahzarin R. Banaji, *Fair Measures: A Behavioral Realist Revision of "Affirmative Action,"* 94 CAL. L. REV. 1063 (2006).

57. Germine H. Awad, Kevin Cokley & Joseph Ravitch, *Attitudes toward Affirmative Action: A Comparison of Color-Blind Versus Modern Racist Attitudes*, 35 J. APPLIED SOC. PSYCHOL. 1384 (2005); CROSBY, *supra* note 13; Crosby, Iyer & Sincharoen, *supra* note 2; Garcia, Desmarais, Branscombe & Gee, *supra* note 49; Harrison, Kravitz, Mayer, Leslie & Lev-Arey, *supra* note 40.

58. Hing, Bobocel & Zanna, *supra* note 47; D. Ramona Bobocel, Leanne S. Son Hing, Camilla M. Holmvall & Mark P. Zanna, *Policies to Redress Social Injustice: Is the Concern for Justice a Cause of Support and of Opposition*, in THE JUSTICE MOTIVE IN EVERYDAY LIFE 204–25 (Michael Ross & Dale T. Miller eds., 2002).

59. JAMES R. KLUEGEL & ELIOT R. SMITH, BELIEFS ABOUT INEQUALITY: AMERICANS' VIEWS OF WHAT IS AND WHAT OUGHT TO BE, SOCIAL INSTITUTIONS AND SOCIAL CHANGE (1986).

60. Aberson & Haag, *supra* note 47; Reyna, Tucker, Korfmacher & Henry, *supra* note 47.

61. Harrison, Kravitz, Mayer, Leslie & Lev-Arey, *supra* note 40.

62. Kravitz, Klineberg, Avery, Nguyen, Lund & Fu, *supra* note 39.

63. David R. Kinder, *The Continuing American Dilemma: White Resistance to Racial Chance 40 Years after Myrdal*, 42 J. SOC. ISSUES 151 (1986); Donald Kinder & David Sears, *Prejudice and Politics: Symbolic Racism Versus Racial Threats to the Good Life*, 40 J. PERSONALITY & SOC. PSYCHOL. 414 (1981); David O. Sears & P.J. Henry, *The Origins of Symbolic Racism*, 85 J. PERSONALITY & SOC. PSYCHOL. 259 (2003).

64. John F. Dovidio, Kerry Kawakami & Samuel L. Gaertner, *Reducing Contemporary Prejudice: Combating Explicit and Implicit Bias at the Individual and Intergroup Level*, in REDUCING PREJUDICE AND DISCRIMINATION 137–63 (Stuart Oskamp ed., 2000).

65. Faye J. Crosby & John F. Dovidio, *Discrimination in America and Legal Strategies for Reducing it*, in PSYCHOLOGICAL SCIENCE IN COURT: BEYOND COMMON KNOWLEDGE (Eugene Borgida & Susan Fiske eds., in press).

66. Paul M. Sniderman, Thomas Piazza, Philip E. Tetlock & Ann Kendrick, *The New Racism*, 35 AM. J. POL. SCI. 423 (1991).

67. *Id.*; Dovidio, Kawakami & Gaertner, *supra* note 64; Kinder, *supra* note 63.

68. Lawrence Bobo, *Race and Beliefs About Affirmative Action: Addressing the Effects of Interests, Group Threat, Ideology and Racism*, in RACIALIZED POLITICS: THE DEBATE ABOUT RACISM IN AMERICA 137–64 (David O. Sears, James Sidanius & Lawrence Bobo eds., 2000).

69. Lawrence Bobo & James R. Kluegel, *Opposition to Race-Targeting: Self-Interest, Stratification Ideology, or Racial Attitudes?*, 58 AM. SOC. REV. 443 (1993).

70. Jim Sidanius, Felicia Pratto, Colette van Laar & Shana Levin, *Social Dominance Theory: Its Agenda and Method*, 25 POL. PSYCHOL. 845 (2004).

71. CROSBY, *supra* note 13.

72. Crosby & Cordova, *supra* note 1.

12. Behavioral Realism in Employment Discrimination Law: Implicit Bias and Disparate Treatment

Linda Hamilton Krieger and Susan T. Fiske

1. OLIVER WENDELL HOLMES, THE COMMON LAW 167 (1963).

2. *Id.*

3. 529 U.S. 598, 655 (2000) (Souter, J., dissenting) [. . .].

4. David M. O'Brien, *The Seduction of the Judiciary: Social Science and the Courts*, 64 JUDICATURE 8, 11 (1980).

5. Linda Hamilton Krieger, *The Intuitive Psychologist Behind the Bench: Models of Gender Bias in Social Psychology and Employment Discrimination Law*, 60 J. SOC. ISSUES 835 (2004).

6. Lee Ross, *The Intuitive Psychologist and His Shortcomings: Distortions in the Attribution Process*, in COGNITIVE THEORIES IN SOCIAL PSYCHOLOGY 337 (Leonard Berkowitz ed., 1978).

7. § 703(a)(1), Title VII of the Civil Rights Act of 1964, as amended, 42 U.S.C. § 2000e-2(a)(1).

8. § 703(m), Title VII of the Civil Rights Act of 1964, as amended, 42 U.S.C. § 2000e-2(m).

9. 490 U.S. 228 (1989).

10. *Id.* at 250.

11. *Id.*

12. ANTHONY G. AMSTERDAM & JEROME BRUNER, MINDING THE LAW: HOW COURTS RELY ON

STORYTELLING, AND HOW THEIR STORIES CHANGE THE WAYS WE UNDERSTAND LAW—AND OURSELVES 110 (2000).

13. Desert Palace, Inc. v. Costa, 539 U.S. 90, 100 (2003).

14. Celotex Corp. v. Catrett, 477 U.S. 317 (1986); CHARLES ALAN WRIGHT, ET AL., § 2727 10A (3d ed. 1998).

15. Reeves v. Sanderson Plumbing Prods., 530 U.S. 133, 150 (2000).

16. 163 U.S. 537 (1896).

17. 347 U.S. 483 (1954).

18. [. . .] Plessy v. Ferguson, 163 U.S. 537, 544, 551 (1896).

19. Brown v. Bd. of Educ., 347 U.S. 483, 494 (1954). [. . .]

20. 505 U.S. 833, 863 (1992).

21. 208 U.S. 412 (1908).

22. 539 U.S. 244 (2003).

23. 539 U.S. 306 (2003).

24. Faragher v. City of Boca Raton, 524 U.S. 775 (1998).

25. Burlington Indus. v. Ellerth, 524 U.S. 742 (1998).

26. *Faragher*, 524 U.S. at 807–8; *Ellerth*, 524 U.S. at 764–65.

27. *Faragher*, 524 U.S. at 804.

28. *Id.* at 806.

29. THERESA M. BEINER, GENDER MYTHS V. WORKING REALITIES: USING SOCIAL SCIENCE TO REFORMULATE SEXUAL HARASSMENT LAW (2005); Joanna L. Grossman, *The Culture of Compliance: The Final Triumph of Form Over Substance in Sexual Harassment Law*, 26 HARV. WOMEN'S L.J. 3 (2003); Susan Bisom-Rapp, *Fixing Watches with Sledgehammers: The Questionable Embrace of Employee Sexual Harassment Training by the Legal Profession*, 24 U. ARK. LITTLE ROCK L. REV. 147 (2001); Susan Bisom-Rapp, *An Ounce of Prevention Is a Poor Substitute for a Pound of Cure: Confronting the Developing Jurisprudence of Education and Prevention in Employment Discrimination Law*, 22 BERKELEY J. EMP. & LAB. L. 1 (2001); Theresa M. Beiner, *Sex, Science and Social Knowledge: The Implications of Social Science Research on Imputing Liability to Employers for Sexual Harassment*, 7 WM. & MARY J. WOMEN & L. 273 (2000); Linda Hamilton Krieger, *Employer Liability for Sexual Harassment—Normative, Descriptive, and Doctrinal Interactions: A Reply to Professors Beiner and Bisom-Rapp*, 24 U. ARK. LITTLE ROCK L. REV. 169 (2001)

30. *See generally* ADVANCES IN BEHAVIORAL ECONOMICS (Colin F. Camerer et al. eds., 2004).

31. 509 U.S. 579 (1993).

32. *Id.* at 593–94. [. . .]

33. Brian Mullen, Rupert Brown & Colleen Smith, *Ingroup Bias as a Function of Salience, Relevance, and Status: An Integration*, 22 EUR. J. OF SOC. PSYCHOL. 103 (1992).

34. Charles Stangor & David McMillan, *Memory for Expectancy-Congruent and Expectancy-Incongruent Information: A Review of the Social and Social Developmental Literatures*, 111 PSYCHOL. BULL. 42 (1992).

35. Thomas M. Ostrom & Constantine Sedikides, *Out-Group Homogeneity Effects in Natural and Minimal Groups*, 112 PSYCHOL. BULL. 536 (1992).

36. *See* Robert F. Bornstein, *Exposure and Affect: Overview and Meta-Analysis of Research, 1968–1987*, 106 PSYCHOL. BULL 265 (1989) [. . .].

37. *See generally* ELIZABETH F. LOFTUS, EYEWITNESS TESTIMONY (2d ed. 1996) [. . .].

38. *See generally* ELIZABETH LOFTUS & KATHERINE KETCHAM, THE MYTH OF REPRESSED MEMORY (1994) [. . .]; Timothy D. Wilson & Elizabeth W. Dunn, *Self-Knowledge: Its Limits, Value, and Potential for Improvement*, 55 ANN. REV. PSYCHOL. 493, 497–98 (2004) [. . .].

39. This principle derives from the U.S. Supreme Court's decision in *Barefoot v. Estelle*, 463 U.S. 880, 901–3 (1983), which is still good law.

40. *See generally* John Monahan, *The Scientific Status of Research on Clinical and Actuarial Predictions of Violence*, in DAVID L. FAIGMAN ET AL., MODERN SCIENTIFIC EVIDENCE: THE LAW AND SCIENCE OF EXPERT TESTIMONY 423 (2d ed. 2002); Robert Menzies et al., *The Dimensions of Dangerousness Revisited: Assessing Forensic Predictions About Violence*, 18 LAW & HUM. BEHAV. 1 (1994); David Faust & Jay Ziskin, *The Expert Witness in Psychology and Psychiatry*, 241 SCI. 31 (1988).

41. John A. Bargh, *The Automaticity of Everyday Life*, in 10 ADVANCES IN SOCIAL COGNITION 1 (Robert S. Wyer Jr. ed., 1997).

42. *See* LEE ROSS & RICHARD E. NISBETT, THE PERSON AND THE SITUATION: PERSPECTIVES OF SOCIAL PSYCHOLOGY 59–89 (1991); Jerome S. Bruner, *On Perceptual Readiness*, 64 PSYCHOL. REV. 123, 123–27 (1957); Lee Ross & Donna Shestowsky, *Contemporary Psychology's Challenges to Legal Theory and Practice*, 97 NW. U. L. REV. 1081, 1088 (2003).

43. *See* Timothy D. Wilson & Nancy Brekke, *Mental Contamination and Mental Correction: Unwanted Influences on Judgments and Evaluations*, 116 PSYCHOL. BULL. 117, 130 (1994). [. . .]

44. Roy F. Baumeister & Mark R. Leary, *The Need to Belong: Desire for Interpersonal Attachments as a Fundamental Human Motivation*, 117 PSYCHOL. BULL. 497, 497 (1995).

45. *See generally* Solomon E. Asch, *Studies of Independence and Conformity: I. A Minority of One Against a Unanimous Majority*, in 70 Psychological Monographs: General and Applied 1 (Herbert S. Conrad ed., 1956).

46. Rod Bond & Peter B. Smith, *Culture and Conformity: A Meta-Analysis of Studies Using Asch's (1952b, 1956) Line Judgment Task*, 119 Psychol. Bull. 111 (1996).

47. Ross, *supra* note 6, at 337–84; Ross & Nisbett, *supra* note 42.

48. 42 U.S.C. § 2000e-2(a)(1) (2000).

49. 539 U.S. 90, 101 (2003).

50. 490 U.S. 228, 250 (1989).

51. Dr. Fiske testified as an expert witness for the plaintiff, Ann Hopkins. For a description of that testimony and the circuit and Supreme Court's reactions to it, see generally Martha Chamallas, *Listening to Dr. Fiske: The Easy Case of* Price Waterhouse v. Hopkins, 15 Vt. L. Rev. 89 (1990).

52. *Price Waterhouse*, 490 U.S. at 250.

53. Gilbert Ryle, The Concept of Mind 13–14 (1949).

54. John F. Kihlstrom, *The Cognitive Unconscious*, 237 Sci. 1445, 1445 (1987).

55. *See generally* Patricia G. Devine, *Automatic and Controlled Processes in Prejudice: The Role of Stereotypes and Personal Beliefs*, in Attitude Structure & Function 181, 182–84 (Anthony R. Pratkanis et al. eds., 1989); *see also* Mary Ellen Goodman, Race Awareness in Young Children (rev. ed. 1964); Phyllis A. Katz, *The Acquisition of Racial Attitudes in Children*, in Toward the Elimination of Racism 125 (Phyllis A. Katz ed., 1976).

56. The amygdala is a small bilateral structure, each half about the size of an almond, located in the temporal lobe. It plays a significant role in emotional learning and evaluation, and particularly in the evocation of emotional responses to fear or aggression-inducing stimuli. Ralph Adolphs et al., *The Human Amygdala in Social Judgment*, 393 Nature 470 (1998).

57. Elizabeth A. Phelps et al., *Performance on Indirect Measures of Race Evaluation Predicts Amygdala Activation*, 12 J. Cog. Neuroscience 729, 730 (2000).

58. *See generally* Bargh, *supra* note 41; Mark Chen & John A. Bargh, *Nonconscious Behavioral Confirmation Processes: The Self-Fulfilling Consequences of Automatic Stereotype Activation*, 33 J. Experimental Soc. Psychol. 541 (1997); James S. Uleman et al., *People as Flexible Interpreters: Evidence and Issues from Spontaneous Trait Inference*, in 28 Advances in Experimental Soc. Psychol. 211 (Mark P. Zanna ed., 1996) [. . .].

59. Michael I. Norton et al., *Casuistry and Social Category Bias*, 87 J. Personality & Soc. Psychol. 817, 821–22, 829 (2004).

60. Gordon Hodson et al., *Processes in Racial Discrimination: Differential Weighting of Conflicting Information*, 28 Personality & Soc. Psychol. Bull. 460 (2002); Christopher K. Hsee, *Elastic Justification: How Unjustifiable Factors Influence Judgments*, 66 Organizational Behav. & Hum. Decision Processes 122 (1996).

61. Gary S. Becker, The Economics of Discrimination 41 (1957).

62. Yuichi Shoda et al., *Intraindividual Stability in the Organization and Patterning of Behavior: Incorporating Psychological Situations into the Idiographic Analysis of Personality*, 67 J. Personality & Soc. Psychol. 674 (1994); Icek Ajzen, *Nature and Operation of Attitudes*, 52 Ann. Rev. Psychol. 27 (2001).

63. Ross & Nisbett, *supra* note 42, at 13.

64. *See, e.g.*, Timothy D. Wilson et al., *A Model of Dual Attitudes*, 107 Psychol. Rev. 101 (2000); Patricia G. Devine, *Stereotypes and Prejudice: Their Automatic and Controlled Components*, 56 J. Personality & Soc. Psychol. 5, 6–7 (1989).

65. Wilson, *supra* note 64, at 104.

66. 945 F.2d 796 (4th Cir. 1991).

67. Susan T. Fiske & Steven L. Neuberg, *A Continuum of Impression Formation, from Category-based to Individuating Processes: Influences of Information and Motivation on Attention and Interpretation*, in 23 Advances in Experimental Soc. Psychol. 1 (Mark P. Zanna ed., 1990).

68. Jacques-Philippe Leyens, et al., *The Social Judgeability Approach to Stereotypes*, in 3 Eur. Rev. of Soc. Psychol. 91 (Wolfgang Stroebe & Miles Hewstone eds., 1992).

69. Vincent Y. Yzerbyt, et al., *Social Judgeability: The Impact of Meta-Informational Cues on the Use of Stereotypes*, 66 J. of Personality and Soc. Psychol. 48 (1994).

70. Alexander v. Gardner-Denver Co., 415 U.S. 36, 44 (1974); McDonnell Douglas Corp. v. Green, 411 U.S. 792, 800 (1973); Franks v. Bowman Transp. Co., 424 U.S. 747, 763 (1976) [. . .].

71. St. Mary's Honor Ctr. v. Hicks, 509 U.S. 502, 526 (1993) (quoting *Green*, 411 U.S. at 801); [. . .].

72. 42 U.S.C. § 2000e-2(m).

73. Webster's Third New International Dictionary of the English Language, Unabridged 1475 (2002).

74. Reeves v. Sanderson Plumbing Prods., Inc., 530 U.S. 133, 151–52 (2000) [. . .].

75. *Id.* at 151.

76. Patterson v. McLean Credit Union, 491 U.S. 164, 188 (1989) [. . .].

77. *Green*, 411 U.S. at 804–5.

78. *Reeves*, 530 U.S. at 151–52 [. . .].

79. Tex. Dep't of Cmty. Affairs v. Burdine, 450 U.S. 248, 254 (1981).

80. *Reeves*, 530 U.S. at 147 [. . .].

81. Price Waterhouse v. Hopkins, 490 U.S. 228, 251 (1989).

82. *Id.*

13. African American Families, Child Maltreatment, and Parental Rights Termination Litigation

Matthew B. Johnson, Kideste M. Wilder, and Misha S. Lars

Authors' Note: The authors acknowledge Delores Jones-Brown, JD., Ph.D., Todd Clear, Ph.D., Daniel Williams, Ph.D., Bernado W. Henry, Esq, Christine Baker, Ph.D. and others who provided support and arrangements to facilitate the completion of this manuscript.

1. Bryan A. Garner, A Dictionary of Modern Legal Usage (2d ed. 2001).

2. *See* John Hope Franklin & Alfred A. Moss Jr., From Slavery to Freedom: A History of African Americans (8th ed. 2000); Samella B. Abdullah, *Transracial Adoption Is Not the Solution to America's Problems of Child Welfare*, 22 J. Black Psychol. 254 (1996).

3. Dorothy Roberts, Shattered Bonds: The Color of Child Welfare (2002).

4. Twila L. Perry, *The Transracial Adoption Controversy: An Analysis of Discourse and Subordination*, 21 N.Y.U. Rev. L. & Soc. Change 33 (1995); Roberts, *supra* note 3, at 228–66.

5. C. Henry Kempe, Frederic N. Silverman, Brandt F. Steele, William Droegemuller & Henry K. Silver, *The Battered Child Syndrome*, 181 J. Amer. Med. Assoc. 17 (1962). For a discussion of the earlier history of the "child protection" and "child saving" movement, see generally Richard Wexler, Wounded Innocents: The Real Victims of the War Against Child Abuse (1995).

6. Pub. L. No. 93-247.

7. Wexler, *supra* note 5.

8. Adoption Assistance and Child Welfare Act, Pub. L. No. 96-272.

9. Roberts, *supra* note 3, at 8. *See generally* Jill Quadagno, The Color of Welfare: How Racism Undermined the War on Poverty (1994); Barry Feld, *The Politics of Race and Juvenile Justice: The "Due Process Revolution" and the Conserv-*ative Reaction, 20 Just. Q. 765-80 (2003); William J. Wilson, The Truly Disadvantaged (1987).

10. *See* Matthew B. Johnson, Christine Baker & Angelina Maceira, *The 1997 Adoption and Safe Families Act and Parental Rights Termination Consultation*, 19 Amer J. Forensic Psychol. 15–28 (2001).

11. Pub. L. No. 105-89; *See* National Coalition for Child Protection Reform Web site, *available at* http://www.nccpr.org (last visited April 14, 2007).

12. *See* Roberts, *supra* note 3.

13. Richard P. Barth, Fred Wulczyn & Tom Crea, *From Anticipation to Evidence: Research on the Adoption and Safe Families Act*, 12 Va. J. Soc. Pol'y & L. 155 (2005); *see generally* Marsha Garrison, *Reforming Child Protection: A Public Health Perspective*, 12 Va. J. Soc. Pol'y & L. 590 (2005); Roberts, *supra* note 3, at 7–24; Brenda Smith, *After Parental Rights Are Terminated: Factors Associated with Existing Foster Care*, 25 Child. & Youth Services Rev. 969 (2003); Valora Washington, Adoption and Support of Abused Children, Testimony before the United States Senate Committee on Finance (Oct. 8, 1997).

14. *See generally* Andrea J. Sedlak & Diane D. Broadhurst, Third National Incidence Study of Child Abuse and Neglect (1996); *see* Toshio Tatara, *Overview of Child Abuse and Neglect, in* Child Welfare: An Africentric Perspective 187, 190 (Joyce E. Everett, Sandra S. Chipungu & Bogart R. Leashore eds., 1991).

15. Roberts, *supra* note 3.

16. Wilson, *supra* note 9, at 58.

17. *See generally* U.S. Department of Health and Human Services, Children's Bureau, National Study of Protective, Preventive, and Reunification Services Delivered to Children and Their Families (1997).

18. Roberts, *supra* note 3 (citing Brett Drake & Sushma Pandey, *Understanding the Relationship Between Neighborhood Poverty and Specific Types of Child Maltreatment*, 22 Child Abuse & Neglect 79, 88 [1998]).

19. Thomas D. Morton, *The Increasing Colorization of America's Child Welfare System*, 57 Pol'y & Prac. of Pub. Hum. Servs. 23, 25 (December 1999).

20. *See generally* Carole Jenny, Lt. Col. Kent P. Hymel, Alene Ritzen, Steven E. Reinert & Thomas C. Hay, *Analysis of Missed Cases of Abusive Head Trauma*, 281 J. Amer. Med. Assoc. 621 (1999); Ira J. Chasnoff, Harvey J. Landress & Mark E. Barrett, *The Prevalence of Illicit-Drug or Alcohol Use During Pregnancy and Discrepancies in Mandatory Reporting in Pinellas County, Florida*, 322 New Eng. J. Med. 1202, 1204 (1990).

21. ROBERTS, *supra* note 3 (citing Norma Harris, *Dealing with Diverse Cultures in Child Welfare*, PROTECTING CHILDREN 6, 7 [Fall 1990]).

22. U.S. DEPT. OF HEALTH AND HUMAN SERVICES, ADMINISTRATION FOR CHILDREN AND FAMILIES, The AFCARS Reports 1999–2005, *available at* http://www.acf.hhs.gov/programs/cb/stats_research/index.htm. Data regarding foster care are based on current estimates from states reporting to the AFCARS database, formed under a federal mandate requiring states to collect and submit data for all children in foster care. *Id.*

23. The Adoption Assistance and Child Welfare Act (AACWA) was passed in 1980 and required states to make reasonable efforts for family reunification and preservation. AACWA was also the first federal law to provide federal aid for subsidized adoption.

24. U.S. DEPT. OF HEALTH AND HUMAN SERVICES, ADMINISTRATION FOR CHILDREN AND FAMILIES, *Analysis of State Child Welfare Data: VCIS Survey Data from 1990–1994, Population Flow Exhibit 8: Substitute Care Trends 1980–1994*, available at http://www.acf.hhs.gov/programs/cb/stats_research/afcars/vcis/iio8.htm.

25. U.S. DEPT. OF HEALTH AND HUMAN SERVICES, *supra* note 22. Racial disparities are more pronounced when examining foster care statistics of major cities. *See* ROBERTS, *supra* note 3, at 8–10; *see generally* Martin Guggenheim, *The Effects of Recent Trends to Accelerate the Termination of Parental Rights of Children in Foster Care: An Empirical Analysis in Two States*, 29 FAM. L. Q. 121–40 (1996).

26. U.S. DEPT. OF HEALTH AND HUMAN SERVICES, *supra* note 22.

27. Guggenheim, *supra* note 25, at 127–32; *see generally* Ruth McRoy, *Expedited Permanency: Implications for African-American Children and Families*, 12 VA. J. SOC. POL'Y & L. 475–92 (2005).

28. U.S. DEPT. OF HEALTH AND HUMAN SERVICES, *supra* note 22.

29. *See generally* Susan P. Kemp & Jami M. Bodonyi, *Beyond Termination: Length of Stay and Predictors of Permanency Outcomes of Legally Free Children*, 81 CHILD WELFARE 58–86 (2002); Smith, *supra* note 13, at 965–85.

30. U.S. DEPT. OF HEALTH AND HUMAN SERVICES, *supra* note 22.

31. *Id.*

32. Guggenheim, *supra* note 25, at 121; *see generally* NANCY MARKER & JOE MAGRUDER, ADOPTIONS IN CALIFORNIA: AGENCY, INDEPENDENT, AND INTERCOUNTRY ADOPTION PROGRAMS, ANNUAL STATISTICAL REPORT (2001); BARBARA NEEDLEMAN, PERFORMANCE INDICATORS FOR CHILD WELFARE IN CALIFORNIA (2001), *available at* http://crrs.berkeley.edu/PIReports/index.html.

33. U.S. DEPT. OF HEALTH AND HUMAN SERVICES, *supra* note 22.

34. *Id.*

35. *Id.*

36. McRoy, *supra* note 27, at 475–89; ROBERTS, *supra* note 3, at 49–54; *see also* Chasnoff et al., *supra* note 20, at 1202–6; Robert Hampton, *Race, Ethnicity, and Child Maltreatment and Analysis of Cases Recognized and Reported By Hospitals*, in THE BLACK FAMILY: ESSAYS AND STUDIES 172 (R. Hampton ed., 1991).

37. McRoy, *supra* note 27; *see generally* Daniel R. Neuspiel & Terry Martin Zingman, *Custody of Cocaine-Exposed Newborns: Determinants of Discharge Decisions*, 83 AMER. J. PUB. HEALTH 1726 (1993).

38. Hampton, *supra* note 36; Jenny et al., *supra* note 20, at 621–26; *see* ROBERTS, *supra* note 3, at 47–51; *see* Loren Siegel, *The Pregnancy Police Fight the War on Drugs*, in CRACK IN AMERICA: DEMON DRUGS AND SOCIAL JUSTICE 249 (Craig Reinarman & Harry G. Levine eds., 1997).

39. Delores D. Jones-Brown, *Race as a Legal Construct: The Implications for American Justice*, in THE SYSTEM IN BLACK AND WHITE [hereinafter THE SYSTEM] 138–52 (Michael W. Markowitz & Delores D. Jones-Brown eds., 2000); KATHERYN K. RUSSELL, THE COLOR OF CRIME: RACIAL HOAXES, WHITE FEAR, BLACK PROTECTIONSIM, POLICE HARASSMENT, AND OTHER MACROAGGRESSIONS 14–25 (1998); *see generally* Daniel E. Georges-Abeyie, *Race, Ethnicity, and the Spatial Dynamic: Toward a Realistic Study of Black Crime, Crime Victimization, and Criminal Justice Processing of Blacks*, 16 SOC. JUST. 35–54 (1989); Becky L. Tatum, *Deconstructing the Association of Race and Crime: the Salience of Skin Color*, in THE SYSTEM 31–46.

40. U.S. DEPT. OF HEALTH AND HUMAN SERVICES, *supra* note 22.

41. *Id.*

42. *See* Matthew B. Johnson, *African-American Youth and the Juvenile Justice System*, N.J. ADVISOR, Fall 2001, at 14–18.

43. *See generally* GARY B. MELTON, JOHN PETRILA, NORMAN G. POYTHRESS & CHRISTOPHER SLOBOGIN, PSYCHOLOGICAL EVALUATIONS FOR THE COURTS: A HANDBOOK FOR MENTAL HEALTH PROFESSIONALS AND LAWYERS (2d ed. 1997).

44. *See generally* Rodney Clark, Norman B. Anderson, Vernessa R. Clark & David R. Williams, *Racism as a Stressor for African-Americans: A Biopsychosocial Model*, 54 AMER. PSYCHOL. 805 (1999).

45. Garrison, *supra* note 13, at 590; *see also* Rodney Hammond, *Public Health and Child Maltreatment Prevention: The Role of the Centers for Disease Control and Prevention*, 18 Child Maltreatment 81 (2003).

46. *See* Johnson, Baker & Maceira, *supra* note 10, at 20–22.

47. Garrison, *supra* note 13, at 595.

48. *Id.*

49. *Id.* at 612.

50. Wilson, *supra* note 9.

51. *See generally* Adolph Reed Jr., Stirrings in the Jug: Black Politics in the Post-Segregation Era (1999) (critiquing pathology language).

52. Michael L. Penn & Christina Coverdale, *Transracial Adoption: A Human Rights Perspective*, 22 J. Black Psychol. 240 (1996).

53. *Id.* at 241.

54. *Id.* at 243.

55. *See* Cynthia G. Hawkins-Leon, *The Indian Child Welfare Act and the African-American Tribe: Facing the Adoption Crisis*, 36 J. Fam. L. 201 (1997); Roberts, *supra* note 3.

56. Perry, *supra* note 4.

57. *See* Johnson et al., *supra* note 10, at 15–27.

58. *See* In the Matter of KHO, 161 N.J. 337, 346 (1999).

59. *See* Theodore Millon, Millon Clinical Multi-Axial Inventory Manual (3d ed. 1994). This instrument has received much criticism. *See* Richard Rogers, Randall T. Salekin & Kenneth W. Sewell, *The MCMI-III and the Daubert Standard: Separating Rhetoric from Reality*, 24 Law & Hum. Behav. 501 (2000).

60. Joel S. Milner, The Child Abuse Potential Inventory: Manual (1986).

61. *Id.* at 4.

62. *See* Matthew B. Johnson, *Examining Risks to Children in the Context of Parental Rights Termination Proceedings*, 22 N.Y.U. Rev. L. & Soc. Change 397 (1996); Matthew B. Johnson, *Psychological Parent Theory Reconsidered: The New Jersey "JC" Case, Part II*, 17 Amer. J. Forensic Psychol. 41 (1999); Matthew B. Johnson & Luis Torres, *Bonding and Contested Parental Rights Termination: The New Jersey "JC" Case, Part I*, 12 Amer. J. Forensic Psychol. 37 (1994).

63. *See* Charles F. Johnson, *Physical Abuse: Accidental Versus Intentional Trauma in Children*, in 2 The APSAC Handbook on Child Maltreatment (John E.B. Myers et al., eds., 2002).

64. *See* Brief for Appellant E.L at DYFS v. RL & EL, 388 N.J. Super. 81 (App. Div. 2006).

65. *See* Wexler, *supra* note 5.

66. *See* Johnson et al., *supra* note 10, at 20.

67. For instance, it has been reported that reforming the system of financial incentive in Illinois to reward permanence via reunification or adoption resulted in a substantial reduction in the foster care population. *See* Richard Wexler, Fatal Errors: Rudolph Giuliani, Nicholas Scoppetta and the Fate of New York's Most Vulnerable Children, *A Report from the National Coalition for Children Protection Reform, available at* www.nccpr.org; Illinois Department of Child and Family Services, *available at* www.state.il.us/dcfs/adoption/index.shtml; Richard Wexler, "Fatal Errors"; Ten Ways to Do Child Welfare Right, *available at* http://www.nccpr.org.

68. *See generally* Maxine Eichner, *Children, Parents, and the State: Re-Thinking Foster Care Relationships*, 12 Va. J. Soc. Pol'y & L. (2005).

69. Garrison, *supra* note 13, at 590; Roberts, *supra* note 3; Wilson, *supra* note 9.

70. *See* Cynthia C. Swenson and Mark Chaffin, *Beyond Psychotherapy: Treating Abused Children by Changing Their Social Ecology*, 11 Aggression & Violent Behav. 120 (2006).

71. Eichner, *supra* note 68.

14. The Law of Implicit Bias

Christine Jolls and Cass R. Sunstein

1. Motor Vehicle Mfrs. Ass'n v. State Farm Mut. Auto. Ins. Co., 463 U.S. 29, 56 (1983).

2. *See, e.g.*, Chlorine Chemistry Council v. EPA, 206 F.3d 1286, 1290–91 (D.C. Cir. 2000).

3. *See, e.g.*, David A. Strauss, *The Law and Economics of Racial Discrimination in Employment: The Case for Numerical Standards*, 79 Geo. L.J. 1619, 1623 (1991).

4. *See, e.g.*, Linda Hamilton Krieger, *The Content of Our Categories: A Cognitive Bias Approach to Discrimination and Equal Employment Opportunity*, 47 Stan. L. Rev. 1161, 1164 (1995).

5. *See* Anthony G. Greenwald & Linda Hamilton Krieger, *Implicit Bias: Scientific Foundations*, 94 Calif. L. Rev. 945, 955–56 (2006).

6. *See id.* at 957–58.

7. *See, e.g.*, Anthony G. Greenwald, Debbie E. McGhee & Jordan L.K. Schwartz, *Measuring Individual Differences in Implicit Cognition: The Implicit Association Test*, 74 J. Personality & Soc. Psychol. 1464 (1998); Brian A. Nosek, Mahzarin R. Banaji & Anthony G. Greenwald, *Harvesting Implicit Group Attitudes and Beliefs from a Demonstration Web Site*, 6 Group Dynamics: Theory, Research, & Practice 101 (2002).

8. *See* Greenwald & Krieger, *supra* note 5, at 955–58; Greenwald, McGhee & Schwartz, *supra* note 7, at 1474; Nosek, Banaji & Greenwald, *supra* note 7, at 105.

9. *See* Greenwald & Krieger, *supra* note 5, at 956.

10. *See id.* at 956, 959–60.

11. *See, e.g.*, Alexander R. Green, Dana R. Carney, Daniel J. Pallin, Kristal Raymond, Lisa I. Iezzoni & Mahzarin R. Banaji, The Presence of Implicit Bias in Physicians and its Prediction of Thrombolysis Decisions for Black and White Patients (2006) (unpublished manuscript, on file with authors); Jeffrey J. Rachlinski, Sheri Johnson, Andrew J. Wistrich & Chris Guthrie, Does Unconscious Bias Affect Trial Judges? (2005) (unpublished manuscript, on file with authors).

12. *See* John F. Dovidio, Kerry Kawakami & Samuel L. Gaertner, *Implicit and Explicit Prejudice and Interracial Interaction*, 82 J. Personality & Soc. Psychol. 62, 66 (2002); Allen R. McConnell & Jill M. Leibold, *Relations Among the Implicit Association Test, Discriminatory Behavior, and Explicit Measures of Racial Attitudes*, 37 J. Experimental Soc. Psychol. 435, 439–40 (2001).

13. McConnell & Leibold, *supra* note 12, at 439.

14. *See, e.g.*, Tristin K. Green, *Discrimination in Workplace Dynamics: Toward a Structural Account of Disparate Treatment Theory*, 38 Harv. C.R.-C.L. L. Rev. 91, 99–108 (2003).

15. The relationship between measures of implicit bias and people's actual behavior is discussed further in R. Richard Banks, Jennifer L. Eberhardt & Lee Ross, *Discrimination and Implicit Bias in a Racially Unequal Society*, 94 Cal. L. Rev. 1169, 1187–89 (2006); Greenwald & Krieger, *supra* note 5, at 953–55; Jerry Kang & Mahzarin R. Banaji, *Fair Measures: A Behavioral Realist Revision of "Affirmative Action,"* 94 Cal. L. Rev. 1063, 1072–75 (2006).

16. For an in-depth discussion of "behavioral realism," see Linda Hamilton Krieger & Susan Fiske, *Behavioral Realism in Employment Discrimination Law: Implicit Bias and Disparate Treatment*, 94 Calif. L. Rev. 997, 997–1026 (2006).

17. *See, e.g.*, Christine Jolls, Cass R. Sunstein & Richard Thaler, *A Behavioral Approach to Law and Economics*, 50 Stan. L. Rev. 1471 (1998); Russell B. Korobkin & Thomas S. Ulen, *Law and Behavioral Science: Removing the Rationality Assumption from Law and Economics*, 88 Cal. L. Rev. 1051 (2000); Jeffrey J. Rachlinski, *The "New" Law and Psychology: A Reply to Critics, Skeptics, and Cautious Supporters*, 85 Cornell L. Rev. 739 (2000).

18. On heuristics and biases, see generally Heuristics and Biases: The Psychology of Intuitive Judgment (Thomas Gilovich et al. eds., 2002) [hereinafter Heuristics and Biases]; Judg-

ment Under Uncertainty: Heuristics and Biases (Daniel Kahneman et al. eds., 1982) [hereinafter Judgment Under Uncertainty].

19. For general discussion of heuristics, see Daniel Kahneman & Shane Frederick, *Representativeness Revisited: Attribute Substitution in Intuitive Judgment*, in Heuristics and Biases, *supra* note 18, at 49–50.

20. *See id.* at 62 (discussing the study).

21. *See id.* at 49–50.

22. *See id.* at 53.

23. *See* Amos Tversky & Daniel Kahneman, *Availability: A Heuristic for Judging Frequency and Probability*, 5 Cognitive Psychol. 207, 208 (1973).

24. *See generally* Dual-Process Theories in Social Psychology (Shelly Chaiken & Yaacov Trope eds., 1999).

25. A qualification is that a bad deliberative process might, of course, produce more errors than rapid intuitions.

26. *See* Kahneman & Frederick, *supra* note 19, at 51.

27. *See* Paul Rozin, *Technological Stigma: Some Perspectives from the Study of Contagion*, in Risk, Media, and Stigma: Understanding Public Challenges to Modern Science and Technology 31, 32 (James Flynn et al. eds., 2001).

28. *See id.*

29. *See, e.g.*, Joseph LeDoux, The Emotional Brain: The Mysterious Underpinnings of Emotional Life 138–78 (1996).

30. *See, e.g.*, Greenwald, McGhee & Schwartz, *supra* note 7, at 1474–75.

31. The legal literature on implicit bias is by now enormous. Recent work emphasizing the IAT in particular includes Ian Ayres, Pervasive Prejudice? Unconventional Evidence of Race and Gender Discrimination 419–25 (2001); Mijha Butcher, *Using Mediation to Remedy Civil Rights Violations When the Defendant is Not an Intentional Perpetrator: The Problems of Unconscious Disparate Treatment and Unjustified Disparate Impacts*, 24 Hamline J. Pub. L. & Pol'y 225, 238–40 (2003); Mary Anne Case, *Developing a Taste for Not Being Discriminated Against*, 55 Stan. L. Rev. 2273, 2290–91 (2003) (book review); Theodore Eisenberg & Sheri Lynn Johnson, *Implicit Racial Attitudes of Death Penalty Lawyers*, 53 DePaul L. Rev. 1539, 1542–56 (2004); Blake D. Morant, *The Relevance of Gender Bias Studies*, 58 Wash. & Lee L. Rev. 1073, 1080 n.35 (2001); Lateef Mtima, *The Road to the Bench: Not Even Good (Subliminal) Intentions*, 8 U. Chi. L. Sch. Roundtable 135, 155–58 (2001); Marc R. Poirier, *Is Cognitive Bias at Work a Dangerous Condition on Land?*, 7 Emp. Rts. & Emp. Pol'y J. 459, 489–91 (2003); Deana A. Pollard, *Unconscious Bias and Self-Critical Analysis: The Case for a Qualified Evidentiary Equal Employment Opportunity Privilege*, 74

WASH. L. REV. 913, 959–64 (1999); Evan R. Seamone, *Judicial Mindfulness*, 70 U. CIN. L. REV. 1023, 1051 n.144 (2002); Michael S. Shin, *Redressing Wounds: Finding a Legal Framework to Remedy Racial Disparities in Medical Care*, 90 CALIF. L. REV. 2047, 2066–68 (2002); Megan Sullaway, *Psychological Perspectives on Hate Crime Laws*, 10 PSYCHOL. PUB. POL'Y & L. 250, 256 (2004); Joan C. Williams, *The Social Psychology of Stereotyping: Using Social Science to Litigate Gender Discrimination Cases and Defang the "Cluelessness" Defense*, 7 EMP. RTS. & EMP. POL'Y J. 401, 446–47 (2003).

32. *See* sources cited *infra* note 45.

33. *See* Banks, Eberhardt & Ross, *supra* note 15, at 1178–89.

34. *See, e.g.*, David A. Strauss, *Discriminatory Intent and the Taming of Brown*, 56 U. CHI. L. REV. 935 (1989).

35. *See* Christine Jolls & Cass R. Sunstein, *Debiasing Through Law*, 35 J. LEGAL STUD. 199, 199–201 (2006).

36. *See* Jeffrey J. Rachlinski, *A Positive Psychological Theory of Judging in Hindsight*, 65 U. CHI. L. REV. 571, 619–23 (1998).

37. *See, e.g.*, Jolls & Sunstein, *supra* note 35, at 207–08.

38. The seminal work is Baruch Fischhoff, *Debiasing*, *in* JUDGMENT UNDER UNCERTAINTY, *supra* note 18, at 422.

39. *See* Jolls & Sunstein, *supra* note 35, at 200–01.

40. *See id.* at 209–16.

41. *See* FRANK A. SLOAN, V. KERRY SMITH & DONALD H. TAYLOR, JR., THE SMOKING PUZZLE: INFORMATION, RISK PERCEPTION, AND CHOICE 157–79 (2003).

42. *See* Jolls & Sunstein, *supra* note 35, at 202, 206–24.

43. 42 U.S.C. §§2000e–2000e17 (2000).

44. Linda Hamilton Krieger nicely summarizes this effect of existing antidiscrimination law:

[On the traditional view], if an employee's protected group status is playing a role in an employer's decisionmaking process, the employer will be aware of that role. . . . Equipped with conscious self-awareness, well-intentioned employers become capable of complying with the law's proscriptive injunction not to discriminate. They will monitor their decisionmaking processes and prevent prohibited factors from affecting their judgments.

Krieger, *supra* note 4, at 1167.

45. The scholarly literature critiquing existing antidiscrimination law, both constitutional and statutory, for its general failure to address the problem of implicit bias is voluminous. *See, e.g.*, Samuel R. Bagenstos, *The Structural Turn and the Limits of Antidiscrimination Law*, 94 CAL. L. REV. 1, 3 (2006) ("Unconscious bias, interacting with today's 'boundaryless workplace,' generates inequalities that our current antidiscrimination law is not well equipped to solve.") (citation omitted); Barbara J. Flagg, *Fashioning a Title VII Remedy for Transparently White Subjective Decisionmaking*, 104 YALE L.J. 2009, 2018–30 (1995) (concluding that existing employment discrimination law would not provide relief for an employee who was disadvantaged by the implicit use of criteria that are more strongly associated with whites than nonwhites); Barbara J. Flagg, *"Was Blind, But Now I See": White Race Consciousness and the Requirement of Discriminatory Intent*, 91 MICH. L. REV. 953, 958 (1993) (stating that existing Equal Protection Clause doctrine "perfectly reflects" whites' failure to "scrutinize the whiteness of facially neutral norms") [hereinafter Flagg, *White Race Consciousness*]; Green, *supra* note 14, at 111 ("[E]xisting Title VII doctrine . . . is ill-equipped to address the forms of discrimination that derive from organizational structure and institutional practice in the modern workplace."); Krieger, *supra* note 4, at 1164 (arguing that the way in which employment discrimination law "constructs discrimination, while sufficient to address the deliberate discrimination prevalent in an earlier age, is inadequate to address the subtle, often unconscious forms of bias" prevalent today); Charles R. Lawrence III, *The Id, the Ego, and Equal Protection: Reckoning with Unconscious Racism*, 39 STAN. L. REV. 317, 323 (1987) (stating that existing Equal Protection Clause doctrine "ignores much of what we understand about how the human mind works" and "disregards . . . the profound effect that the history of American race relations has had on the individual and collective unconscious"); R.A. Lenhardt, *Understanding the Mark: Race, Stigma, and Equality in Context*, 79 N.Y.U. L. REV. 803, 878 (2004) (recognizing the "limitations inherent in the Supreme Court's current approach to racial stigma" under the Equal Protection Clause); Ian F. Haney López, *Institutional Racism: Judicial Conduct and a New Theory of Racial Discrimination*, 109 YALE L.J. 1717, 1830–43 (2000) (describing the gap between subtle forms of discriminatory conduct and current Equal Protection Clause doctrine); David Benjamin Oppenheimer, *Negligent Discrimination*, 141 U. PA. L. REV. 899, 972 (1993) (stating that while "much employment discrimination" results from unintentional behavior, "the courts have looked at employment discrimination as a problem of conscious, intentional wrong-doing"); Antony Page, *Batson's Blind-*

Spot: Unconscious Stereotyping and the Peremptory Challenge, 85 B.U. L. REV. 155, 179–80 (2005) (arguing that existing Equal Protection Clause doctrine in the context of peremptory challenges to jurors fails to respond in an effective manner to implicitly biased behavior); Poirier, *supra* note 31, at 459–63 (criticizing, in light of evidence of implicitly biased behavior, the focus of employment discrimination law on various forms of intentional misconduct); Reshma M. Saujani, *"The Implicit Association Test": A Measure of Unconscious Racism in Legislative Decision-Making*, 8 MICH. J. RACE & L. 395, 413 (2003) (asserting that existing Equal Protection Clause doctrine is "incapable of rooting out racial discrimination where it is most pernicious"); Reva Siegel, *Why Equal Protection No Longer Protects: The Evolving Forms of Status-Enforcing State Action*, 49 STAN. L. REV. 1111, 1137 (1997) (stating that "the empirical literature on racial bias" suggests that "most race-dependent governmental decisionmaking will elude equal protection scrutiny"). For further discussion of many of these critiques, see Christine Jolls, *Antidiscrimination Law's Effects on Implicit Bias, in* BEHAVIORAL ANALYSES OF WORKPLACE DISCRIMINATION (Mitu Gulati & Michael Yelnosky eds., forthcoming 2006).

46. *See* Krieger & Fiske, *supra* note 16, at 1027–52.

47. *See id.* at 1034–36.

48. *See id.* at 1036–38.

49. *See, e.g.*, Johnson v. Transp. Agency, 480 U.S. 616 (1987); Grutter v. Bollinger, 539 U.S. 306, 334 (2003).

50. *See* Kang & Banaji, *supra* note 15, at 1066, 1082–90.

51. Ann McGinley and Michael Selmi have also discussed the problem of implicit bias and noted that affirmative action is a way to ensure that employment opportunities of protected groups do not suffer as a result of such bias. *See* Ann C. McGinley, *The Emerging Cronyism Defense and Affirmative Action: A Critical Perspective on the Distinction Between Colorblind and Race-Conscious Decision Making Under Title VII*, 39 ARIZ. L. REV. 1003, 1044–46, 1048–49 (1997); Michael Selmi, *Testing for Equality: Merit, Efficiency, and the Affirmative Action Debate*, 42 UCLA L. REV. 1251, 1284–89, 1297 (1995).

52. Kang and Banaji, however, ultimately limit their discussion to specific forms of (what is conventionally regarded as) affirmative action. *See* Kang & Banaji, *supra* note 15, at 1067.

53. *See, e.g.*, *Johnson*, 480 U.S. at 626–42 (framework under Title VII); *Grutter*, 539 U.S. at 322–43 (framework under the Constitution).

54. *See* sources cited *supra* note 45.

55. *See* Jolls, *supra* note 45.

56. Leading studies include Nilanjana Dasgupta & Shaki Asgari, *Seeing Is Believing: Exposure to Counterstereotypic Women Leaders and Its Effect on the Malleability of Automatic Gender Stereotyping*, 40 J. EXPERIMENTAL SOC. PSYCHOL. 642, 649–50, 651–52 (2004); Brian S. Lowery, Curtis D. Hardin & Stacey Sinclair, *Social Influence Effects on Automatic Racial Prejudice*, 81 J. PERSONALITY & SOC. PSYCHOL. 842, 844–45, 846–47 (2001); Jennifer A. Richeson & Nalini Ambady, *Effects of Situational Power on Automatic Racial Prejudice*, 39 J. EXPERIMENTAL SOC. PSYCHOL. 177, 179–81 (2003). Kang and Banaji provide additional discussion of supportive evidence, including a recent meta-study by Thomas Pettigrew and Linda Tropp. *See* Kang & Banaji, *supra* note 15, at 1102–05.

57. *See* Lowery, Hardin & Sinclair, *supra* note 56, at 844–45, 846–47.

58. *See* Richeson & Ambady, *supra* note 56, at 181, table 1.

59. *See* Paul Slovic, Melissa Finucane, Ellen Peters & Donald G. MacGregor, *The Affect Heuristic, in* HEURISTICS AND BIASES, *supra* note 18, at 397, 397–400.

60. *See* Jolls, *supra* note 45.

61. *See, e.g.*, 42 U.S.C. § 2000e-2(j) (2000) ("Nothing contained in [Title VII] shall be interpreted to require any employer . . . to grant preferential treatment to any individual or to any group because of the race, color, religion, sex, or national origin of such individual or group on account of an imbalance which may exist with respect to the total number or percentage of persons of any race, color, religion, sex, or national origin employed by any employer . . . in comparison with the total number or percentage of persons of such race, color, religion, sex, or national origin in any community, State, section, or other area, or in the available work force in any community, State, section, or other area. . . ."). For discussion of the ways in which some types of explicit preferential treatment of particular groups can increase bias against these groups, see Linda Hamilton Krieger, *Civil Rights Perestroika: Intergroup Relations after Affirmative Action*, 86 CAL. L. REV. 1251, 1263–70 (1998).

62. *See* Jolls, *supra* note 45.

63. *See, e.g.*, Irene V. Blair, Jennifer E. Ma & Alison P. Lenton, *Imagining Stereotypes Away: The Moderation of Implicit Stereotypes Through Mental Imagery*, 81 J. PERSONALITY & SOC. PSYCHOL. 828, 832–33 (2001).

64. *See* Doug McKenzie-Mohr & Mark P. Zanna, *Treating Women as Sexual Objects: Look to the (Gender Schematic) Male Who Has Viewed Pornography*, 16 PERSONALITY & SOC. PSYCHOL. BULL. 296, 303–04 (1990), discussed in Jolls, *supra* note 45.

65. *See supra* note 59 and accompanying text.

66. *See, e.g.*, Harris v. Forklift Sys., 510 U.S. 17 (1993) (addressing workplace environment under Title VII); Davis v. Monroe County Bd. of Educ., 526 U.S. 629 (1999) (addressing school environment under Title IX of the Education Amendments of 1972); Minn. Stat. §363A.11 subd. 1 (2004) (addressing voluntary organization environment under state law); Jolls, *supra* note 45 (citing and discussing cases, including the renowned *Robinson v. Jacksonville Shipyards, Inc.* case, involving visual media specifically).

67. *See* Jolls, *supra* note 45.

68. *See id.*

69. *See, e.g.*, Faragher v. City of Boca Raton, 524 U.S. 775, 807–09 (1998).

70. *See* Nilanjana Dasgupta & Anthony G. Greenwald, *On the Malleability of Automatic Attitudes: Combating Automatic Prejudice with Images of Admired and Disliked Individuals*, 81 J. PERSONALITY & SOC. PSYCHOL. 800, 803–04 (2001).

71. *See id.*

72. *See* Greenwald & Krieger, *supra* note 5, at 964 (raising caution about longer term effects of positive imagery).

73. *See supra* note 59 and accompanying text.

74. *See supra* note 61 and accompanying text.

75. *See* sources cited *supra* note 69.

76. *See supra* note 49 and accompanying text.

77. *See* Christine Jolls & Cass R. Sunstein, Debiasing Through Law (Nov. 18, 2003) (unpublished manuscript, Yale Legal Theory workshop, on file with authors).

78. *See* Krieger, *supra* note 61, at 1275–76.

79. *See id.* at 1263–70.

80. *See id.*

81. Analyses of affirmative action and implicit bias in the existing legal literature have often not been specific about which sort of mechanism—"insulating" or "debiasing" in our terms—produces the effect of an affirmative action plan; both mechanisms may be contemplated. *See, e.g.*, Michael J. Yelnosky, *The Prevention Justification for Affirmative Action*, 64 OHIO ST. L.J. 1385 (2003); *cf.* Cynthia L. Estlund, *Working Together: The Workplace, Civil Society, and the Law*, 89 GEO. L.J. 1, 7, 26–29, 77–94 (2000) (discussing how population diversity from affirmative action may reduce various forms of bias including conscious bias, but expressing pessimism about the possibility of altering implicit bias).

82. *See* Krieger, *supra* note 61, at 1279.

83. *See* Krieger & Fiske, *supra* note 16, at 1056–61; Kang & Banaji, *supra* note 15, at 1111–15.

84. *See* sources cited *supra* note 45.

85. *See, e.g.*, Flagg, *White Race Consciousness*, *supra* note 45, at 991–1017; Krieger, *supra* note 4, at 1186–1217,

1241–44; Krieger & Fiske, *supra* note 16, at 1056–61; Lawrence, *supra* note 45, at 355–81; Poirier, *supra* note 31, at 478–91; Saujani, *supra* note 45, at 413–18.

86. Green, *supra* note 14, at 147. Green also notes, consistent with the previous paragraph, that employers might seek to construct "heterogeneous work and decisionmaking groups." *See id.*

87. *See* Susan Sturm, *Second Generation Employment Discrimination: A Structural Approach*, 101 COLUM. L. REV. 458, 496 (2001).

88. *See* Kang & Banaji, *supra* note 15, at 1111–15. For an initial discussion of the idea that legal policy in the form of government affirmative action reduces implicit bias through increased population diversity, see Jolls & Sunstein, *supra* note 76.

89. *See* Kang & Banaji, *supra* note 15, at 1110.

90. *See id.* at 1108.

91. *See* Gary Blasi & John T. Jost, *System Justification Theory and Research: Implications for Law, Legal Advocacy, and Social Justice*, 94 CAL. L. REV. 1119, 1136–37 (2006).

92. *See generally* JON ELSTER, SOUR GRAPES (1983).

93. *See* George A. Akerlof & William T. Dickens, *The Economic Consequences of Cognitive Dissonance*, 72 AM. ECON. REV. 307 (1982).

94. AMARTYA SEN, DEVELOPMENT AS FREEDOM 63 (1999).

95. GORDON S. WOOD, THE RADICALISM OF THE AMERICAN REVOLUTION 29–30 (1991).

96. *Id.* at 30.

97. *See supra* note 9 and accompanying text.

98. *See* Jolls & Sunstein, *supra* note 35, at 232.

99. *See id.*

100. For discussion in the context of risky consumer products, see *id.*

101. *See* JOHN RAWLS, A THEORY OF JUSTICE 133 (1971); Jolls & Sunstein, *supra* note 35, at 231–32.

102. *See, e.g.*, J.M. Balkin, *Free Speech and Hostile Environments*, 99 COLUM. L. REV. 2295, 2304–06 (1999); Richard H. Fallon, Jr., *Sexual Harassment, Content Neutrality, and the First Amendment Dog That Didn't Bark*, 1994 SUP. CT. REV. 1, 21–51.

103. *See supra* note 30 and accompanying text.

104. *See* Jolls & Sunstein, *supra* note 35, at 226, 228–30.

105. *See supra* note 37 and accompanying text.

106. *See* Jolls & Sunstein, *supra* note 35, at 228–30.

107. We noted above, for instance, that substantial numbers of African-Americans do not show significant levels of implicit bias. *See supra* note 9 and accompanying text.

108. *See supra* notes 50–53 and accompanying text.

109. Again, Kang and Banaji ultimately limit their analysis to specific forms of affirmative action,

see *supra* note 52, so this problem would not be significant under their analysis.

110. Note, however, that as the example of government affirmative action illustrates, the same measure may sometimes have both insulating and debiasing features; our point here is that the debiasing features distinctively hold out the promise of leaving unchanged the decisionmaking of those who were not biased in the first place.

111. *See* Blasi & Jost, *supra* note 91, at 1157.

15. Toward a Radical Psychology: Psychology, Race, Environment, and Crime

Shayne Jones and Michael J. Lynch

1. *See, e.g.*, SHELDON GLUECK & ELEANOR GLUECK, 500 CRIMINAL CASES (1930).

2. *See generally* Avshalom Caspi, Terrie E. Moffitt, Phil A. Silva, Magda Stouthamer-Loeber, Robert F. Krueger & Pamela S. Schmutte, *Are Some People Crime-Prone? Replications of the Personality-Crime Relationship Across Countries, Genders, Races, and Methods*, 32 CRIMINOLOGY 163 (1994).

3. *See generally* ADRIAN RAINE, THE PSYCHOPATHOLOGY OF CRIME: CRIMINAL BEHAVIOR AS A CLINICAL DISORDER (1993).

4. *See generally* MICHAEL LYNCH & RAYMOND MICHALOWSKI, PRIMER IN RADICAL CRIMINOLOGY: CRITICAL PERSPECTIVES ON CRIME, POWER, AND IDENTITY (2006).

5. *See generally* Nicole Hahn Rafter, *The Social Construction of Crime and Crime Control*, 27 J. RES. CRIME AND DELINQ. 376 (1990).

6. JEFFREY REIMAN, THE RICH GET RICHER AND THE POOR GET PRISON: IDEOLOGY, CLASS, AND CRIMINAL JUSTICE (7th ed. 2004).

7. Kenneth A. Dodge & David Schwartz, *Social Information Processing Mechanisms in Aggressive Behavior*, in HANDBOOK OF ANTISOCIAL BEHAVIOR 171 (David M. Stoff et al. eds., 1997).

8. *See generally* Joshua D. Miller & Donald R. Lynam, *Structural Models of Personality and Their Relation to Antisocial Behavior: A Meta-Analytic Review*, 39 CRIMINOLOGY 765 (2001).

9. *See generally* DANIEL F. CONNER, AGGRESSION AND ANTISOCIAL BEHAVIOR IN CHILDREN AND ADOLESCENTS: RESEARCH AND TREATMENT (2002).

10. Bill Henry & Terrie E. Moffitt, *Neuropsychological and Neuroimaging Studies of Juvenile Delinquency and Adult Criminal Behavior*, in HANDBOOK OF ANTISOCIAL BEHAVIOR 280 (David M. Stoff et al. eds., 1997).

11. *See generally* Kerry L. Jang, W. John Livesley & Philip A Vernon, *Heritability of the Big Five Personality Dimensions and Their Facets: A Twin Study*, 64 J. PERSONALITY 577 (1996).

12. *See generally* DEBORAH W. DENNO, BIOLOGY AND VIOLENCE (1990); Robert O. Phil & F. Ervin, *Lead and Cadmium Levels in Violent Criminals*, 66 PSYCHOL. REP. 839 (1990); Herbert L. Needleman, Julie A. Riess, Michael J. Tobin, Gretchen E. Biesecker & Joel B. Greenhouse, *Bone Lead Levels and Delinquent Behavior*, 275 JAMA 363 (1996); Paul B. Stretesky & Michael J. Lynch, *The Relationship Between Lead Exposure and Homicide*, 155 ARCHIVES OF PEDIATRICS AND ADOLESCENT MED. 579 (2001) [hereinafter Stretesky & Lynch, *Homicide*]; Paul B. Stretesky & Michael J. Lynch, *The Relationship Between Lead and Crime*, 45 J. HEALTH AND SOC. BEHAV. 214 (2004) [hereinafter Stretesky & Lynch, *Crime*]; Kim N. Dietrich, M. Douglas Ris, Paul A. Succop, Omer G. Berger & Robert L. Bornschein, *Early Exposure to Lead and Juvenile Delinquency*, 23 NEUROTOXICOLOGY & TERATOLOGY 511 (2001); Nina G. Pabello & Valerie J. Bolivar, *Young Brains on Lead: Adult Neurological Consequences?*, 86 TOXICOLOGICAL SCI. 211 (2005); Stacey E. Holmes, James R. Slaughter & Javad Kashani, *Risk Factors in Childhood that Lead to the Development of Conduct Disorder and Antisocial Personality Disorder*, 31 CHILD PSYCHIATRY AND HUM. DEV. 183 (2001); Rick Nevin, *How Lead Exposure Relates to Temporal Changes in IQ, Violent Crime, and Unwed Pregnancy*, 83 ENVTL. RES. 1 (2000).

13. *See generally* E.C. Banks, L.E. Ferrettim & D.W. Shucard, *Effects of Low Level Lead Exposure on Cognitive Function in Children: A Review of Behavioral, Neuropsychological and Biological Evidence*, 18 NEUROTOXICOLOGY 237 (1997).

14. *See* Angela C. Anderson, Siegfried M. Pueschel & James G. Linakis, *Pathophysiology of Lead Poisoning*, in LEAD POISONING IN CHILDHOOD (S.M. Pueschel et al. eds., 1996); David Bellinger, *Learning and Behavioral Sequelae of Lead Poisoning*, in LEAD POISONING IN CHILDHOOD (S.M. Pueschel et al. eds., 1996); Kim W. Dietrich, *Low Level Lead Exposure During Pregnancy and its Consequences for Fetal and Child Development*, in LEAD POISONING IN CHILDHOOD (S.M. Pueschel et al. eds., 1996).

15. Stretesky & Lynch, *Homicide*, supra note 12; Stretesky & Lynch, *Crime*, supra note 12; Michael J. Lynch, Herman Schwendinger & Julia Schwendinger, *The Status of Empirical Research in Radical Criminology*, in TAKING STOCK: THE STATUS OF CRIMINOLOGICAL THEORY (Transaction, Advances in Criminological Theory, vol. 15) (Francis T. Cullen et al. eds., 2006); Michael J. Lynch, *Towards a Radical Ecology of Urban Violence: Integrating Medical, Epidemiological, Environmental and Criminological*

Research On Class, Race, Lead (Pb) and Crime, in VI-
OLENCE: FROM THEORY TO RESEARCH (Margaret
Zahn et al. eds., 2004).

16. *See generally* Paul B. Stretesky, *The Distribution of Air Lead Levels Across US Counties: Implications for the Production of Racial Inequality*, 23 SOC.
SPECTRUM 91 (2003).

17. *See generally* David W. Allen, *Social Class, Race
and Toxic Releases in American Counties, 1995*, 38 SOC.
SCI. J. 13 (2001); Daniel R. Farber & Eric J. Krieg,
*Unequal Exposure to Ecological Hazards: Environ-
mental Injustices in the Commonwealth of Massachusetts*, 110 ENVTL. HEALTH PERSP. 277 (2002); Paul B.
Stretesky & Michael J. Lynch, *Environmental
Hazards and School Segregation in Hillsborough,
1987–1999*, 43 SOC. Q. 553 (2003); Paul Stretesky &
Michael J. Lynch, *Corporate Environmental Violence
and Racism*, 30 CRIME, L. AND SOC. CHANGE 163
(1999); Paul B. Stretesky & Michael J. Lynch, *Environmental Justice and the Prediction of Distance to Accidental Chemical Releases in Hillsborough County,
Florida*, 80 SOC. SCI. Q. 830 (1999).

18. KAREN PIPER, LEFT IN THE DUST: HOW
RACE AND POLITICS CREATED A HUMAN AND EN-
VIRONMENTAL TRAGEDY IN L.A. (2006).

19. *See, e.g.*, HAN GERTH & C. WRIGHT MILLS,
CHARACTER AND SOCIAL STRUCTURE: THE PSY-
CHOLOGY OF SOCIAL INSTITUTIONS (1964); ERICH
FROMM, FEAR OF FREEDOM (1942).

20. Miller & Lynam, *supra* note 8.

21. *See generally* Donald R. Lynam, Avshalom
Caspi, Terrie E. Moffitt, Per-Olof H. Wikstrom, Rolf
Loeber & Scott S. Novak, *The Interaction Between
Impulsivity and Neighborhood Context on Offending:
The Effects of Impulsivity Are Stronger in Poorer
Neighborhoods*, 109 J. ABNORMAL PSYCH. 563 (2001).

22. Miller & Lynam, *supra* note 8.

23. MARVIN ZUCKERMAN, BEHAVIORAL EXPRES-
SIONS AND BIOSOCIAL BASES OF SENSATION SEEK-
ING (1994).

24. Caspi et al., *supra* note 2.

25. Lynam et al., *supra* note 21.

26. *See generally* Bradley R. Entner Wright,
Avshalom Caspi, Terrie E. Moffitt & Phil A. Silva,
*The Effects of Social Ties on Crime Vary by Criminal
Propensity: A Life-Course Model of Interdependence*,
39 CRIMINOLOGY 321 (2001).

27. WILLIAM JULIUS WILSON, THE TRULY DISAD-
VANTAGED: THE INNER CITY, THE UNDERCLASS,
AND PUBLIC POLICY (1987).

28. Dodge & Schwartz, *supra* note 7.

29. *See generally* ELIJAH ANDERSON, STREET-
WISE: RACE, CLASS AND CHANGE IN AN URBAN
COMMUNITY (1990).

30. *See generally* SHANNAN M. CATALANO, NA-
TIONAL CRIME VICTIMIZATION SURVEY: CRIMI-
NAL VICTIMIZATION, 2005 (2006).

31. REIMAN, *supra* note 6.

32. EDWIN H. SUTHERLAND, WHITE COLLAR
CRIME 7 (1949).

33. *See generally* DAVID O. FRIEDRICHS, TRUSTED
CRIMINALS: WHITE COLLAR CRIME IN CONTEM-
PORARY SOCIETY (2d ed. 2004).

34. *See generally* Michael J. Lynch, Danielle
McGurrin & Melissa Fenwick, *Disappearing Act: The
Representation of Corporate Crime Research in Crimi-
nological Literature*, 32 J. CRIM. JUST. 389 (2004).

35. FRIEDRICHS, *supra* note 33.

36. REIMAN, *supra* note 6.

37. *Id.*

38. Lynch et al., *supra* note 34.

39. *See generally* Belinda Jane Board & Katarina
Fritzon, *Disordered Personalities at Work*, 11 PSY-
CHOL. CRIME AND L. 17 (2005); Judith M. Collins,
J.M. Schmidt & Frank L. Schmidt, *Personality, In-
tegrity, and White Collar Crime: A Construct Validity
Study*, 46 PERSONNEL PSYCHOL. 295 (1993).

40. *See generally* Tage Alalehto, *Economic Crime:
Does Personality Matter?*, 47 INT'L J. OFFENDER
THERAPY AND COMP. CRIMINOLOGY 335 (2003).

41. *See generally* J. Michael Rayburn & L. Gayle
Rayburn, *Relationship Between Machiavellianism
and Type A Personality and Ethical-Orientation*, 15 J.
BUS. ETHICS 1209 (1996); Robert A. Giacalone &
Stephen B. Knouse, *Justifying Wrongful Employee
Behavior: The Role of Personality in Organizational
Sabotage*, 9 J. BUS. ETHICS 55 (1990); Willem Ver-
beke, Cok Ouwerkerk & Ed Peelen, *Exploring the
Contextual and Individual Factors on Ethical Decision
Making of Salespeople*, 15 J. BUS. ETHICS 1175 (1996);
Gwen E. Jones & Michael J. Kavanagh, *An Experi-
mental Examination of the Effects of Individual and
Situational Factors on Unethical Behavioral Intentions
in the Workplace*, 15 J. BUS. ETHICS 511 (1996).

42. *See generally* ROBERT D. HARE, WITHOUT
CONSCIENCE: THE DISTURBING WORLD OF THE
PSYCHOPATHS AMONG US (1993); C.A. Widom, *A
Methodology for Studying Noninstitutionalized Psy-
chopaths*, 45 J. CONSULTING AND CLINICAL PSY-
CHOL. 674 (1977).

43. *See generally* Paul Babiak, *When Psychopaths Go
to Work: A Case Study of an Industrial Psychopath*,
44 APPLIED PSYCHOL.: INT'L REV. 171 (1995).

44. *Id.*

45. *See generally* Scott J. Dickman, *Functional and
Dysfunctional Impulsivity: Personality and Cognitive
Correlates*, 58 J. PERSONALITY AND SOC. PSYCHOL. 95
(1990).

46. *See generally* G. Blickle, A. Schlegel, P. Fass-
bender & U. Klein, *Some Personality Correlates of*

Business White-Collar Crime, 55 APPLIED PSYCHOL. INT'L.REV. 220 (2006).

47. *See generally* Serge Moscovici & Marisa Zavalloni, *The Groups as a Polarizer of Attitudes*, 12 J. PERSONALITY AND SOC. PSYCHOL. 124 (1969).

48. Irving Janis, *Counteracting the Adverse Effects of Concurrence-Seeking in Policy-Planning Groups: Theory and Research Perspectives*, in GROUP DECISION MAKING (Hermann Brandstatter et al. eds., 1982).

49. *See generally* Leon Festinger, Albert Pepitone & Theodore Newcomb, *Some Consequences of Deindividuation in a Group*, 47 J. ABNORMAL AND SOC. PSYCHOL. 382 (1952).

50. Steven Prentice-Dunn & Ronald Rogers, *Deindividuation and the Self-Regulation of Behavior*, in PSYCHOLOGY OF GROUP INFLUENCE (Paul B. Paulus ed., 1989).

51. *See generally* DAVID G. MYERS, EXPLORING SOCIAL PSYCHOLOGY (1994).

52. *See generally* Diane Vaughan, *Rational Choice, Situated Action, and the Social Control of Organizations*, 32 LAW & SOC'Y REV. 23 (1998).

53. Ronald C. Kramer, *The Space Shuttle Challenger Explosion: A Case Study of State-Corporate Crime*, in WHITE COLLAR CRIME RECONSIDERED (Kip Schlegel & David Weisburd eds., 1992).

54. *See generally* FRANK T. CULLEN, WILLIAM MAAKESTAD & GRAY CAVENDER, CORPORATE CRIME UNDER ATTACK: THE FORD PINTO CASE AND BEYOND (1997).

55. FRIEDRICHS, *supra* note 33.

56. Janis, *supra* note 48.

57. *See generally* SAMUEL WALKER, SENSE AND NONSENSE ABOUT CRIME AND JUSTICE: A POLICY GUIDE (5th ed. 2001).

58. FRIEDRICHS, *supra* note 33.

59. LYNCH & MICHALOWSKI, *supra* note 4; REIMAN, *supra* note 6.

60. LYNCH & MICHALOWSKI, *supra* note 4.

16. The Psychology of Hate Crime Law, Victims, and Offenders

Megan Sullaway

1. FEDERAL BUREAU OF INVESTIGATION, CRIME IN THE UNITED STATES 2004: UNIFORM CRIME REPORTS, 2006, *available at* http://www.fbi.gov/ucr/cius_04/documents/CIUS2004.pdf (last visited July 15, 2006).

2. Hate Crime Statistics Act, 28 U.S.C. § 534 (1990).

3. Wisconsin v. Mitchell, 508 U.S. 476 (1993).

4. FEDERAL BUREAU OF INVESTIGATION, *supra* note 1.

5. KEVIN J. STROM, HATE CRIMES REPORTED IN NIBRS, 1997–99 (2001); Yoshio Akiyama & James J. Nolan, *The Hate Crime Statistics Act of 1990: Developing a Process for Measuring and Predicting the Occurrence of Hate Crime*, Paper presented at the meeting of Hate Crimes: Research, Policy and Action, Los Angeles, CA (Oct. 1999).

6. *See generally* William B. Rubenstein, *The Real Story Of U.S. Hate Crime Statistics: An Empirical Analysis*, 78 TUL. L. REV. 1213–46 (2003).

7. Eric A. Posner, *Law and the Emotions*, U. CHI. L. & ECONOMICS, Olin Working Paper No. 103 (September 2000), *available at* http://ssrn.com/abstract=241389 (last visited July 20 2006).

8. *See generally* Terry A. Maroney, *Law and Emotion: A Proposed Taxonomy of an Emerging Field*, 30 LAW & HUM. BEHAV. 119–42 (2006).

9. *See generally* Phyllis B. Gerstenfeld, *Smile When You Call Me That! The Problems with Punishing Hate Motivated Behavior*, 10 BEHAV. SCI. & L. 259–85 (1992); Brian Levin, *Hate Crimes: Worse by Definition*, 15 J. CONTEMP. CRIM. JUST. 6–21 (1999); Anthony S. Winer, *Hate Crimes, Homosexuals and the Constitution*, 29 HARV. C.R.-C.L. L. REV. 387 (Spring 1993).

10. Maroney, *supra* note 8.

11. *See generally* example taken from James Morsch, *The Problem of Motive in Hate Crimes: The Argument Against Presumptions of Racial Motivation*, 82 J. CRIM. L. & CRIMINOLOGY 659 (1991).

12. U.S. HOUSE COMMITTEE ON THE JUDICIARY. HATE CRIMES PREVENTION ACT OF 1999: TESTIMONY ON H.R. 1082, Testimony by Heidi M. Hurd, 106th Congress, 1st session, AUG. 4, 1999.

13. Morsch, *supra* note 11.

14. U.S. HOUSE COMMITTEE ON THE JUDICIARY, *supra* note 12.

15. U.S. HOUSE COMMITTEE ON THE JUDICIARY. HATE CRIMES PREVENTION ACT OF 1999: TESTIMONY ON H.R. 1082, Testimony by Frederick M. Lawrence, 106th Congress, 1st session, Aug. 4, 1999.

16. U.S. HOUSE COMMITTEE ON THE JUDICIARY, *supra* note 12.

17. *See, e.g.*, Ralph Civil Rights Act. California Civil Code 51.7 and 52.; Cal. Penal Code §1170.75 & §190.2(a)(16) (1999).

18. Meredith Watts, personal communication (Oct. 2 , 2001); *see generally* Meredith Watts, *Aggressive Youth Cultures and Hate Crime: Skinheads and Xenophobic Youth in Germany*, 45 AM. BEHAV. SCIENTIST 600–615 (2001).

19. *See generally* Michael Billig, *Prejudice, Categorization and Particularization: From a Perceptual to a Rhetorical Approach*, 15 EURO. J. SOC. PSYCHOL. 79–103 (1985); HOWARD J. EHRLICH, THE SOCIAL

PSYCHOLOGY OF PREJUDICE (1973); David L. Hamilton, *Stereotyping and Intergroup Behavior: Some Thoughts on the Cognitive Approach, in* COGNITIVE PROCESSES IN STEREOTYPING AND INTERGROUP BEHAVIOR (David L. Hamilton ed., 1981); HENRI TAJFEL, HUMAN GROUPS AND SOCIAL CATEGORIES: STUDIES IN SOCIAL PSYCHOLOGY (1981).

20. EHRLICH, *supra* note 19.

21. *See generally* Megan Sullaway & Edward Dunbar, *Clinical Manifestations of Prejudice in Psychotherapy: Toward a Strategy of Assessment and Treatment*, 3 CLINICAL PSYCHOL. SCI. & PRAC. 296 (1996); Megan Sullaway, *Psychological Perspectives on Hate Crime Laws*, 10 PSYCHOL. PUB. POL'Y & L. 250 (2004).

22. *See generally* William A.V. Clark, *Neighborhood Tipping in Multiethnic/Racial Context*, 15 J. URB. AFF. 161 (1993); George C. Galster, *White Flight from Racially Integrated Neighborhoods in the 1970s: The Cleveland Experience*, 27 URB. STUD. 385–99 (1990); John R. Ottensmen & Michael E. Gleeson, *The Movement of Whites and Blacks into Racially Mixed Neighborhoods: Chicago, 1960–1980*, 73 SOC. SCI. Q. 645–63 (1992).

23. Edward Dunbar, Tom King & Karen Umemoto, *Geo-Mapping Hate Crimes and Aggression Analysis: Partnering Behavioral Science with Law Enforcement*, Paper presented at the meeting of the American Psychological Association, Boston, MA (Aug. 1999).

24. R.B. Mison, *Homophobia in Manslaughter: The Homosexual Advance as Insufficient Provocation*, 80 CAL. L. REV. 133 (1992), *quoting* ROLLIN M. PERKINS & RONALD N. BOYCE, CRIMINAL LAW 86 (1982).

25. MODEL PENAL CODE §210.3(1)(b) (1985).

26. *Hate Crime Statistics Act*, *supra* note 2.

27. FEDERAL BUREAU OF INVESTIGATION, HATE CRIME DATA COLLECTION GUIDELINES, REVISED (1999).

28. FEDERAL BUREAU OF INVESTIGATION, *supra* note 27, at 4.

29. *See generally* GERTRUDE J. SELZNICK & STEPHEN STEINBERG, THE TENACITY OF PREJUDICE: ANTI-SEMITISM IN CONTEMPORARY AMERICA (1969).

30. *See generally* Lester W. Wright, Henry E. Adams & Jeffrey Bernat, *Development and Validation of the Homophobia Scale*, 21 J. PSYCHOPATHOLOGY & BEHAV. ASSESSMENT 337–47 (1999).

31. John B. McConahay, *Modern Racism, Ambivalence and the Modern Racism Scale, in* PREJUDICE, DISCRIMINATION AND RACISM (John F. Dovidio & Samuel L. Gaertner eds., 1986); *see generally* John B. McConahay, Betty B. Hardee & Valerie Batts, *Has Racism Declined? It Depends Upon Who's Asking and What Is Asked*, 25 J. CONFLICT RESOL. 563–79 (1981).

32. *See generally* Thomas F. Pettigrew & Roel W. Meertens, *Subtle and Blatant Prejudice in Western Europe*, 25 EUR. J. SOC. PSYCHOL. 57 (1995).

33. *See generally* John H. Duckitt, *The Development and Validation of a Subtle Racism Scale in South Africa*, 22 S. AFR. J. PSYCHOL. 147 (1991).

34. *See generally* Harrison G. Gough, *Studies of Social Intolerance II: A Personality Scale of Anti-Semitism*, 33 J. SOC. PSYCHOL. 247 (1951).

35. Harrison G. Gough & Pamela Bradley, *Personal Attributes of People Described by Others as Intolerant, in* PREJUDICE, POLITICS, AND THE AMERICAN DILEMMA (Paul M. Sniderman, Philip E. Tetlock & Edward G. Carmines eds., 1993).

36. *See generally* Edward Dunbar, *The Assessment of the Prejudiced Personality: The Pr Scale Forty Years Later*, 65 J. PERSONALITY ASSESSMENT 270 (1995); Edward Dunbar, Jose L. Saiz, Karina Stela & Rene Saez, *Personality and Social Group Value Determinants of Outgroup Bias: A Cross-National Comparison of Gough's Pr/To Scale*, 31 J. CROSS-CULTURAL PSYCHOL. 267 (2000).

37. *See generally* Patricia G. Devine, *Stereotypes and Prejudice: Their Automatic and Controlled Components*, 56 J. PERSONALITY & SOC. PSYCHOL. 5 (1989); Russell H. Fazio, David M. Sanbonmatsu, Martha C. Powell & Frank R. Kardes, *On the Automatic Activation of Attitudes*, 50 J. PERSONALITY & SOC. PSYCHOL. 229 (1986); Russell Fazio, Joni R. Jackson, Bridget C. Dunton & Carol J. Williams, *Variability in Automatic Activation as an Unobtrusive Measure of Racial Attitudes: A Bona Fide Pipeline?*, 69 J. PERSONALITY & SOC. PSYCHOL. 1013 (1995).

38. *See generally* Andrew Karpinski & James L. Hilton, *Attitudes and the Implicit Association Test*, 81 J. PERSONALITY & SOC. PSYCHOL. 774 (2001); Allen R. McConnell & Jill M. Leibold, *Relations Among the Implicit Association Test, Discriminatory Behavior, and Explicit Measures of Racial Attitudes*, 37 J. EXPERIMENTAL SOC. PSYCHOL. 435 (2001).

39. MARVIN R. GOLDFRIED & GERALD C. DAVISON, CLINICAL BEHAVIOR THERAPY 10 (1976).

40. Megan Sullaway & Andrew Christensen, *Couples and Families as Participant Observers of Their Interaction, in* ADVANCES IN FAMILY INTERVENTION, ASSESSMENT AND THEORY 3 (John P. Vincent ed., 1983).

41. INTERNATIONAL ASSOCIATION OF CHIEFS OF POLICE, RESPONDING TO HATE CRIMES: A POLICE OFFICER'S GUIDE TO INVESTIGATION AND PREVENTION (June 1998), *available at* http://www.theiacp.org/documents/index.cfm?fuseaction=document&document_type_id=1&document_id=141 (last visited June 6, 2006).

42. JACK McDEVITT, JENNIFER M. BALBONI, SU-

san Bennett, Jean C. Weiss, Stan Orchowsky & Lisa Walbolt, Improving the Quality and Accuracy of Bias Crime Statistics Nationally: An Assessment of the First Ten Years of Bias Crime Data Collection (2000), *available at* http://www.ojp.usdoj.gov/bjs/abstract/iqabcsn.htm.

43. *See generally* Edward Dunbar, *Symbolic, Relational and Ideological Signifiers of Bias Motivated Offenders: Toward a Strategy of Assessment,* 73 Am. J. Orthopsychiatry 203 (2003).

44. Christopher D. Webster, Kevin S. Douglas, Derek Eaves & Stephen D. Hart, HCR-20: Assessing the Risk for Violence (Version 2) (1997).

45. *See generally* Richard A. Berk, *Thinking About Hate-Motivated Crimes,* 5 J. Interpersonal Violence 334 (1990).

46. *Id.*

47. Dunbar, *supra* note 43.

48. Smith v. Collin, 439 U.S. 916 (1978).

49. Texas v. Johnson, 491 U.S. 397 (1989).

50. People v. Superior Court, 896 P. 2d 1387 (1995).

51. *See generally* Sara B. Reeves & Craig T. Nagoshi, *Effects of Alcohol Administration on the Disinhibition of Race Prejudice,* 17 Alcoholism: Clinical & Experimental Res. 1066–71 (1993); Edward Dunbar, Megan Sullaway & Desiree Crèvecoeur, When Words Alone Don't Suffice: Employing a Systematic Approach in Measuring Offender Bias-Motivation, *available at* http://edunbar.bol.ucla.edu/research.html (last visited Aug. 9, 2007).

52. Edward Dunbar, *Signs and Cultural Messages of Bias Motivated Crimes: Analysis of the Hate Component of Intergroup Violence, in* Law Enforcement, Communication and the Community (Howard Giles ed., 2002).

53. Edward Dunbar, *Examining the Bias Motivation of Hate Crime Offenders: The Relationship of Motivation and Victim Target with Instrumental Aggression* (unpublished manuscript, on file with the author).

54. *See generally* Leonard Berkowitz, Aggression: Its Causes, Consequences and Control (1993).

55. *See generally* Jack Levin & Jack McDevitt, Hate Crimes: The Rising Tide of Bigotry and Bloodshed (1993).

56. McDevitt et al., *supra* note 42.

57. Akiyama & Nolan, *supra* note 5; Rubenstein, *supra* note 6; Federal Bureau of Investigation, *supra* note 1.

58. U.S. House Committee on the Judiciary. Hate Crimes Prevention Act of 1997: Testimony on H.R. 3081, Testimony by Jack McDevitt, 105th Congress, 1st session, July 22, 1998.

59. *See generally* Gregory Herek, J. Roy Gillis &

Jeanine Cogan, *Psychological Sequelae of Hate-Crime Victimization Among Lesbian, Gay, and Bisexual Adults,* 67 J. Consulting & Clinical Psychol. 945 (1999).

60. *Id.* at 949.

61. *See generally* John C.Weiss, Howard Ehrlich & Barbara Larcom, *Ethnoviolence at Work,* 18 J. Intergroup Relations 28 (1991–92).

62. Jack McDevitt, *Plenary Keynote Address,* Paper presented at the meeting of Hate Crimes: Research, Policy and Action, Los Angeles, CA (Oct. 1999).

63. *See generally* Herek et al., *supra* note 59; Karen M. Ruggiero & Donald M. Taylor, *Why Minority Group Members Perceive or Do Not Perceive the Discrimination That Confronts Them: The Role of Self Esteem and Perceived Control,* 72 J. Personality & Soc. Psychol. 373 (1997).

64. *See generally* Ronnie Janoff-Bulman, *Characterological Versus Behavioral Self-Blame: Inquiries into Depression and Rape,* 37 J. Personality & Soc. Psychol. 1798 (1979).

65. *See generally* Ronnie Janoff-Bulman, *Esteem and Control Bases of Blame: "Adaptive" Strategies for Victims Versus Observers,* 50 J. Personality 180 (1982).

66. Janoff-Bulman, *supra* note 64.

67. *See generally* Julie L.Hill & Alex J. Zautra, *Self-Blame Attributions and Unique Vulnerability as Predictors of Post-Rape Demoralization,* 8 J. Soc. & Clinical Psychol. 368 (1989).

68. *See generally* Robert J. Boeckmann & Carolyn Turpin-Petrosino, *Understanding the Harm of Hate Crime,* 58 J. Soc. Issues 207 (2002).

69. National Coalition of Anti-Violence Programs, Anti-lesbian, Gay, Bisexual and Transgender Violence in 2005 (2006), *available at* http://www.avp.org/publications/reports/2005ncavphvrpt.pdf (last visited July 23, 2006).

70. *See generally* Edward Dunbar, *Race, Gender and Sexual Orientation in Hate Crime Victimization: Identity Politics or Identity Risk?,* 21 Violence & Victims 323 (2006).

71. *See generally* Dewey G. Cornell, Janet Warren, Gary Hawk, Ed Stafford, Guy Oram & Denise Pine, *Psychopathy in Instrumental and Reactive Violent Offenders,* 64 J. Consulting & Clinical Psychol. 783 (1996).

72. Dunbar, *supra* note 70.

73. Edward Dunbar, Megan Sullaway & Harold Krop, *Behavioral, Psychometric and Diagnostic Characteristics of Bias-Motivated Homicide Offenders,* Paper presented at the meeting of Hate Crimes: Research, Policy and Action, Los Angeles, CA (Oct. 1999).

74. *See generally* Jack McDevitt, Jack Levin & Susan Bennett, *Hate Crime Offenders: An Expanded Typology,* 58 J. Soc. Issues 303 (2002).

75. *See generally* Raphael Ezekial, The Racist

MIND: PORTRAITS OF AMERICAN NEO-NAZIS AND KLANSMEN (1995).

76. FEDERAL BUREAU OF INVESTIGATION, *supra* note 1.

77. EZEKIAL, *supra* note 75

78. *See generally* Eugene Hightower, *Psychosocial Characteristics of Subtle and Blatant Racists as Compared to Tolerant Individuals*, 53 J. CLINICAL PSYCHOL. 369 (1997).

79. *See generally* Carolyn Turpin-Petrosino, *Hateful Sirens . . . Who Hears Their Song? An Examination of Student Attitudes Toward Hate Groups and Affiliation Potential*, 58 J. Soc. ISSUES 281 (2002).

80. *Id.* at 284.

81. Karen Umemoto & C. Kimi Mikami, *A Profile of Race-Bias Hate Crimes in Los Angeles County*, 2 W. CRIMINOLOGY REV. (2000), *available at* http://wcr.sonoma.edu/v2n2/umemoto.html; *see generally* Donald P. Green, Dara Strolovitch & Jannelle Wong, *Defended Neighborhoods, Integration, and Racially Motivated Crime*, 104 AM. J. Soc. 372 (1998).

82. *See generally* Ian McGregor, Mark P. Zanna, John G. Holmes & Steven J. Spencer, *Compensatory Conviction in the Face of Personal Uncertainty: Going to Extremes and Being Oneself*, 80 J. PERSONALITY & Soc. PSYCHOL. 472 (2001).

83. *See generally* Donald P. Green, Jack Glaser & Andrew Rich, *From Lynching to Gay Bashing: The Elusive Connection Between Economic Conditions and Hate Crime*, 75 J. PERSONALITY & Soc. PSYCHOL. 82 (1998).

84. Donald P. Green, Robert P. Abelson & Margaret Garnett, *The Distinctive Political Views of Hate Crime Perpetrators and White Supremacists*, in CULTURAL DIVIDES: UNDERSTANDING AND OVERCOMING GROUP CONFLICT (Deborah Prentice & Dale T. Miller eds., 1999).

85. NATIONAL COALITION OF ANTI-VIOLENCE PROGRAMS, *supra* note 69.

86. COUNCIL ON AMERICAN-ISLAMIC RELATIONS, *Number of Incidents by Category Since September 11*, 2001 (2002), *available at* http://www.cairet.org/html/by category.htm (last visited Aug. 9, 2007).

87. Rubenstein, *supra* note 6.

88. *See generally* Michael A. Tesner, *Racial Paranoia as a Defense to Crimes of Violence: An Emerging Theory of Self Defense or Insanity?* 11 B.C. THIRD WORLD L. J. 307 (1991).

89. Commonwealth v. Gilchrist, No. 06-9763, 06-9764 (Suffolk Super. Ct., MA, April 17, 1989).

90. Tesner, *supra* note 88.

91. Mubarak Dahir, *Homosexual Panicking*, THE ADVOCATE, June 22, 1999, at 27; Kathleen Kelleher, *The Case Against the Notion of "Homosexual Panic,"* LOS ANGELES TIMES, Nov. 8, 1999, at E1; Kevin Toolis, *License to Hate*, THE GUARDIAN, Aug. 30, 1997, at T36.

92. Robert W. Black, *Judge Criticizes Gay Panic Defense*, ASSOCIATED PRESS, *available at* http://www.lexisnexis.com/lawschool/.

93. *See generally* Henry T. Chuang & Donald Addington, *Homosexual Panic: A Review of its Concept*, 33 CANADIAN J. PSYCHIATRY 613 (1988).

94. *See generally* Gary David Comstock, *Dismantling the Homosexual Panic Defense*, 2 L. & SEXUALITY: A REV. LESBIAN & GAY LEG. ISSUES 81 (1992), *quoting* Edward J. Kempf, PSYCHOPATHOLOGY (1976).

95. *See generally* Burton S. Glick, *Homosexual Panic: Clinical and Theoretical Considerations*, 129 J. NERVOUS & MENTAL DISEASE 20 (1959).

96. Chuang & Addington, *supra* note 93.

97. Barry W. Wall, *Criminal Responsibility, Diminished Capacity and the Gay Panic Defense*, 28 J. AM. ACAD. PSYCHIATRY & L. 454–59 (2000).

98. R. Bradley Sears & Elizabeth Kukura, *Constitutional Analysis of AB 1160: Validity of Due Process Challenges to Legislation Eliminating Gay and Trans Panic Defenses in California*, *available at* http://www.law.ucla.edu/williamsinstitute/publications/Policy-HateCrimes-index.html (last visited July 23, 2006).

99. Robert B. Mison, *Homophobia in Manslaughter: The Homosexual Advance as Insufficient Provocation*, 80 CAL. L. REV. 133–78, 133–34 (1992).

100. Schick v. State, 570 N.E.2d 918 (Ind. Ct. App. 1991).

101. *See generally* Gerstenfeld, *supra* note 9; James B. Jacobs & Kimberly Potter, HATE CRIMES: CRIMINAL LAW AND IDENTITY POLITICS (1998).

102. HATE CRIME STATISTICS ACT, *supra* note 2.

103. Hate Crime Sentencing Enhancement Act. Violent Crime Control and Law Enforcement Act, p 280003 (Public Law 103-322), 108 Stat. 1796, 2096.

104. Church Arson Prevention Act of 1996, 104th Congress, Second Session H.R. 3525, amending 18 U.S.C. § 247.

105. John H. Duckitt, *Prejudice and Behavior: A Review*, 11 CURRENT PSYCHOL.: RES. & REV. 11 291–307 (1992–93).

106. MCDEVITT ET AL., *supra* note 42.

107. Dan M. Kahan, *The Anatomy of Disgust in Criminal Law*, 96 MICH. L. REV. 1621, 1628 (1998).

108. Watts, *supra* note 18.

109. *See generally* Brian Levin, *From Slavery to Hate Crime Laws: The Emergence of Race and Status-Based Protection in American Criminal Law*, 58 J. Soc. ISSUES 227 (2002).

110. *See generally* Lawrence D. Bobo, *Prejudice as Group Position: Microfoundations of a Sociological Approach to Racism and Race Relations*, 55 J. Soc. ISSUES 445 (1999), quoting Herbert Blumer, *Race Prejudice as a Sense of Group Position*, 1 PAC. Soc. REV. 3 (1958).

111. Bobo, *supra* note 109, at 447

112. Bobo, *supra* note 109, *citing* Herbert Blumer, *Industrialization and Race Relations*, in Industrialization and Race Relations: A Symposium 247 (Guy Hunter ed., 1965).

113. Carl Bell, *African American Responses to 9-11*, Paper presented at the annual meeting of the American Psychological Association, Chicago, IL (Aug. 2002); *see generally* Gregory Herek, Jeanine Cogan & J. Roy Gillis, *Victim Experiences in Hate Crimes Based on Sexual Orientation*. 58 J. Soc. Issues 319 (2002); Mari J. Matsuda, Charles R. Lawrence III, Richard Delgado & Kimberlé W. Crenshaw, Words That Wound: Critical Race Theory, Assaultive Speech, and the First Amendment (1993).

17. Prejudice and Police Profiling

Roger G. Dunham and George Wilson

1. Jeffrey Fagan, Measurement and Analysis of Racial Profiling in Law Enforcement (2002) (unpublished manuscript, on file with authors).

2. *See id.* at 3.

3. Lori A. Fridell, By the Numbers: A Guide for Analyzing Race Data from Vehicle Stops vii (2004).

4. *See generally* Gordon Allport, The Nature of Prejudice (1954); Larry Bobo, James Kluegel & Ryan Smith, *Laissez-Faire Racism: The Cystallization of a Kinder, Gentler, Antiblack Ideology*, in Racial Attitudes in the 1990's 15–44 (Stephen Tuch & Jack Martin eds., 1997); Howard Schuman, Charlotte Steeh & Larry Bobo, Racial Attitudes in America: Trends and Interpretations (1985); Thomas Pettigrew, *New Black-White Patterns: How Best to Conceptualize Them*, 11 Ann. Rev. Soc. 329 (1985).

5. Bobo, Kluegel & Smith, *supra* note 4.

6. *Id*; Schuman, Steeh & Bobo, *supra* note 4.

7. Bobo, Kluegel & Smith, *supra* note 4.

8. David Sears, *Symbolic Racism, in* Eliminating Racism 11–24 (Philip Katz & David Taylor eds., 1988); *see generally* James McConahay & James Hough, *Symbolic Racism*, 32 J. Soc. Issues 23 (1976).

9. Pettigrew, *supra* note 4.

10. Schuman, Steeh, & Bobo, *supra* note 4.

11. Bobo, Kluegel, & Smith, *supra* note 4.

12. Allport, *supra* note 4.

13. Larry Bobo & Michael Massagli, *Stereotyping and Urban Inequality, in* Urban Inequality 89, 94 (Alice O'Connor, Chris Tilly & Larry Bobo eds., 2001).

14. Sears, *supra* note 8; Allport, *supra* note 4.

15. *See generally* Michael Omi & Howard Winant, Racial Formation in the United States: From the 1960s to the 1990s (1994).

16. Bobo & Massagli, *supra* note 13; Allport, *supra* note 4.

17. Allport, *supra* note 4.

18. Bobo & Massagli, *supra* note 13; Sears, *supra* note 8.

19. Martin Gilens, Why Americans Hate Welfare (1999); *see generally* George Wilson, *Pathways to Power: Racial Differences in the Determinants of Job Authority*, 44 Soc. Probs. 38 (1997).

20. Allport, *supra* note 4; Bobo & Massagli, *supra* note 13.

21. Schuman, Steeh & Bobo, *supra* note 4.

22. Bobo & Massagli, *supra* note 13.

23. *Id.*

24. Susan Fiske, *Stereotyping, Prejudice, and Discrimination, in* Handbook of Social Psychology 125–43 (David Gilbert, Susan Fiske & Gardiner Lindzey eds., 1998); Pettigrew, *supra* note 4.

25. Fiske, *supra* note 24.

26. Pettigrew, *supra* note 4.

27. *See generally* Elijah Anderson, Streetwise: Race, Class and Change in an Urban Community (1990); Philip Moss & Chris Tilly, Stories Employers Tell: Race, Skill, and Hiring in America (2001); Robert Lake, The New Suburbanites: Race and Housing in the Suburbs (1981); Katherine Newman, No Shame in My Game: The Working Poor in the Inner City (1999); Joleen Kirschenman & Kathryn Neckerman, *We'd Love to Hire Them But . . . : The Meaning of Race for Employers, in* The Urban Underclass 110–32 (Christopher Jencks & Paul Peterson eds., 1991); Camille Charles, *Processes of Racial Residential Segregation, in* Urban Inequality 217–71 (Alice O'Connor, Chris Tilly & Larry Bobo eds., 2001); Reynolds Farley, Charlotte Steeh, Maria Krysan, Thomas Jackson & Kent Reeves, *Stereotypes and Segregation: Neighborhoods in the Detroit Area*, 100 Am. J. Soc. 750–80 (1994); George Galster & Marie Keeney, *Race, Residence, Discrimination, and Economic Opportunity: Modeling the Nexus of Urban Racial Phenomena*, 24 Urb. Affairs Q. 87–117 (1988); Diana Pearce, Black, White, and Many Shades of Gray: Real Estate Brokers and Their Racial Practices (1976) (unpublished Ph.D. Dissertation, University of Michigan, on file with authors).

28. Anderson, *supra* 27.

29. Moss & Tilly, *supra* note 27.

30. Farley, Steeh, Krysan, Jackson & Reeves, *supra* note 27; Galster & Keeney, *supra* note 27.

31. Anderson, *supra* 27; Kirschenman & Neckerman, *supra* note 27; Moss & Tilly, *supra* note 27.

32. Bobo, Kluegel & Smith, *supra* note 4.

33. Gilens, *supra* note 19; *see generally* Mark Peffley, James Hurwitz & Paul Sniderman, *Racial Stereotypes and Whites Political Views of Blacks in the Context of Welfare and Crime*, 41 Am. J. Pol. Sci. 30 (1997); Mark Peffley & James Hurwitz, *Public Perceptions of Race and Crime: The Role of Racial Stereotypes*, 41 Am. J. Pol. Sci. 375 (1997).

34. *See generally* Samuel Walker, Cassia Spohn & Miriam DeLone, The Color of Justice: Race, Ethnicity, and Crime in America (2004).

35. *See generally* Thomas Pettigrew & Joanne Martin, *Shaping the Organizational Context for African American Inclusion*, 43 J. Soc. Issues. 41 (1987).

36. *See generally* George Wilson, Ian Sakura-Lemessy & Jonathon West, *Reaching the Top: Racial Differences in Mobility Paths to Upper-Tier Occupations*, 26 Work & Occupations 165 (1999).

37. Anderson, *supra* 27; Newman, *supra* note 27.

38. Allport, *supra* note 4.

39. Pettigrew & Martin, *supra* note 35.

40. Kirschenman & Neckerman, *supra* note 27; Moss & Tilly, *supra* note 27.

41. Moss & Tilly, *supra* note 27.

42. Wilson, Sakura-Lemessy & West, *supra* note 36.

43. Pettigrew & Martin, *supra* note 35; Wilson, *supra* note 19.

44. Pettigrew & Martin, *supra* note 35; Wilson, *supra* note 19.

45. Pettigrew, *supra* note 4.

46. *See generally* Randy Hodson & Teresa A. Sullivan, The Social Organization of Work (2001).

47. Kirschenman & Neckerman, *supra* note 27; Moss & Tilly, *supra* note 27.

48. *See generally* Sharon M. Collins, Black Corporate Executives: The Making and Breaking of a Black Middle Class (1997).

49. *See generally* John Yinger, Closed Doors, Opportunities Lost: The Continuing Cost of Housing Discrimination (1995); George Galster, *Research on Discrimination in Housing and Mortgage Markets: Assessment and Future Directions*, 3 Housing Pol'y Debate 639 (1992)

50. Yinger, *supra* note 49.

51. David Thatcher, From Racial Profiling to Racial Equality: Rethinking Equity in Police Stops and Searches, Address at the 2001 American Society of Criminology Annual Meetings (2002).

52. Thatcher, *supra* note 51.

53. *See generally* Anne Rawls, *Race as an Interaction Order Phenomenon*, 18 Soc. Theory 241 (2000).

54. *See generally* David Barlow & Melissa Barlow, Police in a Multicultural Society: An American Story (2000).

55. *Id.* at xiii.

56. *See generally* David D. Powell, *A Study of Police Discretion in Six Southern Cities*, 17 J. Police Sci. & Admin. 1–7 (1990); Douglass Smith & Laura Davidson, *Equity and Discretionary Justice: The Influence of Race on Police Arrest Decisions*, 75 J. Crim. L. 234 (1984); Douglas Smith & Cristy Visher, *Street Level Justice: Situational Determinants of Police Arrest Decisions*, 29 Soc. Probs. 167–78 (1981).

57. *See generally* David A. Klinger, *More on Demeanor and Arrest in Dade County*, 34 Criminology 61 (1996); Douglas Smith, *The Organizational Aspects of Legal Control*, 22 Criminology 19–38 (1984).

58. Mark Blumberg, *Race and Police Shootings: An Analysis in Two Cities*, *in* Contemporary Issues in Law Enforcement (J.J. Fyfe ed., 1981); *see generally* James J. Fyfe, *Geographic Correlates of Police Shootings: A Microanalysis*, 17 Crim. & Delinquency 101 (1980); William A. Geller & Kevin Karales, *Shootings of and by Chicago Police: Uncommon Crises. Part I: Shootings by Chicago Police*, 72 J. Crim. L. & Criminology 1813–66 (1981).

59. Roger Dunham & Geoffrey Alpert, *The Effects of Officer and Suspect Ethnicity in Use-of-Force Incidents*, *in* Policing and Minority Communities: Bridging the Gap 102–14 (Karen Terry & Delores Jones-Brown eds., 2004); *Getting It Right: Study Says Miami-Dade PD Has a Handle on the Use of Force*, Law Enforcement News, March 15, 2000, at 1.

60. National Research Council, Fairness and Effectiveness in Policing: The Evidence, 3 (2003).

61. *See generally* Kathryn Russell, *"Driving While Black": Corollary Phenomena and Collateral Consequences*, 40 B.C. L. Rev. 717 (1999).

62. Criminal Careers and "Career Criminals" (Vols. 1–2) (Al Blumstein, Jacqueline Cohen, Jeffrey Roth & Christie Visher eds., 1986); *see generally* Delbert Elliott, *Serious Violent Offenders: Onset, Developmental Course, and Termination*, 32 Criminology 1 (1994).

63. *See generally* Michael Tonry, Malign Neglect (1995).

64. American Civil Liberties Union Web site, http://www.aclu.org (last visited Oct. 16, 2007).

18. The Influence of Criminal Defendants' Afrocentric Features on Their Sentences

William T. Pizzi, Irene V. Blair, and Charles M. Judd

1. *See* Samuel Walker, Cassia Spohn & Miriam DeLone, The Color of Justice: Race, Ethnicity, and Crime in America 262 tbl.9.1 (2000).

2. MICHAEL TONRY, MALIGN NEGLECT—RACE, CRIME, AND PUNISHMENT IN AMERICA 68 (1995). Tonry argues powerfully in his book that the real culprit in the heavy racial imbalance in U.S. prisons is the "malign neglect" of the war on drugs on African Americans.

3. *See generally* Irene V. Blair, Charles M. Judd & Kristine M. Chapleau, *The Influence of Afrocentric Facial Features in Criminal Sentencing*, 15 PSYCH. SCI. 674 (2004).

4. Professor Trina Jones, in an article about discrimination based on shades of skin color among African Americans, traces the term "colorism" to the writer Alice Walker. *See* Trina Jones, *Shades of Brown: The Law of Skin Color*, 49 DUKE L. J. 1487, 1489 (2000). Professor Jones demonstrates in her article a long history of economic and social discrimination against darker-skinned African Americans as compared to those with lighter skin coloring. *See generally id.*

5. The generally likable description, stereotypic of African Americans, presented a person who grew up in rural Georgia, was close to an extended family, was attending junior college in Atlanta, and wanted to be an entertainer. The more negative African-American-stereotypic description presented a person who grew up in inner-city Detroit, was attending college on a basketball scholarship, had failed several classes, had been involved in fights on the basketball court, and was accused of dealing drugs. The white-stereotypic likable description presented a Harvard undergraduate who was a star pre-med student, enjoyed classical music, and wrote music reviews for the school newspaper. And finally, the more negative white-stereotypic description presented a person who was a Princeton undergraduate, was introverted and socially inept, had few friends, and came from a privileged but sheltered background. The complete text of these descriptions can be found in Irene V. Blair, Charles M. Judd, Melody S. Sadler, and Christopher Jenkins, *Afrocentric Features in Person Perception: Judging by Features and Categories*, 83 J. PERSONALITY & SOC. PSYCHOL. 5 (2002).

6. *See generally* Irene V. Blair, Charles M. Judd & Jennifer L. Fallman, *The Automaticity of Race and Afrocentric Facial Features in Social Judgments*, 87 J. OF PERSONALITY & SOC. PSYCH. 763 (2004).

7. *See generally* Irene V. Blair, Kristine M. Chapleau & Charles M. Judd, *The Use of Afrocentric Features as Cues for Judgment in the Presence of Diagnostic Information*, 35 EUR. J. SOC. PSYCH. 59 (2004).

8. For the judgment, subjects were told that the individual was involved in a rough basketball game and a fight with another player loomed as a result.

The question was whether the individual would in fact initiate a fight on the court or would turn and walk away. The four prior situations in which the individual acted either aggressively or nonaggressively involved aggression on the highway, aggression against a rude person in a nightclub, getting angry at his girlfriend for flirting at a party, and getting angry when some personal property was damaged at a party that roommates gave.

9. The Florida Department of Corrections Web site from which data on offenders can be accessed is located at http://www.dc.state.fl.us/index.html (last visited June 26, 2007).

10. *See* Irene V. Blair, Charles M. Judd & Kristine M. Chapleau, *The Influence of Afrocentric Facial Features in Criminal Sentencing*, 15 PSYCHOL. SCI. 674, 675 (2004).

11. For this research on the Florida criminal statutes, we are grateful to Sandy Schmeider, who was at the time a law student at the University of Colorado at Boulder.

19. Fear and Fairness in the City: Criminal Enforcement and Perceptions of Fairness in Minority Communities

Richard R. W. Brooks

1. United States v. Rosenberg, 195 F.2d 583, 608 (1952), *cert. denied*, 344 U.S. 838 (1952).

2. *See* CAROL J. DeFRANCES & STEVEN K. SMITH, U.S. DEP'T OF JUSTICE, SPECIAL REPORT: PERCEPTIONS OF NEIGHBORHOOD CRIME (1995).

3. *See* CALLIE MARIE RENNISON, U.S. DEP'T OF JUSTICE, NATIONAL CRIME VICTIMIZATION SURVEY: CRIMINAL VICTIMIZATION 1999, at 6, 9–11 [. . .].

4. *See* JAMES ALAN FOX & MARIANNE W. ZAWITZ, U.S. DEP'T OF JUSTICE, CRIME DATA BRIEF: HOMICIDE TRENDS IN THE UNITED STATES 2 (1999). [. . .]

5. *See, e.g.*, Randall Kennedy, *The State, Criminal Law, and Racial Discrimination: A Comment*, 107 HARV. L. REV. 1255, 1278 (1994) [. . .].

6. For lists of surveys and empirical research supporting this view, *see* JULIAN V. ROBERTS & LORETTA J. STALANS, PUBLIC OPINION, CRIME, AND CRIMINAL JUSTICE 127–54 (1997); KATHERYN K. RUSSELL, THE COLOR OF CRIME 26–46 (1998); [. . .]; William J. Stuntz, *Race, Class, and Drugs*, 98 COLUM. L. REV. 1795, 1797 (1998).

7. Dan M. Kahan & Tracey L. Meares, *The Coming Crisis of Criminal Procedure*, 86 GEO. L.J. 1153, 1163 (1998).

8. *Id.* at 1166. [. . .]

9. *See* Albert W. Alschuler & Stephen J. Schulhofer, *Antiquated Procedures or Bedrock Rights?: A Response to Professors Meares and Kahan*, 1998 U. CHI. LEGAL. F. 215, 215–16; David Cole, *The Paradox of Race and Crime: A Comment on Randall Kennedy's "Politics of Distinction*," 83 GEO. L.J. 2547 (1995); JACK R. GREENE & RALPH B. TAYLOR, COMMUNITY-BASED POLICING AND FOOT PATROL: ISSUES OF THEORY AND EVALUATION, IN COMMUNITY POLICING: RHETORIC OR REALITY 195, 216 (Jack R. Greene & Stephen D. Mastrofski eds., 1988); Carol S. Steiker, *More Wrong Than Rights*, BOSTON REV., Apr.–May 1999, at 13; Gary Stewart, *Black Codes and Broken Windows: The Legacy of Racial Hegemony in Anti-Gang Civil Injunctions*, 107 YALE L.J. 2249 (1997).

10. *See* Saundra Lee Browning, Francis T. Cullen, Liqun Cao, Renee Kopache & Thomas J. Stevenson, *Race and Getting Hassled by the Police*, 17 POLICE STUD. 1, 8 (1994); Francis T. Cullen, Liqun Cao, James Frank & Robert H. Langworthy, *"Stop or I'll Shoot": Racial Differences in Support for Police Use of Deadly Force*, 39 AM. BEHAVIORAL SCIENTIST 449 (1996) [hereinafter Cullen et al., *"Stop"*] [. . .].

11. David Kocieniewski, *Success of Elite Police Unit Exacts a Toll on the Streets*, N.Y. TIMES, Feb. 15, 1999, at A1. [. . .]

12. The principal data source is the 1993–94 National Black Politics Survey—a nationwide survey of adult African Americans concerning their perceptions of politics, race, and religion.

13. *See* Hubert Williams & Antony M. Pate, *Returning to First Principles: Reducing the Fear of Crime in Newark*, 33 CRIME & DELINQ. 53 (1987).

14. *Id.* at 67–68; *see also* WESLEY G. SKOGAN, DISORDER AND DECLINE: CRIME AND THE SPIRAL OF DECAY IN AMERICAN NEIGHBORHOODS 109–24 (1990).

15. The Uniform Crime Reporting Program provides data on arrests for so-called Part I offenses (which include murder, rape, robbery, aggravated assault, burglary, larceny, auto theft, and arson) and the Part II offenses of forgery, fraud, embezzlement, vandalism, weapons violations, sex offenses, drug and alcohol abuse violations, gambling, vagrancy, curfew violations, and runaways. *See* U.S. DEP'T OF JUSTICE & FED. BUREAU OF INVESTIGATION, UNIFORM CRIME REPORTING PROGRAM DATA [UNITED STATES]: COUNTY-LEVEL DETAILED ARREST AND OFFENSE DATA, 1996, at 1–4 (Inter-university Consortium for Political and Soc. Research No. 2389, 2d ed. Sept. 1998).

16. *See* James Q. Wilson & George L. Kelling, *Broken Windows: The Police and Neighborhood Safety*, ATLANTIC MONTHLY, Mar. 1982, at 29, 31–32 [. . .].

17. SKOGAN, *supra* note 14, at 118. [. . .]

18. *See* David Rohde, *Jurors' Trust in Police Erodes in Light of Diallo and Louima*, N.Y. TIMES, Mar. 9, 2000, at B1.

19. *See, e.g.*, TIMOTHY J. FLANAGAN & MICHAEL S. VAUGHN, PUBLIC OPINION ABOUT POLICE ABUSE OF FORCE, *in* POLICE VIOLENCE 113, 128 (William A. Geller & Hans Toch eds., 1996). [. . .]

20. *See, e.g.*, Timothy J. Flanagan, Edmund F. McGarrell & Edward J. Brown, *Public Perceptions of the Criminal Courts: The Role of Demographic and Related Attitudinal Variables*, 22 J. RES. CRIME & DELINQ. 66 (1985).

21. *See, e.g.*, Phoebe C. Ellsworth & Lee Ross, *Public Opinion and Capital Punishment: A Close Examination of the Views of Abolitionists and Retentionists*, 29 CRIME & DELINQ. 116 (1983) [. . .]; Austin Sarat & Neil Vidmar, *Public Opinion, the Death Penalty, and the Eighth Amendment: Testing the Marshall Hypothesis*, 1976 WIS. L. REV. 171 (1976).

22. *See, e.g.*, TOM. R. TYLER, WHY PEOPLE OBEY THE LAW (1990).

23. *See, e.g.*, National Opinion Survey, *supra* note 12.

24. *See* DAVID H. BAYLEY & HAROLD MENDELSOHN, MINORITIES AND THE POLICE: CONFRONTATION IN AMERICA 42 (1969); ROBERTS & STALANS, *supra* note 6, at 173–75; Ronald Weitzer, *Racial Discrimination in the Criminal Justice System: Findings and Problems in the Literature*, 24 J. CRIM. JUST. 309 (1996).

25. *See* John Hagan & Celesta Albonetti, *Race, Class, and the Perception of Criminal Justice in America*, 88 AM. J. SOC. 329 (1982); CORMARAE R. MANN & WILLIAM WILBANKS, RACISM IN THE CRIMINAL JUSTICE SYSTEM: TWO SIDES OF THE CONTROVERSY, IN CRIMINAL JUSTICE: CONCEPTS AND ISSUES (Chris W. Eskridge ed., 2d ed. 1996); Charles W. Peek, George D. Lowe & Jon P. Alston, *Race and Attitudes Towards Local Police: Another Look*, 18 J. BLACK STUD. 361, 361 (1981); Steven A. Tuch & Ronald Weitzer, *Racial Differences in Attitudes Towards the Police*, 61 PUB. OPINION Q. 642 (1997).

26. *See, e.g.*, KATHERINE MCFATE, JOINT CTR. FOR POLITICAL AND ECON. STUDIES, 1996 NATIONAL OPINION POLL: SOCIAL ATTITUDES.

27. *See* Michael A. Fletcher, *Study Tracks Blacks' Crime Concerns: African Americans Show Less Confidence in System, Favor Stiff Penalties*, WASH. POST, Apr. 21, 1996, at A11.

28. Regina Austin, *"The Black Community," Its Lawbreakers, and a Politics of Identification*, 65 S. CAL. L. REV. 1769, 1770 (1992). [. . .]

29. [. . .] *See* Tracey L. Meares, *Charting Race and Class Differences in Attitudes Toward Drug Legalization and Law Enforcement: Lessons for Federal*

Criminal Law, 1 Buff. Crim. L. Rev. 137, 156–64 (1997).

30. *See* Ellis Cose, Rage of a Privileged Class (1994); Michael C. Dawson, Behind the Mule: Race and Class in African-American Politics (1994); NBPS Survey, *supra* note 12; Jennifer L. Hochschild, Facing Up to the American Dream: Race, Class, and the Soul of the Nation (1995); Howard Schuman, Charlotte Steeh, Lawrence Bobo & Maria Krysan, Racial Attitudes in America: Trends and Interpretations (1997). [. . .]

31. *See* Hagan & Albonetti, *supra* note 25; Raymond J. Murphy & James W. Watson, *The Structure of Discontent: Relationship Between Social Structure, Grievance, and Riot Support, in* The Los Angeles Riots: A Socio-psychological Study 140 (Nathan Cohen ed., 1970); Peek et al., *supra* note 25; Walter J. Raine, *The Perception of Police Brutality in South Central Los Angeles, in* The Los Angeles Riots: A Socio-psychological Study 380 (Nathan Cohen ed., 1970); Ronald Weitzer & Steven A. Tuch, *Race, Class and Perceptions of Discrimination by the Police*, 45 Crime & Delinq. 494 (1999); Scot Wortley, John Hagan & Ross Macmillan, *Just Des(s)ert? The Racial Polarization of Perceptions of Criminal Injustice*, 31 Law & Soc'y Rev. 637, 649 (1997). [. . .]

32. [. . .] Amy Farmer & Dek Terrell, Crime Versus Justice: Is There a Tradeoff? 29 (1999) (unpublished manuscript, on file with author).

33. *Id.* [. . .]

34. *See* 21 U.S.C. § 841 (1994).

35. *See* Paul Butler, *(Color) Blind Faith: The Tragedy of Race, Crime, and the Law*, 111 Harv. L. Rev. 1270, 1276 (1998). [. . .]

36. *See* Kate Stith, The Government Interest in Criminal Law: Whose Interest Is It Anyway?, *in* Public Values in Constitutional Law 137, 153 (Stephen E. Gottlieb ed., 1993).

37. Randall Kennedy, *The State, Criminal Law, and Racial Discrimination: A Comment*, 107 Harv. L. Rev. 1255, 1278 (1994).

38. Tracey L. Meares & Dan M. Kahan, *When Rights Are Wrong*, Boston Rev., Apr.–May 1999, at 4.

39. *Id.*

40. 687 N.E.2d 53 (Ill. 1997)., *aff'd*, 527 U.S. 41 (1999).

41. *See* Meares & Kahan, *supra* note 38, at 8. [. . .]

42. *Id.* at 1183. [. . .]

43. *See* Debra Livingston, *Police Discretion and the Quality of Life in Public Places: Courts, Communities, and the New Policing*, 97 Colum. L. Rev. 551, 595–697 (1997).

44. Kahan & Meares, *supra* note 7, at 1162.

45. *Morales*, 527 U.S. at 114–15 (Thomas, J., dissenting).

46. [. . .] *See* David Cole, *The Paradox Race and Crime: A Comment on Randall Kennedy's "Politics of Distinction"*, 83 Geo. L.J. 2547, 2560–62 (1995). [. . .]

47. Alschuler & Schulhofer, *supra* note 9, at 215–16 (1998). [. . .]

48. *See* Hochschild, *supra* note 30, at 73. [. . .]

49. *See* Dawson, *supra* note 30. [. . .]

50. Schuman et al., *supra* note 30, at 271.

51. *See* Hagan & Albonetti, *supra* note 25, at 352. [. . .]

52. *See* Wortley et al., *supra* note 31.

53. *See* Weitzer & Tuch, *supra* note 31.

54. Alexis de Tocqueville, Democracy in America 145 (1966) (1835). [. . .]

55. *Id.* at 146–47.

56. Hochschild, *supra* note 30, at 102.

57. Cose, *supra* note 30, at 49 (quoting interviewee).

58. *See* Erik Olin Wright, *Race, Class and Income Inequality*, 83 Am. J. Soc. 1368, 1387–88 (1978).

59. Hagan & Albonetti, *supra* note 25, at 352.

60. *See* Nancy Apple & David J. O'Brien, *Neighborhood Racial Composition and Residents' Evaluation of Police Performance*, 11 J. Police Sci. & Admin. 76, 83 (1983).

61. *Id.*

62. *See* Mary R. Jackman & Robert W. Jackman, Class Awareness in the United States (1983). [. . .]

63. Robert J. Boeckmann & Tom R. Tyler, *Commonsense Justice and Inclusion Within the Moral Community: Why Do People Receive Procedural Protection from Others?*, 3 Psychol. Pub. Pol'y & L. 362, 377 (1997).

64. Joanne Martin, *The Tolerance of Injustice, in* Relative Deprivation and Social Comparison 238 (James M. Olson et al. eds., 1986).

65. *See* William Julius Wilson, The Declining Significance of Race: Blacks and Changing American Institutions (1978).

66. *See* Ellsworth & Ross, *supra* note 21; Sarat & Vidmar, *supra* note 21.

67. Ellsworth & Ross, *supra* note 21, at 116.

68. *See* Donald R. Kinder & David O. Sears, *Prejudice and Politics: Symbolic Racism Versus Racial Threats to the Good Life*, 40 J. Personality & Soc. Psychol. 414, 422 (1981). [. . .]

69. Cullen et al., *"Stop", supra* note 10, at 458.

70. *See* Ronald Weitzer, *Citizens' Perceptions of Police Misconduct: Race and Neighborhood Context*, 16 Just. Q. 819, 840 (1999).

OTHER NEW PRESS TITLES ON RACE AND THE LAW

After the Storm: Black Intellectuals Explore the Meaning of Hurricane Katrina
Edited by David Dante Troutt

All Alone in the World: Children of the Incarcerated
Nell Bernstein

Black Judges on Justice: Perspectives from the Bench
Linn Washington

Brown v. Board: The Landmark Oral Argument Before the Supreme Court
Edited by Leon Friedman

Class Notes: Posing as Politics and Other Thoughts on the American Scene
Adolph Reed Jr.

The Color of Politics: Race and the Mainsprings of American Politics
Michael Goldfield

Conned: How Millions Went to Prison, Lost the Vote, and Helped Send George W. Bush to the White House
Sasha Abramsky

Enemy Aliens: Double Standards and Constitutional Freedoms in the War on Terrorism
David Cole

Good Courts: The Case for Problem-Solving Justice
Greg Berman and John Feinblatt

Invisible Punishment: The Collateral Consequences of Mass Imprisonment
Edited by Marc Mauer and Meda Chesney-Lind

Lawyers: A Critical Reader
Edited by Richard L. Abel

Less Safe, Less Free: Why America Is Losing the War on Terror
David Cole and Jules Lobel

A Matter of Law: A Memoir of Struggle in the Cause of Equal Rights
Robert L. Carter

May It Please the Court: Live Recordings and Transcripts of Landmark Oral Arguments Made Before the Supreme Court Since 1955
Edited by Peter Irons

The Monkey Suit: And Other Short Fiction on African Americans and Justice
David Dante Troutt

No Equal Justice: Race and Class in the American Criminal Justice System
David Cole

Profiles in Injustice: Why Racial Profiling Cannot Work
David A. Harris

Race to Incarcerate
Marc Mauer

Remembering Jim Crow: African Americans Tell About Life in the Segregated South
Edited by William H. Chafe, Raymond Gavins, Robert Korstad, and the staff of the Behind the Veil Project

Remembering Slavery: African Americans Talk About Their Personal Experiences of Slavery and Emancipation
Edited by Ira Berlin, Marc Favreau, and Steven F. Miller

See You in Court: How the Right Made America a Lawsuit Nation
Thomas Geoghegan

Unchecked and Unbalanced: Presidential Power in a Time of Terror
Frederick A.O. Schwarz Jr. and Aziz Z. Huq